The Sösdala Horsemen

and the equestrian elite of fifth century Europe

The
Sösdala
Horsemen

and the equestrian elite
of fifth century Europe

—

Edited by Charlotte Fabech & Ulf Näsman

Jutland Archaeological Society

The Sösdala horsemen
– and the equestrian elite of fifth century Europe

Edited by Charlotte Fabech & Ulf Näsman

© The authors 2017

English revision by Alan Crozier
Russian summaries by Nikita Khrapunov (except chapter 13 and 15)

Cover, layout and prepress by Depot 1
Cover photo: detail of the pendant Sösdala I no. 1. Photo Lovisa Dal/Christoffer Fägerström
Printed in Denmark by Narayana Press, Gylling
Type: Arno Pro, FF Mark and Avenir Next
Paper: Galerie Art Volume 135 gram

ISBN 978-87-93423-15-2
ISSN 0107-2854
Jutland Archaeological Publications Vol. 99
Published by Jutland Archaeological Society
Moesgård
DK-8270 Højbjerg
Denmark

Distributed by
Aarhus University Press
Finlandsgade 29
DK-8200 Aarhus NV
Denmark
www.au.dk/unipress

Published with the financial support of
Anders Althins Stiftelse
Beckett-Fonden
Berit Wallenbergs Stiftelse
Dronning Margrethe II's Arkæologiske Fond
Ebbe Kocks stiftelse
Stiftelsen Konung Gustaf VI Adolfs fond för svensk kultur
Lennart J Hägglunds Stiftelse
Letterstedtska föreningen
Magnus Bergvalls Stiftelse
Stiftelsen Oscar Montelii fond
Sven och Dagmar Saléns Stiftelse

Contents

Preface

Some objects in our museums attain with time a status as national treasures, and we find them often depicted in standard handbooks about our prehistory. In spite of frequent exposure, the underlying context and the find circumstances as well as the significance of this information may be almost unknown and unpublished. The find of spectacular equestrian equipment at Sösdala is an example of this. The Sösdala finds – in reality two separate depositions – remained mainly known in the 20th century as eponym of one of the decorative styles during the Iron Age, while questions about context and significance received little scholarly attention. Now Charlotte Fabech and Ulf Näsman have set this omission right with an impressive monograph that is the outcome of six years of work. The source-critical review of the find recovery and the rather confusing archaeological investigations that followed is exemplary and exciting. The finds from Sösdala also became pawns in a political struggle between the museums in Lund and Stockholm. The question was whether the finds should be incorporated in the national collections of the Swedish History Museum in Stockholm or be a valuable supplement to the regional collections at the Historical Museum at Lund University? After much debate and both private and official correspondence the Museum in Lund prevailed and the finds, together with the Fulltofta finds, were permanently placed in a table display case in the Iron Age exhibition hall. Here generations of archaeology students learned about the Sösdala style. In 2007 the finds became part of a new exhibition "Barbaricum – Uppåkra and the Iron Age of Scania".

With fresh eyes and knowledge and curiosity in ample measure, Charlotte and Ulf have studied the unique artefacts and had them analysed with new methods and approaches. Analyses of metal alloys and niello as well as microscopic study of the punched decoration have given new clues to the technology and origin of the equestrian equipment. Scholars first interpreted the finds as religious offerings but today much speaks in favour of considering the depositions as part of a funerary ritual for a dead mounted warrior. Probably South Scandinavian horsemen, who served in Germanic hosts in the wide realm of the Huns, are behind the Sösdala and Fulltofta depositions. During their journeys on the Continent they met mounted nomads and became acquainted with their strange funerary rituals. The rituals were performed some distance from the burial place and included the destruction of the dead warriors' horse tack. The ideas of such rituals were brought home by returning Scandinavians and eventually transferred to Scanian soil, plausibly in an attempt to assert new power positions. Perhaps Charlotte and Ulf have identified a once owner of horse tack from Sösdala in a male burial at the nearby Vätteryd cemetery. Obvious similarities in horse tack and context of the Fulltofta find, 15 km south of Sösdala, also indicate that the respective owners ought to have known one another.

The closest parallel to the parade bridle of Sösdala was found at Kačin in Ukraine. In the same way as Sösdala speaks about far-reaching cultural contacts in the 5th century, Charlotte and Ulf have established an international research team of scholars from Sweden in the north, Germany and France in the west and Poland and Russia in the east. All have contributed valuably to an understanding of the equestrian elite during the Migration Period. The book

The Sösdala horsemen – and the equestrian elite of fifth century Europe gives Sösdala and Fulltofta their justified place in European history. In connection with the publication, the finds from Sösdala and Fulltofta will be displayed temporarily but then they will be given their proper place in the permanent exhibition of the Iron Age in Scania.

Lund, 20 May 2017
Per Karsten
Museum Director
Head of the Historical Museum at Lund University

Резюме

Предисловие

В Предисловии директор музея говорит о значении находок в Сёсдале и Фультофте, *ныне являющихся частью собрания* Исторического музея Лундского университета. Он дает высокую оценку колоссальной работе, проделанной при подготовке этой публикации группой исследователей и редакторами проекта – Шарлоттой Фабек и Ульфом Несманом. Благодаря книге «Всадники Сёсдалы и всадническая элита Европы V в.» Сёсдала и Фультофта займут заслуженное место в истории Европы. После этой публикации находки из Сёсдалы и Фультофты займут надлежащее место в постоянной экспозиции, посвященной Железному веку на территории Скании.

Лунд, 20 мая 2017 г.
Пер Карстен
Директор Исторического музея
Лундского университета

Introduction

Charlotte Fabech & Ulf Näsman

In 1929 the history of the Sösdala find began when workers discovered a large number of mounts of horse tack in a gravel pit. The lucky story of how the Sösdala find was saved reminds us of how much of our knowledge about early history is based on accidental circumstances. Most archaeological objects are in fact lost before they are noticed, recorded, stored in a museum and perhaps exhibited. And many arrive at museums with little if any information about find circumstances. So it is important that there are people outside universities and cities, who have an interest in history and who are actively involved in their community. Without the efforts of Carl Mellton, the elementary school-teacher in Sösdala, the find would have been lost.

The Sösdala find rapidly became internationally famous after a paper in German written by John-Elof Forssander appeared in 1937. He coined the term "Sösdala style" that soon became established in the art history of the Migration Period. But most of the objects remained unpublished and the fame of the name threw them in deep shade.

In 1986 Charlotte saw the Sösdala find for the first time in the exhibition at the Historical Museum at Lund University. She was there to prepare her MA thesis. Realising that the find spot is situated near the large Vätteryd cemetery with stone ships, she also went to Sösdala to experience the local setting of the find. Both the artefacts and the ritual deposition point from Sösdala towards south-eastern Europe. Since that year she hoped once to be able both to publish the find and to discuss the find context internationally.

Significantly, Sösdala artefacts were absent when a large exhibition "Germanen, Hunnen und Awaren. Schätze der Völkerwanderungszeit" opened in 1988 at the museums in Nuremberg and Frankfurt am Main. The only existence of "Sösdala" was as a style concept. The peripheral position of Scandinavia was also obvious in the research programme "The Transformation of the Roman World". But the archaeological record of Migration Period Scandinavia can tell another story, one of Scandinavian involvement in European history, as attempted by Ulf at a workshop in 1996 in Strasbourg.

The bridle from Sösdala is a centrepiece of interaction between South Scandinavia and south-eastern Europe. The complete publication of the Sösdala find demonstrates that South Scandinavia in the Migration Period was an integral part of Europe. We hope it will contribute to changing the view that South Scandinavia is an uninteresting periphery outside the real Europe.

That a Sösdala publication should not be a monograph but a volume of studies became clear after Charlotte's visit in 2001 to Kunsthistorisches Museum in Vienna. There she bought a new book *Barbarenschmuck und Römergold. Der Schatz von Szilágysomlyó*. It was read on the train back to Denmark. It is a collection of interesting papers about a significant find and has excellent artefact photographs. It became our ideal for a publication of Sösdala. But other research projects, easier to finance, came first and years would pass before Sösdala came on the agenda.

In 2008 Charlotte received a grant to investigate whether a project to publish the Sösdala find could be realised. In the years 2009–2012 the possibilities of a Sösdala publication project was investigated but it was only when Charlotte and Ulf in 2012, independently of one another, received an invitation to contribute to a conference, *Inter Ambo Maria*,

in the Crimea (Ukraine) that the Sösdala project began to materialise. We decided to cooperate and to give a joint paper about Sösdala, subsequently published in the conference proceedings in 2013. To present Sösdala seemed appropriate at a conference in south-eastern Europe. The reception after our presentation was overwhelming. For the first time archaeologists understood the exceptional qualities of both the content and the context of the Sösdala find. We concluded that many scholars in Central and Eastern Europe would also appreciate a full Sösdala publication. After the conference we stayed a couple of days in Istanbul and realised that our next step had to be a workshop in Lund where we could discuss a publication project with invited scholars of importance. To publish a find of such international significance we needed support of scholars with greater knowledge of the archaeological record of Western and Eastern Europe as well as domestic scholars with special expertise. We received economic support to arrange a workshop and a number of scholars were invited; all promised to participate.

In May 2013 we gathered at the Historical Museum at Lund University to study the Sösdala finds and to discuss the possibilities for future collaboration concerning a Sösdala publication (fig. 1). The museum generously opened its doors to us and arranged that the whole find complexes from Sösdala I and II as well as Fulltofta were available for close study. All invited were positive and we are grateful that they accepted our invitation to contribute of their time, engagement and knowledge. We promised to apply for money for the necessary preparatory work: scientific

Fig 1. Participants in the 2013 Sösdala workshop in front of the Historical Museum at Lund University.
From left to right: Svante Fischer, Jerry Rosengren, Anneli Sundkvist, Per Karsten, Lovisa Dal, Michel Kazanski, Anna Bitner-Wróblewska, Bengt Nordqvist, Charlotte Fabech and Ulf Näsman. Photo unknown passer-by.

Fig 2. Ulf Näsman, Charlotte Fabech and Lovisa Dal discuss the Sösdala objects in the library of the Historical Museum at Lund University. Photo Daniel Lindskog.

analyses, artefact cleaning and new colour photography, drawings of bridle and saddle reconstructions and artefact cross-sections, layout and printing as well as a second workshop (fig. 2). Fortunately, many foundations viewed our applications favourably, and after some time the economy of the project was consolidated. We are grateful to the foundations that granted our requests.

In November 2015 a second workshop was held in Lund for a final discussion of finds, interpretations and conclusions. The authors presented their contribution, and discussions were lively during fruitful days in Lund. To make the find places Sösdala and Fulltofta and their surrounding landscapes more present to the participants we went to visit the sites. It was a risky business at that time of the year; the weather forecast said cloudy, 6 degrees Celsius and maybe snow. We did get a little snow, but everything went fine (fig. 3)!

It is hard to understand how difficult it is to finance a project like Sösdala. The large research foundations do not support this kind of research, so we had to find support in smaller private foundations. The foundations that generously contributed to the publication are:

Anders Althins Stiftelse
Beckett-Fonden
Berit Wallenbergs Stiftelse
Dronning Margrethe II's Arkæologiske Fond
Ebbe Kocks stiftelse
Stiftelsen Konung Gustaf VI Adolfs fond för svensk kultur
Lennart J Hägglunds Stiftelse
Letterstedtska föreningen
Magnus Bergvalls Stiftelse
Stiftelsen Oscar Montelii fond
Sven och Dagmar Saléns Stiftelse

Working with Sösdala has been like opening Pandora's Box. New unexpected questions appeared constantly. We have tried to catch them and find answers, but sometimes it felt overwhelming with more questions than answers. Finds such as Sösdala represent only the tip of an iceberg of unknown material. Other similar finds are other tips but we do not know whether they belong to the same iceberg or are separate. In fact we think this is a positive result – our main goal is to give Sösdala its just place in the discourse about the epoch-making centuries in the middle of the first millennium AD. Now the Sösdala and Fulltofta finds are put to work. Other scholars will have access to the complete material from Sösdala and Fulltofta and hopefully they will find new questions to ask and new interpretations to present. The lack of a full publication explains why the Sösdala finds have been largely overlooked; another explanation is linguistic difficulties. In the workshops discussions were polyglot with comments in Danish, English (dominating), French, German, Russian and Swedish. In an attempt to remedy this we publish in English with résumés and captions in Russian.

Another complication in our scholarly communication was that similar chronological concepts have different content in Scandinavia and on the Continent (fig. 4). On the Continent the Migration Period phase D1 is roughly contemporary with the later part of Scandinavian Late Roman Iron Age phase C3, Continental D2 corresponds to

Fig 3. *The participants of the second workshop 2015 at the Sösdala gravel pit.*
From left to right: Bengt Nordqvist, Svante Fischer, Olle Andersson, Anneli Sundkvist, Per Karsten, Dieter Quast, Ulf Näsman, Anna Bitner-Wróblewska, Bertil Helgesson, Anna Mastykova, Michel Kazanski, Charlotte Fabech and Lovisa Dal. Photo Stig Jensen, the coach driver.

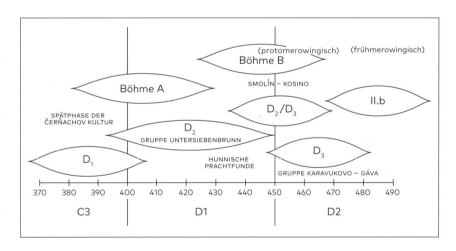

Fig 4. *The relation between Scandinavian chronological phases C3, D1 and D2 (bottom) and Continental chronological concepts.*
After fig. 20 in Kristoffersen, S. & Magnus, B. 2010. Spannformete kar. Udvikling og variasjon. Stavanger. Summary. and Abb. 30 in Tejral, J. 1997. Neue Aspekte der frühvölkerwanderungszeitlichen Chronologie im Mitteldonauraum. In: Tejral, J. et al. (eds). Neue Beiträge zur Erforschung der Spätantike im mittleren Donauraum. Brno: 321-391. Cf. Abb. 41 in Rau, A. 2010. Nydam mose 1. Die personengebundenen Gegenstände. Grabungen 1989–1999. Aarhus/Højbjerg: Summary.

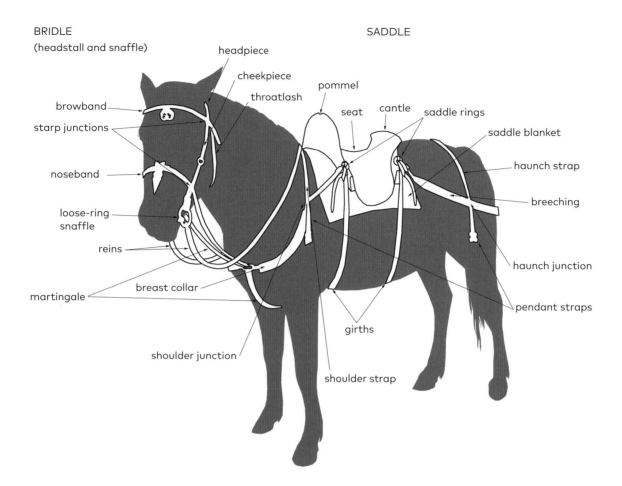

BRIDLE
(headstall and snaffle)

SADDLE

headpiece
cheekpiece
throatlash
pommel
browband
starp junctions
noseband
loose-ring
snaffle
reins
martingale
breast collar
shoulder junction
seat
cantle
saddle rings
saddle blanket
haunch strap
breeching
haunch junction
pendant straps
girths
shoulder strap

Fig 5. The terminology of horse tack used in the Sösdala publication is applied to a reconstruction of a "Sösdala horse". For corresponding term in Russian, see résumé. Drawing Erika Rosengren.

Scandinavian D1 and Scandinavian D2 to Continental D3 and Early Merovingian phases *Alte Merowingerzeit* I–II. To avoid misunderstandings we use the terms Scand-D1 and Cont-D1.

For scholars who never mounted a horse the terminology of the many mounts and straps necessary to bridle and saddle up a horse was a challenge. After good advice from Anneli Sundqvist and Alan Crozier as well as much surfing on the Internet we decided on a terminology of horse tack (fig. 5). The localisation of the main sites treated in the book is found on a map (fig. 6).

In this publication of the finds from Sösdala and Fulltofta the artefacts are reproduced on the scales of 1:1 or 3:4 (75%) in the catalogues. All other illustrations are reproduced on various scales when nothing else is stated.

Many individual persons and scholars have helped us in various ways. We owe them all many thanks: Hans Chr. Andersen, Kent Andersson, Olle Andersson, Anders Andrén, Maria Panum Baastrup, Jan Bemmann, Jenny Bergman, Ruth Blankenfeldt, Audronė Bliujienė, Hampus Cinthio, Sophia Cinthio, Lisbeth Eilersgaard Christensen, Lars Ersgård, Nicolo Dell'Unto, Lotta Fernstål, Marei Hacke, Jan Peder Lamm, Kristina Jansson, Kristina Jennbert, Stig Jensen, Igor' Khrapunov, Birgit Körge, Per Lagerås, Nina Lau, Maxim Levada, Ulla Mannering, Magnus Mårtensson, Mats Mogren, Björn Nilsson, Anders Ödman, Chatarina Ödman, Karl Erik Olsson, Ingvar Ottosson, Jonas Paulsson, Karen Stemann Petersen, Peter Vang Petersen, Andreas Rau, Judyta Rodzińska, Jerry Rosengren, Tom Sandström, Arne Sjöström, Frans-Arne Stylegar, Kaj Thuresson and Helena Victor.

And warm thanks to Per Karsten, head of the Historical Museum at Lund University, who accepted our suggestions and gave us free hands in our work with the exceptional Sösdala find complex, indeed a great privilege.

Finally our many thanks to those who contributed as authors, drawer, editors, photographers or translators: Anna Bitner-Wróblewska, Enrico Cappellini, Alan Crozier, Lovisa Dal, Svante Fischer, Bertil Helgesson, Per Karsten, Michel Kazanski, Jesper Laursen, Nikita Khrapunov, Daniel Lindskog, Meaghan Mackie, Anna Mastykova, Bengt Nordqvist, Snorre Näsman, Dieter Quast, Per Ramqvist, Erika Rosengren, Konstantin Skvortsov, Anneli Sundkvist and Ola Svensson.

This publication never had the goal of covering all aspects of the Sösdala finds. Our focus is to present the artefacts of the three finds, Sösdala I–II and Fulltofta, and to expose the outstanding craftsmanship. Another purpose is an update of the information about classical questions such as chronology, provenance, style and interpretation of find context. We also make an attempt to write the biography of the parade bridle of Sösdala I. Now we hope other scholars will use the publication to put forward new questions and interpretations. A few scientific analyses were made with good results. Obviously other scholarly and scientific analyses will bring further discoveries, analyses we had neither the time nor the resources to carry out. It has been very rewarding to handle and study such rich and exciting archaeological find material. The Sösdala-Fulltofta complex offers new routes to an understanding of the societal changes in a tumultuous period when the classic world collapsed and a new Europe was formed.

Fig 6. The localisation of the main sites treated in this volume.

Резюме

Введение

Шарлотта Фабек, Ульф Несман

История находки в Сёсдале началась в 1929 г., в гравийном карьере. Находка погибла бы, если бы не усилия Карла Мельтона, учителя начальных классов из Сёсдалы. Международную известность Сёсдальской находке принесла статья Йона-Элофа Форссандера, опубликованная в 1937 г. на немецком языке. Он предложил выделить стиль «Сёсдала», но большая часть находок осталась неопубликованной. В 1986 г. Ш. Фабек впервые увидела находку из Сёсдалы в Историческом музее

Лундского университета. С тех самых пор она надеялась опубликовать находку и информацию о ее контексте в издании, которое привлекло бы внимание международной аудитории.

В 2008 г. Ш. Фабек получила грант для изучения вопроса о том, возможна ли реализация проекта по изданию находки из Сёсдалы. Когда в 2012 г. Ш. Фабек и У. Несман независимо друг от друга получили приглашение принять участие в конференции «Inter Ambo Maria» в Крыму, то решили сделать совместный доклад о Сёсдале (опубликован в сборнике материалов конференции в 2013 г.). Доклад был встречен с энтузиазмом. Стало ясно, что многие исследователи из Центральной и Восточной Европы оценят полную публикацию комплекса из Сёсдалы.

В мае 2013 г. небольшая группа исследователей собралась в Историческом музее Лундского университета для изучения находок из Сёсдалы и обсуждения соответствующей публикации (рис. 1). В ноябре 2015 г. в Лунде прошел второй семинар, на котором снова обсуждались эти находки, их интерпретации и результаты исследования. Чтобы познакомить участников проекта с местом, где были открыты находки из Сёсдалы и Фультофты, была предпринята экскурсия на эти памятники (рис. 3).

Задачу осложняло то обстоятельство, что близкие хронологические концепты в Скандинавии и на Европейском континенте имеют разное наполнение (рис. 4). Чтобы избежать непонимания, мы будем использовать такие термины, как, например, «период D1 по скандинавской хронологии» («Scand-D1») и «период D1 по европейской хронологии» («Cont-D1»). Терминология, описывающая различные накладки, зажимы и ремни, использовавшиеся в узде и седлах, представляла собой отдельную проблему, и потому пришлось определиться с терминами, описывающими конскую упряжь (рис. 5; см также русскую терминологию в нижеприведенном списке). Местоположение основных памятников, о которых пойдет речь в этой книге, отмечено на карте (рис. 6).

BRIDLE (headstall and snaffle)	УЗДА (оголовье и удила)
browband	налобный ремень
cheekpiece	нащёчный ремень
headpiece	затылочный ремень
loose-ring snaffle	трензель
cheek-bar snaffle	мундштук
noseband	носовой ремень
reins	поводья
strap junction	распределитель ремней
throatlash	шейный ремень

SADDLE	СЕДЛО
breast collar	нагрудный ремень
breeching	шлея
cantle	задняя лука
girth	подпруга
haunch junction	распределитель ремней (на крупе коня)
haunch strap	спинной ремень
martingale	мартингал
pendant strap	подвесочный ремень
pommel	передняя лука
saddle blanket	потник
saddle ring	подпружное кольцо
seat	сиденье
shoulder junction	распределитель ремней (на плече коня)
shoulder strap	плечевой ремень

Эта публикация не ставит целью дать всесторонний анализ находок в Сёсдале. Наша задача – опубликовать вещи из трех памятников: Сёсдалы I–II и Фультофты. Другая задача – уточнить информацию по таким «классическим» вопросам, как хронология, происхождение, стиль и интерпретация контекста находки. Будем надеяться, что другие исследователи используют эту публикацию, чтобы сформулировать новые вопросы и предложить новые интерпретации. Комплекс Сёсдалы-Фультофты предлагает новые возможности для понимания социальных изменений в бурное время гибели античного мира и формирования новой Европы.

Подписи к иллюстрациям

Рис. 1. Участники Сёсдальского семинара 2013 г. на фоне Исторического музея Лундского университета. Слева направо: Сванте Фишер, Джерри Росенгрен, Аннели Сундквист, Пер Карстен, Ловиса Даль, Михаил Казанский, Анна Битнер-Врублевская, Бенгт Нордквист, Шарлотта Фабек, Ульф Несман. Фото неизвестного прохожего.

Рис. 2. Ульф Несман, Шарлотта Фабек и Ловиса Даль обсуждают вещи из Сёсдалы в библиотеке Исторического музея Лундского университета (фото Даниэля Линдскога).

Рис. 3. Участники второго семинара 2015 г. у гравийного карьера в Сёсдиле. Слеви направо: Бенгт Нордквист, Сванте Фишер, Олле Андерссон, Аннели Сундквист, Пер Карстен, Дитер Кваст, Ульф Несман, Анна Битнер-Врублевская, Бертиль Хельгессон, Анна Мастыкова, Михаил Казанский, Шарлотта Фабек, Ловиса Даль. Фото Стига Йенсена, водителя автобуса.

Рис. 4. Соотношение между фазами C3, D1 и D2 по скандинавской (внизу) и европейской хронологии (по: Kristoffersen, Magnus 2010 fig. 20 (Spannformete kar. Udvikling og variasjon. Stavanger. Summary); Tejral 1997 Abb. 30 (Neue Aspekte der frühvölkerwanderungszeitlichen Chronologie im Mitteldonauraum // Neue Beiträge zur Erforschung der Spätantike im mittleren Donauraum / ed. J. Tejral et alii. Brno: 321–391); ср.: Rau 2010 Abb. 41 (Nydam mose 1. Die personengebundenen Gegenstände. Grabungen 1989–1999. Aarhus; Højbjerg: Summary).

Рис. 5. Термины, описывающие конскую сбрую, использованные в публикации комплекса Сёсдалы, на графической реконструкции «коня из Сёсдалы». Соответствующая русская терминология дана в тексте выше (рисунок Эрики Росенгрен).

Рис. 6. Местоположение основных памятников, упомянутых в этой книге.

Chapter 1

The finds from Sösdala and Fulltofta

A story of rescue, musealisation and oblivion

Charlotte Fabech

At Sösdala the most comprehensive and complete find of horse tack from the Migration Period in Europe was discovered in 1929–1930. It is also one of the most important finds elucidating the relations between Scandinavia and Continental Europe. Here the story is told of how the finds were uncovered and rescued for posterity. Only after a fierce struggle with the central authorities in Stockholm were the Sösdala finds incorporated in the collections of the Historical Museum at Lund University. However, a publication corresponding to the historical significance of the Sösdala finds never appeared. The smaller and less well-known find from nearby Fulltofta is also treated.

Fabech, C. 2017. The finds from Sösdala and Fulltofta – a story of rescue, musealisation and oblivion. In: Fabech, C. & Näsman, U. (eds). The Sösdala horsemen – and the equestrian elite of fifth century Europe. Jutland Archaeological Society.

The Sösdala finds, like many archaeological discoveries, were unearthed by workers extracting gravel. And like many other finders, the workers believed they had discovered a treasure. That the "treasure" did not disappear like so many other prehistoric finds is a coincidence. The coincidence is that a local elementary-school teacher Carl Mellton (1886–1940) had an interest in archaeology and history (fig. 1). He immediately realised the value of the finds and shouldered the responsibility for the situation. He also contacted the Historical Museum at Lund University (LUHM). Mellton's efforts not only rescued the artefacts for posterity, he also informed the museum about find circumstances in text, photos and measurements. As a result it is not only possible for us to discuss the artefacts of an important find, we can also discuss how and why bridles and saddles were dismantled and the remains deposited on top of a gravel ridge near

Fig. 1. Carl Mellton, 1886–1940. Photo studio Herman Piil, Hässleholm.

Fig. 2. Sösdala and Fulltofta are find places near one another in central Scania.

Sösdala. The finds can be dated to the early 5th century AD. The find place is in central Scania (fig. 2).

But it is not a coincidence that the objects are now part of the Lund collection and not in the central Swedish History Museum in Stockholm. The explanation is great efforts to keep the finds in Scania by Professor Otto Rydbeck (1872–1954), director of the museum in Lund, and research assistant John-Elof Forssander (1904–1944). The story also reflects the ability of their opponent *Riksantikvarie* Sigurd Curman (1879–1966) to set short-sighted goals aside in favour of far-sighted strategies. (As *Riksantikvarie* Curman began his work of organising national heritage management in 1923 and in 1938 he became head of the new National Heritage Board). The drama can be followed in partly preserved letters that illuminate the museum order of Sweden in the 1920s–1930s.

From the moment in June 1929 when the gilt silver objects slid down in the gravel pit after 1500 years in darkness, the Sösdala finds aroused great attention and interest. Already in July Otto Rydbeck decided to give the responsibility for publishing the Sösdala finds to Rune Norberg (1906–1977). It was an obvious task for Norberg, who as curator at the Swedish History Museum had catalogued similar saddle mounts found in 1927 in Kanalgatan, Jönköping, Småland, and he had also published two papers about saddles (Norberg 1929a,b). He was evidently the scholar best informed on the subject. The offer was accepted but Norberg never honoured it.

The less well-known mounts of horse tack from Fulltofta were found by a local worker in 1896, also during gravel extraction. The finder delivered the objects to his employer, the owner of the Fulltoftagård estate, who donated them to the museum in Lund. Here they were incorporated in the collection without discussion. Rune Norberg's intention was to include also Fulltofta in his publication but it never materialised.

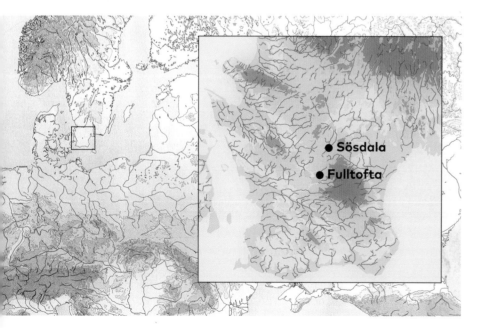

Based on reports, preserved letters, original find catalogues and early publications an attempt is made to tell the story of the discovery and rescue of the Sösdala finds in 1929–30, how the finds became part of the archaeological collection in Lund and why they have remained unpublished to this day. The less well-known Fulltofta finds are also presented in this context. A preliminary study was published in 1991 (Fabech 1991).

Sösdala I, 1929–30, LUHM no. 25 570

In early June 1929 a man entered the bookshop in Sösdala, a village at a railway station in central Scania. He showed a couple of objects to the shopkeeper Svante Nilsson and asked what they were made of and what value they could have. In their conversation it became clear that the man together with other workers was extracting gravel in a gravel pit, leased by the road association of Västra Göinge Hundred (fig. 2). During the work they had stumbled on a treasure and distributed the spoils among themselves. Nilsson immediately reported to the local elementary-school teacher Carl Mellton. He acted at once and hurried to the find place, where he contacted the workers and began to gather the dispersed finds. The rumour about a treasure had spread in the area and people flocked to the pit to look for more. Some also searched on the road where the gravel was spread and a few were lucky. The "treasure" consisted of bronze and gilt silver mounts of horse tack; the silver mounts had been found in gravel that had slid down to the bottom of the pit; the bronzes were found in gravel on the top of the ridge.

The workers handed over eleven mounts to Mellton and asked him to go to Lund and show them to Otto Rydbeck at the museum. Rydbeck realised that the objects were exceptional and contacted the archaeologist Olle Källström (1900–1983), who was excavating in the medieval town of Luntertun, near Ängelholm, north-west Scania. Källström was ordered to go immediately to Sösdala and rescue the finds.

Källström came to the find place on 11 June. He began screening the gravel and organised work in the gravel pit to protect the site against plundering (fig. 3). He also collected the finds that Mellton had gathered from the workers and other treasure-hunters (fig. 4). In all about 100 mounts

Fig. 3. The archaeologist Olle Källström and unknown boy screen gravel in the pit at Sösdala. Photo Carl Mellton 11 June 1929.

Fig. 4. Carl Mellton's photo of bridle and saddle mounts he recovered from the workers. Photo 11 June 1929.

Fig. 5. Objects found when Carl Mellton screened gravel at find spot II; note that a large saddle mount was only found in the screen. Photo Carl Mellton June 1929.

and fragments were handed over to Källström. The workers who found the treasure received 50 Swedish kronor as advance payment for the finds (corresponding to roughly 1,400 SEK today).

Källström sent a preliminary report to *Riksantikvarie* (Custodian of National Antiquities) Curman on 12 June. He asked Curman to confirm Källström's instruction to the district police superintendent O. Ebbeson to secure the find place against plunder and to stop access by outsiders. The landowner and his wife had promised to look after the find place. As soon as the investigations were concluded, the blocking of access to the site could be lifted. Källström left it to Mellton to continue the screening of both the gravel slide in the pit and the loose gravel on the top of the ridge. He asked Curman to authorise Rydbeck and his representative (i.e. LUHM) to carry out the investigations necessary. Since the gravel pit would not be used in the coming months no more action was needed in his opinion. Already on 14 June Rydbeck received the permission of the *Riksantikvarie* to investigate at the site during 1929.

Mellton carried out the investigations 17 June and screened gravel at the bottom of the pit where the gilt silver mounts had been found, but he found only one fragment of a gilt silver mount. Two rivets of silver at one end held a back plate of bronze and a fragment of a leather strap in between (it can be identified as find no. I:37). He also found

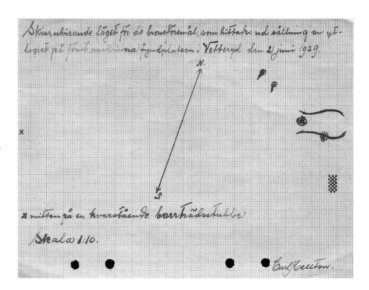

Fig. 6. Carl Mellton's photo and measurement of saddle mounts and saddle rings found in situ at find spot III, 21 June 1929. The position of the long mounts indicates that they were still fastened to the leather cover of the saddle when thrown on the ground.

three back plates of copper, 6–7 cm long and 9–14 mm wide (now unidentifiable). After four more hours of screening without results, Mellton concluded that nothing more was to be found and stopped the investigation of the gravel slide.

Mellton continued his investigations and on 21 June he began to screen the loose gravel on the top of the ridge where the workers had found bronze mounts from dismantled saddles. According to the workers the find spot was 3 m east of the spot where the silver mounts had been deposited before they slid down in the gravel pit. In a letter of 24 June, Mellton reports that he had retrieved several overlooked objects: 5 copper rivets, 4 with roves of iron, 3 strap mounts of copper and 2 iron fragments that perhaps once made up a strap buckle. That he found a 13 cm long bronze mount in the screen tells us how careless the workers had been. On a photo attached to his letter (fig. 5), all the finds mentioned above are to be seen as well as a fourth strap mount and five rivet caps of Cu-alloy, all found by screening (the identifiable objects are nos. I:74, 81–82, 84, 95–99, 131, 177, 186–189 and no. I:37, found earlier in the gravel slide).

To make sure that all loose gravel was screened and to recover objects that the workers had dropped around, the uppermost layer of untouched gravel was also investigated. As a result Mellton found some objects *in situ* 3 m east of the centre of find spot II: two long saddle mounts and four saddle rings (fig. 6). The upper end of the long saddle mounts was found only 2–3 cm deep in the gravel (the vegetation layer had previously been removed by the work-

Fig. 7. The find spot on the gravel ridge at Sösdala from the South. Photo John-Elof Forssander July 1929.

ers). The other end lay 10 cm deep. In the letter he regretted that he had removed the objects, but he could not get in touch with the museum. And he had carefully recorded the find circumstances in photo and measurement.

Mellton's report was received by Otto Rydbeck on 24 June. Mellton writes that one of the workers had informed him that silver and bronze objects were not found at the same place. First they found gilt silver mounts in the gravel slide at the bottom of the pit. Then they searched for more treasure on top of the ridge and found many bronze mounts approx. 3 m east of the place from where they reckoned that the silver objects had slid down. Mellton combined this information with his own observations and concluded that the mounts had been dug down at three different places with approx. 3 m in between.

Forssander visited the place to make his own investigations on 5 and 10–11 July but we do not know what he did there, other than that he photographed the site and sketched a plan of the area (fig. 7–8). Källström instructed the district police superintendent on 21 August that the protection of the site could be annulled since the investigations were finished.

On behalf of Professor Rydbeck Forssander send a report on 17 October to *Riksantikvarie* Curman about his investigations. He described the location of the find place, situated on the top of a small hill that forms the end of a high gravel ridge running roughly east–west. The gravel hill is separated from the ridge by a short hollow, a couple of metres deep and long. Westward the terrain slopes down quickly but after some hundred metres towards the south-west it rises again towards another large gravel ridge. Northward the terrain slopes gently down to the main road. Southward the ground rises after a hollow a few metres broad to a level corresponding to the find place. A photo shows find place and gravel hill from the south (fig. 7). Finally Forssander mentioned that the find place is located less than 500 m south of the unusually large number of erected stones at Vätteryd (the well-known cemetery).

Concerning how the finds were brought forth and how they were rescued, Forssander referred to the preliminary report by Källström and to Mellton's report about the screening. Based on these reports and his autopsy of the site, he sketched the investigated area with the three find spots according to statements by workers and Mellton (fig. 8). In the west the silver objects had once been deposited at find spot I before they followed the gravel slide to the bottom of the pit. Three metres further to the east workers found many bronze objects at find spot II. A hollow left by the workers' digging could still be seen when Forssander arrived in July. How deep the objects were deposited could not be established but it was less than 1 m below the surface. However, Mellton's observations at find spot III, where four saddle rings and two long saddle mounts were uncovered *in situ*, indicate that the objects were deposited just under the vegetation layer and only a few centimetres down in the gravel, perhaps in very shallow hollows (fig. 6).

No new finds were made by Forssander. He summarised that the Sösdala find consisted of more than a hundred objects, mainly silver and bronze mounts. Decoration and shape date the finds to the early Migration Period. Practically all objects were badly deformed. Deep cut marks reveal that sharp weapons had been used. Other objects were broken or violently distorted. The surface of other objects showed that they had been smashed between stones.

He wrote that the silver mounts – strap mounts, strap ends and buckles – belong to a bridle. The bronze mounts with rings and staples belong to saddles. They are made of

massive bronze, sometimes with thin silver covers. Finally he assumed that a lance head of iron (no. I:172) possibly belongs to the find context. It was found (unfortunately we are not informed by whom) 50 m away from the other finds among stone taken from the find place.

Interesting information concerning the find circumstances in 1929 is to be read in Carin Bunte's publication of the find in 1961 of a second bridle at Sösdala: "Information given by the finders, the landowner Nils Weneryd and his father Oscar Jönsson. The latter also came upon and took charge of the 1929 find and regarding the circumstances surrounding that find he now says that there was an oval layer, about 5 × 2.5 metres, of stones about as big as a man's head lying over the four pits" (Bunte 1961 footnote 4). On Mellton's photo of the gravel pit a lot of removed stones are lying on the bottom of the pit, some probably naturally present in the gravel ridge, others perhaps coming from the stone setting. Presumably it was among these stones that the lance head was found.

Forssander not only reported the result of the investigations at the find place, he also emphasised the importance of Mellton, who had rescued the find and informed the museum. Already before a representative of the museum had arrived, Mellton stopped the plundering of the site and began to gather the dispersed objects. He took the responsibility to screen the loose gravel and recorded his observations in exemplary fashion.

As late as 20 January 1930 Mellton sent four more objects that he had received from different persons to Forssander (who catalogued them as nos. I:111–114). In the accompanying letter Mellton related that he had read in the paper *Sydsvenska Dagbladet* that Professor Rydbeck would be supervising the road works at the dairy at Sösdala and wondered who would do the job. He also noticed that activities in the Sösdala gravel pit now were approaching "the find hill, if such an expression is allowable". Mellton demonstrates that he still was interested in the Sösdala finds and that someone ought to keep an eye on the site.

Sösdala nr. 16, N. Mellby sn. V. Göinge hd.
Skala 1:1600

ej odlad mark
odlad mark
dike
fyndplats
undersökt område.

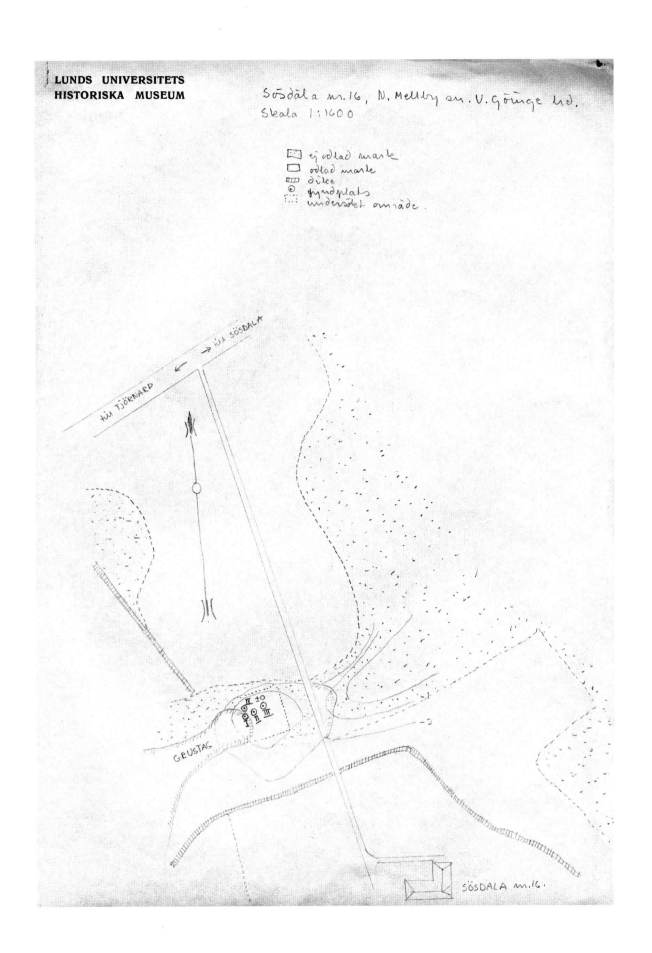

Fig. 9. Objects found 9 April 1930 by workers at find spot IV: saddle mounts and rings with silver inlays; to the left two gilt silver fragments fitting a pendant from find spot I; in the upper left corner a stump of a leather strap with a silver mount and silver-capped rivets. Photo Carl Mellton 9/13 April 1930.

On 29 January Rydbeck sent all the finds from Sösdala 1929 with a find list to the *Riksantikvarie* (the listed finds cannot be identified in Forssander's catalogue).

Obviously Mellton was not asked to supervise the gravel extraction in the Sösdala pit. So on 9 April 1930 workers made a new exclusive find of horse tack, unfortunately in a gravel slide. Mellton's importance is demonstrated once more. His letter of 13 April to Rydbeck reports that he had successfully gathered all objects that were spread among several persons. A find list and a photo were enclosed (fig.

9). The finds are an almost complete set of saddle mounts (see catalogue Sösdala I "Saddle 1"), two gilt silver fragments fitting a pendant from find spot I (no. I:7), and a stump of a leather strap with a double silver-bronze mount and rivets with silver caps (no. I:229).

The new find place was labelled "find spot IV" and was localised approx. 3 m north of the assumed find spot I, 1929. Our only sources are three letters from Mellton of 13 April, 13 and 15 October, information in Forssander's find catalogue, a mark IV added to his sketch of the find place (fig. 8), and a short note added by Rydbeck to Forssander's report of 17 October 1929.

All finds from find spot IV were mailed by Rydbeck 25 June to the *Riksantikvarie*. In the letter he writes that the finds were made in gravel slide in the same gravel pit as in 1929, and he assumed that they had been lying approx. 25 cm deep in pure gravel. This was his explanation of how the representative of the museum missed them during the investigations in 1929; then only the uppermost few centimetres of pure gravel were investigated since the objects of find place III had been found near the gravel surface.

In the same parcel Rydbeck included about 80 mounts and fragments that different persons had found and sent to the museum over some time. Rydbeck listed the finds in three groups, A, B and C, reflecting the find circumstances as far as he was informed.

The 41 objects of find group A came from find spot IV, 3 m north of find spot I and 3.25 m north-west of find spot II. Find group B contains objects that Rydbeck assumed came from the same find spot IV, but because the objects had "wandered" between people in the area before they were delivered to the museum, he finds it impossible to be sure about it. Finally he included 60 objects, find group C, which belong to the finds from 1929 since they came from the road where the gravel from the pit was spread. They were delivered to the museum by different persons confidentially. Rydbeck ended his letter expressing his hope that all finds would be returned to Lund by August.

As late as 13 October 1930 Mellton wrote to Rydbeck to tell him that he had now begun his supplementary investigation at find spot IV. With the help of two boys he planned to screen gravel from an area 5 × 10 m large and 20–39 cm deep. With the letter he sent two silver pieces, one riveted to a back mount of copper. Already on 15 October he told Rydbeck that the screening had yielded little – a small piece of copper was their only find. When nothing had been found on a third day of toil, he expected it would continue that way. After this letter nothing more is heard from Mellton concerning the Sösdala finds.

All finds from 1929 and 1930 were described and catalogued by Forssander as LUHM no. 25 570, in all 247 entries. With a lance head as the only exception, all finds can be interpreted as parts of a bridle and between 7 and 13 saddles (Näsman chapter 7). The find is called Sösdala I.

Sösdala II, 1961, LUHM no. 32 492

At the end of August 1961 archaeological finds appeared once more in a gravel pit at Sösdala. The finds were reported to the authorities by the local representative of the National Heritage Board, Nils J. Jacobsson. The archaeologist

Fig. 10. Lidar map of the find place in 2014 with find places of Sösdala I (1929–1930) and Sösdala II (1961) marked. The map clearly shows that much of the gravel ridge is dug away where the two finds were made. © Lantmäteriet.

Carin Bunte was sent to the site. She made investigations on 22 and 25 August to ascertain the find circumstances. She called the find Sösdala II (Bunte 1961).

The find consists of mounts of a bridle and was made when the land owner Nils Weneryd and Mr Oscar Jönsson were taking gravel from an old gravel pit. They told Bunte that gravel had not been extracted there for the last ten years, but that gravel had previously been carted away from the site for use as road ballast in the neighbourhood. The find place is approx. 60 m north-east of the find place 1929–1930. A recent lidar map reveals that the two finds were made in the same long gravel ridge and that a considerable section of the ridge has disappeared due to gravel extraction (fig. 10).

The finders recovered 16 metal objects and a fragment of a leather strap. They told Bunte that the objects were found within an area just under 1 m in diameter and approx. 1 m below original ground surface. But Bunte could see that the finds came from an old landslide and that nothing was found *in situ*. In her opinion the mounts originally came from a level just below the original heather-covered surface just like the Sösdala I finds. She had gravel from a 3 m broad zone of the slope screened. Fourteen more metal objects were found as well as a stump of leather. The vegetation layer was removed from a 2 × 7 m large area at the top of the pit and the area was searched with a metal detector but nothing was found. She considered it likely that parts of the find were lost in earlier gravel extraction.

The bridle mounts are made of bronze with details of silver sheet. The snaffle is bimetallic of bronze and iron. All finds, 30 items, were described and published in English by Bunte the same year (Bunte 1961). There are no remains of saddles. For new photos see the summary catalogue in this volume.

Bunte stopped further digging in the pit since she believed, considering the four depositions of Sösdala I, that more depositions could be expected nearby. The county custodian of antiquities asked the *Riksantikvarie* in Stockholm for permission to continue investigations of the find place. Whether or not such permission was granted we do not know. But we have found nothing about excavations or any other investigation at the site. And gravel extraction continued.

The whole ridge was metal detected in 2017 on behalf of The County Administrative Board of Skåne without any significant finds.

The Fulltofta finds, 1896, LUHM no. 14 080

In October 1896 the farm hand Måns Olsson was sent to get gravel in a pit belonging to Fulltoftagård in an area with several gravel hills. When he was working he found a number of bronze objects and according to him they were found about 90 cm below the surface. He observed mouldered leather but nothing resembling bone. The find was noticed and mentioned in the papers *Helsingborgsposten* and *Göteborgs Aftonpost*. Here it was told that the gravel pit was now protected and that excavations were planned to take place in spring 1897 (they never took place). The find was donated to the museum in Lund by the landowner, the district judge C.A. Trolle, Fulltoftagård. In October 1897 the director of the museum, Professor Sven Söderberg, visited the find place but no investigations were made. Not until 2002, 105 years later, was the site investigated, now

with metal detector. The purpose was to protect the site and locate the exact find spot, registered as ancient monument Fulltofta no. 98:1. In a gravel pit Jonas Paulsson found two fragments which are very similar to finds from 1896. In 2017 the whole area was metal detected carefully once more on behalf of The County Administrative Board of Skåne. Only two small fragments of attachment plates belonging to the bridle were found.

The find consist of 24 mounts from a bridle and a saddle; some have silver details and two silver-on-bronze covers are partly gilt. A fine find catalogue with text and drawings was made by Söderberg (fig. 11) but astonishingly he did not make any remarks about the function of the mounts; so we don't know whether he ever understood that he was describing an important find of Migration Period horse tack. The Fulltofta mounts were forgotten and only after 1929 did they become part of the archaeological discourse after Norberg gave the Fulltofta find its proper place in a discussion of prehistoric saddles (Norberg 1929b fig. 14; cf. 1931 Abb. 2–3).

The find place is situated approx. 2 km east of Lake Ringsjön, approx 2 km north of Fulltoftagård, and approx. 150 m west of the road between Fulltofta and Häggenäs (fig. 12). The area is characterised by hills covered by heather and forest. South of the find place a brook Hejdebäcken runs in a deep valley. Several ancient monuments are recorded in the area: graves, settlements, remnants of ancient field systems and many clearance cairns. The impression is that the area was intensively used during the Iron Age. A small cemetery with a stone circle and erected stones is found only 300 m south-east of the find place on a pronounced hill (Fulltofta no. 99:1). In a landscape opened by intense grazing the graves were visible from the find place. This relation resembles the relation between Sösdala and Vätteryd, where there is approx. 200 m between find place and burials. If you follow the brook two kilometres westward you come to Lake Ringsjön and a well-known cemetery at Nunnäs with about 60 graves including 9 stone ships and 2 stone circles (Fulltofta no 2:1).

Conclusion

At Sösdala finds of horse tack were made on three occasions, 1929, 1930 and 1961, all caused by gravel extraction.

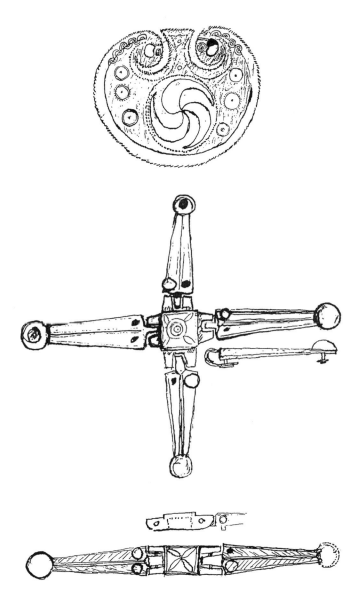

Fig. 11. Three examples of the detailed catalogue drawings of objects from Fulltofta (nos. F:1, F:2 and F:9), 2:3. Drawn in the catalogue of Historical Museum at Lund University by its director Professor Sven Söderberg 1897.

On all occasions the finds were rescued because finders talked about their finds to local persons who informed the authorities. Without any doubt much disappeared on all three occasions, and we can assume a loss of finds before 1929, between 1930 and 1961 as well as after 1961. The parade bridle from Sösdala I is almost complete, but the many saddle mounts represent possibly as many as 13 saddles, many represented by only a single mount or ring. Also the bridle

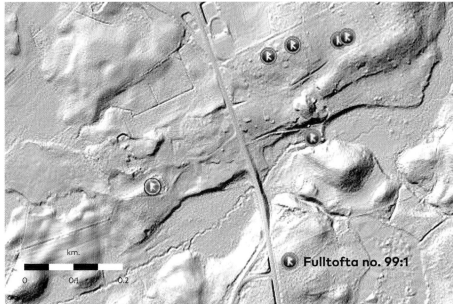

Fig. 12. Lidar map of the find place in 2014 with the Fulltofta deposition marked. On the opposite side of the brook a small cemetery is placed on a hill. © Lantmäteriet.

from Sösdala II is almost complete, but unlike the contexts of Sösdala I and Fulltofta no saddle mounts were found here. The snaffle of the Fulltofta bridle is missing and most pieces of the saddle were lost.

The first time I visited the find place at Sösdala was the spring of 1986. As is evident from a photo from the summer 1989, gravel was still being taken out of the ridge (fig. 13). A later photo reveals that 23 years later more gravel had been extracted but that the gravel pit seemed to be closed; a shed for calves had been built in the pit. A lidar map (fig. 10) from 2014 supplements the picture and shows that some 20 m of the ridge seems to have been removed since 1961.

We find the information left by Mellton 1929 trustworthy: the silver and bronze objects were not found together in one place. The workers found concentrations of bridle mounts of silver at one place and saddle mounts of bronze at another, 3 m apart (find spots I and II). During his investigation Mellton found saddle mounts at a third "find spot" 3 m east of find spot II, the only mounts found *in situ*. He concluded that the objects had been buried at three dif-

Fig. 13. The gravel pit where the Sösdala II find was made in 1961. The photo to the left records active gravel extraction in 1989. The photo to the right reveals that the pit has been enlarged but also that gravel extraction seems to have stopped in 2012. Photos Charlotte Fabech.

ferent places. Based on this information Forssander drew his sketch of the find place (fig. 8). In April the following year gravel extraction continued and a new find of saddle mounts was made in gravel slide. It is an almost complete set from one exclusive saddle. The distance from the new find place called IV to find places I and II was approx. 3 m. Since the earlier find places were dug away, the estimates are of course uncertain.

It is very uncertain whether the find spots were pits or shallow hollows. The various estimates of how deep the objects were found vary between 1 m and 1 cm. Bridles and saddles were dismantled at different places near one another. Perhaps most destroyed mounts were simply dropped at the site, but bits and pieces were also spread around on the trampled-down surface (fig. 6). It is hard to tell, since most finds, except at find spot III, were found in secondary position in gravel slides (Sösdala I find spots I and IV; Sösdala II and probably also Fulltofta). And we have almost no information about the large number of saddle mounts found at find spot II where workers rummaged the top of the ridge for treasure. What we know is that Mellton retrieved several objects when he screened loose gravel left behind by the workers and that Forssander saw a hole where the workers' treasure-hunt took place.

We do not know on what grounds Rydbeck assumed that the objects from find spot IV had been deposited at a depth of 25 cm. In the context, a letter to critical colleagues in Stockholm, it appears to be an attempt to explain away the fact that the representatives of the museum in Lund (Mellton, Källström and last but not least Forssander) missed this remarkable deposition in their investigations of the find area. The fact is that find spot IV is placed well inside an area that Forssander labelled "Investigated area" in his map (fig 8). So if Rydbeck was right, deposition IV had been dug down to a level below what was investigated in 1929, or every square metre of the "investigated area" was not searched. Based on Mellton's letters we conclude that he focused his efforts on a zone from find spot I to find spot II. He obviously became troubled when he found mounts *in situ* 3 m from find spot II (at find spot III). So possibly he stopped his investigations at a radius of 3 m from find spot II. So we suppose that much of the area north and south of find spot II was never investigated by him. What kind of investigations Forssander performed we do not know since he does not tell us in his report; we know he sketched a map that possibly makes the Lund investigations look better than they were; plausibly the dashed square "Investigated area" reflects more an archaeological convention than a reality. In 1930 Mellton made a supplementary investigation on the top of the ridge where find IV had slid down. It affected an area 5 × 10 m and went 20–30 cm down in the gravel. This supports our assumption that this area was not investigated in 1929.

The only reliable information we have about the depth of the deposited objects is Mellton's record of saddle mounts and rings at find spot III. The rings were found only a couple of centimetres down in the gravel, and the long mounts lay between 2 and 10 cm below the surface of

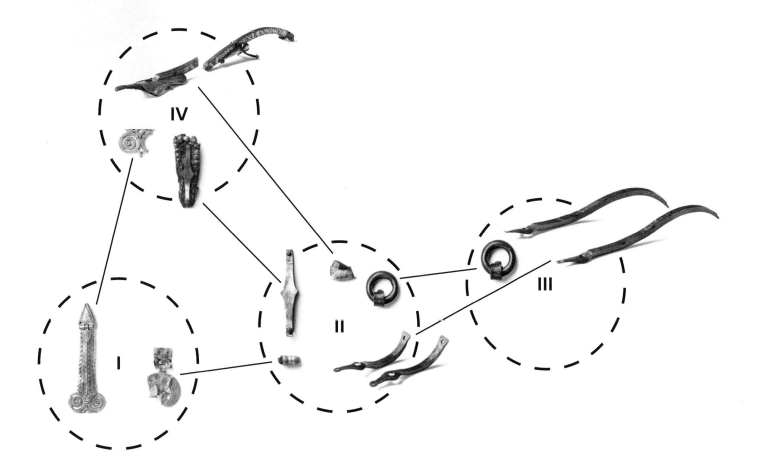

the gravel; the workers had removed vegetation layer ear-lier. This means that the finds were made less than a spade spit deep. So either the dismantled parts of a saddle were put in very shallow hollows or they were thrown directly on the naturally uneven surface of the ridge and the offering scene was then covered with gravel and stones.

What does the find distribution, as we know it, reflect? Many mounts became more or less distorted when the bridle and saddles were dismantled. Sharp tools were used to cut mounts to pieces. Other mounts were brutally broken or crushed between stones. The damage demonstrates how mounts were torn off the saddles. Stumps of leather are preserved and reveal that probably many mounts were still riveted to the leather when deposited. The destruction has nothing to do with battle damage but has similarities to the destroyed military equipment offered in lakes and bogs in South Scandinavia (Ilkjær 2000:138–139; Fabech chapter 2; Nordqvist chapter 11). Obviously it was a ritual destruction of horse tack that took place here: A bridle and many saddles were slaugh-

Fig. 14. Fragments and objects found in different "find spots" that fit fragments or objects in other find spots indicate that bits and pieces were spread over the ritual scene during the destruction of bridle and saddles. Photo montage Charlotte Fabech.

tered within an area less than 10 × 10 m. Based on decoration and shape, the objects can be dated to the early 5th century AD (Näsman chapter 7 and others in this vol.). Judging by the heavy wear and some repairs, the equipment had been in use for some years. It was not made for ritual use.

That the bridle and saddles were dismantled and deposited at one single event is supported by the way in which fragments and mounts were distributed in different find spots (fig. 14). A silver sheet was found 1929 at find spot II (no. I:176), but it once decorated a saddle mount from find spot IV (no. I:213), which was not found until 1930. Two fragments of a gilt silver pendant, according to Mellton, were found in 1930 together with saddle mounts at find

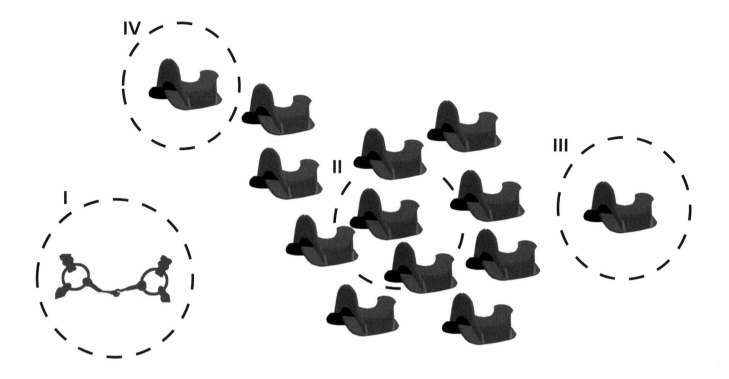

Fig. 15. The four find spots in the find area represent ritual activities that resulted in four concentrations of artefacts. Find spots I and II reflect the main activity area while find spots III and IV are peripheral. Drawing Erika Rosengren.

spot IV (no. I:238). They fit a fragmentary pendant found in 1929 at find spot I (no. I:7). Mounts and rings torn off the same saddle were found at both find spots II and III (see "Saddle 2" in Näsman chapter 7). It is our impression that during the destruction bits and pieces of horse tack were spread outside the four find spots/concentrations. Obviously we can regard the area of find spots I–IV as a single ritual scene.

The centre of the ritual scene was the two find spots/concentrations I and II where a parade bridle and many saddles were dismantled. Some parts fell more or less far off outside the "find spots". Pieces missing today can have lain in areas between the concentrations, where the workers did not notice them. Mellton told Rydbeck that the workers had dropped objects here and there around find spot II; perhaps Mellton simply observed how objects had scattered around the "slaughtering-block" (fig. 15). After

the destruction was finished the ritual was brought to an end and the scene closed by a carpet of gravel and stones, perhaps as Oscar Jönsson remembered it by a 5 × 2.5 m large setting of stones as large as a man's head (Bunte 1961 footnote 4).

This event took place in the first half of the 5th century but was not the first performed here on the ridge at Sösdala. A bridle (Sösdala II) deposited 60 m eastward on the same ridge can be dated to the end of the 4th century (Näsman chapter 7). It is a simpler bridle than the Sösdala I parade bridle and it was dismantled a generation earlier. At Fulltofta, 15 km south-west of Sösdala, a similar destruction of bridle and saddle took place. The saddle mounts have similarities to saddle mounts of "Ejsbøl type" from period Scand-C2/C3 and were probably cast before AD 400. The bridle is of higher quality than that of Sösdala II but not as exclusive as the parade bridle of Sösdala I. The bronze mounts were perhaps cast already in the Late Roman Iron Age but the bridle was upgraded in the early Migration Period by pelta-shaped silver-on-bronze covers in Sösdala style. The Fulltofta ritual event took place more or less simultaneously with that of Sösdala I. The three depositions reveal that violent and fierce

destructions form part of powerful rituals, probably of great social significance. For an attempt to understand the rituals see Fabech chapter 2.

The musealisation
– the struggle for Sösdala

Carl Mellton rescued one of the most remarkable Scandinavian finds from the Migration Period. The museum in Lund was responsible for the supplementary investigations of the find place at Sösdala. But it was not a matter of course that the objects should stay in Scania and become part of the archaeological collection in Lund. The finds from Sösdala I were extraordinary and according to the policy of the time they were to be incorporated in the collections of the national museum in Stockholm.

Only after long and hard negotiations between *Riksantikvarie* Sigurd Curman (the strong director of the history museum in Stockholm) and Professor Otto Rydbeck (director at the Historical Museum at Lund University), did the Royal Swedish Academy of Letters, History and Antiquities (KVHAA) renounce its right to have the Sösdala finds in its collections at the Swedish History Museum (SHM) in Stockholm. Several letters of both official and private character elucidate the negotiations between the parties in Lund and Stockholm; Curman and Rydbeck were seconded by two of the most prominent archaeologists of the time, T.J. Arne and J.E. Forssander (fig. 16).

The museum in Lund was founded in 1805 and is considered the second largest archaeological museum in Sweden. Headed by Professor Otto Rydbeck, when it opened in its present building in 1918 it had become one of the

Fig. 16. *The four main figures in the Sösdala musealisation drama; from the left:* Riksantikvarie *Sigurd Curman, director of the National Heritage Board in Stockholm, Professor Otto Rydbeck, director of the Historical Museum at Lund University, Mr John-Elof Forssander, Fil.Lic. and research assistant at Historical Museum at Lund University (later Dr, Professor and director of the museum), and Dr Ture J. Arne, curator at the Swedish History Museum, Stockholm. Photo Curman: A. Tuulse after Baudou 2004:242;* Rydbeck: *Akademiska föreningens arkiv,* Lund; Forssander *and* Arne: *Svenskt biografiskt lexikon.*

most modern. According to a preserved letter, Rydbeck's ambition was that the museum should not be only a university museum but should serve as the central museum of Scania. As a consequence finds from Scania ought to be kept in Lund, not in Stockholm. Now the finds from Sösdala became the touchstone of his goal.

The struggle began at the end of Forssander's report of 17 October 1929 to the *Riksantikvarie* about the investigations at Sösdala. After Forssander's signature he added, on behalf of Rydbeck: "On behalf of the Historical Museum [in Lund] I hereby ask that the find in its entirety be added to the collections of the museum".

An answer followed on 8 November 1929 in a letter from Sigurd Curman to Otto Rydbeck, which was a formal letter from the *Riksantikvarie* to the Director of the Historical Museum at Lund University. In it Rydbeck could read that the objects found at Sösdala seemed to be of such a character that they should be offered to SHM in Stockholm for redemption, and that the find was of great scholarly value. The question of redemption would be decided by the executive committee of KVHAA. For these reasons the *Riksantikvarie* requested that the find in its entirety be sent to SHM.

Simultaneously with this official and very formal letter, private correspondence took place between Forssander and Olle Källström, who now was research assistant at the History Museum in Stockholm. Here they expressed themselves in blunt and unvarnished sentences that could not be used in official letters. On 13 November Källström wrote a letter to Forssander about sentiments and opinions at the centre of heritage management in Sweden, i.e. the *Riksantikvarie* in Stockholm. The staff at the central museum was indignant with the behaviour of Rydbeck and Forssander, deploring their lack of etiquette. "Here it is the opinion that it is the director who should sign a request that the find should be given to Lund. An excavation report can be signed by the official who did the fieldwork, but it is a museum affair to begin negotiations about the acquisition right. Perhaps you find this formalistic. But for comparison I may mention that even the blind O. Almgren [professor of archaeology at Uppsala University] himself signs all his letters to the *Riksantikvarie*, written by others. [Other prominent scholars like] von Frisen, Wessén, Sune Lindqvist, etc. do the same."

Rydbeck wrote a reply to the *Riksantikvarie* on 5 December and wondered whether it really was necessary to send all the many objects to Stockholm; objects could be damaged, photos of all objects were sent to Stockholm and the finds had already been examined by Rune Norberg, the expert in this field at SHM.

He adds that if the *Riksantikvarie*, in spite of Rydbeck's arguments, insists on his request that the entire find be sent to Stockholm, it can only be the objects of precious metal. Objects of bronze and iron do not fall under the jurisdiction of the Academy (KVHAA), and since from a scholarly point of view it must be out of the question to divide such a find between Lund and Stockholm, he asks whether the question cannot be settled without sending half the find to Stockholm.

Finally Rydbeck complains that the out-of-date ancient monuments law of 1867 was to blame for the fact that the museum in Lund has a relatively insignificant collection of artefacts from the Iron Age. Almost all finds of gold or silver found in Scania were incorporated in the collections of the History Museum in Stockholm. So in his opinion these arguments should make the *Riksantikvarie* consider leaving the Sösdala find to Lund without sending it to Stockholm first. But if this does not happen, he will dutifully send to Stockholm that part of the find over which the Academy has authority, i.e. the finds of silver.

In private correspondence between Källström and Rydbeck, the latter explained on 28 January 1930 why he did not want to send the find to Stockholm. It was not because he feared that the find would remain in Stockholm, but a reaction against the unnecessary formalism in the *Riksantikvarie*'s request. Obviously he now saw a possibility to get out of a situation which had come to a deadlock, and be able to act as a generous director of the research institution and central museum of Scania. So he wrote that he understood that Stockholm was interested in the find also from a scholarly point of view and of course that entailed a study of the find in its entirety. So Rydbeck wrote to Källström that he had changed his mind. The whole find was sent to the *Riksantikvarie* the next day.

Letters from March 1930 between Rydbeck, Curman and Arne reveal that Curman, in an attempt to reach an amicable solution, asked Rydbeck whether an exchange could take place: the Sösdala find in exchange for a find now in the collections of SHM. Rydbeck was not willing to renounce Sösdala, but instead of rejecting the *Riksantikvarie*'s proposal outright, he pretended to negotiate with the museum in Stockholm. His offer was to exchange Sösdala for a 12th century sarcophagus from Löderup, Scania, richly decorated with reliefs (SHM no. 16 100). Since the museum in Stockholm did not answer, he concluded that his proposal was unacceptable. So now he suggested an exchange with a Migration Period neck ring of gold from Skabersjö (fig. 17) plus a Bronze Age find that could illustrate contacts between Sweden and the Continent. He asked for a find from Fjälkinge (SHM no. 12 525) containing a couple of gold rings and bronze axes from England, Italy and Sweden. He realised that this wish probably would not be fulfilled, so he asked for other equivalent offers to choose between.

An answer came from the museum in Stockholm in the form of a private letter from Arne. Acting like a merchant, he tried to persuade Rydbeck to accept an exchange with the Skabersjö ring alone. Rydbeck was told that in Arne's opinion the gold ring was of higher value than the Sösdala find and that it would stand out splendidly in a museum with so few gold objects. The offer to exchange Sösdala for Skabersjö was so good, according to Arne, that Rydbeck was unwise if he did not accept it.

Rydbeck answered Arne promptly. It was not Rydbeck's proposal to barter Sösdala for something else. His offers were only meant to demonstrate compliance on the part of the museum in Lund. The museum preferred to keep the Sösdala find. So his clear message was: The Historical Museum at Lund University has requested to keep the Sösdala find in Lund.

At a meeting on 6 May 1930 the Royal Academy discussed the question of whether the Sösdala find should be redeemed. The Academy found the character of the find to be such that it should be offered to SHM, but considering the circumstances the Academy had decided that it would waive its rights. Arne had it recorded in the minutes of the Academy that he had a dissenting opinion. In the minutes we can read that after his remark: "Mr Arne rose and departed."

Obviously Curman had changed his mind and contrary to his staff he accepted the request that the Sösdala find become part of the archaeological collection in Lund. Curman did not yield to Rydbeck out of weakness; his decision rather expresses his ambition and intuition to achieve superior goals. In these years he was working hard to reform the antiquarian system of Sweden and wished to integrate archaeology in the cultural policy of the Swedish state (Baudou 2004:241–246). Intuitively he understood that if he was to succeed in reorganising the management of the national heritage, the county museums and the central Swedish History Museum, he could not afford a conflict with the museums, politicians and university in Scania. Cooperation was necessary.

Rydbeck's letters show how he too worked for a change of the old-fashioned ancient monuments law. He conferred with the influential politician Karl Schlyter, member of *Riksdagen* (social democrat), president of the court of appeal of Blekinge and Scania (1929–1946) and Minister of Justice (1932–1936). Rydbeck told him that he feared that the centralistic thinking in Stockholm would prevail forever regardless of a reformed ancient monuments law;

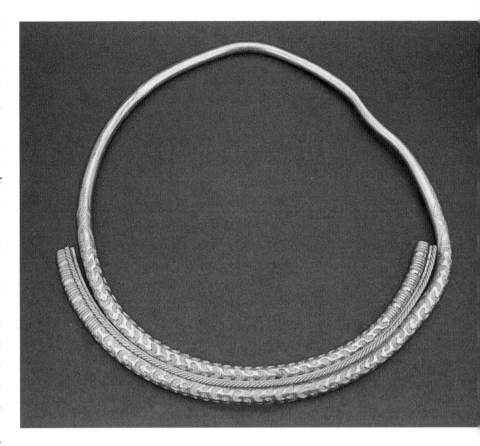

Fig. 17. A neck ring of gold from the Migration Period. Found at Skabersjö in Scania, it was used in the haggling over Sösdala between the museums in Lund and Stockholm. ©Swedish History Museum, photo Ulf Bruxe, SHM no. 13 651.

he argued that LUHM should be give a status equivalent to that of SHM in Stockholm.

After the Sösdala find was given to LUHM the matter was peacefully settled. But the decision of the Academy did not form a precedent; important Scanian finds still went to Stockholm, a couple of examples near the Sösdala find place: Göingeholm (Arne 1937) and Vätteryd (Strömberg 1961). A remark in a paper by Rydbeck (1943:43) about archaeological research at the Historical Museum makes it clear that equal status between Lund and Stockholm was not yet attained. "In the back a showcase was placed that contained finds of early Migration Period depositions, among which one notes the very remarkable offering from Sösdala 16, N Mellby parish, with its wealth of horse tack, mounts of bridles and saddles of bronze, silver and gold.

Fig. 18. Rune Norberg, curator at the Swedish History Museum, Stockholm, was the first to publish finds from Sösdala. Copyright the National Heritage Board, Stockholm.

Only after much trouble with the central authorities could the find be added to the Lund collection". He continued with a complaint about how Scanian gold finds ended up in SHM in Stockholm.

The publication of finds from Sösdala and Fulltofta

As early as July 1929 Otto Rydbeck made up his mind: he entrusted Rune Norberg (fig. 18) to publish the find of bridle and saddle mounts made just a month before at Sösdala. Norberg was research assistant at the Swedish History Museum in Stockholm, and in that capacity he had in 1927 catalogued and in 1929 published Migration Period saddle mounts found in Kanalgatan, Jönköping, Småland (Norberg 1929a,b). So he was undoubtedly the most knowledgeable in Sweden about ancient horse tack. Norberg studied the new finds at the museum in Lund and accepted Rydbeck's offer with enthusiasm. The Fulltofta find of a fragmentary bridle and mounts of a saddle was not part of the deal.

From February 1930 the entire Sösdala find was in Stockholm and Norberg had free access to study the objects. New finds were made in April 1930 and sent to Stockholm on 25 June. In an accompanying letter Rydbeck wrote to the *Riksantikvarie*: "Research assistant R. Norberg was promised soon after the find was made [in 1929] that he could publish the find; this promise is still valid. … If Norberg for some reason is prevented from publishing the find, it seems to me most proper that LUHM should make the arrangements for its publication." This indicates that Rydbeck was not absolutely sure that Norberg could accomplish the task and obviously he considered the possibility that someone else in Stockholm could be interested in taking over – Arne? In August Norberg wrote to Rydbeck that he had almost finished his study of the find and would do his best to prove trustworthy. But he added: "It is not every day that the material for a licentiate thesis becomes more than doubled – both quantitatively and qualitatively – by a single find complex." Here we notice for the first time a clash of interests; on one side we have Rydbeck's and LUHM's wish to get the Sösdala find published for a national and international scholarly public, on the other we have Norberg's ambition to get a university degree based on a licentiate thesis about all finds of offerings from the Migration Period in Scania.

Remains of a bridle and a saddle from Fulltofta were given to LUHM already in 1896 but were still unpublished when Norberg mentioned the saddle mount in his first paper about saddles (1929a:16). It appears that he had not studied it closely and he characterised it (erroneously) as a bog find. In his next paper he published a photo of the saddle mount and in a footnote he mentions that a new find had been made at Sösdala with magnificent mounts of bronze and silver (1929b:106–107, fig. 14, footnote 25). Two years later Norberg presented the Sösdala and Fulltofta finds in a short paper in German about Migration Period bog finds and hoards in Scania. Interestingly he noted that the two finds were made in gravel hills and questioned their affiliation to bog finds, but did not elaborate on the problem (Norberg 1931:111).

He defended his licentiate thesis at the archaeological department of Uppsala University (Norberg 1933). It was entitled (in Swedish) "Scanian offering finds from the Migration Period". According to his bibliography, the thesis was duplicated but never printed (Liivrand 1978), and unfortunately we have been unable to trace a copy (evidently the archaeological department discarded most old licentiate theses). So we do not know his results but can be certain that the finds from Sösdala and Fulltofta were discussed. Norberg published nothing more about the Scanian Migration Period finds. Forssander did so in 1937 (see Näsman chapter 5). He respected Norberg's publication plans, however, and published only general descriptions and a few photos. With the exception of a review of the Snartemo publication in 1937, Norberg published only papers on high and late medieval subjects for the rest of his career.

A few letters are preserved from a voluminous correspondence between Norberg and Forssander between 1942 and the sudden death of the latter in 1944; after that Norberg exchanged letters with Mårten Stenberger, Forssander's replacement. Norberg's letters are a reiterated story about lack of support, money and time. His daily duties as curator at SHM and serious family problems made it impossible for him to finish his study of "the unhappy offering finds". But the story is also about different goals. The museum in Lund would have been content with a long paper about the Sösdala find in *Meddelanden från Lunds Universitets Historiska Museum*: find history, content, dating, reconstructions, etc. Norberg had larger ambitions than a straightforward material publication. In his opinion the deal was that he should publish Sösdala in a comprehensive study including other South Swedish offering finds and put Sösdala into a large culture-historical frame – a monograph that he called (in Swedish) "The Scanian offering finds of the 5th century AD". His ambition was supported by Sune Lindqvist, his professor of archaeology at Uppsala University, who encouraged him to write a doctoral thesis. The thesis would be a "modernisation" of his licentiate thesis from 1933. Norberg wrote that he was happy it remained unpublished because he had changed his opinion about several important questions since 1933 and he expected to get more new ideas before he finished the doctoral thesis.

In May 1944 Stenberger insisted that Norberg had to send an account of the work he had done before he could

Disposition daterad 21/5 1944

R. Norberg: De skånska offerfynden från 400:talet e.Kr.

Inledning

Avd. I:

✓ 1 Offerfynd från jää utom Norden

✓ 2 Offerfynd från jää i Danmark

✓ 3 Offerfynd från jää i Södra Sverige

Avd. II: De skånska offerfynden

    1 Skåne c:a 350-500

✓ 2 Hassle-Bösarp

✓ 3 Sösdala

✓ 4 Fulltofta

✓ 5 Onslunda

✓ 6 Sjörup

✓ 7 Smärre fynd

    8 Förh. & nutida skånska fynd etc.

Avd. III:

✓ 1 Stilstudier (prov.romerskt – nordiskt, uppkomst av stil I)

✓ 2 Formstudier (hästutstyrsel, vapen)

✓ 3 Fyndomständigheterna

✓ 4 Offerfyndens innebörd

✓ 5 Dateringsfrågor

Avd. IV: Sammanfattning (även incl. ett försök att klarlägga en del av Vendelkulturens rötter i 400-talet)

————

✓ Forskningsarbetet klart. Betr. II 3, 4, 7 återstår kontroll av uppgifter (material, mått etc.).

Fig. 19. Fair copy of the handwritten outline of Rune Norberg's planned doctoral thesis. In a letter of 21 May 1944 to Professor Mårten Stenberger.

receive the requested payment from a research foundation. Norberg's answer was to send an outline of his planned thesis to Stenberger (fig. 19). He explained that he almost had finished his research. Forssander had promised to help him to supplement his material for *Avd.* II ch. 1 and 8, but for natural reasons (Forssander's unexpected death) he had not written the two chapters. That work would be financed by the money he had applied for. According to his application he also planned to visit the most important find places in Scania to photograph and map them. When he had finished this work, the grant he had requested would be consumed. Then all that remained was to edit the manuscript and have fair copies of manuscript and drawings made, etc. He should be able to clear off that in about six weeks.

He asks Stenberger whether a manuscript existed of Forssander's planned publication about the Iron Age in Scania. If not, everything had to be done from the beginning. After Forssander became professor of archaeology at Lund University his interest in Iron Age research had grown. When he suddenly died he was busy with a comprehensive study of the Iron Age in Scania from 400 to 1000 (Althin 1944:45–47). Stenberger had to disappoint Norberg that no such a manuscript had been left by Forssander; a short cut was closed.

It seems surprising that Norberg stated that he could finish his doctoral thesis within six weeks but was unable to enclose samples of his manuscript. It is hard not to get the impression that Norberg had no finished text, still 15 years after he first saw the Sösdala find in Lund. How Stenberger acted we do not know. The last we hear from Norberg and his thesis is that he told Stenberger at the end of the letter "that the whole thing is going fairly well and that is not too early". The rest is silence.

After this letter in 1944 and until his death in 1977 Norberg published more than 100 papers on mainly late medieval church art and secular material culture (Liivrand 1978). But nothing about Sösdala or Fulltofta. He never finished his thesis, and the unfortunate consequence is that the two finds never became as important for Migration Period research as they deserve. Fulltofta was more or less forgotten and Sösdala became eponymous for the Sösdala style and bound to Iron Age style studies (Karlsson 1983:163; Bitner-Wróblewska chapter 12; Näsman chapter 5). The name of Sösdala became more famous than the objects found,

and they sank into oblivion. Norberg's reconstruction of a saddle based on the mounts from Kanalgatan (Norberg 1929a fig. 14) came to represent the Sösdala saddles as well.

The funding of studies for a doctoral degree in the 1930s was very limited and economic problems were a serious obstacle for Norberg. His ambition to write a doctoral thesis about all Scanian finds blocked the publication of a paper about Sösdala alone. Now many years later it is a wonder that Norberg's right to publish Sösdala was respected so long and that several scholars refrained from entering deeply into the study of the Sösdala artefacts. As late as 1951 Wilhelm Holmqvist discussed saddle mounts with silver inlays from Sösdala and explained his short presentation with reference to Norberg's planned thesis (1951:111).

In a review of Helmut Geisslinger's dissertation *Horte als Geschichtsquelle* (Hoards as a source of history), Ulf Erik Hagberg praised him for publishing excellent photos of the Sösdala finds "which we Swedes never could agree to publish" (1969). Hagberg refers to nine plates which depict all objects from Sösdala I (Geisslinger 1967 Taf. 10–18). But the catalogue text is very short, there is no verbal description attached to the depicted artefacts, nor can one find a discussion of their function. You will find no reference from his numbering of objects on the plates to the numbers in Forssander's catalogue. The photos are not used at all by Geisslinger in his argumentation about how to interpret the *Horte*. One wonders whether he had other plans when he ordered the photos to be taken in Lund 1965.

So the Sösdala find remained like Fulltofta, in reality unpublished till this day. In several publications you will find the name Sösdala as a dot on distribution maps or you will see one or two photos of the most well-known mounts reproduced over and over again with only short descriptions of find and site. Finally, a full publication is now available.

References

Althin, C.-A. 1944. John-Elof Forssander: in memoriam. *Fornvännen* 39: 45–47.

Arne, T.J. 1937 Ett skånskt fynd från folkvandringstiden. [Göingeholm]. In: *Från stenålder till rokoko. Studier tillägnade Otto Rydbeck*. Lund: 81–95.

Baudou, E. 2004. *Den nordiska arkeologin – historia och tolkningar*. Stockholm.

Bunte, C. 1961. A New Bridle Find from Sösdala. *Meddelanden från Lunds universitets historiska museum* 1961: 194–207.

Fabech, C. 1991. Neue Perspektiven zu den Funden von Sösdala und Fulltofta. *Studien zur Sachsenforschung* 7: 121-135.

Forssander, J.-E. 1937. Provinzialrömisches und germanisches. Stilstudien zu den schonischen Funden von Sösdala und Sjörup. *Kungl. humanistiska vetenskapssamfundet i Lund. Årsberättelse* 1936–37: 183–272 (also in *Meddelanden från Lunds universitets historiska museum* 8: 11–100).

Geisslinger, H. 1967. *Horte als Geschichtsquelle*. Neumünster.

Hagberg, U.E. 1969. Anmälan av Helmut Geisslinger 1967, Horte als Geschichtsquelle. *Fornvännen* 1969/1: 47–48.

Holmqvist, W. 1951. *Tauschierte Metallarbeiten des Nordens aus Römerzeit und Völkerwanderung*. Stockholm.

Ilkjær, J. 2000. *Illerup Ådal – archaeology as a magic mirror*. Højbjerg.

Karlsson, L. 1983. *Nordisk form, om djurornamentik*. Stockholm. Summary pp. 178–189: *Nordic Form – on Animal Ornament*.

Liivrand, L. 1978. Rune Norbergs skrifter 1925–1977. *Fornvännen* 73/1: 25–38.

Norberg, R. 1929a. Ett folkvandringstidsfynd från Jönköping. *Meddelanden från Norra Smålands Fornminnesförening* 9: 5–24. Zusammenfassung.

Norberg, R. 1929b. Om förhistoriska sadlar i Sverige. *Rig* 12: 97–113.

Norberg, R. 1931. Moor- und Depotfunde aus dem 5. Jahrhundert nach Chr. in Schonen. *Acta Archaeologica* 2: 104–111.

Norberg, R. 1933. *Skånes offerfynd från folkvandringstiden*. Licentiate thesis in archaeology at Uppsala University [unpublished/duplicated/missing].

Rydbeck, O. 1943. Den arkeologiska forskningen och historiska muséet vid Lunds universitet under tvåhundra år, 1735–1937. *Meddelanden från Lunds Universitets Historiska Museum* 1943: 1–129.

Strömberg, Märta 1961. *Untersuchungen zur jüngeren Eisenzeit in Schonen 1–2*. Lund.

Letters and other unpublished document studied for this publication:

No.	Date	Sender	Addressee	Archive
1	11-06-1929	Olle Källström	Finders of objects	LUHM
2	12-06-1929	Olle Källström	Sigurd Curman	LUHM
3	14-06-1929	Sigurd Curman	Otto Rydbeck	LUHM
4	24-06-1929	Carl Mellton	Otto Rydbeck	LUHM
5	22-07-1929	Otto Rydbeck	Sune Lindqvist	LUHM
6	21-08-1929	Olle Källström	H. Ebbeson	LUHM
7	17-10-1929	J.E. Forssander	Sigurd Curman	LUHM
8	08-11-1929	Sigurd Curman	Otto Rydbeck	LUHM
9	13-11-1929	Olle Källström	J.E. Forssander	LUHM
10	05-12-1929	Otto Rydbeck	Sigurd Curman	LUHM
11	10-01-1930	Otto Rydbeck	Karl Schlyter	LUHM
12	20-01-1930	Carl Mellton	J.E. Forssander	LUHM
13	27-01-1930	Otto Rydbeck	Olle Källström	LUHM
14	28-01-1930	Otto Rydbeck	Olle Källström	LUHM
15	29-01-1930	Otto Rydbeck	Riksantikvarien	LUHM
16	13-02-1930	Carl Mellton	Otto Rydbeck	LUHM
17	27-02-1930	Otto Rydbeck	Sigurd Curman	ATA
18	10-03-1930	Otto Rydbeck	Sigurd Curman	LUHM
19	17-03-1930	T.J. Arne	Otto Rydbeck	LUHM

No.	Date	Sender	Addressee	Archive
20	18-03-1930	Otto Rydbeck	T.J. Arne	LUHM
21	06-04-1930	Otto Rydbeck	Sigurd Curman	ATA
22	13-04-1930	Carl Mellton	Otto Rydbeck	LUHM
23	03-05-1930	Otto Rydbeck	Sigurd Curman	ATA
24	04-05-1930	Otto Rydbeck	T.J. Arne	ATA
25	06-05-1930	Otto Rydbeck	Sigurd Curman	ATA
26	06-05-1930	Excerpt of KVHAA minutes	The Sösdala find is given to LUHM	LUHM
27	07-05-1930	Otto Rydbeck	Sigurd Curman	LUHM
28	25-06-1930	Otto Rydbeck	Riksantikvarien	LUHM
29	26-06-1930	Olsson	SHM	LUHM
30a	15-08-1930	Olle Källström	LUHM	LUHM
30b	15-08-1930	Olle Källström	LUHM	LUHM
31	20-08-1930	Rune Norberg	Otto Rydbeck	LUHM
32	13-09-1930	Otto Rydbeck	Sigurd Curman	ATA
33	17-09-1930	Otto Frödin	Otto Rydbeck	LUHM
34	13-10-1930	Carl Mellton	Otto Rydbeck	LUHM
35	15-10-1930	Carl Mellton	Otto Rydbeck	LUHM
36	26-01-1931	Otto Rydbeck	T.J. Arne	LUHM
37	11-09-1961	Carin Bunte	National Heritage Board	LUHM
38	21-01-1942	Rune Norberg	J.E. Forssander	LUHM
39	13-02-1943	Rune Norberg	J.E. Forssander	LUHM
40	28-02-1943	Rune Norberg	J.E. Forssander	LUHM
41	13-03-1944	Rune Norberg	Mårten Stenberger	LUHM
42	13-04-1944	Rune Norberg	Mårten Stenberger	LUHM
43	17-04-1944	Mårten Stenberger	Rune Norberg	LUHM
44	??-04-1944	Rune Norberg	Mårten Stenberger	LUHM
45	19-05-1944	Mårten Stenberger	Rune Norberg	LUHM
46	21-05-1944	Rune Norberg	Mårten Stenberger	LUHM
47	??-05-1944	Rune Norberg	Mårten Stenberger	LUHM
48	03-02-1965	Helmut Geisslinger	Holger Arbman	LUHM
49	31-03-1965	Helmut Geisslinger	Märta Strömberg	LUHM

Резюме

Находки из Сёсдалы и Фультофты: история спасения, музеефикации и забвения

Шарлотта Фабек

Подобно многим археологическим открытиям, находки в Сёсдале были сделаны рабочими, добывавшими гравий (рис. 2). И, подобно многим другим находчикам, рабочие думали, что нашли клад. Случайность в том, что «клад» этот не исчез, подобно многим другим находкам доисторического времени. Случайность в том, что учитель местной начальной школы Карл Мельтон (1886–1940 гг.) интересовался археологией и историей (рис. 1). Он сразу же понял ценность находок и взял на себя ответственность за ситуацию и сами вещи (рис. 3–5). Кроме того, он связался с Историческим музеем Лундского университета (ИМЛУ). Мельтон не только сохранил находки для потомков, но и сообщил в музей об условиях находки в письменном виде с приложением фотографий и обмеров (рис. 6). В результате мы можем обсуждать не только вещи из этого важнейшего комплекса, но и вопрос о том, почему уздечки и седла были разломаны, а их фрагменты оказались на вершине гравийной гряды близ Сёсдалы (рис. 7). Элементы конской сбруи обнаруживали трижды, в 1929, 1930 и 1961 гг., всякий раз в результате добычи гравия. Находки можно датировать концом IV – началом V вв. н. э. Место находки находится в центральной Скании (рис. 2).

Сёсдала I, 1929–1930 гг., ИМЛУ, № 25 570.

Серебряные и бронзовые предметы из Сёсдалы I не были найдены одновременно и в одном месте. Рабочие обнаружили, что серебряные уздечные зажимы были сосредоточены в одном месте, а бронзовые оковки седел – в другом, на расстоянии 3 м (пункты I и II). Проводивший исследование Мельтон обнаружил оковки седел в новой точке, в 3 м от пункта II, – это были единственные вещи, обнаруженные *in situ*. На основании этой информации Форссандер выполнил зарисовку места находок (рис. 8). В апреле 1930 г. во время продолжавшейся выемки гравия из завала была найдена очередная группа седельных оковок в пункте IV (рис. 9). Это практически полный набор фурнитуры для одного богатого седла.

Многие вещи получили большие или меньшие повреждения, когда узду и седла разламывали на части. Очевидно, в этом месте происходило ритуальное повреждение конской упряжи, причем узда и несколько седел были разломаны на площади менее чем 10х10 м.

Узда и седла были разломаны и археологизированы в результате одного события – это подтверждается тем, что их фрагменты оказались в разных местах (рис. 14). Очевидно, зону находок I–IV можно считать ареной одной ритуальной сцены. Центром обряда были два места (зоны концентрации) находок (пункты I и II), где были уничтожены парадная узда и несколько седел (рис. 15). Находки залегали на глубине менее чем в штык лопаты. Таким образом, либо детали разломанных седел сложили в очень неглубокие углубления, или их попросту бросили на естественную неровную поверхность гравийной гряды. После того, как все вещи были сломаны, ритуал подошел к концу и его место скрылось под ковром из гравия и камней.

Сёсдала II, 1961 г., ИМЛУ, № 32 492

Произошедшее в первой половине V в. событие было не первым, случившимся на гравийной гряде в Сёсдале. В конце августа 1961 г. в 60 м к востоку, на той же гряде была найдена еще одна узда, получившая название «Сёсдала II». Ее можно датировать концом IV в. (рис. 10). Она проще, чем парадная узда комплекса Сёсдала I, и была разломана поколением раньше. К тому же, хотя узда из Сёсдалы II сохранилась почти полностью, здесь, в отличие от контекстов Сёсдалы I и Фультофты, не были найдены оковки седел.

Во всех трех случаях многие вещи, несомненно, были утрачены, к тому же можно думать, что какие-то артефакты исчезли до 1929 г., между 1930 и 1961 гг., а также после 1961 г. Фотография (рис. 13) и съемка с помощью лазерного дальномера 2014 г. (рис. 10) показывают, что после 1961 г. исчезло около 20 м гравийной гряды.

Находки в Фультофте, 1896 г., ИМЛУ, № 14 080

В 15 км к юго-западу от Сёсдалы, в Фультофте, открыто место, где точно также были разломаны узды и седла (рис. 11, 12). Эта менее известная находка конской сбруи сделана местным рабочим в 1896 г., также во время разработки гравия. Находчик передал находки своему хозяину, который передал их в Лундский музей. Там их без обсуждений включили в состав коллекции. Хотя Руне Норберг хотел использовать вещи из Фультофты в своей публикации, этого сделано не было. Оковки седла близки седельным оковкам типа «Айсбёль» периода C2/C3 скандинавской хронологии – вероятно, они были сделаны до рубежа IV–V вв. Качество исполнения узды выше, чем находки в Сёсдале II, но не настолько выдающееся, как парадная узда из Сёсдалы I. Здесь нет удил, а большая часть деталей седла утрачена. Оковки и накладки из литой бронзы были, вероятно, изготовлены в Позднеримское время, причем узду переделали в начале Эпохи переселения народов, добавив к ней серебряные пельтовидные пластины в стиле «Сёсдала». В Фультофте ритуальные действия совершили более или менее одновременно с обрядом в Сёсдале I. Три анализируемых комплекса показывают, что жестокое и безжалостное уничтожение вещей было частью обрядов власти, вероятно, имевших большое общественное значение (попытка интерпретации этих ритуалов представлена в другой статье автора в этом томе).

Музеефикация – борьба за Сёсдалу

Однако не случайно то, что сегодня эти вещи являются частью коллекции Лундского музея, а не центрального Шведского исторического музея в Стокгольме. Это объясняется теми огромными усилиями, которые приложили профессор Отто Рюдбекк (1872–1954 гг.), директор Лундского музея, и научный сотрудник Йон-Элоф Форссандер (1904–1944 гг.) для сохранения находок в Скании. Эта история рассказывает, что их оппонент – *Riksantikvarie* (глава Совета по национальному наследию) Сигурд Курман (1879–1966 гг.) имел возможность отбросить краткосрочные цели ради дальновидных стратегических интересов. Курман начал работу по организации системы управления национальным наследием в 1923 г., а в 1938 г. возглавил Совет по национальному наследию. Происходившие драматические события можно восстановить по частично сохранившимся письмам, раскрывающим ситуацию в музеях Швеции в 20-е – 30-е гг. XX в. (рис. 16, 17).

Публикация находок из Сёсдалы и Фультофты

С того самого июньского дня 1929 г., когда в гравийном карьере блеснули вещи из позолоченного серебра, проведшие полторы тысячи лет в полной темноте, внимание и интерес к находкам из Сёсдалы не ослабевает. Уже в июле Отто Рюдбекк решил поручить издание находок из Сёсдалы Руне Норбергу (1906–1977 гг.). Это решение было очевидным, ведь Норберг (рис. 18), будучи научным сотрудником Шведского исторического музея в Стокгольме, составил каталог подобных обкладок седел, найденных в 1927 г. в Канальгатане (Йёнчёпинг, Смоланд). Кроме того, он опубликовал две статьи о седлах (Norberg 1929a, b). Ясно, что он лучше других исследователей представлял себе эту тему. Предложение было принято, но обещания своего Норберг не сдержал (рис. 19).

Подписи к иллюстрациям

Рис. 1. Карл Меллтон, 1886-1940 г. Фото студии Херман Пиил, Хесслехольм.

Рис. 2. Места находок в Сёсдале и Фультофте, расположенные неподалеку друг от друга, в центральной Скании.

Рис. 3. Археолог Олле Чельстрём и неизвестный молодой человек расчищают гравий в карьере близ Сёсдалы. Фото Карла Мельтона, 11 июня 1929 г.

Рис. 4. На фотографии Карла Мельтона – узда и оковки седла, которые он получил от рабочих. Фото 11 июня 1929 г.

Рис. 5. Вещи, обнаруженные Карлом Мельтоном в результате просеивания гравия в пункте II; отметим, что именно при просеивании найдена большая оковка седла. Фото Карла Мельтона, июнь 1929 г.

Рис. 6. Выполненные Карлом Мельтоном фото и обмеры оковок седла и подпружных колец, найденных in situ в пункте III 21 июня 1929 г. Положение длинных оковок показывает, что в момент археологизации они по-прежнему были прикреплены к кожаному чехлу седла.

Рис. 7. Место находки на гравийной гряде в Сёсдале вид с севера. Фото Йона-Элофа Форссандера, июль 1929 г.

Рис. 8. На рисунке Йона-Элофа Форссандера 1929 г. представлена территория вокруг гравийной гряды в Сёсдале, с указанием зоны исследований, а также мест, где были сделаны находки, отмеченных пунктами I, II и III. В 1930 г. Отто Рюдбекк добавил место находок IV.

Рис. 9. Вещи, найденные рабочими 9 апреля 1930 г. в пункте IV: оковки седел и подпружные кольца с инкрустацией серебром; слева – два фрагмента из позолоченного серебра, соединяющиеся с подвеской, найденной в пункте I; в верхнем левом углу – обрывок кожаного ремня с серебряным держателем и заклепками с серебряными колпачками. Фото Карла Мельтона, 9/13 апреля 1930 г.

Рис. 10. Съемка места находок с помощью лазерного дальномера в 2014 г. с указанием пунктов, где были обнаружены находки Сёсдалы I (1929–1930 г.) и Сёсдалы II (1961 г.). Карта ясно показывает, что значительная часть гравийной гряды, где были сделаны эти две находки, ныне срыта. Съемка с помощью лазерного дальномера, 2014 г., © Lantmäteriet.

Рис. 11. Три примера подробных рисунков в каталоге, на которых изображены находки из Фультофты. Рисунки из каталога Исторического музея Лундского университета, подготовленного его директором профессором Свеном Сёдербергом, 1897 г.

Рис. 12. Съемка места, где были найдены вещи из Фультофты, с помощью лазерного дальномера. На противоположной стороне ручья – небольшое кладбище на вершине холма. © Lantmäteriet.

Рис. 13. Гравийный карьер, где в 1961 г. была сделана находка Сёсдала II. На фотографии слева показаны работы по добыче щебня, которые велись в 1989 г. На фотографии справа видно, что размеры карьера увеличились, однако добыча щебня, кажется, прекратилась в 2012 г. Фото Шарлотты Фабек.

Рис. 14. Фрагменты и целые вещи, обнаруженные в разных пунктах, соединяющиеся с фрагментами и целыми вещами из других пунктов, показывают, что удила и другие детали разбрасывались по территории, где происходил обряд, в процессе уничтожения узды и седел. Фотомонтаж Шарлотты Фабек.

Рис. 15. Четыре пункта в зоне находок являются свидетельствами ритуалов, в результате которых образовались четыре зоны концентрации вещей. Пункты I и II указывают основную зону обрядовых действий, тогда как пункты III и IV находятся на периферии. Чертеж Эрики Росенгрен.

Рис. 16. Четыре основных участника драматичной истории с музеефикацией Сёсдалы. Слева направо: Riksantikvarie Сигурд Курман, директор Совета по национальному наследию (Стокгольм); профессор Отто Рюдбекк, директор Исторического музея Лундского университета; г-н Йон-Элоф Форссандер, лиценциат, научный сотрудник Исторического музея Лундского университета (позднее – доктор наук, профессор, директор этого музея); доктор Туре Й. Арне, куратор Шведского исторического музея (Стокгольм). Фото Svenskt biografiskt lexikon.

Рис. 17. Золотая гривна Эпохи переселения народов. Эту находку из Скабершё в Скании использовали в споре Лундского и Стокгольмского музеев по вопросу о вещах из Сёсдалы. Фото Ульфа Брюксе (Шведский исторический музей, № 13 651).

Рис. 18. Руне Норберг, куратор Шведского исторического музея в Стокгольме, был первым издателем находок из Сёсдалы. © Совет по национальному наследию (Стокгольм).

Рис. 19. Черновик рукописного плана-проспекта докторской диссертации Руне Норберга. Из письма профессору Мортену Стенбергеру от 21 мая 1944 г.

Chapter 2

Sösdala and Fulltofta: the ritual depositions

Charlotte Fabech

A study of the horse tack found at Sösdala I reveals that a complex ritual destruction of bridle and saddles took place before deposition. The find spot is situated on top of a gravel ridge near the Vätteryd cemetery. An earlier deposition Sösdala II was discovered nearby and a contemporary deposition was made in a gravel hill at Fulltofta 15 km south of Sösdala. The best parallel to the Sösdala I bridle is not found in Scandinavia, but far away at Kačin in Ukraine. Both Kačin and Sösdala belong to a group of exclusive bridle finds, which characterise the superregional warrior elite that developed in the early Migration Period. The two finds are constituents of the material culture of peoples living in central and Eastern Europe, exemplified by bridles from Untersiebenbrunn, Jakuszowice, Kačin, Bar, and Coşoveni. Striking similarities between the Sösdala find circumstances and those of Nomadic funeral depositions open for an interpretation of the Scanian finds as depositions following funerary rituals.

Fabech, C. 2017. Sösdala and Fulltofta: the ritual depositions. In: Fabech, C. & Näsman, U. (eds). *The Sösdala horsemen – and the equestrian elite of fifth century Europe.* Jutland Archaeological Society.

Near Sösdala in central Scania extraordinary finds of horse tack were made during gravel extraction in 1929 and again in 1930 (Fabech chapter 1). The finds are labelled Sösdala I and consist of equestrian equipment – mounts of gilt silver for a parade bridle, bronze mounts for between seven and thirteen saddles and a lance head of iron. In all the finds contain objects catalogued as 247 find numbers. Based on decoration and shape the finds can be dated to the early 5th century AD (Näsman chapter 7).

The finds from Sösdala I were made less than a spade spit deep and the objects were not found together in one place. According to the workers in the gravel pit they found a concentration of bridle mounts of silver at one place and saddle mounts of bronze were found at three other places a few metres away. Many mounts became more or less distorted when bridle and saddles were dismantled before deposition. Sharp tools were used to cut mounts to pieces. Other mounts were brutally broken or crushed between stones. After these actions the silver and bronze objects were deposited in very shallow hollows or they were thrown directly on the naturally uneven surface of the ridge, and then covered with gravel and stones.

In the same gravel ridge another bridle was found in 1961, Sösdala II. Distorted mounts had been deposited 60 m east of Sösdala I. The find catalogue has 30 entries. The mounts are made of bronze and decorated with details in silver and probably from the end of the 4th century. It is simpler than the Sösdala I parade bridle and it was probably dismantled a generation earlier (Näsman chapter 7).

Fifteen kilometres south-west of Sösdala a similar destruction and deposition of bridle and saddle took place on the top of a gravel hill at Fulltofta. Today only 24 objects are preserved, 18 belong to a bronze bridle with details in silver and 6 items represent a cut-up saddle. The bridle was possibly produced in the late 4th century but not deposited until the early 5th century (Näsman chapter 7).

"Bog finds" or "war booty offerings"

Observing that the Sösdala I find contained horse equipment and a lance head, and noting that the objects were deliberately destroyed before deposition, Rune Norberg soon after the discovery attributed the finds to the category "bog finds" (1931). This concept was the common designation of offerings of "war booty" in lakes and bogs. On the basis of excavations in bogs at Thorsbjerg, Nydam, Kragehul and Vimose by Conrad Engelhardt (1863, 1865, 1867 and 1869) in which weapons and other military equipment from the Iron Age were found (2nd–5th century AD), the archaeologist J.J.A. Worsaae presented an interpretation that soon became dominating. He interpreted the "bog finds" with analogies to written classical sources and ethnographical examples as evidence of thank offerings of spoils taken from a conquered enemy at the battlefield (Worsaae 1865:55–60). After thorough discussions his interpretation won general acceptance among contemporary scholars. In the discussion other possible interpretations had been treated. The "bog finds" could be hidden treasure, deserted battlefields or stashed metal. But the alternative interpretations could not explain the mixed composition of the material, the deliberate destruction, the sorting of the material, the wide distribution of the objects at the find place and not least the deposition in lakes or bogs. Worsaae's interpretation is – with some modifications – still valid and supported by later excavations of offerings of military equipment in bogs at Porskær,

Ejsbøl, Illerup and Nydam in Denmark and Skedemosse, Hassle-Bösarp and Finnestorp in Sweden (Fabech 1996; Ilkjær 2003; Nordqvist chapter 11).

The Danish "bog finds" rapidly gained international fame due to their voluminous and well-preserved martial content and were significant in the development of Scandinavian Iron Age research (Ørsnes 1969). Impressed by the wealth of information offered by "bog finds", scholars compared the Sösdala and Fulltofta finds to Danish weapon deposits like Nydam and Porskær and Swedish ones like Finnestorp, Kanalgatan and Åmossarna, all of which were deposited in wetland. They were looked upon as "bog finds" without consideration of the find context.

Bernhard Salin noted in his discussion of which find type the Sjörup finds belonged to that it seemed to be a treasure, but he was so influenced by the recently published bog find from Porskær (Engelhardt 1881) that in the end he left the question open (Salin 1894:96–97). After the publication of the so-called Nydam II find, Sjörup was sorted into a new group of "bog finds", substitute offerings, the so-called *pars-pro-toto* offerings (Kjær 1902:193). Today the *pars-pro-toto* interpretation has become obsolete. My research on the South Scandinavian "bog finds" demonstrated that the offered military equipment had been sorted and that the sorted materials were deposited separately at different places in the same bog; and together they reflect all conquered equipment (Fabech 1990:112; 1991b:91–92). New excavations in Nydam and Ejsbøl have supported these arguments (Jørgensen & Petersen 2003). Consequently the comparison of Sösdala and Nydam II has lost its relevance.

The first time Norberg mentioned the Fulltofta find he assumed that "it is probably of a bog find nature" (1929:106). But three years later he concluded his paper *Moor und Depotfunde aus dem 5. Jahrhundert nach Chr. in Schonen* in *Acta Archaeologica* with his doubt as to whether the "sorgfältig 'getötete' Pferdegeschirre" (thoroughly "killed" horse tack) of the Sösdala and Fulltofta finds which are deposited on gravel hills really belong to the same category as the bog finds (Norberg 1931:111).

Unfortunately Norberg never accomplished his investigations about Scanian offering finds, so we cannot know what he believed. However, his doubts were overlooked by most scholars and no one discussed the problem seriously. For example Birger Nerman called the Sösdala find a bog find against his better judgement (1935:85). In the same book he made the interesting find from Tune in Väte on Gotland into a bog find and consequently an offering, despite the fact that all the objects were found on dry ground in the garden of a farm (Nerman 1935:85, 94; Fabech 1999; 2006:27).

In a popular survey of the prehistory of Sweden by John-Elof Forssander we see among the illustrations finds from Sösdala and Sjörup (1938:202–203, 208). Forssander gives the reader a vivid picture of the ritual destruction of bridle and saddles but he left the find circumstances without comment. Since he quotes the Roman author Livy's description of how Germanic troops destroyed spoils taken from the Romans to celebrate their victory we can assume that he considered the Sösdala deposition as an offering of conquered spoils from a battlefield.

After his retirement as director of Historical Museum at Lund University, Otto Rydbeck published a broad survey of prehistory in Scania (1944). Of course he included the finds from Fulltofta and Sösdala. He added that the two depositions were made in the vicinity of two large cemeteries, Vätteryd and Nunnäs, with erected stones, ship settings, stone circles and stone squares but based no conclusions on this observation. He interpreted the depositions as offerings after a victorious battle and suggested that the fighting could have been about the control of iron production in northern Scania (1944: 60).

In her dissertation Märta Strömberg interpreted the finds from Hassle-Bösarp, Åmossarna, Sösdala, Fulltofta, Tormestorp, Sjörup and Ankhult as offerings to celebrate a victory on the battlefield. For her it was of no importance whether the offering was made in wet or on dry land (1961:83–84). Mårten Stenberger did not distinguish between Migration Period offerings from wet or dry land; for him all were offerings to a war god; on the map, however, different symbols distinguish between finds from dry ground and wet land (1964:496–500, fig. 209; 1977:332–335, Abb. 216).

An alternative interpretation was proposed by Helmut Geisslinger in his 1967 dissertation. He sees all depositions of weaponry and horse equipment as offerings made by a military detachment or company to celebrate some spe-

cial occasion. The offering could be part of conquered war booty or parts of their own equipment. He called them *Gefolgschaftsopfer* (retinue offerings). In his opinion it did not matter whether the finds were deposited in wet land or on dry ground. That simply reflected the specific situation and local circumstances. So he considered also the Sösdala deposition to be a retinue offering (1967:108–110); "einmalige Kollektivopfer hocharistokratischen Characters" (once-only collective offering of high aristocratic nature).

In the same year Ulf Erik Hagberg presented a survey of Swedish "votive deposits" in his dissertation about offerings of battlefield spoils in Skedemosse bog on Öland (1967:63–78). The Sösdala find is interpreted as a special South Swedish *pars-pro-toto* sacrifice that contained only horse tack but no horse bones. And he suggests that the Sösdala offerings like the finds from Fulltofta and Kanalgatan were made to a horse god. With reference to Geisslinger (1967) he adds that such offering could be made both in wetlands and on dry land.

These examples demonstrate that the find contexts did not matter when the character of the Sösdala and Fulltofta finds was discussed. The specific situation and the local conditions determined whether the participants decided to make their offering on dry ground or in wetland. The significance of place for how rituals and other religious actions were carried out was not considered. The focus of scholars was on studies of art, style, chronology and provenance. As late as in 1979 Helmut Roth assumed that the Sösdala find was a bog find (1979:56). The physical setting of finds in their landscape was yet not part of the archaeological agenda. But when finds treated in the same manner but made at different sites all are considered to be the result of sacrifices and the same ritual practice, we cannot see *nor understand* important differences. If we wish to understand differences and similarities of religious practice in time and space, we have to observe the characteristics of religious sites and finds closely.

In 1986 I studied the Sösdala and Fulltofta material in connection with my studies for a *magister* thesis about South Scandinavian offering of military equipment (Fabech 1987). I found it impossible and unqualified to see Sösdala as a *pars-pro-toto* offering deposited on dry land by accident as interpreted by Forssander, a retinue offering as suggested by Geisslinger or an offering to a horse god as Hagberg believed. The Sösdala finds represent something else. In order to try to understand the context of the Sösdala depositions, I realised that I had to visit the find place. On my arrival I was surprised when I saw the surrounding landscape and realised how close the find spot was to the large Vätteryd Iron Age cemetery, only 200–300 m away. Could there be connections between the depositions and the cemetery?

Could it be a horse grave or a grave with horse equipment? The Sösdala finds have too many saddles, and the destruction of the objects, and the lack of horse bones are arguments against the interpretation as a horse grave. The deposition in the topsoil, the lack of human bones and the destruction of the objects are arguments against an interpretation as a human grave with horse equipment.

Searching the literature for finds that could explain the rituals performed at Sösdala and Fulltofta, I found relevant reading only in East and Central Europe. The parade bridle Sösdala I also points in that direction (Näsman chapter 7). Forssander had already pointed in that direction for influences, but I found also a new way to interpret the depositions (Fabech 1991a). New finds made in Hungary were associated with the mounted nomadic Hun culture. They consisted of depositions of destroyed metal objects, including mounts of horse tack. They did not contain any bones or other indications that it could be graves. Hungarian archaeologists interpreted them as remains of *Totenopfer,* deposited after a ritual performed in connection with the funeral of a Hun chief in the neighbourhood (Bóna 1979). Graves and funeral depositions are thus found in the vicinity of each other, but in different places. So I suggested that the Sösdala and Fulltofta finds together with a similar but more questionable find from Vennebo in Västergötland could reflect similar rituals and that contacts with Nomadic cultures in Eastern and Central Europe could be a background (Fabech 1991a-b).[1]

New theories and ideas – A new agenda

In 2012 we presented the finds from Sösdala, a famous name but an almost unknown content and context, at a conference in the Crimea: *Inter Ambo Maria – Tribes and Cultures between Scandinavia and the Black Sea in the Ro-man and Great Migration Periods* (Fabech & Näsman 2013). Our lecture was received with enthusiasm and our conversations with the participants convinced us to work for a complete publication of the Sösdala finds so that the finds could at last be integrated in the European discourse – you are holding the result in your hands.

Thirty years have passed since I presented my interpretation of the Sösdala finds, an interpretation that had great impact on our view on South Scandinavian society in the Migration Period. But much has happened on the archaeological stage during the last 30 years. Important new contributions to our understanding of Migration Period horse tack have been made: the Högom grave and the offering of military equipment at Finnestorp (Ramqvist chapter 10; Nordqvist chapter 11; Näsman chapter 7). But 90 years after the Sösdala discovery and in spite of a surge of metal detecting and excavations at "productive sites", not a single find has been made in Scandinavia that has the character of Sösdala and Fulltofta.

A few old stray finds of bridle or saddle mounts are the only weak indications we have of other similar finds:

A pelta-shaped pendant of bronze with attachment plate and terminals shaped as heads of birds of prey turned inwards found during gravel extraction at Norra Åsum, Scania. The bird heads are similar to heads in Salin's style I (Salin 1904 Fig. 515:i–l).

A saddle ring with staple found in the 19th century during gravel extraction on the 47 m. high haunted hill called Lundebjerg, at Haarslev, Funen (NM no. 15 987, Nationalmuseet, Copenhagen). The staple has been torn out of the saddle, like many staples found at Sösdala, indicating that a saddle was once dismantled here in a similar way (Thrane 1983).

A half loose-ring snaffle with bimetallic bit and two mounts shaped as animal heads (NM no. C4354) found at Hessel, Jutland. It belongs to Ørsnes's bridle type OF1 and he dated it with hesitation to Scand-D2 (1994 Fig. 42:1). Found during digging in a slope of a deep valley, it possibly comes from gravel or sand extraction.

A half loose-ring snaffle with a mount shaped as an animal head (NM no. C1737) found at Hellum Bakker, Jutland. The mount is decorated with inlaid silver, lines and circled dots. It belongs to Ørsnes's bridle type OF1 and he dated it with hesitation to Scand-D2 (1994 Fig. 42:2). It was found during digging in Hellum Bakker (= hills of gravel and sand) and could be the result of gravel extraction.

New theories and ideas in other academic disciplines have inspired new archaeological investigations. Our debates with geographers, historians, place-name researchers, and other scholars widened the study of sites and settlements (Fabech *et al.* 1999:17–22). The introduction of the concept of "chaîne opératoire" in archaeology began a critical and significant step away from traditional studies in artefact morphology, typochronology and function in favour of an interest in the dynamics of artefacts, their "life stories" (Kopytoff 1986; Dobres 1994). Instead of a focus on questions about time and place, there was a greater interest in answering the questions how and why. The artefacts of material culture were no longer considered lifeless things but regarded as objects with inherent power to influence and manipulate (Theuws 2009:292). Settlement archaeology, in its extended form called landscape archaeology, has been able to accommodate the overwhelming amount of objects found at the so-called central places. When the qualities and quantities of the archaeological record revealed hitherto unknown sites of societal significance, the interpretative power of archaeological finds was demonstrated. This development was linked to the interest of post-processual archaeology in artefacts as symbols. The focus moved away from settlement, economy, technology and ecology to landscape, mentality, rituals, warfare and power. A consequence of landscape archaeology has been that scholarly boundaries between archaeological specialities have dissolved. There is now a greater interest in the connections between landscape, sacral places, rituals and the biographies of things (e.g. Bradley 2000).

To understand rituals and ritualisation it is important to understand the physical and spatial setting – the choice of place will have decisive importance for the perception

Fig. 1. The extinct volcano Lönnebjär rises over the landscape. Photo from the east, Charlotte Fabech 2016.

and remembrance of ritual acts. "Places, pathways and human subjectivities mediate each other to create an understanding of the nature of social being. This is always a present-past because places in landscapes gather together histories, experiences, thoughts, events and associations. They are physical, cultural and historical" (Tilley 1999:180). In this perspective I cannot imagine that the "collective" that performed the ritual destruction of bridles and saddles on top of a marked gravel ridge had chosen that site by coincident. Against this background I realised that I had to visit the find place at Sösdala again to look upon the context with new eyes.

Sösdala revisited

The geography of the find area can be described as follows: The Sösdala area is situated in the densest setting of extinct volcanoes in Sweden, characterising the landscape with marked basalt plugs and worn-down volcanoes. Basalt polygons have always fascinated and stories have been told to explain them (fig. 1). Two kilometres south-east of and visible from the find place, the impressive remains of a volcano rise 145 m at Lönnebjär. This landmark is the highest spot in the area. The main traits of the present landscape were formed by the glaciers of the last Ice Age. It is a moraine landscape dominated by sediments formed by a glacial ice stream that ran from the north-east

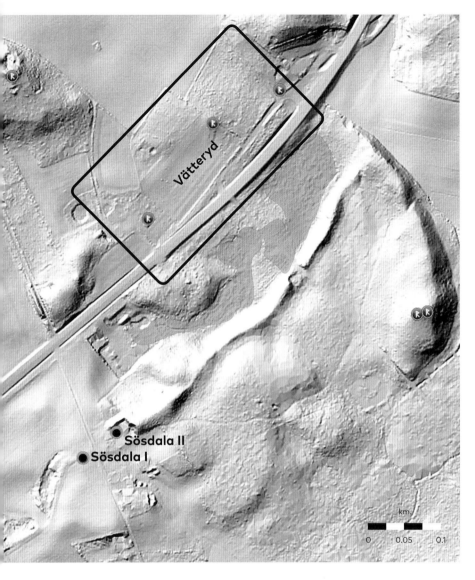

Vätteryd

Sösdala II
Sösdala I

Fig. 2. Lidar map of the area around Sösdala I–II and Vätteryd.
© Lantmäteriet.

towards the south-west and left the gravel ridge where the Sösdala finds were deposited. In low-lying areas between moraine formations smaller wetlands have formed. Tilled fields are mainly found on the glacial silt west of the ice stream. The area is drained by the Mellby Stream that runs from south to north, following the gravel ridges; it flows into Lake Finja.

My new visit to the find place, seen through my new glasses, made a deep impression. The horse tack was "slaughtered" on the top at the southern end of a long, ap-

prox. 10 m high gravel ridge (fig. 2). On the lidar map one can see the scars left by gravel pits where Sösdala I and II were found. At the curved north-eastern end of the ridge two stone-settings are recorded approx. 5 m wide. They are not excavated and consequently undateable. North-west of the ridge the largest preserved Iron Age cemetery of Scania, Vätteryd, is situated between three volcanic hills and an area of small bogs that in the Iron Age could have been shallow meres at the foot of the ridge. The distance to the find places Sösdala I and II is only 200–300 m. Many of the erected stones are arranged as ship-settings. Today only 375 raised stones are still in place, but when Nils Henrik Sjöborg made a drawing published in 1822 more than 600 were visible in a very open landscape (fig. 3). The cemetery was in use from at least the Migration Period to the Viking Age. Graves excavated 1955–1957 were, with one exception, all cremations (Strömberg 1961 II:73–88, Taf. 45:7). In a destroyed cremation a bridge-mount of a sword scabbard was found (fig. 4). It is contemporary with Sösdala I. Bridge mounts of Nydam/Porskær type were a characteristic element of the weaponry of the martial elite from Scandinavia to the Black Sea during period Scand D1 (Rau 2010:286–287, map Abb. 203; Fabech & Näsman chapter 18 fig. 11).

North of the Vätteryd cemetery on the other side of the Mellby Stream undated traces of settlement are found: fireplaces, iron slag, pottery, post holes and pits all indicate Iron Age activities. An old road runs through the eastern part of the cemetery; it is now replaced by a new road for which excavations of the eastern part took place in 1957. To the east the cemetery ends at the wetland below the gravel ridge.

It is probable that the Iron Age landscape was more open and grazed (cf. Lagerås 2002:388–403) than today so from the ridge there was a marvellous prospect as demonstrated by the viewshed (fig. 5). Towards the west and north-west you have a natural stage within a 500 × 500 m large area. Below the ridge there are wetlands, then follows the cemetery framed by three marked volcanic hills and further north contemporary settlements may have been placed. Looking east from the find spot, the tip of Lönnebjär rises above a range of hills. The stage is set.

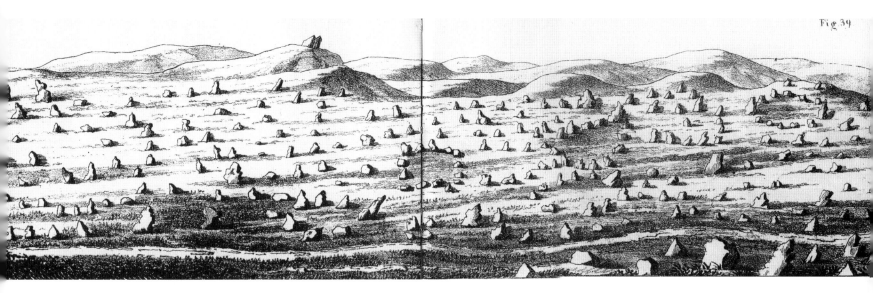

Fig. 39

Fig. 3. Drawing of Vätteryd cemetery published as fig. 39 in Sjöborg 1822.

Sacral places

The surroundings of Sösdala I–II and Vätteryd contain several features that characterise sacral places. Religious practices must happen in special locations where the sacred world is revealed. Such places are known as "hierophanies": places where the holy appeared to people (Bradley 2000:29). This is the manifestation or appearance of the holy to human beings: an event that took place. An archaeological problem of importance is the difficulty of localising a site where a hierophany took place, to find "the interface of the earthly and supernatural worlds" (Green 1995:90).

Any place where the holy appeared could become sacral. Consequently, one has to expect a broad spectrum of sites associated with the holy (Vikstrand 2001:20–24; Andrén 2002). Some sites were important in the mythical history of the society, while elsewhere, victories won made many battlefields sacral. Other sites were used for sacrifices to gods, some served as gateways to the spiritual world and at others one could communicate with ancestors. Initiation rites and other rituals had their own sites. Some sites were public and well known, others were reserved for the few and secret. Thus sacral sites probably varied considerably in form, size and location. Hierophanies can take place anywhere, so in principle any place can be sacral. In reality,

Fig. 4. Vätteryd. Fragment of bridge mount of sword scabbard from a destroyed cremation. Punch-decorated silver-plated bronze. 1:1. (SHM inv.no. 27 124). After Strömberg 1961 II Taf. 45:7.

however, man preferred some landscape settings over others (Svensson chapter 5).

Richard Bradley compared Arthur Evans's studies of sacral places in ancient Greece with the work by Pausanias from the 2nd century AD. He demonstrates that certain types of natural places seem to have been preferred as sacral sites: conspicuous cliffs, hill tops, large boulders, lakes and bogs, watercourses, springs and wells, caves, trees and groves, etc. (Bradley 2000:18–32).

That the inhabitants of Scandinavia had the same apprehension of holy places is revealed by Norse written sources and place names (Brink 2013). Written sources from the period after the conversion give examples of

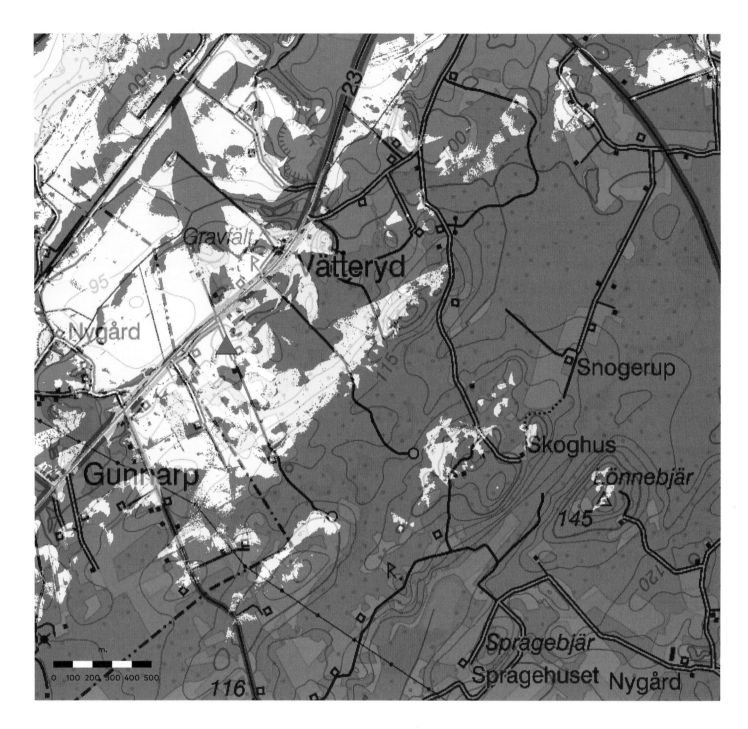

Fig. 5. Recent map of the surroundings of Vätteryd superimposed by a viewshed from the find spot Sösdala I to show its relation to Vätteryd and Lönnebjär. Viewshed Nicolo del'Unto, Lund University. Map SD-terrängkarta, ©Lantmäteriet.

how heathen sacral places and phenomena were still remembered (fig. 6). Natural places mentioned are stony outcrops, stones, groves, and a single well. To evaluate whether the medieval texts give a trustworthy picture of the sacral landscape of the preceding heathen centuries one can compare with the picture presented by place names which reflect an earlier situation (Fabech & Näsman 2013:66–67). Many names of sacral places signify natural features, for example: woodland, trees, hills, islands, rivers and lakes.

The surrounding context of the Sösdala depositions has many of the elements mentioned above: stones, cliffs, hilltops, large boulders, bogs, trees and groves. It cannot have been accidental that horse tack was destroyed and deposited twice on top of the gravel ridge instead of in the small bogs/lakes, nor explained by a specific situation. Had a deposition in wetland been preferred it would have been possible in the local setting. So the choice of the sharp top of a gravel ridge for the ritual was deliberate.

Back to content

Considering an open grazed landscape in the Migration Period, the location close to the Vätteryd cemetery offered an ideal place for rituals. But what kind of rituals? For whom? And why? Acts connected to funerals, ancestor cult, rites of passage or offerings? Of course it is hazardous to try to understand the meaning of rituals, but the attempt has to be made.

In order to answer the questions I had to turn back to the finds themselves to try to understand what the depositions in Sösdala actually represented. "Deposition" is a heterogeneous and difficult category, in archaeology often too quickly subdivided into either secular treasures/ hoards or a sacral interpretation, usually as offerings. As long as the Sösdala and Fulltofta finds were considered to be "bog finds" they were automatically labelled offerings. But not all ritual depositions are offerings.

In pre-Christian Scandinavian societies, religion and profane life were interlaced and virtually impossible to separate from one another. Political and religious power was inseparable (cf. Bradley 2005). Consequently, it is often very difficult to distinguish whether finds have a profane or a sacred background. Most of us know this.

Source	Written sources	Place-names
Natural places	hult lund stenar källa	skog lund träd berg fjäll ö näs vik å/älv sjö
Constructed and cultivated places	ställning (stallr) sal stavgård högar	hem hus sal bo hov hög hamn vin (äng) vang (åkergärde) tun åker
Sacral sites of uncertain character	vi stav (stafr) hörg/harg	vi stav (stafr) hörg/harg

Fig. 6. Based on Scandinavian written sources and place names words characterising sacral sites are listed.
After Fabech & Näsman 2013:66–67.

Anyhow, it is surprising that we archaeologists are so imprecise when classifying finds of religious significance; most of them are simply labelled "offering". To put the labels "offering" or "sacrifice" on various religious depositions is to simplify the often very complex religious acts, the chain of events (Näsström 2004). The sacrifice of a horse, for example, started long before the slaughter, when the animal was chosen and captured. Then the selected animal was perhaps adorned and dedicated to the gods. Slaughter followed – the sacrifice proper – and the body was quartered, the meat prepared for a ritual meal, the hide and cut-off parts like the skull could have been put on stakes, and eventually the bones remaining after the meal were deposited in a proper place. We have to consider this whole process and thus the biography of our find (Kopytoff 1986). We must not base our interpretation only on the final result that is the archaeological record. We must, for example, see animal bones, not primarily as an offering, but maybe as a deposition of

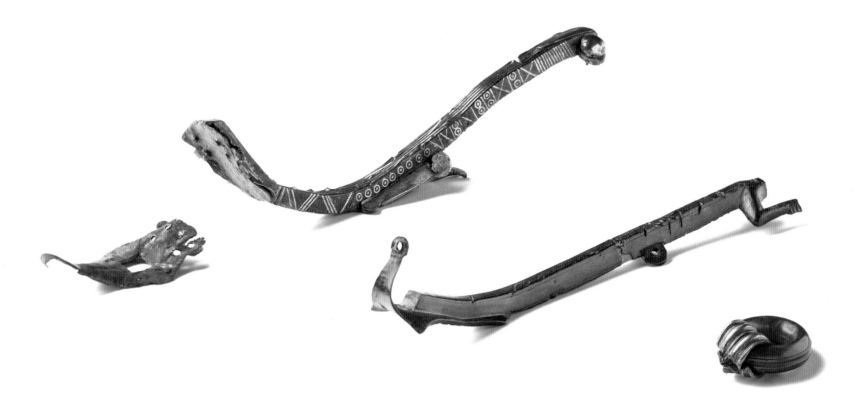

matter too loaded to be thrown among the daily household refuse. And we have to ask to whom the rituals were performed.

I will use the term "deposition", since it covers both secular and sacral contexts as well as finds that include both sacral and secular intentions (Berggren 2006; Fabech 2006). The broad concept "ritual deposition" helps us to identify more finds of interest in a sacral landscape than what the traditional focus on the more limited category of "offerings" can deliver.

The deposition Sösdala I

Find content: exclusive mounts and buckles of silver and bronze for a bridle and up to 13 saddles. A lance head of iron may have been part of the context. No human or animal bones were found.

Treatment: violent destruction of many mounts that were torn off the straps of bridle and saddles (fig. 7). The mounts are bent and broken; some even smashed between stones. Other mounts are cut up with blows of swords or axes, for example many saddle rings are cut off the staple. No objects are burnt or show traces of fire.

Find context: deposited in the sandy topsoil of a gravel ridge in shallow hollows in an area less than 10 × 10 m. The deposition was then covered by a stone layer.

Find surroundings: the deposition took place 60 m from the earlier deposition Sösdala II on top of the same gravel ridge. The find spot is situated with a view of a contemporary cemetery 200–300 m away. Here a bridge-mount of a sword scabbard was found in a destroyed cremation, which is contemporary with Sösdala I. To the west there are smaller bogs/wetlands at the foot of the ridge and to the east peaks of conspicuous remains of extinct volcanoes.

Dating: Early Migration Period or the early 5th century AD (Näsman chapter 7).

The deposition Sösdala II

Mounts and buckles of bridle of bronze with details in silver and copper. No human or animal bones were found. The objects were violently destroyed before deposition. No traces of fire. Deposited in the sandy topsoil inside a small area on top of a gravel ridge, 200–300 m from a contemporary cemetery and smaller bogs/wetland. Dated to

Fig. 7. Ritually destroyed horse tack from Sösdala I. Left: saddle mounts (nos. 215, 119, 154). Right: bridle mounts (nos. 11, 16, 88–90). Photo Daniel Lindskog.

the end of the Late Roman Iron Age, the late 4th century AD or c. AD 400 (Näsman chapter 7).

The deposition at Fulltofta

The find spot at Fulltofta is situated approx. 15 km south-west of Sösdala. The find circumstances are less well known but there are conspicuous similarities in content and context between Fulltofta and Sösdala. The find consists of exclusive mounts of bronze with details in silver, some gilt, for a bridle and a saddle. No human or animal bones were found. The mounts were violently destroyed and bridle and saddle "slaughtered" before deposition. No object has been damaged by fire. They were deposited in a smaller area in the sandy topsoil on the top of a gravel hill with a view of a small cemetery 200–300 m away. The bridle and saddle may have been produced in the Late Roman Iron Age or the late 4th century AD, but the bridle is brought up to date and deposited with a saddle in the early Migration Period or early in the 5th century AD (Näsman chapter 7). This is the backdrop to my conclusion that the Fulltofta find represents rituals like those that took place at least twice at Sösdala.

A scenario

The bridle from Sösdala I belongs to a group of exclusive bridle finds which characterise the superregional warrior elite in Europe in the early Migration Period. Add to this the extraordinary qualities of some saddle mounts that indicate that the horseman must have belonged to the contemporary Scanian elite (Näsman chapter 7; Fabech & Näsman chapter 17). Altogether the character of the social setting that performed the rituals is delineated. The bridle from Sösdala II and the bridle and saddle from Fulltofta are simpler. Both, however, have ornamental details in silver, and riding a horse with bridles and saddles fitted with metal mounts was in itself a sign of high social standing.

The condition of the objects in the Sösdala I deposition demonstrates that they were used in complex rituals before deposition. They were "slaughtered" in choreographed systematic action. The finds were made in shallow hollows inside a limited area and subsequently covered up with sand, gravel and stones. The observations tell us that destruction, deposition and covering are a sequence of events that took place at the same site and time (Fabech chapter 1 fig. 14).

Looked upon from the perspective of action theory, relations between phenomena determine the meaning and

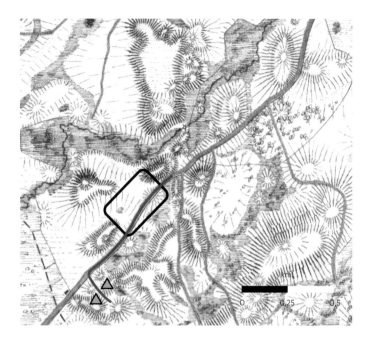

Fig. 8. On the Scanian reconnaissance map from 1812–1820 the Vätteryd cemetery and the two Sösdala find spots are marked as well as a suggested route between them. Detail of map sheet IVÖ 201.

significance of action. So it is impossible to separate action, things and place from one another. The site – where actions took place and where things were used – is as important as the persons who performed the rituals (Berggren 2010:104–113). That the rituals at both Sösdala and Fulltofta took place within sight of contemporary graves and that the place was on top of a gravel ridge or hill with wide views over the surrounding landscape seem essential for understanding the backdrop to the rituals.

From the Vätteryd cemetery you have to go south of the wetlands to reach the gravel ridge (fig. 8). According to Forssander's description in 1929 a short hollow, a couple of metres deep, facilitated passage between two sections of the ridge, a southern one on top of which Sösdala I was deposited and a northern one where Sösdala II was found 1961. This hollow gave a natural access that made it possible to reach the top of the ridge without too much difficulty. Easy access may have been as decisive when this part of the long gravel ridge was chosen for ritual depositions as when Västra Göinge Hundred placed its gravel pit here, 1400 years later.

Events on the ridge could be followed from the cemetery and the burial of a dead person could be seen from the place of deposition. The grave with a sword scabbard mount was established roughly at the time of the Sösdala I deposition. So perhaps it was the horse tack of this warrior that was ritually deposited on the top of the ridge above. Maybe the lance head that was found shows that a lance was thrust into the ground to mark the site; the lance was also a well-established symbol of authority (Theuws 2009:303–304, 307). That the gravel ridge twice became the stage for the same kind of ritual suggests that the relation between cemetery and ritual sites was of decisive significance.

The different dates of the two depositions Sösdala I and II reveal that the top of the ridge was used at least twice as a ritual stage for slaughter and deposition of horse tack; the first time at the end of the 4th century and a second time at the beginning of the 5th. The events seem to be separated by about a generation. Ritual continuity underlines the assumption that the place was not chosen by coincidence and that there has to be a connection in the biographies of the two finds. Considering that the deposition at Fulltofta is more or less contemporary with Sösdala I and that only 15 km separate the two find spots, there may be a connection between the biographies of Fulltofta and Sösdala I – the two horsemen were undoubtedly acquainted with one another.

The introduction of a new and foreign ritual in the traditional Iron Age setting of central Scania is coincident with a settlement change (Carlie 1994:164; Fabech, Helgesson & Näsman chapter 4). The previous period was characterised by a trivial material culture so the seemingly sudden occurrence of new cemeteries and prestigious finds in central Scania suggests the establishment of a new order of power. The deposition Sösdala II represents a new ritual, possibly performed in connection with the burial of a dead warrior and perhaps the aim of the ritual was to prop up the claims of the heirs to an insecure power position. An ancestor was created (cf. Theuws 2009 note 153). The deposition Sösdala I reflects that the next generation also needed a ritual manifestation. The warrior in a contemporary grave at Vätteryd could be the horseman whose equipment was ritually deposited at Sösdala I, and he could actually be "the creator of the ancestor" at Sösdala II.

The ritual destruction and deposition of horse tack during the early Migration Period took place among people with new ideas who knew one another and in a social setting characterised by the impact of a martial culture of multicultural European horsemen. The conclusions based on our new analysis of find contents and contexts increase the relevance of seeing the funeral depositions of mounted nomads as analogies to the Sösdala and Fulltofta finds (Fabech & Näsman chapter 17).

The impact of mounted nomads

The discovery of Hunnic finds at e.g. Zovtnev Velkotokmac, Ukraine, and Pannonhalma, Hungary, as well as new studies and interpretations of old finds like Jędrzychowice (Höckricht), Poland, and Szeged-Nagyszéksós, Hungary, have given an insight into some of the funerary rituals of the Huns (Bóna 1979; 1991). Hungarian archaeologists interpreted them as remains of *Totenopfer*, deposited after rituals performed in connection with the funeral of a Hun chief in the neighbourhood of the burial. Grave and funeral depositions are thus found near one another but in different places (Bóna 1979:311–313, 1991; Kürti 1987; Tomka 1987a, 1987b).

The depositions consisted of destroyed metal objects. The finds typically contain highly ornamented mounts of horse tack, garments with applied gold decoration, a few weapons, and occasional metal vessels. There are some striking similarities between the attributes of the Sösdala finds and those of the Hunnic funeral depositions. Both contain bridles, saddle mounts and weapons. The objects show traces of intentional destruction. They were deposited on dry land close to the surface and in the immediate proximity of contemporary graves. They contain no bones or other indications that it could be graves.

Ethnological analogies that can explain the rituals of such finds are known from later mounted nomads like Avars, Turks and other peoples from Inner Asia. The rites change with time and space, but some phenomena bring them together (Tomka 1987a; 2007). A funeral ceremony consisted of several phases: first the burial of the dead and the funeral feast, after that the erection of a symbol for the dead. Here the wandering soul/spirit of the dead could find shelter in the symbolic effigy for a period, when the dead

had not yet reached the realm of the dead. A doll could be used, or a pole. Sometimes the symbol was a lance with a pennon, placed either at the grave or where the funeral feast was celebrated. Then followed a destruction and subsequent deposition of objects that in this way was sent after the dead to the other world. The objects could be from horse tack or weaponry but vessels and remains from the feast could also be used: this took place at the grave or a short distance from it (Kürti 2007; Tomka 2007).

The ritual comprised the transition from one condition to another, a ritual that reached back in time as well as pointed forward. The rituals seem to be more like *rites de passage* than typical sacrifices. The practice is characteristic of mounted nomads such as Sarmatians, Huns and Alans. In our attempt to understand the occurrence in Scania of similar rituals we have to consider the special importance of the horse as an indicator of power and prestige. Contacts with peoples in Eastern Europe brought Scandinavians in touch with the culture of nomadic pastoralists for whom the horse was central to power and status as well as in ritual (Fabech 1991a-b). Perhaps Scandinavian warriors attended funerary rituals according to nomadic customs or at least heard stories about such rituals. The Fulltofta and Sösdala finds can reflect similar ritual activities performed at a site where it was possible to overlook the burial ground where the dead warrior was buried. Such a ritual could include burial, funeral feast, ritual destruction of horse tack and subsequent deposition of the remains and a designation of the site with a lance.

If we compare the parade bridle of Sösdala I to the bridles in Hunnic funeral depositions like Szeged-Nagyszéksós, some shapes of mounts have similarities. But technique and style are very different – thus Huns' polychrome mounts are of gold with inlaid stones – garnets or almandines. But not everyone in the area dominated by Huns surrendered to this style. "Huns" was an ethnically heterogeneous group in which alongside the "proper" Asian people were included of Iranian stock such as Alans and Sarmatians as well as some Germanic-speaking groups, including Goths and Gepids (Tomka 2007:256–257). The other ethnic groups could maintain much of the individual character of their material culture at the same time as they adopted Hunnic traits, as demon-

Fig. 9. Selected finds from the Fürstengrab *(princely grave) at Ja-kuszowice, Poland. Left: bridle mounts in "Sösdala" style. Right: gold mounts in "Hunnic" polychrome style. © Muzeum Archeologiczne w Krakowie.*

strated in the mixed equipment in graves at Jakuszowice (fig. 9) and Untersiebenbrunn, weaponry and dress are "Hunnic", horse tack "Germanic" (Godłowski 1995; Nothnagel 2008; 2013).

The best parallel to the Sösdala I bridle is not found in Scandinavia, but far away at Kačin in Ukraine (Kazanski & Mastykova chapter 15 fig. 2–7). Both Kačin and Sösda-la belong to a group of exclusive bridle finds, which char-acterise the superregional warrior elite that developed in the early Migration Period. The two finds are constit-uents of the material culture of peoples living in Central and Eastern Europe, exemplified by bridles from Unter-

siebenbrunn, Jakuszowice, Kačin, Bar, and Coşoveni. The remarkable similarities between the Scandinavian and Continental finds, but also the dissimilarities, are import-ant when discussing whether Scanian horsemen served in Germanic contingents within the Hun Empire or outside. Social contacts established long before were important for the recruitment of Scandinavian warriors to war bands in the South. When returning home they brought home new culture – material and immaterial (Fabech & Näsman chapter 17).

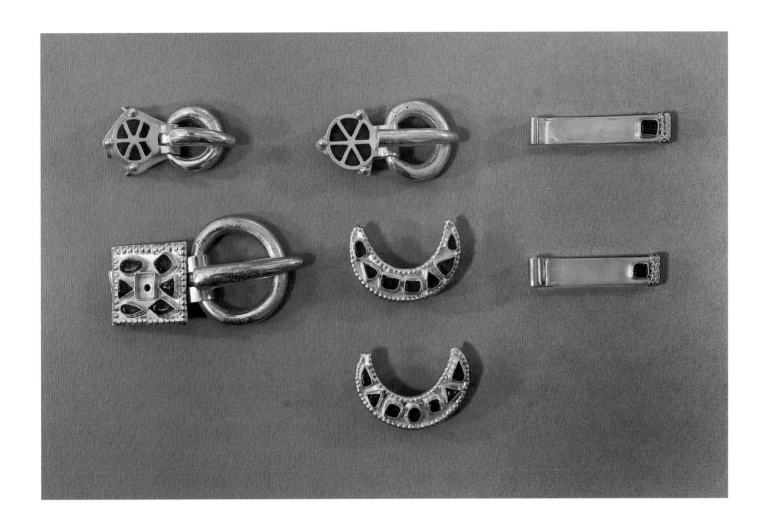

Note

1   In my *magister* thesis 1987 I compared Sösdala and Fulltofta to finds made at Vennebo, Västergötland (SHM inv. no. 6511). The finds consist of exclusive bronze and silver mounts of at least four bridles, two saddles and two lance heads, all from the beginning of the 5th century. The objects were deliberately destroyed before deposition. The finds were made on three occasions in 1874 during fieldwork east of Lake Vennebo. Unfortunately the exact find spot was not recorded so it is uncertain whether the finds were made on dry ground or in ancient, now cultivated wetland. But according to local people the finds came mainly from two fields east of the lake near the border with Redslared parish, an area described as "upland" (Hagberg 1967:75). Based on this information I decided to treat the find as a possible "funeral sacrifice" like Sösdala and Fulltofta (Fabech 1991a &b). However, a detector survey in 1987 of the indicated find place ended without results. In November 2002 Bengt Nordqvist made a detector survey near the lake that yielded finds of horse tack: a saddle mount and a strap buckle of bronze were found in dry ground while a saddle ring of bronze with silver inlays was found in wetland at the lake (Karlsson 2002). A consequence of the new information is that the find context can no longer be regarded as dry ground and it cannot be characterised as "funeral sacrifice". Vennebo will be left out of the discussion until archaeological excavations of the site can settle the question.

References

Andrén, A. 2002. Platsernas betydelse. Norrön ritual och kultplatskontinuitet. In: Jennbert, K., Andrén, K. & Raudvere, C. (eds). *Plats och praxis. Studier av nordisk förkristen ritual.* Lund: 199–342.

Berggren, Å. 2006. Archaeology and sacrifice. In: Andrén, A., Jennbert, K. & Raudvere, C. (eds). *Old Norse religion in long-term perspective.* Lund: 303–307.

Berggren, Å. 2010. *Med kärret som källa. Om begreppen offer och ritual inom arkeologin.* Lund. Summary.

Bóna, I. 1979. Die archäologischen Denkmäler der Hunnen und der Hunnenzeit in Ungarn. Spiegel der internationalen Hunnenforschung. In: Vonbank, E. (ed.). *Nibelungenlied. Ausstellung zur Erinnerung an die Auffindung der Handschrift A des Nibelungenliedes im Jahre 1779 im Palats zu Hohenems.* Bregenze: 297–339.

Bóna, I. 1991. *Das Hunnenreich.* Stuttgart.

Bradley, R. 2000. *An archaeology of natural places.* London.

Bradley, R. 2005. *Ritual and domestic life in prehistoric Europe.* London.

Brink, S. 2013. Myth and ritual in pre-Christian Scandinavian landscape. In: Nordeide, S. Walaker & Brink, S. (eds). *Sacred Sites and Holy Places: Exploring the Sacralization of Landscape through Time and Space.* Turnhout/ York: 33–51.

Carlie, A. 1994. *På arkeologins bakgård. En bebyggelsesarkeologisk undersökning i norra Skånes inland baserad på synliga gravar.* Lund. Summary.

Dobres, M.-A. 1994. Technology's links and *chaînes*: the processual unfolding of technique and technician. In: Dobres, M.-A. & Hoffman, C. (eds). *The social dynamics of technology.* Washington/London: 124–146.

Engelhardt, C. 1863. *Thorsbjerg Mosefund.* Copenhagen.

Engelhardt, C. 1865. *Nydam Mosefund.* Copenhagen.

Engelhardt, C. 1867. *Kragehul Mosefund.* Copenhagen.

Engelhardt, C. 1869. *Vimose Fundet.* Copenhagen.

Engelhardt, C. 1881. Jernalderens Gravskikke i Jylland. *Aarbøger for Nordisk Oldkyndighed og Historie:* 79–184.

Fabech, C. 1987. *Krigsbytteoffer – religiøs ceremoni eller politisk manifestation.* Aarhus [Unpublished *magister*-thesis, Aarhus University].

Fabech, C. 1990. Sjörup – an old problem in a new light. *Meddelanden från Lunds Universitets Historiska Museum. New series 8, 1989–1990:* 101–119.

Fabech, C. 1991a. Neue Perspektiven zu den Funden von Sösdala und Fulltofta. *Studien zur Sachsenforschung 7:* 121–135.

Fabech, C. 1991b. Booty sacrifices in Southern Scandinavia. A reassessment. In: Garwood, P. et al. (eds). *Sacred and profane.* Oxford: 88–99.

Fabech, C. 1996. Booty sacrifices in Southern Scandinavia – a history of warfare and ideology. In: *Roman Reflections in Scandinavia.* Rome: 135–138.

Fabech, C. 1999. Fra offer til boplads – Tune i nyt perspektiv. In: Fuglestvedt, I. *et al.* (eds). *Et hus med mange rom. Vennebok til Bjørn Myhre på 60-årsdagen.* Stavanger: 239–248.

Fabech, C. 2006. Centrality in Old Norse mental landscapes. In: Andrén, A., Jennbert, K. & Raudvere, C. (eds). *Old Norse religion in long-term perspective.* Lund: 26–32.

Fabech, C., Hvass, S., Näsman, U. & Ringtved, J. 1999. Settlement and Landscape – a presentation of a research programme and a conference. In: Fabech, C. & Ringtved, J. (eds). *Settlement and Landscape.* Højbjerg/Aarhus: 13–28.

Fabech, C. & Näsman, U. 2013. Ritual landscapes and sacral places in the first millennium A.D. in South Scandinavia. In: Nordeide, S. Walaker & Brink, S. (eds). *Sacred Sites and Holy Places. Exploring the Sacralization of Landscape through Time and Space.* Turnhout /York: 41–97.

Forssander, J.-E. 1938. Sveriges förhistoriska bebyggelse. In: Wrangel, E. *et al.* (eds). *Svenska folket genom tiderna.* Malmö: 17–293.

Geisslinger, H. 1967. *Horte als Geschichtsquelle.* Neumünster.

Godłowski, K. 1995. Das "Fürstengrab" des 5. Jhs. und der "Fürstensitz" in Jakuszowice in Südpolen. In: Vallet, F. & Kazanski, M. (eds). *La noblesse romaine et les chefs barbares du IIIe au VIIe siècle.* Condé-sur-Noireau/Saint-Germain-en-Laye: 155–179.

Green, M. 1995. *Celtic goddesses. Warriors, virgins and mothers.* London.

Hagberg, U. E. 1967. *The archaeology of Skedemosse 2. The votive deposits in the Skedemosse fen and their relation to the Iron-Age settlement on Öland, Sweden.* Stockholm.

Ilkjær, J. 2003. Danish war booty sacrifices. In: Jørgensen, L. *et al.* (eds). *The spoils of victory. The North in the shadow of the Roman Empire.* Copenhagen: 44–64.

Jørgensen, E. & Petersen, P. Vang. 2003. Nydam Bog – New finds and observations. In: Lars Jørgensen et al. (eds). *The spoils of victory. The North in the shadow of the Roman Empire.* Copenhagen: 258–285.

Karlsson, B. 2002. Arkeologer spårade praktfynd i Sjuhärad. In: *Hallands Nyheter* 8 November 2002. Varberg.

Kjær, H. 1902. *Et nyt fund fra Nydam Mose.* Nordiske Fortidsminder 1. Copenhagen.

Kopytoff, I. 1986. The cultural biography of things. In: Appadurai, A. (ed.). *The social life of things. Commodities in cultural perspective.* Cambridge: 64–91. Reprinted 1988, 1990, 1992, 1997, 1999, 2000.

Kürti, B. 1987. Fürstliche Funde der Hunnenzeit aus Szeged-Nagyszéksós. In: *Germanen, Hunnen und Awaren. Schätze der Völkerwanderungszeit.* Nuremberg: 163–180.

Kürti, B. 2007. Fürstliche Funde der Hunnenzeit aus Szeged-Nagyszéksós. In: Anke, B. & Externbrink, H. (eds). *Attila und die Hunnen*. Speyer/Stuttgart: 258–261.

Lagerås, P. 2002. Skog, slåtter och stenröjning. Paleoekologiska undersökningar i trakten av Stoby i norra Skåne. In: Carlie, A. (ed.). *Skånska Regioner*. Stockholm: 362–411.

Näsström, B.-M. 2004. *Blot. Tro och offer i det förkristne Norden*. Stockholm.

Nerman, B. 1935. *Die Völkerwanderungszeit Gotlands*. Stockholm.

Norberg, R. 1929. Om förhistoriska sadlar i Sverige. *Rig* 12: 97–113.

Norberg, R. 1931. Moor- und Depotfunde aus dem 5. Jahrhundert nach Chr. in Schonen. *Acta Archaeologica* 2: 104–111.

Nothnagel, M. 2008. *Die völkerwanderungszeitlichen Bestattungen von Untersiebenbrunn, Niederösterreich*. Wien (Diplomarbeit). Online: http://othes.univie.ac.at/1440/1/2008-09-18_0100192.pdf – Checked 6 April 2017.

Nothnagel, M. 2013. *Weibliche Eliten der Völkerwanderungszeit. Zwei Prunkbestattungen aus Untersiebenbrunn*. St. Pölten.

Ørsnes, M. 1969. Om forfatteren [Conrad Engelhardt]. Om jernalderns opdagelse. Om Torsbjergfundet. In: *Sønderjyske og fynske mosefund II. Thorsbjerg Mosefund*. By Engelhardt, C. 1863. Copenhagen: v–xviii.

Ørsnes, M. 1994. Zaumzeugfunde des 1.–8. Jhrh. nach Chr. in Mittel- und Nordeuropa. *Acta archaeologica* 64/2, 1993: 183–292.

Rau, A. 2010. *Nydam mose 1–2. Die personengebundenen Gegenstände. Grabungen 1989–1999*. Aarhus/Højbjerg. Summary.

Roth, H. 1979. *Kunst der Völkerwanderungszeit*. Frankfurt a.-M./Berlin/Wien.

Rydbeck, O. 1944. Monument och människor i forntidens Skåne. *Meddelanden från Lunds Universitets Historiska Museum* 1944: 23–153.

Salin, B. 1894. Fynd från Finjasjöns strand, Skåne. *Vitterhetskademiens månadsblad* 1894: 84–106.

Salin, B. 1904. *Die altgermanische Thierornamentik*. Stockholm. (2nd ed. 1935. Stockholm).

Sjöborg, N.H. 1822. *Samlingar för Nordens fornälskare*. A selection with introduction and comments by M. Odelberg. Stockholm 1978.

Stenberger, M. 1964. *Det forntida Sverige*. Uppsala.

Stenberger, M. 1977. *Nordische Vorzeit 4. Vorgeschichte Schwedens*. Neumünster.

Strömberg, M. 1961. *Untersuchungen zur jüngeren Eisenzeit in Schonen I Text. II Katalog und Tafeln*. Lund.

Theuws, F. 2009. Grave goods, ethnicity, and the rhetoric of burial rites in Late Antique Northern Gaul. In: Derks, T. & Roymans, N. (eds). *Ethnic constructs in antiquity. The role of power and tradition*. Amsterdam: 283–319.

Thrane, H. 1983. En lille broncering fra Vedel Simonsens samling. *Fynske minder* 1983: 51–64. Zusammenfassung.

Tilley, C. 1999. *Metaphor and Material Culture*. Oxford/Malden.

Tomka, P. 1987a. Der hunnische Fundkomplex von Pannonhalma. *Acta Archaeologica Hungarica* 38, 1986: 423–488.

Tomka, P. 1987b. Der hunnische Fundkomplex von Pannonhalma. In: *Germanen, Hunnen und Awaren. Schätze der Völkerwanderungszeit*. Nuremberg: 156–161.

Tomka, P. 2007. Über die Bestattungssitten der Hunnen. In: Anke, B. & Externbrink, H. (eds). 2007. *Attila und die Hunnen*. Speyer/Stuttgart: 253–257.

Vikstrand, P. 2001. *Gudarnas platser. Förkristna sakrala ortnamn i Mälarlandskapen*. Uppsala. Summary.

Worsaae, J. J. A. 1865. *Om Slesvigs eller Sønderjyllands Oldtidsminder*. Copenhagen.

Резюме

Сёсдала и Фультофта: ритуальные комплексы

Шарлотта Фабек

Уникальные находки конской сбруи близ Сёсдалы в центральной Скании (Швеция) были сделаны во время добычи гравия в 1929 и потом в 1930 гг. Эти находки, получившие название «Сёсдала I», представляют собой снаряжение всадника и железный наконечник копья. Их можно датировать началом V в. н. э. В 1961 г. на той же самой гравийной гряде обнаружили еще одну узду – «Сёсдалу II». Эти преднамеренно поврежденные накладки найдены в 60 м к востоку от Сёсдалы I. Данные вещи, вероятно, относятся к концу IV в. Вероятно, эту узду уничтожили на поколение раньше, чем вещи в Сёсдале I. В 15 км к юго-западу от Сёсдалы, на вершине гравийного холма в Фультофте, аналогичным образом были испорчены и захоронены уздечка и седло.

Учитывая то, что находки Сёсдалы I включали предметы конской сбруи и наконечник копья, причем эти вещи были преднамеренно испорчены до того, как были помещены в землю, многие исследователи сравнивали находки в Сёсдале и Фультофте с комплексами оружия с территории Дании и Швеции, которые во всех случаях были найдены в заболоченных местах. Потому их рассматривали в числе «болотных находок», не учитывая контекст. Особенности ситуации и местных условий определяли желание участников ритуала сделать приношение на сухой земле или в болоте. Взаимосвязь между конкретной местностью и ходом ритуалов и других культовых действий не принималась во внимание. В фокусе внимания исследователей были вопросы, связанные с мастерством ремесленников, стилем, хронологией и происхождением вещей. До сих пор на археологическую повестку дня не выносились вопросы, связанные с физическим положением находок в рамках ландшафта.

В 1986 г. я изучила материалы из Сёсдалы и Фультофты. Мне показалось невозможным и непрофессиональным интерпретировать находки из Сёсдалы как приношение, случайно оказавшееся на сухой земле. Находки из Сёсдалы представляли собой нечто иное. Чтобы понять контекст комплексов из Сёсдалы, я выехала на место находки, и была удивлена, когда поняла, как невелико расстояние, отделяющее ее от большого могильника Железного века в Веттерюде, отстоящего всего на 200–300 м. Не могли ли приношения и могильник быть связанными между собой?

Не могло ли здесь находиться погребение лошади или могила с конской сбруей? В находках из Сёсдалы было слишком много седел, потому ритуальное повреждение вещей и отсутствие конских костей свидетельствуют не в пользу их интерпретации как погребения лошади. Положение в верхнем слое грунта, отсутствие человеческих костей и преднамеренное повреждение вещей свидетельствуют против интерпретации находок как погребения человека, сопровождавшегося конским снаряжением.

Пытаясь отыскать публикации находок, которые помогли бы объяснить ритуалы в Сёсдале и Фультофте, я смогла найти соответствующую литературу лишь для Центральной и Восточной Европы. Новые находки на территории Венгрии связаны со всаднической культурой кочевых гуннов. Они представляли собой комплексы поврежденных металлических вещей, среди которых были накладки на конскую сбрую. Здесь отсутствовали кости и другие индикаторы погребений. Венгерские археологи интерпретировали их как погребальное жертвоприношение (Totenopfer), археологизированные следы ритуала, совершенного в связи с погребением гуннского вождя поблизости. В результате могила и погребальное приношения были обнаружены в непосредственной близи друг от друга, но в разных местах. Потому я высказала предположение, что находки в Сёсдале и Фультофте могут отражать близкие ритуалы на фоне контактов с кочевническими культурами Центральной и Восточной Европы.

С тех пор, как мною была представлена оригинальная интерпретация находок в Сёсдале, интерпретация, которая оказала существенное влияние на наше понимание общества южной Скандинавии в Эпоху переселения народов, прошло 30 лет. Но за это тридцатилетие на археологической сцене появилось много нового.

Для понимания обрядов и обрядности следует учитывать физико-географические условия местности и взаимное расположение памятников – выбор места имел решающее значение для восприятия ритуальных действий и памяти о них. В этом отношении мне сложно представить, чтобы «коллектив», осуществивший ритуальную порчу уздечек и седел на вершине заметной гравийной гряды, случайно выбрал это место. Исходя из этого, стала ясна необходимость вновь отправиться на место находки в Сёсдале, чтобы взглянуть на ее контекст свежим взглядом.

Новая поездка на место находки и осмотр окружающего ландшафта оставили глубокое впечатление. Конскую упряжь уничтожили на вершине южной оконечности длинной гравийной гряды, в высоту достигавшей около 10 м (рис. 2). К северо-западу от гряды находится Веттерюд – крупнейший из сохранившихся на территории Скании могильников Железного века. Он расположен между тремя вулканическими холмами и зоной небольших болот, которые в Железном веке могли представлять собой неглубокие озера у подножья упомянутой гряды. Расстояние до места находок Сёсдала I и II составляет всего 200–300 м. Многие из находящихся здесь вертикальных камней образуют каменные ладьи. Сегодня на месте сохранились лишь 375 камней, тогда как в 1822 г. на открытой местности было видно более 600 (рис. 3). Могильник использовался, начиная, по крайней мере, с Эпохи переселения народов до Эпохи викингов. В разрушенной кремации обнаружена так называемая «молотовидная» портупейная скоба от ножен меча (рис. 4). Она одновременна Сёсдале I. «Молотовидные» портупейные скобы были характерным элементом вооружения воинской элиты в зоне от Скандинавии до Черного моря в период D1 по скандинавской хронологии.

К северу от могильника Веттерюд обнаружены следы недатированного поселения – очаги, железный шлак, посуда, столбовые и другие ямы, являющиеся показателем деятельности, которая велась здесь в Железном веке. Через восточную часть могильника проходят древние дороги. На востоке могильник заканчивается у заболоченной местности под гравийной грядой. С вершины гряды открывается замечательный вид (рис. 5). В западном и северо-западном направлении на площади 500 х 500 м можно видеть: под самой грядой – заболоченную местность, далее – могильник в окружении трех вулканических холмов, еще дальше к северу могли находиться поселения того же времени. На восток от места находки, над грядой холмов видна вершина Лённебьера (рис. 1). Такой была обстановка.

В окрестностях Сёсдалы I–II и Веттерюда имеется ряд деталей, свойственных священным местам: бросающиеся в глаза утесы, вершины холмов, крупные валуны, озера и болота, водные потоки, источники и колодцы, пещеры, деревья и рощи (рис. 6). Отнюдь не случайно конскую сбрую разломали и дважды оставили на вершине данной гравийной гряды, а не в небольших болотах или озерах, причем это нельзя объяснить и географическими особенностями местности. Если бы вещи захотели бросить в болото, здесь это было бы нетрудно сделать. Выбор острой вершины гравийной гряды для ритуала был преднамеренным. Но какого рода были эти обряды? Кто исполнял их? И почему? Разумеется, попытки понять суть ритуалов рискованны, но сделать их необходимо.

Сценарий

Узда из Сёсдалы I принадлежит к группе выдающихся находок уздечек, характеризующих межрегиональную воинскую элиту Европы в начале Эпохи переселения народов. Состояние вещей показывает, что перед археологизацией их использовали в сложных обрядах. Они подверглись ритуальной порче в ходе систематического хореографического действа (рис. 7). Наблюдения говорят о том, что вещи были разрушены, помещены на землю и покрыты грунтом в результате последовательных действий, проходивших в одном месте и в одно время.

Чтобы попасть от могильника Веттерюд к гравийной гряде, нужно обойти болота с юга (рис. 8). Небольшое понижение в несколько метров глубиной облегчает переход между двумя отрезками гряды – южной, на вершине которой находится Сёсдала I, и северной, где в 1961 г. нашли Сёсдалу II. Это понижение образует естественный подъем, по которому забраться на вершину гряды можно без особого труда. Легкая доступность могла оказаться решающим фактором при выборе этой части длинной гравийной гряды для ритуального жертвоприношения.

За происходившими на вершине гряды событиями можно было следить с могильника, а за погребением умершего можно было наблюдать с места, где осуществляли приношения. Фрагмент ножен меча свидетельствует о том, что кремация воина случилась примерно тогда же, когда возник комплекс Сёсдала I. Вероятно, принадлежавшую этому воину конскую упряжь принесли в жертву на вершине гряды.

Разные датировки комплексов Сёсдалы I и Сёсдалы II свидетельствуют о том, что на вершине гряды не менее двух раз происходили обряды, в ходе которых были уничтожены и захоронены предметы конской упряжи. Кажется, эти события разделило одно поколение. Преемственность обрядов подтверждает предположение, что данное место было избрано не случайно, и что существует связь между «биографиями» двух находок. Учитывая, что приношение конской упряжи на гравийном холме в Фультофте более или менее одновременно Сёсдале I, и что расстояние между двумя памятниками составляет всего 15 км, нельзя исключить и связь между «биографиями» Фультофты и Сёсдалы I, ведь эти два всадника, несомненно, были знакомы.

Появление нового обряда, внешнего по происхождению, в традиционной обстановке центральной Скании Железного века совпало с изменением поселенческой структуры. Первый комплекс (Сёсдала II) представлял новый обряд, возможно осуществленный в связи с погребением умершего воина. Вероятно, целью обряда было подкрепить претензии наследников, положение которых в структурах власти было нестабильным. Появление комплекса Сёсдала I показывает, что и следующему поколению понадобилось проведение данного обряда. Воин, похороненный в синхронной могиле в Ветерюде, мог быть всадником, чье снаряжение было ритуально принесено в жертву в Сёсдале I, а потому он мог оказаться тем, кто «сотворил предка» в Сёсдале II. Чем же он вдохновлялся? На это указывает парадная узда в стиле «Сёсдала».

Ритуальная порча и захоронение конской упряжи в Раннесредневековое время происходило в среде, где возникли новые представления, причем их носители были знакомы друг с другом. Для данной социальной среды характерно было влияние военизированной культуры поликультурных всадников Европы (рис. 9). Выводы, основанные на новом исследовании состава находок и их контекста, повышают достоверность того, что погребальные комплексы конных кочевников можно рассматривать как аналогию находкам в Сёсдале и Фультофте.

Имеется поразительное сходство между характеристиками находок в Сёсдале и гуннских погребальных комплексов.

И те, и другие включали уздечки, оковки седел и оружие. Эти вещи имеют следы преднамеренной порчи. Их поместили на участки сухой земли, в непосредственной близи от одновременных могил. Здесь нет костей и других следов того, что это могли быть погребения.

Погребальный обряд был переходным от одних условий к другим, то есть он был одновременно устремлен назад и направлен вперед во времени. Такие ритуалы, как представляется, больше чем обычные жертвоприношения напоминали обряды перехода (Rites de passage). Эта практика типична для таких конных кочевников, как сарматы, гунны или аланы. Анализируя появление в Скании подобных ритуалов, нужно учитывать особое значение лошади как показателя власти и престижа. Контакты с жителями Восточной Европы привели скандинавов к контактам с кочевыми скотоводами, у которых лошадь находилась в центре представлений о могуществе и общественном положении, что нашло отражение в обряде. Находки в Фультофте и Сёсдале могут отображать подобные обрядовые действия, выполненных в месте, откуда можно было видеть могильник, где хоронили умерших воинов. Такой обряд мог включать погребение, погребальный пир, ритуальную порчу конской сбруи и последующее захоронение ее остатков, а также обозначение этого места с помощью копья.

Подписи к иллюстрациям

Рис. 1. Потухший вулкан Лённебьер возвышается над окружающим ландшафтом. Фото с востока Шарлотты Фабек, 2016 г.

Рис. 2. Снятая при помощи лазерного дальномера карта территории вокруг Сёсдалы I–II и Веттерюда. © Lantmäteriet.

Рис. 3. Рисунок могильника Веттерюд (по: Sjöborg 1822 fig. 39).

Рис. 4. Веттерюд. Фрагмент портупейной скобы от ножен меча из разрушенной кремации. Бронза, плакированная серебром, со штампованным орнаментом (Шведский исторический музей, № 27 124; по: Strömberg 1961 II Taf. 45: 7).

Рис. 5. Современная карта окрестностей Веттерюда и мест находок Сёсдала I–II, на которую наложен снимок зоны видимости (viewshed) в Сёсдала I, показывающий ее расположение относительно Веттерюда и Лённебьера. Съемка зоны видимости (viewshed) Николы дель'Унто, Лундский университет. Карта: SD-terrängkarta © Lantmäteriet.

Рис. 6. Список слов, характеризующих священные места, составленный на основе скандинавских письменных источников и топонимов (по: Fabech & Näsman 2013: 66–67).

Рис. 7. Ритуально поврежденная конская сбруя из Сёсдала I. Слева: оковки седел (№ 119, 154, 215). Справа: уздечные накладки (№ 11, 16, 88–90). Фото Даниэля Линдскога.

Рис. 8. Карта разведок в Скании 1812–1820 гг., на которую нанесены могильник Веттерюд и две находки в Сёсдале, а также предполагаемый путь между ними.

Рис. 9. Избранные находки из княжеской могилы (Fürstengrab) в Якушовице (Польша). Слева: уздечные накладки в стиле «Сёсдала». Справа: золотые изделия в «гуннском» полихромном стиле. © Muzeum Archeologiczne w Krakowie.

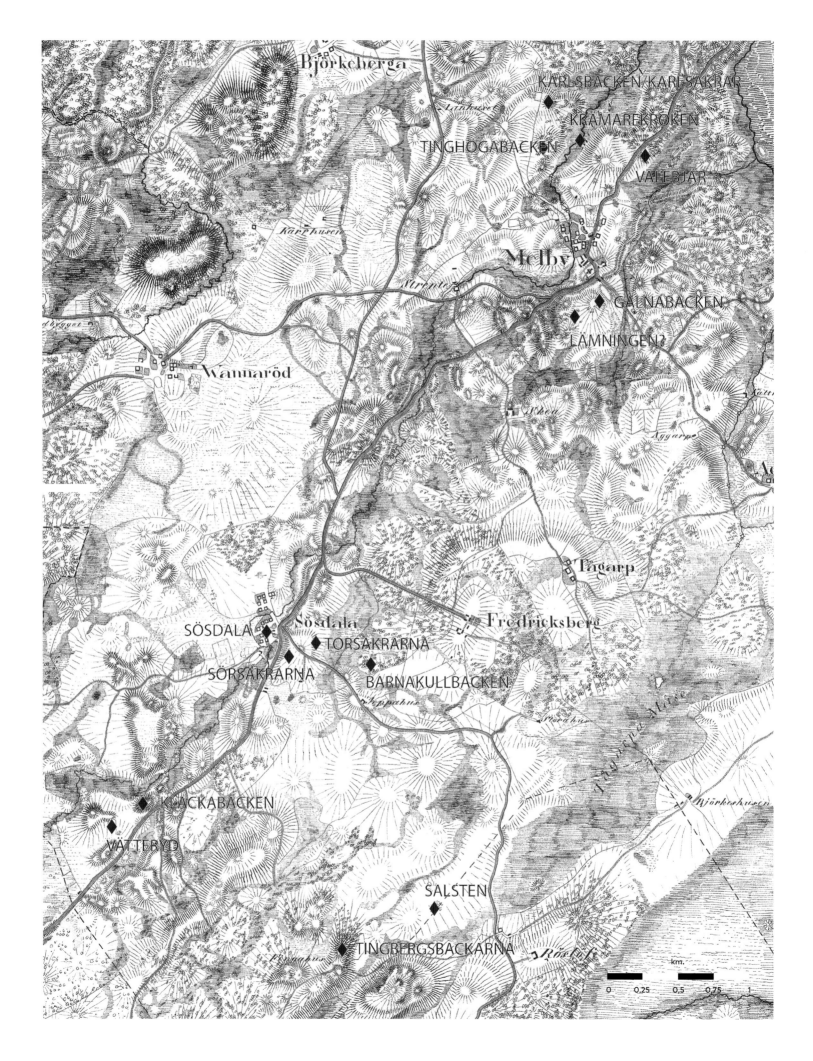

Björkeberga

KARLSBACKEN/KARLSAKRAR

KRAMAREKROKEN

TINGHÖGABACKEN

VALEBJAR

Karrhusen

Melby

GALNABACKEN

LÄMNINGEN?

Wannaröd

Aggarp

Pagarp

SÖSDALA

Sösdala

Fredricksberg

TORSAKRARNA

SÖRSAKRARNA

BARNAKULLBACKEN

Tjockarpa Mosse

Björkeshusen

KLACKABACKEN

VÄTTERYD

SALSTEN

TINGBERGSBACKARNA

Roskbf.

km.

0   0,25   0,5   0,75   1

Chapter 3

Names, place and space
Visualising the landscape of Sösdala

Ola Svensson

Sösdala has been a part of the medieval hundred of Göinge, a geographically vast district with prehistoric roots. Districts like Göinge have had their central places of assembly. These places have recurrent features concerning topography, ancient monuments, accessibility, and local myths reflected in place names. Such features characterise the area around Sösdala. But Sösdala is situated on the periphery of Göinge, in a borderland. Here it is suggested, through data assembled from geography, history, archaeology, and onomastics, that the Sösdala area constituted a separate district at some administrative level which created group identity during the medieval period (c. 1050–c. 1520), but also earlier. The interpretation of place names is a central part of the argumentation, especially the name Sösdala and the occurrence of two field names containing the word ting ('thing', 'assembly').

Svensson, O. 2017. Names, place and space. Visualising the landscape of Sösdala. In: Fabech, C. & Näsman, U. (eds). *The Sösdala horsemen – and the equestrian elite of fifth century Europe*. Jutland Archaeological Society.

Sösdala is situated in Västra Göinge *härad* (an administrative district roughly equivalent to the English 'hundred'), that is to say, in the very extensive area that, before the hundreds of Västra Göinge and Östra Göinge were established in 1637, was called *Göinge härad*. This district is mentioned for the first time in 1085. At that time it is called *Guthisbo* (DD 1R 2:50). It can be assumed that a *Guthir*, regarded by older generations of researchers as a personal name, constitutes the base of *Guthis-* in *Guthisbo*. The last element of the name has usually been interpreted as *bo* 'district, province' (SOL:372; Ringdahl 2008:21). But since it must be questioned whether personal names occur at all in older Nordic district names, one should be open to other interpretations (Andersson 1986:111ff.). One such to consider is *guthir* a title of a ceremonial leader or a priest, compounded of *guth/gudh* 'god' and *ver* (<germ. *wihaz*) 'priest' (Brink 1998:317; Peterson 2007:86, 88).

Guthisbo is one of the few districts in the former Denmark that is equivalent to later known hundreds, and it is also mentioned without the addition *härad* 'hundred' in the oldest sources. Traditionally these districts have been seen as older than those hundreds which already in the oldest records are compounded with the word *härad*. They have been said to be more or less nature-given districts of very old age, which during the early Middle Ages (*c*. 1050–1200) simply were amalgamated into the system of hundreds (Andersson 1982, 1984). This view can be discussed and modified, but regardless of how the hundreds are dated and how one looks upon chronological layers among district names, it is hardly controversial to imagine the existence of a district equivalent to Göinge even before the medieval period (*c*. 1050–*c*. 1520). Tribe names corresponding to Scanian names of hundreds do exist already in late antiquity in the writings of Jordanes (Svennung 1964, 1965).

For a long time it has been an established opinion that the name *Göinge härad* contains the genitive of *gydingar*, a plural inhabitant name based on the district name *Guthisbo* (Lindroth 1911; Ståhle 1946; Andersson 1965; Ringdahl 2008). The umlaut of the stem indicates that the word *gyding* is old, from the Viking Age at the latest.

Assemblies, place names, and landscape

Within the districts known as *härad* (the word is compounded of *här* 'army' or 'crowd of people' and *råd* 'assembly' or 'power') special places existed, having the function of local courts, Da. *Tingsted*, Swe. *Tingsplats* (cf. Svensson 2015:27ff. with refs). The exact location of those places is usually not recorded with certainty until the 17th century, when the "things" moved indoors and from which time we also have a large amount of preserved judgement books. Regarding southern Scandinavia, however, we can still get a relatively clear picture of earlier communal places of assembly, not least though place names associated with law. The major part of those names are names of fields, meadows, and ancient monuments, attested from the 16th century onwards.

The places of assembly and their landscape settings visualised, constructed and supported society at a time when aspirations for more common and public community were not yet manifested through established institutions, the use of writing, or public buildings. They were located at spots in their districts where communications were good, and were, as a rule, topographically special places, for example the end points of ridges or eskers, sites where the land is elevated, or spots close by stream fords – plac-

es where the landscape changes its characteristics. Often they are situated near borders between medieval parishes, probably on prehistoric shared commons predating the establishing of parishes. Normally they are also associated with rich ancient monument contexts, most typically cemeteries, but frequently also at places where prehistoric hoards or deposits from the Neolithic onwards have been found. Sometimes there are springs associated with local folklore traditions near the places of assembly. In some cases a very long continuity of the place chosen for assemblies seems likely. In other cases, however, we see examples of a return to old assembly places – a recycling of history. In the vicinity of the old places of assembly there are not only places with names associated with law. There are usually also places with names containing reminiscences of other kinds of myths and legends. One can think about these areas as epic. Stories of kings, gods, ghosts, and saints gave a certain status to the acts of law, at the same time as the law also contributed new material to the myths and legends. The special status of these places seems to have remained long after the "things" moved to special houses (Sanmark & Semple 2010; Svensson 2015).

The general picture of landscape, name and medieval/prehistoric place of assembly concords to a high degree with the conditions around Sösdala. At one important point, however, the Sösdala area differs from the areas where we normally find medieval and older places of assembly: it is situated on the periphery of Göinge, not in its centre.

Göinge härad, Guthisbo, and Gudingsbackarna

Centrally located in the old district of Göinge we instead find a few sites north-east of Lake Finjasjön which ought to have been of special importance for the Göinge district. Röinge, outside Hässleholm, is well attested as a place of assembly (*tingsplats*) in early modern days; buildings associated with the assembly activities still remain at the place (Ringdahl 2008; Löfgren 2011). Close to Röinge there are also a number of sites whose names have provided the neighbourhood with remarkable stories, from the spheres of law and folklore (DAL; Svensson unpublished excerpts).

Taking place names and topography into account, there is also another place, about 6 km north of Röinge, but still in the same part of the vast Göinge, that has to be mentioned in conjunction with places with the potential of creating and supporting local or regional identity. This is *Gudingsbackarna* (Gudingsbackarne 1815, DAL, Lmh) at Tullstorp, Vankiva parish. These hills are situated at a very distinct narrowing of a river valley, which, for topographical reasons, may have been a strategic node in a prehistoric context. At Gudingsbackarna there is also an archaeological context of cup marks and fossil fields.

The name is interesting. The first element is genitive singular of *guding*, a word whose resemblance to the first elements of *Guthisbo* and *Gydinge herret* is striking. A few dozen sites with names containing *guding* exist in Sweden, but almost all of those are situated along the coast of the Baltic. They correspond with the extension of the etymologically obscure dialect word *guding* 'male eider'.

A connection to 'male eider' at this inland place can be excluded. Instead, the name may be compared to *Gudingshög*, Finspångs läns härad, Östergötland. This name, denominating a mound-like hill, is somewhat difficult to approach since it has various forms attested late. But the resemblance of the name to the nearby village and parish centre *Godegård* (in Guthagarthom 1295) is worth noticing.

One can imagine *Gudingshög* relating in similar ways to *Guthagarthom* as does *Gudingsbackarna* to *Guthisbo*. In both cases the hills are *ing*-derivatives of names containing the word *gudh* 'god'. In both instances there is also reason to discuss whether the first elements of the names represent a name or a title. Regarding *Godegård* one has to consider the personal name *Gudhi* (the most commonly accepted interpretation) or instead a title corresponding to Norse *goði* 'cult leader', chieftain'. Regarding *Guthisbo* we have, as mentioned above, to choose between the less likely name *Guthir* and a title **gudhver* 'priest of god'. The *ing*-derivatives doubtless express some form of close connection, 'the one associated with' or 'the one descending from'. The *ing*-derivatives also tend not to be semantically far from the words they are derived from. In this context we may remind ourselves that a word *goting* 'cult leader, priest', actually did exist in Old High German (Green 2004:437). If the names of the hills containing *guding* are titles, these names prob-

ably reflect a view that the hills in question were places of assembly where a pre-Christian priest fulfilled his duties for and with those associated or in some way connected to him. It must however be stated that *gudhing* is not attested as an appellative in East Norse. *godhi* 'cult leader, priest' is, on the other hand, thought to have existed also in East Norse, but the examples are very few (Andersson 2014). This leads to the thought that *Guding-* in *Gudingsbackarna* (and *Gudingshög*) may well be a personal name, although this must remain an open question. If they are personal names they should rather be seen as the names of mythical historical characters, vital for identity-creating myths of origin relevant to Göinge (and Godegård).

Historicising naming drawing on already existing names is a common feature at prehistoric central places. Often such names are based on district names, but they can also emanate from field names that become the basis of new names or simply are provided with a new historical content. The age of these names varies a great deal. Many are presumably relatively young and a result of an antiquarian discourse in early modern times. But the phenomenon as such is timeless; such names can also be very old. There are names of this type, such as *Vemmenhögarna* 'the mounds of Væmundr', predating and constituting the basis of very old district names, such as *Vemmenhögs härad* (Wæmundhøgheret 1231) (Svensson 2007, 2015).

Finally, it cannot be totally excluded that *Gudingsbackarna* derives directly from the name of the hundred, Old Danish *Gydinge herreth*. But although in both cases we are considering *ing*-derivatives of *gudh*, the absence of umlaut and the singular form of the first element of the name *Gudingsbackarna* speak against such a connection.[1]

What is to be added to the discussion with the interpretations sketched here is the possibility to keep together the district name *Göinge* with the small but distinctive group of district names which are relating to the sacral part of life. In this *Göinge härad* resembles the nearby hundreds *Onsjö härad*, containing the name of the god *Odin*, and *Luggude härad*, in which the last element contains an inflected form of the word *gudh* 'god' (Brink 1998; Svensson 2015). Moreover, there is also material for a discussion about a connection between the name of the district and the name of a particular site: *Gudingsbackarna*.

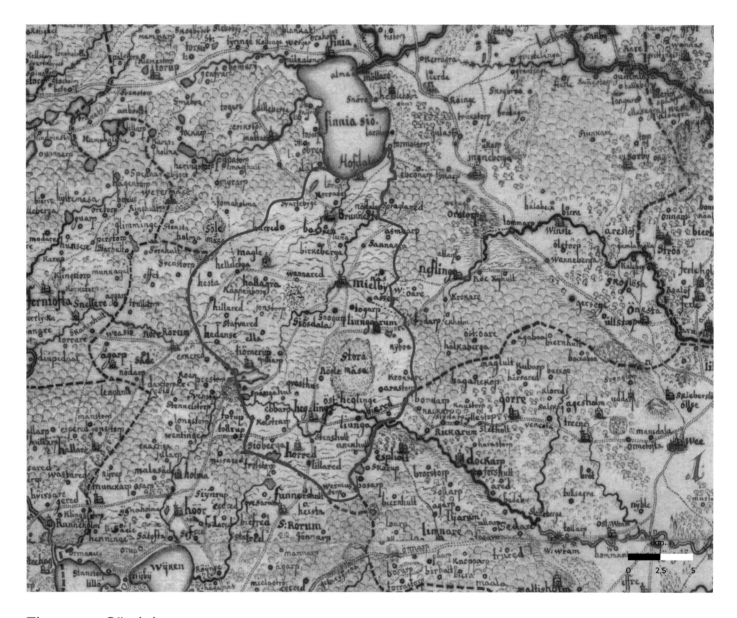

The name Sösdala

The name *Sösdala* (Systaala 1358 reg. c. 1685) have not been given a fully satisfying interpretation. The last element, the word *dal* in the plural, is clear, but the initial *sys-* (>*sös*) is an unusual phonetic combination, so there are few comparable parallels. Most reasonable is to concentrate the discussion on three main tracks. Either the first element of the name contains a word composed from the root of the verb *sjuda* 'seethe, boil', or it contains a cognate to the adjective *sur* 'wet'. Those are the two most important previous suggestions. To those one could also add the possibility of a lost hydronym, the name of a stream or brook, perhaps of onomatopoeic nature. In connection to the

Fig. 1. A proposed domain – a Sösdala "territory" – based on place names and natural geography. A part of Gerhard von Buhrmann's map of Scania, 1684 is used as background. Military Archives, Stockholm. Reproduced and printed by Generalstabens litografiska anstalt, Stockholm 1969.

sur-track an unattested alternative form *sös of the noun *sör* 'dirt' has been suggested (Ringdahl 2008). As for name typology and factual circumstances, this causes no problem, but the fact that the word is unattested raises some doubts. Considering the *sjuda*-track it has been suggested that the first element of the name *Sösdala* is instead a personal name *Sö(i)r, originally meaning 'the one who prepares the [boiling] sacrifice' (Ringdahl 2008).[2] Here too there is a lack of sources, but the name is composed in a well-known manner with many parallels. Here, instead, the typological aspect of the name causes a problem. The last element -dal 'valley' is commonly the generic element of names whose specific element describes the location, topography, flora, size etc. of the dal. -dal-names with personal names as the first element exist, but they are not old. The third suggestion, that the first element of Sösdala contains the name of a stream or brook, requires an explanation of how a name element sus-, which is not entirely uncommon in hydronyms, would develop into sys- (later sös-). Parallels to this seem hard to find.

A possible solution to the problem is to see Sösdala not primarily as a name of a valley and later a settlement, but as a name of a domain, serving both as a district name and as a name of a settlement (fig. 1). This interpretation would fit into an ongoing discussion about certain very old settlement names, most typically names containing the last element -hem 'home, home district' (Vikstrand 2013:19ff.). The obstacle to interpreting the first element as *Sö(i)r is thus removed. *sö(i)r would then not primarily be regarded a personal name, but rather as the title of a cult leader or priest, just like *Guthir in Guthisbo and maybe *Liudhgudha in Luggude härad. One difference is of course the fact that bo and härad, but not dal, are known as administrative district terms. -dal, on the other hand, is a frequently occurring element in district names.

There are also factual circumstances speaking strongly in favour of regarding Sösdala as a very old extensive domain or estate. Already around AD 1065 50 bol (bol 'farm') in Göinge, corresponding to later attested Sösdala län and Mjölkalånga län (län 'fief') were donated to Roskilde Cathedral by the Danish royal family (Ödman 1992:3, footnotes 7 and 8). As we will see, there are also several places with a name that includes the word ting 'thing', 'assembly' near Sösdala, furthermore indicating the status of a district of its own. The second element of the name Sösdala, -dal 'valley', if the interpretation of the first element mentioned above is accepted, most likely refers to the streams, brooks and crack formations which reach from the south-west towards the north-east and characterise this part of central Skåne, from Lake Tjörnarp in the south-west to Lake Finja in the north-east and along the fault that constitutes the north end of the esker Linderödsåsen. The most extensive and visible of these valleys is the one that starts at Tjörnarp, stretches up to Sösdala and further on towards Lake Finjasjön. In this valley not only Sösdala but also Nösdala and Hovdala testify that the association with dal 'valley' is an easy one to make.

Taking vegetation and farming as well as traditional place-name chronology into account, one can imagine a cohesive district, surrounded by forests and reaching from Ynglingarum in the south to Brönnestad in the north and from Ljungarum in the east to Hädensjö in the west (picture). Centrally located in this district there is a vast wetland and forest area. Just at the border of this, exactly in the centre of the suggested district, Sösdala and the Vätteryd cemetery are located. In this context also Mellby 'mid village' gets a very clear meaning: this village is located in the middle of the district between a few of its historically largest and presumably most important settlements, such as Sösdala, Lunnahöja and Brönnestad.

Vätteryd

The name of the Vätteryd cemetery (fig. 2), adjacent to the site where the Sösdala hoard was found, is another name arousing associations with old supernatural beliefs. In this case, however, there is reason to be sceptic. The first element seems to be vätt or vätte 'supernatural (minor) being in the shape of a human person, elf' and the last element looks like ryd 'clearance' (Ringdahl 2008; SOL). It is not remarkable that a field scattered with raised stones is associated with supernatural beings. But names that contain vätt/vätte are extremely rare and the last element -ryd normally has another form in Skåne, namely -röd. Neither is the compound itself completely convincing: clearances are not the type of field or biotope that is the first to be associated with vättar. There is thus reason to believe that the name Vätteryd is young or corrupt. We find the oldest record of the name in the writings of the antiquarian N.H. Sjöborg in 1822. According to Sjöborg's description, the grave-field now called Vätteryd is situated on the Wettery hed (hed 'heath, moor'). However, in a land survey document from 1816, the name is Slätte hed.

Fig. 2. The Vätteryd cemetery consists today of around 250 erected stones – graves of various shapes, some dated from c. AD 400 to c. 900. Two hundred years ago the number of stones was around 600. Photo Ola Svensson 2017.

The combination *Sl* is written in a way that can easily be interpreted as *W*. There could be a misunderstanding or a deliberate interpretation by Sjöborg, or a mistake in the drawing of the map. On the same map a relatively large area – grazing land – that surrounds and includes the grave-field, is called *Väder Grydsmarken*. The phonetic resemblance to *Vätteryd* together with the geographical vicinity raises the suspicion that *Väder Grydmarken* and *Vätteryd*, as well as, perhaps, *Slätte hed*, in one way or another should be kept together when interpreted. *Väder* as in *Väder Grydmarken* would most easily be read as either *väder* as in 'wind' or *vädur* 'sheep' (both pronounced [væːr] in local dialect). Since the last element seems to be the word *gryt* (dial. *gryd*) 'den', the first suggestion is more adequate. The name hence means 'windy den' and has a substantial number of semantic parallels in Skåne, such as *Väderkulan* 'windy den', *Väderpåsen* 'windy bag', and maybe also *Vädergapet* 'windy gap' (DAL: Skånsk ortnamnsdatabas).

The name *Vätteryd* hence seem to have emerged from a confusion of **Vädergryd* and (the misread) *Slätte hed*. The emergence of the name was favoured by the fact that the site was known as a very special ancient monument.

Field names containing stories

Around Sösdala there are localities with names that are linked to myths and legends (frontispiece). Regarding this aspect, the area resembles other areas where ancient monuments and places which were of special importance in the distant past are continuously given new meaning in local place-creating practices. Examples that belong to this category of names are *Torsåkrarna* (DAL, Lmh 1816), *Salsten* (DAL, Lmh 1798), and *Barnabacken* (DAL, Lmh 1816), reminding us of the god or folkloristic figure Thor, a hidden hall for trolls, or the like, underneath a stone, and a hill that a child or children may have haunted. Just as typical is the name of a site on the outskirts of Vätterydsfältet: *Klacker*, *Klackabacken*, *Klacks stenhäll*, or *Klacks hög* (klack 'heel'). The name itself is prosaic; it describes the topography – a steep slope with flat top that ends the Vätterydsfältet to the east, upon which there used to be a now missing rock of diabase. The many forms of the name, its folk etymological interpretation, and the myths with which the name is associated, are typical of names connected to sites of ancient monuments. It is told that a king called *Klack* is buried in the Klackabaken hill (DAL 1926 no. 5362). According to another writer a battle took place in the 7th century AD on the Klackabacken between King Snio of Göinge and King Adils of Uppsala. The story is said to be confirmed by a local poem: "frau Vettery till Mäla by (Mellby) där hördes ett gny te himla sky" (DAL nr 2020:2, 1933), which can be interpreted as "From Vätteryd to Mellby, a mourning sound was heard, all the way to the sky".

Between Sösdala and Fredriksberg there are a couple of fields named *Tingbergsbackarna*. Apparently, the name corresponds to *Tingbergs torp*. It has been suggested that Tingbergs torp was been named after a person called *Tingberg*, and the slopes secondarily after the person (Ringdahl 2008). However, as long as there is no person with that name shown to be connected to the place, it is more plausible to interpret *Tingbergs torp* as assigned to a nature locality or a field: **Tingbjär* 'thing hill' or 'hill near the thing'.

As mentioned above, it has been shown that a majority of the many names of fields in Skåne containing the word *ting* can be connected to places where there is reason to believe that judicial assembly were held during the Middle Ages, and, in many cases, even earlier (Svensson 2015). Typically, we find clear geographical clusters of names of justice, where both the court and the execution function appear. But there is also a small group of more isolated localities with names associated with law that, in one way or another, attest to prehistoric or medieval centrality. **Tingbjär* in Norra Mellby parish is an example of that. As mentioned, a vast property in and around Sösdala formed a separate domain, the Sösdala fief, a circumstance that can be traced back to a royal donation in the 11th century. At this time several donations of farms in Göinge were made by members of the royal family to Roskilde Cathedral. I believe it is not unlikely that the Sösdala property, as well as other larger properties connected to the king or church, also functioned as a court district of its own during early medieval times (11ᵗʰ–12ᵗʰ centuries) and possibly earlier. It is known that many estates in the late medieval era and early 17th century were detached from the hundred's juridical sphere, but the phenomenon is considerably older (Lerdam 2004; Svensson 2015). Most likely the concepts of the medieval *härad*, representing a general practice of law, and *birk*, representing the administration of justice at single estates, had counterparts far back in time (Svensson 2015).

Although there is no vast cluster of law-indicating names near Sösdala, there is yet another name. Just a few kilometres from Tingbergsbackarna there is a site close to Mellby called *Tinghögabacken* (DAL, Lmh 1829:17). There are several ways to interpret the two closely situated hills containing the word *ting-*. They can imply that a thing at some point was moved. **Tingberg* and *Tinghöja* can also be seen as two different expressions of a common memory, or a local myth, implying that a long time ago the area had a thing of its own. One of the names might be secondary to the other, or the names could simply indicate that people could not agree on the exact location of the former *ting*.

Also around Mellby, we find fields with names associated with legends or indicating centrality. *Gallnabacken* most likely contains the adjective *galen* 'mad'. *Ingerör* is probably a cairn where someone called *Inga* or possibly *Inge* (both

names associated with high status) was believed to have been buried. *Karlsåker* (Karls agir 1569) as well as *Karlsbacken* may associate to a mythic person called Karl, or maybe indicate a gathering place for free men (Svensson 2015:218). *Krämmare krokarne* (Lmh 1829) might imply a market place. *Leffningen* (1569 Lb2:119) is likely to be the name of a visible ancient monument. **Valebjär* is an interesting but difficult name to interpret, indirectly proved by the name of a field Valebjärsåker (Hwalebjersåker Mellby 1829:17, Vaallebierg agir/Vaalebierg agir Lb2 120:1). The name resembles the quite large number of names containing the compounds *vall* 'fortification' and a word for a height. But the initial long vowel is unexpected. Perhaps the name originally contains something other than *vall*, e.g. **vale* n. collective of *val* m. 'round stick' (Old Icelandic 'magic stick', compare Modern Icelandic *vala* 'völva'). Both interpretations imply that Valebjär was a high spot provided with a built structure of one kind or another.

The names and the age of settlements

Historical sources indicate that the formation of estates in the late Viking Age, due to royal enfeoffment, had an impact on the area around Sösdala. An important question is of course what the royal power was based upon and what the structures of society and power looked like before the early Middle Ages. Even though the scope of onomastics is limited in this context, something can be said. The region was scarcely populated before the Middle Ages, but it was not unpopulated. Besides archaeological monuments there are also a few place names indicating this, and implying a continuity of settlement until today. *Häglinge*, the name of a neighbouring village south-east of Sösdala, is an example of a name that is dated to before the Viking Age. *Brönnestad* represents another type of name that was common before the Viking Age. *Rösslöv* has been described as a false *-lev*-name (Ringdahl 2008), but this interpretation is based on a couple of very late sources and may be questioned. It cannot be altogether excluded that *Rösslöv* actually is a genuine *-lev*-name. In that case, it would be one of the oldest place names in the area.

Typical for the area otherwise are village names based on elements in nature, names which are very hard to date. They probably vary in age, but nothing argues against quite a few of them being very old – the names *Sösdala, Nösdala,* and *Hovdala* can certainly be some of the oldest place names in the area. Near the places with pre-medieval names we find a large amount of young place names; medieval or younger. These are both village and farm names containing *-torp, -röd, or -hult,* and names of cottages from early modern and modern times. A remarkably large proportion of parish names in this part of Skåne are relatively young place names, that is, from the Viking Age or the Middle Ages: *Matteröd, Tjörnarp, Västra Torup* etc. Since these parishes generally contain settlements with young names, the young parish names probably are a reflection of early medieval colonisation of the woodlands, and late formation of parishes. But concerning the parish names ending with *-arp* and *-rup,* Old Danish *-thorp* 'moved-out farm', it is also plausible that these names bear witness to spatial and social reorganisation – something is broken out and moved away from something else.

The fact that the new settlement was provided with a church may indicate that a rich person or group of people initiated the establishing of the *torp*; people who probably had a prominent position in that society during the late Viking Age and early Middle Ages (Anglert 2006; Karlsson 2011). Social reorganisation is indicated by the donations of property attested in the historical sources. It does not seem farfetched to regard the parish formation as part of the same historical phase as the royal donations in the 11th century. But the situation is complex. It is worth noticing that the two largest royal donations in the area during the 11th century – the estates later known as Sösdala län and Mjölkalånga län – both represent relatively large settlements that were not provided with churches. A possible reason for this would be that the estates were taken over by an elite closely connected to the Danish king at a time when the majority of the formation of parishes had already taken place.

All in all, the place names of the area indicate substantial colonisation and possibly, in addition, social change within the elite, in the early Middle Ages. However, there are exceptions to the general picture: names of district- and settlement names showing that conceptions of certain districts divisions and organisation of settlements have survived from prehistory until today.

There is also a sporadic occurrence of field and nature names giving a very archaic impression. One such name is *Bolmaren/Bolmaremossen,* a name of a vast bog near Häglinge. No absolute dating is possible, but the hydronyms containing *bolm* are in any case part of an ancient Nordic onomasticon. In the same way, *Sörlebäcken,* the name of a brook close to Mellby, is timeless but in accordance with a very old onomasticon.

An attempt to interpret this partly contradictory view can build on the people for whom the various place names were of the greatest importance. What could be said, then, is that the relative permanency of some of the names connected to local settlement, local natural geography and central administration speaks in favour of some sort of unbroken chain passed down among the local users of land as well as among the elite of society – the people organising the country. But the dominant impression of relatively young names nevertheless points at significant changes in settlements and social structure in the area during the late Viking Age, the High and Late Middle Ages, and in early modern times.

Since there are historically large settlements with presumably pre-Viking Age names relatively well spread over the parishes of Norra Mellby, Brönnestad, and Häglinge, it seems reasonable to interpret the stock of younger names in the same area as an expression of an inner expansion.

Notes

1 It is however also in theory possible that the ing-derivative originally was an ung-derivative, which is not expected to course umlaut.

2 See also DS 11 p. 195; Jørgensen 1994:282, about *Systofte,* Denmark.

Sources

DAL *Dialekt- och ortnamnsarkivet i Lund*. Ortnamnsexcerpter. Kept at Lands-arkivet in Lund. Some parts available online: Sprakochfolkminnen.se.

DD *Diplomatarium danicum*. Ed. by *Det danske Sprog- og Litteraturselskab* […] København 1938–.

DS 11 *Danmarks Stednavne*. 11. Stednavneudvalget. Københavns universitet. Institut (Afdeling) for Navneforskning. København: 1922 –. Online 15 September 26: http://danmarksstednavne.navneforskning.ku.dk/

Lb 2 *Lunds stifts landebok*. II. Ljunggren, K.G. & Ejder, B. (eds) *Skånsk senmedeltid och renässans 6*. Lund: 1952.

Lmh *Lantmäterihandling* According to excerpt in DAL.

Skånsk ortnamnsdatabas. Some of the DAL's place-name excerpts are available online at Sprakochfolkminnen.se.

SOL *Svenskt ortnamnslexikon*. 2003. Ed. Wahlberg, M. Uppsala.

Svensson unpublished excerpts. Unpublished excerpts held by Ola Svensson.

References

Andersson, T. 1965. *Svenska häradsnamn*. Uppsala.

Andersson, T. 1982. Danska häradsnamn. Olika typer i formellt hänseende. *Namn och bygd* 70: 46–76.

Andersson, T. 1984. Danska bygde- och häradsnamn. *Namn och bygd*. 72: 90–100.

Andersson, T. 1986. Personnamn i distrikts- och bygdenamn. In: Sandnes & Stemshaug, O (eds). *Personnamn i stadnamn. Artikkelsamling från NORNAs tolvte symposium*. Flatåsen: 111–125.

Anglert, M. 2006. Vidinge, torpnamn och kristen gårdskult. In: Larsson, S. (ed.). *Centraliteter. Människor, strategier och landskap*. Stockholm: 77–100.

Brink, S. 1998. Land, bygd, distrikt och centralort i Sydsverige. Några bebyggelsehistoriska nedslag. In: Larsson, L. & Hårdh, B. (eds). *Centrala platser. Centrala frågor. Samhällsstrukturen under järnåldern. En vänbok till Berta Stjernquist*. Lund: 297–236.

Green, D. H. 2004. *Language and history in the early Germanic world*. Cambridge.

Jørgensen, B. 1994. *Stednavneordbog*. 2nd ed. Copenhagen.

Karlsson, M. 2011. Jordar – teknologi – aktörer. Några tankar om bebyggelse och odling kring Lund och Uppåkra i övergången mellan yngre järnålder och medeltid. *Utskrift* 11: 25–47.

Lerdam, H. 2004. *Birk, lov og ret. Birkerettens historie i Danmark indtil 1600*. Copenhagen.

Lindroth, H. 1911. Göinge härads gårdnamn. *Fornvännen* 6: 175–196.

Löfgren, E. 2011. *Rummet och rätten. Tingshus som föreställning, byggnad och rum i användning 1734–1970*. Gothenburg.

Ödman, A. 1992. Järnskatt och borglän. Presentation av ett påbörjat projekt rörande Nordskånes medeltid. *Ale* 1992/4: 1–14.

Peterson, L. 2007. *Nordiskt Runnamnslexikon*. 5th rev. ed. Uppsala. Online 17 March 29: https://www.sprakochfolkminnen.se/download/18.6dffb94c-149794d926e379/1415279748920/Runnamnslexikon_T+141106.pdf

Ringdahl, C. 2008. *Skånes ortnamn. Serie A 22. Västra Göinge härad med Hässleholms stad*. Lund.

Sanmark, A. & Semple, S. 2010. The topography of outdoor assembly sites in Europe with reference to recent field results from Sweden. In: Lewis, H. & Semple, S (eds). *Perspectives in Landscape Archaeology*. Oxford: 107–119.

Sjöborg, N.H. 1822. *Samlingar för Nordens fornälskare*. Vol. 2. Stockholm.

Ståhle, C.I. 1946. *Studier över de svenska ortnamnen på –inge. På grundval av undersökningar i Stockholms län*. Uppsala/Stockholm.

Svennung, J. 1964. Jordanes beskrivning av ön Scandia. *Fornvännen* 1964:1–23.

Svennung, J. 1965. Jordanes Scandia-kapitel. *Fornvännen* 1965: 1–41.

Svensson, O. 2007. Skånska ortnamn i anslutning till rättsutövning. In: Eggert B., Holmberg B.L. & Jørgensen, B. (eds). *Nordiske navnes centralitet og regionalitet. Rapport fra NORNAs 35. Symposium på Bornholm 4–7 maj 2006*. Uppsala: 191–219.

Svensson, O. 2015. *Nämnda ting men glömda. Ortnamn, landskap och rättsutövning*. Växjö. Summary.

Vikstrand, P. 2013. *Järnålderns bebyggelsenamn. Om bebyggelsenamnens uppkomst och ålder i Mälarlandskapen*. Uppsala. – Online at: Sprakochfolkminnen.se.

Резюме

Географические названия, место и пространство.

Визуализация ландшафта Сёсдалы

Ола Свенссон

Сёсдала находится в Йёинге-херад (Göinge *härad*; *härad* по-шведски «сотня»). Этот округ впервые упоминается в 1085 г. н. э., когда он назывался Гутисбо (*Guthisbo*). Ее название образовано сочетанием *gudhver* («церемониальный вождь» или «[до-христианский] жрец») и *bo* («округ»). Естественно будет предположить, что округ, соответствовавший Йёинге, существовал и до Эпохи средневековья (ок. 1250 – ок. 1520 гг.). Уже Иордан в середине VI в. упомянул несколько топонимов, соответствующих названиям сотен в регионе Скания.

В округах, известных начиная с Эпохи средневековья как *härader* («сотни»), имелись особые места собраний («тинг»). Для южной Скандинавии ясное представление об этих местах дает изучение топонимов, в состав которых входят слова, связанные с законом.

Места собраний и их положение в окружающем ландшафте дают представление об обществе в эпоху, когда община еще не проявила себя в государственных учреждениях, в использовании письменности или общественных сооружениях. Места собраний обнаружены там, где происходило общение – в центре соответствующих сотен (*härader*). Как правило, они выразительны в топографическом отношении, находясь там, где меняется характер ландшафта. Зачастую они находились на границах между средневековыми церковными приходами, вероятно, на доисторических общинных выгонах, предшествовавших делению на приходы. В некоторых случаях они связаны с древними памятниками, например, курганными могильниками или с местами, где осуществляли приношения вещей или прятали клады. В местах древних собраний имеются объекты, названия которых связаны с законом, а также обычно и такие, названия которых содержат воспоминания о мифах и легендах. Их окрестности связаны с эпосом, в котором фигурируют истории королей, богов, призраков,

святых и пр. Места собраний обычно сохраняли подобные статусные признаки на протяжении долгого времени после того, как они перестали быть местом отправления законов.

Общее представление о ландшафте, топонимах и средневековом (доисторическом) месте собраний в высокой степени соответствует условиям Сёсдалы. Однако Сёсдала находится не в центре, а на периферии области Йёинге.

Название «Сёсдала» (*Sösdala*) интерпретировать достаточно сложно, но в нем может заключаться титул *sö(r)ir* («тот, кто готовит вареную жертву»), ставший видовым элементом. Последний элемент, *-dal* («долина»), обычно является родовым элементом слов, видовой элемент которых описывает растительность, размер, топографию и так далее, имея в виду указанную долину. Возможное решение проблемы заключается в интерпретации *Sösdala* как названия домена, служившего одновременно названием области и поселения. Оно соответствует продолжающейся дискуссии о некоторых очень древних названиях поселений. В таком случае название *Sösdala* будет напоминать название округов Гутисбо (*Guthisbo*) и Луггуде-херад (*Luggude härad*), которые, предположительно, включают в себя титулы предводителей культов. Предложенную интерпретацию названия *Sösdala* можно назвать спекулятивной. Но, принимая во внимание всю совокупность фактов, по моему мнению, ее стоит принять во внимание.

Есть и другие основания считать Сёсдалу доменом или поместьем, существовавшим не только в Эпоху средневековья, но и в более раннее время. Около 1065 г. член датской королевской семьи сделал очень богатый подарок кафедральному собору в Роскильде, заключавшийся в фермах, позднее известных как фьефы (*län*) Сёсдала и Мъёлькалонга в Йёинге.

Близ Сёсдалы находятся два отдельных холма с названиями на *Ting-* («собрание»), что дополнительно подчеркивает статус данной области как самостоятельного округа определенного административного уровня.

В окрестностях Сёсдалы можно отыскать разнообразные эпические названия холмов, полей, камней и пр., связывающие местность с историями о различных событиях и более или менее сверхъестественных существах. Один из топонимов, вызывающий в памяти сверхъестественное существа – название могильника Веттерюд, которое толкуется как «лесная поляна *vättar* (эльфов)». Но в этом случае название исказили, чтобы связать его с замечательными конструкциями из вертикальных камней.

Наконец, утверждают, что существенная часть поселений в окрестностях Сёсдалы имеет сравнительно молодые названия, относящиеся к Эпохе средневековья или еще более позднему времени. Но здесь же находится и группа поселений, названия которых датированы Эпохой викингов или имеют еще более древнее происхождение, причем они рассеяны по округе. Этот феномен интерпретируют как показатель преемственности поселенческой структуры начиная со времени перед Эпохой викингов, причем эта структура была частично реорганизована и изменена в ходе внутренней экспансии в Эпоху викинга и Эпоху средневековья.

Подписи к иллюстрациям

Рис. 1. Предполагаемый домен – «территория Сёсдала» – выделенный на основании топонимов и природно-географических условий (на основе карты Герхарда Бурманна 1684 г.).

Рис. 2. Сегодня могильник Веттерюд состоит из 375 вертикальных камней, образующих погребальные монументы разных размеров, некоторые из которых датируются в пределах V–IX вв. н. э. Двести лет тому назад здесь было около 600 камней (фото Олы Свенссон, 2017 г.).

Chapter 4

The Migration Period landscape of central Scania

The local context of the Sösdala and Fulltofta finds

Charlotte Fabech, Bertil Helgesson & Ulf Näsman

A background is given for six exclusive Migration Period finds from central Scania (Tormestorp, Sösdala, Göingeholm, Sjörup, Fulltofta and Claestorp). The area is delimited by uninhabitable horsts and situated in the northern more forested part of Scania. There is long settlement continuity but the archaeological record is relatively poor in comparison to the plains in southern and north-eastern Scania. The six finds mark something new in the area, a presence of warriors connected to the south-east European martial elite. The area is placed at the interface between two major polities in the south-west and north-east. Various reasons why elite warriors were placed here are discussed.

Fabech, C., Helgesson, B. & Näsman, U. The Migration Period landscape of central Scania. In: Fabech, C. & Näsman, U. (eds). *The Sösdala horsemen – and the equestrian elite of fifth century Europe.* Jutland Archaeological Society.

The Sösdala area is famous because of a number of unique finds from the 5th century that demonstrate close connections to eastern and central Europe (Fabech 1990, 1991a, 1991b, 1993; Fabech & Näsman 2013a). The finds include three funeral depositions of splendid horse tack at Sösdala and Fulltofta, an exclusive bridge mount of a sword scabbard, a silver belt buckle and a pelta-shaped pendant from Tormestorp, a silver hoard from Sjörup and an offer-ing from Göingeholm, an eagle-shaped gold plaque from Claestorp as well as a number of large cemeteries with standing stones, stone circles, stone ships, etc. The area is placed in the centre of the forest zone of northern Scania, in a settlement pocket far from the central settlement areas on the plains at the coasts. Ture Arne was of the opinion that the splendid finds point to "the existence of a Migration Period realm, the extent of which cannot be deter-

77

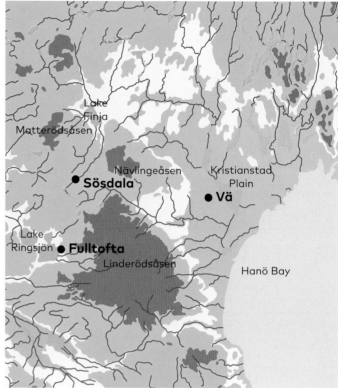

| 0-30 m |
| 30-80 m |
| 80-150 m |
| >150 m |

Fig. 1. The central area of Scania between Lake Finja and Lake Ringsjön along with the Kristianstad plain. Contours at 30 m, 80 m, and 150 m a.s.l. Map after Bredsdorff 1973, digitised by the research project Settlement and Landscape (Fabech, Hvass, Näsman & Ringtved 1999:14).

mined at present" (Arne 1937:94–95; transl.). Indeed, it is remarkable that such exclusive finds were deposited in such remote places, but a satisfactory explanation has not yet been found.

The Sösdala area in Scania

Scania is the southernmost part of Sweden, Swedish since 1658 when Denmark ceded it. Geologically Scania is divided in two parts by a tectonic divide running roughly from north-west to south-east, "the Scanian diagonal" (Emanuelsson *et al.* 1985:11–19; Fabech 1993 figs 2–10; Germundsson & Schlyter 1999:10–18). North-eastern Scania is part of the Baltic shield with bedrock of granite and gneiss. An exception is the Kristianstad plain, which rests on sedimentary rocks (limestone, sandstone, etc.). South-western Scania consists of sedimentary rocks (limestone, sand-

stone, clay slate, etc.) and is connected to the bedrocks of central Europe. The topography is characterised by large faults and horsts following the tectonic divide from north-west to south-east (fig. 1). The horsts determine communication lines through the landscape. For instance, the road northwards from Sösdala has to go through narrow passages between two ridges up to 150 m high, Matterödsåsen to the west and Nävlinge/Göingeåsen to the east. The Sösdala settlement area is bounded to the south-east by another horst, Linderödsåsen. Sösdala is situated in a part of central Scania that is characterised by marked hills consisting of basalt plugs, the eroded remains of extinct volcanoes. The present landscape was shaped much later during the last glacial period when the soil cover was formed. The soil of north-eastern Scania is meagre podsol on coarse moraines poor in clay. Zones of sand and

Fig. 2. A "Sösdala area" is delimited to 16 medieval parishes marked with their churches. A part of Gerhard von Buhrmann's map of Scania, 1684 is used as background. Military Archives, Stockholm. Reproduced and printed by Generalstabens litografiska anstalt, Stockholm 1969.

gravel, including marked gravel ridges, were deposited by ice streams and the ridges run across the landscape from north-east to south-west. The Kristianstad plain is covered with postglacial sand. Numerous depressions became wetlands, lakes or bogs. In contrast, south-western Scania has brown soils of very high agricultural quality on clayey moraine. The geological differences are reflected in the land-use where south-western Scania is highly cultivated with a large population and north-eastern Scania is sparsely populated and in large part covered with forests except in the Kristianstad plain with better agricultural possibilities. Of course there are transition zones between the two landscape types, plains and forests. In historic times, this forest zone was characterised by a mixed economy: husbandry, some cultivation and production of tar, wood, iron, etc.

The Sösdala area (fig. 2) is the southernmost end of an administrative district called Western Göinge *härad* (something like an English hundred) (see Svensson chapter 3). The land between Lake Finja and Lake Tjörnarp was previously called Göingeholmen and its nature with a mild character and deciduous forests differs from the barren northern parts of the district (Stille 1909:860). The area is situated north of the main Scanian watershed and its central part is below 100 m a.s.l. The stream draining Lake Tjörnarp runs northwards past Sösdala to Lake Finja, which discharges into the River Alma, a tributary of River Helge that flows into the Baltic at the Gulf of Hanö. Lake Bosarp with the Sjörup find also drains into the Baltic but through a tributary of the River Vrams that flows eastwards also to River Helge.

The find place of the Fulltofta find is situated on the other side of the watershed Linderödsåsen. It is located near Lake Ringsjön, which is drained by the River Rönne that flows into Skälderviken, a bay of Kattegat. The bedrock and soil quality are about the same as at Sösdala but on the opposite side of the lake we find productive clayey moraine and the find place Claestorp.

A greater settlement area around Sösdala can be marked off in central Scania. Seventeen parishes in three *häraden* are chosen for an extended ancient monuments survey (fig. 2); in Frosta *härad*: Bosjökloster, Fulltofta, Höör, Norra Rörum and Södra Rörum parishes; in Western Göinge *härad*: Brönnestad, Finja, Häglinge, Hässleholm, Ignaberga, Matteröd, Norra Mellby, Nävlinge, Stoby, Tjörnarp and Vankiva parishes; and finally in Gärds *härad* Äsphult parish. All parishes were formed in the High Middle Ages with the exception of the late parish of Hässleholm, a town since 1914 that grew up at a railway junction after 1860. Anne Carlie dealt with the parishes belonging to Western Göinge *härad* in her dissertation (1994).

The remarkable Migration Period finds

In a 10 × 30 km large area around Sösdala, a number of remarkable Migration Period finds were discovered, from North to South Tormestorp, Sösdala, Göingeholm,

Fig. 3. *The find spots from the south: Claestorp, Fulltofta, Sjörup, Göingeholm, Sösdala, Tormestorp. Background map as fig. 2.*

Fig. 4. *Belt buckle and bridge mount found in Tormestorp. 1:1. Photo Daniel Lindskog, Historical Museum at Lund University.*

Sjörup, Fulltofta and Claestorp (fig. 3). The find circumstances and content of the depositions at Sösdala and Fulltofta are presented separately (see the find catalogues; Fabech chapter 1; Näsman chapter 7).

Tormestorp

About 12 km north of Sösdala, two objects were found in 1956 near the beach at Björkviken, a bay of Lake Finja (fig. 4). The intact gilt silver buckle is decorated with geometrical chip-carving classified as Nydam style by Jan Bemmann (1998:237, Fundliste 10:35). The chip-carved decoration of the attachment plate is very similar to the decoration of a strap end found in a woman's grave at Kirchheim am Neckar, Germany (Christlein 1979:153, Taf. 47).The grave is dated to the end of the 5th century but the strap end is consid-

ered to be an heirloom two generations older, which means that it is from the first half of the 5th century, a dating that fits the Tormestorp buckle well. The silver-plated bridge mount of type Nydam-Porskær from a sword scabbard was also found on the same occasion (Strömberg 1961b:73, Taf. 52:2a-b; Bemmann 1998:221–223, Fundliste 9:4). It is damaged by fire, but it is still possible to perceive its outstanding quality. The mount is made of bronze and covered with sheet silver in which a delicate decoration with niello is punched and in the centre a multi-petal flower is incised from deeply punched triangles. Its quality ranks among the highest of all bridge mounts of this type (for mounts of type Nydam-Porskær see now Rau 2010:486–487, Abb. 203). Both buckle and bridge mount indicate the presence

Fig. 5. Pelta-shaped pendant found in Lake Finja at Tormestorp. 1:1. Photo Arne Sjöström.

Fig. 6. Ceramic vessel found at Göingeholm. It contained a selection of a woman's jewellery, see fig. 7. Not to scale. Photo Yliali Asp, SHM no. 21058, Stockholm.

of men of high martial status and indicate close contacts with a European network (Fabech & Näsman chapter 17 fig. 11). Both objects can be dated to Scandinavian period D1.

The two objects were found in secondary position in dug-up sand when a trench for a water pipe was dug. No more finds were made during a metal detecting survey the same year. The water table of the lake was lowered by 3.1 m in the 19th century so the find place probably is old lake bottom. According to uncertain information, sand was once carted to the beach so the find place must be considered problematic.

Some years ago a man was bathing at the Björkviken beach and about 70 m from the present edge of the lake he found a pelta-shaped bronze pendant (fig. 5). It seems to be burnt and has lost both the silver cover and the attachment plate. What is preserved is the outline with two horse heads turning downwards and inwards. It is datable to period Scand-D1 and thus contemporary with the other finds. The burnt surface of the pendant and the burnt bridge mount are very similar, indicating a connection, but unfortunately the precise context of the three finds remains a mystery so the character of the find cannot be settled.

Göingeholm

When levelling a slope during roadworks in 1935 workers found two clay pots four metres apart, buried at a rock outcrop. The site is near the manor of Göingeholm, about 4 km south-east of Sösdala and 2 km from Häglinge church. The site was visited by Ture Arne who recorded the find circumstances (Arne 1937). A simple and crude pot was empty. The other had ribbed and polished decoration (fig. 6) and contained a hoard of a woman's jewellery (fig. 7): three silver dress brooches and an early gilt silver relief brooch in Nydam style, fragments of nine silver clasps (hooks and eyes) and 47 amber beads. Furthermore very rusty iron fragments were found. They represent a knife that had a handle with bronze ring and bronze rivet. The other iron fragments are hard to identify but could be remains of a sword beater used in weaving.

The three dress brooches are untypically made of silver and have details similar to other brooch types datable to period Scand-D1 (cf. Hårdh 2003). The clasps belong to Hines class A and their diameter indicates a date in the early Migration Period (Hines 1993:4–11). The large silver brooch is a unique type intermediate between silver

Fig. 7. Silver jewellery and amber beads found in a ceramic vessel at Göingeholm, see fig. 6. Not to scale. Photo Helena Rosengren, SHM no. 21058, Stockholm.

sheet brooches and relief brooches. It seems to have both chip-carved decoration and decoration punched in sheet silver (cf. Forssander 1937:84). The square head plate has deep geometric decoration but also rows of punch marks. The bow is punch-decorated and ridged silver ribbons are bent around it at the bases. The irregular foot plate is made of sheet silver, roof-shaped and punch-decorated. There are mistakes in the decoration at the end, which is awkwardly cut off. The greatest width is at the end. There are rudimentary hanging animal heads at the base of the bow. All traits indicate early Migration Period and a date in the first half of the 5th century. The decoration is not typical Nydam style, but certainly closely related and it

is included in Bemmann's list of objects in Nydam style (Bemmann 1998 Fundliste 10:28). Arne looked for Norwegian connections to explain brooches and pottery but the lack of contemporary grave finds in Sweden and Denmark made his suggestion problematic. The decoration of pottery from graves at Haraldsted, Zealand, can be compared to the Göingeholm vessel and is dated to early Migration Period (Norling-Christensen 1956:33). In an excavation at Gårdlösa in Scania an inhumation (grave 72) contained a ceramic vessel similar to that of Göingeholm. It is dated to the late Roman Iron Age and early Migration Period, c. AD 350–500 (Stjernquist 1993a:58, pl. 94; 1993b:37–38, 43). The amber beads are probably imports from the south-eastern littoral of the Baltic Sea where similar turned beads are found in several contexts including Kielpino/Kelpin (Arne 1937:93–94). It is worth noting that one of the silver brooches from Kielpino has a foot plate with shape and punched decoration resembling the Göingeholm brooch (see *MPOV* at Kielpino). Jewellery and pots date the hoard to Scandinavian period D1.

The workers observed nothing that could indicate that the two pots are urn graves, and in an inhumation one would not expect jewellery to be put down in a pot. The location of the find spot is the southern end of a marked hill. The old road connects Sösdala, Häglinge and Södra Rörum. It passes an important cemetery at Häglinge. From Södra Rörum a road continued to Fulltofta. How should we understand this deposition of pots in a remote site at an old road? The silver and amber could be a treasure hidden in a nice pot (Fabech 1990:116), but that will leave the empty pot unexplained. That two pots were buried at the foot of a hill where a road passes a rock outcrop can be considered a ritual act (Fabech & Näsman 2013b:77); one pot containing perishable material, the other a woman's jewellery. Perhaps a hierophany once took place here at the road and in commemoration the two urns were deposited here on one or two occasions.

Sjörup

Three finds acquired by the Swedish History Museum (Statens historiska museum, Stockholm) in 1842, 1858 and 1859 have problematic find circumstances (Fabech 1990). The finds were undoubtedly made at the northern end of Lake Bosarpsjön, about 6 km from Sösdala. Unfortunately more precise details of the find circumstances are not known. The find place is situated in a remote location, 3.5 km from Häglinge church and the Iron Age graves preserved in its surroundings. The finds from 1858–1859 were published by Bernhard Salin (1894) but not the buckle found in 1842. It was not published until later by Norberg (1931 Abb. 15) and Fabech (1990 figs 4–5). The more than 200 pieces represent approx. 40 different objects, which are the remains of the equipment of at least twelve warriors and a couple of horses (fig. 8). They are of silver, often gilt and some have niello inlays. A few objects had set stones or glass, still preserved in three objects. The predominant decoration is chip-carved spirals. Only four mounts are decorated in Scandinavian style I but most mounts seem to be decorated in the earlier Nydam style or Sjörup style (Voss 1954:174–176). The collection is not homogeneous but consists of objects brought from

Fig. 8. Hoard of destroyed silver objects found in Sjörup. Not to scale. Photo Sören Hallgren, SHM nos. 1032, 2437 and 2663, Stockholm.

different quarters (cf. Salin 1894:106). The chronological frame for buckles of the Sjörup-Snartemo type is set by Andreas Rau at 455/465–520/530 (Rau 2010:312–313). The last items in the deposition may be four objects decorated in Salin's style I (Salin 1894 figs 44, 45, 47 and 67). The deposition can be dated to the third quarter of the 5th century AD or early Scandinavian period D2a (for the beginning of style I, see Rau 2010:297–301). The objects without style I elements were certainly produced

Object	Found	Missing
Swords	**3**	**9**
Sword pommel	1	11
Hilt mounts	3	21
Mount of sword bead (?)	1	11
Sword scabbards	**12**	**0**
U-shaped chapes	≥12	0
Mouthpieces	3	9
Suspension mounts (?)	2 × 2	10
Edge bindings	Some fragments	Many fragments
Warrior's dress	**5**	**7**
Strap buckles for belts or baldrics	5	7
Strap ends	5	7
Clasp buttons	4	Many
Strap mounts	**1**	**Many**
Double mount	1	Many
Horse tack	**3**	**Much**
Strap junctions	2 + 1	21
Silver ingot	**1**	**–**
A 2 cm long cut off piece	1	–

earlier. A sword pommel decorated in style I shows wear indicating much use.

The Sjörup find is among the most familiar Migration Period finds, mainly due to the fact that it has given its name to one of the styles of the period, the Sjörup style (Voss 1954:174–175; Karlsson 1983:141–142), but also because this silver hoard is rather unique in the Scandinavian source material. The find material exhibits strong connections with central Europe. Since the buckle type lacks Scandinavian prototypes Rau accepts Forssander's idea of a Danubian origin of the type (Forssander 1937:70–81 wrote *gotisch*).

For many years the find was interpreted as a sacrifice of military equipment of the same kind as those at Porskær and Nydam II on Jutland. However the characteristics of the find do not correspond to the traditional "weapon sacrifices", nor to the so-called *pars-pro-toto* offerings (Fabech 1990:111–113). Most of the silver pieces are broken or cut over. The find contained a silver ingot. Probably the many small fragments and objects were deposited close together. There are no weapons in the find itself or in the vicinity of the finding place. A comparison between Sjörup and con-

temporary hacksilver hoards in South Scandinavia (Rau 2010:454–456, Fundliste 26; 2013) shows considerable agreements concerning the treatment and fragmentation of the silver objects. Against this background Sjörup is regarded as a hacksilver hoard on a par with the South Scandinavian hoards at Høstentorp, Simmersted and Hardenberg (Fabech 1990). But there are considerable differences. Roman tableware is missing and there is no domestic female jewellery; there are solely fragments of objects that are easily associated with warriors plus a piece of a silver ingot. Only a location of the exact find spot and a carefully conducted investigation will finally permit us to establish whether the Sjörup find is hoarded wealth or an offering.

The minimum numbers for the equipment of warriors and horses (see table on the left) reveal that the hoard as it is preserved has an unbalanced composition: too many scabbards and too few swords. A comparison with a recent hoard found in England may be illustrative.

In 2009 a sensational find, a mixed gold and silver hoard, was made at Hammerwich near Lichfield in Staffordshire, England (Leahy & Bland 2009; *Staffordshire hoard*). The find place is a tilled field where the plough had scattered the hoard and an area 9 × 13 m was investigated to recover the objects. The weight of the gold objects is 5 kg and 1.4 kg is silver objects. The hoard has a martial character and consists of more than 3,500 pieces of more or less fragmented fittings for swords, shields and helmets as well as remains of four or five Christian processional crosses. As many as 86 different sword pommels are recorded (Fischer & Soulat 2010). Many objects are decorated in Salin's style II or have garnet cloisonné. The deposition is believed to have taken place between AD 650 and AD 700 but many objects are earlier, some as old as the first half of the 6th century. The find place is situated centrally in the Anglo-Saxon kingdom of Mercia that was often in armed conflict with its neighbours.

The publication of the find is not finished and no consensus exists concerning its interpretation. It cannot be clarified whether the hoard represents an offering or whether it was profane treasure, stashed away and never retrieved in connection with warfare. A comparison with the Sjörup deposition seems relevant. Despite the fact that the Sjörup hoard was found in Scania and is about 200 years older, the selection of artefacts and their treatment are similar. Male war-gear dominates in both hoards. The sword fittings were brutally torn off the sword, smashed and cut to pieces. In Sjörup scabbard mounts and strap junctions of bridles are included but are missing in the Staffordshire hoard. Remains of helmets and shields are present in the Staffordshire hoard and missing in Sjörup. But both finds are characterised by strong links to warfare and violence (cf. Halsall 2010).

The unbalanced composition of the two hoards can be the result of how a battlefield was looted by the victorious side. It was important that the looting was performed according to established rules to preserve warriors' willingness to fight. Rituals were a way to ensure that rules were followed. The destruction of battle field loot was a way to demonstrate contempt for the enemy. A ritual was not a single act but a whole chain of various events (Fabech 2011a). To celebrate a victory the weaponry of the defeated was collected and ritually destroyed. In a way the enemy was conquered once more when his exclusive weapons were dismantled and destroyed. This destruction reinforced the victory and outraged the defeated and deprived them of their status as warriors (cf. Rau 2010:512–518). Both the Staffordshire and Sjörup hoards are understandable as results of weapon rituals at the battlefield that took place before final destruction and deposition. After destruction some of the loot was probably distributed among the attending warlords (cf. Tacitus *Annales* I:59). It is easy to understand how the unbalanced composition of the hoards was a result of the circumstances of this distribution. When brought home the loot was transformed to bullion of gold or silver to be used by the warlord and his retainers. The way the silver chapes of sword scabbards in the Sjörup hoard were cut into small pieces illustrates their transformation from weaponry to currency (Fabech 1990 fig. 7). Probably parts of the hoard were already in circulation. So it seems likely that the hoard was hidden as valuable raw material, perhaps due to warfare.

Claestorp

About 20 km from the Sösdala find spot another remarkable find was made in a tilled field 1882 (Holmqvist 1961). It is filigree-decorated gold plaque, approx. 4 cm large,

Fig. 9. Eagle-shaped gold plaque with chains found in Claestorp. Approx. 2:1. Photo Ulf Bruxe, SHM no. 7004, Stockholm.

shaped as an eagle with six gold chains attached (fig. 9). The find spot is near the south-eastern part of the Lake Ringsjön (ancient monument, *FMIS* no. Bosjökloster 38:1), near an old road passing the lake, today route E22. An investigation with metal detector gave a negative result, so the find was perhaps single or the find spot is not correctly mapped. On the opposite eastern side of the lake you find the large Nunnäs cemetery and the Fulltofta find spot. In the neighbourhood an old thing site is recorded (Svensson 2015:148–158; *FMIS* no. Bosjökloster 39:1). A remarkable Bronze Age hoard was made nearby (*FMIS* no. Bosjökloster 23:1). Once this area was outlying land of Bo, an estate centre and nodal place. In the 12th century a nunnery was established on the island Bosön (Bosjökloster).

Holmqvist assumed that the eagle was a late Roman or Byzantine work, perhaps from Italy, and he dated it tentatively to the 6th century in the Migration Period, perhaps earlier, perhaps later. On the back of the eagle there are six loops for gold chains (remains of four are preserved), three at the top and three at the bottom. Possibly the plaque was a chain distributor in a threefold chain of gold, perhaps part of a pectoral. Such objects did not arrive in Scania through normal exchange but were probably brought home as plunder or gifts. The lack of find context makes it impossible to discuss the character of the find: settlement? hoard? grave? offering? But as an indicator of power and connections with south-eastern Europe it is remarkable and the site deserves attention.

To be able to explain the occurrence of these six unusual and exclusive finds in the forested zone of central Scania a survey is needed of the general settlement picture that is delineated by the ordinary archaeological record, place names and later written sources.

The archaeological record

Studies of Iron Age settlement in Scania, and in large parts of northern Europe, once took their starting point in graves and cemeteries (Strömberg 1961a; Carlie 1994). In the last few decades settlements have become an important source in many parts of Europe. In central Scania, however, archaeological excavations are very few and we must rely on other sources such as the visible ancient monuments recorded in the Ancient Monuments Survey in Sweden (*FMIS*). Stray finds in the collections of museums are also a valuable source.

Settlements

In reality no settlements were excavated in the Sösdala area. But settlement remains are recorded. North-west of the Vätteryd cemetery, postholes, fireplaces, pits and finds of iron slag have been excavated; only a rough dating to the Iron Age is given (*FMIS* no. Norra Mellby 261:1, 265:1). Another site was excavated two kilometres to the south of the Tormestorp find place. No dating artefacts were found but there are ^{14}C dates from the late Bronze Age/Early Iron

Age and from the Late Roman Iron Age/Migration Period (*FMIS* no. Brönnestad 49:4). Settlement remains have also been found at Fogdarp, Bosjökloster parish (Strömberg 2013; *FMIS* no. Bosjökloster 118). The site is not precisely dated, but is situated less than a kilometre from the finding place of the gold eagle from Claestorp (see above; *FMIS* no. Bosjökloster 38:1).

Ancient monuments

In his survey of the ancient monuments record of Sweden Åke Hyenstrand mapped all ancient monuments recorded in Scania (1984:125–128, map 49). The Sösdala-Fulltofta area is placed in his "archaeological research area 2c", i.e. Inner Scania. The overall Scanian distribution of ancient monuments shows large areas without or with very few recorded ancient monuments. Two very different explanations offer themselves: first the cultivated plains, where most monuments have disappeared, and second the forested horsts and stone moraines, where settlement has always been sparse. In the forested zone in inner Scania a relative find concentration is found in the broad Sösdala valley.

A map of recorded cemeteries demonstrates extensive destruction of graves on the plains (Hyenstrand 1984 map 51). In contrast, the relatively good preservation in the Sösdala area is visible on a number of maps (Hyenstrand 1984 maps 6–7, 18, 24–25, 29; cf. Helgesson 2002 fig. 13). The most common ancient monuments in central Scania are single graves, cemeteries, rock carvings (cup marks) and ancient field remains. Generally they bear witness to a relatively widespread and stable settlement. Some of these monuments and remains can be typologically dated to the Migration Period and later (cf. Carlie 1994).

Stone settings

Preserved grave monuments are common in central Scania (*FMIS*). Certainly many pre-date the Migration Period. It is obvious that there is a connection between graves from the Late Roman Iron Age and those from the Migration Period. But only at one site, at Vätteryd, can continuity be demonstrated from the Migration Period to the following Vendel and Viking Periods. There are, of course, some fundamental source-critical aspects to consider.

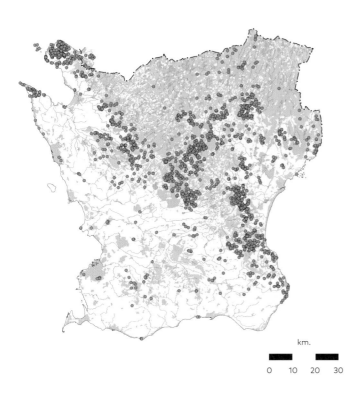

Fig. 10. Round stone settings recorded in Scania. After Helgesson, B. & Lindberg, S. 2017 fig. 1:99.

A common grave form in Scania, as elsewhere in Sweden, is round filled stone settings. The diameter of the stone settings can vary considerably, from less than 5 m up to 35–40 m. However, most of them are less than 10 m (Carlie 1994:61–71). They often appear in isolation, but are also common in cemeteries, sometimes as the only grave form. Stone settings were in use for a long period, from the Late Bronze Age to the Viking Age. This also corresponds to the situation in Blekinge, Halland and Småland. The overall picture is, however, that most round stone settings can be dated to the Pre-Roman and Roman Iron Age. This is confirmed by Tony Björk's survey of Scanian graves (2005:64–66 and catalogue). Therefore, the distribution of round stone settings indicates settled areas during the Pre-Roman and Roman Iron Age but some might be later or earlier.

Most round stone settings are situated in the border zone between plain and forest (fig. 10) and usually close to the basement rock moraines, which today are normally covered with forest. Only a few are preserved in the central agricultural areas where many were removed by cultivation. There are many stone settings in a zone between Lake Finja and Lake Ringsjön, forming a settlement corridor so to speak. Stone settings are also common in the border zone between the Kristianstad plain and the ridge of Linderödsåsen, in the inner parts of the valley of the River Rönne, on the Bjäre peninsula and in the valley of the River Helge north of rapids at Torsebro.

Round stone settings generally pre-date the Migration Period and concentrations of them certainly indicate densely settled areas in the Pre-Roman and Roman Iron Age. In the Sösdala area they indicate that the area had a stable settlement before the deposition of the Migration Period finds dealt with here.

Cemeteries and graves from the Migration Period to the Viking Age

Excavated grave finds from the Migration Period onwards are very few in the area (table 1). The only large excavation was made at the classic and well-known cemetery Vätteryd, the best preserved in Scania (*FMIS* no. Norra Mellby 1:1; Strömberg 1961b:73–86; Carlie 1994:279–280). Today 375 standing stones are preserved but in the 19th century as many as 600 were recorded (Fabech chapter 2 fig. 3). Today they represent 15 stone ships, 2 square stone settings and 183 now single standing stones. Only a few monuments and graves have been excavated. Most excavated graves are simple pits with a few cremated bones (including animal bones such as horse and dog). Unfortunately, the relation between dated grave finds and standing stone monuments is not obvious. Most graves at Vätteryd are poor but some richer ones contained numerous fragments of burnt jewellery such as brooches and beads of glass, silver and carnelian. In two graves finds were made that can be dated to the 5th century. Chronologically grave finds are distributed across the Migration, Vendel and Viking Periods, from the 5th to the 10th century (Carlie 1994:280; Helgesson 2002:77). Thus continuity is probable.

The earliest grave is a cremation, grave 127, that contained a fragmentary bridge mount of type Nydam-Porskær for a sword scabbard (Strömberg 1961b:85; Taf. 45:7; Bemmann

Fig. 11. Graves and cemeteries recorded in the Sösdala area, according to table 2. Blue dots are the find places of fig. 3. Background map as fig. 2.

nia, without counterparts in western Scania (Helgesson 2002:81, fig. 14). The two warrior graves stand out from the rest of the Vätteryd graves.

Other similar cemeteries with stone ships and standing stones are found in the area, for instance at Häglinge, Ljungarum, Mala and Nunnäs (Carlie 1994:228–272). Carlie divides the cemeteries from Western Göinge into seven groups (1994:88–101); four are relevant here (fig. 11; table 2). Group 1 is a *varied type* where stone circles, standing stones, simple stone settings, barrows, cairns, triangular stone settings and stone ships might be included. At an excavated cemetery, at Vannaröd in Norra Mellby parish, a single grave is the earliest from early Pre-Roman Iron Age (or perhaps earlier). Not until the Late Roman Iron Age/Migration Period is another dated grave context found, a stone circle. A third burial is ^{14}C-dated to Vendel/Viking Period. Group 5 is the *stone circle type* and consists solely of stone circles (*domarringar*). Only one cemetery at Arkelstorp in Stoby parish is recorded with an uncertain dating to the Late Roman Iron Age or Migration Period. Group 6 is the *stone ship type* where stone ships dominate, combined with, for instance, standing stones and square stone settings. This cemetery type can be dated from the Migration Period to the Viking Age. The five cemeteries mentioned above all belong to this type. Group 7 is the *standing stone type* and consists solely of standing stones. Probably many cemeteries of group 7 are in fact fragments of larger cemeteries of group 6 and probably once had stone ships. They are also dated to the same periods.

There is of course a fundamental source-critical aspect to bear in mind. Many cemeteries with stone ships and standing stones were damaged or completely removed in modern times and the stones used for roads, bridges and house foundations. A once large cemetery might today only be indicated by one or a few standing stones. That visible remains of graves can be totally removed above ground became obvious during the excavations at Hammar outside Kristianstad in 2011 (Helgesson *et al.* 2013:107ff, 163ff). Here foundations of three standing stones and a 40 metre long stone ship were found in a cultivated field. This cemetery was unknown prior to excavation. So the number of recorded graves is far from the amount that once existed,

1998:221–223, Fundliste 9:5). It is made of bronze and covered with punched decorated sheet silver (Fabech chapter 2 fig. 4); most probably it is contemporary with the Sösdala I find and corroborates the presence of warrior elite at Sösdala. The only inhumation, grave 20, contained a single-edged sword, a lance head and several fittings, rods, sheets, nails and rivets of iron (Strömberg 1961b:79–80, Taf. 42). This weapon grave is dated to the second half of the Vendel period, 7th–8th century (Strömberg 1961a:107; cf. Nørgård Jørgensen 1999:120–130). It belongs to a small group of weapon graves from eastern and central Sca-

and the sparse distribution of such remains in the southern and north-eastern plains is more representative of recent agriculture than it reflects ancient reality.

The cemeteries seem to have been used for a long time. They stand for stability and indicate local societies with long duration. Beginning in the Migration Period the many cemeteries of groups 6 and 7 appear as new forms of burial and reflect changes in society, perhaps combined with new ritual behaviour. The conspicuous grave monuments were visible from far away, in contrast to the low stone settings of the Pre-Roman and Roman Iron Age, so aspects of power and ownership have to be considered.

The distribution of this type of cemeteries is quite even in the Sösdala area. By and large it may be assumed to represent the settled areas. Many cemeteries, especially of groups 6 and 7, are situated in the vicinity of historic farms, hamlets and villages, known from the Middle Ages and the 16th–17th centuries. This indicates that society continuously transformed into the medieval society of the 11th–12th centuries. The graves are situated in areas which were cultivated in the late 17th century, or in the borderland between cultivated and wooded areas. Very few graves are found in woodland. This indicates that the extent of open landscape was more or less the same in the late 17th century as in the second half of the first millennium. Today many marginal fields, meadows and pastures are overgrown and more or less forested due to structural changes in agriculture.

Stray Finds

In central Scania archaeological finds dated to the Pre-Roman and Roman Iron Age are rare, but this is contradicted by a large amount of ancient monuments. The rarity of artefact finds is rather due to two important source-critical aspects. When large areas were pastures and the cultivated fields were small, the result was only a few recovered stray finds. Furthermore this part of Scania has never seen large archaeological excavations.

Norra Mellby, Stoby, Ignaberga, Finja and Häglinge parishes are rather rich in finds from the Bronze Age, corresponding to a distribution of ancient monuments such as cairns. An arm ring from Ignaberga and a neck ring from Norra Mellby can be dated to the Pre-Roman Iron Age. So continuity from the Late Bronze Age may be surmised.

Fig. 12. Distribution of recorded strike-a-light stones. Only approximate find places given as hamlet/village or parish. Background map as fig. 2. Data from Strömberg 1961; Carlie 1994 and FMIS.

Stray finds from the Roman Iron Age are absent with the exception of ceramics from Häglinge (Carlie 1994:273–284). And some of the strike-a-light stones treated below probably are from the Late Roman Iron Age; the rest from the Migration Period. A complete single-jointed snaffle of iron comes from Röinge in Stoby parish (SHM 18006:3; Strömberg 1961a:144, 1961b:86; Carlie 1994:284). Strömberg dated it for unknown reasons to the Viking Age. But in our opinion, similarities to a snaffle from Dallerup in Jutland (Ørsnes 1994 fig. 2) indicate that its long rein

Fig. 13. An example of a pointed oval strike-a-light stone with suspension groove. Stray find from Östergötland. Not to scale. Photo Sara Kusmin, SHM no. 7149, Stockholm.

mounts (Ørsnes's type 4A) and narrow bit rings (type 2C) date it to the early Migration Period, Scand-D1.

Stray finds from the Vendel Period and the Viking Age are uncommon in central Scania (Carlie 1994:273–284). There are for instance a lance head from Finja, glass beads from Finja and Häglinge and iron axes from Häglinge, Hässleholm and Stoby supplemented with an axe from Bosjökloster (Strömberg 1961b:19). Most stray finds are without clear contexts, but they indicate settled areas and are related to late prehistoric cemeteries as well as to historic farms, hamlets or villages of the Middle Ages.

Strike-a-light stones

The exclusive Migration Period finds from Fulltofta, Sjörup, Sösdala and Tormestorp cannot be balanced with corresponding ordinary material. An exception is a number of strike-a-light stones of types that in graves are dated to the Roman Iron Age and Migration Period (fig. 12; table 3). Strike-a-light stones were carried in the belt, either in a pouch, in a leather strap or fixed on the belt with elaborate mounts (Ilkjær 2000:52–57 with figs; Ramqvist 1992:99–103, 111–114 with figs.). The many stray finds demonstrate that they obviously were often lost. Strike-a-lights are useful as indicators of settled areas and their distribution in the landscape complements maps of ancient monuments such as graves. First of all, they are durable. Second, particularly the pointed-oval strike-a-light stones are conspicuous and collectable artefacts, also for laypersons (fig. 13). Graves are preserved most often in areas with little human activity

while most strike-a-lights were found during agricultural work. In many Scanian parishes a strike-a-light stone is the only recorded Iron Age find. Of course representativity is a problem and the degree of collecting and reporting to museums varies considerably between local areas.

Strike-a-light stones from Sweden were discussed and mapped in an early paper by Hanna Rydh (1917). Even though some stones were found in datable contexts, most are stray finds. More recently a typology was presented on the basis of more than one hundred fire-making sets from the offering of military equipment at Illerup, Jutland (Ilkjær 1993:235–242). The pointed elliptic strike-a-lights (Ilkjær types 4 and 5) occur from the Late Roman Iron Age (Scand C2–C3) and became common in the Migration Period (Scand D1–D2). The elaborate stones with a groove along the edges for suspension are hard to make and there might have been specialised production (Grimbe 2001). Strike-a-light stones are found in the large Danish bog finds with military equipment (for instance Ejsbøl and Illerup) and in graves they are always found in male graves with weapons (Ilkjær 1993:343–386). Thus the stones are connected with warriors and elaborate belts with a strike-a-light stone were a symbol of elite warriors (cf. Ramqvist 1992 fig. 68). Thus the stray finds in the Sösdala area indicate settlements and areas where warriors have carried on.

All of the strike-a-lights from central Scania are stray finds and none has a finding place more precise than hamlet/village or parish. The stones belong to two types: oval and pointed elliptic strike-a-lights. Amongst the 23 stones, 6 are oval (Ilkjær type 1–3), 16 pointed elliptic (Ilkjær type 4–5) and one cannot be determined. The majority of the stones are of the pointed elliptic type that can be dated late in the period of use, i.e. some are contemporary with the Migration Period finds at Sösdala and Fulltofta. The distribution of the recorded stones is uneven and found in two clusters, around Häglinge and east of Lake Finja. Sporadic finds of stones occur in other places. The overall distribution reflects settled areas and corresponds roughly to the find places Tormestorp, Sösdala, Göingeholm, Sjörup and Fulltofta. But the two clusters are hard to understand and probably represent the source-critical aspects of any archaeological record.

Ancient field remains

Many ancient field remains are preserved in the forested highlands of southern Sweden where they consist almost entirely of clearance cairns (Gren 2003; Pedersen & Jönsson 2003; Pedersen & Widgren 2011:51). Sometimes also stone walls, terraces and embanked fields occur. It is common to find cleared areas surrounding the clearance cairns. It is assumed that the largest area was used as pasture and that stock-raising dominated the subsistence economy. Clearance cairns are preserved outside the historical infields. Unfortunately, the often extensive areas or systems with ancient field remains are hard to date. The earliest ^{14}C dated remains are from the late Bronze Age and the last are from recent historical times. The same area may have been used for long times and/or during several periods. Dating in some areas with ancient field remains in central Scania reveals an expansion period during the Roman Iron Age and the Migration Period followed by a period with less activity until a new slow expansion later in the Vendel Period and Viking Age (Jacobsson 2000, catalogue nos. 48, 60, 63, 65, 226; Carlie 2002; Lagerås 2002:388–391; 2013 fig. 2; Carlie & Strandmark 2015:32–33). Often a close connection is found between ancient field remains and burial sites from the Pre-Roman and Roman Iron Age, which supports an early dating. Distribution maps demonstrate that stone settings and ancient field remains exist within the same zones and areas, a relationship that can be found throughout most of southern Scandinavia (Gren 2003; Pedersen & Jönsson 2003).

In the Stoby area cultivation in areas with clearance cairns seem to have ceased in the Migration Period but pasture continued (Carlie 2002: 353–355; Lagerås 2002:398–403). This appears to coincide with the shift from dispersed graves to large cemeteries with standing stones, stone ships, etc. mentioned above. Unfortunately there is little information about what rural system followed in the period AD 400–1200, but pollen analysis demonstrates continued grazing and cultivation through the Migration Period. No contemporary field remains are preserved. An explanation may be that the historical infield system was established by then and that all early traces were obliterated by later land use. Or perhaps a strip field system was introduced and the infield system was not established until after AD 1200.

During the Iron Age all settlements of Scania had an economy based on mixed farming with some cultivation and much animal husbandry. All archaeological studies of farming systems in the Migration Period demonstrate that the arable fields were small (a few hectares per farm) while meadows for hay-making and pastures were extensive (Carlsson 1979; Widgren 1983; Fallgren 2006; Fabech & Ringtved 2009; Näsman 2009; Pedersen & Widgren 2011). Probably the obvious differences in historic time between cereal cultivation on the plains and stock-raising in the forested areas were less pronounced during the Iron Age. Certainly the better soils on the plains had more productive grazing, which was reflected in denser settlement and larger population, but it was a difference in degree, not in kind. The central and northern parts of Scania were known in historic times for many complementary economic niches, for instance the supply of wooden products (timber), iron, charcoal and tar. Some division of labour between plains and forests may be assumed also for the Iron Age but not to the same degree. It has for example been suggested that control over the iron supply might have been important for the economy of central Scania also during the Iron Age (Strömberg 1961a:179; Fabech 1993:208).

From northern Scania, southern Halland and Småland there are large depositions of bog ore that was used for low-technology iron production (Hyenstrand 1984 map 31). Traces of extensive iron production are well documented in these areas but only one site at the northern end of the Sösdala area is known to have iron production contemporary with the Sösdala finds, at Vankiva north of Lake Finja (Ödman 2001:136). So for now iron production must be considered as a marginal possibility. An assumed control over long-distance transport of currency bars from inner Småland is still only a hypothesis. Nevertheless it is problematic that we do not know how the supply of raw iron to the central settlement areas of Scania and Zealand was organised (Ödman 1998:205–208; Helgesson 2002:163; Björk 2009; Fabech 2011b:225–227). The martial elite used much iron to acquire and keep up their power. The question is not whether they had access to this strategic resource but from where and in what way they got it.

Place names

The record of archaeological finds and monuments gives a fragmented picture of the settlement development, but supports a general assumption that settlement was continuous through the first millennium. An important supplement to archaeology is offered by place name research. Usually the earliest Scandinavian place names are dated to the Roman Iron Age or Migration Period. Early place names between Lake Finja and Lake Ringsjön are rare (Svensson chapter 3; Lindroth 1911; Carlie 1994:167–175; Wahlberg 2003 *passim*; Ringdahl 2008 *passim*).

Svensson assumes that Sösdala, Nösdala and Hovdala are among the earliest and they reveal a row of old settlements in the valley (*-dal* = valley). In Svensson's opinion Sösdala was "a name of a domain, serving both as a district name and as a name of a settlement" and we think that makes sense. It is possible that the three *-dala* place names once were used for larger domains in the valley. Probably Pre-Roman and Roman Iron Age settlement pattern was unstable with dispersed farms and extensive land use based mainly on pasture. In the Migration Period it is suggested that changes took place with a concentration of farmsteads to a few larger and more stable sites and a cultivation system based on enclosed infields with arable and meadows (Lagerås 2002:401–403; Fabech & Ringtved 2009: 167–173; Näsman 2009:100–107). This change is manifested by the large stone ship cemeteries (Carlie 2002:253–355). From now on the name Sösdala probably designated a settlement near the Vätteryd cemetery.

Another possibly early settlement name is Röslöv, but there is no relevant archaeological record for this site. The name of the parish and church village is Häglinge, an early name and nearby one can find one of the cemeteries with stone ships. Another early name is Brönnestad, a parish south of Lake Finja. Here remains of cemeteries with stone ships are found and the Tormestorp finds were discovered nearby.

In our opinion *Hov-* in Hovdala originally referred to either a pagan sanctuary or a magnate residence (but see Wahlberg 2003:132; Ringdal 2008:35); the two functions were often united in one building (Sundqvist 1998:143–163; 2008). In pagan Scandinavia social leaders were also cult leaders. Of the alternative interpretations of the first element *Sös-* in Sösdala that Svensson presents, we assume that the reference is not to dirt or wetland as usually suggested, but to a person, *Söir*, who had responsibility in the area for the pagan sacrifices. The mounted warriors represented by Migration Period finds on the Vätteryd cemetery and on the Sösdala ridge probably were not only magnates but also cult leaders; it is tempting to believe that they had a relation to the *Söir* mentioned by Svensson. A central obligation of the elite was the administration of law at the thing. So we have to consider also temporary centres such as thing sites. In the Sösdala area a couple of names on hills point only vaguely to a localisation of an early thing site central in an old Sösdala *bygd* or settlement area (Svensson chapter 3).

Usually names ending in *-by* are dated to the later Iron Age, the Vendel and Viking Periods and in the area this group is represented by Mellby, a name indicating a settlement between other places, perhaps Sösdala and Sandåkra. A dating to the Migration Period cannot be excluded (Vikstrand 2013:31). That Mellby became a church village and gave its name to the parish indicates that Sösdala had lost some of its position at the time of Christianisation and subsequent parish organisation. Later names ending in *-torp* are usually interpreted as farmsteads that have moved out from an earlier settlement. Examples in the area are Tormestorp in Brönnestad, Tjörnarp (possibly related to Sösdala) and Sjörup in Häglinge. Numerous names ending in *-röd* and *-hult* emanate mainly from the high medieval colonisation of outlying pastures and forests.

Fulltofta belongs to the name type *-tofta* which is more or less contemporary with the *-by* names. Of course one cannot assume a connection but nevertheless it is interesting that the meaning of the name is something like "the enclosed pasture for horses" (cf. Fabech & Ringtved 2009:171–172). Fulltofta parish is located between two parishes with interesting names: Höör and Hörby. Höör refers directly to a sacral *hørg*, some kind of pagan construction or building. The name Hörby consists of *hørg-* and *–by*, meaning the settlement at the sacral site. On the southern shore of Lake Ringsjön an estate is named Bo, which suggests that it had administrative functions. On the island of Bosön a Benedictine monastery was established in the 11th century on basis of a donation presumably by a captain Tord Thott, a legendary Viking chief. It was on the land owned by Bo that the gold eagle of Claestorp was found.

The early place names mark a well-demarcated settlement corridor southward from Lake Finja. It contains names signifying both secular and pagan power. The Sösdala *bygd* seems to have been oriented north- and eastwards to the Kristianstad plain with its old central place at Vä (*Væ* = cult site). To the south a sparsely populated forested zone separates the Sösdala area from Fulltofta at Lake Ringsjön. Here we also find indications of secular and pagan power. It is possible to see the area between Lake Finja and Lake Ringsjön as one coherent region, but is should preferably be looked upon as two independent *bygder* on either side of a thinly settled borderland. The Sösdala and the Fulltofta areas, have central positions in central Scania with regard to communication between the two main political centres: south-western Scania with Uppåkra as its centre and a *bygd* in north-eastern Scania with Vä as its probably most important centre. Mounted warriors at Sösdala and Fulltofta could control and redistribute iron, animal products, furs, etc. from the northern forests, but probably it was most significant that the two sites watched an interface between two large political entities (Fabech 1999a:467–468).

Written sources

On the basis of the record of archaeology and toponomy we assume settlement continuity in the Sösdala area from the Bronze Age to the Viking Age. A marked change took place in the early Migration Period with the founding of new cremation cemeteries with stone ships, etc. Contemporary with this are the spectacular Migration Period finds. They manifest a marked break with the past. New features are the strong foreign relations, primarily with south-eastern Europe. Also new is the martial character of four of the finds. Mounted warriors seem to have established themselves in this area of interior Scania. Apart from a weapon grave at Vätteryd there is little that allows us to follow this elite through the Vendel and Viking Periods. But the source material is also too weak to support assumptions of discontinuity.

Other studies of spectacular finds from the Migration Period have demonstrated relations to later centres of power (Fabech 1999b). The observations give reason to discuss continuity from power centres in the Migration Period to power centres during the Viking Age and the early Middle

Fig. 14. The Romanesque parish church of Norra Mellby from the north. The tower is an addition from 1917. Photo Charlotte Fabech 2016.

Ages (11th–12th centuries). Consequently it is of interest that there are several sources that reveal the presence of early medieval estates in the Sösdala area consisting of stray farms as well as whole hamlets or villages. Our main sources are ecclesiastic documents of donations of estates to churches and monasteries.

The largest donation, 28 farms in Sösdala village, was given to Roskilde Cathedral, Zealand, *c.* AD 1060–1073. The royal donor was either Queen Estrid, mother of King Svend Estridsen, or Queen Margrethe, wife of King Harald Hen, son of Svend Estridsen. Perhaps the estate was an inheritance from Ulf Jarl, who was father of Svend Estridsen and possibly Earl of Scania (Ödman 2015). Regardless of this, during the late Viking Age most of Sösdala was the property of a member of the highest echelon of contemporary society. We do not know any remains of a manor or an early church in Sösdala. When parishes were organised in the 12th century Sösdala had lost its old central function manifested by the Vätteryd cemetery. The parish centre had moved to Norra Mellby, a settlement north of Sösdala.

The medieval church in Norra Mellby is among the largest in Scania and its masonry indicates that it belong to the first generation of stone churches in Scania (fig. 14; Ödman 2015:16–17). A tie beam found in the present church emanates from a large wooden church, probably erected in the 11th century. According to the medieval archaeologist Erik Cinthio a stone cellar excavated in 1928–1929 north of the church was possibly remains of a medieval stone building (Karlsson 1989). The character of the building is unfortunately unknown, but possibly it is remains of a manor house. The farms of Norra Mellby belonged in the Middle Ages also to the crown but were not dispossessed (Ödman & Ödman 2011:184).

As neighbour to the estates at Sösdala and Norra Mellby another magnate setting is found in the parish of Häglinge. The medieval church was somewhat larger than that in Norra Mellby. The find spots at Sjörup and Göingeholm are both placed on the outskirts of the medieval village. Two ecclesiastical donations are known. Half of the village farms were donated to Dalby monastery; the other half went to the chapter of Lund. The identity of the donors is unknown but they must have belonged to the contemporary elite; the Danish king Harald Hen or his queen are possibilities since he is the only king buried in Dalby church (Ödman & Ödman 2011:169–170). In 1998–2000 remains of an ecclesiastical stone palace were investigated near Häglinge church. It was built in the early Romanesque period, i.e. early 12th century. The building remains are what are left of the Archbishop's *skudgård* or *hovgård* (a manor serving as administrative estate centre). It probably succeeded the old (Viking Age) manor of the Häglinge estate. In the 17th century the *hovgård* was moved out of the village to the place of a hamlet Hörröd where all three farms were closed down. In 1769 it was renamed Göingeholm, originally the name of a larger area between Lake Finja and the border with Frosta *härad* including the parishes of Brönnestad, Häglinge, Matteröd, Norra Mellby and Tjörnarp (Karlsson 1986:92–102).

An analysis of cadastral maps led to the hypothesis that an early medieval manor existed near Brönnestad parish church. It is assumed that it was confiscated by the king in the 13th century. A hypothesis is that the manor was then moved to a site named Hovdala where it developed into a fortified castle (Ödman & Ödman 2011:199). In the Middle Ages many manors were moved out of the villages and located in solitary positions (Skansjö, Riddersporre &

Reisnert 1989). The find spot Tormestorp is placed near the border between Brönnestad and Stoby parishes.

The find spot Fulltofta is situated approx. 2 km from the Fulltofta parish church and manor. In the Middle Ages the manor belonged to the archbishop in Lund and after the Reformation it became property of the Danish crown. In this case the manor stayed at the site of the church village.

Bosjökloster parish church was built in the 12th century as the church of a Benedictine monastery on an island in Lake Ringsjön. It belonged to the manor of Bo on the southern shore of the lake. The monastery was possibly founded as early as the 11th century and it was based on a donation by Tord Thott (above).

Conclusion

The remarkable 5th century finds tell us that men from this area were connected to a European network of mounted elite warriors. They probably took part in dramatic events and returned loaded with glory and wealth. Their presence in central Scania calls for a good explanation, but there is no obvious one. Precursors in the Roman Iron Age are lacking, so the spectacular finds have no local background (Helgesson 2002:128–132). The area had been settled long before, but the 1st–4th centuries AD are poor in finds. The local inhabitants seem not linked to the international elite network in this period. The unusual Migration Period finds in central Scania represent something really new in the area and they coincide in time with the foundation all over Scania of new cemeteries with standing stones and stone ships.

However, the 5th century finds have a background in many finds from central settlement areas, both to the west and to the east (compare Helgesson 2002 fig. 29 and 32). But what reason did members of the Scanian elite have for establishing themselves far from the wealthy plains? It is striking that so many finds are associated with mounted warriors and armed power. Four of the elite sites date to the early Migration Period, Scand-D1. The bridles found at Sösdala I and Fulltofta were possibly brought home by returning warriors and reflect their personal experiences from south-eastern Europe. As suggested by Michel Kazanski at the Lund Workshop in 2015, family relations established long before between South Scandinavian and

Fig. 15. Densely settled areas in Scania in the Migration, Vendel and Viking Periods. After Ödman & Ödman 2011 fig. 205. Redrawn from fig. 6 in Callmer 1991.

south-east European elites can explain the routes followed by young Scanian warriors (cf. Kazanski & Mastykova chapter15). These routes were well-established since the 4th century (Näsman 1984:97–99). It is easy to argue that the elites on the plains sustained such links during the Roman Iron Age, while traces of such relations are virtually absent in central and northern Scania.

The silver hoard from Sjörup is from period Scand-D2 and easily understood as stashed precious metal. The comparison with the gold and silver hoard from Staffordshire makes it possible to interpret Sjörup as a warlord's share of battlefield booty after a victorious battle. For some reason it was hidden and forgotten at the fringe of the Häglinge settlement area. At any rate, the hoard demonstrates that people of the highest echelon had a relation to central Scania also in the second half of the 5th century.

The settlement pattern of Scania in the second half of the 1st millennium AD is characterised by large continuous settlement areas on the plains along the western and southern coasts (fig. 15). Another large settlement area was established in the Kristianstad plain in the north-east.

But horsts and other obstacles to settlement caused a fragmented settlement pattern along "the Scanian diagonal". The area between Lakes Finja and Ringsjön belongs here.

Two different views of the political structure of Scania in this period exist. One uses the Anglo-Saxon kingdoms of the 7th century as an analogy and is based on an application of the Tribal Hidage (Callmer 1991). In this perspective Migration Period Scania was split into several more or less independent polities and the Sösdala area could be either a separate early polity or a part of one, in that case roughly corresponding to Göinge *härad*. This point of view corresponds to Arne's idea of a Migration Period realm in central Scania (Arne 1973:94–95). Only through time were the separate polities united and ended as administrative districts in a Danish kingdom at the end of the first millennium.

As an alternative to the Anglo-Saxon analogy Ulf Näsman (1998; 1999) presented a model based on the concept of peer polity interaction (*sensu* Renfrew 1986) and analogies to the ethnogenesis of the Franks. According to the model south-western Scania was already one unit. Another large polity is surmised to have existed on the north-eastern Kristianstad plain. A smaller polity possibly existed north of the Söderåsen horst in the valley of the River Rönne. In this model the Fulltofta-Sösdala settlement area is placed between two polities with Fulltofta facing south-west and Sösdala towards the north-east (Fabech 1991a:467–469, fig. 11; Helgesson 2002:156 fig. 34).

We suggest that elite warriors established themselves in central Scania around AD 400 where they carried out tasks of importance for central powers in the west (Uppåkra?) and/or in the east (Vä?). The new local leadership did not cease with the 5th century, we believe. We assume (with weak support in the archaeological record, only a Vendel Period weapon inhumation in Vätteryd) that there was power continuity until the 11th and 12th centuries when written sources and building remains substantiate large royal domains in the Sösdala settlement area. It is not necessarily a family continuity but continuous places and positions of power.

The localisation of the find places in a broad corridor between the horsts Matterödsåsen, Linderödsåsen, Nävlingeåsen and Söderåsen suggests that communication can be a decisive factor (figs 10–11). On a map indicating densely settled areas in Scania during the 5th–11th centuries (fig. 15) there seems to be a gap between the Sösdala area and the Fulltofta area. This gap was not uninhabited, however, as demonstrated by the distribution of stone settings, but perhaps a divide and an interface between two polities existed. Is it a coincidence that the historical *härad* boundary runs here?

It was here horsemen at Sösdala and Fulltofta had a mission to control passage. Before Scania became integrated as part of the Danish kingdom we suspect that the route across Linderödsåsen, the present E22, was not yet established as a main road between Uppåkra/Lund and Vä. Old roads went from settlement to settlement; they connected neighbours. To travel safely you followed established routes consisting of interconnected sites where you knew friends and foes (Le Goff 1988:136; Fabech 1999a:458). An alternative route from south-west to Vä passed between the horsts Nävlingeåsen and Linderödsåsen. It can be

followed with archaeological finds and is visible on Buhrmann's map. It passed Claestorp and Fulltofta, continued to Häglinge via Södra Rörum and Ynglingrum, and passed Rickarum and Venestad before reaching Vä on the Kristianstad plain.

What was controlled? Movement of persons and warriors? Transport of produce from the forests? Iron? Furs? We do not know. But for instance the necessity of iron in the Migration Period was great and increasing, and at present we do not know how the supply was organised. Perhaps the reason for control was political. The 5th century in South Scandinavia was a period of unrest where unstable polities contended for power. Twenty-two offerings of military equipment are dated to the 5th century and represent as many battles in South Scandinavia (Fabech 2011a:34). So perhaps the warriors simply watched one another? Was guard duty in a border area a good solution when young hotspurs had to be distanced from the centre of power?

References

Arne, T.J. 1937. Ett skånskt fynd från folkvandringstiden. [Göingeholm] In: *Från stenålder till rokoko. Studier tillägnade Otto Rydbeck*. Lund: 81–95.

Bemmann, J. 1998. Der Nydam-II-Fund. In: Bemmann, G. & Bemmann, J. *Der Opferplatz von Nydam. Die Funde aus den älteren Grabungen: Nydam-I and -II*. Band 1–2. Neumünster: 217–240.

Björk, T. 2005. *Skäran på bålet. Om den äldre järnålderns gravar i Skåne*. Lund.

Björk, T. 2009. Vems var järnet? Om järn och makt i skånsk järnålder. In: Helgesson, B. (ed.). *Järnets roll*. Kristianstad: 33–50.

Bredsdorff, P. 1973. *Kortlægning og historiske studier. Et værktøj?* Copenhagen.

Callmer, J. 1991. Territory and dominion in the Late Iron Age in southern Scandinavia. In: Jennbert, K. *et al.* (eds). *Regions and reflections. In honour of Märta Strömberg*. Stockholm/Lund: 257–273.

Carlie, A. 1994. *På arkeologins bakgård. En bebyggelsesarkeologisk undersökning i norra Skånes inland baserad på synliga gravar*. [Ph.D. thesis]. Lund. Summary.

Carlie, A. 2002. Människor och landskap. Om förhistoriska samhällen i en nordskånsk inlandsbygd. In: Carlie, A. (ed.). *Skånska regioner*. Stockholm: 281–361.

Carlie, A. & Strandmark, F. 2015. *Väg E22 förbi Linderöd. Fossil åkermark, boplatslämningar och gravar på Linderödsåsen Skåne*. Lund.

Carlsson, D. 1979. *Kulturlandskapets utveckling på Gotland. En studie av jordbruk- och bebyggelseförändringar under järnåldern*. Visby.

Christlein, R. 1979. *Die Alamannen. Archäologie eines lebendigen Volkes*. Stuttgart. (2nd rev. ed.; 1st ed. 1978).

Emanuelsson, U. *et al.* 1985. *Det skånska kulturlandskapet*. Lund. 2nd rev. ed. 2002.

Fabech, C. 1990. Sjörup – an old problem in a new light. *Meddelanden från Lunds Universitets Historiska Museum*. New series 8, 1989–1990: 101–119.

Fabech, C. 1991a. Booty sacrifices in Southern Scandinavia. A reassessment. In: Garwood, P. *et al.* (eds). *Sacred and profane*. Oxford: 88–99.

Fabech, C. 1991b. Neue Perspektiven zu den Funden von Sösdala und Fulltofta. *Studien zur Sachsenforschung* 7: 121–135.

Fabech, C. 1993. Skåne – et kulturelt og geografisk grænseland i yngre jernalder og i nutiden. *Tor* 25: 201–245. Summary.

Fabech, C. 1999a. Centrality in Sites and Landscapes. In: Fabech, C. & Ringtved, J. (eds). *Settlement and Landscape*. Højbjerg/Aarhus: 455–473.

Fabech, C. 1999b. Organising the Landscape. A matter of production, power, and religion. In: Dickinson, T. & Griffiths, D. (eds). *The Making of Kingdoms*. Oxford: 37–47.

Fabech, C. 2011a. War and rituals. Changes in ritual and transformations of power. In: Panhuysen, T.A.S.M. (ed.). *Transformations in North-Western Eu-*

rope (AD 300–1000). (Neue Studien zur Sachsenforschung 3). Hannover/Stuttgart: 27–36.

Fabech, C. 2011b. Bidrag till skånsk järnhantering. In: Högberg, A. (ed.). *Södra Kristineberg – hantverk i fokus*. Kristianstad: 215–231.

Fabech, C., Hvass, S., Näsman, U. & Ringtved, J. 1999. Settlement and Landscape – a presentation of a research programme and a conference. In: Fabech, C. & Ringtved, J. (eds). *Settlement and Landscape*. Højbjerg/Aarhus: 13–28.

Fabech, C. & Näsman, U. 2013a. A lonely rider? The finding place of the Sösdala-find and the context of its finds. In: Khrapunov, I. & Stylegar, F.-A. (eds). *Inter Ambo Maria. Northern barbarians from Scandinavia towards the Black Sea*. Kristiansand/Simferopol: 84–106. Резюме.

Fabech, C. & Näsman, U. 2013b. Ritual landscapes and sacral places in the first millennium A.D. in South Scandinavia. In: Nordeide, S. Walaker & Brink, S. (eds). *Sacred Sites and Holy Places. Exploring the Sacralization of Landscape through Time and Space*. Turnhout/York.

Fabech, C. & Ringtved, J. 2009. Arealanvendelse og landskabstyper i det 1. årtusinde. In: Odgaard, B. & Rømer, J. Rydén (eds). *Danske landbrugslandskaber gennem 2000 år – fra digevoldinger til støtteordninger*. Aarhus: 143–176.

Fallgren, J.-H. 2006. *Kontinuitet och förändring. Bebyggelse och samhälle på Öland 200–1300 e Kr*. Uppsala. Summary.

Fischer, S. & Soulat, J. 2011. The typochronology of sword pommels from the Staffordshire hoard. https://finds.org.uk/staffshoardsymposium/papers/svantefischerandjeansoulat – Checked 24 April 2017.

Forssander, J.-E. 1937. Provinzialrömisches und germanisches. Stilstudien zu den schonischen Funden von Sösdala und Sjörup. *Kungl. humanistiska vetenskapssamfundet i Lund. Årsberättelse 1936–37*: 183–272 – Also in *Meddelanden från Lunds universitets historiska museum 8*: 11–100.

Germundsson, T. & Schlyter, P. (eds) 1999. *Atlas över Skåne*. Vällingby/Gävle.

Gren, L. 2003. Hackerör i Njudungs västra härad: regional analys och detaljstudier i Norra sandsjö. In: Widgren, M. (ed.). *Röjningsröseområden på sydsvenska höglandet. Arkeologiska, kulturgeografiska och vegetationshistoriska undersökningar*. Meddelanden nr 117. Kulturgeografiska institutionen, Stockholms universitet. Stockholm.

Grimbe, J., 2001. *Ovala eldslagningsstenar – vad har de använts till? Ett försök att med arkeologiska experiment och analyser utvärdera eldslagningsstenens funktion*. [B.A. thesis in archaeology]. Umeå University.

Halsall, G. 2010. The Staffordshire hoard. Warfare, aggression and the use of trophies. https://600transformer.blogspot.se/2010/05/the-staffordshire-hoard-warfare.html – Checked 30 April 2017.

Hårdh, B. 2003. Uppåkra i folkvandringstiden. In: Hårdh, B. (ed.). *Flera fynd i centrum. Materialstudier i och kring Uppåkra*. Stockholm/Lund: 41–80.

Helgesson, B. 2002. *Järnålderns Skåne. Samhälle, centra och regioner*. Lund.

Helgesson, B., Fabech, C., Linderoth, T. & Skoglund, P. 2013. *Hammar 9:21 m fl. Särskild undersökning 2010–2011*. Kristianstad.

Helgesson, B. & Lindberg, S. 2017. Brons- och järnålder – med en fortsättning i medeltid? In: Brink, K. & Larsson, S. (eds). *Östra Odarslöv 13:5, ESS-området Forntid möter framtid – volym 1. Arkeologisk undersökning 2013*: 102–162.

Hines, J. 1993. *Clasps, hektespenner, agraffen. Anglo-Scandinavian clasps A-C of the 3rd to 6th centuries A.D.* Stockholm.

Holmqvist, W. 1961. En främmande fågel. *Fornvännen* 56: 80–96. Summary.

Hyenstrand, Å 1984. *Fasta fornlämningar och arkeologiska regioner*. Stockholm. Summary.

Ilkjær, J. 1993. *Illerup Ådal 3. Die Gürtel*. Højbjerg/Aarhus.

Ilkjær, J. 2000. *Illerup Ådal – archaeology as a magic mirror*. Højbjerg.

Jacobsson, B. 2000. *Järnåldersundersökningar i Sydsverige. Katalog för Skåne, Halland, Blekinge och Småland*. Riksantikvarieämbetet. Avdelningen för arkeologiska undersökningar. Lund.

Jørgensen, A. Nørgård 1999. *Waffen und Gräber. Typologische und chronologische Studien zu skandinavischen Waffengräber 520/30 bis 900 n. Chr.* Copenhagen.

Karlsson, L. 1983. *Nordisk form, om djurornamentik*. Stockholm. Summary pp. 178–189: *Nordic Form – on Animal Ornament*.

Karlsson, T. 1986. Häglinge hovgård och herresätet Hörröd. *Västra Göinge hembygdsförenings skriftserie* 34: 85–106.

Karlsson, T. 1989. Kapell, kloster eller huvudgård Norra Mellby. *Västra Göinge hembygdsförenings skriftserie* 37.

Lagerås, P. 2002. Skog, slåtter och stenröjning. Paleoekologiska undersökningar i trakten av Stoby i norra Skåne. In: Carlie, A. (ed.). *Skånska Regioner*. Stockholm: 362–411.

Lagerås, P. 2013. Agrara fluktuationer och befolkningsutveckling på sydsvenska höglandet tolkade utifrån röjningsrösen. *Fornvännen* 108: 262–277. Summary.

Leahy, K. & Bland, R. 2009. *The Staffordshire hoard*. London.

Le Goff, J. 1988. *Medieval civilization 400–1500*. Oxford (1st ed. 1964 *La civilisation de l'Occident médiéval*. Paris).

Lindroth, H. 1911. Göinge härads gårdnamn. *Fornvännen* 6: 175–196.

Näsman, U. 1984. *Glas och handel i senromersk tid och folkvandringstid*. Uppsala. Summary.

Näsman, U. 1998. Sydskandinavisk samhällsstruktur i ljuset av merovingisk och anglosaxisk analogi eller i vad är det som centralplatserna är centrala? In: Larsson, L. & Hårdh, B. (eds). *Centrala platser. Centrala frågor. Samhällsstrukturen under järnåldern*. Lund: 1–26.

Näsman, U. 1999. The ethnogenesis of the Danes and the making of a Danish kingdom. In: Dickinson, T. & Griffiths, D. (eds). *The making of kingdoms*. Oxford: 1–10.

Näsman, U. 2009. Jernalderens driftsformer i arkæologisk belysning. In: Odgaard, B. & Rømer, J. Rydén (eds). *Danske landbrugslandskaber gennem 2000 år. Fra digevoldinger til støtteordninger*. Århus: 99–116.

Norberg, R. 1931. Moor- und Depotfunde aus dem 5. Jahrhundert nach Chr. in Schonen. *Acta Archaeologica* 2: 104–111.

Norling-Christensen, H. 1956. Haraldstedgravpladsen og ældre germansk Jærnalder i Danmark. *Aarbøger for Nordisk Oldkyndighed og Historie*: 14–143.

Ödman, A. 1998. Northern Skåne – a resource area for medieval Denmark. In: Andersson, H., Ersgård, L. & Svensson, E. (eds). *Outland Use in Preindustrial Europe*. Lund.

Ödman, A. 2001. *Vittsjö – en socken i dansk järnbruksbygd*. Lund.

Ödman, A. 2015. Ulf Jarl, Knut den Store och Kävlinge bro. *Ale* 2015/3: 10–23. Summary.

Ödman, A. & Ödman, C. [2011]. *Händelser längs en väg. Finjasjöbygden med den medeltida Hovdalaborgen i centrum – från folkvandringstid till stormaktstid*. Lund.

Ørsnes, M. 1994. Zaumzeugfunde des 1.–8. Jhrh. nach Chr. in Mittel- und Nordeuropa. *Acta archaeologica* 64/2, 1993: 183–292.

Pedersen, E.A. & Jönsson, B 2003. Röjningsröseområdet Järparyd i Rydaholms socken, Finnveden, Småland. In: Widgren, M. (ed.). *Röjningsröseområden på sydsvenska höglandet. Arkeologiska, kulturgeografiska och vegetationshistoriska undersökningar*. Stockholm.

Pedersen, E.A. & Widgren, M. 2011. Agriculture in Sweden, 800 BC-AD 1000. In: Myrdal, J. & Morell. M. (eds). *The agrarian history of Sweden*. Lund: 46–71.

Ramqvist, P.H. 1992. *Högom. The excavations 1949–1984*. Umeå.

Rau, A. 2010. *Nydam mose 1–2. Die personengebundenen Gegenstände. Grabungen 1989–1999*. Højbjerg/Aarhus. Summary. Dansk resumé.

Rau, A. 2013. Where did the late empire end? Hacksilber and coins in continental and northern Barbaricum c AD 340–500. In: Fraser, H. & Painter, K. (eds). *Late Roman silver. The Traprain treasure in context*. Edinburgh: 339–357.

Renfrew, C. 1986. Introduction. In: Renfrew, C. & Cherry, J. (eds). *Peer Polity Interaction and Socio-political Change*. Cambridge (= New Directions in Archaeology): 1–18.

Ringdahl, C. 2008. *Skånes ortnamn. Serie A 22. Västra Göinge härad med Hässleholms stad*. Lund.

Rydh, H. 1917. S.k. eldslagningsstenar från järnåldern. *Fornvännen* 12: 172–190.

Salin, B. 1894. Fynd från Finjasjöns strand, Skåne. *KVHAAs månadsblad* 23: 84–106.

Skansjö, S., Riddersporre, M. & Reisnert, A. 1989. Huvudgårdarna i källmaterialet. In: Andersson, H. & Anglert, M. (eds). *By, huvudgård och kyrka*. Stockholm/Lund: 71–133.

Stille, A. 1909. Göinge. *Nordisk familjebok* 10: 860–861.

Stjernquist, B. 1993a. *Gårdlösa. An Iron Age community in its natural and social setting. 2 The archaeological fieldwork, the features and the finds*. Lund.

Stjernquist, B. 1993b. *Gårdlösa. An Iron Age community in its natural and social setting. 3 Chronological, economic, and social analyses*. Lund.

Strömberg, B. 2013. Väg E22 Rolsberga-Fogdarp. Arkeologisk förundersökning. Lund.

Strömberg, M. 1961a. *Untersuchungen zur jüngeren Eisenzeit in Schonen. I Text*. Lund.

Strömberg, M. 1961b. *Untersuchungen zur jüngeren Eisenzeit in Schonen. II Katalog und Tafeln*. Lund.

Sundqvist, O. 1998. Kultledare och kultfunktionärer i det forntida Skandinavien. *Svensk religionshistorisk årsskift* 1998: 76–104. Summary.

Sundqvist, O. 2008. Cult leaders, rulers and religion. In: Brink, S. & Price, N. (eds). *The Viking World*. London: 223–226.

Svensson, O. 2015. *Nämnda ting men glömda. Ortnamn, landskap och rättsutövning*. Växjö. Summary.

Tacitus, C. [2003].*The Annals & the Histories*. Ed. by M. Hadas. New York.

Vikstrand, P. 2013. *Järnålderns bebyggelsenamn. Om bebyggelsenamnens uppkomst och ålder i Mälarlandskapen*. Uppsala.

Voss, O. 1955. The Høstentorp silver hoard and its period. *Acta Archaeologica* 25, 1954: 171–217.

Wahlberg, M. (ed.) 2003. *Svenskt ortnamnslexikon*. Uppsala.

Widgren, M. 1983. *Settlement and farming systems in the early Iron Age*. Stockholm.

Internet references

FMIS– Swedish National Heritage Board, register of ancient monuments: http://www.raa.se/in-english/about-fornsok/

MPOV = Migration Period between Odra and Vistula: http://www.mpov.uw.edu.pl/en/thesaurus – Checked 27 April 2017.

SHM – Swedish History Museum, Stockholm. The easiest way to use the digital collections of the Swedish History Museum is to search for the identification number (*inventarienummer*) in the search engine: http://mis.historiska.se/mis/sok/sok.asp?qtype=invnr&sm=o_1

Staffordshire hoard = http://www.staffordshirehoard.org.uk – Checked 27 May 2017.

Table 1

Parish	Farm/village	Date	FMIS	References
Finja	Mölleröd	LRIA/MIG	83	Bj.:242
Hässleholm	Hässleholm	IA	2	Ca.:276
Hässleholm	Läreda	IA	58?	Ca.:276
Ignaberga	Ignaberga	EPRIA	42	Bj.:242
Ignaberga	Ignaberga	MIG	23	Bj.:242
Ignaberga	Ignaberga	EIA	42	Bj.:242
Ignaberga	Ignaberga	EIA	42	Bj.:242
Ignaberga	Ignaberga	EIA	42	Bj.:242
Ignaberga	Ignaberga	LB/EIA	22,41	Bj.:242
Ignaberga	Ignaberga	LB/EIA	22,41	Bj.:242
Ignaberga	Ignaberga	LB/EIA	22,41	Bj.:242f
Norra Mellby	Vannaröd	MER/VIK	36	Ca.:279
Norra Mellby	Vannaröd	LRIA/MIG	36	Bj.:243
Norra Mellby	Vannaröd	LB/PRIA	36	Bj.:243
Norra Mellby	Vannaröd	EIA	36	Bj.:243
Norra Mellby	Vannaröd	LRIA/MIG	36	Bj.:243
Norra Mellby	Sösdala	LB/EPRIA	27	Bj.:243
Norra Mellby	Lunnahöja	PRIA	–	Bj.:243
Norra Mellby	Vätteryd	MIG/VIK	1	Ca.:279f
Norra Mellby	Björkeberga	IA	44	Ca.:281
Södra Rörum	Ekeröd	EIA	41	Bj.:200
Stoby	Arkelstorp	LRIA/MIG	7	Bj.:243
Stoby	Arkelstorp	LRIA/MIG	7	Bj.:243
Stoby	Arkelstorp	LRIA/MIG	7	Bj.:243
Stoby	Arkelstorp	LB/EPRIA	205	Bj.:243
Stoby	Arkelstorp	LB/EPRIA	206	Bj.:244
Stoby	Kvistalånga	LRIA	–	Bj.:244
Stoby	Grantinge	IA	39	Ca.:284

Table 1. Excavated graves from central Scania. LB = Late Bronze Age; PRIA = Pre-Roman Iron Age; EPRIA = Early Pre-Roman Iron Age; EIA = Pre-Roman and Roman Iron Age; LIA = Late Iron Age; LRIA = Late Roman Iron Age; MIG = Migration Period; IA = Iron Age; MER = Merovingian Period; VIK = Viking Period. FMIS = number in the Ancient Monuments Survey. Bj. = Björk 2005; Ca. = Carlie 1994.

Table 2

Parish	FMIS certain	FMIS uncertain	Carlie 1994 type
Bosjökloster	36		6?
Bosjökloster	40		1?
Brönnestad	2		7
Brönnestad	13, 16, 34, 76		1
Brönnestad	23, 24		1
Brönnestad	52, 53		6?
Brönnestad	121		1?
Brönnestad		133	?
Brönnestad		154	1?
Brönnestad	178		7?
Finja	17		7
Finja	132		7
Fulltofta	2, 3		6
Fulltofta	20, 21, 103		1
Fulltofta	30, 31		1
Fulltofta	84		1?
Fulltofta		99	
Häglinge	1		6
Häglinge	54, 56, 57		7
Hässleholm	2		7
Hässleholm	18		7?
Hässleholm	33		7?
Hässleholm		36	7?
Höör	1		1?
Höör	3		1?
Höör	5		7?
Höör	16		7
Höör	21		5?
Höör		86	7?
Höör	158		7?
Höör	161, 162		1
Höör	200		6?
Höör	335		1
Ignaberga		15	
Ignaberga	18		1
Matteröd		8	1?
Matteröd	74		1?
Nävlinge	1		7
Norra Mellby	1		6
Norra Mellby	5		

Parish	FMIS certain	FMIS uncertain	Carlie 1994 type
Norra Mellby	10, 11		7*
Norra Mellby	16, 17, 18, 19		6*
Norra Mellby		22	7?
Norra Mellby	35		1
Norra Mellby	36		1
Norra Mellby		43	1?
Norra Mellby	121		1
Norra Mellby	173		6*
Norra Mellby	254	252	1
Norra Mellby	287		6*
Norra Rörum	3		1
Norra Rörum	8		1
Norra Rörum	10		7
Norra Rörum	20		1
Norra Rörum		81	1?
Norra Rörum		120	1?
Södra Rörum	1		1
Södra Rörum	4		6
Södra Rörum		35	5?
Södra Rörum	51		1
Stoby	3		1
Stoby	7		5
Stoby	10		7?
Stoby	23		7
Stoby	36		7
Stoby	39		7
Stoby	50		1
Stoby	61		1?**
Stoby	97		1***
Stoby		121	1?
Stoby		170	7?
Vankiva	13, 14		1
Vankiva	17		1
Vankiva	26		7
Vankiva	119		7?

Table 2. Cemeteries, grave groups and graves from the Late Iron Age are recorded according to Carlie's classification system (1994:43, 88). Graves and cemeteries from the relevant parishes in Frosta and Gärds *häraden* are added. That some graves are presented as uncertain in a separate column is due to problems in assessing them.

*These might originally have constituted one and the same cemetery.
**Part of Stoby FMIS 3.
***Part of Stoby FMIS 50. (FMIS; Carlie 1994).

Table 3

Parish	Farm/village	Type	Ref.
Äsphult	Äsphult	PE	Strömberg:24
Äsphult	Äsphult	PE	Strömberg:24
Bosjökloster	The parish	O	SHM 14265:1186
Bosjökloster	The parish	O	SHM 14265:1187
Finja	Mariehill	PE	Strömberg:73
Häglinge	Häglinge	O	Carlie:274
Häglinge	Häglinge	O	Carlie:274f
Häglinge	Häglinge	PE	Strömberg:73
Häglinge	Häglinge	PE	Strömberg:73
Häglinge	Häglinge	PE	Strömberg:73
Häglinge	Häglinge ?	PE	Strömberg:73
Häglinge	Kolstrarp	PE	Carlie 1994:275
Höör	The parish	PE	Strömberg:20
Ignaberga	Gulastorp	PE	Strömberg:73
Ignaberga	Attarp	PE	Carlie 1994:277
Norra Mellby	Sösdala	PE	Strömberg:86
Stoby	Kvistalånga	O	Carlie:283
Stoby	The parish	O	Carlie:283
Stoby	Röinge	PE	Strömberg:86
Stoby	Röinge	PE	Strömberg:86
Stoby	Kvistalånga	PE	Carlie:283
Stoby	Kvistalånga	?	RAÄ 77, 89
Vankiva	The parish	PE	Carlie:284

Table 3. Strike-a-lights from central Scania. O = oval strike-a-light; PE = pointed elliptic strike-a-light. Carlie 1994; RAÄ – Swedish National Heritage Board, the Ancient Monuments Survey in Sweden (*FMIS*); SHM – The Swedish History Museum, Stockholm; Strömberg 1961b.

Резюме

Ландшафт Центральной Скани в Эпоху переселения народов

Местный контекст находок из Сёсдалы и Фультофты

Шарлотта Фабек, Бертиль Хельгессон, Ульф Несман

Местность, где находится Сёсдала, знаменита множеством уникальных находок V в., указывающих на тесные связи с Восточной и Центральной Европой. К их числу относятся три погребальных приношения роскошной конской сбруи в Сёсдале и Фультофте, единственная в своем роде портупейная скоба от ножен меча, серебряная поясная пряжка и пельтовидная подвеска из Торнесторпа (рис. 4–5), клад серебряных изделий из Шёрупа (рис. 8), приношение в Йёингехольме (рис. 6–7) и золотая пластина в виде орла из Клаэсторпа (рис. 9). Здесь сохранилось много крупных могильников с наземными конструкциями в виде вертикальных камней, каменных кругов, каменных ладей и пр. (рис. 2–3). Область Сёсдалы находится в центре лесной зоны северной Скании (рис. 1). Примечательно, что эти уникальные находки обнаружены в труднодоступных местах – пока удовлетворительного объяснения этому феномену так и не найдено.

Для объяснения шести уникальных находок из центральной Скани изучались археологические данные, топонимика и письменные источники. Пространственное распространение древних памятников, сохранившихся на территории Скании, указывает на обширные территории, где древние памятники или отсутствовали, или были единичными. Если на территории сельскохозяйственных угодий большая часть памятников исчезла, то на покрытых лесами моренах поселения во все времена были немногочисленными. На фоне центральной Скани район Сёсдалы был зоной сравнительно высокой концентрации памятников (рис. 10–11).

По мнению О. Свенссон (см. статью в этом томе), Сёсдала, Нёсдала и Ховдала – топонимы древние (-dal = «долина»). Согласно предположению исследователя, первый элемент (Sös-) в слове «Сёсдала» (Sösdala) относится к лицу, Söir, которое отвечало за языческие жертвоприношения.

Древние топонимы указывают на своеобразный коридор из поселений, существовавший к югу от озера Финья (рис. 14).

Находки из Сёсдалы, Фультофты и Торнестропа свидетельствуют о том, что жители этой зоны были связаны с существовавшим в Европе сообществом элитных всадников. Их присутствие в центральной Скани требует надлежащего объяснения, найти которое не так уж просто. Яркие находки не связаны с местным контекстом Римского железного века. Необычные находки Эпохи переселении народов в центральной Скани указывают на появление здесь чего-то действительно нового, причем это происходит синхронно с возникновением новых могильников с вертикальными камнями и каменными ладьями на территории всей Скании.

Какие же причины заставили представителей элиты Скании поселиться вдали от богатых равнин? Показательно, что с конными воинами и военной властью связано много находок – Фультофта, Шёруп, Сёсдала, Торнесторп и Веттерид. Многочисленные кремни от огнив (рис. 12–13) указывают на присутствие здесь большой группы воинов. Найденные в Сёсдале I и Фультофте уздечки, вероятно, привезены возвращавшимися домой воинами, а потому являются отражением личного опыта этих людей, полученного на юго-востоке Европы. По предположению М. М. Казанского, которое он сделал на Лундском семинаре 2015 г., установленные задолго до этого времени семейные связи между элитами южной Скандинавии и юго-восточной Европы могли определять те пути, по которым двигались молодые воины из Скании, пути, хорошо известные с IV в.

Клад серебряных изделий из Шёрупа относится к периоду D2 по скандинавской хронологии (рис. 8) – здесь, очевидно, спрятали вещи из драгоценного металла. Сопоставление с кладом золота и серебра из Стаффордшира в Англии позволяет интерпретировать Шёруп как принадлежавшую военному вождю долю трофеев, взятых в победоносной битве. Клад из Шёрупа показывают, что представители высшего слоя общества поддерживали связи с центральной Сканией и во второй половине V в.

Поселенческая структура Скани во второй половины 1 тысячелетия н. э. характеризовалась обширными протяженными зонами поселений на равнинах вдоль западного и южного побережья (рис. 14). Еще одна крупная зона поселений возникла на равнине Кристианстад на северо-востоке. Но горсты и другие препятствия для расселения людей привели к фрагментации поселенческой структуры на «Сканийской диагонали». К ней относится область между озерами Финья и Рингшён. Можно предположить, что знатные воины утвердились здесь на рубеже IV–V вв. н. э., и что они выполняли задачи, имевшие большое значение для центральной власти на западе и/или на востоке. По нашему мнению, преемственность власти сохранялась здесь до XI–XII вв., когда письменные источники и строительные остатки позволяют выделить обширные королевские домены в зоне поселений Сёсдалы (рис. 15).

Локализация находок в широком коридоре в центральной Скани заставляет предположить, что решающим фактором были коммуникации (рис. 10–11). На карте (рис. 14) показаны зоны, плотно заселенные V–XI вв., и, кажется, заметен разрыв между областью Сёсдалы и областью Фультофты.

Этот разрыв не был совсем не заселенным, на что указывает распространение каменных конструкций (рис. 10), но, вероятно, он разделял и связывал два государственных образования. Именно здесь всадники из Сёсдалы и Фультофты могли контролировать этот переход. Древние дороги шли от поселения к поселению; они связывали соседей. Чтобы избежать опасности в путешествии, нужно было следовать по сложившимся путям, представлявшим собой взаимосвязанные места, где можно было встретить знакомых – друзей и врагов. Древний путь с юго-запада на северо-восток проходил через Клаэсторп и Фультофту, далее шел к Хеглинге, откуда следовал через Йёингехольм и Шёруп, а затем достигал равнины Кристианстадт.

Но что именно было объектом контроля – перемещение людей и воинов? перевозка продукции из лесов? железо? меха? Этого мы не знаем. Потребность в железе в Эпоху переселения народов была велика и все время возрастала, но сегодня не известно, как было организована снабжение. Вероятно, причина для установления контроля была политической. На юге Скандинавии V в. был временем смут, когда нестабильные политические образования боролись за власть. Потому, быть может, воины просто наблюдали друг за другом? Было ли учреждение стражи на пограничной территории хорошим решением в условиях, когда молодые горячие головы требовалось отодвинуть от центров власти?

Подписи к иллюстрациям

Рис. 1. Центральная часть Скании между озером Финья и озером Рингшён, а также равниной Кристианстад (по: Bredsdorff 1973). Горизонталями показаны высоты 30, 80 и 150 м над уровнем моря. Оцифровано в ходе исследовательского проектам «Поселения и ландшафты» (Fabech, Hvass, Näsman, Ringtved 1999: 14).

Рис. 2. В окрестностях Сёсдалы существовало 16 средневековых приходов, отмеченных соответствующими церквями. На основе фрагмента карты Скании Герхарда фон Бурманна (1684 г.). Военный архив, Стокгольм (по: Generalstabens litografiska anstalt, Stockholm 1969).

Рис. 3. Места, где были сделаны находки, с юга на север: Клаэсторп, Фультофта, Шёруп, Йёингехольм, Сёсдала, Торнесторп (на основе той же карты, что и рис. 2).

Рис. 4. Поясная пряжка и портупейная скоба от ножен меча, найденные в Торнесторпе (фото Даниэля Линдскога; Исторический музей Лундского университета).

Рис. 5. Пельтовидная подвеска, найденная в озере Финья близ Торнесторпа (фото Арне Шёстрёма).

Рис. 6. Керамический сосуд, найденный в Йёингехольме. В нем находился набор женских украшений (см. рис. 7; фото Илиали Асп; Шведский исторический музей, Стокгольм, № 21058).

Рис. 7. Серебряные украшения и янтарные бусы, найденные в керамическом сосуде, в Йёингехольме (см. рис. 6; фото Хелены Росенгрен; Шведский исторический музей, Стокгольм, № 21058).

Рис. 8. Клад разломанных серебряных вещей, найденный в Шёрупе (фото Сёрена Хальгрена; Шведский исторический музей, Стокгольм, №№ 1032, 2437, 2663).

Рис. 9. Золотая пластинка в виде орла с цепочками, найденная в Клаэсторпе (фото Ульфа Брюкса; Шведский исторический музей, Стокгольм. № 7004).

Рис. 10. Мегалитические круги на территории Скании (по: Helgesson, Lindberg, 2017 fig. 1: 99).

Рис. 11. Могилы и могильники в окрестнястях Сёсдалы, типы 1, 5, 6, 7 (по: Carlie 1994). Синими квадратами показаны места находок, отмеченных на рис. 3 (на основе той же карты, что и рис. 2).

Рис. 12. Распространение паспортизированных кремней от кресал (на основе той же карты, что и рис. 2; данные по: Strömberg 1961; Carlie 1994; Совет по национальному наследию Швеции).

Рис. 13. Образец миндалевидного кремня от кресала с желобком для подвешивания. Эстергётланд, подъемный материал (фото Сары Кусмин; Шведский исторический музей, Стокгольм, № 7149).

Рис. 14. Плотно заселенные области Скании в Эпоху переселения народов, Вендельский период и Эпоху викингов (по: Ödman, Ödman 2011 fig. 205; перерисовано по: Callmer 1991 fig. 6).

Рис. 15. Романская приходская церковь в Норра-Мельбю, вид с севера. Башня пристроена в 1917 г. (фото Шарлотты Фабек, 2016 г.).

Chapter 5

Sösdala: find and style 1929–1993

Ulf Näsman

The research history of the Sösdala finds from the early Migration Period is reviewed. Many well-preserved mounts of a parade bridle and several saddles were found at Sösdala, Scania, in 1929–1930. The find was not presented internationally until 1937 when J.E. Forssander published his celebrated paper "Provinzialrömisches und germanisches". But only the punch-decorated silver mounts became famous since they were used to define his "Sösdala style". The outlook of other scholars was limited to the material published by Forssander and thematically research was restricted to questions about the origin and chronology of the Sösdala style. Research about the relation of the Sösdala finds to Late Roman provincial arts and crafts and to the Scandinavian "Nydam style" is treated.

Näsman, U. 2017. Sösdala: find and style 1929–1993. In: Fabech, C. & Näsman, U. (eds). *The Sösdala horsemen – and the equestrian elite of fifth century Europe*. Jutland Archaeological Society.

When workers in 1929 found a lot of small "golden" objects in a gravel pit at Sösdala (Fabech chapter 1), they had no idea that they had made a major archaeological discovery, or that the place name would be famous. But that would not happen any time soon.

The Sösdala finds were mentioned for the first time in print already the same year, but only as a footnote in a short paper by Rune Norberg about Migration Period saddle mounts in Sweden (Norberg 1929b:113). But in his first paper on saddle mounts one finds no reference to Sösdala (Norberg 1929a). In this paper he published an often reproduced attempt to reconstruct a saddle, based on Migration Period saddle mounts found in 1927 in Jönköping, Småland (SHM no. 18 359). The Jönköping finds were compared to finds from Västergötland and Scania, finds that since have remained central in the discussions about the Sösdala finds and style (Västergötland: Vennebo SHM No. 6 511, and Finnestorp SHM no. 8 232; Scania: Fulltofta, LUHM No. 14 080, and Åmossarna, Österlens museum no. 2 963). As far as we have observed, this is the first time that such mounts and rings were correctly identified as belonging to saddles. Norberg reconstructed the saddle as a solid tree saddle (cf. Sundkvist chapter 9; Näsman chapter 7). Norberg dated ring saddles to the 5th century in the Migration Period.

This essay presents the research history of chronology and provenance of the bridle and saddle mounts from

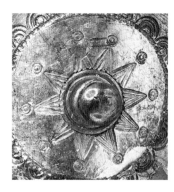

Fig. 1. Left: a punched star on the pelta-shaped pendant from Jakuszowice, Poland. After Åberg 1936:271. Right: a punched star on a strap-junction from Sösdala no. I:14. Photo Daniel Lindskog.

Sösdala and Fulltofta until the early 1990s. It must be noted that the relative chronological concepts C3 and D1 have a different meaning in Scandinavia than in Continental chronologies (see Introduction fig. 4; cf. Rau 2010:65). The two Sösdala finds can be dated to the Late Roman Iron Age period Scand-C3 (Sösdala II) and the early Migration Period Scand-D1 (Sösdala I). In calendar years the Sösdala finds and related phenomena can be dated to a period beginning in the late 4th century and ending before the middle of the 5th century.

As soon as Norberg had been able to study the Sösdala finds from 1929 in Lund and again in 1930, when all Sösdala I finds were at the Swedish History Museum in Stockholm, he hurried to publish a short paper for an international public, including the first published photos of mounts from Fulltofta and Sösdala (Norberg 1931 figs 4–13). The paper signalled his ambition to write a monograph about Scanian Migration Period bog finds and hoards. Norberg noted that the two finds were not bog finds but found in gravel ridges, an observation often overlooked or disregarded by later scholars. He assumed that the Sösdala saddle mounts represented 4–5 saddles similar to his Jönköping reconstruction. In the description of the punched ornamentation on the mounts of the Sösdala I bridle he emphasises that some mounts have classical (= Roman) character and that others show Germanic *horror vacui*. Probably the "classical" objects are those belonging to punch group 1 according to Lovisa Dal (chapter 6) and

those covered with punch marks are found in her punch groups 2 and 3. Norberg assumed a date in the first half of the 5th century, perhaps in its later part due to the presence of what he called shallow chip-carving and punch marks with relief effect. His brief discussion of the origin of the Scanian finds includes the finds from Untersiebenbrunn. Also influences from the Middle Rhine area and *Südrußland* (today Ukraine) are mentioned on the basis of studies by Bernhard Salin (1904) and Nils Åberg (1919a; 1924). Nevertheless, he assumed that the Scanian finds may be local products.

For reasons unknown to us, Norberg never brought his project to a conclusion (see Fabech chapter 1). His licenciate dissertation at Uppsala University (Norberg 1933) remained unpublished (and is unfortunately untraceable). He never returned to the subject in print (cf. Liivrand 1978).

Before the workers dug in the Sösdala gravel pit, Nils Åberg concluded in his study of the punched star ornamentation that its origin was to be found in the Roman provinces on the Rhine from where it reached South Scandinavia (1919a). He was later entrusted with the task of publishing a grave find from Jakuszowice in Poland (1936; cf. Godłowski 1995). Of course he mentioned the similarities to finds from Fulltofta, Sösdala and Vennebo, but he could not deal with them since Norberg was working on the subject. In the short paper Åberg dated the Sösdala parade bridle to the early 5th century with reference to Szilágy-Somlyó, Untersiebenbrunn, and Jakuszowice. He noted the awkwardly punched star on the pelta-shaped pendant from Jakuszowice compared to the accurate stars in Sösdala (fig. 1) and the absence of shallow chip-carving as found in Sösdala (fig. 2).

For studies published in connection with the retirement of Otto Rydbeck, director of Historical Museum at Lund University, Ture J. Arne wrote a paper on a ritual deposition at Göingeholm of a ceramic vessel filled with silver jewellery and amber beads (Arne 1937; Fabech, Helgesson & Näsman chapter 4). He dated the find to the second half of the 5th century or *c.* AD 500 (certainly too late). The striking fact that the find spot is situated in the same area as the finds from Sösdala, Sjörup, and Fulltofta was noted. The finds from Sösdala and Fulltofta were considered to be two or three decades later than the Untersiebenbrunn

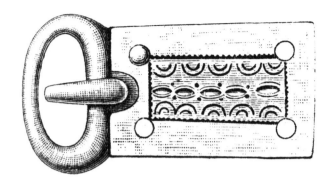

Fig. 2. Deep lens-shaped punch marks on belt buckles from Finnestorp (left, after Åberg 1919a fig. 32), Untersiebenbrunn (centre, photo KHM-Museumsverband 1525/2016, Vienna) and detail of the pelta-shaped pendant from Sösdala, nos. I:19–21 (right, photo Daniel Lindskog).

find and he dated them to the early 5th century. He also noted that the depositions had taken place in hills, not in wetland. He suggested that the remarkable find concentration in central Scania represented a realm with wide connections and he associates this realm with the tribal name *Liothida* in the Gothic history of Jordanes.

John-Elof Forssander

Also in 1937 John-Elof Forssander's celebrated paper on the Sösdala finds appeared, a paper that eventually made the place name Sösdala famous. Forssander had specialised in Stone and Bronze Age archaeology (Arbman 1966; Stjernquist & Ambatsis 1979), so probably the paper was written to make him eligible for the professorship in Lund, which he finally got in 1938. The paper is a very rich study in comparative archaeology, but it has also a very complex and sometimes confusing composition.

Forssander used the Sösdala finds in an archaeological/art-historical project, in which he analysed Scandinavian decorative styles found on silver jewellery and weapon mounts of the early Migration Period in order to trace their origin in Europe. Thus he follows in the steps of Salin (1904:153–161) and Åberg (1919a,b). Forssander was the first to give the style its lasting name, the Sösdala style, but he never defined it unambiguously. Like Norberg before

him, he noticed the similarities between the finds from Sösdala and nearby Fulltofta, both found in gravel ridges, and perhaps Vennebo, the find circumstances of which are too uncertain to allow interpretation. But neither find circumstances nor local context mattered much in his paper.

Forssander found a larger body of material for a study of the Sösdala style in the Scandinavian silver sheet brooches and illustrated the paper with brooches from Eidsten, Roligheden and Mejlby. The silver sheet brooches of the Migration Period are characterised by hanging animal heads at the upper part of the lower plate. The brooch type as well as the punched ornamentation is rooted in simpler silver sheet brooches of the Late Roman Iron Age (Hansen 1970) and ultimately they have, according to Forssander, an origin in "Gothic" silver sheet brooches (1937:33). It has to be emphasised that the number of relevant silver sheet brooches was and still is small, only four in Denmark, two in Norway and one in Sweden (Nielsen 1985:116–117; Bitner-Wróblewska chapter 12; 2001:99).

Punched ornamentation on blank or gilt silver surfaces, a play between dark and light, between undecorated, nielloed and/or punch-decorated, and simple animal depictions are of course fundamental to Forssander's characterisation of the style. But also openwork is prominent on a number of the Sösdala mounts (Sösdala catalogue

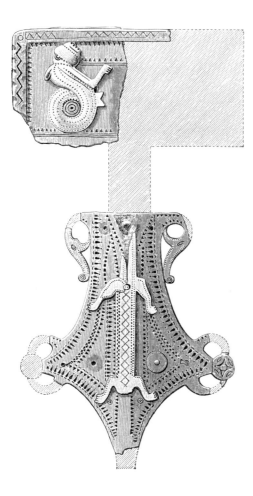

Fig. 3. Silver sheet brooch from Mejlby, Jutland. 1:1. After Salin 1904 Abb. 489.

nos. I:1–5, 19). The openwork of the Mejlby silver sheet brooch was noted by Forssander and he emphasised that the technique of the style is silver smithery, not casting (fig. 3). The plastic hippocampus and lizard on the Mejlby brooch were cast separately and soldered on. (In Sösdala only the three-way connector of no. I:1 has soldered-on details.) Forssander also saw the similarities between horse heads of three Sösdala mount (see catalogue nos. I:1, 10 and 11) and horse heads on a sword chape from Veien in Norway (Arwidsson 1984; it is, however, labelled Nydam style by Jan Bemmann 1998 Fundliste 10 no. 21). A significant contribution to the understanding of the technique of the Sösdala and Nydam styles was offered by Olfert Voss later on in a paper about the Høstentorp hoard (1955a, below).

That the punched ornamentation of the Late Roman Iron Age is crucial for understanding the ornamentation of the early Migration Period had been noted by scholars long before Forssander described the Sösdala style in 1937. Examples are pioneering studies by Bernhard Salin (1904) and Nils Åberg (1919a,b). Punched ornamentation was later on studied by Ulla Lund Hansen (1970), Helmut Roth (1979), Erling Benner Larsen (1984), Jens Nielsen (1985) and Elmer Fabech (1985). In spite of all efforts, it has proved impossible to draw a sharp chronological line between punched ornamentation from periods Scand-C3 and Scand-D1. Now the punched ornamentation of Sösdala is analysed by Lovisa Dal (chapter 6).

Forssander interpreted the punched ornamentation of the Sösdala style as a simplification or translation of "Gothic" filigree decoration from the 4th century, and compared the filigree-decorated pelta-shaped pendants in the Zakrzów (Sackrau) grave to the punch-decorated pelta-shaped pendants from Sösdala I (see catalogue nos. I:19–21) and Vennebo. Consequently he rejected Åberg's suggestion that the punched "star ornamentation" had its origin in provincial Roman workshops of the Rhine provinces (1937:31–33 footnote 1). In his opinion the star punched on a sword bridge mount from the Thorsbjerg weapon deposit (Åberg 1919a fig. 4) was earlier than Åberg's assumed Late Roman prototypes from the Rhine area. Possibly Forssander believed that the mount, like most of the Thorsbjerg finds, was datable to an early phase of the Late Roman Iron Age. But a small number of objects, including the star-decorated bridge mount, are certainly much later; it is now attributed to the late weapon combination group 9, i.e. to the second third of the 4th century or early period Scand-C3 (Matešić 2015:62–63, 258, Taf. 23 M165). So the Thorsbjerg bridge mount is contemporary with many Late Roman punch-decorated belt sets and thus Åberg's idea is brought back to life.

Of course, Forssander knew that there is a large corpus of silver objects of Late Roman types that are punch-decorated with rows of dots, circles, semicircles, etc. He also noted the occurrence of horse heads in profile on provincial Roman objects, a grand example being the strap end from Babenhausen (Quast chapter 14 fig. 4:1; See *Riemenzungen Form C Typ c* in Sommer 1984:53–55, Taf. 22:3a,b). In 1937 the chronological relation between "Germanic" and "Roman" objects was unclear, but he assumed nevertheless that Roman material culture influenced the "Germanic" and not the other way around. He followed the Roman impact by tracing the motif of shallow chip-carved (in reality punched) lens shapes from Mainz to Untersiebenbrunn as well as to Vennebo and Sösdala (1937:62). So Forssander was able to trace both animal heads and punched ornamentation from Scania back to provincial Roman metal crafts in the west. But he emphasised that this Roman impact could not explain what he called *goto-ungarische Züge* in the Sösdala style.

In Forssander's opinion the saddle mounts were without doubt made in Scandinavia. He also supposed that the mounts of the parade bridle were Nordic, and why not made in Scania: "unter allem Umstände Erzeugnisse einer nordischen, warum nicht schonischen Metallindustrie" (1937:64). But the style had its roots elsewhere, and not in the West. So Forssander continued his search for a "Gothic" connection; ideas about the so-called *gotische Rückstrom* were very popular in the early 20th century and central in Bernhard Salin's great work (1904: 12, 41, 136 etc.). On the basis of finds from Brangstrup, Himlingøie, Varpelev, Zakrzów, etc. Forssander argued that contacts with the *gotisch-Südrussische Kunstindustrie* were established already in the Late Roman Iron Age. The Brangstrup hoard was very important when he argued that in the 4th century there existed close links to the Goths on the Black Sea. Joachim Werner confirmed this view in a paper on the relations between Funen and the Černjachov culture (Werner 1988). After the arrival of the Huns in AD 375 some barbaric groups fled westwards into the Danubian basin and from here the relations to Scandinavia continued during the early 5th century, as demonstrated by the finds from Untersiebenbrunn. It escaped Forssander's notice that the distribution of glass vessels with cut decoration could have given further support to the assumed link between Scandinavia and the Black Sea area in the 4th century; obviously he had not yet seen Gunnar Ekholm's first paper on "Oriental" glass vessels (Ekholm 1936).

The obvious similarities between the Sösdala parade bridle and the bridle mounts from Coşoveni and Untersiebenbrunn are central in his argument. The two finds have kept this position in all discussions about the Sösdala find and style (cf. Kazanski & Mastykova chapter 15). In more recent literature a number of name combinations are used to characterise the decorative style: Sösdala-Untersiebenbrunn, Untersiebenbrunn-Sösdala, Sösdala-Coşoveni, Sösdala-Untersiebenbrunn-Coşoveni, Untersiebenbrunn-Coşoveni, Untersiebenbrunn-Kačin, and now Dieter Quast suggests Sösdala-Untersiebenbrunn-Velp (Quast chapter 14). In this way similarities in shape and ornamentation are emphasised, but one also has to acknowledge the differences; regional variation is obvious (Nothnagel 2008:167). Certainly there is a relation between the four bridle finds, to which the bridle from Jakuszowice can be added. But a fact is that close links in shape or style are few. Forssander exemplified similarities with the deep lens-shaped punch marks on a strap buckle in the deposition at Finnestorp and similar punch marks on mounts from Untersiebenbrunn (fig. 2). The Finnestorp buckle, he suggested, is either a direct import or a copy (1937:36–38). In the Sösdala find itself deep lens-shaped punch marks are found on only one object, the pelta-shaped pendant (see catalogue nos. I:19–21). Deep lens-shaped punch marks were important for both Salin (1904:153–161) and Åberg (1919a), who both characterised them as shallow chip-carving and thus they became, in their strict typological thinking, indicators of a relatively late date in the Sösdala style phase.

Forssander concluded that the workshop that produced the parade bridle of Sösdala had a direct or indirect relation to "Gothic" workshops represented by Coşoveni and Untersiebenbrunn. His final proof was the bridle found in the grave at Jakuszowice (with reference to Åberg 1936). The grave was given chronological significance and was dated after the two hoards from Şimleu Silvaniei (Szilágysomlyó) to AD 375–400. Today scholars date the depositions at Şimleu Silvaniei later, to between AD 400 and 450 (*MPOV* 2016 at Şimleu Silvaniei) or to *c.* AD 430–450 (Kiss 1999); Kiss argued that the two Şimleu Silvaniei hoards were hidden by Gepid royalties. The Jakuszowice grave belongs to period Cont-D2 and probably not after *c.* AD 430. Today the dead person and the grave goods are not associated with the Goths (a constituent part of the Wielbark culture) but with the Przeworsk culture (Godłowski 1995; *MPOV* 2016 at Jakuszowice).

Still Forssander had problems in understanding the origin of the Sösdala style. The finds from Coşoveni, Jakuszowice, and Untersiebenbrunn could not help him to solve them (1937:62–63). He had to admit that "Die spezielle Tierornamentik des Sösdala-depots hat keine Gegenstücke im gotischen Stilkreis des 4. Jhs." And indeed, there is no *Tierornamentik* in the Untersiebenbrunn-Coşoveni material. But now horse and bird heads on mounts from Kačin (Kachin) and Bar, both Ukraine, have opened a new entry to discuss this problem that still awaits its solution (cf. Levada 2011 fig. 3, 5; Fabech & Näsman 2013:101 fig. 23, and Kazanski & Mastykova chapter 15).

To find the origin of the Sösdala horse heads Forssander turned again to late provincial Roman belt fittings that he assumed were produced from *c.* AD 350 until the "Germanic" crossing of the Rhine AD 406 (1937:43–62). He discussed the relation between belt mounts produced by Roman *fabricae* for the Roman army and belt mounts that seem to be barbaric copies made for and used by "Germanic" warriors in Roman service. He concluded that the Sösdala style is rooted in provincial Roman "military" belts, but he found it difficult to decide exactly where its development took place along the long Roman border. The Rhine valley seemed most likely, as previously suggested by Åberg (1919a,b). But since mounts are also found in the east along the Danube, he could not exclude the central Danubian area. Much research is invested in the Late Roman belt sets (e.g. Böhme 1974; 1986; Sommer 1984; cf. Quast chapter 14) and Forssander's chronology and chorology are obsolete. Markus Sommer concluded his analyses that late provincial Roman belt mounts were not exclusively military and that the production was based on numerous smaller workshops, not large *fabricae* (1984:87–88, 101–102). In the chaotic 5th century this facilitated the transference of know-how and/or craftsmen to the Barbarians.

At last, Forssander had to make up his mind. He concluded that it was through contacts with provincial Roman handicraft in the late 4th century that barbaric peoples along the Rhine frontier laid the foundation of what in Scandinavia became the Sösdala style. He mentions for example the strap end from Babenhausen with two outward-looking horse heads in profile, similar to those on

the three-way connector of Sösdala no. I:1. From the Rhine area, "Germanic" interpretation of late Roman ornamentation and design was brought to Scandinavia where a style developed as illustrated by the silver sheet brooches and the mounts of horse equipment. This is also the conclusion of Helmut Roth in 1979. Forssander used the similarities to mounts from Untersiebenbrunn to date the Sösdala bridle to *c.* AD 400 or a little before; I guess it was the production time that Forssander dated. In a popular publication he wrote that "Germanic" 5th century art not owed much more than the horse heads in profile to influences from the West Roman provinces, while the rest is connected to "Germanic-Gothic" metal crafts in the East ("southern Russia") during the 4th century and its development on the Danube in the early 5th century (Forssander 1938:198–199).

Another well-known Scanian deposition, the chip-carved mounts from Sjörup, was used by Forssander as a contrast to the punch-decorated Sösdala material. He used the chip-carved, gilt and nielloed silver objects to characterise what he labelled the Sjörup group and later scholars changed to "Sjörup style". But this concept has later been surpassed by the Nydam style of Olfert Voss (1955, below). Cast in silver and decorated with chip-carved spirals in various combinations, the Sjörup mounts represent a more advanced technique. For Forssander the many objects looked homogeneous, but differences in manufacture as well as a few objects with animal ornaments in Salin's Style I indicate that the find has a mixed origin (cf. Salin 1894:106; Karlsson 1983:12, 141). The origin of the Sjörup style could not be found in the area where the Sösdala style was bred, so he looked in another direction and again he found a "Gothic" relation with reference to new finds from "*Westrussland*" (1937 Abb. 27), coin-dated to after AD 350. The find is, as we now know, from Zamość, Poland, and today it is placed much later, late in Continental period Cont-D2 (*c.* AD 380/400–440/450) or in the second quarter of the 5th century (*MPOV* 2016 at Zamość). Forssander knew that his dating of early chip-carved objects in Hungary to *c.* AD 400 was much earlier than that of other scholars like Åberg. It is a mistake caused by his assumption that chip-carved bronzes disappeared from the provincial Roman "market" around AD 400 (1937:74–75). Today chip-carved belt buckles as depicted by Forssander in Abb. 29–32 are dated to after *c.* AD 450 (Rau 2010 fig. 129–132).

The Sjörup style had a chronological function in Forssander's study. With reference to Gothic migration history he argued that the Visigothic passage over the Danube into Roman territory in AD 376 made them familiar with provincial Roman metal crafts and that the distribution in Europe of chip-carved "Gothic" objects ended already in the early 5th century AD. So he dated the beginning of the Sjörup style to the early 5th century and assumed consequently that the Sösdala style ended in the early 5th century (1937:76, 83–86). Forssander, in contrast to many other scholars, realised however that the Sösdala and Sjörup [Nydam] styles overlapped in the first half of the 5th century (cf. Näsman 1984:61, Abb. 1). First the punched Sösdala style came from the provincial Roman West in the late 4th century and then in the early 5th century the chip-carved Sjörup style came from the "Gothic-Hungarian" East (1937:77). But he got this wrong because he assumed a hiatus between the provincial West Roman production of chip-carvings with spirals, rosettes, tendrils, etc. and the Scandinavian Sjörup material. This hiatus he filled with the punch-decorated Sösdala style and the "Gothic-Hungarian" chip-carved material. I will not discuss the Sjörup finds further, only point out that the find spot is situated only 6 km from Sösdala (Fabech; Helgesson & Näsman chapter 4).

When Forssander discussed that the end of the Sösdala style and the beginning of the Sjörup style overlapped in the early 5th century, he referred to finds from Kiełpino (Kelpin) and Świelino (Schwellin), both Poland (1937:84 Abb. 34). Today the two finds are dated towards the middle of the 5th century (*MPOV* 2016 at Kiełpino and Świelino). In this context the square-headed silver brooch found in a ritual deposition at Göingeholm (Arne 1937) is of course important with its combination of punched and shallow chip-carved ornamentation (fig. 4). The find spot is only 4 km from Sösdala. Forssander noted that the brooch was deposited together with many large turned amber beads, which are very similar to those from Kiełpino and in key finds in south-eastern Europe. Anyhow the amber beads reveal cross-Baltic links.

The ideas of Forssander were rapidly integrated in the scholarly discussion concerning the Migration Period in

Fig. 4. A square-headed silver brooch deposited at Göingeholm, Scania, together with other silver jewellery and many amber beads in a ceramic vessel. 1:1. Photo: Helena Rosengren, Swedish History Museum, Stockholm. SHM no. 21 058. For the entire find, see Fabech, Helgesson & Näsman chapter 4 fig. 6–7.

Scandinavia. An example is a short paper by Hans Norling-Christensen on the beginning of the Migration Period in which he used the chronological concepts Sösdala and Sjörup phases (1949). Norling-Christensen accepted Forssander's dating of the beginning of the Sösdala phase to the second half of the 4th century. But he disagreed with Forssander's idea that the Sjörup style had its origin at the "Gothic" Black Sea or in "Gothic" Hungary; he emphasised that late Roman chip-carved belt mounts continued to be produced in the western provinces well into the 5th century, and concluded that the Sjörup style was created on the basis of Late Roman chip-carvings during the first half of the 5th century. Support for the dating of the Sjörup phase he found in the insular Late Roman silver hoards from Coleraine, Ireland, and Traprain, Scotland, but also in the Høstentorp silver hoard, Zealand, later to be published by Olfert Voss (1955a, below). Obviously his general dating of the Sjörup deposition is too early; today the Sjörup deposition is placed in the second half of the 5th century (cf. Rau 2010:312–313).

Holmqvist and Stjernquist

During the 1930s the idea of "Gothic" connections became infected by the Nazi misuse of the concept of *Drang nach Osten* and after the Second World War the *gotische Rückstrom* had become obsolete. So in 1951 the learned scholar Wilhelm Holmqvist dissociated himself from the *gothischen Kulturstrom* and emphasised Scandinavian contacts to provincial West Roman handicrafts; anyhow, he remarked that the silver-inlaid saddle mounts at Sösdala had nothing to do with the Goths (1951:95–97, 109–113, Abb. 51–54). Holmqvist made an observation in his survey of *Tauschierte Metallarbeiten* that is important for the dating of the bit from Sösdala II; according to him all dated inlays with twisted silver and copper wire are from the Late Roman Iron Age and none from the Migration Period (1951:88–92). Recent publications do not change this as far as I have noted (see Näsman chapter 7).

A few years later Holmqvist published a general survey of "Germanic Art" in which he again argued strongly against the "Gothic" connection and in his opinion "the primary home" of "Germanic art" was after all to be found in "southern Scandinavia and the North Sea Basin" under strong impact of provincial West Roman art (Holmqvist 1955:9–16). He refers to Forssander's paper but does not use the concept of Sösdala style and his illustrations do not include any object punch-decorated in Sösdala style. In a popular summary of his life-long devotion to "Germanic art" this omission is total and Forssander's study is ignored (1977:29–32). My guess is that this reflects the fact that Sösdala style objects are very rare in Sweden and only present in south-western Sweden (Bitner-Wróblewska chapter 12 fig. 2). But it can also be explained by the late Roman "classical" character of the Sösdala style in contrast to the "Germanic" Nydam and Sjörup styles.

In her 1955 dissertation on the Roman Iron Age cemetery at Simris, Scania, Berta Stjernquist presented serious criticism of explanations based on "Gothic" connections found in earlier scholarship, including Forssander's 1937 paper. Since Almgren in 1897 and Salin in 1904 several Scandinavian artefact types had traditionally been explained as a result of Gothic influences from the Black Sea area that redistributed a Roman impact in Gothic raiment. Now Stjernquist demonstrated that it was much easier to explain the occurrence of new artefact types by influences directly from the Roman Empire and by interaction with other "Germanic" groups along the Roman borders. Her criticism hits the core of Forssander's paper. It became obvious that his results had to be revised.

Voss and the Nydam style

The Danish scholar Olfert Voss wrote a celebrated paper about Høstentorp, a hoard of hack silver found on Zealand (Voss 1955a,b). It contains many pieces of cut-up Roman tableware of silver but also hacked pieces of Scandinavian jewellery. Voss's paper is famous because he distinguished and defined the Scandinavian Nydam style (cf. more recently Bemmann 1998:233–240). Objects in Nydam style are characterised by deep chip-carving in cast, gilt and nielloed silver and by a frequent use of animals as motifs along the margins of the objects. The animals are rendered closer to their Roman prototypes than the animals of Salin's Style I. Voss also gave a good survey of the Sösdala and Sjörup styles *sensu* Forssander. Many silver fragments of the Høstentorp hoard were cut from pendants and silver sheet brooches in classical Sösdala style. He placed the Sösdala style in the period *c.* AD 400–450 and found it connected to Eastern Europe. Its beginning was dated with reference to the finds from Untersiebenbrunn to *c.* AD 375. The grave from Untersiebenbrunn has recently been dated to the first third of period Cont-D2 (*c.* AD 380/400–440/450) or *c.* AD 400 ±20 years (Nothnagel 2008:190–196, 258; 2013:134; with ref. to Tejral 1997).

Voss rejected Forssander's and Norling-Christensen's suggestions that the Sjörup style appeared already in the early 5th century and instead he placed it after *c.* AD 475 because some of the objects had animal ornamentation in Salin's Style I. Norling-Christensen replied the same year that Voss's late dating of Style I was problematic (1955), since the root of the Nydam style is to be found in the late Roman chip-carvings of the western provinces. But of course Voss had realised that his chronology created a long gap between Sösdala and Sjörup. He filled it with a group of relief brooches that could be placed in a typological sequence between the silver sheet brooches of the Sösdala phase (type Mejlby-Roligheden) and the relief brooches decorated with chip-carving in Salin's Style I (type Tveitane-Gummersmark). He named this phase after the Nydam II find (cf. Bemmann 1998). Among relief brooches in Nydam style Voss mentioned Skerne from Denmark and Hol, Krosshaug (Hauge) and Lunde, all from Norway, and Röra from Sweden (and could have included the brooch from Göingeholm). He noted that the Sösdala and Nydam styles occurred simultaneously in the first half of the 5th century (with reference to the Świelino brooches) but also that the Nydam style dominated the second half of the century until the Sjörup style and Salin's Style I appeared at the end of the 5th century AD. He rejected the "Gothic" connection advocated by Forssander and assumed a direct link to provincial Roman craftsmen.

Voss's analysis of the workmanship of the Høstentorp fragments is important, revealing a gradual development from mainly silver smithery in the Sösdala style to mainly silver casting in the Nydam style and Salin's Style I (in fact already briefly noted by Bjørn Hougen 1936:20). Silver sheet brooches carry punched ornamentation but in some cases beadings along the edges are cast separately and soldered on. Ornamental fields in chip-carving could also be separately cast and soldered on. Obviously the craftsmen didn't yet master casting such large objects as square-headed brooches. The Nydam phase represents an experimental phase of improving know-how in casting, illustrated splendidly by one of the Skerne brooches, which carries typical Sösdala punch marks (fig. 5).

Hans Norling-Christensen made a new attempt (1956) to widen the concepts "Sösdala phase" and "Sösdala circle" and included objects traditionally considered to be from the Late Roman Iron Age. In absolute terms he dated the Sösdala phase to the latter half of the 4th century and around AD 400 – but without much success. His proposals were rejected by, for instance, Helmut Geisslinger (1961:177 footnote 14).

Fig. 5. Silver brooch from Skerne, Falster, with mixed decoration: gilding, gold filigree, mounted stones, punching and chip-carving and niello. Approx. 1:1. Nationalmuseet, Copenhagen no. C288. Photo Lennart Larsen.

Fig. 6. Punch marks combined as a star occur on three objects in Sösdala, strap junction no. I:14 (to the left), pelta shaped pendant nos. I:19–21 (in the middle) and strap buckle no. I:27 (to the right). Photo Daniel Lindskog.

The "star" ornamentation revisited

Twenty years after his paper about Jakuszowice (above), Nils Åberg returned to the question of the origin of punched ornamentation in a comprehensive study about the "historical" relation between the Late Roman and the Migration Periods (1956:151–153). He established that punched ornamentation occurred in large areas of Europe in the 4th and 5th centuries, on the Rhine and the Danube, among "West-Germanic" peoples as well as among "Goths". But the specific star motif has a more restricted distribution. His opinion about the origin of the star motif is of interest in connection with Sösdala, where three very differently punched stars are found (fig. 6). Åberg did not include Forssander's paper among his references, so I guess that he rejected Forssander's assumption that the punched star motif came from "Gothic" filigree ornamentation (above). Objects decorated with punched stars are unknown in the Danube region according to Åberg; outside Scandinavia he only found them in Gallia and along the Rhine. He dated Roman objects with punched stars to after AD 350 and the earliest finds in Scandinavia are seen on four bridge mounts, two from graves in Norway and Sweden (Sætrang, Slomann 1959 Pl. VII:1b; and Tibble, Andersson 1991 Abb. 1) and two from weapon depositions in Jutland (Nydam, cf. Bemmann & Bemmann 1998:166; Taf. 63; and Thorsbjerg, cf. Matešić 2015:62–63, 258, Taf. 23). All four bridge mounts are today dated to Scand-C3. Åberg had no record of punched stars east of the Oder before c. AD 400, so the punched stars that later became frequent in the south-eastern Baltic area are irrelevant in this context (for a later analysis of the south-eastern Baltic material, see Bitner-Wróblewska 2001). Åberg also suggested a western origin for the horse heads of the Sösdala parade bridle, a "Germanic" adaptation of similar motifs in provincial Roman belt sets like that from Ehrenbürg (Quast chapter 14 fig. 4; Åberg 1956 fig. 172 (find spot called Walberla); Koch 1965 Taf. 12; Böhme 1979 Taf. 124).

The 1960s

Märta Strömberg's dissertation (1961) is a broad survey of the "Late Iron Age in Scania", incorporating results of her own excavations in Scania, among them the Vätteryd cemetery near the Sösdala find spot. Her focus was on landscape archaeology, not on deep artefact studies. However, she noted that many extraordinary depositions had taken place in central Scania and discussed how this could be explained (see Fabech, Helgesson & Näsman chapter 4). In her find catalogue the Sösdala finds are summarised on the basis of Forssander's paper 1937. Her review of the art-historical significance of the parade bridle follows his views (1961:89–90, 183). She adds, however, that the high quality of the craftsmanship indicate the presence of *"continental-germanische Hantwerker"*. A number of other finds are mentioned to support the idea of Scanian contacts across the Baltic Sea to south-eastern Europe (cf. Bitner-Wrób-lewska chapter 12; 1991).

A stray find at Dahmker, Germany, of an axe-shaped bronze pendant with punched decoration resembling finds from Untersiebenbrunn and Sösdala was the starting-point for a paper on horse tack and decorative style by Helmut Geisslinger (1961). The pendant itself is important primarily because it has close parallels along the Danube: Grundremmingen (Quast chapter 14 fig. 1), Untersiebenbrunn and Coşoveni (Kazanski & Mastykova chapter 15 figs 3, 4, 7) and since it is the first object in Schleswig-Holstein to be associated with the Sösdala style complex. Geisslinger emphasises that the find place on the southern shore of the Baltic bridges a gap between Danubian and Scandinavian finds of horse tack. He dates the beginning of the Sösdala phase (*Sösdalastufe*) to *c*. AD 350 with reference to coins in the Zamość hoard. Today it is dated to the second quarter of the 5th century (*MPOV* 2016 at Zamość). The end of the phase is dated to just before AD 450 with reference to brooches from Skerne and Świelino, their combination of chip-carving and punched decoration already mentioned by Forssander. Geisslinger tries another way to date the Sösdala phase by comparing its punched decoration to provincial Roman *punzverzierte Gürtelgarnituren* (Roman belt sets); the comparison results in a very wide Sösdala period *c*. AD 350–450 (cf. Quast chapter 14).

In 1961 a new deposition of horse trappings was found during gravel extraction at Sösdala, a bridle with bronze mounts with silver details, much simpler than the parade bridle from 1929. It was published as Sösdala II the same year by Carin Bunte (1961). She dated its manufacture to the late 4th century of the Late Roman Iron Age with reference to Holmqvist's dating of artefacts inlaid with twisted silver and copper wires (above). The mounts are considered to represent one single bridle and all found a place in her reconstruction (fig. 7). She assumed that the bridle is a "Swedish" work. The heavy wear on the bridle indicates a long period of use. Bunte also noted the ritual destruction before its final deposition. The fragile construction of the attachment plates puzzled her and she found the bridle inadequate for a charger but suitable for a "cult horse". A deposition like this is considered to reflect "individual sacrificial ceremonies".

Fig. 7. A reconstruction of the bridle Sösdala II found 1961. After Bunte 1961 fig. 10.

Since scholars had neglected the significance of the belt mounts from Ehrenbürg, Robert Koch wrote a paper to present the mounts and place them in time and space (1965; obviously Åberg's 1956 publication had escaped his attention). He corrected an early mistake, repeated by Åberg; the Ehrenbürg mounts are made of silver, not bronze. Consequently he associates the belt set with a small group of high quality mounts like Babenhausen, Vermand, and Ejsbøl. Characteristic of the Ehrenbürg mounts are pairs of animal heads in profile, which Koch assumed to represent horses (Quast chapter 16 fig. 4). The occurrence of similar animal heads (horses?) in the archaeological record of the period was mapped, including Sösdala (1965 Abb. 3; supplemented in Böhme 1974:124 footnote 574); the distribution was found to be very wide (cf. Quast chapter 14). In the punched ornamentation of the Ehrenbürg mounts he emphasised the zigzag borders of punched triangles which he found to be characteristic of the Sösdala style (in the Sösdala find present on pendants nos. I:2, 3, and 4). Other punch marks of the Sösdala style are analysed, for instance the deep lens-shaped punch marks (in Sösdala only found on pendant nos. I:19–21). The material is dated with reference to finds with coins to *terminus post quem* AD 375–411, i.e. the late 4th and the early 5th century. The question whether the mounts from Ehrenbürg are made by "Germanic" or provincial-Roman craftsmen Koch found impossible to answer. For instance the horse head in profile was a popular motif in provincial Roman as well as in "Germanic" workshops around AD 400. He hoped for a solution in new finds and new analyses of relevant artefact groups in old collections.

In 1967 two dissertations were published in which the Sösdala and Fulltofta finds were included (Hagberg 1967; Geisslinger 1967). In Helmut Geisslinger's publication good photos of almost all bits and pieces of bridle and saddle mounts from Sösdala I are reproduced on Taf. 10–18. Unfortunately they are presented higgledy-piggledy. His find catalogue is astonishingly laconic and there are no references to the photos. There is no discussion of specific artefacts, so it is inconceivable why so many photos were published. But "the excellent pictures of the Sösdala find" were welcomed by Ulf Erik Hagberg since "we Swedes never could agree on its publication" (1967:47–48; my transl.). Neither scholar really discussed chronology or provenance. Instead they focused on the ritual destruction of the horse trappings and tried to understand the background to the offerings (Fabech chapter 2).

New attempts to define a Sösdala style

After more than 30 years Forssander's concept Sösdala style still lacked a proper definition. This was problematic since the "Sösdala" style often was used to define the beginning of the Migration Period in both relative and absolute chronology. Attempts to solve the problem were made by Ulla Lund Hansen (1970) in her publication of a grave with silver sheet brooches from Kvarmløse in Zealand and by Bente Magnus in her publication of a grave with an early square-headed relief brooch from Krosshaug in Jæren, Rogaland (1975). Lund Hansen attempted to distinguish between the punched style of the Late Roman Iron Age and the Sösdala style of the Migration Period. Her attempt to distinguish the latter from the former is based on the presence (or not) of hanging animal heads on silver

sheet brooches and on a high (or low) number of different punched motifs in the ornamentation. One fifth of the different punch marks registered are only known in finds from the Late Roman Iron Age, another fifth are known in finds from both the Late Roman Iron Age and the Migration Period, while three fifths are only known from the Migration Period. She agreed with Voss's opinion that the Sösdala and Nydam styles occurred simultaneously in the early 5th century and that both styles were inspired by decorative mounts made in the Roman Empire.

Bente Magnus, in her publication of a grave find from Krosshaug at Hauge in Rogaland, gave a good review of the chronological problems of the 5th century AD (1975 ch. 4, unfortunately in Norwegian with only a summary in English). She discussed the style problems at length and repeated Forssander in an attempt to present a definition of the Sösdala style. It is used to decorate plane silver surfaces on which undecorated fields alternate with decorated, gilt surfaces with ungilt. Punch marks and line drawing are used in the decoration. Triangles with various fillings and concentric circles with central dot are the most characteristic punch marks. Animals are a motif of minor importance; horse heads in profile seem to be the most popular. Objects made in Sösdala style are found in Denmark, Norway, and Sweden. Magnus added that the main occurrence is found in Sweden (an inconceivable statement considering the few Swedish objects registered by Bitner-Wróblewska chapter 12 fig. 2; 2001 ch. 3). Magnus emphasised that the Sösdala and Nydam styles overlapped in time in the early 5th century. Objects in Sösdala style or Nydam style as well as so-called Nydam brooches and cruciform brooches were used to draw a line between the Late Roman Iron Age and the Migration Period. The Sösdala style was used as an argument in her chronological study of cruciform brooches.

As observed by Jens Nielsen (1985:81–91), neither Lund Hansen nor Magnus could find an unshakable definition of the Sösdala style. In a Sösdala context, Magnus's study of the whirl motif (1975:74–76) is interesting, since a whirl is incised on the back of the strap junction Sösdala no. I:15, until recently unknown but now detected by Lovisa Dal. It is the only whirl in the Sösdala find complex. It is interesting that the craftsman sketched a whirl but then chose not to finish it. But in the Fulltofta find a whirl is the main motif on a pelta-shaped pendant (Fulltofta catalogue no. F:1). Quoting Holmqvist 1952, Magnus concludes that the motif is derived from Roman art. It never became very popular in Scandinavia (except on Gotlandic picture stones) and is restricted to objects in Sösdala and a few objects in Nydam style (more on whirls in Näsman chapter 7).

Kunst der Völkerwanderungszeit

Two decorative styles precede Salin's Style I. They are named after finds at Sösdala and Nydam, but they were never labelled by Salin. Today both concepts are well-established internationally, the Sösdala style according to Forssander (1937) and the Nydam style according to Voss (1955a). They are included in all overviews of the development of art styles during the Late Roman Iron Age and the Migration Period in an area north of the Roman Empire, from the Black Sea to the North Sea. But the relations between the Sösdala, Nydam, and Sjörup styles as well as their relation to Salin's Style I are difficult to make clear. A simple solution was to put the styles in a sequence of boxes; Egil Bakka, for instance, used strict boxes into which the archaeological material was put (1973; 1977). The Sösdala style was placed in a box in the first half of the 5th century with a small overlap with the succeeding Nydam style (fig. 8).

The comprehensive publication *Kunst der Völkerwanderungszeit* (Art of the Migration Period) was really the state of the art in 1979. After a long introductory discussion (1979:17–85) written by the editor Helmut Roth it contained fifteen regional overviews by international specialists, who described and depicted a number of select art works. Roth used the concept Sösdala-Coşoveni style to frame the result of the barbaric adaptation of Late Roman ornamentation that took place in the late 4th century and continued into the early 5th century. Unfortunately, the find circumstances are misunderstood in his description of the Sösdala finds (1979:56). The find was not made "*im Moor*" (in a bog) but on top of a gravel ridge and the many bronze rings are not "*Zügelringe*" (rein rings) but saddle rings. However, the characteristics of the Sösdala-Coşoveni style are well presented and illustrated by a selection of punched motifs (fig. 9). It is strange that neither the editor nor the Swedish specialist (below) found reason to in-

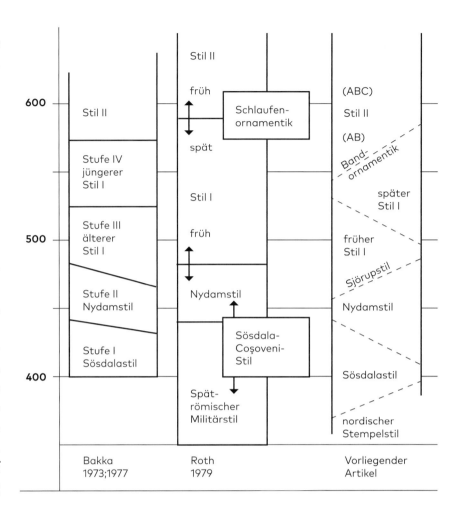

Fig. 8. A comparison of Migration period style chronologies. After Näsman 1984 Abb. 1. Based on Bakka 1973; 1977 and Roth 1979:346.

clude just one photo of objects from Sösdala itself in such a thick book.

Roth's opinion that the style was fully developed already at the end of the 4th century is based on the dating of the finds from Untersiebenbrunn. The origin of the Sösdala-Coşoveni style was found in metal mounts of late provincial Roman manufacture with punched ornamentation, for instance the *Tierkopfschnallen mit Punzverzierung* (Animal head buckles with punched ornamentation). The more common mounts with chip-carving are the backdrop of the Nydam style. Also the horse heads of the Sösdala parade bridle have parallels in late Roman belt and sword fittings. As contact area he mentions a region from lower Rhine to upper Danube (cf. Quast chapter 14). Thus

Fig. 9. Punched motifs of the Sösdala-Coşoveni style according to Roth 1979 Fig. 3.

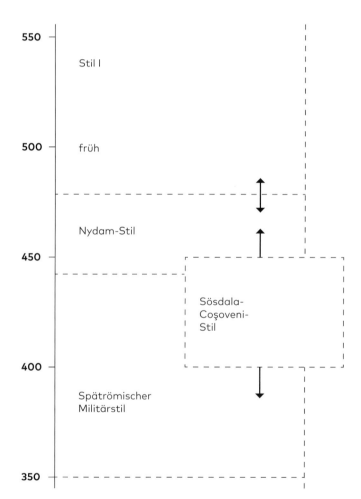

Fig. 10. Style development in the Late Roman and Migration Periods. Detail from Roth 1979:346.

Roth too rejected Forssander's Gothic *Rückstrom* and supported Åberg's provincial-Roman origin. Roth surmised that most objects in Sösdala style like silver sheet brooches were made by "Germanic" craftsmen, but he was not convinced that all mounts from the Sösdala deposition were "Germanic." At the end of the publication a diagram is found in which the various styles were sorted in relation to both relative and absolute chronology on the Continent (fig. 10). The Sösdala-Coşoveni style fills its own box in the early Migration Period. It is interesting to see how Roth let it overlap with late provincial Roman ornamental style (*Spätrömischer Militärstil*) for a long period and only at the end is there a short overlap with the Nydam style. The Sösdala-Coşoveni style began, according to the diagram, at the start of the Migration Period, *c.* AD 400. Arrows indicates that the style was rooted earlier in the 4th century, in Eggers' period C3, and that its overlap with the Nydam style may have lasted into the second half of the 5th century. The Nydam style covers a short period *c.* AD 440–480, followed by Salin's Style I.

The task of presenting the Nordic material entrusted by Roth to two Scandinavian scholars; Egil Bakka took care of the Danish-Norwegian material (1979:243–254) and Birgit Arrhenius the corresponding Swedish, Finnish and Estonian material (1979:254–265). Bakka described the Sösdala style conventionally without any illustration, in contrast to the many photos chosen by him to represent the following styles based on chip-carving. He explicitly denied the assertion that the Sösdala and Nydam styles were more or less contemporary. Arrhenius, with her outlook from Central Sweden, hardly noticed the Scanian Sösdala finds or the south-west Scandinavian Sösdala style (cf. Arrhenius 1994:194).

The 1980s

The great scholar Günther Haseloff was devoted to the study of "Germanic" animal art and wrote very little about the decorative Sösdala style (1981). But he noted briefly that the punched (star) ornamentation of course had a provincial Roman origin (1984:110). An important example of his argument for an origin in provincial Roman craft production was the silver sheet brooch from Roligheden in Norway (considered by both Forssander and Voss to be Sösdala style). The punched animal motif on the square head plate is compared to an original Roman cast bronze mount found at Svenning in Norway that depicts two dolphins in relief (Bakka 1969; Haseloff 1986 Abb. 21–22). He also argued that Roman craftsmen could have made some pieces of work in early Sösdala style. He believed that after the Roman administration of the western provinces had collapsed, "Germanic" warriors not only brought back material loot to the homelands but perhaps also "whole *ateliers* of craftsmen". He was convinced that skilled craftsmen from the Roman provinces could have moved as far as to present-day Denmark (1974:4, 6).

A fierce attack on the dominant archaeological study of style was delivered by Lennart Karlsson in a book about "Nordic form" (1983). It is in Swedish but has an extensive summary in English. His goal was "to illuminate the growth and survival of these specifically Scandinavian forms and to follow the domestic lines of development which begin in the Migration Period and which continue on towards the rune-stone ornamentation of the 11th century" (1983:179). The chapters of the book distribute the various stylistic expressions from the 5th to the 11th century and he totally avoids traditional concepts like Sösdala style, Nydam style, etc. Instead of a fragmentation into "styles" he emphasised the continuity and the overlap from one to another "style". We find as expected the "Sösdala style" contained in his chapter about the 5th century and illustrated by four objects, two from Sösdala itself, a mount and a pendant with horse-like animal heads, and two silver sheet brooches from Norway, Eidsten and Roligheden, which are so often used to represent the "Sösdala style". At the end of the book there is a critical catalogue of about 100 different style concepts. It is interesting to read his description of the "Sösdala style", which follows Forssander closely, and to learn how negatively he appreciated its aesthetic qualities (1983:163). To me it is obvious that his negative attitude is based on his search for a continuously developing, luxuriant and genuine Nordic animal art. The unobtrusive "classic" Sösdala style does not fit in. I see similarities in his attitude to the ideas of the Danish painter Asger Jorn (Magnus, Franceschi & Jorn 2005a,b); among numerous splendid photos by Franceschi, not one

represents the Sösdala style (except punched stars on a copy of the Gallehus horns).

Many scholars like Bakka and Roth placed styles in chronological boxes without much overlap between them. In a paper in 1984 I noted that both find combinations in reliable contexts, and individual artefacts demonstrate that different styles overlapped for a long time (at that time I had not read Karlsson 1983) and that the Nydam style only replaced the Sösdala style gradually in the early Migration Period (fig. 8). Anyhow, Sösdala-style objects were produced from the late 4th and well into the 5th century, but the last elements of the style seem to have disappeared before *c.* AD 450.

In a great exhibition in Nuremberg and Frankfurt a.M. about *Germanen, Hunnen und Awaren* Scandinavia was presented by Birgit Arrhenius (1987). She emphasised that "Germanic" craftsmen learned from skills present in Roman workshops along the *Limes* (cf. Kaltofen 1984:67, 78). Some prestigious artefacts of probable Danubian provenance were supposed to be gifts to Nordic warriors as a kind of *dona militaria* (military rewards) while others may have been part of their pay or simply gifts (and I will add loot). The Sösdala style is only treated briefly in a catalogue text on the bridle and saddle mounts from Vennebo (1987:462). Here it is stated that the Sösdala style developed on the basis of late Roman patterns and that it has a wide distribution in "Germanic" Europe from the Middle Rhine, via the "Elbe Germanic" area, to Poland and the Baltic coast with its main occurrence (*Schwerpunkt*) in South Sweden (the same mistake as in Magnus 1975, above) and further to the Danubian area where the finds from Untersiebenbrunn are well known. It is not entirely clear whether this is a description of a route of distribution or only a list of regions where the style is represented in the archaeological record. The Sösdala style, according to Arrhenius, reflects Nordic contacts with the core area of the Great Migrations from the Hun invasion of south-eastern Europe until the time of Attila.

Sösdala, Baltic star ornamentation, ritual destruction and saddles

In a paper from 1991, a prelude to her book from 2001, Anna Bitner-Wróblewska discussed the relation between

Scanian Sösdala style and its variations on the opposite side of the Baltic, the star ornamentation (for her present opinion, see her contribution in chapter 12). She assumes that the origin of the star ornamentation found in the eastern Baltic region is to be sought in the Scandinavian Sösdala style, which developed from a local tradition of punched ornamentation and influences from Roman punch decorated objects. The divergences between the Scanian Sösdala style and the style of artefacts in the Baltic lands are interpreted as "local variations of two styles which are closely related". The East Baltic star ornamentation is characterised by punch marks, but niello inlays and animal heads occurring in the Scandinavian Sösdala style are missing. The two styles are illustrative of the fact that a number of regional styles of punched ornamentation developed around AD 400, a phenomenon framed by concepts like "Sösdala-Untersiebenbrunn-Coşoveni style".

An important new argument for the south-east European connections was presented by Charlotte Fabech (1991; 1993). In her opinion the ritual depositions of horse trappings at Sösdala and Fulltofta had not been explained satisfactory. Her new interpretation is based on the observation that the horse gear was ritually destroyed and that the remains were deposited not in graves but on top of gravel ridges and not in wetland. She found a possible explanation by analogy with equestrian nomadic burial customs as evinced by written sources as well as the archaeological record of south-eastern Europe. This discussion is not the subject of my paper and instead I refer to her paper in this volume. The importance of her contribution is obvious since it gives further support to old hypotheses that south-east European relations are reflected by both the Scandinavian saddle type and the Sösdala style: it also strengthen the presumed links between the Scanian finds and finds at Bar, Coşoveni, Jakoszowice, Kačin and Untersiebenbrunn.

Per Ramqvist is the first to discuss Scandinavian ring saddles since Norberg in 1931. In his great monograph about the Högom burial mounds (in Medelpad, Northern Sweden) he studied the horse tack found in the very rich grave chamber of mound 2 (1992; cf. Ramqvist chapter 10). It included a battle bridle, a common loose-ring snaffle, as well as a saddle with mounts, rings and girth buckles. The buried man is in fact the only Scandinavian Migration Period warrior we know who can sport a ring saddle in his grave. The battle bridle is not similar to the bridles of Sösdala and Fulltofta, but relatively well preserved leather straps and mounts make its reconstruction interesting. Ramqvist compared his Högom reconstruction to Bunte's reconstruction of the Sösdala II bridle (fig. 7). And like Bunte he assumes a ritual use of the bridle (1992:76–77).

In Högom four saddle mounts and four saddle rings belong to the same saddle type as the Sösdala mounts and rings. Ramqvist assumed that the Högom saddle is contemporary with the Sösdala saddles and thus about 100 years old when put in the grave. But I do not believe so; it may be younger, probably from the second half of the 5th century or period Scand-D2. In Högom the long mounts of Sösdala type on the pommel are replaced by shorter mounts extended by separate bronze rails. Another trait that I consider to be late is that all four saddle mounts have animal heads at both ends, similar to a saddle mount from Finnestorp (Nordqvist chapter 11 fig. 22). Ramqvist also assumes that the origin of the Scandinavian saddle construction is an equestrian nomadic saddle type (cf. Bemmann 2012), adopted long before the 5th century. According to Lau's recent dating, the Thorsbjerg saddle mounts belong to weapon group 9 in period Scand-C2/C3, i.e. early 4th century. The earliest remains of a saddle with four rings are found in Illerup, dated to period Scand-C1b, i.e. early 3rd century (Lau 2014:75–78, Abb. 50). Consequently the saddle type was probably a result of interactions with nomadic horsemen, for instance the Sarmatians (cf. Carnap-Bornheim 2001), but not with the Huns.

A systematic study of Scandinavian bridle finds was presented by Mogens Ørsnes in 1994. In his system the bridle from Sösdala I belongs to type OF1/2 and the two bridles Sösdala II and Fulltofta to type OF1; all three bridles are dated to period Scand-D1 (Ørsnes 1994:249–251; fig. 53a,b). The limited distribution of similar bridles in North and East Europe is according to Ørsnes an indication that the prototypes should be found in the equestrian equipment of princely Huns. His dating of Sösdala II is, however, too late according to Holmqvist 1951 (see above) and should rather be Scand-C3.

Fig. 11. Horse heads decorate the cheek-piece mount from Sösdala (5:3) and the pendant from Kačin (3:2). Similar and different. Sösdala photo Daniel Lindskog; Kačin after Levada 2011 fig. 3.

Ørsnes also assumed an equestrian nomadic origin of the Scandinavian saddles but emphasised that our possibilities to solve the problem are seriously restricted by the very uneven and unrepresentative archaeological record of saddle finds in Europe (for saddles, see Näsman chapter 7).

The transition from the Late Roman Iron Age period Scand-C3 to the Migration Period is placed as early as *c.* AD 375 in a survey of Iron Age chronology (Hansen 1993:168–169). For lack of criteria based on artefact analyses the Migration Period is subdivided according to a sequence of ornamental styles. According to the chronological diagram, the Migration Period began with a Sösdala style phase that ended around AD 450. There was an overlap from *c.* 420/430 with a Nydam style phase, which lasted until *c.* AD 500, followed by a short phase with Sjörup style/Salin's Style I. According to the diagram, the Migra-

tion Period ended already *c.* AD 520/530 with the occurrence of Salin's Style II or the so-called Vendel style B.

Conclusion

Carl Mellton's rescue of the Sösdala I finds in 1929 was the basis of Forssander's idea of a Sösdala style. But the many saddle mounts found at Sösdala did not change the reconstruction of the Scandinavian ring saddle type, which has remained more or less the same since Norberg published the Jönköping saddle mounts in 1929 (cf. Sundkvist, Näsman and Ramqvist chapter 10). Forssander focused on only some of the many mounts of the parade bridle in 1937.

But he made them famous as foundation stones of a European ornamental style north of the Alps; he made the place eponymous of the Sösdala style. Several attempts are made to replace Forssander's original description of the style with accurate definitions but, as could be expected, all have failed. Styles can be described but are difficult to define (cf. Magnus 1975:119–123). You can expect good descriptions but not exact definitions of for example Mannerism, Baroque or Rococo. There will always be a matter of taste in how to evaluate numerous borderline cases. Consequently styles are not good for precise dating and must be avoided in definitions of chronological periods; the overlap in time from one to another style is simply too long (Näsman 1984:70; Bitner-Wróblewska chapter 12). But styles are important for the description and understanding of the material culture of any period. And they are carriers of meaning.

The dating of the Sösdala find to the beginning of Scand-D1, i.e. first half of the 5th century; and Cont-D2 (380/400–440/450) seems to be well established but it is more uncertain when a "Sösdala style" began in the late 4th century and also how long and frequently it was used in relation to the Nydam style in the 5th century.

Forssander's attempt to trace the Sösdala style back to the 4th century Goths north of the Black Sea has not many followers anymore. Instead most scholars have accepted that the origin of the Sösdala style is to be found exactly where Åberg had looked for the origin of the punched "star ornamentation" in 1919, i.e. in late Roman workshops, perhaps mainly in the Rhine provinces. It is also a common assumption that craftsmen, "Roman" or "Germanic", trained in provincial Roman workshops contributed one way or another to the formulation of the "Barbaric" styles Sösdala, Nydam and early Style I. But comprehensive studies of the interaction between "Roman" and "Germanic" craftsmen are missing, a lack explained in part by the very different source material in the regions involved (Quast chapter 14).

Scholars still cannot satisfactorily explain the obvious similarities between the Sösdala parade bridle and bridle finds in Eastern Europe such as Kačin (fig. 11; cf. Bitner-Wróblewska chapter 12; Kazanski & Mastykova chapter 15). Most scholars assume that the Sösdala-Untersiebenbrunn-Coşoveni horizon reflects an impact from the Huns. And of course that impact was felt in various ways. But the characteristics of the Sösdala style are absent in Hunnic material culture and vice versa. The incompatibility of "Hunnic" gold mounts and "Germanic" silver mounts is illustrated by the Jakuszowice grave find (fig. 9 in Fabech chapter 2; cf. Godłowski 1995; Anke & Externbrink 2007:268–269). Still there is an open discussion as to whether the different parts of the Sösdala parade bridle were made in Scania, in Scandinavia or elsewhere. We believe the provenance is one workshop in south-eastern Europe (see Fabech & Näsman chapter 17).

The technological backdrop of silver sheet brooches and punched ornamentation during the Late Roman Iron Age – early Migration Period and the manufacture of objects in Sösdala style on one hand (period Scand-D1) and the cast Nydam style with chip-carving on the other has not been studied since Voss 1955a (cf. Magnus 1975:44–47; Karlsson 1983:163). As a result the second bridle recorded as Sösdala II has not found a place in the scholarly discourse in spite of Bunte's publication (1961), nor has the mostly unpublished Fulltofta bridle. The internal chronology of the three bridles Sösdala I, Sösdala II and Fulltofta has not been discussed until now (see Näsman chapter 7).

The research development the last twenty years is illustrated by papers written by scholars invited for this volume, contributing to a better understanding of the interaction between Scandinavian horsemen and the mounted elite of both Barbaric and provincial Roman regions of Europe (cf. Fabech & Näsman chapter 17).

References

Åberg, N. 1919a. Den germanska stjärnornamentiken under 3- och 400-talet e.Kr. *Antikvarisk tidskrift för Sverige* 21/3: 1–51 – http://runeberg.org/antiqtid/21/0245.html – Accessed November 2016.

Åberg, N. 1919b. *Ostpreussen in der Völkerwanderungszeit*. Uppsala.

Åberg, N. 1924. *Den nordiska folkvandringstidens kronologi*. Stockholm.

Åberg, N. 1936. Till belysande av det gotiska kulturinslaget i Mellaneuropa och Skandinavien. *Fornvännen* 31: 264–277. Zusammenfassung.

Åberg, N. 1956. *Den historiska relationen mellan senromersk tid och nordisk folkvandringstid*. Stockholm. Zusammenfassung pp. 231–254.

Arbman, H. 1966. John-Elof Forssander. *Svensk biografiskt lexikon* 16: 334.

Almgren, O. 1897. *Studien über nordeuropäische Fibelformen der ersten nachchristlichen Jahrhunderte mit Berüchsichtigung der provinzialrömischen und südrussischen Formen*. Stockholm. – 2nd ed. 1923. Leipzig.

Andersson, K. 1991. "Tibblefyndet" – Neues Licht auf einem alten Grabfund im südwestlichen Teil Upplands, Schweden. *Studien zur Sachsenforschung* 7: 1–10.

Anke, B. & Externbrink, H (eds) 2007. *Attila und die Hunnen*. Speyer/Stuttgart.

Arne, T.J. 1937 Ett skånskt fynd från folkvandringstiden. [Göingeholm]. In: *Från stenålder till rokoko. Studier tillägnade O. Rydbeck*. Lund: 81–95.

Arrhenius, B. 1979. Die Nordgermanen im Osten Skandinaviens. In: Roth, H. (ed.) 1979: 254–265, Taf. 192–207.

Arrhenius, B. 1987. Skandinavien und Osteuropa in der Völkerwanderungszeit. In: *Germanen, Hunnen und Awaren. Schätze der Völkerwanderungszeit*. Nuremberg: 441–467.

Arrhenius, B. 1994. Järnåldern. In: *Signums svenska konsthistoria* 1. Lund/Kristianstad: 163–225.

Arwidsson, G. 1984. The splendid sword from Veien in Norderhov. In: *Festskrift til Thorleif Sjøvold*. Oslo: 21–29.

Bakka, E. 1969. A Roman bronze mount from Trøndelag. *Norwegian Archaeological Review* 2: 94–95.

Bakka, E. 1973. Goldbrakteaten in norwegischen Grabfunden: Datierungsfragen. *Frühmittelalterliche Studien* 7: 53–87.

Bakka, E. 1977. Stufengliederung der nordischen Völkerwanderungszeit und Anknüpfungen an die Kontinentale Chronologie. In: Kossack, G. & Reichstein, J. (eds). *Archäologische Beiträge zur Chronologie der Völkerwanderungszeit*. Bonn: 57–60.

Bakka, E. 1979. Die Nordgermanen im Westen Skandinaviens. In: Roth, H. (ed.) 1979: 243–254, Taf. 182–191.

Bemmann, G. & Bemmann, J. 1998. *Der Opferplatz von Nydam. Die Funde aus den älteren Grabungen: Nydam-I und -II*. Band 1–2. Neumünster.

Bemmann, J. 1998. Der Nydam-II-Fund. In: Bemmann, G. & Bemmann, J. 1998: 217–240.

Bemmann, J. (ed.) 2012. *Steppenkrieger. Reiternomaden des 7.–14. Jahrhunderts aus der Mongolei*. Bonn /Stuttgart.

Bitner-Wróblewska, A. 1991. Between Scania and Samland. *Fornvännen* 86/4: 225–241.

Bitner-Wróblewska, A. 2001. *From Samland to Rogaland. East-west connections in the Baltic basin during the Early Migration period*. Warsaw.

Böhme, H.W. 1974. *Germanische Grabfunde des 4. bis 5. Jahrhunderts zwischen unterer Elbe und Loire*. Munich.

Böhme, H.W. 1979. *Die Germanen in der Germania Libera und in Nordgallien*. In: Roth, H. (ed.) 1979: 191–203.

Böhme, H.W. 1986. Das Ende der Römerherrschaft in Britannien und die Angelsächsiche Besiedlung Englands im 5. Jahrhundert. *Jahrbuch des Römisch-Germanischen Zentralmuseums Mainz* 33/2: 469–574.

Bunte, C. 1961. A New Bridle Find from Sösdala. *Meddelanden från Lunds universitets historiska museum*: 194–207.

Carnap-Bornheim, C. von 2001. Das Waffengrab von Geszteréd (Komitat Szabolcs-Szatmár-Bereg) aus "germanischer" Sicht. In: Istvanovits, E. & Kulcsár, V. (eds). *International connections of the Barbarians of the Carpathian Basin in the 1st–5th centuries A.D.* Aszód/Nyíregyháza: 125–138.

Ekholm, G. 1936. Orientalische Glasgefässe in Skandinavien. *Eurasia Septentrionala Antiqua* 10: 61–72. – Reprinted in Ekholm, G. 1974. *Romersk import i Norden jämte bibliografi 1910–1971*. Uppsala.

Fabech, C. 1991. Neue Perspektiven zu den Funden von Sösdala und Fulltofta. *Studien zur Sachsenforschung* 7: 121–135.

Fabech, C. 1993. Skåne – et kulturelt og geografisk grænseland i yngre jernalder og i nutiden. *Tor* 25: 201–245. Summary.

Fabech, C. & Näsman, U. 2013. A lonely rider? The finding place of the Sösdala-find and the context of its finds. In: Khrapunov, I. & Stylegar, F.-A. (eds). *Inter Ambo Maria. Northern barbarians from Scandinavia towards the Black Sea*. Kristiansand/Simferopol: 84–106. Резюме.

Fabech, E. 1985. Teknisk beskrivelse og vurdering af sølvblikfiblen fra Sejlflod grav DI. In: Nielsen, J.N., Jørgensen, L. Bender, Fabech, E. & Munksgaard, E. En rig germanertidsgrav fra Sejlflod, Nordjylland. *Aarbøger for Nordisk Oldkyndighed og Historie* 1983: 101–122. Summary.

Forssander, J.-E. 1937. Provinzialrömisches und germanisches. Stilstudien zu den schonischen Funden von Sösdala und Sjörup. *Kungl. humanistiska vetenskapssamfundet i Lund. Årsberättelse* 1936–37: 183–272 – Also in *Meddelanden från Lunds universitets historiska museum* 8: 11–100.

Forssander, J.-E. 1938. Sveriges förhistoriska bebyggelse. In: E. Wrangel, A. Gierow & B. Olsson (eds) 1938. *Svenska folket genom tiderna*. Malmö:17–293.

Geisslinger, H. 1961. Frühvölkerwanderungszeitliches Zaumzeugzubehör von Dahmker, Krei Herzogtum Lauenburg. *Offa* 17/18, 1959–1961: 175–180.

Geisslinger, H. 1967. *Horte als Geschichtsquelle*. Neumünster.

Godłowski, K. 1995. Das "Fürstengrab" des 5. Jhs. und der "Fürstensitz" in Jakuszowice in Südpolen. In: F. Vallet & M. Kazanski (eds.) *La noblesse romaine et les chefs barbares du IIIe au VIIe siècle*. Condé-sur-Noireau/Saint-Germain-en-Laye: 155–179.

Hagberg, U. E. 1967. *The archaeology of Skedemosse 2. The votive deposits in the Skedemosse fen and their relation to the Iron-Age settlement on Öland, Sweden*. Stockholm.

Hansen, U. Lund 1970. Kvarmløsefundet – en analyse af Sösdalastilen og dens forudsætninger. *Aarbøger for Nordisk Oldkyndighed og Historie* 1969: 63–102. Zusammenfassung.

Hansen, U. Lund 1993. The Iron Age and the Viking Period. In: Hvass, S. & Storgaard, B. (eds.) *Digging into the past. 25 years of archaeology in Denmark*. Copenhagen/Højbjerg: 168–171.

Haseloff, G. 1974. Salin's style I. *Medieval Archaeology* 18: 1–15.

Haseloff, G. 1981. *Die germanische Tierornamentik der Völkerwanderungszeit 1–3*. Berlin/New York.

Haseloff, G. 1984. Stand der Forschung. Stilgeschichte Völkerwanderungs- und Merovingerzeit. In: *Festskrift til Thorleif Sjøvold*. Oslo: 109–124.

Haseloff, G. 1986. Bild und Motiv im Nydam-Stil und Stil I. In: Roth, H. (ed.). *Zum Problem der Deutung frühmittelalterliche Bildinhalte*. Sigmaringen: 67–110.

Holmqvist, W. 1951. *Tauschierte Metallarbeiten des Nordens aus Römerzeit und Völkerwanderung*. Stockholm.

Holmqvist, W. 1952. De äldsta gotländska bildstenarna och deras motivkrets. *Fornvännen* 47: 1–20. Zusammenfassung.

Holmqvist, W. 1955. *Germanic art during the first millennium A.D*. Stockholm.

Holmqvist, W. 1977. *Vår tidiga konst*. Stockholm.

Hougen, B. 1936. *The migration style in Norway*. Oslo.

Kaltofen, A. 1984. *Studien zur Chronologie der Völkerwanderunszeit im südöstlichen Mitteleuropa*. Oxford.

Karlsson, L. 1983. *Nordisk form, om djurornamentik*. Stockholm. Summary pp. 178–189: *Nordic Form – on Animal Ornament*.

Kiss, A, 1999. Historische Auswertung. In: Seipel, W. (ed.). *Barbarenschmuck und Römergold. Der Schatz von Szilágysomlyó*. Vienna: 163–168.

Koch, R. 1965. Die spätkaiserzeitliche Gürtelgarnitur von der Ehrenbürg bei Forchheim (Oberfranken). *Germania* 43: 105–120.

Larsen, E. Benner 1984. Værktøjsspor/på sporet af værktøj. Identifikatiion og dokumentation af verktøjsspor, – belyst ved punselornamenterede genstande fra Sejlflod. *Kuml* 1982–83: 169–180. Summary.

Lau, N. 2014. *Das Thorsberger Moor 1. Die Pferdegeschirre. Germanische Zaumzeuge und Sattelgeschirre als Zeugnisse kriegerischer Reiterei im mittel- und nordeuropäischen Barbaricum*. Schleswig. Summary.

Levada, M. 2011. To Europe via the Crimea: on possible migration routes of the northern people in the Great Migration period. In: Khrapunov, I. & Stylegar, F.-A. (eds). *Inter Ambo Maria. Contacts between Scandinavia and the Crimea in the Roman Period*. Kristiansand/Simferopol: 115–137. Резюме.

Liivrand, L. 1978. Rune Norbergs skrifter 1925–1977. *Fornvännen* 73/1: 25–38.

Magnus, B. 1975. *Krosshaugfundet. Et forsøk på kronologisk og stilhistorisk plassering i 5. årh*. Stavanger. Summary.

Magnus, B. 2005a. *Mennesker, guder og masker – i nordisk jernalderkunst*. In: Magnus, B.; Franceschi, G. & Jorn, A. *10000 års nordisk folkekunst. Nordisk jernalder 1*. Valby.

Magnus, B. 2005b *Fuglen, dyret og mennesket – i nordisk jernalderkunst*. In: Magnus, B.; Franceschi, G. & Jorn, A. *10000 års nordisk folkekunst. Nordisk jernalder 2*. Valby.

Matešić, S. 2015. *Das Thorsberger Moor 3:1–2. Die militärischen Ausrüstungen*. Schleswig. Summary.

Näsman, U. 1984. Zwei Relieffibeln von der Insel Öland. *Praehistorische Zeitschrift* 59/1: 48–80.

Nielsen, J.N. 1985. Sejlflod-udgravningen og grav DI. Blikfibler og kommentarer til Sösdalastilen. *Aarbøger for Nordisk Oldkyndighed og Historie* 1983: 66–101. Summary.

Norberg, R. 1929a. Ett folkvandringstidsfynd från Jönköping. *Meddelanden från Norra Smålands Fornminnesförening* 9: 5–24. Zusammenfassung.

Norberg, R. 1929b. Om förhistoriska sadlar i Sverige. *Rig* 12: 97–113.

Norberg, R. 1931. Moor- und Depotfunde aus dem 5. Jahrhundert nach Chr. in Schonen. *Acta Archaeologica* 2: 104–111.

Norberg, R. 1933. *Skånes offerfynd från folkvandringstiden*. Uppsala [Unpublished and inaccessible licentiate thesis in archaeology Uppsala university].

Norling-Christensen, H. 1949. Germansk Jærnalders Begyndelse i Norden. *Viking* 13: 1–15.

Norling-Christensen, H. 1955. Inlegg i anledning af Olfert Voss' foredrag. [See Voss 1955b]. *Stavanger Museums Årsbok*: 62.

Norling-Christensen, H. 1956. The Haraldsted burial ground and the Early Migration period in Denmark. *Aarbøger for Nordisk Oldkyndighed og Historie*: 76–143.

Nothnagel, M. 2008. *Die völkerwanderungszeitlichen Bestattungen von Untersiebenbrunn, Niederösterreich*. Vienna. – Online: http://othes.univie.ac.at/1440/1/2008-09-18_0100192.pdf – Accessed 14 October 2016.

Nothnagel, M. 2013. *Weibliche Eliten der Völkerwanderungszeit. Zwei Prunkbestattungen aus Untersiebenbrunn*. St. Pölten.

Ørsnes, M. 1994. Zaumzeugfunde des 1.–8. Jhrh. nach Chr. in Mittel- und Nordeuropa. *Acta archaeologica* 64/2, 1993: 183–292.

Ramqvist, P.H. 1992. *Högom. The excavations 1949–1984.* Umeå.

Rau, A. 2010. *Nydam mose 1–2. Die personengebundenen Gegenstände. Grabungen 1989–1999.* Højbjerg/Aarhus. Summary.

Roth, H. (ed.) 1979. *Kunst der Völkerwanderungszeit.* Frankfurt a.-M./Berlin/Vienna.

Salin, B. 1894. Fynd från Finjasjöns strand, Skåne. *KVHAAs månadsblad* 23: 84–106.

Salin, B. 1904. *Die altgermanische Thierornamentik.* Stockholm. – 2nd ed. 1935. Stockholm.

Slomann, W. 1959 *Sætrangfunnet. Hjemlig tradisjon og fremmede innslag.* Oslo.

Sommer, M. 1984. *Die Gürtel und Gürtelbeschläge des 4. und 5. Jahrhunderts im römischen Reich.* Bonn.

Stjernquist, B. 1955. *Simris. On Cultural Connections of Scania in the Roman Iron Age.* Lund.

Stjernquist, B. & Ambatsis, J. 1979. John-Elof Forssander som forskare. Förteckning over John-Elof Forssander tryckta skrifter. *Fornvännen* 74/3: 174–178.

Strömberg, M. 1961. *Untersuchungen zur jüngeren Eisenzeit in Schonen 1–2.* Lund.

Tejral, J 1997. Neue Aspekte der frühvölkerwanderungszeitlichen Chronologie im Mitteldonauraum. In: Tejral, J., Friesinger, H. & Kazanski, M. (eds). *Neue Beiträge zur Erforschung der Spätantike im mittleren Donauraum.* Brno: 321–391.

Voss, O. 1955a. The Høstentorp silver hoard and its period. *Acta Archaeologica* 25, 1954: 171–217.

Voss, O. 1955b. Folkvandringstidens stilproblemer og Høstentorp-fundet. *Stavanger Museums Årsbok*: 59–62. [For comment, see Norling-Christensen 1955].

Werner, J. 1988. Dančeny und Brangstrup. Untersuchungen zur Černjachov-Kultur und zu den 'Reichtumszentren' auf Fünen. *Bonner Jahrbücher* 188: 241–286.

Internet references

MPOV = Migration Period between Odra and Vistula http://www.mpov.uw.edu.pl/en/thesaurus – Checked 27 April 2017.

SHM – Swedish History Museum, Stockholm. The easiest way to use the digital collections of the Swedish History Museum is to search for the identification number (*inventarienummer*) in the search engine: http://mis.historiska.se/mis/sok/sok.asp?qtype=invnr&sm=0_1

Резюме

Сёсдала: находка и стиль, 1929-1993 гг.

Ульф НесманКогда в 1929 г. благодаря усилиям Карл Мельтона находки из Сёсдалы I были спасены, это обстоятельство дало Йону-Элофу Форссандеру возможность выделить стиль «Сёсдала» (Forssander 1937). Однако многочисленные находки оковок седел в Сёсдале не изменили предложенную реконструкцию седла скандинавского типа с подпружными кольцами, которая остается в более или менее неизменном виде с тех пор, как в 1929 г. Руне Норберг опубликовал седельные оковки из Йёнчёпинга (см. статьи Аннели Сундквист, Ульфа Несмана и Пера Рамквиста в этом томе). Хотя Форссандер говорил о некоторых из множества зажимов от парадной узды, он сделал их знаменитыми, превратив в фундамент для выделения орнаментального стиля, распространенного в Европе к северу от Альп. Благодаря ему, место находки стало эпонимным для стиля «Сёсдала». Было сделано несколько попыток заменить первоначальное описание по Форрссандру более точными дефинициями, но, как и следовало ожидать, все они провалились. Стили можно описать, но трудно определить (ср.: Magnus 1975: 119–123). Вопрос о том, как оценивать многочисленные пограничные случаи, всегда оставался делом вкуса. Потому стили не вполне подходят для точных датировок и, следовательно, ссылок на них стоит избегать при выделении хронологических периодов: наложения стилей друг на друга в хронологическом отношении слишком велики (рис. 8; см. также статью Анны Битнер-Врублевской в этом томе). Тем не менее, стили сохраняют свое значение для описания и изучения материальной культуры любого времени. И они несут определенный смысл.

Датировка находки в Сёсдале началом периода D1 по скандинавской хронологии, т. е. первой половиной V в., или периодом D2 по континентальной шкале (380/400–440/450 гг.) кажется хорошо аргументированной, однако значительно менее ясно, когда именно в конце IV в. возник стиль «Сёсдала» и насколько долго и часто он использовался в связи со стилем «Нидам» после первой трети V в.

Попытки Форссандера проследить стиль «Сёсдала» начиная с культуры северопричерноморских готов IV в. в настоящее время не пользуются популярностью. В противоположность этому, большинство исследователей согласны с тем, что истоки стиля «Сёсдала» должны находиться там, где в 1919 г. Оберг искал истоки «звездчатого декора», т. е. в позднеримских мастерских, вероятно, главным образом в рейнских провинциях. Кроме того, общепринято, что «римские» или «германские» мастера, обучавшиеся в провинциально-римских мастерских, тем или иным образом повлияли на формирование варварских стилей «Сёсдала», «Нидам» и ранний «Первый звериный стиль» (по Бернхарду Салину). Однако всестороннего исследования взаимосвязей между «римскими» и «германскими» мастерами не существует; отчасти это объясняется чрезвычайным разнообразием источникового материала в исследуемых регионах (см. статью Дитера Кваста в этом томе).

До сих пор исследователи не могут удовлетворительным образом объяснить очевидное сходство между парадной уздой из Сёсдалы и уздечками из Восточной Европы (ср. статьи Михаила Казанского и Анны Мастыковой, а также Анны Битнер-Врублевской в этом томе). Большинство исследователей полагает, что горизонт «Сёсдала–Унтерзибенбрунн–Кошовени» отражает гуннское влияние. Разумеется, это влияние ощущалось в разных моментах. Но характеристики стиля «Сёсдала» отсутствуют в материальной культуре гуннов, и наоборот. Находки из погребения в Якушовице демонстрируют несовместимость золотых «гуннских» и серебряных «германских» накладок (Godłowski 1995; Anke & Externbrink 2007: 269–269). До сих пор не решен вопрос о том, были ли различные элементы парадной узды из Сёсдалы сделаны в Скании, в Скандинавии в целом или еще где-либо (см. статьи Ульфа Несмана, а также Шарлотты Фабек и Ульфа Несмана в этом томе).

Технологии, на фоне которых возникли серебряные фибулы со щитком и изделия со штампованным орнаментом Позднеримского времени – начала Эпохи переселения народов, а также производились вещи в стиле «Сёсдала» (период C3–D1 по скандинавской хронологии) с одной стороны, и литой стиль «Нидам» с кербшнитным орнаментом (период D1 по скандинавской хронологии) с другой, не исследовались со времени работы Фосса 1955 г. (Voss 1955; ср.: Magnus 1975: 44–47). В итоге вторая узда, зафиксированная в Сёсдале II, несмотря на публикацию Бунте (Bunte 1961), так и не нашла себе место в научном дискурсе, подобно практически не изданной узде из Фульстофты. До настоящего времени не обсуждалось хронологическое соотношение трех уздечек из Сёсдалы I, Сёсдалы II и Фульстофты (см. вторую статью Ульфа Несмана в этом томе).

Публикуемые в данном томе статьи демонстрируют результаты исследований последних двадцати лет, способствующие лучшему пониманию взаимодействий между скандинавскими всадниками и конной знатью как варварских, так и провинциально-римских регионов Европы (см. статью Шарлотты Фабек и Ульфа Несмана в этом томе).

Подписи к иллюстрациям

Рис. 1. Слева: выполненная штампом звезда на пельтовидной подвеске из Якушовице (Польша) (по: Åberg 1936: 271). Справа: выполненная штампом звезда на распределителе ремней из Сёсдалы (№ I, 14; фото Даниэля Линдскога).

Рис. 2. Глубокие линзовидные отпечатки штампа на поясных пряжках из Финнесторпа (слева; по: Åberg 1919a fig. 32), Унтерзибенбрунна (в центре; фото Музея истории искусств, № 1525/2016, Вена), и фрагмент пельтовидной подвески из Сёсдалы (справа; № I, 19–21; фото Даниэля Линдскога).*

Рис. 3. Серебряная фибула со щитком из Мейльбю (Ютландия; по: Salin 1904 Abb. 489).

Рис. 4. Серебряная фибула со щитком из комплекса в Йёинъехольме (Скания), включавшего серебряные украшения и множество янтарных бусин, помещенных в керамический сосуд (фото Хелены Росенгрен, Шведский исторический музей, № 21 058; о комплексе в целом см. статью Фабек и Бертеля Хельгессона в этом томе).

Рис. 5. Серебряная фибуле из Скерне (Фальстер), со смешанным декором: позолота, золотая филигрань, вставки из камней, штампованный и кербшнитный орнамент, чернение (фото Леннарта Ларсена, Национальный музей, Копенгаген).

Рис. 6. Отпечатки штампа, образующие комбинацию в виде звезды, на трех предметах из Сёсдалы: распределителе ремней № I, 14 (слева), пельтовидной подвеске № I, 19–21 (в центре) и ременной пряжке № I, 27 (справа) (фото Даниэля Линдскога).

Рис. 7. Реконструкция узды из Сёсдалы II, находка 1961 г. (по: Bunte 1961 fig. 10).

Рис. 8. Сопоставление стилей Эпохи переселения народов в хронологическом отношении (по: Näsman 1984 Abb 1; на основе: Bakka 1973; 1977 и Roth 1979: 346).

Рис. 9. Нанесенные штампом орнаментальные мотивы стиля «Сёсдала–Кошовени» (по: Roth 1979 Fig. 3).

Рис. 10. Развитие орнаментальных стилей в Позднеримское время и Эпоху переселения народов (деталь из: Roth 1979: 346).

Рис. 11. Головки лошадей на зажиме, удерживавшем нащечный ремень, из Сёсдалы, и на подвеске из Качина имеют как сходства, так и различия (фото находки из Сёсдалы Даниэля Линдскога; подвеска из Качина по: Levada 2011 fig. 3).

Chapter 6

Scientific analyses of Sösdala objects

Lovisa Dal[1]

Scientific analyses of objects from Sösdala I are presented. Punch marks on 57 gilt silver mounts were examined under microscope, revealing a high quality of craftsmanship. In all, 27 different punched motifs have been described. By comparative studies, objects with punch marks made by the same tools have been identified. By interlinking the objects, three different sets of tools have been identified, plausibly representing three different craftsmen/workshops. One pendant is a loner of lower quality and probably a replacement. Trial marks are punched on the back of some objects and on others motifs are sketched. Analyses of a sample of 12 silver mounts revealed that the alloy consisted of 85–95% silver. Some alloy variations support the grouping based on punch analysis. One object with niello inlays was mapped with SEM/EDS. The niello was shown to consist of pure silver sulphide according to Roman tradition, indicating the manufacturing date to before the end of the 5th century AD.

Dal, L. 2017. Scientific analyses of Sösdala objects. In: Fabech, C. & Näsman, U. (eds). *The Sösdala horsemen – and the equestrian elite of fifth century Europe.* Jutland Archaeological Society.

Even to the naked eye it is obvious that the objects from Sösdala I are a result of high-quality craftsmanship. The strikingly designed pendants, mounts, and strap ends are made of shining silver with gilded surfaces. Additionally the excellent shapes are generously decorated with geometric patterns to make them even more exquisite and glittering.

Nevertheless it is still more breathtaking to put the same objects under a microscope. There, the magnified surfaces clearly show consistent quality all the way down to the smallest details – the stamps. Micro triangles, concentric semicircles, stars and dots are only a few of the motifs that have been accurately manufactured and punched. In some cases even the punches themselves are decorated. The great variety and effort put into the decorations at the time had no reason but beauty. Today, however, they may also fill a scholarly function, since the punches actually are loaded with information, directly from the craftsman's hand.

1   Contributions by Marei Hacke and Kaj Thuresson, the Swedish National Heritage Board.

Fig. 1. Details of punched decoration on mounts nos. 41 and 43. Photo Lovisa Dal and Christoffer Fägerström.

By studying the objects in general and the stamps in particular, more about how the objects were manufactured has been found out, including the possibility to determine whether some objects have been decorated with the same tools, and by extension in the same workshop (fig. 1).

The stamps

Altogether 57 objects in the Sösdala I find are decorated with stamps (fig. 2). Typically a line is punched along the edge, often with a row of geometric figures along the centre line. Most ornaments consist of decorative, geometric patterns, but concentric circles are also put as eyes on objects shaped as horse heads or curved bird's heads. Objects with a square shape often have circles, stars or rosettes at the centre.

In total 27 different punched motifs have been used for decoration (fig. 3). They are punched singly or in combi-nations. Shapes such as circles, concentric semicircles and dots are common, and appear in one way or another on all objects. Others such as triangles, triangles with a knob on top, spiny triangles and concentric semicircles with cogs on the outside can be seen on a smaller number. Six of the stamps are found on one piece only. It should be remarked that most semicircles are actually more than half a circle.

At most 12 different punches have been used on the same object – which is no. 1, a mount made of four joined parts. It is also the only piece with niello inlays. Among the 12 punches used you find a unique pelta-shaped stamp, three different double concentric circles, two different double concentric semicircles and two different triangles with knob on top (fig. 4).

All stamps are small and most of them very small. The largest stamp of all is a sixfold concentric circle with a di-ameter of 12.5 mm (on nos. 12 and 13), which is more than twice as big as the second largest stamp, a common four-fold concentric circle measuring 4.5 mm/diameter. The frequent concentric semicircles vary between 1.2 and 1.8 mm in radius.

The most common stamp of all is the dotted line, which is typically used along the edges of the objects (fig. 5). The tiny line is only 0.5 mm wide, and is made by a 6 mm long rectangular stamp, with up to 16 dots placed in a row. Shorter stamps with fewer dots were used when punch-ing curved lines. On some of the objects a straight line is punched instead of the dotted line. However, the decora-tion is so delicate; you can hardly see a difference with the naked eye.

Other common detailed stamps are triangles and trian-gles with a knob on top (fig. 6). Many of them are further decorated with internal lines. One of them is perhaps the most impressive stamp of all, an equilateral triangle with a side of only 1.3 mm. The tiny surface has a waffled pat-tern made of five perfectly parallel lines in each direction. Considering the lines are not thicker than a single hair, it's impossible not to be impressed by the skill involved in manufacturing this punch!

Thanks to the high ambitions to make detailed punch-es, our chances to find characteristic features on them in-crease. In the microscope details of how a line ends, the shape of a curve or a small defect work like unique finger-

prints. By identifying and recognising the different elements, it is possible to compare stamps with the same motif on different objects and determine whether they were punched by the same tool.

However, since there is an impending risk of confusion when studying 27 types of stamps punched on 57 objects, it is necessary to work with one motif at the time. To get a basic impression of the material, a suitable stamp to begin with has to occur on as many objects as possible. The dotted line previously described is the most abundant stamp used, but because the imprints are very thin, are punched unevenly deep and often overlap, these stamps are hard to use for comparative studies.

Fig. 2. Overview of the gilded silver objects with punched decorations. Photo Lovisa Dal.

The second most common motif is the double concentric semicircle. The stamp is often punched in a row directly within the edge line, but on 12 of the rectangular strap mounts, many are also arranged together as triangles. All objects, except for 19 pieces, have been decorated with a double concentric semicircle, which makes it a suitable stamp to use for the initial studies.

Fig. 3. Drawings of the different motifs on the stamps. Drawing Lovisa Dal.

Fig. 4. Detail of a horse head on mount no. 1. Photo Lovisa Dal and Christoffer Fägerström.

Sorting into groups

Starting off by systematically comparing the concentric semicircles, it was established that five different punches had been used to produce the motif. Using them, the first objects could be divided into basic groups (fig. 7).

By continuing with cross-comparing less common but significant stamps such as triangles, triangles with a knob on top, concentric circles and spiny concentric semicircles, object by object, known connections were verified and further new ones established. Eventually it was established that all objects could be sorted into three groups. All objects, that is, except one.

Group 1 consists of 11 objects (nos. 1, 3, 4–6, 10, 11, 17, 18, 22, 24, 25, 26) including the mount with niello (no. 1) mentioned above (fig. 8). The objects clearly share a ho-

mogeneous design with outward-looking horse heads, voluminous loops and triangular plates. In this group all objects have drawn lines around the edges and no punch with dotted line has been used. The stamps are firmly punched with distinct shapes. Altogether ten different stamp motifs have been used within the group.

Group 2 consists of 5 objects (nos. 7–9, 14, 15, 16, 19–21) of which two are pendants with strap mounts, and three strap junctions (fig. 9). On the objects several stamps are combined to form larger patterns like stars, flowers and circles. On the cross-shaped strap junctions the decorations are emphasised by alternately gilded and silvery areas.

Altogether 15 different stamps have been used in this group. The stamps are even smaller and with finer details than on the other objects. For example a fourfold concentric circle with a diameter of only 1.8 mm can be seen as well as a tiny 1 mm wide double concentric semicircle and of course the exquisite waffled triangle already described. The small stamps are punched with a light hand, but with great accuracy. In this group both straight and dotted lines are used.

Group 3 is the largest group with 39 objects (nos. 12, 13+245, 27, and all mounts nos. 28–70), consisting of 1 buckle, 2 pendants(?), 26 strap mounts, 7 fragments of three ring-

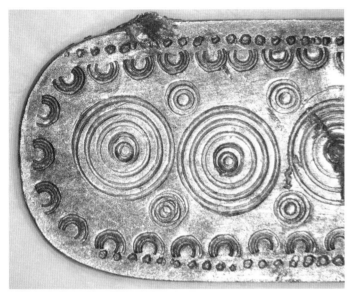

Fig. 5. The two types of dotted lines, ring-link mount no. 33, strap end no. 35. Photo Lovisa Dal and Christoffer Fägerström.

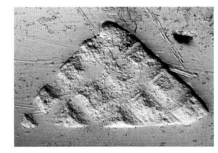

Fig. 6. Various punched triangles, with and without knob on top; from nos. 1 (x20), 3 (x20), 14 (x24 and x26), 19 (x30), and 35 (x47). Various magnifications. SEM photo Lovisa Dal.

link connectors and 3 strap ends (fig. 10). The objects are of a few different types, but the decorated part is most often a rectangular gilded sheet. The decoration is typically composed of a dotted line around the edge. Within it, concentric semicircles, spiny concentric semicircles or spiny triangles follow the long sides and along the very centre line is a row of fourfold concentric circles (6 mm in diameter). Since the objects are made of sheet silver, it is sometimes possible to see deformations from the imprint on the back. The stamps are punched with high precision, but in the microscope both overlapping and double punching are revealed.

The only object really sticking out in the large Group 3 is no. 27, being the only buckle. By the stamps, it is closely connected to three strap ends that all pass through its frame (nos. 35, 36 and 38). They are all decorated with a concentric semicircle from another punch than the rest of the objects in Group 3. The objects also share a waf-

Fig. 7. The same motif but different punches. When comparing double concentric semicircles in microscope, it was established that the motif originates from five different punches. Details of nos. 18, 1, 14, 47 and 27. Photo and drawings Lovisa Dal.

fled triangle (not as perfectly manufactured as the one described earlier) and have a dotted edge line where the dots are slightly bigger and placed further apart.

For a long time, therefore, the buckle and three strap ends were thought to be a group of their own. However, the coarse dotted line was also seen on a double strap mount (no. 39), whose other stamps clearly belonged to Group 3. As previously established, though, dots are too imprecise to build a result upon and it was not until a small skew double concentric circle was reviewed among objects in both groups that they were interlinked (the skew concentric circles can be seen on the pictures in fig. 5).

The loner

The three groups include all of the objects, except for a single pendant with strap mount (no. 2). As regards material, design and shape it is very similar to no. 3 in Group 1. Even the motifs of the stamps and the very places they are punched onto the object match completely. The only – though striking – difference is the quality of the stamps and the skill of punching (fig. 11). Compared to the decorations on the pendant from Group 1, the tools used on no. 2 seem to be blunt and perhaps even damaged. The way they are punched seems slipshod. This can be seen in the flat triangular field near the loop where triangles with a knob on top are punched in a V-shape.

On pendant no. 2 the craftsman seems to have started punching at one end with hard and determined strikes, to begin with almost in a straight line, but along the way the blows became lighter and more irregular. The knob on top, which appears to have a crack in it, becomes more and more vague, and in the last punch mark it is not even visible.

Another example of using a bad quality punch can be seen in the eyes of the horses. On the similar pendant in group 1, a double concentric circle is punched. However, on no. 2 it looks as if the punch used is incomplete, since only about half of its outer circle is present. To make a whole circle, the eyes therefore have been punched with several strikes while turning the punch, giving a muzzy look.

The triangular punch used to stamp two rows along the centre line is likewise badly manufactured with uneven sides. Again the tool has not been held and turned steadily, and it has been hit with different force from different angles, causing an irregular row – not to mention the surroundings.

Considering the striking similarities between pendant nos. 2 and 3, it is easy to believe that they were manufactured in the same place, but on a closer look this seems unlikely and it cannot be confirmed by the stamps. One possibility could be that they are the result of a master teaching an apprentice, but it seems strange to let a slipshod piece like this follow the other exquisite objects. A more plausible explanation might be that there originally were two high-quality pendants, of which one was damaged and had to be remade by someone who did not have access to the same set of punches, and who was not as skilled as the first craftsman (cf. Fabech & Näsman chapter 17).

Similar objects in different groups

Among the objects, there are two more pendants with strap mounts, nos. 4 and 7, which in many ways resemble one another, but belong to different groups based on their stamps. The objects are very like the previously described nos. 2 and 3 as they have about the same size and design, but with the main difference that four openwork double concentric circles replace the horse heads at the end of the pendant. Both nos. 4 and 7 have wavy long sides with a hole in each arch. While the overall impression of nos. 4 and 7 is uniform, the details, however, are completely different. Pendant no. 4 is decorated with dots around the holes as well as triangles and triangles with a knob on top, sorting it into Group 1.

Group 1 no. 25570:	○	○	◎	◎	⌒	⬯ (triangle/bulb)	⬯ (triangle/bulb)	△	⌓⌓	—
1	X	X	X	X	X	X	X		X	X
3	X		X	X		X		X		X
4,5,6		X	X	X		X		X		X
10	X	X		X	X	X	X			X
11	X	X		X	X	X	X			X
17	X			X		X				X
18	X			X		X				X
22	X					X				X
24				X						X
25						X				X
26				X						X

Fig. 8. Objects decorated with the same stamps are sorted into the same group. Here objects in Group 1 and their stamps: nos. 1, 3, 4–6, 10, 11, 17, 18, 22, 24, 25, and 26. Photo and drawing Lovisa Dal.

Pendant no. 7 lacks the dots around the holes and has instead a zigzag line punched along the holes. Its concentric semicircles and mini-triangles belong to Group 2.

There are thus no decoration elements in common, except for a detail on no. 7 (fig. 12). At the edge of the first arches three very small circles are punched on one side, and three equally small dots on the opposite. Since the decorations is symmetrical throughout the material, this stands out. It is almost as if the craftsman made a test, had a change of mind and decided not to continue. What more is, this is the only place where a small circle, as well as a dot, are used on objects in Group 2. In Group 1, however, both are common and appear on almost every object. Un-

fortunately both dots and circles are too small and simple to be used to determine whether the two groups possibly belong together.

On the back

One more object has what may be a punch test by the craftsman (fig. 13). At least that might explain why there are three stamps in a row on the back of the strap mount (no. 19) belonging to the pelta-shaped pendant (nos. 20, 21). No other objects have stamps on their back. The stamp is square with an X in the middle and small cavities in the sides. Punched side by side in a repetitive pattern, it gives a line of crosses and dots. The same stamp is found in a row

Group 2 no. 25570:	○	○	◎	◎	◎	◎	⌒	⌒⌒	⌒⌒⌒	▲	△	▫▫▫▫	—	▱	◍	✕
7, 8, 9, 238	X	X		X	X			X	X			X	X	X		
14			X			X (hole in the middle)	X	X		X	X	X				
15							X					X				
16							X					X				
19			X			X					X	X	X	X		X (backside)
20, 21			X			X		X				X	X	X	X	X

Fig. 9. Objects that are decorated with the same stamps are sorted into the same group. Here objects in Group 2 and their stamps: nos. 7–9, 14, 15, 16, and 19–21. Photo and drawing Lovisa Dal.

Fig. 10. Objects that are decorated with the same stamps are sorted into the same group. Here objects in Group 3 and their stamps: nos. 12, 13, 27, 28–70. Photo and drawing Lovisa Dal.

Group 3 no. 25570:	○	◎	◎	◎	⌒	⬙	⬙	◁	⋀	▱▱▱
12	X	X	X	X	X					X
13	X	X	X	X	X					X
27	X	X	X		X			X		X
28,61	X		X		X				X	X
29					X					
31	X		X		X				X	X
32	X		X		X					X
33	X	X	X		X	X				X
34	X	X	X		X	X				X
35	X	X	X		X			X		X
36,37,69,70			X		X					X
38	X							X		X
39,67	X		X			X				X
40	X		X		X					X
41	X		X						X	X
42	X		X		X					X
43	X		X				X			X
44	X		X		X					X
45	X		X		X					X
46	X		X		X					X
47	X		X		X					X
48	X		X		X					X
49			X		X		X			X
50	X		X		X					X
51	X		X		X					X
52	X		X			X				X
53	X		X			X				X
54	X		X		X					X
55	X		X		X					X
56	X		X		X					X
57	X		X		X					X
58	X		X			X				X
59	X	X	X			X				X
60,66	X		X		X					X
62	X		X			X				X
64	X		X			X				X
65,68	X		X						X	X
245	X		X		X					X

The loner no. 25570:	○	⊙	⊙	⩗	—	△
2	X	X	X	X	X	X

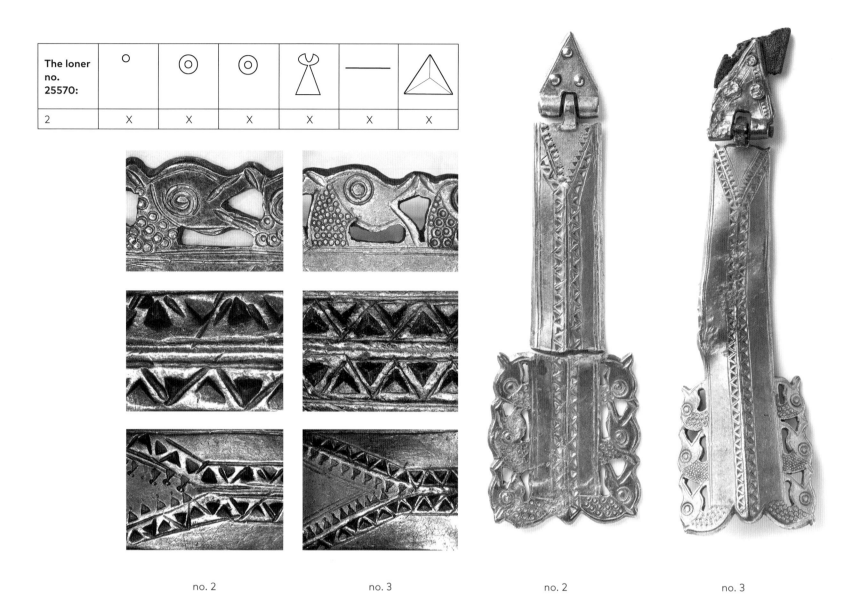

no. 2   no. 3   no. 2   no. 3

Fig. 11. At first sight the pendants nos. 2 (The loner) and 3 (Group 1) are very much alike, but a closer look reveals striking differences in the quality of both punches and punching. Photo Daniel Lindskog. Detail photo and drawing Lovisa Dal.

between two dotted lines along the edge on the front of the pelta shaped pendant.

The only other objects with something on the back are the three cross-shaped strap junctions (nos. 14, 15, 16), which also belong to Group 2. On their back, thin lines have been scratched, hardly visible to the naked eye. In the microscope, however, the lines turn out to be sketches and reveal three different geometric shapes; a rosette, a whirl

and a pentagram (fig. 14). The shapes are enclosed in circles on which points are marked as guidelines for spokes and tips.

The scratched rosette on the back of no. 16 is almost identical to the one fully implemented up front on nos. 15 and 16. It is a geometrically drawn floral rosette made of one circle and the arches from another 12 evenly-spaced, overlapping circles.

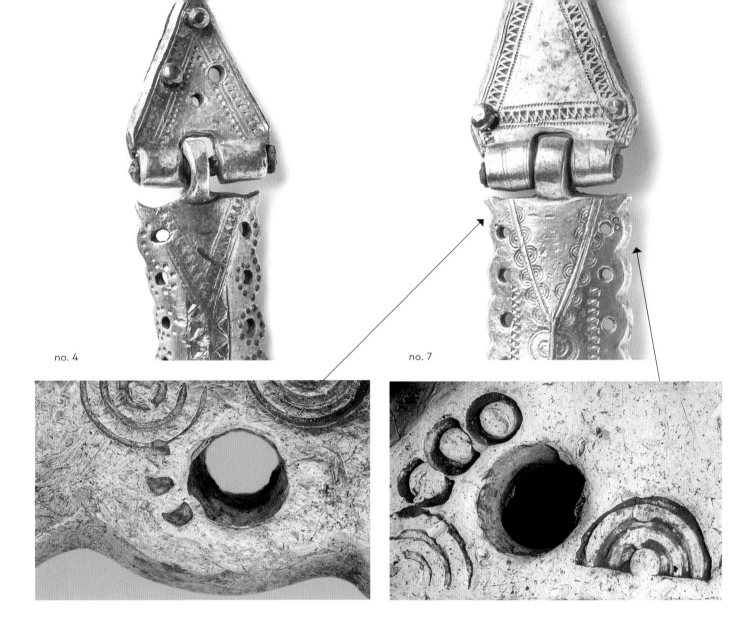

no. 4

no. 7

Fig. 12. Upper part of pendants nos. 4 and 7. On pendant no. 7, three dots and three rings are punched in an asymmetric way, see close-ups. This is the only place these stamps are used on objects sorted into group 2. Photo Daniel Lindskog, detail photo Lovisa Dal and Christoffer Fägerström.

The whirl on the back of strap junction no. 15 has 12 curved spokes meeting in the centre of the circle. The pentagram on no. 14 is a five-pointed star made of continuous straight lines, with a centre area shaped as a pentagon.

Also on the fronts of the strap junctions, traces of scratched lines and points are visible among the stamps. The sketches correspond to the punched decoration and show how the craftsman has used them as benchmarks.

Further traces from the craftsmen

Sketches and punch tests are traces from the craftsmen's workflow, trying to do their best. The assignment is characterised by concentration and patience. An ordinary strap mount from Group 3 contains about 110 stamps (a dotted edge line, a row of concentric circles in the middle and concentric semicircles in between). On the bigger and more complex mount no. 1 more than 600 punch strokes

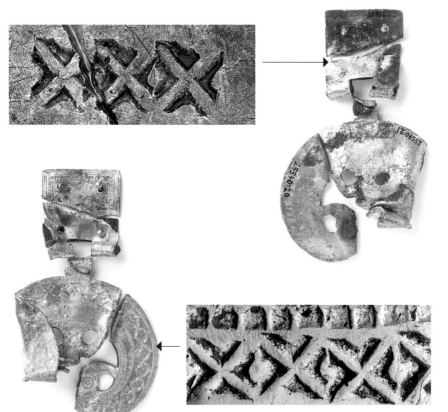

Fig. 13. On the back of the strap mount no. 19 are three punch marks of the repetitive motif that can also be seen on the front of the associated pendant nos. 20–21. They are to be considered as a punch test. Photo Lovisa Dal and Christoffer Fägerström.

Fig. 14. On the back of strap junctions nos. 14, 15 and 16 vague sketches of complex geometrical patterns are scratched. Photo Daniel Lindskog. Drawing Lovisa Dal.

have been required to complete the decorations. Thinking about the craftsmen who made these objects, it is impossible not to imagine how they sometimes must have felt tired, unfocused, stressed or hungry during work. We all know that such feelings cause mistakes, which might be an explanation for irregularities and faults in the decoration, even if asymmetry on purpose cannot be ruled out. The following have been noticed.

Missing line: The strap buckles nos. 24 and 26 are very similar objects when it comes to both shape and decoration. On the triangular plates a single line follows the edges in a V-shape. Along it a row of concentric semicircles is punched, and innermost runs a double line. But for some reason one of the innermost lines on no. 24 is single (fig. 15). Asymmetric lines occur on more pieces.

Inaccurate orientation: The cheek-piece mount (no. 10) is shaped like two outward-looking horse heads with eyes and ears. To emphasise the mane and curve of the neck, several rows of stamps and lines follow the edges of the object (fig. 16). They are carefully punched and follow every change of direction. The craftsman must have turned the

punch, or the piece, countless times, and that is why it is surprising to see that the last three concentric semicircles in a row are punched at the wrong angle, since the craftsman failed to turn the punch.

Omitted centre circle: In some cases stamps are combined to make more complex patterns. For example tiny concentric circles are punched on top of triangles to form stars (see fig. 6 and Näsman chapter 5 fig. 6), or to punch a small circle in the centre of a bigger concentric circle to give it an extra ring. The latter is done on almost every object in Group 3, or more particularly on 34 out of 37 objects. Only three different objects (nos. 31, 36, 49) are left with a flat centre (fig. 17). Since the group is so homogeneously decorated otherwise, it raises the question whether they were simply forgotten.

Other observations show cases where stamps overlap in a way that reveals the order in which they were punched, and sometimes even from which direction the craftsman started working. Looking closely at how the objects were made, it is also obvious that the holes for rivets were made after the object was decorated, since they often go through stamps.

no. 14

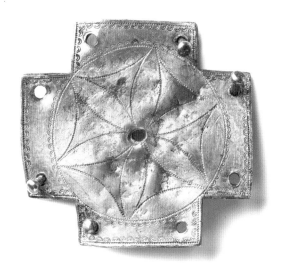

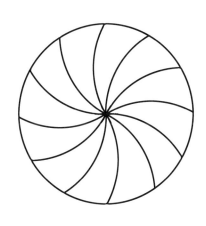

no. 15

no. 16

Fig. 15. An example of irregularities among the otherwise symmetrical and accurate decorations is the missing double line on strap buckle no. 24 to the left; cf. the double lines on buckle no. 26 to the right. Photo Lovisa Dal.

Fig. 16. Concentric semicircles punched at a wrong angle, strap mount no. 10. Photo Lovisa Dal and Christoffer Fägerström.

Stamps on fragments of copper alloy

In this article stamps on objects of gilded silver have been investigated. It needs to be mentioned, however, that among the objects in the Sösdala find, punched concentric semicircles also were found on three fragments of thin copper alloy plate (nos. 84, 193 and 195). The fragments probably belong together, but the edges are without fit. The stamp mostly resembling one used in Group 1, but the metal is too corroded to draw conclusions from. Unfortunately, it is not possible to determine which kind of artefact the fragments come from.

Method development and analyses
Lovisa Dal, Marei Hacke and Kaj Thuresson

Prior to this work, it was not known whether it would be possible to identify characteristic features on the stamps, distinct enough to determine whether the same punch had been used on more than one object. It was also uncertain what it would take to distinguish the very small details required. In a corresponding study of punch marks by Larsen (1984:169–180) successful comparisons were made. In his work 11 stamps on 3 objects from Sejlflod, Denmark,

were cast in silicon and examined in SEM. The method undoubtedly proved to work well, but because of the extent, it would be unwieldy to fully implement on the many objects from the Sösdala find. Since an easier and faster method was needed, the question was how much could be seen directly on the object in an ordinary microscope, compared to using highly advanced equipment as scanning electron microscope (SEM).

To sort out possibilities and limitations, the initial work was therefore done in cooperation with the Swedish National Heritage Board in Visby. With their great help and equipment, 20 selected objects were subject to examination. By taking photographs of the stamps in a microscope and comparing them with further magnifications in SEM, it was established that for the more complex motifs the magnification in an ordinary microscope was accurate enough to distinguish one punch used from another. However, simpler punch marks, such as dots and pits, require higher magnification and studies in the SEM to find the necessary characteristics and features. Thanks to the large number of stamps and the rich variety of motifs in Sösdala, enough stamps with

Fig. 17. Concentric circle with or without extra centre circle, mount no. 49, mount no. 43. Photo Lovisa Dal and Christoffer Fägerström.

sufficient details could be chosen for studies in an ordinary microscope.

No silicone castings turned out to be necessary in the work, but in the case of comparing the bottom structure of the relatively deep triangles punched along the centre line of nos. 2 and 3, small imprints were made with Farcolina (brand name for modelling clay without sulphur, made in Denmark). The imprints gave a rapid and easy way of telling the differences between the tips of the triangles in an ordinary microscope.

Besides the work with identification of the stamps, staff at the Swedish National Heritage Board also provided expertise considering analyses of metal compositions, niello content, fibre identification and leather identification.

Metallurgic analyses

The main aim of metallurgic analyses was to ascertain the alloy components in the silver and by extension investigate the possibilities to separate or connect different objects by the metal. In all, 12 of the silver objects with stamps were analysed with μXRF (ARTAX 800). The objects had been cleaned in advance, to remove any layers of corrosion, glue and lacquer. Nevertheless presence of dirt or corrosion, inhomogeneous metal alloy, differences in penetration depth of X-ray beam as well as deviations within standards and references, are some of the error sources that must be considered. Each surface chosen was therefore measured on five individual points, to obtain a more reliable result.

The analyses showed that the metal alloy consists of approximately 85–95% silver with small amounts of copper and gold. The values, however, differed a great deal between the five measurements on each surface, due to the error sources. Because of the variations, it was judged impossible to group the objects from the relatively few analyses made. All objects were also positively detected for trace amounts of lead and some surfaces also for sulphur, iron, bismuth, zinc and mercury. The trace elements are likely to originate from the metal ore and manufacturing. The mercury, however, might be a residue from the gilding process.

It is interesting to notice that the objects with clearly detectable zinc content belong to Group 2. Only one object (no. 47) from Group 3 was selected to be analysed (at that time the groups were unknown), but it also showed presence of zinc. Very little zinc was detected in the metal from objects in Group 1. This may indicate different sources of metal and is a support for the assumption that the mounts in group 1 were produced in another workshop than the mounts in group 2 and 3. However, zinc is also present in the alloy of a fragment of a snaffle ring, no. 108, the snaffle being associated with the bridle mounts of group 1. The alloy of the ring also differs, with a higher occurrence of lead.

Niello

As previously mentioned, the mount pendant no. 1 is not only decorated with stamps, but also with niello inlay. In the middle of the gilded pendant an elongated silvery area is defined by a border line and filled with lines and loops in a row – possibly stylised three-leaved plants. At the end

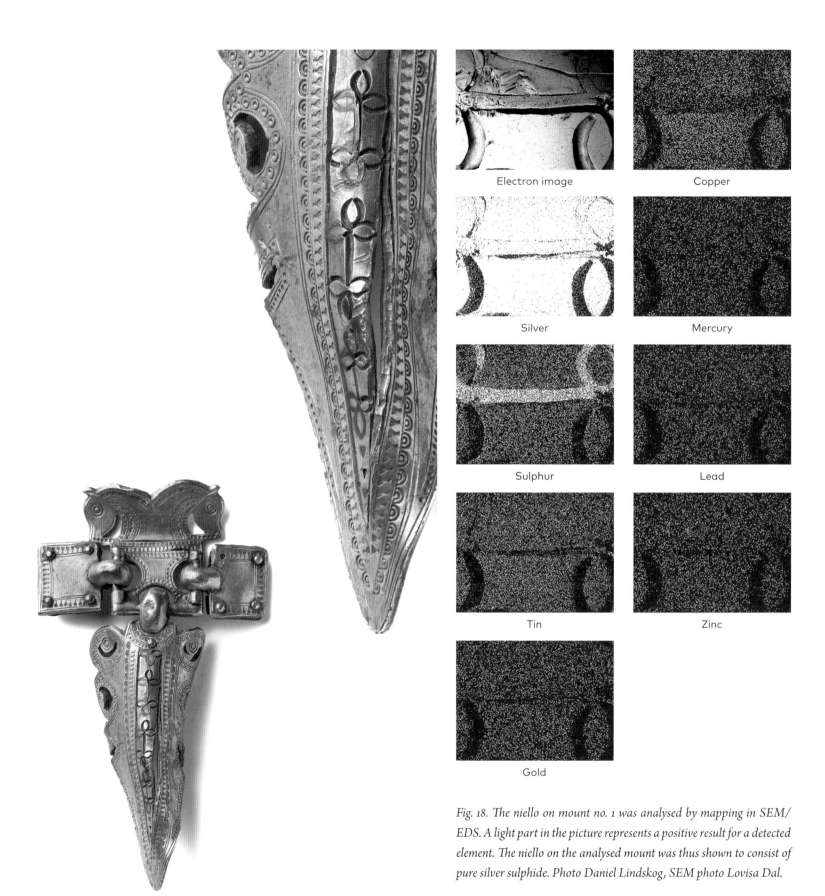

Fig. 18. The niello on mount no. 1 was analysed by mapping in SEM/ EDS. A light part in the picture represents a positive result for a detected element. The niello on the analysed mount was thus shown to consist of pure silver sulphide. Photo Daniel Lindskog, SEM photo Lovisa Dal.

point the decoration is finished by three small triangles. The black niello gives an effective colour contrast to the surrounding silver and gold. The substance has been inlaid into cavities, and even though some pieces have fallen out, about half of it is still in place.

Niello is composed of one or more metal sulphides, usually from silver, copper or a mixture of both. When containing sulphides from one metal only, it is usually the same as the metal of the object in which the inlays are made. Susan La Niece analysed eight Migration Period artefacts at the Swedish History Museum, Stockholm (1983:279–297); only one, a Cu-alloy clasp button from Helgö, turned out to have niello of pure silver sulphide, while the other objects (including some from the Scanian Sjörup find) contained mixed silver-copper sulphide. La Niece concludes that niello with sulphides from one metal only belong to the Roman tradition, while a mixture of both silver and copper does not appear until the end of the 5th century. Further on, in Eastern Europe during the early 11th century AD, lead was added, to make the melted niello more fluid.

Corresponding niello analyses were made on 21 Iron Age artefacts by Karen Stemann Petersen at the National Museum of Denmark, Copenhagen (Petersen 1998). The result supported La Niece's conclusion since the two artefacts from the Late Roman Iron Age had niello inlays of silver sulphide, compared to only two of eight from the Migration Period (the well-known relief brooches from Skerne and Gummersmark). The other objects showed a mixture of silver-copper sulphide (cf. Rau 2010 note 281).

To examine the type of niello used on the mount pendant no. 1, a 5 × 8 mm surface was analysed by mapping with SEM/EDS (LEO 1455VP). The result clearly pointed out silver sulphide as the single component in the niello and thereby assigns the object(s) to Roman tradition (fig. 18).

Thus the Sösdala pendant belongs to a small exclusive group of Scandinavian Migration Period objects, indicating relatively close contacts to Roman craftsmen (see Fabech & Näsman chapter 17 for further discussion).

Leather analysis

Among the metal objects found in Sösdala, there are also fragments of leather. A few pieces are loose and others are still fixed with rivets in mounts. All of them are heavily frag-

Fig. 19. Detail of a preserved seam on leather strap no. 93. Magnification x54. Photo Lovisa Dal.

mented and deteriorated, but a survey in microscope and SEM showed possibilities to find both hair pores and hair. Three samples from Sösdala I (from nos. 93, 94 and 149) were provided for proteomic analysis. The purpose was the identification of the animal species used as biological sources to produce the skin chosen. The analyses were made in 2017 at Centre for GeoGenetics, University of Copenhagen, by Assistant Professor Enrico Cappellini and Research Assistant Meaghan Mackie (report at LUHM). A number of proteins and peptides were confidently identified for each sample. Two samples (nos. 94 and 149) were determined to have been made from *Bos taurus* (cow), while the last sample of a thin leather cover (no. 93) is ovine. It was not possible to discriminate whether the sample originated from either *Ovis aries* (sheep) or *Capra hircus* (goat).

Fibre analysis

Some of the leather pieces hold remains of seams and stitches. The initial investigation in microscope and SEM showed that the fibres were deteriorated and heavily soaked in cellulose nitrate, giving a smooth and glossy appearance that did not reveal anything about the origin. A cleaned sample (no. 93) was run in FTIR which indicated vegetable fibre (fig. 19). Further analyses in microscope finally revealed the sample to be of bast fibre, i.e. hemp, nettle or flax. According to an e-mail of 1 March 2016 from

Ulla Mannering, University of Copenhagen, flax is the most suitable vegetable fibre for seams in leather.

Conclusion

In the Sösdala find there are 57 gilded silver objects decorated with punched geometric patterns. Among the 27 different types of stamps that have been used, motifs such as circles, concentric semicircles, dots and triangles are the most common. Six motifs, however, are uniquely punched onto one object only. The items are decorated with several stamps in different combinations. The most decorated object is a mount (no. 1) that has been worked with no less than 12 different punches and 600 hammer blows. The same object is the only one in the Sösdala find with niello inlays.

The stamps are very small, most often only a few millimetres, showing great skill in craftsmanship, as regards both the manufacture and the use of the tools. Based on careful microscope studies, it has been possible to identify significant features of the stamps. Details such as the shape of a curve, a pointy end of a line or a defect in the surface work as fingerprints, as is repeated every time the punch is used. By comparing the stamps on different objects it is possible to determine whether more than one object has been decorated with the same tool and thus likely in the same workshop. In this way the objects from Sösdala have been interlinked in three groups.

However, considering the striking similarities between some objects sorted into different groups, it is tempting to assume they too were made in the same workshop, but perhaps by different craftsmen who all had their individual sets of tools.

Only one object, the pendant no. 2, does not fit into any group. The object is at first sight very like another pendant, no. 3, but the stamps and craftsmanship are of much lower quality than the rest of the objects. It is therefore suggested that there originally were two equally high-quality pendants, of which one was damaged and had to be remade. The new craftsman obviously did not have access to the same set of punches, and was not as skilled as the first.

On a few of the objects, traces can be seen how the craftsmen performed their work. On the back of the pendant mount no. 19 is found what is suggested to be a triple punch test of a repetitive stamp, fully used on the front of the associated pendant no. 21. This punch is used on this object only. Also on the back of three strap junctions, sketches of complex geometric patterns are lightly scratched. Only one of the sketches was finally implemented on the front.

The punched patterns have a symmetrical design throughout, but occasionally irregularities have been noticed. Considering that an ordinary mount from Group 3 is decorated with approximately 110 punch marks, it is likely that an uneven number of lines, irregular direction of stamps or omitted details are simply mistakes.

Studies of how the stamps overlap can also reveal the order in which the motifs were punched, and at times even from which direction the craftsman started working. It has also been observed that the holes for rivets were made after the object was decorated, since they often go through the metal without considering the decorations.

Twelve objects were selected for metallurgical analysis with μXRF (ARTAX 800). The main aim was to ascertain the alloy components in the silver and by extension investigate the possibilities of separating or connecting different objects by the metal. The analyses show the objects to have a high silver content with a low percentage of copper and gold. Trace elements of zinc were clearly detected in the objects corresponding to Group 2, but almost nothing at all in Group 1. Only one object from Group 3 was analysed, but it too showed positive for zinc. This may indicate different sources of metal and possibly that the workshop used different silver alloys or that the mounts in group 1 were produced in another workshop than the mounts in groups 2 and 3.

SEM analysis of the niello on no. 1 proves it to consist of pure silver sulphide, which links the objects to Roman tradition and dates the manufacture to before the end of the 5th century.

Initial examinations of the heavily deteriorated leather showed possibilities to find both hair pores and remaining hair. By proteomic analysis three leather samples were determined to be of cow and sheep/goat. The identification of a bast fibre (hemp, nettle or flax) from remains of stitching also indicates the potential of further investigations.

Acknowledgement

The analyses were financed by a generous grant from Anders Althins Stiftelse. The Sösdala analyses were supported by the Swedish National Heritage Board in Visby where it was included in its Research & Development Programme. Thanks for assistance to Marei Hacke, Magnus Mårtensson, Tom Sandström and Kaj Thuresson.

References

La Niece, S. 1983. Niello. An historical and Technical Survey. *The Antiquaries Journal* 63: 279–297.

Larsen, E. Benner 1984. Værktøjsspor/På sporet af værktøj. Identifikation og dokumentation af værktøjsspor, – belyst ved punselornamenterede genstande fra Sejlflod. *Kuml* 1982–83: 169–180.

Petersen, K. Stemann 1998. Danish niello inlays from the Iron Age. *Journal of Danish archaeology* 1994–1995: 133–149.

Rau, A. 2010. *Nydam mose 1. Die personengebundenen Gegenstände. Grabungen 1989–1999.* Højbjerg/Aarhus. Summary. Dansk resumé.

Резюме

Естественнонаучное исследование вещей из Сёсдалы

Ловиса Даль

В состав находки в Сёсдале входят 57 предметов из позолоченого серебра, украшенные штампованным геометрическим орнаментом (рис. 2). Из 26 использованных здесь штампов разных типов наиболее популярны мотивы в виде круга, концентрических полукругов, точек и треугольников (рис. 3). Шесть мотивов уникальны – они присутствуют только на одном предметы. Изделия украшены различными комбинациями несколькими штампами. Более всего декорирован зажим налобного ремня (№ 1), декор которого выполнен как минимум 12 разными штампами и 600 ударами молотка. Этот предмет – единственный из найденных в Сёсдале, инкрустированный чернью (рис. 4).

Все штампы очень небольшого размера, чаще всего не более нескольких миллиметров; тем самым они демонстрируют выдающееся мастерство, проявленное изготовителями как при производстве инструментов, так и при их применении (рис. 6).

На основе тщательного исследования под микроскопом можно выявить ряд важных характеристик штампов. Детали наподобие формы дуги, заостренного окончания линии или дефект в обработке поверхности являются своего рода «отпечатками пальцев», так как они возникали всякий раз при использовании конкретного штампа. Сравнивая оттиски штампов на разных предметах, можно определить, использовался ли один и тот же инструмент для украшения нескольких вещей, и, следовательно, сделаны ли они в одной мастерской (рис. 7).

Таким образом, вещи из Сёсдалы были объединены в три группы (рис. 8–10). Однако учитывая поразительное сходство некоторых предметов, отнесенных к разным группам, соблазнительно будет предположить, что и они изготовлены в одной мастерской, но, вероятно, разными мастерами, причем каждый из них пользовался индивидуальным набором инструментов (рис. 12).

Находка № 2 одна-единственная не соответствует ни одной группе. Хотя, на первый взгляд, это изделие очень похоже на находку № 3, использованные на изделии № 2 штампы и качество изготовления куда более низкого качества, чем на остальных вещах. Потому можно предположить, что первоначально были две высокохудожественные подвески, одну из которых повредили, и потому пришлось сделать новую. Новый ремесленник, очевидно, не имел доступа к первоначальному набору штампов и не был настолько искусным, как первый (рис. 11).

На нескольких предметах можно увидеть следы, показывающие, как работали мастера. На оборотной стороне изделия № 19 находятся, надо думать, три пробных отпечатка одного и того же штампа, выполненный которым декор целиком покрывает лицевую часть связанной подвески № 21 (рис. 13). Данный штамп нанесен только на эту вещь.

Также на оборотной стороне трех соединителей ремней едва прочерчены наброски сложных геометрических орнаментов. Лишь один из этих черновиков был в итоге нанесен на лицевую часть (рис. 14).

Нанесенные штемпелем орнаменты полностью симметричны, но иногда отмечены и отступления от этого принципа. Если учесть, что обычный зажим группы 3 украшен примерно 110 отпечатками штампа, то, думается, придется сделать вывод, что случаи с нечетным количеством линий, несимметрично выставленными штампами и пропущенными деталями стали результатом ошибок, хотя нельзя исключать и того, что здесь асимметрия задумывалась изначально (рис. 15–17).

Изучение наложений штампов может также выявить порядок, в котором наносили орнаментальные мотивы, а иногда даже направление, по которому начинал работу мастер. Также отмечено, что отверстия для заклепок проделывали уже после нанесения декора, поскольку они зачастую не учитывают орнаментацию.

Был проведен рентгенофлюоресцентный анализ металла по выборке из 12 вещей (с помощью спектрометра «ARTAX 800»). Основной целью было выявление состава серебряного сплава и, исходя из него, изучение возможности для разделения вещей на группы или выявления связей между ними по свойствам металла. Поверхность каждой вещи исследовалась в пяти различных точках. Анализ показал, что вещи имеют высокое содержание серебра с незначительными примесями меди и золота. Незначительное, но явное присутствие цинка выявлено на изделиях, отнесенных к группе 2, причем в группе 2 цинк практически отсутствует. Хотя в исследовании участвовала только одно изделие из группы 3, в этом случае реакция на цинк также оказалась положительной. Это может указывать на разные источники металла; не исключено и то, что зажимы группы 1 изготовлены в другой мастерской по сравнению с зажимами групп 2 и 3.

Изучение черни, нанесенной на изделие № 1, под растровым электронным микроскопом доказало, что она выполнена из чистого сульфида серебра, что связывает предмет с римской традицией и позволяет датировать его производство временем до конца V в. (рис. 18).

Первоначальное исследование сильно поврежденной кожи продемонстрировало, что здесь можно выявить как устья волосяных фолликулов, так и сохранившиеся волоски. На потенциальную возможность для будущих исследований указывают фрагменты лубяного волокна (конопли, крапивы или льна), обнаруженные в остатках стежков (рис. 19).

Данное естественнонаучное исследование велось в сотрудничестве со Шведским советом по национальному наследию в Висбю (Готланд).

Подписи к иллюстрациям

Рис. 1. Детали штампованного орнамента на зажимах № 41 и 43 (фото Ловисы Даль).

Рис. 2. Общий вид предметов из позолоченного серебра со штампованным орнаментом (фото Ловисы Даль).

Рис. 3. Прорисовки различных мотивов на штампах (рисунок Ловисы Даль).

Рис. 4. Деталь головы коня на зажиме налобного ремня № 1 (фото Ловисы Даль).

Рис. 5. Два типа точечных линий: на уздечном зажиме № 33 (слева) и наконечнике ремня № 35 (справа) (фото Ловисы Даль).

Рис. 6. Разные виды нанесенных штампом треугольников, с точкой наверху или без таковой. С вещей № 1 (х20), 3 (х20), 14 (х24 и х26), 19 (х30), 35 (х47) (фото с помощью электронного микроскопа Ловисы Даль).

Рис. 7. Тот же мотив, выполненный другими штампами. Изучение двойных концентрических полукругов под микроскопом показало, что этот мотив выполнен пятью разными штампами. Детали изделий № 18, 1, 14, 47, 27 (фото и рисунки Ловисы Даль).

Рис. 8. Вещи с декором, выполненным одинаковыми штампами, отнесены к одной группе. На рисунке показаны изделия группы 1 и их штампы: № 1, 3, 4–6, 10, 11, 17, 18, 22, 24–26 (фото и рисунки Ловисы Даль).

Рис. 9. Вещи с декором, выполненным одинаковыми штампами, отнесены к одной группе. На рисунке показаны изделия группы 2 и их штампы: № 7–9, 14–16, 19–21(фото и рисунки Ловисы Даль).

Рис. 10. Вещи с декором, выполненным одинаковыми штампами, отнесены к одной группе. На рисунке показаны изделия группы 3 и их штампы: №. 12, 13, 27, 28–70 (фото и рисунки Ловисы Даль).

Рис. 11. Хотя на первый взгляд подвески № 2 и 3 очень похожи, при более тщательном осмотре обнаруживаются разительные отличия как между качеством самих штампов, так и в их нанесении (фото Даниэля Линдскога; макросъемка и рисунки Ловисы Даль).

Рис. 12. В верхней части подвески № 7 имеются три точки и три кольца, нанесенные с помощью штампа в ассиметричном порядке. Это единственный случай, когда эти штампы декорируют изделие из группы 2 (фото Даниэля Линдскога; макросъемка Ловисы Даль).

Рис. 13. На оборотной стороне зажима ремня № 19 находятся три отпечатка штампа с повторяющимся мотивом, который можно увидеть также на передней части связанных с ней подвесок № 20–21. Их следует считать пробой штампа (фото Ловисы Даль).

Рис. 14. На оборотной стороне распределителей ремней № 14–16 процарапаны неразборчивые наброски сложных геометрических изображений (фото Даниэля Линдскога; рисунок Ловисы Даль).

Рис. 15. Пример неправильно нанесенного декора, который в других случаях симметричен и аккуратен: на пряжке ремня № 24 (слева) отсутствует двойная линия – ср. двойные линии на пряжке № 26 (справа) (фото Ловисы Даль).

Рис. 16. Концентрические полукруги, оттиснутые под неверным углом, на зажиме ремня № 10 (фото Ловисы Даль).

Рис. 17. Концентрические круги с дополнительным кружком в центре или без такового, на зажимах № 49 (слева) и № 43 (справа) (фото Ловисы Даль).

Рис. 18. Чернение на зажиме налобного ремня № 1 исследовалось путем микросъемки с помощью электронного микроскопа. Светлая часть снимка отраажет положительный результат для выявленного элемента. Таким образом, выясняется, что чернение на исследуемом зажиме налобного ремня состоит из чистого сульфида серебра (фото Даниэля Линдскога; фото с помощью электронного микроскопа Ловисы Даль).

Рис. 19. Деталь сохранившегося шва на кожаном ремне № 93. Увеличение х54 (фото Ловисы Даль).

Chapter 7

Sösdala and Fulltofta: bridles and saddles

Ulf Näsman

The typochronology of selected mounts of bridle and saddles found at Sösdala and Fulltofta in Scania is discussed. The parade bridle Sösdala I has mounts from different sources, one closely related to late Roman craftsmanship, the others to "Barbarian" settings. It is dated to the early Migration Period. The bridle Sösdala II is of lower quality and probably from the end of the Late Roman Iron Age. The Fulltofta bridle was probably produced in the Late Roman Iron Age but updated with silver covers in "Sösdala" style and deposited in the early Migration Period. Between seven and thirteen saddles were cut to pieces at Sösdala I. At Fulltofta only few remains of a saddle were recovered. The Sösdala mounts define a common "Sösdala saddle type" and the Fulltofta mounts define a rare "Fulltofta type". The two types are placed in between earlier saddles of "Ejsbøl type" and later saddles of "Högom type".

Näsman, U. 2017. Sösdala and Fulltofta – bridles and saddles. In: Fabech, C. & Näsman, U. (eds). *The Sösdala horsemen – and the equestrian elite of fifth century Europe.* Jutland Archaeological Society.

At Sösdala and Fulltofta, two adjacent places in central Scania, remains of bridles and saddles from the Migration Period were found during gravel extraction (for find circumstances, see Fabech chapter 1). All finds are kept in the collections of Historical Museum at Lund University (Sösdala I LUHM inv.no. 25 570, Sösdala II LUHM inv.no. 32 492, Fulltofta LUHM inv.no. 14 080). There are similarities as well as differences between the bridles and saddles which are of interest for a discussion of function, chronology and provenance. Not all small finds will be discussed below, only mounts that will contribute to an understanding of chronology and provenance. For the rest, see the find catalogues.

The gilt silver mounted parade headstall places the Sösdala I bridle in an exclusive category of high quality (fig. 1). The mounts have a rich decoration with horse heads in profile and an abundance of different punch marks (Dal chapter 6). Most prominent is a nose mount, the pendant of which has a niello-decorated central panel (no. I:1).

The use of silver in its bimetallic snaffle is unique in Scandinavia (Ørsnes 1994:235) and comparable iron/silver bits are only to be found as far away as at Jakuszowice in Poland, Kačin in Ukraine and Untersiebenbrunn in Austria, all contemporary with Sösdala I in early period Scand-D1 (Kazanski & Mastykova chapter 15 figs 1–4; see

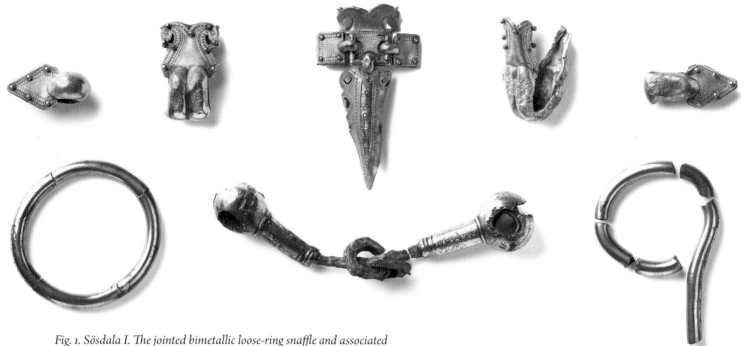

Fig. 1. Sösdala I. The jointed bimetallic loose-ring snaffle and associated mounts. Photo Daniel Lindskog.

also Godłowski 1995; Levada 2011; Nothnagel 2013). Exclusive decoration in silver is also present among the many fragmentary saddles found at Sösdala I.

Only very special circumstances can explain how the unequalled bridle came to remote Sösdala. The person who brought the bridle here must have had an unusual background. But a biography of the bridle from manufacture till deposition at Sösdala can only be reconstructed hypothetically (Fabech & Näsman chapter 17).

The bridles from Sösdala II and Fulltofta are simpler. Both, however, have ornamental details in silver but the decoration is simple. The attachment plates of Sösdala II are hammered out from rods while those of Fulltofta are cast. The snaffle is completely missing in Fulltofta but completely preserved in Sösdala II, although ritually destroyed. No traces were found of a saddle at Sösdala II, but two important saddle mounts are included in the Fulltofta find.

It is worth noting that none of the three bridles had rein chains but reins of leather. In the Migration Period rein chains, Ørsnes type 6C2, are very rare (Ørsnes 1994:224–226, 251, fig. 14i). A probable Migration Period type is so far only known from one place, the offering of military equipment at Finnestorp, Västergötland (Nord-

qvist chapter 11 fig. 2, 14). Nina Lau does not discuss Migration Period horse tack but the rein chains of Finnestorp figure in her illustrations as the last type (Lau 2014 Abb. 14:7, 18).

The find from Sösdala is the largest assortment of saddle remains in Scandinavia. Only the offering of battlefield spoils at Finnestorp has a larger number of fragmented saddle mounts. But in contrast two almost complete sets of mounts and rings for saddles are preserved in Sösdala and two more saddles can be reconstructed on the basis of preserved mounts. In all the mounts come from as many as seven saddles, to which may be added six more represented by saddle rings only. The thirteen Sösdala saddles date to period Scand-D1 and are typologically earlier then the well-preserved saddle from Högom from period Scand-D2a (Ramqvist chapter 10). The relation between the ring saddles from the Migration Period and the saddle finds from the Late Roman Iron Age has been unclear. But an analysis of saddle mounts from Fulltofta demonstrates that the Fulltofta find is a missing link connecting saddle mounts from period Scand-C2/C3 (e.g. Ejsbøl and Thorsbjerg) and Scand-D1 (Sösdala I). The origin of the Migration Period ring saddle can be traced back to the early 3rd century, period Scand-C1b.

Fig. 2. Sösdala II. The double-jointed bimetallic loose-ring snaffle. Photo Daniel Lindskog.

Snaffles

Loose-ring snaffles are preserved in both Sösdala I and II; Sösdala I is single-jointed (nos. I:100 –110, fig. 1) and Sösdala II is double-jointed (nos. II:1–2, fig. 2); unfortunately nothing remains of the bit in Fulltofta. Probably single-jointed loose-ring snaffles are the most common bit today and were so also in the past; the archaeological record contains numerous bits of the type from the Early Roman Iron Age onwards (e.g. Ørsnes 1994:242–252, 268; Bitner-Wróblewska 2007:81; Lau 2014: 132–133, Abb. 85:2,4; 86:4 and Sundkvist chapter 9). Double-jointed snaffles are also common, and opinions among riders differ concerning the advantages and disadvantages of the two bit types (according to my surfing on the Web. For a discussion of snaffles from a rider's point of view, see Sundkvist chapter 9).

Both snaffles are bimetallic: iron/silver in Sösdala I and iron/bronze in Sösdala II. The bit itself consists of an iron rod, square in cross-section. It is single in Sösdala I and folded double in Sösdala II. The looped ends that hold the bit rings are encased in silver (Sösdala I) or bronze (Sösdala II). Bimetallic bits are known since the Roman Iron Age; e.g. such bits are at Illerup dated to *c.* AD 200, period Scand-C1 (Carnap-Bornheim & Ilkjær 1996:275–7, 472–4,

Taf. 5 & 40). The bit ends from Sösdala I and II have very different shapes. The casings of the Sösdala I bit ends have rounded cross-section and the loops are also nicely rounded, similar to the loops of the bit ring mounts (nos. I:10–11 and I:17–18). The Sösdala II bit ends have a square cross section and the loops have flat facets. There is no typochronology of Scandinavian bit end casings from the Migration Period, and since the number of preserved bit ends is small and they vary considerably in shape, no typology will be attempted here. So at present the Sösdala bits cannot be dated on this criterion.

Michel Kazanski has discussed a group of European Migration Period snaffles with bit end casings that have loops and mounts with sharp longitudinal facets (Kazanski 1991:137–9, fig. 9). They include snaffles from Jakuszowice, Kačin and Untersiebenbrunn, and it is assumed that the type was introduced by the Huns. Such loops are not represented at Sösdala but are to be found on other Scandinavian snaffles, e.g. in Denmark at Hessel (Ørsnes 1994 fig. 42:1) and in Sweden at Finnestorp (Nordqvist chapter 11 fig. 12), both possibly from Scand-D2.

The snaffle of Sösdala I has relatively large plain bit rings (Ørsnes type 2B) while Sösdala II has small bit rings (Ørsnes type 2C) that are decorated with an external

Fig. 3. Sösdala II. A connecting link between bit ring and headstall with inlays of twisted copper and silver wire. Photo Daniel Lindskog.

moulding between lines. The snaffles are classified by Mogens Ørsnes as his bridle type OF1 (Sösdala II) and OF1/2 (Sösdala I); both are dated to period Scand-D1.

However, inlays of twisted copper and silver wire inlays on the connecting links of the snaffle Sösdala II (fig. 3), according to a study by the Swedish scholar Wilhelm Holmqvist (1951:88–92), should not be dated later than Scand-C3, the Late Roman Iron Age in Scandinavia. In a recent publication of military equipment offered at Kragehul, the metal inlays on a mouth guard are erroneously described as rhombic inlays of copper and niello (Iversen 2010:91–92, 132–133). The guard is dated to weapon group 11 or Scand-C3, and presumably deposited *c.* AD 400. Holmqvist convincingly described the same inlays as a twisted copper and silver wire hammered into a groove (1951 Abb. 41). From the weapon deposition at Ejsbøl, strap mounts decorated with inlays of twisted copper and silver wire are dated to weapon group 8/9 or Scand-C2/C3. The twisted inlays are strangely described as *gewundene Silbereinlagen* and as *gewundenen Furchen die Silbereinlagen aufweisen* (Jørgensen & Andersen 2014:137–140, Abb. 89). Another example is a bridge mount for a sword scabbard included in the offering of military equipment at Thorsbjerg, Schleswig. It belongs to weapon combination 9 and is dated to *c.* AD 300–350 (Matešić 2015:62–63, 258, Taf. 23: M165). So the twisted copper and silver wire of the Sösdala

II snaffle indicates that it is the earliest known deposition at Sösdala.

The focus in Nina Lau's Thorsbjerg publication (2014) is on horse tack from Roman Iron Age offerings of military equipment. The bits are mostly ported snaffles with loose rings (called *Kandarengebisse,* which is curb bits; but the Thorsbjerg bits may have given only limited curb function, see Sundkvist chapter 9; 1992:120). But loose-ring jointed snaffles are present in Lau's material. She briefly mentions that Migration Period snaffles like Sösdala I and Vennebo, Västergötland, may be derived from her bridle type "Thorsbjerg", that is, loose-ring jointed snaffles from Scand-C2/C3 (2014:58–63, 257–8, Abb. 47, 49). Ørsnes likewise assumed that snaffles like those from Sösdala are a continuation of Late Roman Iron Age snaffles of his types OD and OE. The Migration Period bridles are distinguished from those dating to the Roman Iron Age by their characteristic strap mounts (1994:249).

It is worth noting that the parade bridle Sösdala I was not fitted with a ported snaffle but a milder single-jointed one. Looking at Ørsnes's table (1994 fig. 53) one gets the impression that an explanation could be chronological, assuming that ported bits (his types OA, OB and OC) fell out of use after the Late Roman Iron Age. However, Ørsnes noted three Swedish finds demonstrating a continued use of ported snaffles well into the Migration Period, Finnestorp and Vennebo (Nordqvist chapter 11; Ørsnes 1994:268, fig. 48c) and Högom, Medelpad (Ramqvist chapter 10; 1992 pl. 35). Perhaps the rider who used the Sösdala parade bridle preferred a looser "nomadic" riding style (cf. Sundkvist chapter 9). In the Högom grave two bits were present; one ported snaffle bit with cheek bars (Ørsnes type OC/OH) and one double-jointed loose-ring snaffle (Ørsnes type OD). The combination in Högom of ported snaffle and cheek bars is unique according to Ørsnes (1994:236). Ramqvist assumes that the ported bit was used in a battle bridle (1992:66), and I guess that this implies that the simple iron snaffle was for daily use.

The Sösdala II snaffle is furnished with extra connecting links between bit rings and headstall. This is a rare solution. We only know that construction in two snaffles, Sösdala II and a double-jointed snaffle from Vennebo (Arrhenius 1987 Taf. 74, Ørsnes 1994 Fig. 48,1; Lau 2014 Abb.

49:1). The cheek bars of the ported bit from Högom are connected to the cheekpieces of the headstall with connecting links; being simple loops of iron, however, they differ a lot from those of Sösdala II (Ramqvist chapter 10 fig. 11; 1992:70–71 fig. 41:18,23, pl 35, 41). Links with a similar function are also found in the Fulltofta find, but there they belong to the headstall and are not part of the snaffle (below, nos. F:7–8).

Bit lengths seem to be related to the size of other bridle mounts and thus horse size (Lau 2014:132–133 Tabelle I; cf. Sundkvist 2001:105–107). In Sösdala I it can be measured as approx. 148 mm, i.e. longer than the various bit lengths presented by Lau as being from 95 to 133 mm, while the Sösdala II bit is 120 mm, i.e. in the middle of the field. According to modern tables of horse sizes a bit length of approx. 140 mm fits full horses while 120 mm fits a cob or a large pony (cf. Rosengren chapter 8). It was a stout horse that once carried the parade bridle.

Sösdala I – the Headstall of a Parade Bridle

The many decorative silver mounts from Sösdala I probably belong to the headstall of a bridle including the snaffle described above. During the Migration Period decorative mounts were used in the headstalls of East and North European bridles of Ørsnes type OF1 (Ørsnes 1994:191; mount types 9C–E). Numerous decorated silver mounts are included in the material from find spot I at Sösdala I. Since nothing indicates that more than one bridle is represented by the material, it is assumed that all silver mounts had a place in the same headstall. But still, it is a matter of discussion whether they all belong to the parade bridle or whether some may have embellished breast collar or breeching for the saddle of the same horse (reconstructions in Fabech & Näsman chapter 17).

Careful analysis has demonstrated that the mounts are produced with four different sets of punches (Dal chapter 6; cf. similar results in unpublished BA-thesis, Ersgård 1974). It is of course an open question whether they represent four different craftsmen in the same workshop or four different workshops. Based on the quality of silver plate and punched decoration, the following mounts are assumed to be a set of bridle mounts produced in the same workshop: nose mount no. I:1, pendants nos. I:3–4,

No. I:	Artefact type	Width mm
10–11	Cheekpiece mounts; strap fragment	33
19	Attachment plate of pelta-shaped pendant	30
22	Tongue-less buckle with triangular attachment plate	29
17–18	Rein mounts	25
15	Strap junction	22
27	Strap buckle	21
7, 14	Pendant; strap junction	20
1, 25	Nose mount; strap buckle	18
4, 24	Pendant; strap buckle	17
12–13	Strap ends/pendants(?)	15
94	Fragment of leather strap	>14
2–3	Pendants; strap fragment	14
93	Fragment of leather strap	14
28–34	Ring-link connectors	14
40–65	Rectangular strap mounts (24=14 mm, 1=13 mm, 1=15 mm)	14
35–38	Strap ends	12
39	Strap mount	10

bit ring mounts nos. I:10–11, rein mounts nos. I:17–18 and strap buckles no. I:22, 24–26 (fig. 4; for punch group 1, see Dal chapter 6).

Many mounts from the assumed headstall are made of thinner silver plate and all are decorated with another set of punches; they were made by another craftsman or they come from another workshop (punch group 2): pendant no. I:7, strap junctions nos. I:14–16 and a pelta-shaped pendant with attachment plate nos. I:19–21 (fig. 5; for punch group 2, see Dal chapter 6). Pendant 7 is similar to but not identical to no. I:4 in punch group 1; it probably replaced a lost counterpart.

A large group of mounts are decorated with a third set of punches: mounts nos. I:12–13, strap buckle no. I:27 and mounts nos. I:28–70 which include more than 23 rectangular strap mounts, at least three ring-link connectors and three strap ends (fig. 6; for punch group 3, see Dal chapter 6).

Pendant no. I:2 is very similar to pendant no. I:3 in punch group 1. However, it lacks punch identities to other mounts and can be considered to be a copy of inferior quality to replace a lost counterpart to no. I:3 (Dal chapter 6 fig. 11).

Fig. 4. Sösdala I. Mounts produced in the same workshop, punch group 1. Photo Daniel Lindskog.

Leather straps

Only seven stumps of leather straps are preserved in Sösdala I (plus a number of small remains still in place in some of the attachment plates). Only four strap fragments are from find spot I. The best-preserved stump is no. I:93, made of a thicker core wrapped in thinner leather. A seam along both edges held the leathers together (cf. similar straps in Högom, Ramqvist chapter 10). It is 4 mm thick and only 14 mm wide and consequently too narrow and too thick for most of the mounts in find spot I. It has no traces of metal mounts. In the attachment plate of pendant no. I:3 remains are preserved of an approx. 14 mm broad one-layer leather strap without seams. In a cheekpiece mount (no. I:10) a broad one-layer leather strap, approx. 2.7 mm thick is preserved. The two fragments reveal that the straps of the headstall were made from one-layer leather, so no. I:93 hardly belongs here. A function as reins is a good guess. This seems to tally with a proteomic analysis which showed that ovine (goat/sheep) leather was used for the cover (Dal chapter 6).

Strap fragment no. I:94 comes from a leather strap without seams that once was more than 14 mm wide. It has two rivet holes with impressions left by washers, one round, and one square. It probably belongs to the headstall. A pro-

teomic analysis has determined no. I:94 to have been made from *Bos taurus* (cow).

Using the width of the attachment plates as guide one can assume a plausible width of matching straps, see table.

Possibly strap breadth varied considerably depending on the function in the bridle. The headstall found in the Högom grave consisted of narrow, 10 mm broad straps but at several places the straps widened from 10 mm to 17, 20, 21 or 22 mm to fit attachment plates and mounts (Ramqvist 1992:66–72).

Connector mounts for cheekpieces and reins

We can be certain that most mounts in punch group 1 belong to the same bridle. The elegant silver mounts nos. I:10–11, the attachment plates of which are decorated with horse-heads in profile, probably connected the cheekpieces of the headstall to the bit rings of the snaffle (nos. I:102–110). They represent type 4 (*Gebißbeschläge* = bit mounts) in Ørsnes's system but were not included (1994:190; 277), perhaps because they are unique. Obviously the horse-heads are related to the occurrence of similar horse-heads on provincial Roman objects, e.g. the strap end from Babenhausen (Quast chapter 14 fig. 4:1). Ilia Akhmedov mentions the horse-heads of the Sösdala mounts in his

Fig. 5. Sösdala I. Mounts produced in the same workshop, punch group 2. Photo Daniel Lindskog.

Fig. 6. Sösdala I. Select mounts produced in the same workshop, punch group 3. Photo Daniel Lindskog.

discussion of Bosporan finds of snaffles with zoomorphic cheek bars (Akhmedov 2001:369–372, fig. 4–5). He notes the provincial Roman background of the animal heads and emphasises the stylistic differences between the horse-heads on mounts from Kačin and Sösdala and the Bosporan beast heads.

The leather straps were once approx. 33 mm wide at the mounts and must have tailed away to the assumed strap junctions (nos. I:14–16) where the straps may once have been only approx. 20–22 mm wide. Nor were simpler but equally well-made mounts (nos. I:17–18) that fastened the reins to the bit rings classified by Ørsnes; the width of the attachment plates indicates that the reins were approx. 25 mm wide near the snaffle.

It is worth a remark that the best parallels to the Sösdala I bridle from Jakuszowice, Kačin, Untersiebenbrunn and other bimetallic bits (Kazanski 1991 fig. 9), including Bar, Ukraine (Levada 2011 fig. 6; Kazanski & Mastykova chapter 15), are connected to the headstall with mounts that have rectangular attachment plates (Ørsnes 1994:235, type 4E). Exceptions are a snaffle from northern Italy (Kazanski 1991 fig. 9) and one from Kerch, Crimea, with rhombic attachment plates (Akhmedov 2001 fig. 4:1,3) but for lack of context information they are hard to evaluate. Later (6th

century) snaffles from Hauskirchen, Austria (Friesinger & Adler 1979 fig. 12) and Veszkeny, Hungary (Bóna 1976 pl. 77), have triangular attachment plates for headstall and reins. For a discussion of triangular attachment plates, see Strap buckles below.

Pendants

Three remarkable pendants come from the workshop represented by punch group 1. One is hung from a three-way connector connected to the straps with two attachment plates (no. I:1). The three-way connector is crowned with two horse-heads in profile, similar to those at the cheek-piece mounts (nos. I:10–11; above). A similar three-way connector is part of a 5th century silver hoard found at Bar, Ukraine (Levada 2011 fig. 5, 10:7; Fabech & Näsman chapter 17 fig. 8). This connector is however crowned by two heads of birds. The niello inlays in the central panel of the Sösdala pendant are unusual, depicting three-petal leaves. The same motif is found chip-carved on the Roman strap end from Babenhausen mentioned above because of its horse-heads (Quast chapter 14 fig. 4:1). An assumed Roman connection of the Sösdala pendant is supported by the fact that pure silver sulphide in Roman tradition was used in the niello (Dal chapter 6). This precious adornment certainly had a central position in the headstall; we suggest at the noseband near the cheekpiece mounts with similar horse-heads (for reconstructions, see Fabech & Näsman chapter 17).

Two pendants (nos. I:3–4) made in the same workshop may also belong to the headstall (fig. 4). They differ in length and shape. Pendants nos. I:2 and I:7 are obvious replacements of their counterparts; no. I:7 was made by the craftsman who punched mounts in group 2 and no. I:2 is a loner of lower quality. It seems unlikely that the longer pendants nos. I:4 and 7 were hung at the end of the browband and the shorter nos. I:2 and 3 at the noseband (see how strap ends are placed in the Högom bridle, Ramqvist chapter 10 fig. 9–10, 14; 1992 fig. 41, 44–45). Rather they were used in a breast collar or a breeching (reconstructions in Fabech & Näsman chapter 17).

A demolished but once very elegant pelta-shaped pendant belongs to punch group 2 (fig. 7). It has an attachment plate decorated with a punched star motif. A profiled knob on an iron axle (no. I:185) is catalogued as coming from find spot II, but likely belongs to this pendant; a similar arrangement is found on lunate pendants in the grave find from Hauskirchen (fig. 8; Friesinger & Adler 1979:46–48, Abb. 13; Menghin 1985:63–64; Taf. 22).[1]

It seems important to differentiate between lunula-shaped and pelta-shaped pendants since the meanings of the symbols have very different backgrounds. However, both were used for apotropaic purposes. Pendants are lunate when they are shaped like a crescent and outlined by segments of two circles, one convex and one concave, with different diameter. The symbolic meaning was originally based on associations with the moon and femininity (Bishop 1988:107). Pelta is a Latin word based on a Greek word for shield; pelta-shields could have different shapes. Eventually some oval shields were given two symmetrical openings at the upper rim to improve the visibility of the warrior behind the shield. Depictions of the mythical Amazons often show them using such shields but as an apotropaic symbol it is used also in male contexts. Pendants are here considered to be pelta-shaped when the inner concave outline is broken by a central projection; sometimes the ends of the pelta and the projection meet, sometimes in elaborate openwork like Sösdala nos.

Fig. 7. Sösdala I. The pelta-shaped pendant (nos. I:19–21) in photographic reconstruction with added knob (no. I:185). Photo Daniel Lindskog.

I:19–21. In other cases the inner outline is simply double concave, e.g. in Finnestorp (Nordqvist chapter 11 fig. 28) and such open pendants can be characterised as lunate pelta-shapes.

Pelta-shaped and lunate pendants in horse tack are discussed by Ørsnes as his type 9E (1994:240). He listed the following Migration Period pendants, which belong to horse tack: Finnestorp, Fulltofta, Sösdala I; Sösdala II and Vennebo all (Sweden), Jakuszowice (Poland), Černâhovsk (former Insterburg, Kaliningrad Oblast, Russia), Hauskirchen (Austria) and Veszkeny (Hungary). To this can now be added two pelta-shaped pendants in gilt bronze from a bridle found in a grave at Šosseynoe (former Maulen, Kaliningrad Oblast), which are decorated in Salin's style I and dated to *c.* AD 475–550 (Skvortsov chapter 13 fig. 2). Of these the pendants from Fulltofta, Sösdala II, Jakuszowice, Černâhovsk, Šosseynoe and Veszkeny were probably placed in a bridle. But according to the published

Fig. 8. Hauskirchen, Austria. One of four lunate pendants in gilt bronze from a rich grave. 4:5. After Friesinger & Adler 1979 Abb. 13.

reconstruction of horse tack found in a chamber grave at Hauskirchen, the four lunate pendants hung from the breast collars of two draught horses (Friesinger & Adler 1979; 46–48, Abb. 14).

Both pelta-shaped and lunate pendants occur in horse tack from the Roman Iron Age (Bitner-Wróblewska 2007:82; Lau 2014:143 Abb. 95; cf. Kazanski & Mastykova chapter 15). Possibly pelta-shaped pendants were not introduced in Scandinavian horse tack until period D1, in phase 2 of Bitner-Wróblewska's Sösdala horizon (Bitner-Wróblewska 2001:118, fig. 26, 32). Pelta-shaped pendants also occur in other contexts as ornaments in women's necklaces and as decorations on sword scabbards (Bitner-Wróblewska chapter 12; Magnus 1975 fig. 27–28; Gebers & Hinz 1977:23–24, Abb. 5:1–2). That the pelta originally acquired its apotropaic qualities since it symbolised an Amazon shield may have been unknown in Northern Europe, but probably its protective qualities were familiar.

The contemporary use of lunate pendants can explain why the peltas are so often turned upside-down (more below at the Fulltofta headstall). It also deserves to be remembered that the pelta was not a heathen symbol; Christians could use it too as an apotropaic symbol, see for example a sarcophagus from Nablus, the West Bank (Goldmann fig. 11). A lunate pendant from Sösdala II and two pelta-shaped pendant covers from Fulltofta are treated below.

The Sösdala I pelta-shaped pendant matches the strap junctions of the headstall and it could have an apotropaic position at the browband (reconstructions in Fabech & Näsman chapter 17). But perhaps it was used elsewhere, for example at a breast collar, a common position of lunate and pelta-shaped pendants in Roman horse tack where it also had a symbolic apotropaic function (Hagberg 1957; Bishop 1988:passim).

Strap buckles

Four strap buckles, nos. I:22, 24, 25 and 26, belong to punch group 1 and plausibly all were used in the headstall. They have a loose attachment plate shaped as an isosceles triangle, which at the three very similar buckles nos. I:24–26 ends in a roundel with a rivet (fig. 9). The corners at the base of the triangle are cut off, giving the buckles a distinct polygonal shape. There are plenty of straps in a headstall where adjustability could be practical; the three buckles nos. I:24–26 could be inserted in, for example, the two cheekpieces and in the throatlash. The strap ends nos. I:35, 36 and 38 from punch group 3 that pass through the frame of these buckles will however cover the decorated attachment plate and were probably used at the ends of browband and noseband as in the Högom headstall (reconstruction in Fabech & Näsman chapter 17).

Buckle no. I:22 is a peculiar loner (fig. 4). It has no tongue and its oval frame is much worn in a way that is difficult to understand. It may have been a kind of slider for an up to 34 mm broad strap but so far we have not been able to find where to place it. The buckle is gilt and punch-decorated so it was not placed in a hidden position. Perhaps the buckle once connected a strap from the saddle girth to a two-piece breast plate and a martingale (reconstruction in Fabech & Näsman chapter 17). A simple tongue-less buckle is also found among the bridle

Fig. 9. Sösdala I. Strap buckle (no. I:26), cf. fig. 4. Photo Daniel Lindskog.

Fig. 10. Sösdala I. Two small silver buckles (nos. I:23 and I:111). Photo Daniel Lindskog.

mounts from Jakuszowice (Kazanski & Mastykova chapter 15 fig. 1).

Scandinavian Migration Period strap buckles rarely have triangular attachment plates – for example, only one is included among many buckles from Gotland; it lacks, however, cut-off corners (Nerman 1935 no. 489). A buckle from a rich grave at Skottsund, Medelpad, has a punch-decorated triangular attachment plate with a roundel at the end; it lacks, however, cut-off corners and has a frame of different type. Among other finds in this remarkable grave, a scabbard bridge mount deserves to be mentioned. The grave is dated to Scand-D1 (Straume 1987:114, Taf. 95). Two buckles with cut-off corners are found in the offering of military equipment at Nydam, Jutland (Rau 2010:304–305, Taf. 19:6–7), but they are small and have integral attachment plates. They are nevertheless of interest since they are made of gilt silver and have simple punched decoration with niello. They were found in the offering Nydam IV, which is dated to period Scand-D2a, i.e. *c.* AD 450–475. Rau interprets them as shoe buckles. He compares the Nydam buckles to other Migration Period buckles but they seem less relevant here since all have integral attachment plates and lack cut-off corners. A more relevant silver buckle is found in the Kačin find (Kazanski & Mastykova chapter 15 fig. 2; Levada 2011 fig. 3); its attachment plate has the same triangular shape with end roundel but lacks cut-off corners and punched decoration.

The Sösdala buckles are considered by Jan Bemmann the most similar to a fragmentary buckle from the Nydam II find (Bemmann 1998:230; Taf. 234:69). Its attachment plate is described as rhombic with small roundels for rivets in the three corners. It is punch-decorated in a way resembling "Sösdala style" (Franzén 2009 fig. 4 after Kjær 1902:189). Rhombic attachment plates seem to be very rare in Western and Central Europe. In fact they are absent in Scandinavian contexts dated to the Late Roman Iron Age, so a domestic origin of the Nydam and the Sösdala buckles seems to be out of the question. Bernhard Salin and later scholars mention similar buckles from the Crimea and the middle and lower Danubian regions dated to Cont-D1–D2 (Franzén 2009; Rau 2010:318). Of course the Nydam buckle and the Sösdala buckles are related, for example the tongues have similar shapes, but there are differences as well. The Nydam buckle has a "rhombic" attachment plate and lacks the large roundel at the end. It is thus more related to later south-east European buckles with chip-carved rhombic attachment plates from the second half of the 4th century (Rau 2010 Abb. 130–132).

The Sösdala buckles are in my opinion not rhombic but triangular with cut-off corners and they have a large roundel at the end and lack the small roundels at the corners. So better prototypes are known from Late Roman provincial contexts for buckles with loose triangular attachment plates with cut-off corners and roundel at the end, for instance at sites as far from one another as Dunaújváros in Hungary, Vermand in France (Kazanski & Mastykova chapter 15 fig. 10:8, 10; cf. Tejral 2010: 101) and Straubing in Germany (Prammer 1987:599, Abb. 3). The triangular attachment plate of a buckle from Mainz, Germany, has cut-off corners and is decorated with a chip-carved rosette and is certainly of Roman manufacture (Sommer 1984; 18, 21 Taf. 1:10). So our good guess is that the Sösdala buckles were not made in Scandinavia and that their background is to be sought among buckles made in late Roman workshops distributed from the Rhine to the Danubian basin in Hungary.

Buckles with loose triangular attachment plate are known in finds from the Danubian basin, often associated with the Huns (Tejral 2010 Abb. 10, 11, 13). But they have a differently shaped frame and mostly lack cut-off corners and the roundel at the end. But a gold buckle with a roundel at the end attributed to the Huns was found in a grave at Árpás in Hungary (Wieczorek & Périn 2001:36,120; Anke & Externbrink 2007:182–183); Jaroslav Tejral considers it to be an isolated example (2010:100–101, Abb. 11:8). These buckles are hardly the prototypes of the Sösdala buckles but reflect the same origin, the products of provincial Roman workshops.

The cast buckle with integral plate no. I:27 is unique (fig. 6). It belongs to punch group 3 including three strap ends I:35, 36 and 38 that pass through the frame of the buckle, but it is unlikely they are functionally related. Simpler buckles with triangular integral plate are known in the Migration Period, but none resembles no. I:27; see for example a buckle found in the deposition of military equipment at Porskær, Jutland (Jørgensen 2008:174). Perhaps more relevant is a buckle from Lovö, Uppland, which is dated to period Scand-D1, but instead of a roundel it ends in a rudimentary animal head (Lamm 1973: 21, 58; pl. 10:8; Straume 1987 Taf. 93:8). Triangular buckles with end roundel probably have an origin in late Roman buckles (above and Kazanski & Mastykova chapter 15). They are known from Gallia to the Danubian area (Sommer 1984:18, 38).

Two small silver buckles with rounded integral plate may also be part of the bridle (nos. I:23 and 111). They are simple but well made (fig. 10). Two small buckles are also included in the Sösdala II bridle and Bunte assumed that they buckled the reins to the snaffle rings (nos. II:19–20; Bunte 1961 fig. 9–10). A similar function could be assumed for two small buckles in the Fulltofta bridle (nos. F:18–19), but this cannot be the case for Sösdala I since two gilt and punch-decorated mounts better fulfil the function

Fig. 11. Åmossarna, Scania. Recovered objects of offered horse tack: a double-jointed snaffle with cheek bars, three saddle rings, a strap buckle, and a bronze ring. © Österlens museum, Simrishamn.

(above, nos. I:17–18). The two silver buckles would rather have been used in a more hidden position, for instance at throatlash, headpiece or martingale.

Buckles with loose rounded attachment plate are common in contemporary finds across Europe but buckles with a rounded integral attachment plate are rare. In an offering of horse tack in Åmossarna, Scania, a similar bronze buckle was found (Österlens museum no. 2963e). It had three rivets, two with preserved silver caps (fig. 11). The find probably dates to Scand-D1. In the offering of military equipment at Illerup, Jutland, a similar buckle is assigned to offering C, dated to early period Scand-D1 (Ilkjær 1993:140–142, Taf. 78). A bronze buckle found at the large cemetery at Sejlflod, Jutland, has a D-shaped frame and a rounded integral attachment plate with three rivets (Nielsen 2000 grave IC x3373). The grave pottery is dated by Jytte Ringtved to her phase d, corresponding to Scand-D1 (Ringtved 1988 fig. 31 and appendix C).

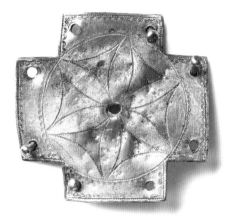

Fig. 12. Sösdala I and Untersiebenbrunn, Austria. Punched six-petal flowers decorate a strap junction (Sösdala no. I:15) and a strap mount (Untersiebenbrunn, no. ANSA U40). 5:4. Photo Daniel Lindskog and © KHM Museumsverband, Antikensammlung, Vienna.

Strap junctions

It is striking that strap junctions are missing in the mount set of punch group 1. In a headstall four straps meet on each side of the horse-head: headpiece, cheekpiece, browband and throatlash (for terminology, see Introduction). At this point strap junctions, one on each side, could accentuate and support the four-strap meeting. If a noseband is included two more strap junctions could find their place. Four cross-shaped strap junctions of a headstall were recorded *in situ* in grave 79 excavated at Netta, Poland (Bitner-Wróblewska 2007:82, Pl. 38; Lau 2014 Abb. 107; cf. Abb. 112); the grave is dated to period Cont-C2. In Sösdala I only three suitable strap junctions were found, so it seems that one was lost (nos. I:14–16). All belong to punch group 2. It is reasonable to assume, as Ørsnes did, that the strap junctions were used in the parade bridle to supplement the mounts of punch group 1.

I do not know any other finds of similar strap junctions. They are included in Ørsnes type 9D1 (1994:238; 277), which contains mounts of varying shapes, very loosely defined as "cross-shaped". Stylistically the mounts are excellent Sösdala style and firmly dated to early Scand-D1 by the similarity to the punch-decorated mounts from Untersiebenbrunn (fig. 12).

Strap ends

The many mounts of punch group 3 (fig. 6) include three similar strap ends that pass the frame of the strap buckles mentioned above (nos. I:35, 36, 38). Probably they were used in the headstall of the parade bridle at the ends of brow- and noseband. Two more strap-end-like mounts are present, nos. I:12–13 (fig. 6), but they do not fit the buckles nos. I:24–27 easily and are assumed to have another function as decoration of a martingale (reconstruction in Fabech & Näsman chapter 17).

The only strap ends included in Ørsnes's system (type 9F) are later, from period Scand-E1 . The shape of the three Sösdala strap ends is very simple and similar ones cast in bronze are found in Migration Period graves on Gotland (Nerman 1935 nos. 473–479). Whether the simple shape was influenced or not by gold strap ends in so-called Hunnic grave finds, e.g. at Szekszárd-Bal-Parászta, Hungary (Tejral 2007:111), is anyone's guess. The gilt silver strap end with punched decoration found in the grave at Jakuszowice has a simple shape that is only superficially similar (Kazanski & Mastykova chapter 15 fig. 1).

Strap mounts and ring-link connectors

Exquisitely punched rectangular mounts and similar ring-link connectors probably decorated the straps of the parade bridle. At least three pairs of ring-link connectors are part of the Sösdala I bridle (fig. 13); probably at least one pair is lost. The use of ring-link connectors in headstalls is evidenced by the find Sösdala II (below); several linked mounts of a different type are found in the Fulltofta bridle (below).

In total the strap mounts of Sösdala I measure 190 cm, which can be compared to the 209 cm of leather straps preserved of the Högom headstall (Ramqvist 1992:67–72, fig. 41). So we suggest that all ring-link connectors, rectangular strap mounts and strap ends decorated the headstall of the Sösdala I bridle.

We do not know any other Scandinavian Migration Period bridle with similar decorative mounts. But stray finds of similar bridle mounts are found in Finnestorp (Nordqvist chapter 11 fig. 4, 7–10). The Högom headstall is decorated with Cu-alloy studs with domed silver caps (cf. Quast 2007:57). A number of bridles from Illerup dated to *c.* AD 200 are decorated with various types of mounts, not considered by Ørsnes (Carnap-Bornstein & Ilkjær 1996). Roman Iron Age bridles with long rectangular mounts are known, for example at Babięta (former Babienten), Chrustal'noe (former Wiekau) and Povarovka IV (former Kirpehnen), all Kaliningrad Oblast, Russia, and dated to B2–C1 (La Baume 1944: Abb. 8a,b; 10; Lau 2014:42, 158, Abb. 30; 105:2). Another interesting find of headstall mounts from Mödring, Austria, is dated to period C1b (Lau 2014:45, Abb. 34). A better comparative find is grave 17 at Tumiany (former Daumen) (Poland) where the bridle for horse 30 is of great interest for a reconstruction of the bridle Sösdala I. The horse graves at Tumiany are generally dated to the 6th century, corresponding to Polish period E2 (Baranowski 1996). An excavation of a cemetery at Nowinka, northern Poland, uncovered 130 cremations from the second half of the 6th century to the early 7th century. Numerous Scandinavian artefacts, including mounts of horse tack (strap junctions) of Scandinavian type, reveal strong relations to Scandinavia. In several cases a horse was inhumed below a cremation, the horse often furnished with bridles. Some had plenty of bronze mounts. The bridles of graves 78, 83, 118 and 121 that could be reconstructed demonstrate that the straps could be covered with mounts (Kontny, B.; Okulicz-Kozaryn, J. & Pietrzak, M. 2011 pl. 114–115).

Ørsnes assumed that the frequent use of mounts in the Sösdala I headstall reflects an impact from Hunnic horsemen (1994:268), but his statement is undocumented since no references are given. Of course, examples of headstalls decorated with rectangular mounts are known in the area dominated by Huns in the early 5th century, e.g. a rich *Totenopfer* (funeral sacrifice) found at Pannonhalma-Szélsőhalom (Wieczorek & Périn 2001:50, 132). But references given above to earlier and later bridles make it reasonable to assume that among equestrians there simply was a latent possibility to decorate parade bridles with decorative mounts when wealth allowed. Dieter Quast suggests that the frequent use of richly decorated horse tack in the Roman Empire indicates that Roman workshops were more important than Nomadic or "Germanic" for the spread of decorated straps in Europe (2007:63). Certainly the punched decoration of the Sösdala silver mounts conveys a "classic" impression (cf. Norberg 1931:108).

Fig. 13. Sösdala I. A ring-link connector cut in two (nos. I:33–34). Photo Daniel Lindskog.

Summary

The remarkable headstall of Sösdala I is in many ways unique but it has similarities to contemporary finds from Jakuszowice, Kačin, Untersiebenbrunn and other finds from Eastern and Central Europe. Comparative finds are to be found in both West and East Roman provinces as well as in settlement areas of "barbarian" *gentes*. The analyses of shape and design as well as technology make it obvious that the headstall is composed of mounts from different artisans. It is very likely that the mounts belonging to punch group 1 were made in a workshop with close relations to Roman production. Mounts belonging to punch group 2 and 3 also represent high-quality handicraft but are made in a more "barbarian" style, possibly in the same workshop. The loner no. I:2 is a simple copy made by a less competent craftsman. The mounts were probably produced early in the 5th century but wear and repairs indicate a deposition later in the century. For an attempt to reconstruct a biography of the bridle, see Fabech & Näsman chapter 17.

The Sösdala II headstall

Remains of a second bridle were found by workers at Sösdala in 1961 and published the same year by Carin Bunte (1961). This bridle is much simpler and the mounts are made of Cu-alloy with details in silver (fig. 14). The attachment plates are slipshod smithery and seem to be breakable, while the bimetallic snaffle is of higher quality with a decoration of inlaid twisted copper and silver wire (fig. 3), while only simple lines decorate the mounts of the headstall.

Fig. 14. Sösdala II. Select mounts of the bridle; for snaffle see fig. 2. Photo Daniel Lindskog.

Leather straps

A piece of the leather strap is preserved (no. II:29), on to which a buckle (no. II:19) was riveted. The leather strap is single without seams; 14 mm wide and 2.7 mm thick. An indeterminable leather fragment was also found together with the buckles (no. II:30). The leather fragments represent the reins.

Connector mounts for cheekpieces and noseband

The headstall is connected to the bit rings via connecting links. A loop in one end held the bit ring and at the other end another loop held two triangular attachment mounts (fig. 2–3), longer for the cheekpiece and shorter for the noseband. The mounts are shaped as isosceles triangles with a roundel at the end; they belong to Ørsnes type 4A (1994: 235, 277; Abb. 2, 42a, 46), a type that in his material never is dated earlier than period Scand-D1. However, similarities to triangular attachment plates in provincial Roman contexts make an earlier date possible (see above at the Sösdala I headstall, Strap buckles). A bit from northern Italy (Kazanski 1991 fig. 9) has mounts with similar attachment plates, but for lack of context information it is hard to evaluate.

The Sösdala plates are decorated with simple edge lines and a strip of silver sheet; the rivets have silver caps. The remarkably weak construction of the attachment plates was noted by Bunte (1961: 207). The slipshod quality of the smith's work differs strongly from the high quality of corresponding mounts in Sösdala I and Fulltofta. In my opinion craftsmanship and decoration indicate a production date not later than the Late Roman Iron Age period Scand-C3.

Strap buckles

The two buckles have a square frame and an integral attachment plate shaped as an isosceles triangle with a roundel at the end (fig. 15). Bunte saw parallels in two finds from the Late Roman Iron Age (1961:204), a grave from Havor, Gotland (Almgren & Nerman 1923 no. 529) and an offering of military equipment at Kragehul, Jutland. Both the Kragehul and Havor buckles are included by Rasmus Iversen in a rather heterogeneous group, dated to weapon group 11 or period Scand-C3/D1 (Iversen 2010:112, Abb. 43, Taf. 74, Fundliste 6). Another similar buckle from Havor is dated to the early Migration Period (Nerman 1935 no. 141). In the offering of military equipment from Skedemosse, Öland,

Fig. 15. Sösdala II. Two strap buckles (nos. II:19–20). Photo Daniel Lindskog.

an undated buckle has a similarly shaped frame but lacks a roundel at the end of the triangular attachment plate (Hagberg 1967 pl. 5:F915). It is included in Iversen's find list, but the buckles from Sösdala II or Fulltofta are not, unfortunately. A date of the Sösdala II buckles to around AD 400 seems reasonable (cf. the strap buckles of Sösdala I, above). As suggested by Bunte they probably fastened the reins to the bit rings (Näsman chapter 5 fig. 7).

Pendants

Two very different pendants were once part of the Sösdala II bridle, one lunate, the other shaped as a strap end (fig. 14). The simple lunate pendant is undecorated and fastened to a ring-link connector with a bronze strip forming a slip-shod loop (no. II:10). The attachment plates have the same shape as those for cheekpieces and noseband (see above).

A pendant that is similar to the Sösdala II pendant was recorded *in situ* when grave 79 at Netta was excavated. It is lunate but a tip at the centre of the double concave inner outline makes it a pelta-like lunula or a lunate pelta. The Netta record demonstrates that lunate pelta-shaped pendants could be fastened to browbands. The grave is dated to period Cont-C2 (Bitner-Wróblewska 2007:82, fig. 6, pl. 38–40; Lau 2014 Abb. 95:1, 107:3). The find strongly supports Bunte's reconstruction of the Sösdala II headstall (Näsman chapter 5 fig. 7). Among the Polish finds mentioned by Bitner-Wróblewska, a lunate pendant of Cu-al-

loy from Kosewo (former Kossewen) deserves attention (Nowakowski 1998:10, Taf. 6:84). Another Roman period find in which a lunate pendant is assumed to have adorned the browband was found at Beuningen, the Netherlands (Lau 2014 Abb. 95:4). A recent and unpublished find of a lunate pelta-shaped pendant comes from occupation layers in a house in the Sandby ringfort, Öland (Gunnarsson *et al.* 2017). It is of Cu-alloy and covered with a silver sheet with lines along the edges as its only decoration. The occupation layer is dated to the 5th century.

Lunate pelta-shaped pendants can according to Joachim Werner be traced back to the 1st century AD when Sarmatians north of the Danube adopted the shape from the Roman Empire (Werner 1988:266; on lunate pendants in the Roman army in the 1st century AD, see Bishop 1988:*passim*, fig. 47). In the Late Roman Iron Age and in the first half of the 5th century AD lunate pelta-shaped pendants spread to "Germanic" contexts including Scandinavia. As symbols a lunula represented of course the moon and, like a pelta, also had an apotropaic purpose in the horse tack (Bishop 1988:107).

The pendant shaped as a strap end is hinged to a rectangular attachment plate (no. II:26). It is vaguely shaped like an animal (?snake) head with eyes rendered as circled dots. The front of the attachment plate is covered with a silver sheet. Concentric circled dots decorate both pendant and attachment plate. I do not know any good parallels to this pendant. Bunte placed it at the noseband but this is of course very uncertain. Its function could well have been as strap end somewhere (cf. hinged strap ends in Nydam, Rau 2010 Abb. 123:2–3).

Strap junctions

Only one strap junction is preserved (fig. 14), classified as type 9C in Ørsnes's system. It consists of four attachment plates fastened to a ring. (It could also be described as a four-way ring-link connector.) The attachment plates have the same shape and decoration as the other attachment plates in the Sösdala II bridle. The only relevant parallel in Ørsnes's catalogue is a strap junction from Bregentved, Zealand (Ørsnes 1994 Fig. 35). It is dated to period Scand-D1, probably on the basis of its decoration. The Sösdala II strap junction is likely earlier.

Fig. 16. Fulltofta. Select mounts of the headstall. Photo Daniel Lindskog.

Strap junctions with a central ring are not unknown in the Migration Period or earlier. In the earlier offering of military equipment at Ejsbøl, Jutland, a strap junction with ring and four simple attachment plates was found (Ørsnes 1988 Taf. 64:21). It is not commented upon in the new Ejsbøl publication (Jørgensen & Andersen 2014:148–154) but probably it had a function in a belt. Strap junctions for three straps (three-way ring-link connectors) are also part of belt sets in the Nydam find (Rau 2010 Taf. 23).

In Gotland junctions for three straps are found in Migration Period grave contexts, probably for use in belts (Nerman 1935 nos. 177, 512). The attachment plates are triangular and have a roundel at the end, but the long sides are concave; they are well made but have similarities to the simpler attachment plates of Sösdala II.

Strap mounts and ring-link connectors
No strap end is preserved in the Sösdala II find (but note remark about pendant no. II:26 above). At least eight ring-link connectors were fitted into the headstall (fig. 14; nos. II:4–9, II:11–18). The attachment plates are similar to those discussed above. Ring-link connectors used in military belts to suspend various objects demonstrate that the technique was known in period Scand-C2–C3 but they are not considered further here, e.g. belt sets at Nydam and Ejsbøl (Rau 2010 Taf. 8, 10, 16, 18; Jørgensen & Andersen 2014:148, 154, Abb. 102, Taf 55–56). More relevant ring-link connectors that join parts of the same leather belt are found in

Kragehul (*Ringverbindungsbeschläge*, Iversen 2010:116–117, Taf. 75), dated to weapon group 11 or period Scand-C3/D1, and in Migration Period graves in Gotland (Nerman 1935 nos. 173–177, 507).

Four simple ring mounts (fig. 14; nos. II:21–25) have good parallels in the headstall found at Netta, where three are found *in situ* at browband and noseband among other mounts (Bitner-Wróblewska 2007:82, Taf. 39:9), perhaps with a function as in the reconstruction of the Sösdala II bridle (Fabech & Näsman chapter 17). The Netta grave is dated to period Cont-C2.

Summary
The headstall of Sösdala II is much simpler in material and craftsmanship than the headstall of Sösdala I. The lack of comparative material makes a discussion about provenance hazardous. There are indications that the craftsman was influenced from outside Scania, but at present it seems most reasonable to suggest that the bridle is a South Scandinavian product. The shape and design of snaffle and headstall are difficult to date precisely. Ørsnes dated the bridle to Scand-D1, but probably the snaffle should be dated earlier, to Scand-C3. Perhaps the snaffle is older and the mounts of the headstall added later. The bridle was probably deposited before the deposition of bridle and saddles at Sösdala I.

Fig. 17. Fulltofta. One of two silver-on-bronze covers for axe-shaped pendants in the headstall (no. F:1). Photo Daniel Lindskog.

Fig. 18. Vennebo. Rounded bronze pendant with fitting silver cover, part-ly gilt and punch-decorated in a pelta-like shape. Approx. 1:1. Photo SHM no. 6 511:4.

The Fulltofta headstall

Back in 1896 remains of a headstall and a saddle were found at the top of a gravel hill at Fulltofta, 15 km from Sösdala. Strangely enough, Sven Söderberg did not recognise it as horse tack when he described in detail the finds in the museum catalogue. The Fulltofta headstall, like that of Sösdala II, consists of bronze mounts with simple linear decorations and details in silver sheet, but the quality is much higher (fig. 16). Attachment plates are not made of sheet metal but cast. The different parts of the mounts are not ring-linked but connected to one another with precisely cast hinges. The casting is good and the many attachment plates have standardised dimensions. Sheets of silver are applied on the centre pieces of the mounts and decorated with incised simple four-petal flowers and circled dots. This decoration has nothing to do with "Sösdala style".

Three pendants have punched decoration, two of them in rich "Sösdala style" (fig. 17; nos. F:1, F:2cum25). The two pelta-shaped silver-on-copper plates date the find to Migration Period Scand-D1. Since the first publication by Rune Norberg (1931 Abb. 3) it has been assumed that they were applied to the axe-shaped pendants that hang in the strap connectors (fig. 16; nos. F:5–6). This is reasonable,

but since it cannot be proven whether they are an original or a later addition, one has to look for other criteria to date the bronze mounts. It is interesting to compare the Fulltofta silver covers with a pendant from Vennebo which is decorated with a punched pelta (fig. 18). The pendant consists of a silver cover and a back plate of bronze with the same shape. This comparison makes it obvious that the axe-shape of the Fulltofta pendants was not originally made to be covered with a very deviant pelta-shaped silver sheet (fig. 19).

Ørsnes's dating of the Fulltofta bridle to Scand-D1 (1994:238 Fig. 36) probably rests primarily on the "Sösdala style". But possibly also on the triangular attachment plates, which have a superficial similarity to other "contemporary" headstall mounts (his types 4A and 9C). However, an earlier date seems possible since triangular attachment plates with a roundel at the end also are well known in Roman provincial buckles from the 4th and 5th centuries (above at the Sösdala I headstall, Strap buckles).

The construction of the Fulltofta mounts with cast hinges connecting the different parts is unique in the bridle material as far as I have noted. Ørsnes (1994:238) grouped hinge-linked and ring-linked connectors together (his type 9C), but the Fulltofta construction is much stiffer and

Fig. 19. Fulltofta. Green verdigris on the back of one of the silver-on-copper covers (no. F:2) fits the axe-shaped pendant (no. F:5). Photo Daniel Lindskog.

Fig. 20. Fulltofta. Hinge-linked mounts connected bit-ring to cheekpieces and noseband in the headstall (no. F:7). Photo Daniel Lindskog.

more complicated to produce. Analogues to cast hinges are found in belt sets from Gotland and Norway (in some cases it is uncertain whether the illustrated hinges are cast). Two graves from the Late Roman Iron Age (Almgren & Nerman 1923 nos. 544–545) are dated to weapon groups 10 and 11 or Scand-C3 (Ilkjær 1990:267, Abb. 193–194), and several graves are from the Migration Period (Nerman 1935 nos. 158–172, 467, 508–509). Hinged belt mounts are used in parade belts from Norway and Sweden in period Scand-D1 and D2 (Ramqvist 1992 pl. 71, 76; Bemmann & Hahne 1994:497 Abb. 100). Thus the technology was available to a possibly Scandinavian workshop. It was used with great skill to create a complete set of different strap connectors in a very convincing design.

Hinge-linked mounts for bit rings, cheekpieces and noseband

Unfortunately, nothing remains of the snaffle, but an almost complete mount and a much fragmented similar one reveal how the bit was connected to the headstall (fig. 20; nos. F:7–8). Two triangular attachment plates (Ørsnes type 4A), one for the cheekpiece, one for the noseband, are hinged to the central piece. A third hinged arm ends in a loop for the bit ring. This connector arm had the same function as the connecting links of the Sösdala II snaffle (above), but in Fulltofta as part of the headstall, not the

snaffle. On the fourth side there is an integral triangular projection.

Strap buckles

The two buckles have a square frame with concave sides and a square integral attachment plate with two rivets and a third rivet in a rounded projection (fig. 16; nos. F:18–19). Small integral buckles are common in Scand-C3–D1, see above at Sösdala I and Sösdala II (nos. I:23, 111; II:19–20). No exactly similar buckle is known, but a buckle from Modvo in Norway has an attachment plate with a third rivet in an angular projection at the end (Straume 1993:222, fig. 42f); it is dated to weapon group 10 or Scand-C3 (Ilkjær 1990 Abb. 193). Integral buckles with square frame that have concave sides are considered typical of weapon group 11 that dates to the end of Scand-C3 and the beginning of Scand-D1 (Iversen 2010:112, Abb. 43). Two buckles with integral attachment plates from the Sejlflod cemetery are of interest; one has a square frame with concave sides and a triangular plate (Nielsen 2000 grave IP x 3598), while the other has an D-shaped frame and a plate with an irregular triangular shape (Nielsen 2000 grave UA x 2473). It is notable that its base has cut corners. Sejlflod grave IP is dated by Ringtved to Scand-C3 (Ringtved 1988:141, fig. 49) and grave UA to Scand-D1 (Ringtved 1988: 141, fig. 31 and appendix C).

Pendants

Two pendants shaped as strap ends are entirely covered with undecorated silver sheet (fig. 16; nos. F:11–12). Only one is preserved completely; the other is represented only by the attachment plate. No similar pendants can be cited.

Two axe-shaped pendants belong to the headstall (fig. 16; nos. F:5–6), where they probably served as apotropaic symbols at the brow- and noseband. [2] They hang from the central piece of a hinge-linked strap connector. On the opposite side of the central piece there is an integral triangular projection. The Fulltofta pendants seem to correspond to axe-shaped pendants type 4 in Kokowski's typology: flat pendants with a massive suspension loop, an anchor-like outline, and a much curved edge (Kokowski 1998:100; after Schuster 2006:73–74). Similar pendants in silver or Cu-alloy have a wide distribution in Europe from Germany to the Carpathian basin, but are rare in Scandinavia; to my knowledge the only Scandinavian representation is the Fulltofta pendants. Finds date to the Late Roman Iron Age and the Migration Period, e.g. the famous grave finds at Haßleben, Germany (Jankuhn 1973). The distribution in time and space indicates an origin in south-eastern Europe in the Dacian-Sarmatian region on the lower Danube (Gebers & Hinz 1977:27, 31–32; Kokowski 1998:102; after Schuster 2006). The symbolic meaning of axes varies; they could for instance be seen as a sun symbol (Montelius 1900, 1917). However, axes are naturally associated with strength and power, so in the context and position of the Fulltofta headstall the axe-shaped pendants may simply be apotropaic.

A pelta-shaped silver-on-bronze plate was presumably affixed to each axe-shaped pendant after some time (fig. 19). The silver covers have a rich punched decoration and are party gilt. Like the Sösdala I pelta-shaped pendant (nos. I:19–21) the ends are shaped as bird heads. Despite the lack of niello, the decoration is a much better representative of the "Sösdala style" than the Sösdala I pelta pendant. The central motif of the completely preserved pelta no. F:1 is a punched whirl with curved spokes subdividing the circle into three areas which are left in blank silver, and three which are punch-decorated and gilt. At both sides of the whirl there are three roundels, a gilt one in the middle that is flanked by two in silver (see box on whirls).

Hinge-linked strap junctions

Four hinge-linked strap junctions are preserved, including the two mounts connecting bit rings, cheekpieces and noseband mentioned above. Two strap junctions with four attachment plates (fig. 16; nos. F:3–4) connected cheekpieces to browband, headpiece and throatlash. They are classified as type 9C by Ørsnes (1994:238, 277, Fig. 36).

Strap ends

Only one strap end is preserved (fig. 16; no. F:13). The front is covered with a punch decorated silver sheet. The concentric semicircles are identical to those of the pelta-shaped silver covers (nos. F:1–2, F:25) and it cannot be excluded that they were punched into the silver plate only when the pelta-shaped silver plate was fastened to the axe-shaped pendants. It is unknown whether there was one or more strap ends. We have not found parallels to its shape.

Hinge-linked strap connectors

Including the already mentioned strap connectors with axe-shaped pendants, the headstall had four strap connectors. The other two (fig. 16; nos. F:9–10) were probably placed in the check-pieces (reconstruction in Fabech & Näsman chapter 17). They are constructed like the other strap mounts but their centre piece is rectangular.

Summary

The headstall of Fulltofta is unique. It sports two axe-shaped pendants, which are unknown elsewhere in the Scandinavian record. The date of the bridle probably is late 4th or early 5th century, period Scand-C3/D1. The bridle is not much worn but has a repair. The pelta-shaped silver covers, which are decorated in developed "Sösdala style", reveal that the deposition took place in Scand-D1. For lack of comparative material the provenance of the bronze bridle is difficult to discuss: Scanian, Scandinavian, Continental, or provincial Roman? The two axe-shaped pendants indicate a production on the Continent, possibly in the Danubian basin. However, the two silver covers are probably a later Scanian contribution.

Whirls

Interestingly a whirl is found sketched on the back of one of the strap junctions of the headstall Sösdala I (no. I:15). It has twelve curved spokes (Dal chapter 6 fig 14). The whirl (*Wirbelrosette* in German) is an old sun motif in Mediterranean art and was introduced to Scandinavia in the middle of the 4th century, carved in a curved wooden plank from one of the Nydam boats. It is decorated with a chip-carved four-petal flower and a whirl (Rieck 2003 fig. 10). It is supposed to belong to the so-called fir-ship and it is now assumed that it was deposited on the same occasion as the better-preserved "Nydam boat", which according to dendro-dates was built AD 310/320 and deposited just before or around the middle of the 4th century AD (Rieck 2016). Whirls decorate typical carriers of "Sösdala style": mounts of horse tack from Sösdala and Fulltofta, a silver sheet brooch from Eidsten, Norway (Salin 1904 Abb. 493; Hougen 1936 fig. 8; Magnus 2015 fig. 6), and a number of shield-shaped pendants (Magnus 1975:74,78, fig. 19, 21, 23; 2015 fig. 7). Bente Magnus dates the pendants to early 5th century (Scand-D1) and does not know a use of the symbol later than the middle of the century. In her opinion the function was apotropaic. Whirls have the most well-known Scandinavian occurrence on the famous picture stones of Gotland (Lindqvist 1941–42:91; Fig. 1–29; Nylén & Lamm 1988). Lindqvist dismissed interpretations of the whirl as a depiction of a shield. He also rejected the assumption that it is sun symbol, but Nylén & Lamm accept this, but neither goes into any depth. So did Wilhelm Holmqvist in an analysis of the background of the Gotlandic whirls (1952). The material available to him consisted mostly of publications of Roman floor mosaics and there he found a fitting background. He concluded that one or a few craftsmen from Gotland had travelled in the Roman world and later composed their pictures on the basis of what they remembered having seen. But he did not discuss the meaning contemporary spectators may have given the Roman motif. Today a much more varied archaeological record can be searched. However, this is not the place for an in-depth study of whirls, so I will restrict myself to a number of examples.

Whirls are known since long before the Birth of Christ, e.g. six-spoked whirls in the bottom of Greek sieves found in south Russia (Pfommer 1983 Abb. 1, 6). A whirl is found at the centre of a richly decorated silver plate from a hoard of ritual silver vessels found at Wettingen in Switzerland and buried around AD 250 (Simonett 1946 Taf. 1). The whirl is interpreted as *Sinnbild des Lebens* (symbol of life). A sarcophagus from Jerash, Jordan (ancient Gerasa), has two peltae and two whirls in relief on its side (photo *Rome Art Lover*). In the archaeological museum of Split a pagan Roman grave-stone from the 2nd/3rd century AD has a whirl in a central, probably apotropaic position (photo *Ubi erat lupa*). Also in early Christian art, whirls are used as an apotropaic symbol, found e.g. at the entry to Syrian dwellings and on capitals and chancel slabs in Syrian churches (Wulff 1914 Abb. 252, 256, etc.). In the Roman world the whirl was a widespread decorative and apotropaic sun symbol; it is obviously not an exclusively heathen symbol.

Among whirls that in time and space are more relevant to Sösdala and Fulltofta one can mention a whirl decorating a typical provincial Roman belt set from Oudenburg, Belgium, from a 4th century grave (Böhme 1979 fig. 121a) and a whirl on the grip of a comb found in an early 5th century grave at Grafenwörth, Lower Austria (Stadler 1987 Taf. 54).

Recently Anders Andrén interpreted the punched decoration of the pelta-shaped pendant cover of Fulltofta "as a kind of abbreviated version of the Gotlandic solar cycle" referring to his analysis of the picture stones of Gotland (Andrén 2014:140) The argument is part of an update of the long since assumed sun cult of the Nordic Bronze Age with continuation until AD 535–536 (but without any reference to the studies of Montelius 1900; 1917). Andrén's ideas are followed up by Magnus (2015). Roman connections are mentioned but Andrén does not follow this track further. This is a pity, since it seems obvious to us that the whirl motif is part of a "package" of Roman influences. The Roman impact on "barbarian/Germanic" decorative handicraft is the root of the "Sösdala style" in the second half of the 4th century. And the whirl motif disappeared with the "Sösdala style" around the middle of the 5th century as a result of the growing popularity of chip-carved decoration of the Nydam style that ended in the dominating style I of Salin. The whirl was replaced by chip-carved spirals arranged as "rosettes" The only later occurrence mentioned by Magnus is two small chip-carved whirls on an early relief brooch from Gotland (Nerman 1935 no. 347; Näsman 1984 Anhang 2, Nr. 12). By then Roman motifs had lost the support of a strong Roman empire.

Apart from the interpretation of whirls as sun symbols, one should not neglect the obvious association of shield-shaped pendants and some strap junctions with real shields (Sösdala I no. I:14; Finnestorp see Nordqvist chapter 11 fig. 9–10; Untersiebenbrunn see Kazanski & Mastykova chapter 15 fig. 3). The pelta shape itself was originally derived from a Greek shield type and when applied on other objects by long tradition carrying an apotropaic meaning. The strength of the pelta as an apotropaic symbol was doubled when the object was decorated with shield-like motifs such as concentric circles, whirls, four or six-petal flowers, etc.

Introduction to saddles

After more than 20 years it is still true that our knowledge about saddles in Late Roman and Migration Period Europe is very fragmentary (Ørsnes 1994:272: cf. Kiss 1984; Quast 1993:445). The first publications devoted to finds of prehistoric saddle remains in Sweden came in 1929 but the saddle finds at Sösdala were only mentioned in a footnote (Norberg 1929b footnote 25). None of the finds that Norberg treated came from informative contexts; they were all accidental finds made by laymen and gave few hints as to how the saddles were constructed. Not until 1949–51 a complete set of saddle mounts was found *in situ* during the excavation of a burial mound at Högom; unfortunately it would take 40 years before the well-documented excavation was published (Ramqvist chapter 10; 1992). This is the only excavated find of a Scandinavian ring saddle and as a grave find very informative. The saddle remains found at Sösdala clearly belong to a saddle constructed like the Högom one.

The mounted warrior was buried at Högom one or two generations after the Sösdala I saddles were dismantled. However, it is assumed that the saddle was old when put in the grave in the late 5th century (Ramqvist 1992:85), so maybe less than a generation separates the production of the saddles. Ramqvist has described the remains of the Högom saddle in detail. Based on his description and reconstruction the saddle can be deconstructed in its functional parts. There remain large parts of the pommel and smaller parts of the cantle (Ramqvist chapter 10 fig. 2–5). Pommel and cantle were given stability by wooden laths. The pommel wood was approx. 4 cm thick at the top and wider at the base. A leather cover was stuffed with cereal straw. No indisputable traces of saddle bars were recorded during the excavation but are assumed in the reconstruction drawings of pommel and cantle. Consequently it is not known how the seat was worked out and Ramqvist refrained from a reconstruction of a complete saddle. But it seems certain that it consisted of a leather cover stuffed with straw with wooden bows in pommel and cantle, and it can be assumed that it also had horizontal wooden bars of a kind, laths or boards.

Saddle rings were stapled to pommel and cantle, one on each side and four in all. They do not penetrate the saddle boards but are fastened only to the pommel and to the cantle. Four short cast bronze mounts helped to keep the rings in place and they are decorative as well. All have ends shaped like animal heads. They are similar but only identical in pairs, at the pommel and at the cantle. On the pommel the short mounts were extended with bronze rails to protect the leather on the upper part. The combination of short saddle mounts and rails at the pommel of the Högom saddle is approx. 27 cm long and can be compared to whole long saddle mounts in other finds: Finnestorp 28 cm, Fulltofta approx. 28 cm, Hassle-Bösarp 26 cm, Sösdala 27–30 cm and Vennebo 27 cm. They are all bent in more or less similar curves and probably had the same function at a high pommel (Finnestorp: Nordqvist chapter 11 fig. 18; Fulltofta no. F:24; Hassle-Bösarp: Stjernquist 1974:28,38, fig. 20; Sösdala nos. I:115, 117–118, 122–129, 201–202, 213, 215; Vennebo: Stjernquist 1974 fig. 26; Arrhenius 1987 no. XI,7i).

At Högom remains of a leather strap were found on one of the saddle rings (Ramqvist chapter 10 fig. 7), indicating that something was tied to the saddle rings; Ramqvist suggests that it could be breast collar or breeching. As many as four girth buckles were found, grouped two by two. Ramqvist does not explain how the girths were fastened to the saddle. I guess two of the buckles can be accounted for by two girths. The other two may have been used to regulate breast plate and breeching.

The metal parts of the Högom saddle can be summarised as follows

- two short saddle mounts-cum-rails for the pommel
- two short saddle mounts for the cantle
- four saddle rings with staples
- four strap buckles

Ramqvist's analysis of the finds at Högom and his reconstruction of the saddle contradict the first and often reproduced reconstruction of a ring saddle by Rune Norberg (fig. 21), which he based on finds from Kanalgatan in Jönköping, Småland (1929a:10–11 fig. 14–16; 1929b fig. 7–8; 1931 fig. 14). He placed the long saddle mounts at a higher cantle and the short ones at a lower pommel, i.e. the opposite of Högom. He assumed erroneously that all

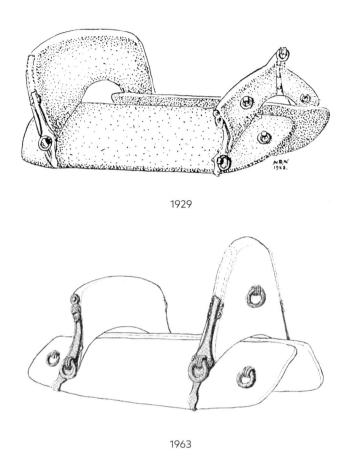

1929

1963

Fig. 21. Kanalgatan. Reconstructions of the tree of a ring saddle based on the mounts found in Jönköping. After Norberg 1929a fig. 14 and Arbman 1963 fig. 45.

five mounts and eleven saddle rings came from the same saddle. In a Sösdala perspective, it seems more likely that at least three saddles are represented.

Many years later Norberg was given the possibility to revise his reconstruction when Holger Arbman wished to use a reconstruction by Norberg to illustrate his contribution to a popular book about the history of Jönköping (1963:78–84). Unfortunately this publication was mainly of local interest and Norberg's much revised reconstruction never received the scholarly attention it deserved.

Now Norberg placed the short mounts on the cantle and the long mounts on a high pommel (fig. 21b). In Arbman's text one can read that the Kanalgatan finds represent more than one saddle. Norberg's own explanation of the 1963 reconstruction is missing, but now it is in accordance with Ramqvist's Högom reconstruction that consequently

can replace the Kanalgatan reconstruction as a "ring saddle standard". On the basis of a saddle of "Högom type", an attempt will be made to sort the large Sösdala material of saddle remains into individual saddles (see below and find catalogue). Among many saddle mounts from Finnestorp, at least one seems to represent a saddle of "Högom type" (Nordqvist chapter 11 fig. 22).

In 1929 Norberg suggested that the large saddle rings were placed in the heavy saddle mounts and used to keep the saddle in place (1929b:104). However, because he then believed all eleven rings came from the same saddle, he added later in the paper that perhaps additional rings once were used to tie baggage to the saddle (1929b:112).

An archaeological experiment using Norberg's first saddle reconstruction took place at Lejre in 1970 (Krogh 1970). Unfortunately Krogh used Norberg's reconstruction uncritically. Later studies of saddle remains from Ejsbøl (below) and Högom (above) make the results of the experiment a thing of the past, however interesting some of the practicalities of his experimental reconstruction are (see also criticism in Sundkvist 1992:131–132). Krogh followed Norberg and fastened all eleven saddle rings to the saddle. Four were used to fasten breast collar and breeching. Three were used for the baggage at the pommel. The last four at the cantle were used to fasten sword and quiver to the saddle. The low pommel of the Norberg/Krogh reconstructions is contradicted by the many long saddle mounts found at Sösdala and other sites. And as reported above, Norberg had himself already revised this detail years before Krogh made his experiments.

Norberg's use of historic Swedish packsaddles as a prototype for his 1929 reconstruction of Migration Period ring saddles was uncritically accepted by Birgit Arrhenius and she described them as "a kind of packsaddle characterized by its many ring-mounts in which burdens could be fastened" (1983:63). Later saddles from the Vendel Period with high pommels have no rings and they are differently interpreted as parade saddles "for a warrior, needing a steady seat to be able to handle a spear while mounted." She assumes that the saddle type with high pommel ("high frames") was derived from the Huns but only indirectly, since she believed – based on the low pommel of Norberg's first reconstruction – that saddles with high pommel did not occur in Scandinavia before the Vendel Period, i.e. the late 6th and early 7th century (obviously the Högom saddle was not known to her in 1983). She suggested that post-Hunnic saddles like the one from a late 5th century grave II at Apahida, Romania (Horedt & Protase 1972), formed the background to the Vendel Period saddles in Sweden. Similar views are expressed by Henrik Thrane in a publication of stray finds of a saddle mount and a saddle ring from Funen (1983).

Informed by Högom and analyses of earlier Scandinavian saddle mounts like Ejsbøl and Sösdala, it now seems certain that the Scandinavian Vendel Period saddles grew from a domestic saddle tradition deeply rooted in the Late Roman Iron Age (Scand-C1b–C2) and that the saddle type continuously changed its appearance following international stylistic trends (cf. Ramqvist chapter 10). The early introduction of saddles with high pommel was according to Sundkvist (chapter 9) a greater improvement for riding than the later introduction of the stirrup.

Mounts and rings of nine ritually distorted saddles found at Ejsbøl are important for the understanding of how Scandinavian ring saddles developed (Ørsnes 1988:93–95, pl 184–190; 1994:272, Fig. 56–57). According to Ørsnes's analysis only two saddles had both rings and mounts, seven had rings but no mounts. In an early popular publication an Ejsbøl saddle was reconstructed with a low cantle and a pommel that is only slightly higher (Ørsnes 1984:31). Later he suggested, unfortunately without reconstruction drawings, that the short mounts (13–14 cm long) because of the bend were placed on a high pommel and the long flatter mounts (22–25 cm long) were placed on a lower rounded cantle (echoed by Lau 2014:190–191; Fundliste 33); he presented no real argument for how he reached a conclusion opposite to the evidence of Högom. A reconstruction drawing based on Ørsnes's ideas was produced in the 1990s by Jørgen Andersen for the archaeology exhibition at Museum Sønderjylland in Haderslev; it was preceded by literature studies and discussed with several archaeologists (fig. 22). On the evidence of Högom and with the support of saddles from Sösdala and Fulltofta (see below), I suggest nevertheless that the long mounts from Ejsbøl were placed on a high pommel and the short ones on a low cantle.

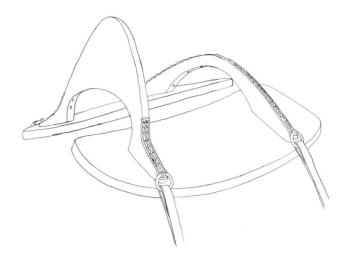

Fig. 22. Ejsbøl. A reconstruction of the tree of "Sattel I". ©Jørgen Andersen, Museum Sønderjylland – Arkæologi Haderslev.

The Ejsbøl mounts are made of ribbon-like bronze sheets. The edges are raised by narrow bronze strips which are soldered on. As decoration a row of studs with lens-shaped heads are placed in the central groove. A few of them are longer rivets that fastened the mount to the pommel or cantle. Presumably it is correct when Ørsnes wrote that the weak mounts of thin bronze plate mainly were decorative, but they were nevertheless firmly attached to the pommel and cantle with 2–3 long rivets with washers. The lower end of each mount is rounded with a central hole for a saddle ring, which Ørsnes assumed was used to fasten the saddle (fig. 22). Rings without mounts were used on simpler saddles. The staples of the rings show that the wood of the pommel and cantle was approx. 3–4 cm thick. Based on photos of mounts with staples and rivets I estimate that the wooden laths of the pommel and cantle were between 3 and 6 cm thick.

In a later paper Ørsnes briefly discussed similar mounts in the depositions of military equipment in Jutland at Vingsted, Vingre Mølle and Thorsbjerg, to which may be added a similar mount found at Hassle-Bösarp in Scania (1994:272; cf. Stjernquist 1974: 43). The length of the long ribbon-like mounts is at Ejsbøl 22–25 cm, at Hassle-Bösarp 26 cm, Thorsbjerg 27 cm and Vingsted 24–25 cm (Lau 2014 Fundliste 33). They belong to the same saddle type, an "Ejsbøl type", dated to period Scand-C2/C3 (Lau 2014:191, however, dates Vingsted to Scand C1b/

C2). The long mounts, according to Ørsnes (and Lau), were placed on the cantle, the short ones on the pommel. The publication of new finds of saddle mounts and rings from Ejsbøl (Jørgensen & Andersen 2014:130–132) does not add much to the discussion. Important is Ørsnes's chronological observation (1994:272) that the early ring saddles with high pommel and cantle are more than 100 years earlier than the appearance of mounted Huns in Europe. So the often reiterated opinion that the Scandinavian saddle type had its origin in Hunnic saddles is simply erroneous.

The last contribution to the typochronology of Scandinavian ring saddles is found in a publication of the offering of military equipment at Thorsbjerg (Lau 2014:66–78; 179–193). Two 27 cm long ribbon-like mounts are of interest in this context. They are similar to the Ejsbøl mounts (Lau 2014:420, Taf. 62). The lower end is rounded with a central hole for a staple with a saddle ring. The raised edges and the groove are punch decorated. In the groove a row of studs with lens-shaped heads is inserted; a few of them are longer rivets that fastened the mount to the pommel (I believe) or to the cantle (Lau's opinion). The rivets demonstrate that the wooden lath was originally between 2 and 5 cm thick. The two mounts are dated to Scand-C2/C3 (Lau 2014:257).

Lau's review of saddle development takes us far back in the Roman Iron Age. The earliest evidence of saddles is indirect, mounts that decorated and strengthened breast collars and breechings, which are pointless without a saddle. In Illerup the earliest saddle finds are dated to weapon group 5–6, period Scand-C1b, c. AD 200. The earliest evidence of a saddle with rings is four rings with round mounts and staples that were found with mounts for breast-plate and breeching (fig. 23; Carnap-Bornheim & Ilkjær 1996:112–117). According to the publication of the Illerup saddles, the rings were used to fasten the saddles. Based on the rich assemblage of early saddle tack in Illerup two different saddle types are assumed: a simple stuffed (?leather) cushion, and a more complex saddle that consisted of a stuffed cushion of leather, strengthened by a slender frame of wooden laths and furnished with four saddle rings (Carnap-Bornheim & Ilkjær 1996:272–272). Also somewhat later saddles with rings but no mounts

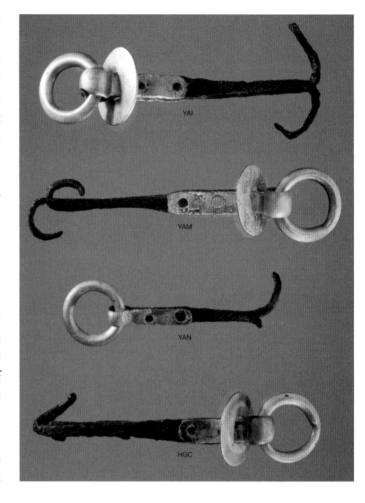

Fig. 23. Illerup. The earliest known saddle rings from c. AD 200. Approx. 3:5. After Carnap-Bornheim & Ilkjær 1996 Taf. 115. Photo Preben Dehlholm, ©Moesgård Museum.

are present in Ejsbøl (above) and Skedemosse (Hagberg 1967:73,77; Taf. 6). Saddles with saddle rings with small round mounts or no mounts at all are here called the "Illerup type".

The saddle type with high pommel and lower cantle is generally assumed to have been introduced in Europe by mounted nomads. Since it now is a fact that the Huns of the late 4th and early 5th centuries came too late, the Sarmatians have emerged as an attractive alternative. Contacts between Sarmatians and "Germanic" elites are recorded for the 3rd century, and the central Danubian basin in present-day Hungary stands out as an important contact zone (Lau 2014:76–78; 256–258). The role of the

Roman cavalry as a conceivable intermediary between Nomadic and sedentary "Germanic" horsemen is at present enigmatic (cf. Ramqvist chapter 10). Hard saddles with metallic mounts existed in the Roman Empire, as exemplified by a grave find at Sarry in Gaul (Kazanski & Mastykova chapter 15 fig. 11).

In our opinion, however, it seems probable that the Scandinavian ring saddle is an internal development of external prototypes. Possibly cushion saddles of Roman origin transformed under the influence of Nomadic (?Sarmatian) saddles and developed into saddles with some kind of wooden support (Sundkvist chapter 9). At present it seems to be a South Scandinavian idea that saddles could be fastened by tying straps to metal rings.

A number of saddle finds are dated to the Late Roman Iron Age in a recent survey (Lau 2014:66–78; cf. Quast 1993:443–445) but the evidence is only indirect, consisting of girth buckles and mounts of breast collars and breechings; nothing seems to remain of the saddles (Lau 2014 Abb. 54, 111, 116). From the early Migration Period a large number of saddles are recorded in Nomadic ("Alanic" or "Hunnic") contexts; the evidence consists of decorative gilt silver or gold sheets that give an idea of how the front and pommel of the saddle were shaped (Bóna 1991:177–179; 244–245; Abb. 23–24). In the post-Hunnic second half of the 5th century only few saddles are recorded. In the wealthy burial at Blučina (South Moravia) mounts are preserved that were nailed to a presumably high pommel (Kiss 1984 Abb. 3). In the second grave from Apahida, three snaffles and mounts for a saddle with straps were found in the remains of a wooden box (Horedt & Protase 1972). The saddle mounts are all ornamental and tell very little about the construction apart from the two large eagle mounts which indicate that the pommel was high. From the late 5th and the 6th century some saddles are recorded in graves, but in most cases the only trace of a saddle is a girth buckle (Quast 1993:446). Well-preserved remains of pommel and cantle were found in a 6th century grave at Oberflacht (Baden-Württemberg). Holes for leather thongs indicate they were tied to boards, so the basic structure of the saddle tree is the same as the Nomadic saddles mentioned above, but the pommel and cantle are very low (Quast 1993 Abb. 1–3).

Sösdala saddles

Framed by early Illerup and Ejsbøl saddle types and a late Högom type, the saddle remains from Sösdala and Fulltofta will be discussed below. The best Sösdala evidence about ring saddles is offered by Carl Mellton's excavation in 1929 of mounts from the so-called find spot III and by saddle mounts found together in 1930 at the so-called find spot IV (Fabech chapter 1). Based primarily on the shape of eleven long saddle mounts, the term "Sösdala type" will be used to characterise an early Migration Period phase in ring saddle development. Other long mounts belonging to saddles of "Sösdala type" are found at Finnestorp, Hassle-Bösarp and Vennebo (cf. Stjernquist 1974:38). Two more finds of long mounts of this type demonstrate that the saddle type was relatively common. Two long mounts found at Kanalgatan have the upper end cut off and unfortunately lost (Norberg 1929a fig.1:I–II). In a cairn at Snosarve, Gotland, two fragments of saddle mounts were found in 1857 (Norberg 1929b fig. 15–16; Nerman 1935 nos. 555–556). One has a shape so similar to the Sösdala mount no. I:121 that it can be included in the "Sösdala" type. The saddle mounts from Fulltofta are however considered to belong to a "Fulltofta type" (below). The shape of a saddle mount from Tranemo, Västergötland, is unique and does not belong to the "Sösdala type" (SHM no. 8 232; Norberg 1929a fig. 12; Stjernquist 1974:43, fig. 27).

Many small objects and fragments found at find spots II and IV cannot be placed in saddles with certainty; they are described and depicted in the catalogue.

Saddle 1

At find spot IV an apparently almost complete set of saddle mounts was found by workers (fig. 24; cf. find catalogue Saddle 1). The homogeneity of the material speaks in favour of the assumption that a saddle with straps was cut to pieces here (cf. Norberg 1931:108). What remains are two 29–30 cm long saddle mounts for the pommel, one 13 cm short bent saddle mount for the cantle, six almost identical saddle rings, four with a diameter of 46–47 mm and up to 82 mm long staple legs, two with a diameter of only 43 mm and staple legs up to 66 mm. The four larger rings were presumably held in place by saddle mounts on the pommel and the cantle. Where the two extra saddle rings

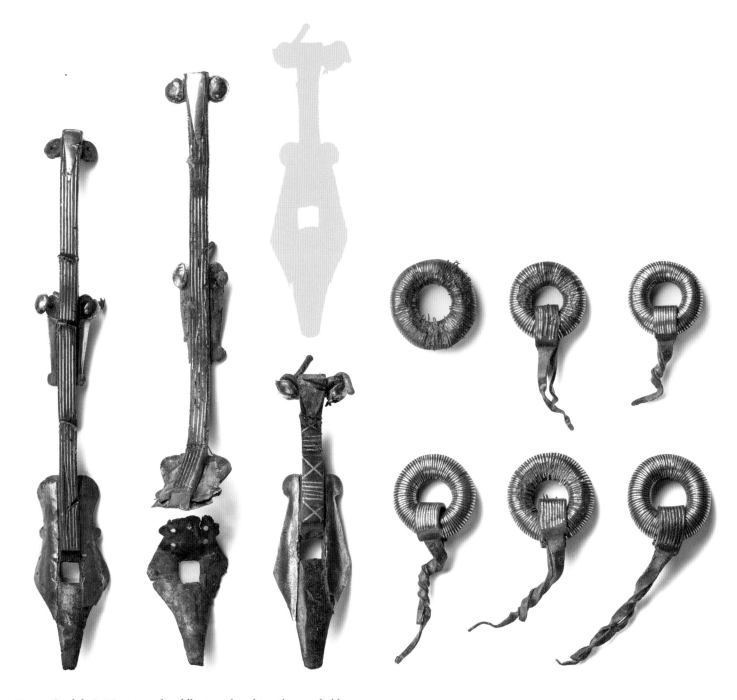

Fig. 24. Sösdala I. Mounts and saddle rings found together, probably from the same saddle, "saddle 1". A short mount is missing. Photo Daniel Lindskog.

were placed is unknown, as is their function; perhaps they were stapled to the pommel or cantle to fasten baggage. One of the silver sheets (no. I:176) that decorate mount no. I:213 was found in 1929 at find spot II. Two fragments of a gilt silver pendant (no. I:238) from find spot IV fit a fragmented pendant in find spot I (no. I:7). This demonstrates that bits and pieces of horse tack were spread over a larger area during the ritual activity. At find spot IV a combination of mounts comparable to the Högom saddle is found:

- two long saddle mounts for the pommel
- two short saddle mounts (one missing) for the cantle
- four saddle rings with staples for the saddle mounts

- two somewhat smaller saddle ring with staples (for ?baggage)
- strap buckles are absent (A possible pin of a buckle (no. I:114) and two rust lumps (now unidentified) that Mellton labelled "possible buckle" are the only weak evidence of girth buckles. In our reconstruction buckles are replaced by two hooks and by straps tied to the rings (Fabech & Näsman chapter 17)

Saddles with mounts shaped like the long mounts of "saddle 1" are called "Sösdala type". The lengths of the preserved rivets give us an indication how thick the wood in pommel and cantle was. A rivet on no. I:213 was once driven through wood 31 mm thick, and a rivet in no. I:215 went through a pommel 29 mm thick (fig. 25). This is in accordance with observations from Högom and Ejsbøl (above).

The finds of horse tack from Vennebo include an intact long saddle mount of bronze, decorated in silver (SHM 6 511:20) with similarities to the mounts of "saddle 1". Both the size and the bend of the Vennebo mount (SHM 6 511:20) resemble other long mounts (Finnestorp, Hassle-Bösarp) and they certainly belong to the same saddle type, the "Sösdala type".

The short mount has a sharp bend like the cantle mounts found at Högom (fig. 26). It probably held a saddle ring at the cantle. The cantle remains of Högom do not tell us much about the shape or whether it leaned back to give the rider a better seat (Ramqvist chapter 10; 1992:82). Based on old nomadic saddles (Bemmann 2012) and old depictions of saddled horses, e.g. Emperor Taizong's horses, we assume that the cantle leaned back (fig. 27).

Among the finds from find spot IV an important stump of leather strap is remarkable (no. I:229, fig. 28). It is an end of a strap, 28 mm broad, decorated with studs with silver caps and a silver-on-bronze mount (for straps decorated with *Silbernieten*, see Quast 2007:57). A narrower 20 mm broad strap is riveted to the underside. It seems to be a narrower, probably undecorated continuation of the broad strap. The strap fragment reveals that the many silver-on-bronze mounts probably once decorated leather straps of a saddle (from find spot II nos. I:113, I:134–144 and from find spot IV nos. I:242–243, I:247) We believe the leather strap end comes from a breast collar or a breeching of "saddle

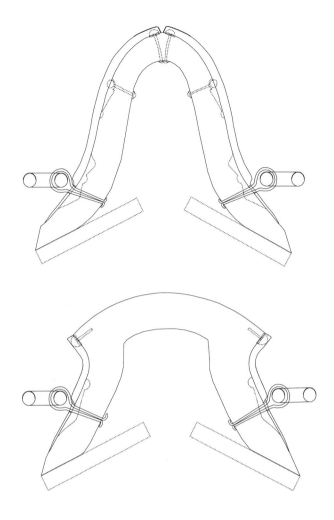

Fig. 25. Sösdala I. The mounts and saddle rings with staples of "saddle 1" applied on pommel and cantle based on the Högom find. The presence of saddle boards is uncertain. Drawing Erika Rosengren.

1". Probably also two hooks (nos. I:132–133) are from find spot IV. We suggest that they were used to facilitate the saddling; one end of the breast collar and breeching was hooked to a saddle ring, and a narrow strap at the other end was tied to a ring on the opposite side (reconstruction in Fabech & Näsman chapter 17). A sample of leather strap no. I:149 was determined to have been made from *Bos taurus* (cow) and the strap may be from the saddle tack (for analyses, see Dal chapter 6).The short distance between finds spots I and IV as well as crossing finds make it tempting to assume that the exclusive "saddle 1" was used on the same horse as the parade bridle.

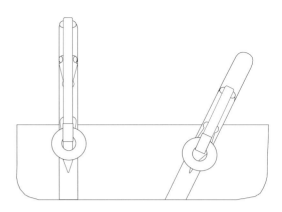

Fig. 26. Sösdala I. A short mount for the cantle of "saddle 1" (no. I:217). Photo Daniel Lindskog.

Fig. 27. Sösdala I. Reconstruction of the tree of "saddle 1". The presence of saddle boards is uncertain. Drawing Erika Rosengren.

Saddle 2

When investigating at find spot II, Mellton found and recorded remains of a saddle approx. 3 m away at a site later called find spot III. He found *in situ* two saddle rings, which had been cut-off from the saddle and thrown on the ground together with two 27 cm long saddle mounts that seem still to have been kept together by the leather cover (Fabech chapter 1 fig. 6). The combination of mounts and rings belongs to the "Sösdala type" and was probably used on a high pommel of "Högom type". Two smaller saddle rings that had been pulled out were also found *in situ* nearby (nos. I:205–206); possibly they belong to the same saddle (fig. 29).

The shape of the lower end of the long mounts have their only match in two short saddle mounts found by workers at the nearby find spot II (nos. I:125–126). The assumption that they come from the cantle of the same saddle finds support in the fact that two of the saddle rings from find spot II (nos. I:170–171) are identical to the one Mellton found at find spot III (nos. I:203–204). Thus saddle remains found at find spots II and III can be combined in a way comparable to Sösdala "saddle 1" (and Högom):

- two long saddle mounts for the pommel
- two short saddle mounts for the cantle
- four saddle rings with staples for the saddle mounts
- two smaller saddle ring with staples (for ?baggage)
- strap buckles are absent

The long mounts of Sösdala "saddle 2" are simply hammered out of heavy Cu-alloy rods, 7/9 × 11 mm thick. But the size and bend is the same as the more elaborate mounts of Sösdala "saddle 1" and Vennebo and they certainly represent the same "Sösdala type". Simple long mounts of iron with the same size and bend are known from Finnestorp (Nordqvist chapter 11 fig. 18) and Hassle-Bösarp (Stjernquist 1974 fig. 20), reinforcing the impression that such long mounts were the standard type of mounts for a pommel in period Scand-D1 of the early 5th century AD.

Saddle 3

A third saddle consists of two 30 cm long mounts from find spot II for the pommel (nos. I:117, 119); they also belong to the "Sösdala type". The lower end of a third broken mount is similar (no. I:127); it is uncertain but possible that the mount comes from the cantle of the same saddle (fig. 30).

The upper end of the long mounts is given a simple stylised shape of an animal with two legs and a head; for a modern spectator it looks like a lizard. Lizard-like animals are found on some objects from Scand-D1 such as the Mejlby brooch, Jutland (Näsman chapter 5 fig. 3), the golden neckring from Hannenov, Falster (Brøndsted 1963:292) and the golden neck collar from Ålleberg, Västergötland (Salin 1904 Abb. 499). Similar simple animal heads appear on brooches from Scand-D1 and D2 but for lack of thorough studies I refrain from a deeper chronological discussion. A broken saddle mount from Finnestorp (Nordqvist chapter 11 fig. 25) is a distant parallel to the Sösdala "lizard". More or less related animal heads are found on other Finnestorp saddle mounts (Nordqvist chapter 11 fig. 19–22), some are simple as the Sösdala heads, others are more detailed and resemble the mounts of Högom; perhaps this reflects the time span of manufacture of the Finnestorp mounts.

Saddle 4

This saddle is a very simple smithery product like "saddle 2"; the two long mounts of "Sösdala type" were hammered out of 5 × 10 mm thick rods of Cu-alloy (nos. I:122, 129). Both mounts are cut to pieces but the most complete was once at least 28 cm long. A short saddle mount (no. I:124) is hammered out of a 4 × 8 mm thick Cu-alloy rod. It looks like the two short mounts included in "saddle 2" above, but its lower end has a different shape resembling what is left of the end of the long mount no. I:122. So tentatively I assume that it comes from the cantle of the same saddle.

Saddles 5, 6 and 7

Three saddles are represented only by a single long mount, probably all of "Sösdala type". "Saddle 5" is represented by a worn and repaired long mount from an exclusive saddle with mounts decorated with silver sheets and delicate incrustation (fig. 31). It can be compared to "saddle 1" in quality. The saddle rings were also probably decorated in silver. The upper end of a long mount of "saddle 6" is cut off (no. I:121). The end of the preserved lower part is shaped like an animal nose but there is no animal head. A saddle ring with staple is left in place, revealing that the wood of the pommel had been approx. 27 mm thick. Similar saddle rings are not found among the loose saddle rings. The saddle was of high quality. Only the cut-off upper half of a long mount is left of "saddle 7" (no. I:131; it does not fit no. I:121). It is well formed and probably this saddle too was of high quality.

Saddle rings

In all 33 saddle rings were found at Sösdala I. Six were found together with matching mounts as part of "saddle 1".

Fig. 28. Sösdala I. Front and back of the preserved end of a leather strap (no I:229). Decorated with a double bronze and silver mount and studs with silver caps. Photo Daniel Lindskog.

Six other rings probably belong to "saddle 2". A single ring is still sitting in its long mount, labelled "saddle 6". The remaining 20 saddle rings cannot be attributed to any of the specific saddles above. Similar rings occur in combinations of four (twice), three and two (twice) and probably come from five different saddles (fig. 32). Five single rings lack equals and could represent as many saddles. Four of the seven saddles represented by saddle mounts lack saddle rings, but unfortunately it is not possible to match loose mounts with loose rings. It must also be remembered that one cannot exclude the possibility that some saddles had rings but no mounts (cf. mountless saddles of "Illerup type" above). So the 33 saddle rings may come from as many as thirteen different saddles, but one cannot exclude that saddle rings with different shape were used on the

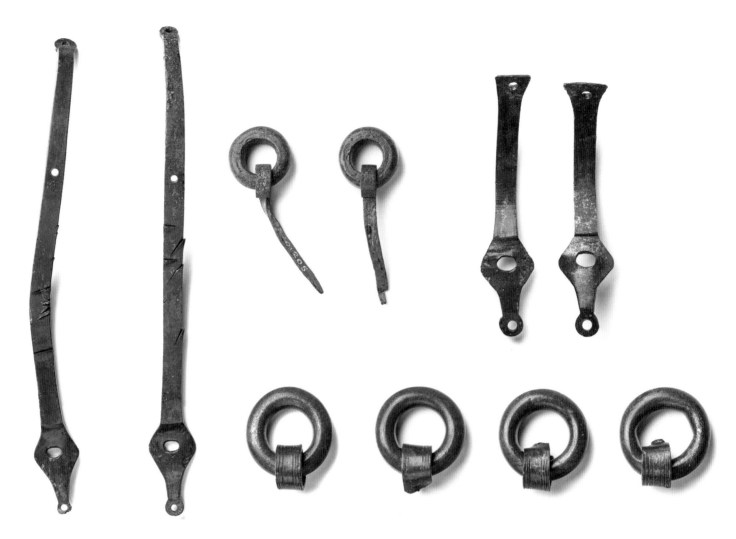

Fig. 29. Sösdala I. Mounts and saddle rings from the same saddle, "saddle 2". Left finds from find spot III (nos. I:201–206). Right finds from find spot II (nos. I:125, 126, 170, 171). Photo Daniel Lindskog.

same saddle (cf. the fourth different saddle ring at Högom; Ramqvist 1992:80 and the deviating rings nos. I:205–206 of "saddle 2").

A complete set of four similar rings come from the same saddle (nos. I:154–157) but it is not possible to identify matching mounts with certainty. They have staple loops decorated with sheet silver and with the same moulding. Two more saddle rings have the staple loops covered with silver sheet and they represent a saddle of different quality (no. I:112, 159). A saddle ring without staple (no. I:164) looks like the preceding one and may belong the same set. Four simpler saddle rings may come from the same saddle (nos. I:153, 158, 160, 168). Their staples are similar, but only one

has a loop covered with a now loose plain silver sheet (no. I:158). So possibly they all once were covered with silver sheet. Three sets of silver decorated saddle rings thus come from exclusive saddles; perhaps one set belongs to the silver decorated "saddle 5", but it is impossible to tell which one.

Three saddle rings are similar (nos. I:163, I:165–166); two of them have staples with an unusual cast honeycomb pattern and certainly come from the same saddle. Two saddle rings from the same saddle have a heavy triangular cross-section and a staple loop with moulding (nos. I:151–152). Four rings are single and perhaps they are all that is left of four saddles (nos. I:161, 162, 167, 169).

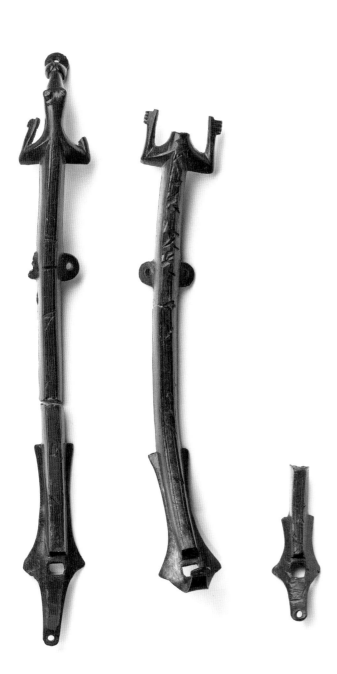

Fig. 30. Sösdala I. Mounts, two long and one short, of "saddle 3" (nos. I:117, 119, 127) and the "lizard" from the front. Photo Daniel Lindskog.

The Fulltofta saddle

At Fulltofta a distorted short saddle mount was found in 1896 (no. F:23) and a photo was published by Norberg (1929b fig. 14) but the significance of the mount remained unnoticed (fig. 33). In fact it is a kind of missing link in between saddles of "Ejsbøl type" and "Sösdala type". Its ribbon-like upper part has remarkable similarities to early saddle mounts of "Ejsbøl type" but the lower end is not rounded but is given a flat rhomboid shape like Migration Period saddle mounts of "Sösdala type" (Finnestorp, Hassle-Bösarp, Kanalgatan and Vennebo). The ribbon-like up-

per part is not made of bronze sheet like the "Ejsbøl type" but is cast. The decoration is similar with a central row of lens-shaped studs as on saddle mounts dated to Scand-C2/ C3 (Ejsbøl, Hassle-Bösarp, Thorsbjerg, Vingre Mølle and Vingsted). The studs are covered with lens-shaped silver caps. Its original bent shape is distorted as a result of the ritual destruction. It is only approx. 14–15 cm long and probably it originally had a bend that once fitted a cantle like the three short mounts from Sösdala (nos. I:124–126). In 1896 some other finds from the saddle were recovered: two saddle rings, one with staple (nos. F:21–22) and two

Fig. 31. Sösdala I. Only a long mount is preserved of "saddle 5" (no. I:115). Photo Daniel Lindskog.

strap hooks (nos. F:16–17). We know only one other find with strap hooks, Sösdala I (see above Sösdala "saddle 1" nos. I:132–133), a lucky coincidence supporting a date of the deposition of the Fulltofta saddle to the early Migration Period, Scand-D1, but its manufacture could well be in the 4th century, in Scand-C3.

In an authorised metal detecting survey in 2002 Jonas Paulsson found the upper part of a long saddle mount (no. F:24) in secondary position in the old gravel pit. It has the same ribbon-like shape as the short mount and the same decoration with lines and a central row of lens-shaped studs in groups of three between rivets that fastened the mount to the pommel (fig. 33). The lower end is cut off between the second and third stud, so using no. F:23 as a model for the lost end the original length can be estimated to approx. 28 cm, corresponding to the long mounts of "Sösdala type". During the destruction of the saddle the mount was bent out of shape.

From a typological point of view the upper part of the two Fulltofta saddle mounts has great similarities to sheet mounts of "Ejsbøl type" while the lower part corresponds to the lower part of the "Sösdala type". Thus the Fulltofta saddle seems to be a connecting link between saddles of "Ejsbøl" and "Sösdala" types (fig. 34). Interestingly an unnoticed short saddle mount of similar type is included in the Kanalgatan find. It was published by Norberg, who placed it on the pommel of the same saddle as the other mounts (1929a fig. 14–16); erroneously in our opinion. It

is ribbon-like and has a central furrow with a row of four holes for studs/rivets (compare four holes for three studs and one rivet on Fulltofta no. F:23). Its lower end has a different shape, however. In our opinion it is a short cantle mount from another saddle. It is 112 mm long, to be compared to the 118–130 mm of short cantle mounts from Sösdala (nos. I:124–126) and the approx. 150 mm of the short Fulltofta mount (no. F:23). The Fulltofta and Kanalgatan mounts are intermediate between saddles of "Ejsbøl" and "Sösdala" type and deserve their own designation, the "Fulltofta type".

Summary Saddles

It is assumed that the Scandinavian saddle type, the ring-saddle, developed on the basis of influences from both Roman and Nomadic saddles. The earliest archaeologically observed saddles in Scandinavia are from the early Late Roman Iron Age, around AD 200, so a mixed Roman/Sarmatian origin is plausible. The Sösdala saddles are the result of a 200-year-long development. Our understanding of the use of the many metal saddle mounts found at Sösdala is based on well-preserved saddle remains from a chamber grave at Högom. The saddles had wooden bows in a high pommel and a lower cantle, both – like the seat – covered with leather and stuffed with straw. It can be assumed that there were also horizontal wooden bars of a kind, laths or boards, to which the bows were tied with leather thongs (see preserved 14th and 17th century saddles from Mongolia, Bemmann 2012:201, 212) . Mounts riveted to pommel and cantle held four saddle rings which were used to hold the saddle in place with girths, breast collar and breeching. The saddle mounts from Fulltofta are a missing link in a sequence of finds from Illerup, Ejsbøl, Fulltofta, Sösdala and Högom, for the first time arranged in a coherent ring-saddle typology covering the 3rd to 5th centuries AD. The saddle type continued into the 6th–7th centuries of the Vendel Period when the characteristic rings and mounts were abandoned but the high pommel and low cantle were kept.

Conclusion

It is noteworthy that the exclusive bridle mounts from Sösdala I are made of solid gilt silver while the simple mounts

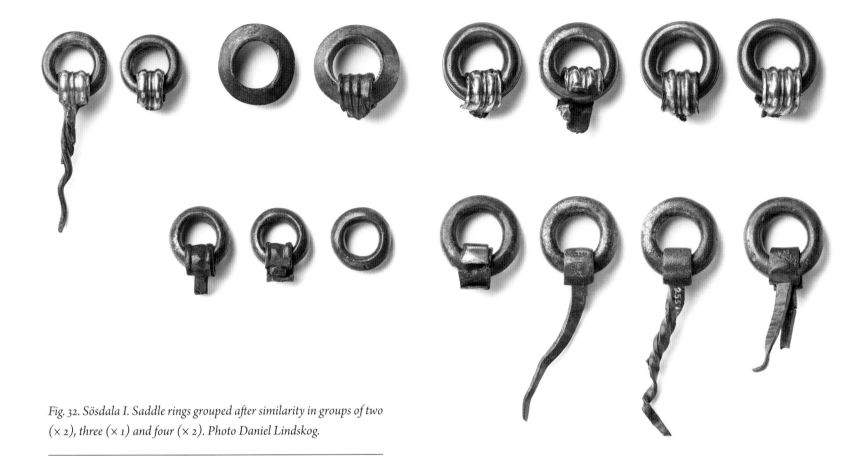

Fig. 32. Sösdala I. Saddle rings grouped after similarity in groups of two (× 2), three (× 1) and four (× 2). Photo Daniel Lindskog.

from Sösdala II and Fulltofta are made of Cu-alloy with details covered with silver sheet. The Fulltofta bronze bridle has two pendant covers of silver.

The bridle Sösdala I was the last to be demolished and deposited on the crest of the gravel ridge. It is much worn so an assumed production date *c*. AD 400 means that the deposition can be dated some decades into the 5th century A.D. The provenance of the bridle mounts will be discussed later (Fabech & Näsman chapter 17). the origin of the "Sösdala style" is discussed in other papers (Bitner-Wróblewska chapter 12; Fabech & Näsman chapter 17; Kazanski & Mastykova chapter 15; Näsman chapter 5; Quast chapter 14). For the origin and meaning of the sacrificial ritual, see Fabech chapter 2.

It is assumed that the bridle Sösdala II was produced towards the end of the late Roman Iron Age but possibly deposited only at the very beginning of the Migration Period. Probably two succeeding generations of horsemen are represented by the bridles Sösdala II and Sösdala I. The Fulltofta bridle with axe-shaped pendants may have been pro-

duced in the Late Roman Iron Age, Scand-C3, but it was brought up to date in period Scand-D1 with pelta-shaped silver-on-bronze covers decorated in "Sösdala style", probably locally produced. Possibly it was deposited at roughly the same time as the more exclusive bridle at Sösdala I. The three horsemen probably knew one another.

The many saddles dismantled at the top of the Sösdala gravel ridge once had different worth, but the mounts are equal from a utility point of view. The silver-incrusted saddles were the most exclusive ("saddles" 1 and 5). The exclusive silver-inlaid saddle 1 found near the parade silver bridle could have been used on the same horse. The animal-shaped end on the long mounts of "saddle 3" also indicates high quality, as do the remains of "saddles" 6 and 7. Only two saddles have a simple functional design ("saddles" 2 and 4). We can only speculate as to whether the dismantled saddles once belonged to one or more horsemen (cf. "biography" by Fabech & Näsman chapter 17).

The Fulltofta saddle was probably produced before any of the Sösdala saddles and it was "old-fashioned"

when deposited. The Fulltofta mounts support the assumption that Migration Period ring saddles of "Sösdala" and "Högom" types developed from the "Ejsbøl type" of period Scand-C2/C3. So far only two finds and three mounts represent saddles of "Fulltofta type" (Fulltofta and Kanalgatan) while mounts of saddles of "Sösdala type" are found at six places (Finnestorp, Hassle-Bösarp, Kanalgatan, Snosarve, Sösdala and Vennebo). The Högom type is only known at its eponymous site but is probably present also in Finnestorp.

Notes

1 Benita Clemmensen (2014:132) has for unknown reasons labelled the Sösdala I and the Høstentorp pelta-shaped pendants as bæltesmykke (belt ornament). In endnote 46 a pendant from Finnestorp is also labelled bæltesmykke.

2 Benita Clemmensen (2014 endnote 48) has for unknown reasons labelled the Fulltofta pendant as et rasleblik af bronze med sølvbelægning (a rattle plate of bronze with silver cover).

References

Akhmedov, I. R. 2001. New data about the origin of some constructive parts of the horse-harness of the Great Migration Period. In: Istvánovits, E. & Kulcsár, V (eds). *International connections of the barbarians of the Carpathian basin in the 1st – 5th centuries A.D.* Aszód/Nyíregyháza: 363–388.

Almgren, O. & Nerman, B. 1923. *Die ältere Eisenzeit Gotlands. Zweites Heft.* Stockholm.

Andrén, A. 2014. *Tracing Old Norse cosmology.* Lund.

Anke, B. & Externbrink, H. (eds). 2007. *Attila und die Hunnen.* Speyer/Stuttgart.

Arbman, H. 1963. Jönköpingstrakten under förhistorisk tid. In: *Jönköpings stads historia I. Från äldsta tid till stadens brand 1612.* Jönköping.

Arrhenius, B. 1983. The chronology of the Vendel graves. In: Lamm, J.P. &

Nordström, H.Å. (eds). *Vendel Period Studies.* Stockholm: 39–70.

Arrhenius, B. 1987. Skandinavien und Osteuropa in der Völkerwanderungszeit. In: *Germanen, Hunnen und Awaren. Schätze der Völkerwanderungszeit.* Nuremberg: 441–467.

Baranowski, T. 1996. Pochówki koni z Tumian, w woj. Olsztyńskim. *Archeologia Polski* 41/1–2: 65–128. Summary: Horse burials at Tumiany, Olsztyn voivodeship. *Archeologia Polski* 41/1–2: 128–130.

Bemmann, J. 1998. Der Nydam-II-Fund. In: Bemmann, G. & Bemmann, J. 1998. *Der Opferplatz von Nydam. Die Funde aus den älteren Grabungen: Nydam-I and II.* Band 1–2. Neumünster: 217–240.

Bemmann, J. (ed.) 2012. *Steppenkrieger. Reiternomaden des 7. – 14. Jahrhunderts aus der Mongolei.* Bonn/Stuttgart.

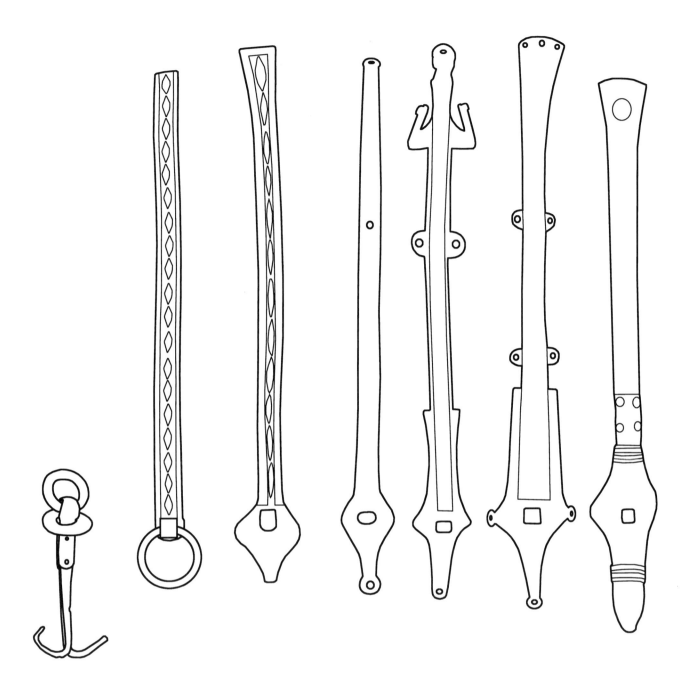

Fig. 34. Five stages/types in the development of the Scandinavian ring saddle represented by mounts, from left 1) Illerup, period C1b, 2) Ejsbøl C2/C3, 3) Fulltofta C3/D1, 4) Sösdala D1 (nos. I:201,117, 115), 5) Högom D2a. Drawing Erika Rosengren.

Bemmann, J. & Hahne, G. 1994. Waffenführende Grabinventare der jüngeren römischen Kaiserzeit und Völkerwanderungszeit in Skandinavien. Studie zur zeitlichen Ordnung anhand der norwegischen Funde. *Bericht der Römisch-Germanischen Kommission* 75: 284–640.

Bishop, M.C. 1988. *Cavalry equipment of the Roman army in the first century AD.* Oxford.

Bitner-Wróblewska, A. 2001. *From Samland to Rogaland. East-west connections in the Baltic basin during the Early Migration period.* Warsaw.

Bitner-Wróblewska, A. 2007. *Netta. A Balt cemetery in Northeastern Poland.* Warsaw.

Böhme, H.W. 1979. Die Germanen in der Germania Libera und in Nordgallien. In: Helmut Roth (ed.). *Kunst der Völkerwanderungszeit.* Frankfurt a.-M./Berlin/Vienna: 191–203, Taf. 116–130.

Bóna, I. 1976. *The dawn of the Dark Ages. The Gepids and the Lombards in the Carpathian Basin.* Prague.

Bóna, I. 1991. *Das Hunnenreich.* Stuttgart.

Brøndsted, J. 1963. *Nordische Vorzeit. 3 Eisenzeit in Dänemark.* Neumünster.

Bunte, C. 1961. A New Bridle Find from Sösdala. *Meddelanden från Lunds universitets historiska museum* 1961: 194–207.

Carnap-Bornheim, C. von & Ilkjær, J. 1996. *Illerup Ådal 5–7. Die Prachtausrüstungen.* Højbjerg/Aarhus.

Clemmensen, B. 2014. Kirkemosegård. Et offerfund med smykker fra ældre germansk jernalder. *Kuml* 63: 109–140.

Ersgård, L. 1974. *Sösdalafyndets stämpelornamentik.* [B.A. thesis in archaeology]. Lund University.

Franzén, R. 2009. The image of Loki from Proosa in Estonia: A Migration Period high status buckle with an elevated circular fastening plate in the light of similar buckles recovered in Scandinavia. *Fennoscandia archaeologica* 26: 53–80.

Friesinger, H. & Adler. H. 1979. *Die Zeit der Völkerwanderung in Niederösterreich.* St. Pölten/Wien.

Gebers, W. & Hinz, H. 1977. Ein Körpergrab der Völkerwanderungszeit aus Bosau, Kreis Ostholstein. *Offa* 34: 5–39.

Godłowski, K. 1995. Das "Fürstengrab" des 5. Jhs. und der "Fürstensitz" in Jakuszowice in Südpolen. In: F. Vallet & M. Kazanski (eds). *La noblesse romaine et les chefs barbares du IIIe au VIIe siècle.* Condé-sur-Noireau/Saint-Germain-en-Laye: 155–179.

Gunnarsson, F. et al. 2017. *Sandby borg – undersökningar 2015, Sandby sn, Mörbylånga kommun, Öland.* Kalmar.

Hagberg, U.E. 1957. Folkvandringstida hängprydnader. *Tor* 3, 1957: 108–120. Zusammenfassung.

Hagberg, U.E. 1967. *The archaeology of Skedemosse 1. The excavations and the finds of an Öland fen, Sweden.* Stockholm.

Holmqvist, W. 1951. *Tauschierte Metallarbeiten des Nordens aus Römerzeit und Völkerwanderung.* Stockholm.

Holmqvist, W. 1952. De äldsta gotländska bildstenarna och deras motivkrets. *Fornvännen* 47: 1–20. Zusammenfassung.

Horedt, K. & Protase, D. 1972. Das zweite Fürstengrab von Apahida (Siebenbürgen). *Germania* 50/1–2: 174–220.

Hougen, B. 1936. *The migration style in Norway.* Oslo.

Ilkjær, J. 1990. *Illerup Ådal 1–2. Die Lanzen und Speere.* Højbjerg/Aarhus.

Ilkjær, J. 1993. *Illerup Ådal 3–4. Die Gürtel.* Højbjerg/Aarhus.

Iversen, R. Birch 2010. *Kragehul mose. Ein Kriegsbeuteopfer aus Südwestfünen.* Højbjerg/Aarhus. Summary.

Jankuhn, H. 1973. Axtkult. In: *Reallexikon der Germanischen Altertumskunde* 1: 562–566.

Jørgensen, A. Nørgård 2008. *Porskjær mosefund.* Højbjerg/Aarhus. Zusammenfassung.

Jørgensen, A. Nørgård & Andersen, H.C. 2014. *Ejsbøl mose. Die Kriegsbeuteopfer im Moor von Ejsbøl aus dem späten 1. Jh.v.Chr bis zum frühen 5 Jh.n.Chr.* Højberg/Aarhus.

Kazanski, M. 1991. A propos des armes er les éléments de harnachement "orienteaux" en Occident à l'époque des Grandes Migrations (IVe–Ve s.). *Journal of Roman Archaeology* 4: 123–139.

Kiss, A. 1984. Archäologische Angaben zur Geschichte der Sättel des Frühmittelalters. *Alba Regia* 21: 189–207.

Kjær, H. 1902. *Et nyt fund fra Nydam Mose.* Nordiske Fortidsminder 1. Copenhagen.

Kokowski, A. 1998. Metalowe wisiorki w ksztalcie topora na terenie Barbaricum na pólnoc i pólnocny-wschod od limesu rzymskiego, w okresie rzymskim i we wczesnym okresie wędrówek ludów. In: Ilkjær, J. &. Kokowski, A. (eds). *20 lat archeologii w Masłomęczu 1. Weterani.* Lublin: 99–116.

Kontny, B., Okulicz-Kozaryn, J. & Pietrzak, M. 2011. *Nowinka, site 1. The cemetery from the Late Migration Period in the northern Poland.* Gdańsk/Warsaw.

Krogh, S. 1970. *Foreløbig rapport over forsøg med rekonstrueret rideudstyr af jernaldertype udført juli 1970.* Lejre.

La Baume, W. 1944. Altpreußisches Zaumzeug. *Alt-Preussen* 9/1–2:1–19.

Lamm, J.P. 1973 *Fornfynd och fornlämningar på Lovö. Arkeologiska studier kring en uppländsk järnåldersbygd.* Stockholm.

Lau, N. 2014. *Das Thorsberger Moor 1. Die Pferdegeschirre. Germanische Zaumzeuge und Sattelgeschirre als Zeugnisse kriegerischer Reiterei im mittel- und nordeuropäischen Barbaricum.* Schleswig.

Levada, M. 2011. To Europe via the Crimea. On possible migration routes of the northern people in the Great Migration Period. In: Igor' Khrapunov & Frans-Arne Stylegar (eds). *Inter Ambo Maria. Contacts between Scandinavia and the Crimea in the Roman Period.* Kristiansand/Simferopol: 115–137.

Lindqvist, S. 1941–42. *Gotlands Bildsteine 1–2.* Stockholm.

Magnus, B. 1975. *Krosshaugfunnet. Et forsøk på kronologisk og stilhistorisk plassering i 5. årh.* Stavanger. Summary.

Magnus, B. 2015. Shield-formed pendants and solar symbols of the Migration Period. In: Lars Larsson *et al.* (eds). *Small things – Wide horizons. Studies in honour of Birgitta Hårdh.* Oxford: 115–120.

Matešić, S. 2015. *Das Thorsberger Moor 3:1–2. Die militärischen Ausrüstungen.* Schleswig. Summary.

Menghin, W. 1985. *Die Langobarden. Archäologie und Geschichte.* Stuttgart.

Montelius, O. 1900. Solgudens yxa och Tors hammare. *Svenska fornminnesföreningens tidskrift* 10, 1900: 277–296.

Montelius, O. 1917. Soldyrkan, Solkult. *Nordisk familjebok* 26:306–307.

Näsman, U. 1984. Zwei Relieffibeln von der Insel Öland. *Praehistorische Zeitschrift* 59/1: 48–80.

Nerman, B. 1935. *Die Völkerwanderungszeit Gotlands.* Stockholm.

Nielsen, J.N. 2000. *Sejlflod – ein eisenzeitliches Dorf in Nordjütland. 1: Text und Pläne. 2: Abbildungen und Tafeln.* Copenhagen.

Norberg, R. 1929a. Ett folkvandringstidsfynd från Jönköping. *Meddelanden från Norra Smålands Fornminnesförening* 9: 5–24. Zusammenfassung.

Norberg, R. 1929b. Om förhistoriska sadlar i Sverige. *Rig* 12: 97–113.

Norberg, R. 1931. Moor- und Depotfunde aus dem 5. Jahrhundert nach Chr. in Schonen. *Acta Archaeologica* 2: 104–111.

Nothnagel, M. 2013. *Weibliche Eliten der Völkerwanderungszeit. Zwei Prunkbestattungen aus Untersiebenbrunn.* St. Pölten.

Nowakowski, W. 1998. *Die Funde der römischen Kaiserzeit und der Völkerwanderungszeit in Masuren.* Berlin.

Nylén, E. & Lamm, J.P. 1988. *Stones, ships and symbols. The picture stones of Gotland from the Viking Age and before.* Stockholm.

Ørsnes, M. 1984. *Sejrens pris. Våbenofre i Ejsbøl Mose ved Haderslev.* Haderslev.

Ørsnes, M. 1988. *Ejsbøl I. Waffenopferfunde des 4.–5. Jahrhundert nach Chr.* Copenhagen.

Ørsnes, M. 1994. Zaumzeugfunde des 1.–8. Jhrh. nach Chr. in Mittel- und Nordeuropa. *Acta archaeologica* 64/2, 1993: 183–292.

Pfommer, M. 1983. Griechische Originale und Kopien unter römischen Tafelsilber. *The J. Paul Getty Museum Journal* 11: 135–146.

Prammer, J. 1987. Germanen in spätrömischen Straubing. In: Pülhorn, W. (ed.). *Germanen, Hunnen und Awaren. Schätze der Völkerwanderungszeit.* Nürnberg: 599–607.

Quast, D. 1993. Das hölzerne Sattelgestell aus Oberflacht, Grab 211. Bemerkungen zur merowingerzeitlichen Sätteln. *Fundberichte aus Baden-Württemberg* 18: 437–464.

Quast, D. 2007. Zwischen Steppe, Barbaricum und Byzanz. Bemerkungen zu praktvollem Reitzubehör des 5. Jahrhunderts n.Chr. *Acta Praehistorica et Archaeologica* 39: 35–64.

Ramqvist, P.H. 1992. *Högom. The excavations 1949–1984.* Umeå.

Rau, A. 2010. *Nydam mose 1–2. Die personengebundenen Gegenstände. Grabungen 1989–1999.* Højbjerg/Aarhus. Summary.

Rieck, F. 2003. The ships from Nydam bog. In: Jørgensen, L. *et al.* (eds). *The spoils of victory: the North in the shadow of the Roman Empire.* Copenhagen: 296–309.

Rieck, F. 2016. Skibene fra Nydam mose. *Skalk* 2016/6: 10–17.

Ringtved, J. 1988. Jyske gravfund fra yngre romertid og ældre germanertid. *Kuml* 1986: 95–231.

Salin, B. 1904. *Die altgermanische Thierornamentik.* Stockholm. (2nd ed. 1935, Stockholm).

Schuster, J. 2006. *Die Buntmetallfunde der Grabung Feddersen-Wierde. Chronologie – Chorologie – Technologie.* Oldenburg/Wilhelmshaven.

Simonett, C. 1946. Der römische Silberschatz aus Wettingen. *Zeitschrift für schweizerische Archäologie und Kunstgeschichte* 8: 1–15.

Sommer, M. 1984. *Die Gürtel und Gürtelbeschläge des 4. und 5. Jahrhunderts im römischen Reich.* Bonn.

Stadler, P. 1987. Die Bevölkerungsstrukturen nach Eugippius and den archäologischen Quellen. In: *Germanen, Hunnen und Awaren. Schätze der Völkerwanderungszeit.* Nuremberg:297–347.

Stjernquist, B. 1974. Das Opfermoor in Hassle Bösarp, Schweden. *Acta Archaeologica* 44, 1973: 19–62.

Straume, E. 1987. *Gläser mit Facettenschliff aus skandinavischen Gräbern des 4. und 5. Jahrhunderts n.Chr.* Oslo.

Straume, E. 1993. Gravene. In: B. Solberg (ed.). *Minneskrift Egil Bakka.* Bergen: 207–247.

Sundkvist, A. 2001. *Hästarnas land. Aristokratisk hästhållning och ridkonst i Svealands yngre järnålder.* Uppsala. Summary.

Tejral, J. 2007. Das Attilareich und die germanischen *gentes* im Mitteldonauraum. In: Anke, B. & Externbrink, H. (eds). 2007. *Attila und die Hunnen.* Speyer/Stuttgart: 107–113.

Tejral, J. 2010. Zur Frage der frühesten hunnischen Anwesenheit in donauländischen Provinzen am Beispiel des archäologischen Befundes. *Slovenská archeológia* 58/1; 81–122.

Thrane, H. 1983. En lille broncering fra Vedel Simonsens samling. *Fynske minder* 1983: 51–64. Zusammenfassung.

Werner, J. 1988. Dančeny und Brangstrup. Untersuchungen zur Černjachov-Kultur und zu den 'Reichtumszentren' auf Fünen. *Bonner Jahrbücher* 188: 241–286.

Wieczorek, A. & P. Périn (eds). 2001. *Das Gold der Barbarenfürsten.* Stuttgart.

Wulff, O. 1914. *Altchristliche und byzantinische Kunst I. Die Altchristliche Kunst.* Berlin.

Internet references

Goldmann http://zeevgoldmann.blogspot.se/ Checked 25 October 2016.

Rome Art Lover http://romeartlover.tripod.com/Jerash02.html Checked 24
  January 2017.

Ubi erat lupa http://www.ubi-erat-lupa.org/monument.php?id=24817
  Checked 9 February 2017.

Резюме

Сёсдала и Фультофта – уздечки и седла

Ульф Несман

В статье обсуждается типохронология отдельных деталей узды и оковок седел, археологизированных в гравийных холмах близ Сёсдалы и Фультофты в регионе Скания. Замечательное оголовье коня из Сёсдалы I уникально во многих отношениях, однако имеет черты сходства с одновременными находками из Якушовице, Качина, Унтерзибенбрунна и других мест в Восточной и Центральной Европе. Сопоставимые вещи следует искать в провинциях Западной и Восточной Римской империи, а также в зонах расселения варварских племен (*gentes*). Изучение форм, декора и технологий дает основания утверждать, что данное оголовье состояло из зажимов, поступивших из разных источников. Весьма вероятно, что зажимы с оттисками штампов группы 1 (рис. 4) седланы в мастерской, имевшей тесные связи с римским производством, а другие, с отпечатками штампов группы 2 (рис. 5), вероятно, выполнены в варварском окружении, которое, тем не менее, испытывало сильное влияние со стороны римской культуры. Зажимы с отпечатками штампов группы 3 (рис. 6) – продукт ремесла высокого уровня, но кажутся менее «классическими», чем группы 1 и 2. «Варварским окружением» можно считать южную Скандинавию. Единственное в своем роде изделие № I, 2 – это копия, вероятно, местная. Все эти зажимы были сделаны, вероятно, в начале V в., но имеющиеся следы износа и ремонта указывают, что их археологизация произошла позже, в течение данного столетия. Позже всех была разломана и археологизирована узда из Сёсдалы I. Она имеет выраженные следы использо-

вания, и потому, если принять за время производства рубеж IV–V вв., то ее археологизацию нужно будет отодвинуть на несколько десятилетий вглубь V в.

Материал и исполнение оголовья из Сёсдалы II гораздо проще, чем у оголовья из Сёсдалы I (рис. 14). Ничто не указывает на то, что сделавший ее мастер испытывал сильное влияние извне, так что эту узду можно считать продуктом исключительно Скании. Оголовья и удила сложно датировать по форме и орнаментации. Эрснес датировал данную узду периодом D1 по скандинавской хронологии, но удила, вероятно, следует отнести к более раннему времени, а именно периоду C3 по скандинавской хронологии. Вероятно, удила более древние, а детали оголовья добавили к ним позже. Считается, что узда из Сёсдалы II была сделана ближе к концу Позднеримского времени, но археологизирована она, возможно, в начале Эпохи переселения народов. Уздечки из Сёсдалы II и Сёсдалы I, вероятно, представляют два поколения всадников, сменившие одно другое.

Уникально оголовье из Фультофты (рис. 16, 20). Узда с топоровидными подвесками могла быть сделана в Позднеримское время, в период C3 по скандинавской хронологии. В период D1 по скандинавской хронологии ее обновили, добавив серебряные пельтовидные накладки с декором в стиле «Сёсдала» (рис. 17). Ее археологизация могла произойти одновременно с богатой уздой из Сёсдалы I. Возможно, эти два всадника были знакомы друг с другом. Отсутствие сопоставимых материалов оставляет открытым вопрос о происхождении бронзовой узды – сделана ли она в Скании, Скандинавии, на Континенте или же в римских провинциях? Однако две серебряные накладки, вероятно, местные, из Скании.

Наши представления о седлах, бытовавших в Европе в Позднеримское время и Эпоху переселения народов, очень фрагментарны. Для седла, бытовавшего в южной Скандинавии, характерно наличие тяжелых подпружных колец. В южноскандинавских вотивных комплексах с воинским снаряжением найдено множество оковок от седел с подпружными кольцами. Эти находки датированы Позднеримским временем (периоды С1–С3 по скандинавской хронологии) и началом Эпохи переселения народов (периоды D1–D2a по скандинавской хронологии), т. е. приблизительно III–V вв. Остатки седел из Сёсдалы и Фультофты рассмотрены на фоне ранних седел типов «Иллеруп» и «Эйсбёль» (рис. 22–23) и позднего типа «Хёгом» (см. статью Рамквиста в этом томе). Основываясь, главным образом, на форме найденных в Сёсдале одиннадцати длинных оковок седла, предложено выделить седла типа «Сёсдала», который характеризует определенную фазу в развитии седел с подпружными кольцами в начале Эпохи переселения народов. Элементами седла с подпружными кольцами были четыре кольца с крепежными шипами, две длинные оковки передней луки и две короткие оковки задней луки. В некоторых случаях добавлялись два дополнительных кольца для крепления багажа. В Сёсдале найдены два, очевидно, полных набора оковок седла

(рис. 24, 27). Еще пять седел представлены неполными наборами оковок или единственной оковкой (рис. 28–29). Отдельные подпружные кольца могли относиться как минимум к тринадцати седлам (рис. 30). Две оковки седла, найденные в Фультофте, что недалеко от Сёсдалы (рис. 31), представляют собой «недостающее звено» между седлами типа «Эйсбёл» Позднеримского времени и седлами типа «Сёсдала» начала Эпохи переселения народов (рис. 32).

На вершине гравийной гряды в Сёсдале разломали несколько седел, имевших разную ценность. Самые выдающиеся из них – седла с инкрустацией серебром (рис. 24–25, 29). На высокое качество указывают также длинные оковки с зооморфными окончаниями от «седла 3» (рис. 28). Лишь два седла имели простой функциональный дизайн (рис. 27).

Седло из Фультофты, вероятно, было сделано раньше, чем седла из Сёсдалы, так что к моменту археологизации оно было «старомодным». Оковки из Фультофты подтверждают предположение, что седла с подпружными кольцами Эпохи переселения народов типа «Сёсдала» и «Хёгом» были результатом эволюции седел типа «Эйсбол», относящихся к периоду С2/С3 по скандинавской хронологии. Оковки седел типа «Сёсдала» найдены в шести местах на территории современной Швеции (в Финнесторпе, Хассле-Бёсарпе, Канальгатане, Сносарве, Сёсдале и Веннебо). Тип «Хёгом» известен только на эпонимном памятнике, но, возможно, присутствовал и в Финнесторпе (см. статью Нордквиста в этом томе; рис. 37).

ПОДПИСИ К ИЛЛЮСТРАЦИЯМ

Рис. 1 Сёсдала I. Биметаллический трензель с двухчастным грызлом и связанные с ним зажимы (фото Даниэля Ландескога).

Рис. 2. Сёсдала II. Биметаллический трензель трехчастным грызлом (фото Даниэля Ландескога).

Рис. 3. Сёсдала II. Соединитель оголовья и кольца удил, инкрустированный скрученной медной и серебряной проволоками (фото Даниэля Ландескога).

Рис. 4. Сёсдала I. Зажимы, вероятно, сделанные в одной мастерской, с оттисками штампов группы 1 (фото Даниэля Ландескога).

Рис. 5. Сёсдала I. Зажимы, вероятно, сделанные в одной мастерской, с оттисками штампов группы 2 (фото Даниэля Ландескога).

Рис. 6. Сёсдала I. Избранные зажимы, вероятно, сделанные в одной мастерской, с оттисками штампов группы 3 (фото Даниэля Ландескога).

Рис. 7. Сёсдала I. Пельтовидная подвеска (№ I, 19–21) на фотореконструкции с добавлением кнопки (№ I, 185) (фото Даниэля Ландескога).

Рис. 8. Хаускирхен (Австрия). Одна из четырех подвесок-лунниц из позолоченной бронзы, найденных в богатом погребении (по: Friesinger & Adler 1979 Abb. 13).

Рис. 9. Сёсдала I. Ременная пряжка (по. I, 26; ср. рис. 4; фото Даниэля Ландескога).

Рис. 10. Сёсдала I. Две малые серебряные пряжки (№. I, 23; I, 111; фото Даниэля Ландескога).

Рис. 11. Омоссарна (Скания). Находки вещей из жертвоприношения конской упряжи: трехчастный мундштук с боковыми щечками, три подпружных кольца, ременная пряжка и бронзовое кольцо (фото Музея Эстерлена, Симрисхамм).

Рис. 12. Сёсдала I и Унтерзибенбрунн (Австрия). Нанесенные штампом изображения шестилепестковых цветков украшают распределитель ремней (Сёсдала №. I, 15) и зажим (Унтерзибен-брунн, № ANSA U40) (фото Даниэля Ландескога и из собрания древностей Музея истории искусства, Вена).

Рис. 13. Сёсдала I. Разрубленный на две части уздечный зажим (№ I, 33–34). фото Даниэля Ландескога).

Рис. 14. Сёсдала II. Избранные уздечные зажимы; удила см. на рис. 2 (фото Даниэля Ландескога).

Рис. 15. Сёсдала II. Две ременные пряжки (№ II, 19–20; фото Даниэля Ландескога).

Рис. 16. Фультофта. Часть зажимов от оголовья (фото Даниэля Ландескога).

Рис. 17. Фультофта. Одна из двух серебряных накладок на топоровидные подвески оголовья (№ F, 1; фото Даниэля Ландескога).

Рис. 18. Веннебо. Закругленная бронзовая подвеска с серебряной плакировкой, частично позолоченная и украшенная штампованным декором, пельтовидной формы (фото Шведского исторического музея; № 6511, 4).

Рис. 19. Фультофта. Следы зеленой патины на оборотной стороне одной из серебряных накладок (№ F, 2) соответствует топоровидной подвеске (фото Даниэля Ландескога).

Рис. 20. Фультофта. Шарнирные накладки соединяли кольцо удил с псалиями и носовым ремнем оголовья (№ F, 7; фото Даниэля Ландескога).

Рис. 21. Канальгатан. Реконструкция деревянного каркаса седла с подпружными кольцами на основе оковок, найденных в Йёнчёпинге (по: Norberg 1929a fig. 14).

Рис. 22. Эйсбол. Реконструкция деревянного каркаса из Саттел I (© Йорген Андерсен, Музей археологии Сондерйюлланна в Хадерслеве).

Рис. 23. Иллеруп. Древнейшие подпружные кольца рубежа II–III вв. н. э. (по: Carnap-Bornheim & Ilkjær 1996 Taf. 115; фото Пребена Дельхольма, Музей Месгорда).

Рис. 24. Сёсдала I. Совместная находка оковок седла и подпружных колец, вероятно, происходивших от одного «седла 1» (фото Даниэля Ландескога).

Рис. 25. Сёсдала I. Оковки и подпружные кольца с крепежными шипами («седло 1»), по аналогии с находкой в Хегоме, крепились на передней и задней луке седла (рисунок Эрики Росенгрен).

Рис. 26. Сёсдала I. Короткая оковка задней луки «седла 1» (№ I, 217; фото Даниэля Ландескога).

Рис. 27. Сёсдала I. Реконструкция деревянного каркаса «седла 1» (рисунок Эрики Росенгрен).

Рис. 28. Сёсдала I. Лицевая и оборотная сторона сохранившегося конца кожаного ремня (№ I, 229), украшенного двойной накладкой из бронзы и серебра, а также гвоздиками с серебряными шляпками (фото Даниэля Ландескога).

Рис. 29. Сёсдала I. Оковки и подпружные кольца от одного «седло 2». Слева – находки из пункта III (№ 201–206), справа – из пункта II (№ 125, 126, 170, 171) (фото Даниэля Ландескога).

Рис. 30. Сёсдала I. Две длинные и одна короткая оковка «седла 3». Справа – верхняя часть оковки в виде ящерицы (фото Даниэля Ландескога).

Рис. 31. Сёсдала I. Единственная уцелевшая оковка (длинная) «седла 5»: а) вид сверху, b) вид сбоку (№ I, 115) (фото Даниэля Ландескога).

Рис. 32. Сёсдала I. Подпружные кольца, объединенные по сходным признакам в группы по два (x 2), три (x 1) и четыре (x 2) (фото Даниэля Ландескога).

Рис. 33. Фультофта. Оковки седла: короткая (слева; № F, 23) и фрагментированная длинная (справа; № F, 24) (фото Даниэля Ландескога).

Рис. 34. Пять стадий развития (типов) скандинавского седла с подпружными кольцами по данным оковок из: 1) Иллерупа, период С1b; 2) Эйсбола, период С2/С3; 3) Фультофты, период С3/D1; 4) Сёсдалы, период D1 (№ I, 201. 117. 115); 5) Хёгома, период D2a (рисунок Эрики Росенгрен).

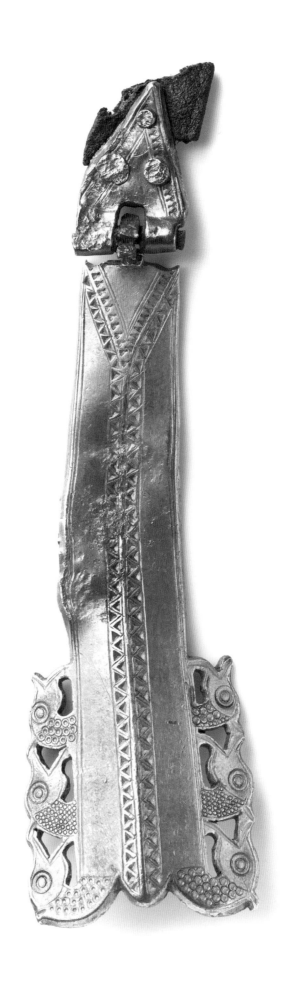

Chapter 8

The Iron Age horse

Erika Rosengren

The Sösdala find with its exquisite horse equipment is spectacular and testifies to the prominent role of the horse in Iron Age society. Although the remains of the horses themselves are absent, information about the animal's physical characteristics can be found in related finds from elsewhere in Scandinavia. It is possible to infer that the horses do not seem to have expressed much phenotypic variation. The horses were around 120–140 cm over the withers and most were black, bay or chestnut in colour. Genetically, modern Nordic horses show abundant diversity both among and within horse breeds, possibly reflecting a bias toward the trading of females already in ancient times. In contrast, local stallions seem to have been highly valued and preferred over imported ones, based on the autochthonous paternal lineages exhibited by the same breeds. At some point in time, an influx of genes from eastern horse populations occurred, possibly mirroring the eastern influences seen in other categories of archaeological material, but this may also be of an earlier or later date.

Rosengren, E. 2017. The Iron Age horse. In: Fabech, C. & Näsman, U. (eds). *The Sösdala horsemen – and the equestrian elite of fifth century Europe.* Jutland Archaeological Society.

The horse is believed to have been domesticated in the Eurasian Steppe 5,000–6,000 years ago (Ludwig *et al.* 2009), and introduced in various parts of Europe in the Late Neolithic/Bronze Age (Bendrey 2012). In addition to having long-lasting impact on human societies by increasing mobility and trade, influencing human lifestyles and profoundly changing warfare (Levine 2000), it is apparent from both archaeological material and written accounts that the horse was a symbol of status and had a prominent role in the cult (Näsström 2002; Fabech & Ringtved 2009). Horses could serve as various offerings, for example as food, gifts, protection, and booty (Vretemark 2013). Consequently, remains of either whole carcasses of horses,

selected body parts or food waste are found in a variety of contexts: wetlands, wells, graves, on settlements and within house structures (Stjernquist 1973; Møhl 1997; Carlie 2004; Vretemark 2013; Dobat *et al.* 2014).

The Sösdala find, dated to the Migration Period (*c*. AD 400), is one of the most interesting finds associated with horses. It consists of exclusive riding gear, saddles and tackle, and has been interpreted as making up a funeral sacrifice (Fabech chapter 2). In this context the Iron Age horse itself is absent, possibly slaughtered and eaten in connection with the burial of its leader (Fabech & Näsman chapter 17). That no physical remains of horses were found in close proximity to the sacrificed horse equipment

Fig. 1. Examples of horses displaying the most prevalent coat colours; chestnut, bay and black. Photo: Photocase/kb-photodesign.

in Sösdala is a major drawback and, although remains of horses were abundant in the graves at the nearby burial site of Vätteryd (Strömberg 1961), they come from cremations and were too fragmented to provide much information. An essential part of the equation is thereby missing, and in order to investigate the physical characteristics of the horse we need to look elsewhere.

Although written contemporary sources from Iron Age Scandinavia are almost non-existent there are a good number of descriptions from foreign writers, for example, Roman chroniclers. Primarily restricted to aristocratic settings, consequently, there are apparent discrepancies between these sources and the abundant archaeological

finds (Vretemark 2013), and comparisons should therefore be treated with caution.

In the written narratives, for example, sacrifices most often involve male animals, but, with the exception of the four sacrificed stallions in Illerup Ådal (Dobat *et al.* 2014), no sex preference seems to have existed for horses in graves or in sacrificial contexts (Götherström 2002; Monikander 2010; Svensson *et al.* 2012). The apparent lack of a preference for stallions compared to mares, in turn, shows that the people conducting the rituals had stronger criteria for the evaluation of a horse than sex, perhaps selecting animals based on capability, breed or aesthetics (Götherström 2002).

Also, the Roman historian Tacitus describes white horses as particularly holy in his *Germania* (chapter 10) and the coat colour of horses is only occasionally mentioned in the written material describing the Viking Age (Sundkvist 2001). When Svensson *et al.* (2012) used genotyping of coat colour SNPs on the horse remains from Skedem-osse (AD 200–500), Valsgärde (AD 450–750) and Ultuna (AD 800–1050) they were able to show that the three basic coat colours, bay, black, and chestnut (fig. 1), seem to have been dominant and equally common at all sites. However, according to the authors, the genes determining various spotting patterns and dilutions believed to have existed are still unknown, or impossible to target in fragmented ge-netic material such as ancient DNA (Svensson *et al.* 2012). Also, the findings of horses with silver dilution, although only in heterozygote state, makes it likely that there were animals expressing the silver phenotype present in Sweden during at least the early Viking Age (Svensson *et al.* 2012).

According to written accounts there existed a large number of different horse breeds within the Roman Em-pire. Selective breeding was practiced and certain horse races were reserved for certain categories within society (Hyland 1990). Different phenotypes of horses based on body size and proportions, possibly constituting different breeds, have been proposed from the Swedish Iron Age (Sundkvist 1992).

The withers heights of the horses recovered from Skedemosse and Hassle-Bösarp ranged between 120 and 140 cm (Stjernquist 1973; Monikander 2010). The horses from Finnestorp were approx. 140 cm (Nordqvist 2006) and the horses from Röekillorna are described as larger than a modern-day Icelandic pony (145 cm: Møhl 1997). The withers heights of the four horses recovered at Illerup Ådal A ranged between 130 and 141 cm (Dobat *et al.* 2014). Overall, this gives an average height of about 130 cm in the Scandinavian Early Iron Age horses (fig. 2).

However, Azzaroli (1985) has previously discussed the problem of separating different horse types based on skeletal morphology in all but extreme cases. One should also keep in mind that only a small portion of the bone material, due to the challenges concerning DNA preserva-tion and additional taphonomic processes, are suitable for genetic or biometric analyses. Bones found in cremation burials, in alkaline wetlands or as refuse material at settle-ments are often too fragmented or deteriorated. Therefore, the results previously cited represent only a limited num-ber of horses originally used in Iron Age society and are thus not based on an unbiased sample.

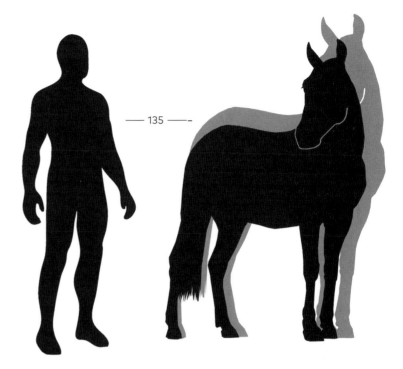

Fig. 2. *Mean withers heights of the Iron Age horses (black) compared to the mean withers heights of modern Nordic horse breeds (grey). Draw-ing Erika Rosengren.*

Interestingly, the estimated withers height agrees well when compared to the measurements of horses from the Continent and the British Isles. Remains of horses from Pre-Roman Iron Age/transitional period (1st century BC–1st century AD) Britain had a mean withers height of 126 cm (Albarella *et al.* 2008). Celtic horses are described as small (110–130 cm withers height), whereas Romans bred larger horses (>140 cm). Therefore, remains of small horses have been considered to come from local animals while larger ones have been proposed to be imported, en-dowed or looted (Elsner *et al.* 2016). It is speculated that the Romans introduced new female lineages to conquered regions (Bower *et al.* 2013) and according to Caesar hors-es were traded over long distances (*De Bello Gallico* 4,2,2). Also, in areas under Roman influence, like Britain, an in-crease in body size and change in body shape over time has been observed, suggesting that horse improvement was likely to have been brought about with new breeding stock (Albarella *et al.* 2008).

Although the body size of horses increased during the Iron Age (Fabech & Ringtved 2009), no significant change has been observed from sites in Northern Europe contemporary with the Roman Empire. Consequently, it has been speculated whether one of the four horses from Illerup Ådal A, interpreted as a surprisingly large animal, might indicate import from either Eastern Europe or the Roman Empire (Lau 2014, Table 1). This would be in accordance with the various elements of riding equipment found in southern Scandinavian weapon sacrifices showing close similarities to riding gear from the northern Danube area or the Roman Empire (Lau 2014). Strontium isotope analysis of enamel of two of the other horses showed a local origin within the region of Denmark, southern Sweden or northern Germany for these horses (Dobat et al. 2014), rendering the issue unresolved.

However, although studying only a small portion of the mtDNA, Elsner et al. (2016) found that smaller and larger individuals from sites in Switzerland (originally identified as local and imported, respectively) did not differ genetically. Persistent gene flow through the domestication process, high mobility of the horse, and its prevalent use for transportation has been evoked to explain the high genetic diversity (in both mitochondrial and autosomal DNA), as well as the absence of strong phylogeographic structuring that exists among horses (Vilà et al. 2001; Petersen et al. 2013).

Unlike the descendants of other domesticated species like cattle, sheep, and goats that are derived from a limited number of animals that were domesticated in just a few places 8,000–10,000 years ago, the horse mitochondrial genomes tell a very different story. The mtDNA of modern horses shows a high diversity in terms of haplogroups, most of which are shared among modern breeds and different geographic areas (Lippold et al. 2011b; Achilli et al. 2012). The genetic data appears to suggest that, in addition to the knowledge of horse breeding, the rapid spread of horse domestication out of western central Eurasia during the Neolithic involved actual population movement (Levine 2002; Achilli et al. 2012).

Within the autosomal DNA (i.e. microsatellites), the divergence between breeds is more marked than was observed with mtDNA sequences, further illustrating that maternal gene flow dominated the genetic exchange between breeds and may reflect a bias toward females in breeding and trade (Vilà et al. 2001).

In contrast, the Y-chromosome diversity found in modern domestic horses is exceedingly low. One hypothesis to explain this has been that the wild horse population from which they were domesticated also lacked diversity, possibly due to the polygynous breeding patterns in wild horses (Wallner et al. 2013). The absence of Y-chromosomal diversity in modern horses is, however, most probably a result of a limited number of stallions initially being domesticated and the breeding practices developed after domestication further reducing the effective number of males (Lippold et al. 2011a). Haplotype 1 is believed to be the only one that survived through domestication and later selective breeding, and it is distributed across almost all breeds and geographic regions. All other haplotypes arose directly or indirectly from haplotype 1. Wallner et al. (2013), studying the genetic variation of the Y-chromosome in extant horse breeds, found that northern European breeds, like the Icelandic Horse, Shetland Pony, and the Norwegian Fjord horse, retained autochthonous Y-chromosome variants (haplotypes 4–6) in high frequencies. Haplotype 4, for example, is found in half of all Icelandic horses, haplotype 6 in 74% of Shetland ponies and haplotype 5 is fixed in Norwegian Fjord horse (Wallner et al. 2013). The autochthonous haplotypes would imply that these horse breeds were either subjected not at al or very little to the introgression of genetic material of stallions from Central Europe and the Near East documented in other breeds. Presumably, if the adaptations of these breeds to local conditions made them valued more highly than imported animals, this could explain their comparatively isolated history. One example is the restriction of import of horses to Iceland established already in AD 930 (Wallner et al. 2013).

The free-roaming horses of the Iron Age were left by themselves in wood- or moorland for large parts of the year where only selected stallions were allowed to run with the mares. This traditional way of keeping horses is recorded for primitive breeds like the Gotland Russ well into historic times (Zimmermann 1999; Sundkvist 2004). Evidence from the written sources, where herds connect-

Fig. 3. A herd of 60 Exmoor ponies is roaming freely on Langeland, Denmark. Photo Turist- og Erhversforeningen Langeland, http://www. langeland.dk/ln-int/langeland/wild-horses-langeland.

ed to specific persons or farms are mentioned, tell us that pedigree was important already in ancient times. A method to influence the stock was to buy a suitable stallion and let him loose. By subsequently removing young colts, probably through castration, there were ways to raise the chances of having foals by the selected stallion (Sundkvist 2004). Aggressive behaviour causing problems to travellers most probably led to the number of loose-running stallions being restricted, as is exemplified by 19th century laws from Norway and Iceland (Sundqvist 2004). Also, this practice of keeping herds of breeding animals free-roaming might initially have been as much out of necessity as convenience(fig. 3). For example, conservationists initially encountered problems such as pacing, excessive aggression, impotence, and infanticide when they tried to breed the wild Przewalski's horse (Boyd & Houpt 1994, Warmuth *et al.* 2012). The area in connection with the Skedemosse bog has been interpreted by Hagberg as a site for annual round-ups of the free-ranging horse herds (1967).

A close genetic relationship between modern northern European breeds (Norwegian Fjord horse, Nordland/ Lyngen horse, Døle horse, Coldblooded trotter, Shetland pony, Finnhorse, North Swedish horse and Icelandic horse) and the Mongolian native horse has been revealed using microsatellite data as well as genome-wide SNP data, indicating a contribution of eastern genes to northern European horse populations (Bjørnstad *et al.* 2003; Petersen *et al.* 2013). This would possibly suggest that these breeds have an ancient and isolated history or were subjected to a more recent influx of eastern genes. Great expansions of the Nomadic Empires, conducted on horseback, under Scythians (8th century BC – 2nd century AD), Sarmatians (2nd century – 4th century AD), Huns under Attila (5th century AD) and Genghis Khan (13th century AD), are known examples of such possible eastern influences. The question of when this occurred could potentially be answered by future analysis of the genomes of ancient remains of Scandinavian horses.

To sum up, the Swedish horses do not seem to have expressed a lot of phenotypic variation. The horses were around 120–140 cm over the withers and most were black, bay or chestnut in colour. Maternally inherited mitochondrial genomes show abundant diversity both among and within horse breeds, possibly reflecting a bias toward the trading of females. In contrast, local stallions seem to have been highly valued, based on the autochthonous paternal lineages exhibited by modern northern European breeds. At some point in time, an influx of genes from eastern horse populations occurred, possibly mirroring the eastern influences seen in other categories of archaeological material (e.g. that described by Fabech 1991), but may be earlier or later.

Glossary

Mitochondrial DNA (mtDNA) is the DNA located in mitochondria, exclusively inherited from the mother.

Y chromosomal DNA is the DNA in the non-recombining part of the male sex chromosome, exclusively inherited from the father.

Autosomal DNA is the DNA in the chromosomes (with the exception of the sex chromosomes) within the cell nucleus.

Single nucleotide polymorphisms (SNPs) are variations at single positions (base pairs) in the DNA sequence among individuals.

An *allele* is one of a number of alternative forms of the same gene occupying a given position, or locus, on a chromosome.

A *haplotype* is a group of alleles that are transmitted together.

A *haplogroup* is a group of closely related haplotypes.

Phylogeography is the study of the processes controlling the geographic distributions of lineages by constructing the genealogies of populations and genes.

References

Achilli, A., Olivieri, A., Soares, P., Lancioni, H., Hooshiar Kashani, B., Perego, U.A., Nergadze, S.G., Carossa, V., Santagostino, M., Capomaccio, S., Felicetti, M., Al-Achkar, W., Penedo, M.C.T., Verini-Supplizi, A., Houshmand, M., Woodward, S.R., Semino, O., Silvestrelli, M., Giulotto, E., Pereira, L., Bandelt, H.-J. & Torroni, A. 2012. Mitochondrial genomes from modern horses reveal the major haplogroups that underwent domestication. *Proceedings of the National Academy of Sciences* 109: 2449–2454.

Albarella, U., Johnstone, C., Vickers, K., 2008. The development of animal husbandry from the late Iron Age to the end of the Roman period. A case study from south-east Britain. *Journal of Archaeological Science* 35/7: 1828–1848.

Azzaroli, A. 1985. *An early history of horsemanship*. Leiden.

Bendrey, R. 2012. From wild horses to domestic horses. A European perspective. *World Archaeology* 44/1: 135–57.

Bjørnstad, G., Nilsen, N. Ø. & Røed, K. H. 2003. Genetic relationship between Mongolian and Norwegian horses? *Animal Genetics* 34: 55–58.

Bower, M.A., Edwards, C.J., Evans, C., Downes, C.S., 2013. Horse husbandry in Iron Age and Romano-British East Anglia. Ancient DNA analysis of horses at Langdale Hale, Cambridgeshire. In: Evans, C., Appleby, G., Lucy, S., Regan, R. (eds). *Process and History. Romano-British Communities at Colne Fen, Earith. An Inland Port and Supply Farm*. Cambridge: 140–143.

Boyd, L. & Houpt, K. A. 1994. *Przewalski's Horse, the History and Biology of an Endangered Species*. Albany: 195–228.

Caesar, Gaius Iulius *De Bello Gallico*. Ed. & transl. by L. Möller 2013. *Der gallische Krieg/Gaius Iulius Caesar*. Wiesbaden.

Carlie, A. 2004. *Forntida byggnadskult*. Stockholm.

Dobat, A.S., Price, T.D., Kveiborg, J., Ilkjær, J. & Rowley-Conwy, P. 2014. The four horses of an Iron Age apocalypse. War-horses from the third-century weapon sacrifice at Illerup Aadal (Denmark). *Antiquity* 88: 191–204.

Elsner, J., Deschler-Erb, S., Stopp, B., Hofreiter, M., Schibler, J. & Schlumbaum, A. 2016. Mitochondrial d-loop variation, coat colour and sex identification of Late Iron Age horses in Switzerland. *Journal of Archaeological Science: Reports* 6:386–396.

Fabech, C. 1991. Neue Perspektiven zu den Funden von Sösdala und Fulltofta. *Studien zur Sachsenforschung* 7.

Fabech, C. & Ringtved, J. 2009. Arealanvendelse og landskabstyper i det 1. år-tusinde. In: Odgaard, B. & Rømer, J. Rydén (eds). *Danske landbrugslandskaber gennem 2000 år – fra digevoldinger til støtteordninger.* Aarhus: 143–176.

Götherström, A. 2002. The value of stallions and mares during the Early Medieval time in upper class Svealand. Molecular sex identifications on horse remains from Vendel and Eketorp. *Journal of Nordic Archaeological Science* 13: 75–78.

Hagberg, U.E. 1967. *The archaeology of Skedemosse II. The votive deposits in the Skedemosse fen and their relation to the Iron-Age settlement on Öland, Sweden.* Stockholm.

Hyland, A. 1990. *Equus. The horse in the Roman world.* London.

Jansen, T., Foster, P., Levine, M.A., Oelke, H., Hurles, M., Renfrew, C., Weber, J. & Olek, K. 2002. Mitochondrial DNA and the origins of the domestic horse. *Proceedings of the National Academy of Sciences* 16: 10905–10910.

Lau, N. 2014. *Das Thorsberger Moor 1. Die Pferdegeschirre. Germanische Zaumzeuge und Sattelgeschirre als Zeugnisse kriegerischer Reiterei im mittel- und nordeuropäischen Barbaricum.* Schleswig.

Levine, M. 1999. Botai and the Origins of Horse Domestication. *Journal of Anthropological Archaeology* 18: 29–78.

Levine, M. 2002. mtDNA and horse domestication. The archaeologist's cut. In: Mashkour, M. (ed.). *Equids in Time and Space.* Durham.

Lippold. S., Knapp, M., Kuznetsova, T., Leonard, J.A., Benecke, N., Ludwig, A., Rasmussen, M., Cooper, A., Weinstock, J., Willerslev, E., Shapiro, B. & Hofreiter, M. 2011a. Discovery of lost diversity of paternal horse lineages using ancient DNA. *Nature Communications* 2: 450.

Lippold, S., Matzke, N.J., Reissmann, M. and Hofreiter, M. 2011b. Whole mitochondrial genome sequencing of domestic horses reveals incorporation of extensive wild horse diversity during domestication. *BMC Evolutionary Biology* 2011/11: 328.

Ludwig, A., Pruvost, M., Reissmann, M., Benecke, N., Brockmann, G.A., Castanos, P., Cieslak, M., Lippold, S., Llorente, L. & Malaspinas, A.S. 2009. Coat Color Variation at the Beginning of Horse Domestication. *Science* 324: 485.

Møhl, U. 1997. The human and animal bones from Röekillorna in Hagestad – zoological light on sacrificial practices. In: Stjernquist, B. *The Röekillorna Spring – Spring cult in Scandinavian prehistory.* Lund: 123–153.

Monikander, A. 2010. *Våld och vatten. Våtmarkskult vid Skedemosse under järnåldern.* Stockholm.

Näsström, B.-M. 2002. 2002. *Tro och offer i det förkristna Norden.* Stockholm.

Nordqvist, B. 2006. *Offerplatsen Finnestorp. Grävningsredogörelse för Offerplatsen Finnestorp 2000–2004.* Gothenburg.

Petersen, J.L., Mickelson, J.R., Cothran, E.G., Andersson, L., Axelsson, S., Bailey, J.E., Bannasch, D., Binns, M.M., Borges, A.S., Brama, P., da Câmara Machado, A., Distl, O., Felicetti, M., Fox-Clipsham, L., Graves, K.T., Guérin,

G., Haase, B., Hasegawa, T., Hemmann, K., Hill, E.W. Leeb, T., Lindgren, G., Lohi, H.H., Lopes, M.S., McGivney, B.A., Mikko, S., Orr, N., Penedo, C.T., Piercy, R.J., Raekallio, M., Rieder, S., Røed, K.H., Silvestrelli, M., Swinburne, J., Tozaki, T., Vaudin, M., Wade, C.M., McCue, M.E. 2013. Genetic diversity in the modern horse illustrated from genome-wide SNP data. *PLOS ONE* 8 (1), e54997.

Stjernquist, B. 1973. Das Opfermoor in Hassle Bösarp, Schweden. *Acta Archaeologica* 44: 19–62.

Strömberg, M. 1961. *Untersuchungen zur jüngeren Eisenzeit in Schonen. Vol I.* Lund.

Sundkvist, A. 1992. *Rida de döda. Vikingatida bett i Valsgärde och Birka.* University of Uppsala. [Unpublished MA thesis].

Sundkvist, A. 2001. *Hästarnas Land. Aristokratisk hästhållning och ridkonst i Svealands yngre järnålder.* Uppsala. Summary.

Sundkvist, A. 2004. Herding horses. A model of prehistoric horsemanship in Scandinavia – and elsewhere? In: Santillo Frizell, B. (ed.). *PECUS. Man and animal in antiquity.* Rome: 241–249.

Svensson, E.M., Telldahl, Y., Sjölin, E., Sundkvist, A., Hulth, H., Sjøvold, T. & Götherström, A. 2012. Coat colour and sex identification in horses from Iron Age Sweden. *Annals of Anatomy* 194: 82–87.

Tacitus. *Germany and its tribes.* Ed. and transl. by A.J. Church & W.J. Brodribb. In: Complete Works of Tacitus. New York 1942. – Online at Perseus Digital Library http://www.perseus.tufts.edu/hopper/text?doc=urn:cts:latinLit:phi1351.phi002.perseus-eng1:1 – Checked 3 October 2016.

Vilà, C., Leonard, J. A., Götherstrom, A., Marklund, S., Sandberg, K., Lidén, K., Wayne, R. K. & Ellegren, H. 2001. Widespread origins of domestic horse lineages. *Science* 291: 474–477.

Vretemark, M. 2013. Evidence of animal offerings in Iron Age Scandinavia. In: G. Ekroth & J. Wallensten (eds). *Bones, behaviour and belief. The zooarchaeological evidence as a source for ritual practice in ancient Greece and beyond.* Athens: 51–59.

Wallner, B., Vogl, C., Shukla, P., Burgstaller, J.P., Druml, T. & Brem, G. 2013. Identification of Genetic Variation on the Horse Y Chromosome and the Tracing of Male Founder Lineages in Modern Breeds. *PLOS ONE* 8(4): e60015.

Warmuth, V., Eriksson, A., Bower, M.A., Barker, G., Barrett, E., Hanks, B.K., Li, S., Lomitashvili, D., Ochir-Goryaeva, M., Sizonov, G.V., Soyonov, V., Manica, A., 2012. Reconstructing the origin and spread of horse domestication in the Eurasian steppe. *Proceedings of the National Academy of Sciences* 109: 8202–8206.

Zimmermann, W. H. 1999. Why was cattle-stalling introduced in prehistory? In: Fabech, C. & Ringtved, J. (eds). *Settlement and Landscape.* Højbjerg/Aarhus: 301–318.

Резюме

Лошадь Железного века

Эрика Росенгрен

Находка в Сёсдале, датирующаяся Эпохой переселения народов (рубеж IV–V вв.), является одним из наиболее интересных археологических открытий, связанных с лошадьми. Однако в непосредственной близости от места жертвоприношения конской упряжи не были найдены останки лошадей. В результате утрачена важнейшая часть уравнения, и для изучения физических особенностей лошади приходится обращаться к другим регионам.

Существует ряд одновременных находке письменных источников, оставленных чужеземными авторами, в том числе римскими хронистами. Согласно им, в жертву приносили чаще всего самцов животных, однако если использовать определение пола на молекулярном уровне, то создается впечатление, что и в погребениях, и в контексте жертвоприношений ни одному из полов животных предпочтений не отдавали. К тому же, в противоположность словам письменных источников о лошадях светлой масти, генетическое исследование останков скандинавских лошадей на мононуклеотидный полиморфизм указало на доминирование вороной, гнедой и рыжей пород, которые, как представляется, были одинаково распространены на всех памятниках. Возможное присутствие доминантного гена-ослабителя, осветляющего окраску серебристыми тонами, отмечено лишь для останков начала Эпохи викингов.

По данным ряда останков, обнаруженных на скандинавских памятниках, более или менее синхронных находке в Сёсдале, высота лошадей в холке определяется как приблизительно 120–140 см. Любопытно, что предполагаемая высота в холке хорошо соответствует данным, полученным для лошадей, живших на Европейском континенте и на Британских островах. Предполагают, что в этих регионах римляне завели новые женские линии лошадей; помимо этого, с течением времени наблюдается увеличение размеров и изменение формы тела животных, что заставляет предположить вероятное улучшение породы в результате использования

нового племенного скота. Однако на синхронных скандинавских памятниках подобных изменений не наблюдается.

Генетические исследования наследуемых по материнской линии митохондриальных ДНК лошадей Железного века показали их большое разнообразие, которое исследователи интерпретируют как отражение тенденции к торговле самками животных. В аутосомных ДНК (т. е. микросателлитах) дивергенция современных пород более выражена, чем наблюдается по последовательностям митохондриальных ДНК, что еще раз подтверждает доминирование потока материнских генов в генном обмене между породами. Наоборот, выявленное у современных домашних пород разнообразие Y-хромосомы весьма ограничено, что, вероятно, является результатом использования очень немногочисленных жеребцов-производителей, одомашненных изначально, причем развивавшиеся после доместикации способы разведения породы в дальнейшем сократили используемое количество самцов. Доказано, что современные североевропейские породы, например, исландская лошадь, шетландский пони и норвежская фьордовая лошадь, очень часто сохраняют автохтонные варианты Y-хромосомы, тесно связанные с гаплотипом предков. По-видимому, если адаптация этих пород к местным условиям повысила их ценность по сравнению с привозными животными, то это обстоятельство могло быть объяснением их сравнительно изолированной истории.

Наконец, исследования микросателлитов и общегеномного мононуклеотидного полиморфизма открыли тесные генетические связи между современными североевропейскими породами и аборигенными монгольскими лошадьми, указав на участие восточных генов в формировании североевропейских популяций лошадей. Это может означать, что данные породы лошадей имеют древнюю, изолированную историю, или же что они недавно испытали приток восточных генов. Известными примерами восточного влияния является экспансия великих кочевых империй, осуществлявшаяся всадниками – скифами (VIII в. до н. э. – II в. н. э.), сарматами (II–IV в. н. э.), гуннами Аттилы (V в. н. э.) и Чингисханом (XIII в. н. э.). Однако этот восточный генетический материал мог быть привнесен одновременно и в более раннее, и в более позднее время, причем ответ на этот вопрос, возможно, позволят отыскать дальнейшие исследования геномов из останков древних лошадей, найденных на территории нынешней Скандинавии.

Подписи к иллюстрациям

Рис. 1. Лошади самых распространенных мастей – рыжей, гнедой и вороной (фото Photocase/kb-photodesign).

Рис. 2. Средняя высота холки лошадей Железного века в сравнении со средней высотой холки современных лошадей скандинавских пород (рисунок Эрики Росенгрен).

Chapter 9

East is East and West is West and never the twain shall meet?

The equestrian context of Sösdala

Anneli Sundkvist[1]

The Migration Period Sösdala find from Scania, Sweden, consists of several horse-related artefacts. The horse equipment is put into its equestrian context. What do the artefacts tell us about the riding they were once made for? The 5th century AD was turbulent and the old Roman values were challenged by riders from the east. Where did the Sösdala riders get their equestrian influences from? The Sösdala saddles and bridles are discussed from a rider's perspective, with emphasis on function and the impact on the horse caused by the pieces of equipment.

Sundkvist, A. 2017. East is East and West is West and never the twain shall meet? The equestrian context of Sösdala. In: Fabech, C. & Näsman, U. (eds). *The Sösdala horsemen – and the equestrian elite of fifth century Europe.* Jutland Archaeological Society.

A horse is not always a horse. In modern western society, where horses are mainly used for recreation (even though there are several exceptions, e.g. police horses), there are several types of horses. Many of the breeds we know today are old, sometimes hundreds of years old (Rosengren chapter 8). They were all bred for a certain purpose and formed by selective breeding and/or physical environment. This has given us a variation in height from less than one metre to 180 cm. Horses differ in size, temperament, conformation, colour etc., and have done so for a very long time. Horses have been bred selectively for thousands of years. Ancient breeders aimed to gain the boldest and strongest war horse, the most smooth-gaited riding horse or the fastest hunter or race horse. These types existed already in antiquity, but then they were not what we today define as a breed of horses. Since the 19th century, breeds are defined by a stud book.

War horses and riding horses

Since horses have been of different use and types for a very long time, one horse was not enough for many people. In the Middle Ages, war horses were led to battle by the

Fig. 1. A collected bullfighting horse in training at the canter. The horse is in the "frame" set by the rider. The purpose of all dressage work is to get the horse off the forehand, to let the hind legs carry more weight in order to make turns, pirouettes etc. in small spaces. Photo: Anneli Sundkvist, Portugal 2004.

squire while the knight rode another horse, preferably a palfrey – a gaited riding horse – while travelling (Gladitz 1997:157; Hyland 1998:15). A fresh horse was vital in battle, and travels could not be allowed to make the *destrier* tired. Also, for travelling, specialised amblers were more comfortable for the rider. The amble is a four-beat gait, preserved in few European breeds today but more common in historic times. Amble is smooth and less tiresome for rider as well as horse.

Cart and draught horses

When the horse once was adopted into war service, it was in front of a chariot. For a thousand years, the majority of war horses would draw chariots (Sidnell 2006:6). The custom was widely spread, from the Far East to the British Isles and Northern Africa. In Scandinavia, the cart or draught horse did not play an important role in transport until early modern time and war chariots were never adopted. Iron Age evidence of cart horses are few in Scandinavia, although horse and wagon have been depicted as far back as the Bronze Age and remains of wagons have been found in Denmark (Schousbo 1987). Parts of harness are found in Late Iron Age graves (e.g. Vendel in Uppland, Stolpe & Arne 1912) and are also pictured on e.g. the 9th century tapestry from the Oseberg ship in Norway (Ingstad 1992:181–186). Oseberg is a grave from which we also have several examples of Viking Age sleighs (Christensen 1992:123–126). Sleighs might have been used for a long time, but summer transport must have been more efficient by boat or using pack horses. In the Roman Empire, with Roman roads, fast cart horses were more important. Horses were not used for agricultural purposes until the Middle Ages. One of the first depictions of an agricultural draught horse is found on the lower margin of the Bayeux Tapestry (scene 10).

Pack horses

Pack horses, also known as sumpters, have been used worldwide for millennia. Animals are still used to carry today. Sumpters are known from Roman times (Junkelmann 1990: Abb. 72), even though the good roads and general organisation probably made them less important than wagon transport. In Scandinavian Iron Age contexts depictions are sparse, but pack horses are mentioned in the Icelandic sagas. A pony with pack saddle identical to those used in Shetland in the early 20th century is depicted on the Bayeux tapestry (scene 41). Pack horses must have been very common in eras when the roads were bad or non-existent, but they are not prominent in the sources before the medieval period. They must have been essential in Scandinavia for travelling outside the waterways and in the summer season. According to Gladitz (1997:155–156) sumpters were more valuable than cart horses in 12th century England. Sumpters were probably sturdy, calm horses with ground-covering walk. In the Middle Ages, a large household on the move needed several horses and horses of different types (cf. Gladitz 1997:156).

Fig. 2. A racehorse in training at the canter. Even though the horse is held back by her rider, the longer, lower shape with stretched neck is visible. Photo: Anneli Sundkvist, Newmarket, England 2015.

Fig. 3. The finish of a race. The horses are galloping on loose reins with their heads and necks stretched forward. Photo: Anneli Sundkvist, Newmarket, England 2015.

Different purpose – different horse

To conclude on the topic of horse types: the sources from the 4th and 5th centuries concerning horse types are scarce. Apart from cult purposes, which are not discussed in this paper, the main use of horses must have been riding and packing. Requirements of a riding horse for transport or war might be different. When on a long journey, a gaited riding horse must have been a big advantage.

The art of riding in the Iron Age

Styles of riding

The art of riding in the first part of the first millennium AD can be divided into two distinct styles; the *western* with the horse collected between the rider's legs and hand (fig. 1), and the *eastern* with the horse moving close to its natural form (fig. 2–3). The styles have been developed from different needs. In general terms, the western style is more suitable for situations when horse and rider need to move slowly in small areas and make tight turns, while the eastern style was shaped for riding fast on wide plains. Already in prehistoric times, the styles were probably mixed. When the Parthians defeated the Romans at Carrhae in 53 BC (Harran in Turkey), their cavalry consisted of light archers as well as heavily armed lancers (Curtis & Tallis 2012:25–27).

Today, the western style is exemplified in e.g. mounted bullfighting, where horse, rider and bull are in a small arena. A bullfighter's horse needs to be able to accelerate to avoid the bull and also to turn 180 degrees in a tight circle (or rather a pirouette) to make it possible for the rider to attack. Mounted bullfighting is still traditional in Portugal, harking back centuries. Training a bullfighter horse takes years, since the horse need to build its strength and balance to make close turns, accelerate, and decrease speed in tight spaces. The horses are bred with the purpose of being easy to collect, to have a very good canter (to be able to move slowly and make the turns) and to have a lot of courage not to flee from the bull. These skills are probably very similar to what was needed from a medieval war horse. In the Middle Ages, horses from the Iberian Peninsula were in high demand as *destriers* (Davis 1989:49–57; Gladitz 1997:162–164).

The eastern style of riding still exists among nomadic riders in the plains of central Asia and among riders performing horseback archery as a sport. The horse is a platform for many activities. Speed is essential, but tight turns in closed areas are not high priority. In mounted combat hit-and-run tactics were used. Horses raced at full speed towards the enemy, letting the riders attack with arrows or

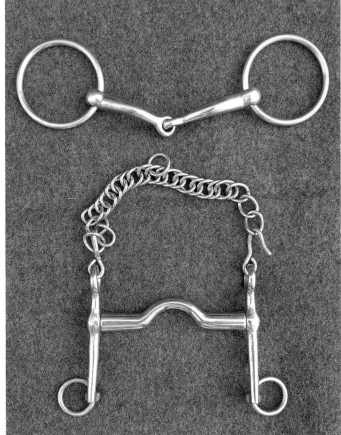

Fig. 4. A Portuguese horseman in the 21st century. Wearing traditional suit, he is on his way to work with fighting bulls. Photo: Anneli Sundkvist, Portugal 2004.

Fig. 5. Modern European jointed snaffle (top) and curb with moderate port and the curb chain attached. Photo: Anna Backman, http://www.hippokultur.se/.

javelins. Once the weapon was launched, the rider raced away and rearmed. Training was not very complicated. The horses needed to be steady, obedient and unafraid. They also needed to continue straight forward while the rider was doing what he had to do (e.g. using his bow) and turn away when the rider either changed his position in the saddle (and moves his weight) or used the reins.

Regardless of style, riders keep the reins in their left hand, leaving the right hand for weapon or tool (fig. 4). A mounted warrior holds reins and shield in his left hand and the sword, javelin or lance in the right. A mounted archer who needs both hands for his weapon must also be able to put the reins down on the neck of the horse while it is continuing forward at high speed. In 53 BC, the Romans first encountered Parthian mounted archers at Carrhae. Roman writers describe the hit-and-run tactics with frustration. The Parthians took to simulated flight, just to turn around in the saddles and shoot backwards, the Parthian shot (Curtis & Tallis 2012:26–27).

In the 4th and 5th centuries, parts of equipment follow the style of riding. This is where archaeology could be used to separate riders of different traditions. Spurs and curb bits are connected to the western, or Roman, style. Eastern riders used a snaffle bit and never wore spurs, but they sometimes had a whip. This might sound promising, but unfortunately the equipment is not standardised. The snaffle bit was the most common bit in the west long after the introduction of the curb during Celtic times (fig. 5; Chenevix Trench 1970:38, cf. Green 1992:208). On Roman monuments cavalry horses are ridden on curb as well as snaffles, and both types survive in the archaeological material (Hyland 1990:136–137; Junkelmann 1992:18–26). Spurs were used, but not by all riders. Whips leave few, if any, archaeological traces. The classic archaeological method, to turn to material culture, is insufficient for determining a certain riding style to which the Sösdala rider can be connected.

Horse combat

The Sösdala finds were deposited long before the stirrup, probably invented in China in the 4th century AD, reached Europe (Sidnell 2006:304–311). In 1962, medieval historian Lynn White argued that the stirrup was the backbone of a change of cavalry technique as well as the entire society in the early Middle Ages. He saw the stirrup as a necessity for organised, mounted shock combat with lances – the fighting style of the medieval knight (White 1962). White's theory was widely accepted and not really challenged until the 1990s when Bernard Bachrach argued that a saddle with a rigid tree and high cantle was what really made the difference rather than the stirrup (Bachrach 1993). Philip Sidnell (2006:304–315) underlines that there is no direct link between the introduction and acceptance of the stirrup in the West in the 8th–9th centuries and the breakthrough for mounted shock combat at Hastings in 1066.

The role of the stirrup in the development of mounted combat has generally been overrated. Already before the birth of Christ, there were many efficient cavalry units. How the units relevant to the Sösdala finds fought is not clear, since we are not sure which these units were. There might have been fights between riders. There were certain riders who attacked enemies on the ground in groups. This can seen on many Roman monuments, e.g. Trajan's Column and Marcus Aurelius' Column, both dated to the 2nd century AD. Equestrians were certainly used for chasing and overrunning the enemy. They might also have fought as mounted archers (Goldsworthy 2003:204–205) and against other mounted archers.

According to Roman depictions (mainly marble carvings), riders sometimes entered close combat. In many cases, the warrior depicted is the emperor, sitting on his war horse in the turmoil of battle (fig. 6). Such battle scenes might be set with the purpose of increasing the glory and heroism of the emperor, rather than to tell a true story of how the battle was fought. On the other hand, Adrian Goldsworthy remarks that in Late Antiquity some cavalry units were more heavily armoured than the infantry. There were more of these warriors in the eastern army, probably because one of their main opponents was the heavily armed Persian cavalry (Goldsworthy 2003:205). Horses were probably used in close combat before the Middle

Fig. 6. Emperor Trajan (AD 98–117) in a small-horned saddle. The marble work is from Trajan's reign but was reused on the Arch of Constantine (AD 315), situated outside the Colosseum in Rome. Note the mounted breast collar. Photo: Anneli Sundkvist.

Ages, even against other cavalry units. In general, however, their role might have been to transport their riders quickly from place to place.

Horses and horse tack as gifts and loot

Horses and their equipment as royal gifts have a long tradition. In *Beowulf*, set in the 6th century, we are told that the hero received eight horses from the Danish king after having killed the monster Grendel (line 1035–1039, Heaney 1999). Beowulf later gave four of them to King Hygelac (line 2163–2165). In his biography of Charlemagne from the 9th century, Notker Balbulus writes that the Emperor gave Spanish horses to the King of Persia. The *Gesta Guillelmi ducis Normannorum et regis Anglorum* (chapter 1, verse 13) tells us that William, Duke of Normandy was given Spanish horses (Davis & Chibnall 1998:17). The tradition, the age of which we do not know, continued into historic times. Charles XI of Sweden was an enthu-

Fig. 7. Long-reining on the tombstone of the cavalry man Longinus Biarta, who died in AD 68. The saddle has prominent horns. Photo: Wikimedia Commons.

siastic rider and horseman. During his reign he received many horses, sometimes with saddles and bridles. Some were loot from foreign campaigns, such as two Arabian stallions the Swedish aristocrat Nils Bielke had taken in Hungary (Larsdotter 2008:97–98). Others were gifts from kings and emperors, most probably given as an act of diplomacy and peace. The Royal Armoury still has large collections of saddles and bridles of foreign origin. The horses are gone, but the monumental paintings the king ordered are still part of the furnishing of some Swedish castles. Horses and their tack as gifts did certainly exist already during the Iron Age. A bridle like the one from the Sösdala 1929 pit I would have been a splendid gift for well-performed duty.

The Sösdala horse equipment

The context and history of the Sösdala find are described by Charlotte Fabech (chapter 1). All artefacts are connected to horses. In all, the Sösdala find consists of five pits or deposits containing at least seven saddles and two mounted bridles (Näsman chapter 7). Unfortunately, little organ-

ic material is preserved and the contexts were destroyed by the finders. Despite this, the shape of the mounts and the bits can be used to discuss what type of horsemanship and riding the Sösdala rider was carrying out.

Saddles

It is not clear where, when and by whom the true saddle was invented, but it changed riding and the use of horses forever. Spacers, wooden constructions over the withers, lift the rider from the back of the horse, which saves both parts muscular ache and wounds caused by friction. To some extent, this is the effect of a stuffed blanket or saddle pad as well, but since these constructions follow the movements of the horse, they do not provide the steady platform needed for someone who is armed and armoured. To do this in a safe and efficient way, a built-up saddle that supports the rider is necessary (cf. Hyland 1990:130–131). Early saddles with wooden spacers are found in Pazyryk, barrow 1 and 2, dating to the 5th–4th centuries BC (Rudenko 1970:129–133, xxxv–xxxvi). The rigid tree saddle, with a full construction of wood, might have been invented by Nomadic tribes in the east, but its introduction in Western Europe is uncertain.

Before 1967 and the publication of the Roman sites of Valkenburg and Vechten (Groenman-van Waateringe 1967:104–121), little was known about the cavalry saddle of Imperial Rome. Finds of leather from these Dutch sites made it possible for the archaeologist Peter Connolly to reconstruct the Roman cavalry saddle two decades after Groenman-van Waateringe's publication (Connolly 1987). The reconstruction was later tested by the historian and professional horse trainer Ann Hyland. She used one of her horses, believed to be similar in type to horses preferred by the Romans (Hyland 1990:131–134). The experiment did result in some clarification of the rigging of the saddle. Concerning function, Hyland concluded that the reconstruction was well suited for a task as a battle saddle and must have increased the capability of the Roman cavalry (Hyland 1990:132). Peter Connolly made two varieties of the saddle, the difference being the size of the horns – the erect knobs on the cantle and pommel (Hyland 1990:134). Many depictions of Roman saddles show horns of modest size (fig. 6), although there are exceptions as on the tombstone of Longinus Biarta from the area of Cologne, dated to the 1st century AD (fig. 7).

Regardless of their size, saddle horns were useful for riding in battle and also served an important role in cross-country riding. Horns made going up- or downhill at speed safer and easier. Larger horns provide more security (and more protection, although Roman saddles do not seem to have been designed to protect the rider as medieval battle saddles were), but also have disadvantages. Larger and more enclosing horns make it harder to mount or dismount the horse quickly. Mounting a large-horned saddle like Connolly's reconstruction without stirrups could have been quite a challenge.

Connolly's reconstruction was also tested by the historian and experimental archaeologist Marcus Junkelmann, who noted that the larger horns gave the rider several problems. One was the chance to break free from the horse in case of a fall; another was the ability to mount and dismount swiftly while in full armour. Also, the saddle was very uncomfortable and the short skirts resulted in blisters and bleeding wounds on the legs of the rider (Junkelmann 1992:47–57). Junkelmann accepted the fittings of the leather cover, but stated that the question of the Roman horned saddle as a rigid tree saddle should be further discussed (Junkelmann 1992:60). While Hyland accepted Connolly's interpretation of the saddle as a rigid tree saddle and discussed the introduction into the west (Hyland 1990:132), Junkelmann sought other solutions. He evaluated several modern European working saddles and new reconstructions. The conclusion was that it is possible that the Roman cavalry saddle was a treeless, padded saddle with the horns sewn to the pommel. If the saddle did have a solid tree, the horns could not have been fastened to it, the way Connolly proposed in his original reconstruction, but must have been flexible to allow the rider to mount and dismount while in armour (Junkelmann 1992:66). Such a saddle would still give support but be more comfortable when travelling over great distances.

When we turn to the Sösdala era, the periods after the re-localisation of Roman power to Constantinople as well as Rome in the late 3rd century, we see visible differences in the type of saddle used in the east compared to the saddle of the Roman cavalry of the 1st and 2nd centuries. In general, saddles built further east had more elaborate cantles and pommels that were closed in "bows" rather than separate horns (Anke 2007:218–219). To judge from the mounts, this was the construction of the Sösdala saddles. During the first millennium, this construction became common in east and west. Research about the construction of later Roman saddles is sparse. Marble carvings, which provide much information about horses and tack in the first couple of centuries AD, are less common from the following centuries. Mosaics, e.g. in the Villa del Casale, Sicily,[2] depict 4th century horsemen. While bridles and breeching are prominent, saddles are hidden under flowing fabric. Some of the mounted hunters seem to be riding bareback. In some respects, e.g. comfort and protection, closed saddle bows might have been superior to horns. During the first millennium the horned saddle slipped into historical obscurity while the model with closed pommel and cantle survives to this day. It is possible that this transformation started in the 4th century, along the eastern frontiers of what was to become the Byzantine Empire. For the horses, the change must have been of little importance.

Migration Period saddles in Sweden were first discussed by Rune Norberg, who made a reconstruction based on saddle mounts found under the Kanalgatan street in the city of Jönköping, province of Småland (Norberg 1929b). The Jönköping saddle was distinguished by quite heavy and crude rings made from copper alloy, which has resulted in the term "ring saddle" (e.g. Ramqvist 1992:78; Fabech & Näsman 2013:93). Similar rings were also known from e.g. Vennebo, Västergötland (Montelius 1884:242; Norberg 1929b:104–106) and Fulltofta, Scania. Later, saddles of this type have been found at Högom, Medelpad (Ramqvist 1992 and chapter 10), and of course Sösdala.

The question about the role of the saddle rings has yet to be answered. The long rivets suggest deep anchoring in the wood. Patterns of wear tell a story of heavy pressure on some rings. A theory suggests that the rings were used to fasten hanging equipment (see e.g. Arrhenius 1983:63), but a study of pack horses through time shows that the desire for a tight profile is evident. Hanging objects are uncomfortable for the rider, might scare the horse, and are prone to be lost if a strap breaks. It is possible that the rings

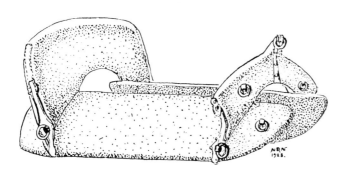

Fig. 8. The reconstruction of the Jönköping saddle made by Rune Norberg. After Norberg 1929a fig. 14.

---

served to lash up equipment, but it seems unlikely that the objects would hang free and move with the horse.

Most ancient saddles, irrespective of culture, were equipped with breast collar and/or breeching (fig. 6). These straps serve to keep the saddle in place in situations when its position is at risk of being altered. Were the rings part of the saddle and used to hold the breeching and/or breast collar together? Norberg suggested this already in his article about the Jönköping saddle (1929b:104), but it is hard to follow his idea when studying the reconstruction (fig. 8). The Jönköping find consisted of several saddle rings. Since neither wood nor leather was preserved, the reconstruction was based upon existing historic saddles in the Swedish Royal Armoury. The artefacts were mounted on a wooden tree. However, since the context of the find was disturbed, the positions of different objects were lost. It is possible, even likely, that the Jönköping find represents more than one saddle. Apart from the cases where rings are still attached to the mounts there is no information on the placements of the rings on the saddles in either Jönköping or Sösdala. Regardless of contextual problems, Norberg's theory about the rings as holds for different straps is – in my opinion – plausible. Breast collar, breeching and even girth could be *tied* to the rings without using a buckle (cf. reconstruction fig. 5 in Fabech & Näsman chapter 17).

Norberg states that he used "the most primitive" saddles in the Royal Armoury – two pack saddles from Småland (Norberg 1929b:103). His choice was probably based on age and provenance. The question I have to ask myself is

whether Norberg's reconstruction is valid. I have already mentioned the possibility that the mounts belonged to more than one saddle. As a matter of fact, Norberg himself had a hard time trying to place all the mounts and rings on a single saddle tree. But what about the wooden tree? The Roman cavalry saddle might not, after all, have been built upon a rigid tree as first reconstructed by Connolly (1987), but according to the research by Junkelmann (1992) it could have been treeless, gaining stability by padding, leather, wooden spacers and craftsmanship. In Scandinavia, the best-preserved Migration Period saddle is the Högom saddle, dated to *c.* AD 500 (Ramqvist 1992:221 and chapter 10), or, according to new research, to AD 455/465–505/515 (Fabech & Näsman 2013:94 with references). Organic material is preserved, but nothing from what Ramqvist mentions as "the boards" – the tree. Ramqvist states that no remains of the tree were found, but a feature visible in one of the photos from the excavation of the saddle might be remains (Ramqvist 1992:83). It strikes me as somewhat strange that no pieces of the tree or the "saddle boards" are preserved from Högom, when we do have braided straw from the padding. But after having gone through Junkelmann's research and studied his pictures of an "undressed" Maremma saddle (Junkelmann 1992: Taf. 70), I am more or less convinced that the Högom saddle never had a rigid tree. Apart from Junkelmann's theories about the Roman saddle (1992:66), there are many examples. For instance, there are treeless saddles from Maremma, Italy (fig. 9–10) built for long days' work with cattle. These saddles still give the rider support and comfort.

For almost ninety years, Norberg's reconstruction has been the model for Iron Age saddles in Sweden. Most likely we should reconsider and look for more alternatives: a softer, more comfortable saddle but still with built-up pommel and cantle that secure the rider and provide support. Migration Period saddles have often been interpreted as "Nomadic" (Krogh 1970; Fabech & Näsman 2013:93). Hunnic saddles are interpreted as "wooden saddles", but are we sure that they had trees? Many mounts from archaeological contexts tell a story about high, wooden, pommel and/or cantle (e.g. Bóna 1991:177, Abb. 23, 48; Anke 2007:224–225) and that interpretation seems solid to me. But an entire wooden tree that con-

Fig. 9. Treeless Maremma saddle. Note the "pillows" that distribute the pressure, the padded, comfortable seat and the built-up wooden pommel. Photo: Anneli Sundkvist, Blera, Italy 2004.

Fig. 10. "Butteri", Italian cowboys with traditional tack and equipment. The high pommels of these saddles probably resemble what the Sösdala saddles might have looked like. These saddles most likely have wooden trees (cf. fig. 9 for a treeless variety of the Maremma saddle). Photo: Anneli Sundkvist, Blera, Italy 2006.

nects pommel and cantle might not be the norm. According to István Bóna, this interpretation is built upon horse burials with golden or gilt mounts fastened to pommel and tree at the front of what is assumed to be solid tree saddles (1991:177–179, Abb. 23). There certainly were saddles of stock saddle type[3] in the 5th–6th centuries (Liesowska 2016), but were they really the only type in Europe and Scandinavia? Nomadic peoples of the east have figured in discussions about Iron Age Scandinavian horsemanship for decades (e.g. Krogh 1970; Nylén 1973; Ørsnes 1994:272; Fabech & Näsman 2013:94 with references) and for good reasons. There are striking examples of obvious influence, such as the Magyar origin of a distinct type of 10th century double cheek bar snaffles found in e.g. the Ladby skip (Thorvildsen 1957) and the Birka graves (Arbman 1940–1943). However, we should not forget about the west. The splendour of the Illerup Ådal breechings and breast collars has clear Roman connections. A built-up saddle was essential for horseback work as well as any type of mounted combat, no matter the choice of weapon. Pommel and cantle kept the rider in a steady position, giving him security when he carried out his duties, in peace and war. Recently, an entire saddle was found in a 6th century tomb in Mongolia (Liesowska 2016). This saddle has

a wooden tree,[4] but also stirrups. A rider who rises in the stirrups will concentrate the pressure of his weight on the spots where the stirrup leathers are fastened. Therefore, a rigid tree is more important when riding with stirrups since it distributes the pressure over the horse back, preventing it from saddle sores. In Europe, examples of fragments of saddle tree are found in a grave from Koroncó, Hungary (László 1943:109–116). Dating to the Magyar period, the saddle was equipped with stirrups and reconstructed as a stock saddle with breast collar and breeching (László 1943: Abb. 12). Before the introduction of stirrups and before mounted shock combat, the tree might have been less important. Later, it became vital.

The Sösdala saddle mounts were probably decoration. Damage that could be fended off by this type of metal mounts on pommel and cantle must have come from cutting and crushing weapons like swords and clubs used in very close combat and from specific angles. As protection,

Fig. 11. Horse with curb on Trajan's column (2nd century) in Rome. A curb bit consists of a mouthpiece with an elaborate part in the middle – the port and shanks with loops for the reins and cheekpieces. The shanks work as a lever, making the bit more efficient and – in the wrong hands – more severe than the old snaffle bit. On the other hand, the bit gives a skilled rider the opportunity to use very fine aids. Photo: Anneli Sundkvist.

the Sösdala saddle mounts were not very efficient, but they must have served their purpose as marking their riders' importance. A mounted, gilded[5] saddle is part of Beowulf's splendid gift after his victory over Grendel (lines 1035–1039, Heaney 1999; cf. Fabech & Näsman chapter 17):

Next the king ordered eight horses
With gold bridles to be brought through the yard
into the hall. The harness of one
included a saddle of sumptuous design,
the battle-seat where the son of Halfdane
rode …

Concerning the rider's skills and demands, the mounts tell us very little. The Sösdala saddles were built for mounted work which could have been battle. In some respects, dif-ferent type of tasks may have required different tightness of the seat. An archer turning around to perform the Parthian shot might need a slightly larger seat than a warrior using his lance against foot soldiers (or an archer firing straight forward or sideways only). A new reconstruction based upon available saddles e.g. Sösdala, Jönköping and Högom, as well as material from the Continent, would most probably spread some light over the Migration Period saddles of Scandinavia including the use of the mysterious saddle rings.

Bits and bridles

According to Charles Chenevix Trench, the curb bit was invented by the Gauls in the 3rd century BC (Chenevix Trench 1970:38). Chenevix Trench does not quote sources and his book has errors, but it is still one of the most thorough works on riding and horsemanship from a historic perspective. The curb bit is a technically advanced construction, giving pressure on the back of the horse's head which makes it yield to the bit and bend the neck in a beautiful arch, almost by the weight of the bit and reins only (fig. 5, 11).

Regardless of where it was invented, the curb was used in Gaul prior to the Roman conquest and in Europe before the birth of Christ. A bronze horse from the treasure of Neuvy-en-Sullias, Loire, France, dated to the era before the Roman conquest (Green 1992:208), is clearly equipped with a bit with long shanks (Green 1992: fig. 4:4). The Romans used curbs from at least the birth of Christ (Junkelmann 1992:20–23). Based on art, snaffles seem to have been common, but many monuments clearly show curbs (fig. 11). Some specimens survive in the archaeological material, e.g. from the Roman fort Newstead in Scotland (Junkelmann 1992: Abb. 11).

Scandinavia, however, provides a different picture. The curb was not introduced until the Middle Ages (Sundkvist 2001:104 with refs). Nomadic riders of the great plains favoured the old snaffle bit too. A snaffle is an efficient way to stop a horse, especially when using the one-rein stop. The rider takes one of the reins, if needed closer to the bit than usually, and drags the rein towards his hip, making the horse bend its neck and come to an immediate halt. The full cheek snaffle[6] is advantageous for this manoeuvre, since the cheek bars keep the bit in place in the horse's mouth. Stopping was the main task for the bit in the eastern style of riding. The distribution of the weight of the rider's body was used to make the turns. When areas were smaller and a collected horse was needed, the curb was favourable.

Some Scandinavian bits from the Roman and Migration Periods might have worked partly as a curb. Snaffles with a port from the Roman Iron Age are found in, e.g. Site A deposition in the war-booty find Illerup-Ådal, Jutland (early Roman Iron Age, Carnap-Bornheim & Ilkjær 1996a,b; Ilkjær 2003:50), and Ejsbølgård E (c. AD 300, Andersen 2003:254–255). Migration Period examples include the exclusive Högom bit (Ramqvist 1992: plate 41a) and Vennebo (SHM 6511:15[7]). The port creates a pressure on the tongue, encouraging the horse to lower its head. I would not classify these bits as curbs, but when examining the material on a visit to Moesgaard in 2002, I came to the conclusion that the mouthpiece together with the large rings and the metal bars under the horse's chin most probably give limited curb function. A bit from Ejsbølgård E, fitted with large bridle chains and small bronze hooks situated between the chains and the rings of the bit, might have worked in the same way. The present reconstruction (Andersen 2003: fig. 13) includes the bronze hooks as connections to the cheekpieces, but they might have been holders for a strap in the same position as a metal bar in the type 2 bits from Illerup Ådal (cf. Ilkjær 2000:109). In general, reconstruction and test riding (by a rider skilled in one-hand riding) would be needed to really analyse these bits and their function.

Snaffles with a port have stiff mouthpieces, but the impact might be achieved using other solutions. Most port-snaffles are known from high-standard deposits. Still we know that bits with ports or a "port" function were used in Sweden during the Roman Iron Age. Bit wear, most probably originating from a port, was discovered on a horse tooth (a p2) found in a well in Gilltuna, Västmanland, close to Lake Mälaren in Sweden. A radiocarbon sample from the well dates it to AD 80–240 (Sundkvist 2014:403–406). In this period, Gilltuna was a pretty large farm, but there are no signs of it being a manor (Sundkvist & Eklund 2014).

The 1929 Sösdala deposit I snaffle is jointed (Näsman chapter 7 fig. 1), but the joint is curved, forming a moderate port. It is possible that the construction of the bit gives some pressure on the tongue. The bit from the 1961 find is a double jointed snaffle. This bit works like an ordinary jointed snaffle (cf. Sundkvist 2001:22–23).

Apart from the bit, the Sösdala bridle parts do not tell much about function. Most mounts are delicate and fragile. They were most probably for decoration, creating a splendid sight when put on a good-looking horse. Maybe those who knew the "language" of the ornaments could also read the story of the rider's past adventures far away.

... and never the twain shall meet? Sösdala in context

As has been put forward by Fabech and Näsman, the Sösdala find might represent homecoming warriors, Scandinavians who came back after having taking part in some of many wars that raged on the European Continent during the turbulent 5th century (Fabech & Näsman 2013:102). As for the warriors who fought close the frontier in the Roman army (which paid them in solidi – cf. Fischer chapter 16 and Fischer *et al.* 2011), what were their equestrian ideals?

Different needs once shaped two distinct styles of riding: with collection to control the horse in a tight space (fig. 1) and without collecting, the rider depending on the horse's own balance and shape, using it as a platform from which missile weapons could be launched (fig. 3). The small gilded horse heads of the Sösdala bridle mounts have prominent, arched necks. They are held back by short reins. Ears are pinned forward, telling us that we are looking at horses interested in what lies in front of them. These are proud and bold horses, but they yield to the bits. Another Scandinavian monument that indicates a western rider's ideal in Scandinavia is the Möjbro runestone, dated to the 6th century (fig. 12). The Möjbro horse is ridden on a loose rein, and the arched neck shows that the horse is yielding to the bit. The position of the hind legs suggests a collected horse.

The best parallels to the Sösdala mounts are found in the east, in a Hunnic grave in Jakuszowice, Poland, and from a hoard found in Kačin, Ukraine (Levada 2011:116–118). The origin might be Roman parade equipment, like

Fig. 12. The Möjbro runestone (U877), Uppland, Sweden. The horse is ridden on a loose rein, yielding to the bit. The leg position is known from several Roman monuments and probably represents a modified two-beat canter or gallop. Photo Sören Hallgren 1996, Historiska museet (SHM), Stockholm.

the 4th century breast collars from the treasure found in 1793 on the Esquiline Hill in Rome (Junkelmann 1992 Abb. 99), which was "barbarised" to fit a somewhat different craftsmanship – or taste. Just like the Sösdala horses, those from Kačin are collected, "on the bit" with beautiful, arched necks.

In Late Antiquity, the Roman cavalry had adapted and introduced horseback archery (Goldsworthy 2003:205). Warriors from the steppe might favour the beauty and versatility of the collected horse. There is no contradic-

tion in the same warrior using both styles, depending on the situation. A good Roman warhorse might be schooled both to work collected, which was needed in close combat, and to continue forward on loose reins while the rider was firing arrows. The Sösdala saddles do not have the Roman horns but closed "bows" forming pommel and cantle, which might have been influenced by nomadic saddles. We have no information about the tree – if there ever was a tree, that is. The bits are snaffles. My conclusion is that the Sösdala material shows traces of two styles of riding and maybe two horse cultures. Our homecoming warrior was a child of his time. Living and riding close to the frontier, he and his brothers in arms picked up influences from east as well as west.

Notes

1 I would like to express my sincere gratitude to the staff of the Library of Vitterhetsakademien for help and excellent service during the research process.

2 This site contains many pictures from the villa: http://www.pbase.com/dosseman_italy/armerina (checked 29 April 2016).

3 A stock saddle is built upon a wooden tree, consisting of two "boards" placed along the back of the horse. It is a common type for working saddles from different parts of the world to this day.

4 Based on the tree, this saddle is a stock saddle.

5 The original sinc is often translated as "gold". According to Bo Gräslund, the true meaning is "treasure" or "luminous".

6 A full cheek snaffle is a snaffle with cheek bars or side bars. They are often referred to as "curb" in archaeological literature, but have no leverage.

7 There are excellent photos as well as some original documentation of the Vennebo find in the digital collections of the Swedish History Museum. The easiest way is to use the identification number (Sw: inventarienummer) 6511 in the search engine: http://mis.historiska.se/mis/sok/sok.asp?qtype=invnr&sm=o_1

References

Andersen, H.C. 2003. New investigation in the Ejsbøl bog. In: Jørgensen, L., Storgaard, B. & Gebauer Thomsen, L. (eds). *The spoils of victory. The North in the shadow of the Roman Empire*. Copenhagen: 246–257.

Anke, B. 2007. Der reiternomadische Steppenkrieger. In: Anke, B. & Externbrink, H. (eds). *Attila und die Hunnen*. Speyer: 218–228.

Arbman, H. 1940. *Birka I. Die Gräber. Tafeln*. Uppsala.

Arbman, H. 1943. *Birka I. Die Gräber. Text*. Uppsala.

Arrhenius, B. 1983. The chronology of the Vendel graves. In: Lamm, J.P. & Nordström, H.Å. (eds). *Vendel Period Studies*. Stockholm: 39–70.

Bachrach, B. 1993. *Charles Martel, Mounted Shock Combat, the Stirrup and Feudalism. Armies and Politics in the Early Medieval West*. Aldershot.

Bóna, I. 1991. *Das Hunnenreich*. Stuttgart.

Carnap-Bornheim, C. & Ilkjær, J. 1996a. *Illerup Ådal 5. Die Prachtausrüstungen. Textband*. Højbjerg/Aarhus.

Carnap-Bornheim, C. & Ilkjær, J. 1996b. *Illerup Ådal 7. Die Prachtausrüstungen. Tafelband*. Højbjerg/Aarhus.

Chenevix Trench, C. 1970. *Ridkonstens historia*. Stockholm.

Christensen, A.E. 1992. Kongsgårdens håndverkere. In: Christensen, A.E., Ingstad, A.S. & Myhre, B. *Osebergdronningens grav. Vår arkeologiske nasjonalskatt i nytt lys*. Oslo: 85–137.

Connolly, P. 1987. The Roman Saddle. In: Dawson, M. (ed). *Roman Military Equipment. The Accoutrements of War. Proceedings of the third Roman Military Equipment Research Seminar*. Oxford: 7–27.

Curtis, J. & Tallis, N. 2012. *The Horse. From Arabia to Royal Ascot*. With contribution by Astrid Johansen. London.

Davis, R.H.C. 1989. *The Medieval Warhorse. Origin, Development and Redevelopment*. London.

Davis, R.H.C. & Chibnall, M. (ed. & transl.) 1998. *The Gesta Guillelmi of William of Poitiers*. Oxford.

Fabech, C. & Näsman, U. 2013. A Lonely Rider? The Finding Place of the Sösdala Find and the Context of its Finds. In: Khrapunov, I. & Stylegar, F.-A. (eds). *Inter Ambo Maria. Northern barbarians from Scandinavia towards the Black Sea*. Kristiansand/Simferopol: 84–106.

Fischer, S., López-Sánchez, F. & Victor, H. 2011. The 5th Century Hoard on Theodosian Solidi from Stora Brunneby, Öland, Sweden. A Result from the LEO Project. *Fornvännen* 106: 189–204.

Gladitz, C. 1997. *Horse Breeding in the Medieval World*. Dublin.

Goldsworthy, A. 2003. *The Complete Roman Army*. London.

Green, M. 1992. *Animals in Celtic Life and Myth*. London/New York.

Groenman-van Waateringe, W. 1967. *Romeins lederwerk uit Valkenburg Z.H. Nederlandse Oudheden II*. Amsterdam.

Heaney, S. 1999. *Beowulf*. London/New York.

Hyland, A. 1990. *Equus. The Horse in the Roman World*. London.

Hyland, A. 1998. *The Warhorse 1250 – 1600*. Stroud.

Ilkjær, J. 2000. *Illerup Ådal – et arkæologisk tryllespejl*. Højbjerg.

Ilkjær, J. 2003. Danish war booty sacrifices. In: Jørgensen, L., Storgaard, B. & Gebauer Thomsen, L. (eds). *The spoils of victory. The North in the shadow of the Roman Empire*. Copenhagen: 44–65.

Ingstad, A. 1992. Tekstilene i Osebergskipet. In: Christensen, A.E., Ingstad, A.S. & Myhre, B. *Osebergdronningens grav. Vår arkeologiske nasjonalskatt i nytt lys*. Oslo: 176–208.

Junkelmann, M. 1990. *Die Reiter Roms. Teil I: Reise, Jagd, Triumph und Circusrennen*. Kulturgeschichte der antiken Welt 45. Mainz.

Junkelmann, M. 1992. *Die Reiter Roms. Teil III: Zubehör, Reitweise, Bewaffnung*. Kulturgeschichte der antiken Welt 53. Mainz.

Krogh, S. 1970. *Foreløbig rapport over forsøg med rekonstrueret rideudstyr af jernaldertype udført juli 1970*. Lejre.

Larsdotter, A. 2008. *Hästens tid. Rid- och stridskonst under stormaktstiden*. Lund.

László, G. 1943. *Der Grabfund von Koroncó und der Altungarische Sattel. Mit 19 Tafeln und 81 Textabbildungen*. Archaeologica Hungarica 43. Budapest.

Levada, M. 2011. To Europe via the Crimea. On possible migration routes of the Northern people in the great Migration Period. In: Khrapunov, I. & Stylegar, F.-A. (eds). *Inter Ambo Maria. Contacts between Scandinavia and the Crimea in the Roman Period. Collected papers*. Kristiansand/Simferopol: 115–137.

Liesowska, A. 2016. Archaeologists find ancient mummy, approximately 1,500 years old in Mongolia. *The Siberian Times*. 9 April 2016. Checked 29 April 2016 at http://siberiantimes.com/science/casestudy/news/n0638-archeologists-find-ancient-mummy-approximately-1500-years-old-in-mongolia/#_ga=1.148405559.1271597417.1460972726.

Montelius, O. 1884. Hvad vi veta om Vestergötland under hednatiden. *Svenska fornminnesföreningens tidskrift* 5: 231–248.

Norberg, R. 1929a. Ett folkvandringstidsfynd från Jönköping. *Meddelanden från Norra Smålands Fornminnesförening* 9: 5–24. Zusammenfassung.

Norberg, R. 1929b. Om förhistoriska sadlar i Sverige. *Rig* 12: 97–113.

Notker Balbulus = Thorpe, L. 1969. *Einhard and Notker the Stammer. Two Lives of Charlemagne*. Harmondsworth.

Nylén, E. 1973. Stridshästens hållning. *Tor* 15: 68–83.

Ørsnes, M. 1994. Zaumzeugfunde des 1.–8. Jahrh. nach Chr. in Mittel- und Nordeuropa. *Acta Archaeologica* 64/2: 183–292.

Ramqvist, P. H. 1992. *Högom. The excavations 1949–1984. Högom part I*. Umeå.

Rudenko, S.I. 1970. *Frozen Tombs of Siberia. The Pazyryk Burials of Iron Age Horsemen*. London.

Schovsbo, P.O. 1987. *Oldtidens vogne i Norden. Arkæologiske undersøgelser af mose- og jordfundne vogndele af træ fra neolitikum til ældre middelalder*. Frederikshavn. Zusammenfassung.

Sidnell, P. 2006. *Warhorse. Cavalry in Ancient Warfare*. London/New York.

Stolpe, H. & Arne, T.J. 1912. *Graffältet vid Vendel*. Stockholm.

Sundkvist, A. 2001. *Hästarnas land. Aristokratisk hästhållning och ridkonst i Svealands yngre järnålder*. Uppsala. Summary.

Sundkvist, A. 2014. Så fick jag se en blekgul hästtand. In: Sundkvist, A. &

Eklund, S. 2014: 403–406. Originally published in SAU Blog 13 June 2011: http://www.saublogg.se/2011/06/sa-fick-jag-se-en-blekgul-hasttand/

Sundkvist, A. & Eklund, S. 2014. *Gilltuna – där man följde traditionen. Den första storskaligt undersökta tuna-gården*. Uppsala.

Thorvildsen, K. 1957. *Ladby-skibet*. With contribution by M. Degerbøl. Copenhagen.

White, L. 1962. *Medieval Technology and Social Change*. Oxford.

Резюме

Запад есть Запад, Восток есть Восток, не встретиться им никогда?

Особенности верховой езды всадников из Сёсдалы

Аннели Сундквист

В Железном веке в Скандинавии лошадей использовали разными способами. Состояние дорог ограничивало использование двух- и четырехколесных повозок, так что основной функцией лошадей были верховая и вьючная езда. В Римской империи тягловые лошади играли бóльшую роль. Находка в Сёсдале представляет собой еще один пример того, как много значили хорошие верховые лошади.

Способ верховой езды различался в зависимости от места и цели. Вообще-то говоря, возникший на Восточных равнинах стиль верховой езды не предусматривал перенесение большей части веса на задние ноги лошади, которую пускали в свободный галоп, тогда как западный стиль подразумевал большую собранность лошади и приспособленность к работе на ограниченном пространстве. Стили могли смешиваться и вероятно смешивались уже в доисторическое время.

Конская упряжь из Сёсдалы демонстрирует влияние обоих стилей. Седла могли не иметь деревянной основы, оставаясь мягкими конструкциями, имевшими составные переднюю и заднюю луки, которые фиксировали всадника в седле. Форма передней и задней луки заставляет думать, скорее, о гуннских седлах, чем о седлах римской кавалерии с раздвоенными луками. Требуются дополнительные исследования, чтобы установить, был ли у седла деревянный каркас. Крупные кольца использовали, вероятно, для фиксации нагрудного ремня и шлеи, позволявших неподвижно зафиксировать седло.

Удила представляют собой составной трензель, за исключением находки 1929 г., судя по форме которой здесь сочленение грызл могло служить портом (изгибом для воздействия на язык и нёбо лошади). Однако они не могли действовать как рычаг и потому данные удила не являлись мундштуком. В Скандинавии удила мундштучного типа появились только в Средневековье.

Комплекс из Сёсдалы интерпретируют как принадлежности воина, вернувшегося домой после службы на Европейском континенте на протяжении бурного V в. На стиль его верховой езды, несомненно, оказал влияние опыт других всадников, вместе с которыми он служил и сражался. К этому времени римская конница приспособилась к условиям пограничья, используя конных лучников и тяжеловооруженных всадников.

Характерный для Сёсдалы стиль верховой езды, вероятно, представлял собой результат смешения приемов, используемых древнеримской кавалерией Запада и кочевниками равнин Востока.

Подписи к иллюстрациям

Рис. 1. Собранная лошадь – участник боя быков, тренирующая средний галоп (кентер). Лошадь находится в установленных всадником «рамках». Смысл дрессуры в том, чтобы заставить лошадь убрать нагрузку с передней части корпуса и перенести основную часть веса на задние ноги, а это дает возможность поворачиваться, делать пируэты и т. д. на ограниченном пространстве (фото Аннели Сундквист, Португалия, 2004 г.).

Рис. 2. Скаковая лошадь, тренирующая кентер. Несмотря на то, что всадник сдерживает лошадь, заметно, что она принимает вытянутую, низкую позу, вытягивая шею (фото Аннели Сундквист, Ньюмаркет, Англия, 2015 г.).

Рис. 3. Финиш скачек. Лошади пущены в галоп, поводья отпущены, головы и шеи вытянуты вперед (фото Аннели Сундквист, Ньюмаркет, Англия, 2015 г.).

Рис. 4. Португальский всадник XXI в. Надев традиционный костюм, он отправляется на работу – участвовать в бое быков (фото Аннели Сундквист, Португалия, 2004 г.).

Рис. 5. Современный европейский составной трензель (вверху) и мундштук с небольшим портом и подгубной цепочкой (фото Анны Бакман, http://www.hippokultur.se).

Рис. 6. Император Траян (98–117 гг. н. э.) в седле с небольшими луками. Хотя это изображение на мраморе выполнено во время его правления, его вторично использовали в Арке Константина (315 г. э.), расположенной за римским Колизеем. Отметим надетый на лошадь нагрудный ремень (фото Аннели Сундквист).

Рис. 7. Управление лошадью с помощью длинных поводьев на надгробии кавалериста Лонгина Биарты, умершего в 68 г. н. э. У седла имеются выступающие луки (фото Wikimedia Commons).

Рис. 8. Реконструкция седла из Йёнчёпинга, сделанная Руне Норбергом (по: Norberg 1929a fig. 14).

Рис. 9. Бескаркасное седло типа «Маремма». Отметим распределяющие давление «подушки», удобное сиденье с набивкой и составную деревянную луку (фото Аннели Сундквист, Блера, Италия, 2004 г.).

Рис. 10. Итальянские пастухи – «буттери» с традиционной упряжью и снаряжением. Высокие луки их седел, вероятно, похожи на седла из Сёсдалы. У этих седел, вероятнее всего, есть деревянный каркас (ср. рис. 8, на котором показано бескаркасное седло типа «Маремма»). (Фото Аннели Сундквист, Блера, Италия, 2004 г.).

Рис. 11. Лошадь в мундштуке, изображенная на Колонне Траяна в Риме (II в.). Мундштук состоит из грызла с фигурной средней частью (портом) и боковых щечек с петлями для крепления повода и нащечных ремней. Щечки мундштука служат рычагом, делая действие удил более эффективным, а в неловких руках – более жестоким, чем у возникшего ранее трензеля. Однако такие удила дают опытному наезднику возможность управлять лошадью с помощью очень легких движений (фото Аннели Сундквист).

Рис. 12. Рунический камень из Мёйбро (U877) (Уппланд, Швеция). Всадник правит лошадью с помощью отпущенных поводьев, прикрепленных к удилам. Положение ног, известное по нескольким римским памятникам, вероятно, указывает на то, что лошадь пущена в род двухтактного кентера или в галоп (фото Сёрена Хальгрена, 1996 г., Шведский исторический музей, Стокгольм).

Chapter 10

Saddle and bridle from Högom, Central Sweden

Per H. Ramqvist

Based on the rich chamber grave from Högom, Medelpad, Central Sweden, dated to c. AD 500, the saddle and the so-called battle bridle are discussed. The well-preserved artefacts could be analysed in detail. The battle bridle can be reconstructed in detail since most of the leather straps were preserved. A reconstruction of the ring saddle is presented. It is also argued that most of the Scandinavian saddle finds had the same construction. The differences are mainly the curvature of the front saddle bow and the style in which the mounts were shaped. There is a large gap in knowledge about what the saddles of high-ranking Roman riders looked like. Since no ring saddles are known among contemporary nomads, the Scandinavian use of ring saddles could either be a regional invention or more plausibly a copy of such elements used by the late Roman aristocracy. The saddle could have been transformed in much the same way as Roman belt mounts were transferred to the Sösdala and Nydam styles and later Style I.

Ramqvist, P. 2017. Saddle and bridle from Högom, Central Sweden. In: Fabech, C. & Näsman, U. (eds). *The Sösdala horsemen – and the equestrian elite of fifth century Europe.* Jutland Archaeological Society.

One of the most famous graves in Northern Europe from the Migration Period was excavated 1949–1951 at Högom just outside Sundsvall, Medelpad in Central Sweden by Dagmar Selling and Sverker Janson from the Central Board of National Antiquities (map fig. 6 in Introduction). In no. 2 of the four large mounds a 5 × 2 m large and unrobbed chamber was found (Ramqvist 1990, 1992; Nockert 1991). Due to advanced excavation methods, long before their time, the unrobbed content of the chamber could be retrieved extraordinarily well (Ramqvist 2014). The unusu-ally rich equipped chamber has been dated to *c.* AD 500, mostly due to the frequent presence of Salin's style I. The chamber in the large mound, its location in the landscape where crossroads met, along with the other extraordinary features on the site (Ramqvist 2016), make the site an important central place of economic, political and probably also of religious power.

The artefacts in the grave show that the buried aristocrats in Högom for several generations were part of a vast interregional network in Europe. This network stretched

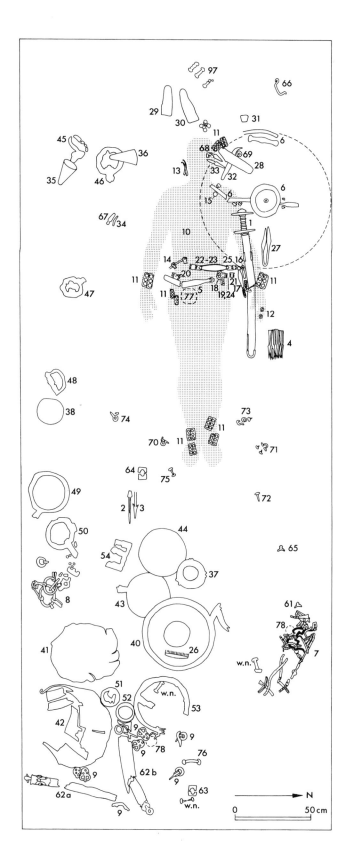

Fig. 1. Plan of the burial chamber in mound no. 2 at Högom. The position of the deceased is interpreted by the author. Finds no. 9 in the bottom part of the plan belong to the saddle and find no. 7 in the low right is the battle bridle.

from western Norway through western and eastern Europe and is reflected in the material remains in the chamber, such as the facetted glasses, bronze cauldron and plate, the sword and its mounts, and not least the fantastic horse equipment such as the saddle and one of the bridles. Note that the populous region of the Mälar Valley does not seem to have been part of these socio-political alliances.

The chamber

Mound no. 2 at the cemetery at Högom contained a 5 × 2 metre large and compressed wooden chamber. Its original height was impossible to determine, but it must have been about 1–1.5 m considering that some of the grave content probably was placed on the walls of the chamber (cf. fig. 1).

The chamber was furnished like a kind of two-room apartment with a "private" part where the deceased was laid on a wooden bed and an "official" room with a saddle and two bridles. Also placed there were most of the containers surrounding a bronze plate with an exclusive comb. It seems as if the official room was intended for two, the deceased and an allied peer. In the private room and also on the bed, full military equipment was placed, with spatha, shield, two axes, a bow (probable) with 36 red-painted arrows, lance and spear. On the chamber floor, on and under the deceased, several kinds of furs were found, including bear, marten, beaver, reindeer/roe deer, sable, polecat, seal, and pinniped or musquash. On the bed personal hygienic utensils were also placed in pouches and wooden cases. The red dress with its decorated termination bands was well preserved (Nockert 1991). A second greenish spare dress was placed under the head of the deceased. Together the two dresses had over seventy clasp buttons of gilded silver and bronze. Gold items occur in the form of two finger rings, two spoonlike pendants; two gold pins (for barter) placed in a leather bag riveted to the belt and one unminted gold tablet on the chest of the deceased, an obol.

b)

c)

Fig. 2. a: Photo of the front bow as it was recovered directly after the excavation. Leather-seams, filling, mounts and rings are in place. There are also parts of a bearskin that covered almost the entire chamber floor visible to the right. – b: Interpretation sketch: front side and – c: Rear side of front bow showing the different materials of the front saddle. 1= wood; 2= bronze; 3= leather-seams; 4= visible straw filling; 5= animal fur (secondary); 6= leather. Drawing: Per H. Ramqvist.

Salin's style I occurs on several objects, most elaborately on the mouthpiece of the sword scabbard and the twelve clasp buttons on the sleeves, but also in a fragmented form on the wooden case for the beard shears. The occurrence of style I is the basis for the dating of the chamber. If we took these objects away the dating would be about one century earlier, meaning that most of the more luxurious objects in the chamber were antiquities at the time of the disposal!

The saddle

General observations and interpretations

The best-preserved saddle in Northern Europe was found in the eastern part of the chamber. Like all the other objects in the chamber it was of course compressed, but substantial parts, especially the front bow, were quite well preserved (fig. 2).

The saddle and its mounts were found on top of two of the saddle-girth buckles. which can indicate that it either was placed that way on the chamber floor, or more probably the saddle was placed on a kind of scaffold, table or the like. In that part of the chamber several rounded, decorated and mounted rods etc. were found, indicating some kind of furniture.

As could be judged from the recovered parts of the saddle it consisted of a front and a rear bow, both equipped with bronze mounts. The front bow was approx. 33 cm high (from the assumed horse to the top of the middle part of the bow). All of the main functional parts of the saddle were preserved.

The skeleton of the saddle bow was made of wood, even though only tiny wooden fragments could be observed by the excavator Dagmar Selling. Partially better preserved, however, was the elaborate wooden lath, running from the

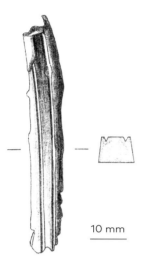

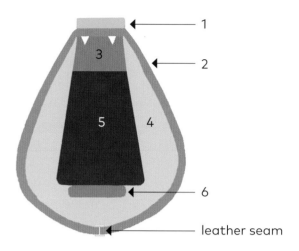

Fig. 3. A loose fragment of the conical wooden lath. The lath was shaped in accordance with the bronze mounts, cf. fig. 4. Drawing: Andrzej Link.

Fig. 4. The "stratigraphic" cross-section of the saddle bows was: 1) on top the bronze mounts; 2) the leather cover; 3) the elaborate wooden lath; 4) the straw filling 5) the wooden skeleton and possibly 6) a simple wooden lath. Drawing: Per H. Ramqvist.

bottom to the crown of the front bow. This lath was well preserved, probably due to the immediate contact with the bronze mounts. It was well adjusted to both the lower animal mounts and to the flat mounts on the upper part of the bow. The wooden lath had a 10 mm wide and flat bottom and an 8 mm wide top, i.e. slightly conical (fig. 3). On the flat top two fine parallel lines were carved about 1 mm inside the edges. The bottom part of the lath was widened and provided with groups of transverse grooves and hence adjusted to the mounts. These details show that the saddle was made by one hand and not a result of secondary additions.

In direct contact with the leather seam on the underside of the front bow, there is one tiny fragment of another light, rectangular wooden lath (fig. 2) about 8 mm wide. This lath is not nearly as well-shaped as the upper one. It has however been impossible to examine it more closely without destroying the saddle, and it is uncertain whether it happens to be a twig from the wooden frame or a lath running all the way on the underside of the wooden skeleton. There are some more hints of the latter.

The front saddle bow was covered with leather. Several preserved seams were found and there were also parts of leather preserved on the flat mounts. Of special interest

are the leather fragments found on the underside of one of the flat bronze mountings. This shows that the wooden lath was once covered with leather (for the "stratigraphic" cross-section, see fig. 4).

These occurrences indicate that the physical front bow was about 40 cm wide at the bottom and approx. 33 cm high. The width of the bow at the top was roughly 5 cm with an increasing width below the mounts to a maximum 15 cm. The saddle blade, which was resting on the horseback, was at least 4 mm thick (cf. fig. 5).

Saddle mounts
On top of the bow all the way around there were metal mounts, on the crown in the form of flat thin bronze rails (10 mm wide and 2.5 mm thick) and lower down towards the horse back each side was terminated with the animal-headed bronze mounts. In the middle of each animal-headed mount there was a rectangular hole through which a staple with cavetto bronze ring had been fastened.

Most details can be provided about the front bow (fig. 2), which contained a two-piece bronze mount on each side of the bow. The lower part of the mount had a hole in the middle for a bronze ring and had terminations in

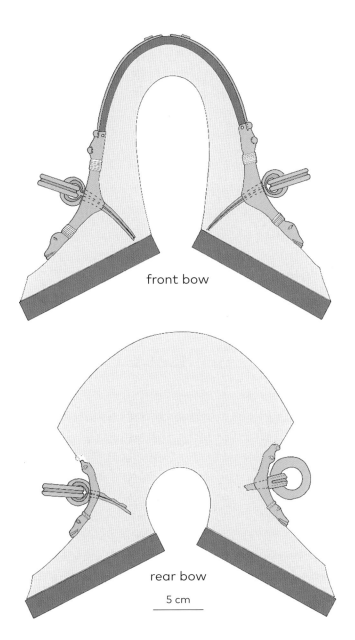

front bow

rear bow

5 cm

Fig. 5. Reconstruction sketch of the front and rear bows of the Högom saddle. Note that the height of the rear saddle bow is just a suggestion. Drawing: Per H. Ramqvist.

Fig. 6. One of the animal-headed bronze mounts from the front saddle bow in Högom. Note that the animal head to the right (upper) is more elaborate with elevated eyes and nostrils. These more elaborate animal-heads were facing the potential rider. Photo SHM.

the form of animal heads. As a collar of the animal heads there were four flat silver wires incrusted in the mount (fig. 6). The animal heads to the right, i.e. the side of the mount turning upwards towards the rider, are somewhat more elaborate with elevated eyes and nostrils compared to the smoother animal head facing down, the left head. According to the excavator Dagmar Selling the flat top of

each eye cylinder was also covered with thin silver sheets with concentric decorations (Ramqvist 1992:79).

The mounts on the back bow were smaller. The ring on the saddle's left back bow is turned vertically, all the others horizontally. The staple of the vertical ring mount also differs from the others as it has only one leg, while all the other have two. The mounts of the back bow were smaller than those of the front bow, but made in the same style. The upper animal head in this case too was more elaborate, with protruding nostrils. Silver inlays, however, only occurred on the rear bow on the lower heads of the mounts and consisted of only one flat silver band.

It is interesting to note that there are no signs of wear on the saddle parts at all. But on the right side of the front saddle bow the wooden lath has been damaged (fig. 2), a sharp cut at approx. 45 degrees apparently caused by a sword or an axe. It has been roughly mended with a not particularly well designed bronze sheet, which has been fastened by bronze rivets hammered into the wooden lath. This is surely enigmatic, a saddle not much used but nevertheless deliberately damaged.

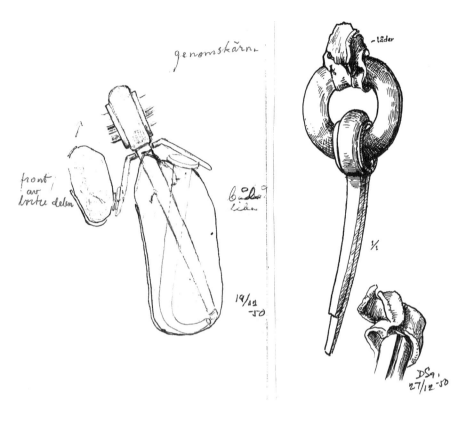

Fig. 7. Original drawings made during the excavations. Left: how the large bronze nails were attached in the saddle, beside the staple. Right: how a leather strap was fixed to one of the bronze rings on the front saddle bow. Drawings: Dagmar Selling.

Fastening of the rings into the front saddle bow

From some of the finds with saddle-rings it is obvious that they were hammered through a wooden skeleton of the saddle and bent to 90 degrees on the rear side, which made them sit properly. From other finds, however, such as some of the rings from Sösdala, it can be seen that they are twisted in different ways. Since many of the finds are ritually deposited the saddles could have been deliberately disassembled and distorted and from a constructional aspect are not necessarily to be trusted. In the undistorted Högom case, however, none of the four staples for the rings have been bent. Instead a separate large bronze nail was used, 82 mm long, with a rounded shaft, 7 mm in diameter at the top and with a flat round head 13 mm in diameter and 2 mm thick (figs 2b-c and 7). These large bronze nails were

hammered in beside the mount at an angle and 22 mm of the point of the nail was hammered back at 90 degrees to clinch the staples of each ring. Such bronze nails were used only for the front saddle bow. This fastening method seems unique, and as far as I know no similar bronze nails have been found together with saddle mounts from the Migration Period finds.

Most of the measurements of the saddle could be estimated from the observations made concerning the front saddle bow. Statements regarding the rear saddle bow are that it was not identical to the front bow. There are no signs of whether the saddle bows were standing straight or leaning.

What can also be said about the saddle bows is that the animal mounts of the front bow are curved at an angle of approx. 143 degrees, while the back mounts indicate a steeper form at roughly 130 degrees (where 180 degrees represents a straight mount). Dagmar Selling mentions in her excavation report, however, that the rear bow had the same filling and leather cover as the front bow. She also states that it consisted of "2 mot varandra vända, lika delar, längre än framkarmen och utan träskena" ("2 equal parts turned towards each other and longer than the front bow and without a wooden lath" my transl.).

What she really means is uncertain, but my interpretation is that the rear bow, like the front bow, under the pressure of the collapsing chamber, had been divided into two parts and that "längre" ("longer") possibly means wider. The rear bow was obviously not as elaborate as the front bow since it missed both the wooden lath and the upper flat bronze mounts. But one conclusion seems clear, namely that it had a "slimmer waist", which allowed an elegant yet broad back support (cf. reconstruction sketch fig. 5). The height of the rear bow is uncertain.

On the original drawings made by Dagmar Selling during the laboratory excavations, she noted that a 15 mm wide leather strap was attached to one of the saddle rings of the front bow (fig. 7). This tells us something about the rings actually having a function and not only being a symbolic ornament. It is plausible that these leather straps had to do with breast-girth and breeching. The saddle rings are not connected to a saddle girth, since this was found in the form of two pairs of sturdy bronze buckles. They evidently show that the saddle girths consisted of two 35 mm broad leather straps (Ramqvist 1992:83, pl. 57–59; Ahlqvist 2008:27ff.).

Notes on the dating, function and reconstruction of the saddle

Concerning the dating of the artefacts in chamber grave no. 2 in Högom, it is obvious that several "antiquities" (heirlooms), were buried with the deceased (Ramqvist 1992:222ff.). Several of the artefacts were about one century old when they were placed in the chamber around AD 500. That is true, for instance, for the Vestland cauldron, the bronze dish, the two facetted glasses. It is therefore no surprise that the saddle and the bridle (below) also both belong to the 5th century AD. Of course it is weak to convey a negative argument such as the lack of Style I ornaments, but it seems fair to say the horse equipment belongs to an older style tradition, formulated under the term "Sösdala style" (Karlsson 1983:163). This seems to be the case in several aristocratic graves, not least in Norway and particularly the example "Lopsthaugen" in Hordaland (Schetelig 1912:83ff.). All the artefacts, including a solidus (375–383) could be dated to *c.* 400 AD, but there were also two tiny fragments of a silver mount. These were ornamented with Salin's Style I and hence dated the grave to the late 5th to the mid 6th century AD. This situation is identical with the Högom chamber and illustrates the archaeological difficulties when, for instance, regional customs favour keeping heirlooms. Today it is impossible to understand what decisions lay behind the final deposition of the antiquities together with an aristocrat. It can possibly be connected to variations in the inter-regional peer polity interactions and relations between peers and how different negotiations between them developed, etc. Let us say that alliances were established AD 400 between Högom and peers in Thüringen. These relations were kept for some generations, when suddenly the political situation in Thüringen changed and the old descendants were killed or dismissed. Then perhaps the oldest to die in Högom at that time were given all the artefacts saved and connected to that relation to follow him in the chamber, so the partners could meet in Valhalla or maybe in Paradise or in Hades and continue their alliance.

Comparable saddle findings

It is easy to believe that the inspiration of the saddle emanated from the eastern and south-eastern nomadic tribes intruding and interacting with Europe during the Late Roman Iron Age and the Migration Period. This also may have been the case regarding the formal construction of the blade saddle, but not when it comes to the embellishment and final expression of the saddles. Metal mounts and rings, etc. that seem relatively common on Scandinavian saddles have never occurred on Hunnic saddles found hitherto (cf. Tkačenko 2010). This seem to be a Scandinavian tradition starting at the latest at the beginning of the Late Roman Period (Carnap-Bornheim & Ilkjær 1996:272–273). The early mountings are round and made of thin forged bronze sheets and the rings are smaller. Later on, as in Sösdala and Högom, the mounts are heavier and cast (cf. Fabech & Näsman 2013). The heavier mounts also require a better and more stable base for attaching the mounts on the saddles. That could be one reason to involve more wood in the construction. I am not convinced, however, that the early saddles e.g. from Illerup did not have a wooden skeleton. Even though the rings, nails and the other mounts are lighter they were nevertheless fastened and hammered into some solid material, probably a little steadier than the wooden laths discussed by Carnap-Bornheim & Ilkjær (1996:115–116). As has been pointed out above, the Högom saddle probably had a framework of a combination of solid wood and wooden laths. A hypothesis therefore could be that the type of saddle found in Scandinavia from the beginning of the Late Roman Period is the same type as we find in Högom and its successors during the Merovingian Period. The differences are mainly the kind of mountings they were equipped with, from light hammered and forged bronze sheets to heavier cast mounts.

The so-called *Prunksätteln* in Continental Europe are few and mostly represented by metal mounts from the front saddle bow. In the known cases they are embellished with cloisonné with almandine or glass stones and gold rivets in a way not found in the Migration Period finds of Scandinavia (cf. Vierck 1972; Arrhenius 1983). This kind of saddles occurs however during the late 6th century boat graves in Vendel and Valsgärde, northern Uppland (Arrhenius 1983). However, the saddles discussed here are about one century

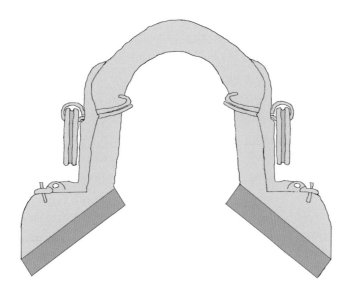

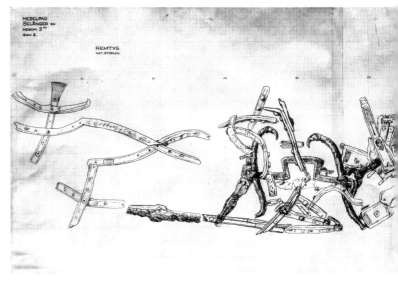

Fig. 8. An example of the placement of the saddle mounts found in Vännebo, Västergötland. Sketch by Per H. Ramqvist after the illustrations in Norberg 1929.

Fig. 9. Drawing of the bridle in situ during the excavation. Drawing: Dagmar Selling.

older. It is important to note that all metal mounted saddles belong to the aristocratic groups of Central and North Europe (e.g. Quast 1993) and that on the Continent and in Högom they are found in graves. In South Scandinavia they are only found as ritual depositions (cf. Fabech 1991; Näsman chapter 7). This circumstance highlights another issue, not in focus here, namely the existence of distant alliances between petty kingdoms and their aristocracies during the Migration Period (cf. Ramqvist 1991).

The number of sites with saddle traces mentioned in Ramqvist (1992:84) is today almost the same, but new knowledge has been obtained since, not least from the sacrifice of military equipment at Finnestorp in Västergötland in Sweden where new excavations have been conducted (*e.g.* Nordqvist 2005; 2006 and chapter 11). Horse trappings (and some other artefacts) found there are also the closest parallels to the Högom horse tack found hitherto. One of the animal headed saddle mounts has much in common (Nordqvist chapter 11 fig. 22). The same goes for some of the bridle parts (see below).

The saddle mounts from Sösdala have their best counterparts in Vännebo, Västergötland (SHM inv.nr. 6511; Norberg 1929). In the latter find, however, two mounts

demonstrate that the lower part of the saddle bow could be terminated at right angles, which contrasts with the normal smooth terminations shown by all the other known saddle mounts (cf. Norberg 1929:106). Compare its 90-degree (fig. 8) termination with the 143 degrees of the front saddle bow in Högom. This difference indicates that the saddles had different appearances and that the Vännebo saddle is divergent. This mount also shows that the earlier reconstructions presented by Norberg (1929) and others, suggesting that the bronze mounts were fastened in both the bow and the saddle board, are wrong. The mounts were fixed only on the bow.

The bridle and snaffle

Two snaffles were found in the Högom chamber. The more simple iron snaffle (a casual snaffle) with loose rings and a tripartite bit was found directly by the southern wall of the chamber, while a more elaborate and well-preserved bridle and snaffle was found along the northern wall of the chamber (cf. fig. 1). The headstall of the snaffle with loose rings is not reconstructable since only tiny fragments of the leather straps were preserved. Two smaller iron rings, a large buckle with two strap attachments, a cavetto ring and

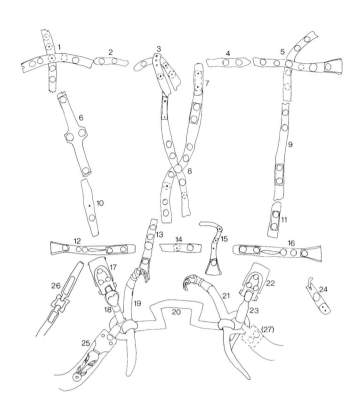

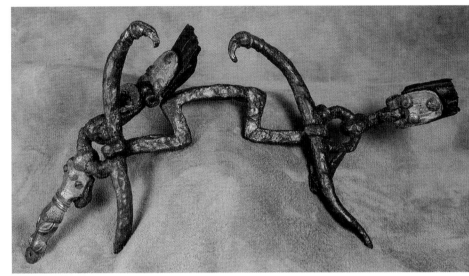

Fig. 11. The bit with related mounts. Note that the right side (to the left on the photo) have an animal-headed rein mount and a human mask (cf. fig. 12). Photo: Gunnel Jansson, SHM.

Fig. 10. Numbered parts of the battle bridle. The arrangement is made according to the interpretation of its design shown in fig. 14. Drawing: Per H. Ramqvist.

eight iron strap end mounts (pendants) also belonged to the snaffle (Ramqvist 1992:77f.; pl. 44–47). The text below, however, only concerns the so-called "battle bridle".

This more elaborate of the two bridles, the "battle bridle", was probably hanging on the northern wall of the chamber. In earlier literature (e.g. Ramqvist 1990:41) this snaffle has wrongly been called a curb, but the right term should be snaffle (cf. Sundkvist 2001:23).

Due to several bronze and silver rivets, nails and mounts on the bridle much of the leather straps was preserved, quite in contrast to the ring snaffle where only fragments of the leather straps were left. The excavation revealed a kind of "structural mess" (fig. 9), although it is quite possible to decode. It had substantial parts left of the leather straps and could be reconstructed in essential parts (fig. 10).

Like all the other artefacts the bridle was heavily compressed and salvaged in 26 different pieces of leather, iron, gilded bronze and silver (figs 9–10). The leather straps were generally made of two 10 mm wide and 2–3 mm thick strips riveted and sawn together to a normally 5 mm thick strap. The straps were 22 mm wide and 8 mm thick where they connect to the hinged mounts (nos. 17 and 22 on fig. 10). The rein straps also seem to have had the same size.

The rivets are made of bronze with domed heads covered with silver sheets. They are grouped in pairs and placed at relatively even intervals on the straps. Where straps meet, the joint is fastened with a somewhat larger bronze rivet with flat head without silver cover. On the right side of the bridle, there is a 111 mm long bronze mount with a widened central part (no. 6 on fig. 10). Along the edge of the mount there is a thin carved line. It is a double mount with bronze top and a bottom part of iron and between these there is a 6 mm thick double leather strap. Both the leather strap and the bottom iron mount are cut in the same form as the upper bronze mount. The bronze and iron mounts and the leather strap are riveted together with four bronze rivets with domed and silver covered heads. There is no counterpart of the left side of the bridle.

The bit is made of iron, made from a rectangular iron bar measuring 9 × 7 mm on the right side and 10 × 10 mm on the left side (fig. 11). It is provided at the centre with a

Fig. 12. *Detail of the iron linking mount of the right side of the bridle. The photo shows the gilded silver oval with the two "eyes" of the human mask. Photo: Gunnel Jansson, SHM.*

Fig. 13. *The rein mount on the right side of the bit showing an animal head covered with punched semicircles and triangle figures. Photo: Gunnel Jansson, SHM.*

forged elliptical port, measuring 64 × 11–20 × 9 mm. Both ends of the bit are bent to form loops, which are attached around the cheek bars. The edges of the iron bar are not rounded, making it a very sharp bit.

The cheek bars are made of iron, gently S-curved 135 and 145 mm long respectively and 10 mm thick at the centre. They have tapering ends and on top each has a gilded bronze sleeve in the form of a plastic head of a bird of prey. On the centre of each bar there is a loop for the rein mounts and the head straps to be attached.

The hinged mounts attached to the loops of the cheek bars are mounted on a 22 mm wide and 4+4 mm thick leather strap. They are made of bronze and riveted to the strap by three silver-covered domed bronze rivets. Between the rivets the semicircular fixing plate of the mount is provided with a gilded silver sheet. These sheets have punched ornaments; the left one in the form of semicircles and the right one with semicircles and triangles. On the right mount punched semicircles form a cross and in each of the four fields of that cross three triangles are punched.

Between the iron loop on the cheek bar and the hinged mounts there is a connecting link of iron. The right one of these linking mounts is more elaborate than the left one. Close to the hinged mount it has been forged out into a form closely resembling a stylised human face or mask measuring 21 × 20 × 3 mm (figs 11–12). Its flat upper surface was gilded and has two, probably drilled, semicircular ornaments close to the place where a human face should have its eyes. The form of this part of the mount and the placement of the semicircular ornaments reinforce the impression of a human face or mask.

Only on the right side of the 21 mm wide rein strap there is an 84 mm long mostly gilded bronze mount in the shape of an animal head (fig. 13). The head itself is 40 mm and has a 6 mm broad "collar" closest to the 23 × 20 mm large fixing plate of the mount. The mount terminates with a ring, which was attached to the loop of the animal-headed cheek bar. The fixing plate has a small ridge running from the collar to the ring. Three rivets, of which the middle one is 8 mm in diameter and has a domed silver-plated head, hold a silver sheet in place as well as the leather rein

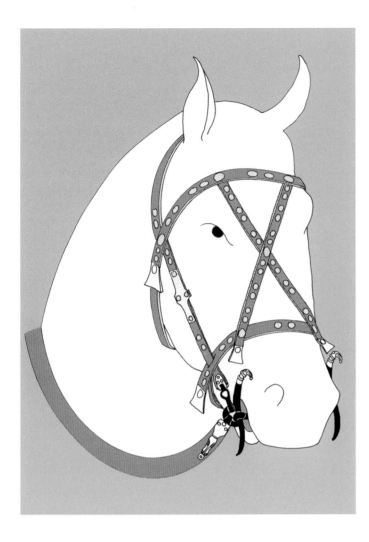

Fig. 14. Reconstruction of the "battle bridle" from Högom. Drawing: Per H. Ramqvist.

beneath the mount. This silver sheet is ornamented with punched ornaments on both sides of the ridge, in the form of semicircles placed with their opening towards each other. The head of the animal is covered with rows of punched alternating triangles and semicircles.

Notes on reconstruction of the "battle bridle"

It is notable that most of its elaborate mounts and ornaments are placed *on the right side* of the bridle. Even if the difference between the two sides is not large it is nonetheless quite obvious in its asymmetry. The extra strap mount, the gilded mask figure and the elaborate rein mount in the form of an animal head are all placed on the right side of the bridle. Even a detail such as the punched ornaments on the otherwise identical hinged mounts are more complex on the right side. What that really means is unclear, but could have to do with certain aspects of ceremonial rites and which side should be exposed to the public, or something of that kind.

There are as always uncertainties with a reconstruction of bridles (fig. 14), but several clear things are present such as the crossing straps in the middle of the horse's forehead. There are no traces left of the upper part of the headpiece and the lower part of the noseband, i.e. the part under the mandible, which probably means that these parts of the bridle were not equipped with bronze mounts. That these straps actually existed is seen on fragments nos. 1, 5, 26 and 24 (fig. 10).

Other bridles

On the whole my reconstruction of the bridle is a close parallel to the ideas presented by Bunte (1961) concerning the Sösdala II bridle and the example from Thorsbjerg (Engelhardt 1863 pl. 13). This, however, represents the older type of horse equipment with rein chains and saddles with lighter, forged sheet mounts, found in several of the offerings of military equipment in South Scandinavia, such as Illerup in Jutland as well as Skedemosse on Öland. Bridles with cheek bars are old and common in the southeast European material (Werner 1985). But there are far fewer with animal-headed cheek bars from the Migration Period. One of the best parallels can be found in the Finnestorp sacrifice in Västergötland, where a plastic bird of prey has its beak rolled in towards the throat (Nordqvist chapter 11 fig. 16). On the Continental examples we often find bits with decorated cheek bars and sometimes stylised, implied animal heads (cf. Akhmedov 2002). Among the central European as well as among the eastern nomadic groups another type of snaffle with loose rings is most common (Akhmedov 2002; Quast 2007). There are no certain opinions about the differences of the two kinds of snaffles (cf. Sundkvist chapter 9), and they can both be equipped with a similar kind of bit, but the more elaborate animal heads certainly belonged to the elite of the communities.

Conclusions

The horse equipment in mound no. 2 in Högom also includes iron spurs, and perhaps some of the wooden artefacts partly preserved in the area of the saddle could have been the handle of a horse whip or the like.

The horse equipment from Högom as a whole shows very few signs of wear; on the saddle hardly anything and on the bridle there are traces of wear on the small bronze loops on fragment 26 (fig. 10). It is of course hard to judge the wear on the iron loops of the bit since they are very rusty and have been conserved. But the few notable wear marks show that the horse equipment was only used occasionally.

In Scandinavia Högom hitherto is unique with its grave goods in the form of horse equipment. The closest parallels are found with some of the elites in contemporary Continental burials such as Krefeld-Gellep, Ravenna, Tournai (Childeric) and similar, i.e. in the top stratum of the late 5th and early 6th centuries. But even though there are similarities, there it is also a large difference in the type of saddle equipment. No saddle rings and associated mounts have been found outside Scandinavia. This means that all the saddle parts found in Scandinavia belong to the kind of saddle represented by the one in Högom. The approximate size, the curvature of the front saddle bow, the tree skeleton, the filling and the leather cover are traits to be found on all Scandinavian saddles. The transition angle on the lower part of the front bow (i.e. where the actual animal headed mounts are placed) vary from the almost straight Sösdala mounts (nos. I:200–201 in the catalogue) via Högom to the steepest with a 90-degree angle, in Vännebo (fig. 8). But these differences are just cosmetic and have nothing to do with the construction of the saddle. Since there are hitherto very few Migration Period finds with saddle mounts (for example none in Norway), it is hard to speculate about what these cosmetic differences actually meant. Geographical, chronological, social?

Even though there are excavated saddles in south-east Europe, not a single element of the so-called ring saddles has as yet been found in any grave from the steppes. The old hypothesis of, for example, Norberg (1929), that the rings and mounts were inspired by the Roman military saddles seems fair. But it is also probable that the idea of the blade saddle and the cheek bar snaffle originated among the Pontic nomads (cf. Akhmedov 2001, 2002). There is however a large knowledge gap concerning the saddles among the Roman top stratum. It is well known that the Romans used different kinds of saddles; they obviously also had parade saddles or the like and high-ranking officers probably also had elaborate saddles. What did they look like? Obviously they existed and were significant since Emperor Leo I (emperor 457–474) banned the decoration of saddles with pearls and gemstones (Quast 2007:50). Even though it is a negative argument it is plausible that the high-ranking Romans had mounted saddles (maybe with rings). Perhaps a similar process took place with the saddles as with the belt mounts of late Roman soldiers in the provinces. These soldiers carried, among other things, belts with cast bronze mounts, often with geometric ornaments in chip-carved technique and punched ornaments. The edges of these mounts and buckles were flanked by animals in a plastic style. The animals could be lions, dolphins, etc. Decorations of this kind were brutally transformed on the South Scandinavian mounts, leading to what we call Nydam and Sösdala styles and to Salin's style I, the very hallmark of the artisans work during approximately one century between AD 450–550. The objects were successively covered with symbols of Old Norse religion. Saddles, bridles, and other martial objects among the aristocracies in Scandinavia were also to a large degree attributed to the martial god Odin.

References

Ahlqvist, J. 2008. *Högomsadeln – funktion och kontext.* [B.A. thesis in archaeology]. Umeå University.

Akhmedov, I.R. 2001. New data about the origin of some constructive parts of the horse-harness of the Great Migration Period. In: Istvánovits, E. & Kulcsár, V (eds). *International connections of the barbarians of the Carpathian basin in the 1st–5th centuries A.D.* Aszód/Nyíregyháza: 363–388.

Akhmedov, I.R. 2002. Cheek-pieces and elements of harness with zoomorphic decoration in the Great Migrations period. In: Tejral, J. (ed.). *Probleme der frühen Merowingerzeit im Mitteldonauraum.* Brno: 11–30.

Arrhenius, B. 1983. The chronology of the Vendel graves. In: Lamm, J.P. & Nordström, H.Å. (eds). *Vendel Period Studies.* Stockholm: 39–70.

Bunte, K. 1961. A new bridle find from Sösdala. *Meddelanden från Lunds Universitets Historiska Museum* 1961: 194–206.

Carnap-Bornheim, C. von & Ilkjær, J. 1996. *Illerup Ådal 5. Die Prachtausrüstungen. Textband.* Højbjerg/Århus.

Engelhardt, C. 1863. *Thorsbjerg mosefund.* Copenhagen.

Fabech, C. 1991. Booty sacrifices in Southern Scandinavia. A reassessment. In: P. Garwood (ed.) *Sacred and profane.* Oxford: 88–99.

Fabech, C. & Näsman, U. 2013. A lonely rider? The finding place of the Sösdala find and the context of its finds. In: Khrapunov, I. & Stylegar, F.-A. (eds). *Inter ambo maria. Northern Barbarians from Scandinavia towards the Black Sea.* Kristiansand/Simferopol: 84–106.

Karlsson, L. 1983. *Nordisk form, om djurornamentik.* Stockholm.

Nockert, M. 1991. *The Högom find and other Migration Period textiles and costumes in Scandinavia. Högom Part II.* Umeå.

Norberg, R. 1929. Om förhistoriska sadlar i Sverige. *Rig:* 97–113.

Nordqvist, B. 2005. Der Kriegsbeuteopferplatz von Finnestorp in Schweden. *Offa* 61/62: 221–238.

Nordqvist, B. 2006. *Offerplatsen Finnestorp. Grävningsredogörelse över de arkeologiska undersökningarna utförda under åren 2000–2004.* Göteborg.

Quast, D. 1993. Das hölzerne Sattelgestell aus Oberflacht Grab 211 – Bemerkungen zu merowingerzeitlichen Sätteln. *Fundberichte aus Baden-Württemberg* 18: 437–464.

Quast, D. 2007. Zwischen Steppe, Barbaricum und Byzanz. Bemerkungen zu prunkvollem Reitzubehör des 5. Jahrhunderts n. Chr. *Acta Praehistorica et Archaeologica* 39: 35–64.

Ramqvist, P.H. 1990. *Högom.* Stockholm.

Ramqvist, P.H. 1991. Über ökonomische und sozio-politische Beziehungen der Gesellschaften der nordischen Völkerwanderungszeit. *Frühmittelalterliche Studien* 25: 45–72.

Ramqvist, P.H. 1992. *Högom. Part I. The excavations 1949–1984.* Umeå.

Ramqvist, P.H. 2014. Burial mound dissection in Sweden. In: Smith, C. (ed.). *Encyclopedia of global archaeology.* New York: 1056–1060.

Ramqvist, P.H. 2016. Grisfest i Fröland? Nya resultat angående hög 3 i Högom, Medelpad – samt något om hög 4. *Arkeologi i Norr* 15: 91–118.

Schetelig, H. 1912. *Vestlandske graver fra jernalderen.* Bergen.

Sundkvist, A. 2001. *Hästarnas dal. Aristokratisk hästhållning och ridkonst i Svealands yngre järnålder.* Uppsala.

Tkačenko, I.D. 2010. Riding horse tack among the cattle-breeders of Central Asia and Southern Siberia in the first and second millennia CE. *Études mongoles et sibériennes, centrasiatiques et tibétaines* 41. https://emscat.revues.org/1552 – Checked 28 October 2016.

Vierck, H. 1972. Prunksättel aus Gellep und Ravenna. *Archäologisches Korrespondenzblatt* 2: 213–217.

Werner, W.M. 1985. Pferdetrensen aus Südosteuropa. Eine Übersicht. *Archäologisches Korrespondenzblatt* 15: 463–479.

Резюме

Седло и узда из Хёгома в центральной Швеции

Пер Х. Рамквист

В этой статье рассматривается так называемая «узда боевого коня» на основании седла и одной из двух уздечек, найденных в богатой и неразграбленной камерной могиле в Хёгоме (Медельпад, центральная Швеция), датируемой рубежом V–VI вв. Выдающаяся сохранность этих вещей позволяет проанализировать ряд деталей, отсутствующих в других находках из Северной Европы. Представлена реконструкция седла с подпружными кольцами, в частности, его передней луки и ее внутренней структуры. Приведены доказательства того, что конструкция большинства седел, найденных на территории Скандинавии, в той или иной степени напоминает седло из Хёгома. Различия затрагивают главным образом изгиб нижней части передней луки седла, оформленной бронзовыми оковками, и стиля этих оковок. Указанный изгиб демонстрирует линию изменений – от почти прямых экземпляров из Сёсдалы, через находку из Хёгома, вплоть до двух оковок седел из Веннебо, завершение которых образует прямой угол.

Узду боевого коня можно реконструировать во всех подробностях. Большая часть кожаных ремней сохранилась благодаря многочисленным бронзовым и серебряным заклепкам. Узда и удила были ассиметричны: справа, если смотреть со стороны всадника, использовались металлические

накладки более тонкой работы и более сложная орнаментация. Это можно интерпретировать как указание на того, что их использовали как в военных, так и в церемониальных целях.

В наших представлениях об облике седел высокопоставленных римских всадников имеется существенный пробел. Поскольку седла с подпружными кольцами в культуре синхронных кочевников до сих пор не обнаружены, подобные седла, бытовавшие в Скандинавии, были либо местным изобретением, либо, что более вероятно, результатом копирования соответствующих элементов, принятых у римской аристократии. Трансформация седла могла напоминать эволюцию римских поясных накладок, результатом которой стали накладки типов «Сесдала» и «Нидам», а впоследствии вещи в «Первом зверином стиле» (по Бернхарду Салину).

Подписи к иллюстрациям

Рис. 1. План погребальной камеры в кургане № 2 в Хёгоме. Положение погребенного реконструировано автором. Находки № 9 в нижней части плана были частями седла, находка № 7 внизу справа – узда боевого коня.

Рис. 2. a) Фотография передней луки седла сразу после окончания раскопок. Фрагменты кожаного чехла со швами, набивка, оковки и подпружные кольца находятся на своих местах. Здесь же – фрагменты медвежьей шкуры, почти полностью покрывавшей пол камеры справа. – b, c) Графические реконструкции передней и задней стороны передней луки седла с указанием материалов, из которых сделана передняя часть седла: 1 = дерево; 2 = бронза; 3 = фрагменты кожаного чехла со швами; 4 = остатки соломенной набивки; 5 = мех животного (от другого элемента погребального инвентаря); 6 = кожа (рисунок Пера Х. Рамквиста).

Рис. 3. Обломанный фрагмент конической деревянной планки. Форма планки соответствует бронзовым оковкам (ср. рис. 4; рисунок Анджея Линка).

Рис. 4. «Стратиграфический» поперечный разрез седельных лук: 1) верхние бронзовые оковки, 2) кожаный чехол, 3) сложная деревян-

ная планка, 4) соломенная набивка, 5) деревянный каркас, 6) вероятно, простая деревянная планка (рисунок Пера Х. Рамквиста).

Рис. 5. Графическая реконструкция передней и задней луки седла из Хёгома. Отметим, что высота задней луки седла предполагаемая (рисунок Пера Х. Рамквиста).

Рис. 6. Одна из оковок передней луки седла из Хёгома с изображением головок животных. Отметим, что головка животного справа (верхняя) – более тонкой работы, с приподнятыми глазами и ноздрями. Такие головы животных более искусной работы смотрели на всадника (фото Шведского исторического музея).

Рис. 7. Оригинальные рисунки, выполненные во время раскопок, показывают, что: a) крупные бронзовые гвозди находились рядом с крепежным шипом подпружного кольца; b) к одному из бронзовых колец на передней луке седла крепился кожаный ремень (рисунок Дагмар Селлинг).

Рис. 8. Вариант реконструкции седла с оковками, найденного в Веннебо в Вестергётланде (чертеж Пера Х. Рамквиста по иллюстрациям в: Norberg 1929).

Рис. 9. Узда in situ в процессе раскопок (рисунок Дагмар Селлинг).

Рис. 10. Пронумерованные детали узды боевого коня, размещенные в соответствии с ее реконструкцией, предложенной на рис. 14 (чертеж Пера Х. Рамквиста).

Рис. 11. Удило с накладками. Отметим, что на правой стороне (на фотографии слева) имеется накладка на повод в виде головки животного и человеческой личины (ср.: рис. 12; фото Гуннел Янссон, Шведский исторический музей).

Рис. 12. Деталь железного зажима, соединявшего удила с оголовьем в правой части узды. На фотографии – овал из позолоченного серебра с двумя «глазками» человеческой личины (фото Гуннел Янссон, Шведский исторический музей).

Рис. 13. Накладка для повода с правой стороны узды с изображением головки животного, покрытая штампованными изображениями полукругов и треугольников (фото Гуннел Янссон, Шведский исторический музей).

Рис. 14. Реконструкция узды боевого коня из Хёгома (рисунок Пера Х. Рамквиста).

Chapter 11

Horse tack from the Finnestorp offering site

Bengt Nordqvist

The offering site of Finnestorp, Västergötland, Sweden, is presented. Offerings of weapons and other types of military equipment took place here following victorious battles. Conquered equipment was offered in a wetland on a few occasions. Approx. 50% of the finds represent horse tack. Artefacts related to bridles and saddles are presented and their chronological distribution is discussed. Several mounts of gilt silver are punch-decorated in Sösdala style. The Finnestorp artefacts are compared to other Scandinavian finds. The deposited objects at Finnestorp date to the Migration Period Scand-D1–D2a, the 5th century AD.

Nordqvist, B. 2017. Horse tack from the Finnestorp offering site. In: Fabech, C. & Näsman, U. (eds). *The Sösdala horsemen – and the equestrian elite of fifth century Europe.* Jutland Archaeological Society.

The offering site at Finnestorp belongs to a type of finds made in lakes or bogs ("bog finds") that are often called war booty offerings, but in reality they mainly contain offerings of military equipment. This type of offerings is known from Denmark, southern Sweden and Schleswig (Fabech 1996; Ilkjær 2003; Rau & von Carnap-Bornheim 2012). Corresponding finds are not known from Finland or Norway, but a few finds of similar character are known in the Baltic States and in Poland. The offerings consist of objects from equipment carried by warriors, sometimes also by their warhorses. Preservation is often excellent. Most finds were deposited between the late 2nd century and the end of the 5th century. About half the number of finds made at Finnestorp belongs to horse tack and several mounts are punch-decorated in high-quality Sösdala style.

The offerings of military equipment are currently interpreted as thank or votive offerings made in sacral lakes or bogs after a victorious battle (Worsaae 1865:65ff.). They contain all or select parts of the equipment gathered on the battlefield: conquered from the enemy, the equipment consists mainly of weapons and warrior's personal outfit but also sometimes horse tack such as saddles and bridles (e.g. Ilkjær 2003:44–64; Hansen 2003:84–89). Before deposition many objects were ritually destroyed and cut in pieces. The offerings not only reflect the ritual events but are also the result of preceding battles between settlement areas and regions in a period characterised by constant conflicts between warlords. The aim of the actions varied

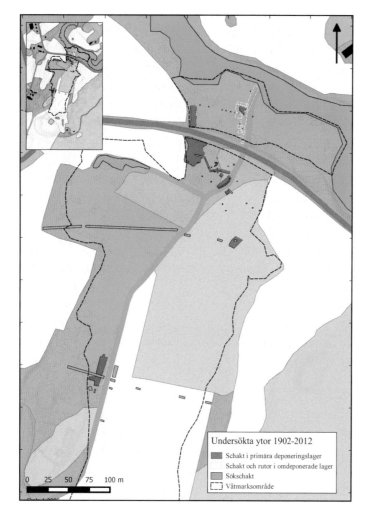

Fig. 1. Find distribution on the offering site. Dashed line delimits the wetland. 1a) Trenches excavated 1902–2012.
Maps © Offering Site Finnestorp.

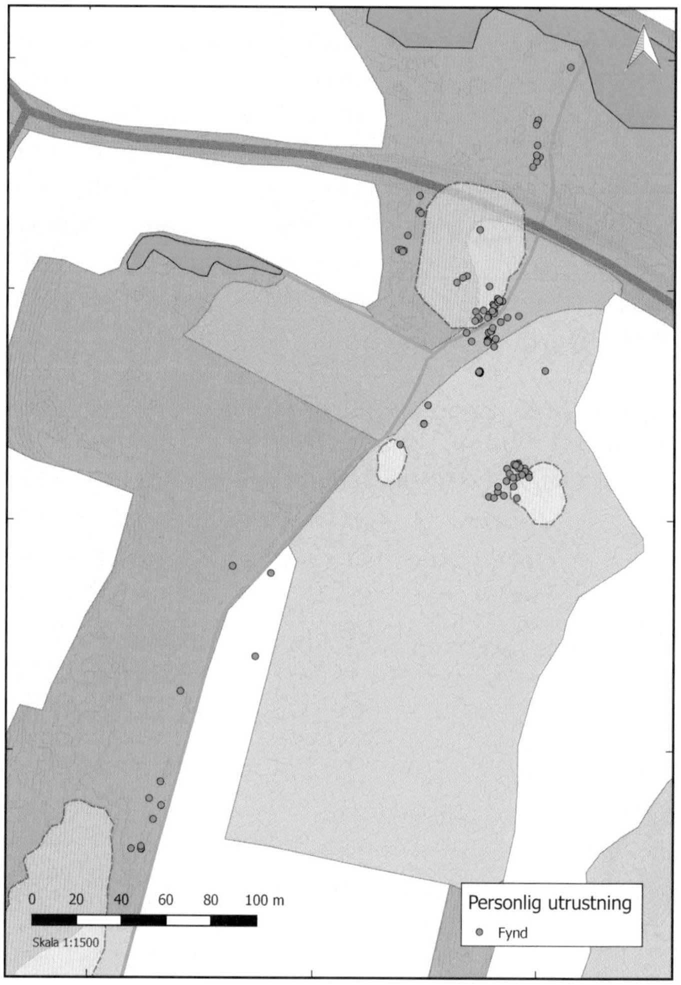

Fig. 1b) Distribution of artefacts of the personal equipment of warriors.

from simple plundering raids to fights for control over resources, people and property.

Research on the very large find material in offerings of military equipment has been in progress since the middle of the 19th century when Conrad Engelhardt excavated and published "bog finds" at Thorsbjerg, Nydam, Kragehul and Vimose in Denmark (Engelhardt 1863; 1865; 1867; 1869). In the second half of the 20th century large excavations took place at Ejsbøl, Illerup and Nydam in Denmark and Skedemosse in Sweden (Hagberg 1967a,b; Ørsnes 1988; Ilkjær 1990; 2003:44–64; 2008). Since 2000 a large project is running with excavations, research and publications on an offering of military equipment at Finnestorp,

Västergötland, south-western Sweden (Nordqvist 2017).

In Sweden Skedemosse and Finnestorp are well-known offerings of military equipment; smaller but similar finds have been made at other Swedish places like Hassle-Bösarp and Åmossarna in Scania and Kanalgatan at Jönköping in Småland; possibly also Vännebo in Västergötland belongs here (Hagberg 1967b:75–76; Norberg 1931; Stjernquist 1974:40; Fabech chapter 2 note 1). The Swedish finds are not as well excavated or studied as the Danish and consequently much less new knowledge has been generated about the Swedish finds compared to studies of Danish and North German finds. The Danish and North German sites contribute more comprehensive material than the Swedish

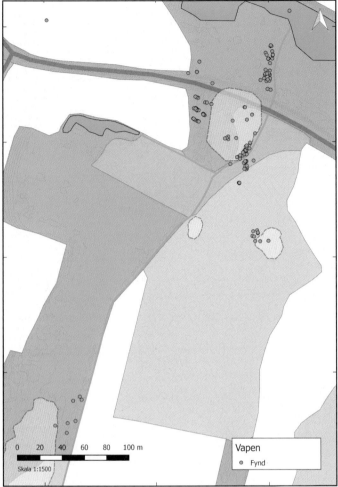

Fig. 1c) Distribution of artefacts related to weaponry.

Fig. 1d) Distribution of artefacts of horse tack.

sites (Rau 2005). There are significant differences concerning the categories of objects that have been found on the different sites; for instance, remains of horse tack are more common in Swedish than in Danish finds (Nordqvist 2008).

Finnestorp: a short research history

The Finnestorp finds were made in a drained wetland in central Västergötland, south-west Sweden (for map see Introduction fig. 6).

In the years 1902–1903 a road was built across this wetland (fig. 1a). During the road construction finds were made of sword fragments, lance heads, gilt mounts, and a gold finger-ring. Furthermore bones in abundance were

found, mainly from horses but also human. A result of this discovery was that the archaeologists Otto Frödin (1881–1953) and Gustaf Hallström (1880–1962) from the Swedish History Museum in Stockholm came to Finnestorp in 1904 to conduct investigations. They excavated only limited parts of the find area. In the coming 70 years various archaeologists visited Finnestorp to undertake small investigations.

In 1973 the road across the wetland was rebuilt and a part of the find area was destroyed. Again the road works were not accompanied by archaeological excavations. But in 1980 a small trial trench was opened by Ulf Erik Hagberg (1932–2012) and Eva Bergström (1941–2013). On that

2

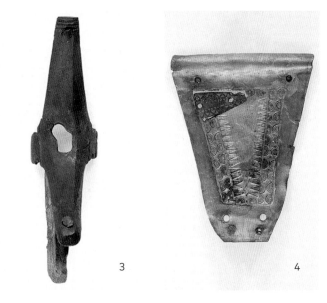

3

4

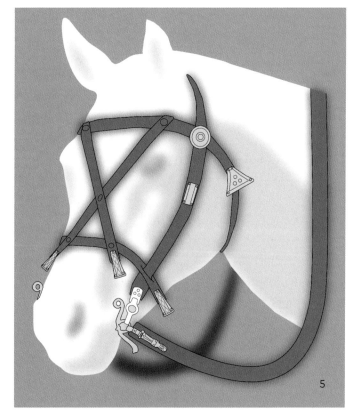

5

Fig. 2. A fragment of a rein chain is in pristine condition. © Offering Site Finnestorp.

Fig. 3. A short saddle mount with much wear in the hole for the staple of a saddle ring, see also fig. 23. © Offering Site Finnestorp.

Fig. 4. A unique find is a repaired strap end of gilt silver sheet. A small gilt silver mount has been riveted to the strap to fill a hole in the strap end. © Offering Site Finnestorp.

Fig. 5. An attempt to fit mounts found at Finnestorp into a bridle, which is based on the bridle from Högom (Ramqvist chapter 10 fig. 9–14). © Offering Site Finnestorp.

occasion bones, a saddle mount and a piece of gilt sheet metal was found.

In 1991 an excavator was used to clear the Händene Stream through the wetland. An excavation followed, led by Ulf Viking (1955–1998). In this excavation some finds were made: bones, lance heads, fragments of sword blades and a saddle mount.

None of these excavations were systematic, comprehensive or continuous and none was followed up. On this backdrop a project Offerplats Finnestorp (Offering Site Finnestorp) was started in 2000.[1] According to a comprehensive research strategy recurrent investigations in the field were planned. The aim was to make smaller excavations spread over the whole find area; it was important to investigate both wet and dry settings. The project was based on two campaigns of fieldwork, a first stage in 2000–2004 and a second in 2008–2012 (Nordqvist 2017).

The setting of the find place Finnestorp

The offering site is situated on the border between the parishes of Larv and Trävattna (Riksantikvarieämbetet's ancient monument no. Larv 121:1). The parish border runs in a depression that is a drained wetland where the Händene Stream falls into the river Lidan, one of the largest watercourses in Västergötland. The site is placed in a central part of the province in a forested area characterised by extensive wetlands – a natural border area between two rich agrarian plains, the Skara Plain to the west and Falbygden to the east.

In the 20th century it was assumed that finds came only from a small part of the wetland, a mistake explained by the small excavations along the road and that all known finds came from an area approx. 25 × 25 m in size. The research project in the early 21st century was able to establish that the find area is as large as approx. 400 × 100 m (for an excavation report, see Nordqvist 2017).

Varying conditions in the wetland have considerably influenced the preservation of the find material. Bronze and silver artefacts are well-preserved in the whole find area, while organic material such as bone and wood is well-preserved only in the northern part. Artefacts of iron such as sword blades, lance and spear heads, snaffles and mounts for saddles are badly preserved in all parts of the find area.

Among the finds different forms of decorative mounts and pendants are present. Other find categories found are clasps, sword pommels, chapes and mouthpieces of sword scabbards, sword beads, saddle mounts and strap mounts and parts of bridles. Furthermore, there are large amounts of unburnt bones, mainly from horse.

Most of the offered objects are connected with elevations in the wetland that seem to have been small islands when offerings took place here. The offering rituals were performed from these islands (see fig. 1b–d). Although single finds are found without connection to the islands, they are few and sparsely spread over the find area. Remains of fireplaces were observed on three of the four discernible islands in the wetland. They are small, irregular, shallow and diffuse. All are placed near the edge of the water at that time.

The many cut-off metal mounts demonstrate that the objects were ritually destroyed and cut in pieces before the artefacts in question were thrown out into the wetland. Even small artefacts such as sword pommels were cut in two.

A different ritual behaviour is associated with four pits, considered to be offering pits (Nordqvist 2017:147–153). They are approx. 20–85 cm in diameter and approx. 20–55 cm deep and found all over the find area. In three pits there were offerings of whole sets of horse bridles, two of which are exclusive, and one contained horse teeth. Two pits contained exclusive mounts that seem to have been still riveted to the strap when deposited. Note that the bit is missing in all these bridles. A common feature of the mounts is that they were not cut in pieces but are whole sets of bridle mounts. At present it can be established that the objects found in offering pits are decorated in Sösdala style and consequently dateable to the period c. AD 375–450.

Finds from Finnestorp

The Finnestorp offering site is characterised by an abundant occurrence of Migration Period finds. But it is important to remember that we only know a small number of what once was offered on the site. So in a summary like this it is problematic to make meaningful estimates of the number of finds of various categories. For example, many objects are fragmentary and cut in pieces. And all iron objects are badly corroded.

In the 20th century approx. 100 metal objects were recorded, mainly very rusty iron objects (for some silver mounts, see Åberg 1919 fig. 31–35). Only a few of them are from archaeological excavations. This changed in the research excavations in 2000–2004 and 2008–2012. In spite of limited excavation efforts the number of recorded metal artefacts increased by approx. 600 items. Among them objects of bronze or silver dominate.

At Finnestorp objects are found made of gold, silver, bronze, iron and wood. Wooden artefacts are a small piece of a saddle tree and poles cut with an axe. The many bones are mainly from horses, but humans, pigs and sheep/goat are also represented. The find material is roughly subdivided into three categories.

1) Personal equipment: finger-ring in gold, clasps, belt mounts (buckles, strap ends), belt bag (mini-buckle and pendant), etc. In all over 100 objects belong to this category (fig. 1b).

2) Weapons: sword (blade, pommel, hilt), sword scabbard (chape and mouthpiece), mounts of sword belt, lance and spear heads, arrow heads and possibly a throwing axe (francisca?). Totally just under 200 objects belong to this category (fig. 1c).

3) Horse tack: mounts of saddles and bridles. Decorative mounts, strap junctions and strap ends come from headstalls. Mounts including rein chains are from the snaffle. Saddle remains are mounts and rings with staples. Probably all of the pelta-shaped pendants belong to saddles. In all nearly 300 objects belong to this category (fig. 1d).

6   7   8

9

10   11

Preliminary analysis of horse tack from Finnestorp

A number of ¹⁴C dates are available for Finnestorp (Nordqvist 2017 bilaga 3). Only relevant and calibrated results are presented here. Three dates of horse bone fall within the interval AD 320–550 (2 sigma) or AD 350–500 (1 sigma). A third radiocarbon date has been obtained from remains of a piece of oak preserved below a short saddle mount of bronze (fig. 3, 23); the radiocarbon date is AD 330–540 (2 sigma). The result of the ¹⁴C dates from Finnestorp is unsurprising: the finds were deposited in the 4th–6th centuries, mainly in the Migration Period. More detailed chronological analysis of the evidence of horse tack must be based on typo-chronological discussions, which are fraught with difficulties.

A central question is whether our dates refer to the production or to the deposition of an artefact. The problem is rendered more difficult by the observation that simple functional designs have a long life while richly decorated mounts like the pelta-shaped pendants have a shorter production time. Another problem is the low number of comparable objects that sometimes leads the discussion into circles; an object in a single well-dated context will be used over and over again.

Sometimes the condition of an object can be helpful. An example from Finnestorp is given by a fragment of a rein chain the links and rings of which appear to be in pristine condition (fig. 2). On the other hand some objects are very much worn. Two examples: due to forces pulling the saddle ring the staple has worn a long hole in the mount (fig. 3, 23). Also repairs deserve to be mentioned in this context. A hole in a triangular strap end of a bridle that was found in one of the offering pits has been closed with a small piece of another mount (fig. 4). The problem is that it is difficult to conclude whether the wear or damage was caused by very long but sporadic use or by short but very intense use.

12   13

Fig. 6. Cross-shaped strap junction covered by sheet silver. Only decoration is edge lines. © Offering Site Finnestorp.

Fig. 7. Strap mount of silver with gilt and punch decorated panel. The rivets have silver caps. © Offering Site Finnestorp.

Fig. 8. Strap end of silver with gilt and punch decorated panel. The punched decoration is varied including three stars and five triquetras of lens-shaped punch marks. Rivets have silver caps. © Offering Site Finnestorp.

Fig. 9. Round strap junction of silver with gilt and punch-decorated panel. Rivets have silver caps. © Offering Site Finnestorp.

Fig. 10. Round strap junction of silver with gilt and punch-decorated panel. In the centre a facetted "shield boss". Rivets have silver caps. Note cut marks. Front and side views. © Offering Site Finnestorp.

Fig. 11. Long strap mount with widened centre. Bronze covered with sheet silver. Cut in pieces. © Offering Site Finnestorp.

Fig. 12. A bit ring with two strap mounts. One cut in two is shaped like an animal head. Both have facetted loops and rivets with silver caps. © Offering Site Finnestorp.

Fig. 13. A fragment of a bimetallic snaffle with loose ring, bit end and two mounts. © Offering Site Finnestorp.

The bridles of Finnestorp

Since we only have fragments of bridles the finds are divided into three groups, A) mounts of the headstall, B) mounts of the bit, and C) the mouthpiece.

A) The headstall

Mounts attached to the straps of the headstall (fig. 5) consist of a bronze plate covered by a gilt silver sheet, but also much simpler mounts are present. Some are covered with thin sheet silver (fig. 6), others are of sheet bronze. The central part of the decorated silver sheets is gilt while the broad edges are left as ungilt silver (figs 7–9). Many mounts have a punched decoration in Sösdala style of high quality, mainly on the gilt surfaces. The decoration

consists of semicircles, circles, stars, triangles, rosettes, etc. All mounts were fastened to the strap with rivets with washers. Some rivets are covered with silver caps. The grave find from Högom is a good guide when discussing where in the headstall different mounts were placed (see Ramqvist chapter 10 figs 9–10, 14). Based on this reference triangular mounts (fig. 8) could have been strap ends at the nose- and browbands. Round and cross-shaped mounts served as strap junctions (fig. 6, 9–10). Rectangular strap mounts were mainly decorative (fig. 7). A few mounts crossed the strap.

As pointed out by Fabech & Näsman (2013:101–102), a shield-shaped strap-junction from Finnestorp (fig. 10) is very similar to round strap-junctions in the important find from Untersiebenbrunn, Austria (Kazanski & Mastykova chapter 15 fig. 3; cf. Nothnagel 2008 Taf. 11–12). The central faceted "shield boss" can be dated with reference to real shield bosses, which are dated to the early Migration Period and found in Central and Eastern Europe but not in Scandinavia (Kazanski 1988:76, fig. 6–7). Patricius Stilicho, depicted on the famous Monza diptych, holds a shield with a faceted shield boss, which underlines both chronology and social setting (Conti 1999:14–16).

The gilt mounts with rich decoration punched in Sösdala style can be dated to the first half of the 5th century (Hansen 1970: 88–89; 93–98). Bitner-Wróblewska places her Sösdala horizon in a period from the second half of the 4th century to the first half of the 5th century (2001:

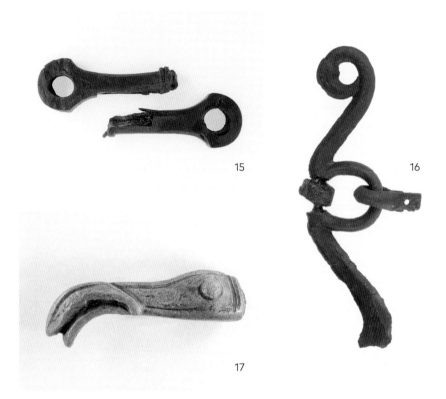

14

Fig. 14. Two fragments of rein chains. Left a fragment of a bimetallic snaffle with bit ring, bit end, hook for the cheekpiece of the headstall as well as links and a ring of the rein chain. Right rings and links of a rein chain. © Offering Site Finnestorp.

Fig. 15. Bit ends of a bimetallic mouthpiece, bronze on iron. © Offering Site Finnestorp.

Fig. 16. A cheek bar of bronze ending in a head of a bird of prey turned downwards. In the loop a fragment of the iron mouthpiece and a simple strap mount of bronze. © Offering Site Finnestorp.

Fig. 17. A bronze casing shaped as a head of a bird of prey interpreted as a terminal of a cheek bar, cf. fig. 16. © Offering Site Finnestorp.

Fig. 18. A corroded but almost intact long saddle mount of iron with ring and staple in place (Finnestorp group 1). Length 28 cm. Note remains of rivets that fastened the mount to the pommel of the saddle. © Offering Site Finnestorp.

15

16

17

18

105). Fabech & Näsman assign the Sösdala finds to period Scand-D1, and with reference to the last contribution to the chronological discussion period D1 is dated to AD 410–455/465 (Rau 2010:119–122, Abb. 41; Fabech & Näsman 2013:100). The general opinion is that the Sösdala style developed in the late 4th century and rapidly faded out again in the second half of the 5th century.

Also simple mounts exist only decorated with lines along the edges. The simple mounts are made of bronze or silver sheet. Some bronze mounts are covered with thin silver sheet. An example is a cross-shaped strap junction of sheet silver (fig. 6). Like most of the cross-shaped strap-junctions that Ørsnes registered as his type 9D1, the Finnestorp strap junction may be dated to period D1 (Ørsnes 1994 find catalogue). In Finnestorp a simple long mount (fig. 11) has an equivalent in the Högom grave (Ramqvist chapter 10 fig. 10:6) so perhaps it is also from c. AD 450–520.

B) The bit mounts

The mouthpiece of a bit has loops at both ends that held loose bit rings or loose cheek bars, to which the mounts of reins and cheekpieces of the headstall were fastened. The mounts are cast in massive bronze. Most are zoomorphic and demonstrate skilled craftsmanship with distinctly shaped muzzles, eyes, ears and necks. Some seem to depict horse heads (fig. 12), cf. the "horse heads" on mounts in the Högom find and in two Danish finds from Hellum and Hessel (Ramqvist chapter 10 fig. 13; Ørsnes 1994 fig. 42). Other mounts are only faintly outlined as animal heads (fig. 13). The strap mounts have a triangular cross-section and belong to Ørsnes's bit mount type 4A–4B and to his bridle type OF1 from the period c. AD 375–550 (Ørsnes 1994:249–251, Fig. 53b). The sculptural qualities of the animal heads resemble a late group of saddle mounts (below), implying a date of the mounts to c. AD 450–520.

In some bridles rein chains of bronze were used. Rein chains consist of rings, links and a terminal mount between chain and leather rein (fig. 14). Instead of fixed mounts between cheekpieces and bit rings, bridles with rein chains had a hook, which made it possible to detach the snaffle from the headstall. Rein chains have been found at other offering sites such as Ejsbøl, Illerup, Skedemosse and Thorsbjerg (Ørsnes 1988 Taf. 167–181; 1994:194–213; Lau 2014:24–66). The different pieces of rein chains found at Finnestorp are relatively similar to one another (fig. 2, 14). Line decoration and facets of the rings as well as the fish-tail-shaped ends of the links distinguish them from rein chains of the Late Roman Iron Age (Ørsnes 1994 fig. 14; Lau 2014 Abb. 14:7). In the most recent survey of rein chains Lau places the Finnestorp type after her so-called Thorsbjerg type from C2/C3, c. AD 250–375 (Lau 2014:58–63 Abb. 18). Rein chains are depicted on medallion copies from Mauland, Norway, and Sundsvall and Aneby, Sweden, and on one of the golden horns from Gallehus, Jutland (Arbman 1936; Ørsnes 1994:226; 251; Lau 2014:260 Abb. 145–147), indicating that rein chains were in use through C3 and still in D1. In Ørsnes's opinion the rein

chains from Finnestorp that belong to his type 6C2 represent a development of his bridle type OC. I agree with Ørsnes that this type of rein chains was used into period D1 (Ørsnes 1994:191, 205, 224–225, Fig. 14:i).

C) The mouthpiece

Only few and rusty fragments are preserved of iron mouthpieces. Fragments of a ported mouthpiece of iron (Ørsnes's bit type 1B3) belong to loose-ring snaffles usually dated to C2/C3 or the 4th century (Ørsnes 1994:190), but the diameter of the bit ring, approx. 60 mm, indicates that it belongs to bit ring type 2C, indicating a date c. AD 375–550. In fact, ported bits were still used in the Migration Period as evidenced by finds from Vännebo and Högom, dated to period D1 (uncertain) and D2, respectively (Ørsnes 1994:278, fig. 48:3; Ramqvist chapter 10 fig. 9–11).

Some mouthpieces from Finnestorp are bimetallic with preserved bit ends of bronze, while the mouthpieces of iron have rusted away more or less completely. The bit ends held a loose bit ring or cheek bar. The shape of bit ends varies but a couple are similar to bit ends found in Ejsbøl, Nydam and Thorsbjerg (fig. 15; Ørsnes 1994 Fig. 40a–b). The Thorsbjerg finds are dated by Lau to period C2/C3 (Lau 2014:58–63, Taf. 4–5; 8–9).The lack of closed finds from both C3 and D1 makes it difficult to estimate the life of this type of bit ends but probably it was in use also after C2/C3. Another bit end of bronze from Finnestorp is still in place on a bit ring with rein chain (fig. 14). For its date to period D1, see rein chains above. A third bimetallic snaffle has faceted bit ends and a loose bit-ring that belongs to Ørsnes's type 2C (fig. 13). With a type 2C bit ring and a long strap mount of Ørsnes's type 4A, the snaffle belongs to his bridle type OF1 and can, like a similar find from Dallerup in Jutland, be dated to D1 (Ørsnes 1994 fig. 2). Bimetallic bits with differently shaped bit ends are found in Vännebo and Sösdala, which Lau adds to her Thorsbjerg type, but she consider them as developed variants dateable to D1 (Lau 2014:63).

At Finnestorp one intact cheek bar and a fragment of another have been found. On the best-preserved the bar curves below and above a central loop in which mouthpiece, rein mount and mount for the cheekpiece were fastened. The upper end of the bar is shaped as a head of a

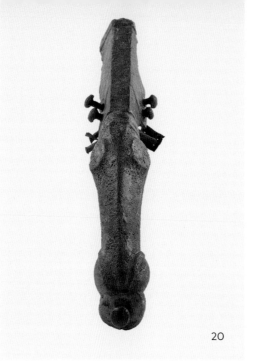

Fig. 19. The cut-off lower end of a saddle mount of bronze (Finnestorp group 3). Note the animal-head-shaped end and the hole for the staple of a saddle ring. © Offering Site Finnestorp.

Fig. 20. Broken-off upper part of saddle mount of bronze (Finnestorp group 6). Shaped as an animal head. © Offering Site Finnestorp.

Fig. 21. A bronze casing shaped as a head of a bird of prey for a saddle mount of iron (Finnestorp group 4). © Offering Site Finnestorp.

---

bird of prey (fig. 16). In the loop a fragment is preserved of the mouthpiece of iron and a facetted strap mount of bronze. The bird head has a slender strongly bent neck and a curved beak, very similar to the bird heads of the cheek-bar snaffle from Högom, dated to period D2 (Ramqvist chapter 10 fig. 11). But there are also differences. The cheek bar of Finnestorp is entirely of bronze and the lower part is flat; the Högom cheek bars are made of a round iron rod. This type of cheek bar, according to Kazanski, is also found on the Continent and he presents examples from north-eastern France and from the Caucasus (Kazanski 2016:26–27, fig. 1). They are dated to the second half of the Migration Period, the late 5th and early 6th century.

Probably also a broken-off bird head of bronze once was the end of a cheek bar (fig. 17). It can be compared to bird heads of bronze on the iron cheek bars of Högom (Ramqvist chapter 10 fig. 10–12) and also to much younger

cheek bars found in grave I at Vendel, Uppland (Arrhenius 1983 fig. 18a–b). Probably both Finnestorp cheek bars can be dated to the second half of the 5th or possibly as late as the early 6th century.

Saddles

A brief introduction to saddles seems necessary (cf. Näsman chapter 7; Sundkvist chapter 9. Ramqvist chapter 10). The Nordic ring saddles have no relation to the Roman four-horned saddle. The consensus among scholars is that the Nordic ring saddle traces its origin from South-eastern Europe. The saddle probably developed in the interaction between Goths and Sarmatians during the 3rd–4th centuries when they lived close together west of the Black Sea (e.g. Ramqvist 1992:86, Ørsnes 1994:271; Anke 1998:109; Lau 2014:76–78; 256–258). Then relatively rapid local developments of saddles followed; for example it was apparently a South Scandinavian idea to furnish saddles with saddle rings. The classical ring saddle is only known in finds from Denmark, Schleswig and Sweden. The earliest dated ring saddles are more than 100 years earlier than the Huns' arrival in Europe (Ørsnes 1994:271–272; von Carnap-Bornheim & Ilkjær 1996:272–273). Seemingly the saddle developed independently in South Scandinavia in the period c. AD 200–500 (Ørsnes 1994:271–272; von Carnap-Bornheim & Ilkjær 1996:272–273).

About half of the saddle mounts found at Finnestorp are forged in iron; the other half are cast in bronze. Some

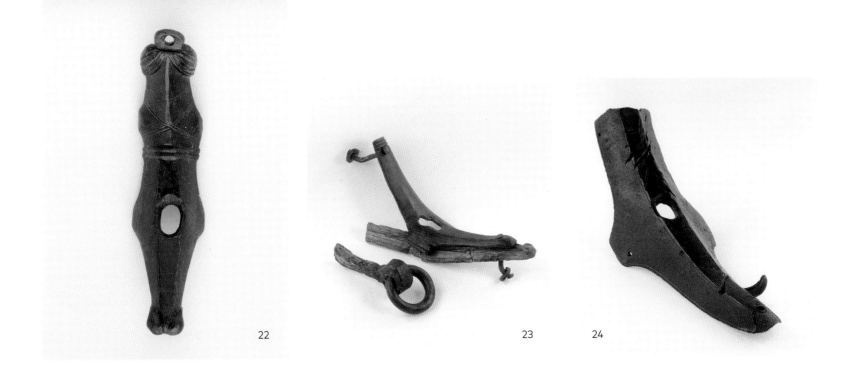

22   23   24

mounts are made in a combination of the two metals. Many mounts are only preserved as fragments. Only some smaller mounts are well-preserved. In cross-section the mounts are hollow to fit the crest of the pommel or cantle. The girth was fastened with buckles and saddle straps were adorned with pelta-shaped pendants.

Two types of saddle mounts of iron occur in Finnestorp (Carlstein 2014 Finnestorp group 1 and 2). Group 1, which consists of iron mounts almost without decoration, is represented by a complete mount (fig. 18). It is bent in a gentle S-curve and was placed on a high pommel. Its shape is very similar to a long saddle mount of iron from Hassle-Bösarp (Stjernquist 1974:28, 38–43, Fig. 20) and also to long bronze mounts from Sösdala (nos. I:201–202). This indicates a date of the Finnestorp mount to period D1. Mounts of group 2 are preserved only as fragments; iron mounts decorated with bronze sheets and inlays. One fragment has preserved inlays of a circled dot and short crossing lines. A survey of inlays in metal established that iron objects with inlaid circled dots (mainly on lance and spear heads) occur as early as the 2nd century AD but are more common in the 3rd century (Holmqvist 1951:77–79) Rein mounts with thin silver inlays found in Skedemosse are dated to c. AD 250–375 (Holmqvist 1951:86, Hagberg 1967a fig. 67; Rau 2005). Circled dots are found as inlays in bronze on saddled mounts from period D1 found at Vännebo (Holmqvist 1951:112, Abb. 47–48) and Sösdala (no. I:213, I:215). Inlays in iron are rare in the Migration Peri-

Fig. 22. An intact short saddle mount of bronze with hole for the staple of a saddle ring (Finnestorp group 5). One end is shaped as a horse head with details depicting a bridle (cf. fig. 5); the other end is perhaps intended to depict the rump of a horse. © Offering Site Finnestorp.

Fig. 23. Short intact saddle mount with rivets, saddle ring and staple. It was found with the staple in the hole and on top of preserved oaken remains of the saddle, see also fig. 3. © Offering Site Finnestorp.

Fig. 24. Cut-off lower end of saddle mount of bronze with hole for the staple of the saddle ring (Finnestorp group 3). Simple lines are the only decoration. © Offering Site Finnestorp.

od; in fact Holmqvist knew none. But now an exclusive lance head with precious metal inlays has appeared in the offering find Nydam IV, which is dated to period D2a, c. AD 450–475. Inlays are found on both sides, on one a silver swastika, on the other a quadruped in gold (Petersen 1998:263 Abb. 107). According to Berta Stjernquist the long saddle mount of iron from Hassle-Bösarp had a rivet with a bronze cap and possibly also inlaid crossing lines (Stjernquist 1974:28, 38); it was dated to the early Migration Period. The iron mounts from Finnestorp are similar to mounts from Vännebo, Sösdala (bronze) and Hassle-Bösarp (iron) and probably from period D1.

All bronze mounts are cast. Some mounts have a hole for the staple of a saddle ring and were placed at the lower

25   26   27

Fig. 25. Cut off upper end of saddle mount of bronze. The end is shaped as a lizard (or dragon) with forelegs (Finnestorp group 6).

Fig. 26. Saddle ring of bronze with inlays of silver wire on the upper side. © Offering Site Finnestorp.

Fig. 27. Girth buckle of bronze with double tongues and B-shaped attachment plate. © Offering Site Finnestorp.

---

end of the pommel or cantle (fig. 19). The depicted animal head has a simple shape like mounts from Högom (Ramqvist 1992 pl. 49–51). Other mounts without staple hole were probably placed at the top of the pommel (fig. 20). It is unclear whether the short Finnestorp mounts were combined with bronze rails like the mounts and rails protecting the Högom saddle (Ramqvist 1992 fig. 48a; pl. 55–56); such rails are simply not found. Three different types of bronze mounts are found at Finnestorp, and it will be argued below that their changing shape is connected to chronology. 1) Bimetallic mounts, bronze mounts which are cast to the end of an iron rod (fig. 21); 2) bronze mounts shaped as animal heads (fig. 20, 22), and 3) mounts decorated with lines only (fig. 23–24).

1) Bronze mounts cast on an iron rod have different shapes. Some are zoomorphic (Finnestorp group 4) and appear either as sculptural animal heads (fig. 21) or are more simplified. A comparable saddle mount of iron with

an animal head in cast bronze comes from the Vännebo find; perhaps it depicts the head of a lizard (Holmqvist 1951 Abb. 47; Carlstein 2014 Appendix 2:17). Carlstein places the group in the period c. AD 450–500, but in my opinion this type of mounts should be dated to c. AD 400–450. This is in accordance with Åberg's dating of the Vännebo find (Åberg 1936:274–275; Holmqvist 1951:112).

2) The most advanced type of saddle mounts have a sculptural shape, often formed as a horse head, and a few short intact mounts have the other end shaped as a rump (fig. 22; Finnestorp groups 5 and 6). The details are often well formed, for example as muzzle, eyes, ears and neck. Lines and narrow ridges seem to depict bridles and neckrings. The mounts are dated to c. AD 450–500 (Carlstein 2014:46). Similar mounts are known from the Högom saddle where they are placed at the lower end of pommel and cantle; the Högom grave is dated to c. AD 500 (Ramqvist chapter 10). In the opinion of Fabech and Näsman the chamber grave can be dated to period D2a that according to Rau's analysis give a date to c. AD 455/465–505/515 (Rau 2010:120; Fabech & Näsman 2013:94).

A probably cut-off mount shaped as an animal head was probably placed at the top of a high pommel (fig. 20); only a rough date to the 5th century is possible. The upper end of a mount is shaped as the forepart of an animal body, a lizard (or dragon) with legs stretching out from the mount (fig. 25). The lower end is cut-off so that the part that probably had a hole for a saddle ring staple is miss-

28

Fig. 28. Lunate pelta-shaped pendant of silver still attached to its strap mount. Silver with gilt and punch decorated panel. © Offering Site Finnestorp.

Fig. 29. Open pelta-shaped pendant of silver with ends shaped as bird heads in silhouette. Silver with gilt and punch decorated panel. © Offering Site Finnestorp.

Fig. 30. Pelta-shaped pendant of silver. Gilt lunate punch decorated panel. Ends shaped as heads of birds of prey. © Offering Site Finnestorp.

Fig. 31. Pelta-shaped pendant of silver with gilt lunate pelta-shaped panel surrounded by punch decoration. Ends shaped as in-turned bird heads with open beaks. Niello inlays along the edges and on the bird heads.

29

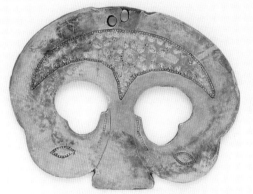

30

ing. The upper end has some similarity to two long saddle mounts from Sösdala (nos. I:117, I:119). There are similar lizard-like figured on a golden neck collar from Ålleberg, Västergötland, and a neck-ring from Hannenov, Falster in Denmark (Haseloff 1981 Abb. 136–137). Haseloff dates the rings to the middle or a little later of the 5th century. The Finnestorp lizard has an ornamental detail, a characteristic shape of the shoulder, which is found in animals drawn in Haseloff's style IB (Haseloff 1981 Abb. 98c). The transition from Sösdala/Nydam style to Salin's style I is placed around AD 475 by Haseloff (1981:17) In Salin's study of the shoulder shapes of animal figures in his style I (Salin 1904 Fig. 516), shoulders shapes d–f seem to give a relevant comparative material. To conclude, the saddle mounts in question seem to belong to a period AD c. 450–520.

3) The third group is saddle mounts of cast bronze with a widened part and a hole for the staple of the saddle ring (fig. 23–24). The only decoration is simple lines and ridg-

31

es. The well-preserved short mount found with staple and saddle-ring in place was still riveted to the remains of an oaken lath. Finnestorp group 3 is dated by Carlstein to c. AD 400–450 (Carlstein 2014:44; 46).

Also belonging to saddles there are rings and staples. The rings and staples found at Finnestorp are of more or less corroded iron or of well-preserved bronze. Many saddle rings are still attached to their staple. Only a couple of saddle rings have silver inlays (fig. 26) like saddle rings from Vännebo (Holmqvist 1951 Abb. 47) and Sösdala (nos. I:207–212).

Strap buckles fastened the girth of the saddles. Buckles found are of bronze with a large integral attachment plate and a strong frame. Some have double tongues (fig. 27). Similar girth buckles are found in the Högom grave (Ramqvist 1992 pl. 59) and in the Vännebo offering (SHM nos. 6511:3, 22).

Pelta-shaped pendants

At Finnestorp seven different pelta-shaped pendants have been found (fig. 28–31; and chapter 12 fig. 1f). One still has its attachment plate preserved. They may have decorated either straps holding the saddle, such as breast collar or breeching, or they hung, for example, from the browband of the headstall (Hagberg 1957:108; Ørsnes 1994:241). The development of these pendants seems to go from open lunate pelta-shapes to proper pelta-shaped pendants with bird-head terminals. In Finnestorp the most common type is the open (lunate) pelta-shape. Three have a punched star as decoration and are without animal-head terminals (fig. 28; an old find in Åberg 1919 fig. 31). Punched stars cannot be dated more accurately than to period C3–D1, c. 300–450. Only one of the lunate pendants seems to take an intermediate position with terminals formed as bird heads in profile and a star as central motif in the punched decoration (fig. 29). The lunate pelta-shaped pendants have a shape like other pendants, for example from Varpelev, Denmark, dated to C2, c. AD 250–320 (Jørgensen et al. 2003:396) and Brangstrup, Funen, dated to C3, c. AD 310–375 (Andersson 1995:41; Jørgensen et al. 2003:425). But lunate pelta-shaped pendants are also known from period D1 of the Migration Period, for example at Birkeland and Skreros in Norway (Magnus 1975 fig. 27–28),

and Sandby fort on Öland (Gunnarsson et al. 2017). The lunate pelta-shaped pendants from Finnestorp can probably be dated to the early Migration Period.

Three pelta-shaped pendants have a central panel in lunate pelta-shape and punch marks in Sösdala style (fig. 30–31; and Bitner-Wróblewska chapter 12 fig. 1f), but only one has a punched star. The two without star have terminals shaped as in-turned bird heads with curved beaks and round eyes. The bird heads are made in deep relief, almost chip-carved, perhaps indicating a later date. Both pendants have niello inlays and were possibly produced later than the lunate pelta-shaped pendants but still within the 5th century. The pelta-shaped pendants from Finnestorp have similarities to pendants in Migration Period horse tack from Vännebo, Fulltofta and Sösdala, (Sweden), Jakuszowice (Poland) and Černâhovsk (former Insterburg, Kaliningrad, Russia) (Ørsnes 1994:240–242; Bitner-Wróblewska 2001: 92–95).

Conclusion

In Finnestorp there is a discrepancy between the amount of horse bone recovered and the estimated number of bridles and saddles. There are too many bones and too little horse tack. Today we cannot quantify the number of horsemen whose equipment was offered, but it can be established that there is no evidence of common warriors on foot. Nor was equipment of whole contingents of defeated cavalry offered. The horse tack recovered in the Finnestorp swamp represents the elite of contemporary horsemen. The arsenal of weaponry and horse tack that seems to have been produced by the most skilled craftsmen supports this assumption.

At present we believe that the recorded finds represent a couple of victorious battles. Conquered objects were brought from a battlefield to be offered in the wetland around the Händene Stream at river Lidan on a few occasions over less than a hundred years.

Note

1   Project Finnestorp is funded by Torsten Söderbergs Stiftelse.

References

Åberg, N. 1919. Den germanska stjärnornamentiken under 3- och 400-talet e.Kr. *Antikvarisk tidskrift för Sverige* 21/3: 1–51.

Åberg, N. 1936. Till belysande av det gotiska kulturinslaget i Mellaneuropa och Skandinavien. *Fornvännen* 31: 264–277. Zusammenfassung.

Andersson, K. 1995. *Romartida guldsmide i Norden 3. Övriga smycken, teknisk analys och verkstadsgrupper.* Uppsala. Summary.

Anke, B. 1998. *Studien zur reiternomadischen Kultur des 4. bis. 5. Jahrhunderts 1–2.* Berlin /Weisbach.

Arbman, H. 1936. En barbarisk guldmedaljong från Småland. *Fornvännen* 31: 58–59.

Arrhenius, B. 1983. The chronology of the Vendel graves. In: Lamm J. P. and Nordström, H.-Å. (eds). *Vendel Period Studies.* Stockholm: 39–70.

Bitner-Wróblewska, A. 2001. *From Samland to Rogaland. East-West connections in the Baltic basin during the Early Migration Period.* Warsaw.

Carlstein, C. 2014. *Krigarens säte i striden?* [B.A. thesis in archaeology]. University of Gothenburg. – On-line: http://www.academia.edu/11006457/ Krigarens_sate_i_striden_Caj_Carlstein.

Carnap-Bornheim, C. von & Ilkjær, J. 1996. *Illerup Ådal 5–7. Die Prachtausrüstungen.* Højbjerg/Århus.

Conti, R. 1999 (1st ed. 1993). *Il tesoro. Guida alla conoscenza del Tesoro del Duomo di Monza.* Monza.

Engelhardt, C. 1863. *Thorsbjerg Mosefund.* Copenhagen.

Engelhardt, C. 1865. *Nydam Mosefund.* Copenhagen.

Engelhardt, C. 1867. *Kragehul Mosefund.* Copenhagen.

Engelhardt, C. 1869. *Vimose Fundet.* Copenhagen.

Fabech, C. 1996. Booty sacrifices in Southern Scandinavia – history of warfare and ideology. In: *Roman Reflections in Scandinavia.* Rome: 135–138.

Fabech, C. & Näsman, U. 2013. A lonely rider? The finding place of the Sösdala-find and the context of its finds. In: Khrapunov, I & Stylegar, F.-A. (eds). *Inter Ambo Maria. Northern barbarians from Scandinavia towards the Black Sea.* Kristiansand/Simferopol: 84–106. Резюме.

Gunnarsson, F. et al. 2017. *Sandby borg – undersökningar 2015, Sandby sn, Mörbylånga kommun, Öland.* Kalmar.

Hagberg, U.-E. 1957 Folkvandringstida hängprydnader. *Tor* 3: 108–120.

Hagberg, U.-E. 1967a. *The archaeology of Skedemosse 1. The excavations and the finds of an Öland fen, Sweden.* Stockholm.

Hagberg, U.-E. 1967b. *The archaeology of Skedemosse 2. The votive deposits in the Skedemosse fen and their relation to the IronAge settlement on Öland, Sweden.* Stockholm.

Hansen, U. Lund 1970. Kvarmløsefundet – en analyse af Sösdalastilen og dens forudsætninger. *Aarbøger for Nordisk Oldkyndighed og Historie* 1969: 63–102. Zusammenfassung.

Hansen, U. Lund 2003. 150 years of weapon-offerings finds. Research and interpretation. In: Jørgensen, L. et al. (eds). *The spoils of victory. The North in the shadow of the Roman Empire.* Copenhagen: 84–89.

Haseloff, G. 1981. *Die germanische Tierornamentik der Völkerwanderungszeit 1–3.* Berlin/New York.

Holmqvist, W. 1951. *Tauschierte Metallarbeiten des Nordens aus Römerzeit und Völkerwanderung.* Stockholm.

Ilkjær, J. 1990. *Illerup Ådal 1–2. Die Lanzen und Speere.* Højbjerg/Aarhus.

Ilkjær, J. 2003. Danish war booty sacrifices. In: Jørgensen, L. et al. (eds). *The spoils of victory. The North in the shadow of the Roman Empire.* Copenhagen: 44–64.

Ilkjær J. 2008 Die Funde aus Illerup Ådal – Der Stand der Forschung im Jahr 2006. In: Abegg-Wigg, A. & Rau, A. (eds). *Aktuelle Forschungen zu Kriegsbeuteopfern und Fürstengräbern im Barbaricum.* Neumünster: 19–24.

Jørgensen, L. et al. (eds). 2003. *The spoils of victory. The North in the shadow of the Roman Empire.* Copenhagen.

Kazanski, M. 1988. Quelques parallèles entre l'armement en Occident et a Byzance (IVᵉ–VIIᵉ s.). In: Landes, C. (ed.). *Gaule mérovingienne et monde méditerranéen.* Lattes: 75–87.

Kazanski, M. 2016. Les mors de cheval à décor zoomophe de l'époque des Grands Migrations. *Bulletin de liaison de l'Association française d'archéologie mérovingienne* 40: 26–32.

Lau, N. 2014. *Das Thorsberger Moor 1. Die Pferdegeschirre. Germanische Zaumzeuge und Sattelgeschirre als Zeugnisse kriegerischer Reiterei im mittel- und nordeuropäischen Barbaricum.* Schleswig.

Magnus, B. 1975. *Krosshaugfunnet. Et forsøk på kronologisk og stilhistorisk plassering i 5. årh.* Stavanger. Summary.

Norberg, R. 1931. Moor- und Depotfunde aus dem 5. Jahrhundert nach Chr. in Schonen. *Acta Archaeologica* 2: 104–111.

Nordqvist, B. 2008 Der Kriegsbeuteopferplatz von Finnestorp in Schweden. *Offa* 2004/5. 61/6 221–238.

Nordqvist, B. 2017. *Offerplats Finnestorp. Grävredogörelse åren 1902–2012.* Gothenburg.

Nothnagel, M. 2008. *Die völkerwanderungszeitlichen Bestattungen von Untersiebenbrunn, Niederösterreich.* [Mag.phil. thesis] University of Vienna. – On-line: http://othes.univie.ac.at/1440/1/2008-09-18_0100192.pdf – Checked 18 April 2017.

Ørsnes, M. 1988. *Ejsbøl I. Waffenopferfunde des 4.–5. Jahrhundert nach Chr.* Copenhagen.

Ørsnes, M. 1994. Zaumzeugfunde des 1.–8. Jahrh. nach Chr. In Mittel- und Nordeuropa. *Acta Archaeologica* 64: 183–292.

Petersen, P. Vang 1998. Der Nydam-III und Nydam-IV-Fund. In: Bemmann, G. & Bemmann, J. 1998. *Der Opferplatz von Nydam. Die Funde aus den älteren Grabungen: Nydam-I and II. Band 1–2.* Neumünster: 241–265.

Ramqvist P. 1992. *Högom. The excavations 1949–1984.* Neumünster.

Rau, A. 2005. Skedemosse §4. Kriegsbeuteopfer. *Reallexikon der Germanischen Altertumskunde* 28: 632–635.

Rau, A. 2010. *Nydam mose 1–2. Die personengebundenen Gegenstände. Grabungen 1989–1999.* Højbjerg/Aarhus. Summary. Dansk resumé.

Rau, A. & Carnap-Bornheim, C. von 2012. Die kaiserzeitlichen Heeresaus-

rüstungsopfer Südskandinaviens In: *Altertumskunde – Altertumswissenschaft – Kulturwissenschaft: Erträge und Perspektiven nach 40 Jahren Reallexikon der Germanischen Altertumskunde.* Berlin: 515–540.

Salin, B. 1904. *Die altgermanische Thierornamentik.* Stockholm. (2nd ed. 1935 Stockholm).

Stjernquist, B. 1974. Das Opfermoor in Hassle Bösarp, Schweden. *Acta Archaeologica* 44, 1973: 19–62.

Worsaae, J. J. A. 1865. *Om Slesvigs eller Sønderjyllands Oldtidsminder.* Copenhagen.

Резюме

Конская сбруя из жертвенного места Финнесторп

Бенгт Нордквист

Осушенное болото, где были сделаны Финнесторпские находки, расположено в центральном Вестергётланде, на юго-западе Швеции (см. карту во Введении). Жертвенное место Финнесторп относится к группе памятников в озерах или болотах (*bog finds*, «болотные находки»), которые интерпретируются как приношения, сделанные из благодарности или по обету. Захваченное у врага военное снаряжение доставляли с поля битвы и приносили в жертву после победы в сражении. Предварительно многие вещи в ходе обряда разрушали и разрубали на части. Подобные приношения известны в Дании, южной Швеции и Шлезвиге. Несколько близких по характеру находок известно в государствах Прибалтики и в Польше. Приношения состояли из снаряжения, которое носили воины, а иногда – их боевые кони. Такие приношения появились в результате сражений между разными поселенческими зонами или регионами в период, характеризующийся перманентными конфликтами между военными вождями. Их действия преследовали различные цели, начиная от простых грабительских набегов и заканчивая сражениями, которые должны были обеспечить контроль над ресурсами, населением и собственностью. Большая часть находок археологизирована в конце II – конце V в.

В Финнесторпе найдено много элементов конской упряжи, а некоторые из них имеют нанесенный с помощью штампа декор в стиле «Сёсдала». Находки в Финнерсторпе делались неоднократно и при разных обстоятельствах начиная с 1992 г., но широкомасштабные раскопки велись только в ходе реализации проекта 2000–2004 и 2008–2012 гг. Сейчас установлено, что приношения совершались на большой площади, приблизительно 400 х 100 м (отчет о раскопках: Nordqvist 2017). Памятник находится в центральной части Вестергётланда, в лесной зоне, характеризуемой обширными заболоченным пространством – на естественной границе между двумя богатыми аграрными равнинами, Скара на западе и Фалбюгденом на востоке.

Среди находок присутствуют различные декоративные накладки и подвески. Другие категории находок – зажимы, бутероли и оковки устьев ножен мечей, темляки мечей, оковки седел и накладки на ремни, а также большое количество необожженных костей, главным образом конских. Большая часть принесенных в жертву вещей связана с возвышенностями на болотах, которые, как представляется, были небольшими островками. Обряды жертвоприношения осуществлялись с этих островков (см. рис. 1, b–d). На трех островках обнаружены остатки кострищ.

Жертвенное место Финнесторп характеризуется большим количеством находок, датирующихся Эпохой переселения народов. Недавние раскопки увеличили количество документированных металлических вещей приблизительно до 600. Металлические вещи, сделанные из золота, серебра, бронзы и железа, можно ориентировочно поделить на три категории: 1) личное снаряжение (рис. 1, b; всего к этой категории относится 100 предметов); 2) оружие (рис. 1, c; фрагменты мечей и ножен, накладки на портупею меча, наконечники копий, дротиков, стрел и, вероятно, метательный топор; к этой категории относятся не менее 200 предметов); 3) конская сбруя (рис. 1, d; оковки седел и накладки на уздечные ремни; к этой категории принадлежит около 300 предметов).

Уздечки представлены исключительно фрагментами трех категорий: A) накладки на ремни оголовья, B) детали удил, C) грызло. Большая часть накладок на ремни оголовья (рис. 5) представляют собой бронзовую пластину, покрытую позолоченной серебряной пластинкой (рис. 7–10). Многие из них украшены в стиле «Сёсдала». Некоторые заклепки имеют серебряные шляпки. Треугольные накладки (рис. 8) могли быть наконечниками носового и налобного ремня (рис. 5). Круглые и крестовидные накладки служили распределителями ремней (рис. 6, 9–10). Прямоугольные накладки на ремни имели главным образом декоративную функцию (рис. 7). Кроме того, простые накладки, выполненные из бронзовой или серебряной пластины, были декорированы простой линией вдоль края (рис. 6, 11). Распределители ремней в виде щита (рис. 10) очень похожи на распределители ремней из знаменитой находки в Унтерзибенбрунне в Австрии (Fabech & Näsman 2013: 101–102). Фасетированный «умбон щита» можно датировать началом Эпохи переселения народов по сходству с настоящими умбонами щита (Kazanski 1988: 76, fig. 6–7). Накладки с декором в стиле «Сёсдала» можно отнести к первой половине V в.

К концам грызл крепились подвижные кольца или подвижные псалии, к которым присоединялись зажимы, удерживавшие повод и нащечные ремни оголовья. Бронзовые зажимы зооморфной формы; на некоторых из них, кажется, изображены головы лошадей (рис. 12). Другие зажимы имеют более простую форму (рис. 13). Накладки на ремни принадлежат к типу OF1 по типологии узды из Эрснеса, датирующемуся последней четвертью IV – серединой VI вв. (Ørsnes 1994: 249–251, fig. 53b). Обнаружены фрагменты поводьев в виде бронзовой цепи (рис. 2, 14). Поводья, часть которых, крепившаяся к удилу, представляла собой

металлическую цепь, известны на других памятниках, например, в Эйсбеле и Торсбьерге (Lau 2014: 24–66). Согласно недавнему исследованию, тип «Финнесторп» бытовал после типа «Торсбьерг» периода C2/C3, то есть середины III – рубежа третьей и четвертой четверти IV в. (Lau 2014: 58–63 Abb. 18). Цепные поводья использовались на протяжении периода C3 и в периоде D1 (Ørsnes 1994: 191, 205, 224–225, fib. 14). Лишь несколько фрагментов сделаны из железа, в том числе и грызло с портом. Удила с портом использовались в Эпоху переселения народов, как следует из находок в Веннебо и Хёгома (Ørsnes 1994: 278, fig. 48:3; см. также статью Х. Рамквиста в этом томе, рис. 9–11). Другие грызла из Финнесторпа – биметаллические, причем концы железного грызла помещены в бронзовые футляры (рис. 13–15). Фасетированный конец грызла с подвижным кольцом и длинным зажимом для ремня относится к типу OF1 по типологии уздечек из Эрснеса, который датируется периодом D1 (ср: Ørsnes 1994: fig. 2). Верхний конец полностью сохранившегося псалия в виде головы хищной птицы (рис. 16) очень похож на псалий из Хёгома, датированный периодом D2 (см. статью Х. Рамквиста в этом томе, рис. 11). Вероятно, оконечностью псалия была и отломанная голова птицы (рис. 17).

Большинство железных оковок седел фрагментированы; полностью сохранилась лишь одна находка (рис. 18). По сходству с оковками из Хассле-Бёсарп и Сёсдалы ее можно датировать периодом D1. Несколько бронзовых оковок седла имеют отверстия для шипа, с помощью которого крепилось подпружное кольцо, – они располагались у нижнего конца передней или задней луки седла (рис. 19, 23–24). Поломанные оковки без крепежного отверстия, вероятно, помещались у верхнего края передней луки седла (рис. 20). В Финнерсторпе найдены три типа бронзовых оковок: 1) биметаллические, из бронзы и железа (рис. 21); 2) бронзовые, в виде голов животных (рис. 20, 22); 3) с простым декором в виде линий (рис. 23–24). Оковки первой группы должны быть датированы первой половиной V в. Оковки второй группы часто имеют форму конской головы (рис. 22). Они напоминают оковки седла из Хёгома и датируются второй половиной V в. Верхний конец еще одной поломанной оковки выполнен в форме протомы ящерицы (рис. 25). Ее плечо соответствует формам d–f по типологии, предложенной Б. Салином в исследовании I Скандинавского стиля (Salin 1904 fig. 516), и, вероятно, относится к середине V – первому двадцатилетию VI в. Оковки третьей группы (рис. 23–24) датируются первой половиной V в. Найденные в Финнесторпе подпружные кольца и крепежные шипы сделаны из железа и бронзы. Многие подпружные кольца по-прежнему соединены с соответствующими шипами. Некоторые подпружные кольца инкрустированы серебром (рис. 26). Подпруги седел застегивались с помощью пряжек (рис. 27).

Найдено семь разных пельтовидных подвесок (рис. 28–31). Вероятно, они украшали седельные ремни или, может быть, оголовье. Самый распространенный в Финнерсторпе тип – это открытая (имеющая форму полумесяца) пельтовидная подвеска (рис. 28–29), вероятно, датирующаяся началом Эпохи переселения народов. У трех пельтовидных подвесок имеется центральная зона в форме пельты-полумесяца, декорированная штампом в стиле «Сёсдала» (рис. 30–31). Два изделия инкрустированы чернью – они, вероятно, сделаны позже, в V в.

Обнаруженные элементы конской сбруи представляют культуру, принадлежавшую элите живших в одно и то же время всадников. Это предположение подтверждается арсеналом оружия и набором конской сбруи, которые, как представляется, были сделаны самыми умелыми мастерами. Зафиксированные находки говорят о нескольких победоносных сражениях. Несколько раз на протяжении менее ста лет с поля битвы доставляли захваченные вещи и приносили их в жертву в болоте.

Подписи к иллюстрациям

Рис. 1. Расположение находок на месте, где проводились жертвоприношения. Пунктиром отмечена зона болота. 1a) Раскопы 1902–2012 гг. 1b) Места находок личного снаряжения воинов. 1c) Места находок вещей, связанных с вооружением. 1d) Места находок элементов конской сбруи. Карты: © Offering Site Finnestorp.

Рис. 2. Фрагмент поводьев, крепившийся к удилу и представлявший собой металлическую цепь, в его первоначальном виде. © Offering Site Finnestorp.

Рис. 3. Короткая оковка седла со следами значительного износа на отверстии для шипа, крепившего подпружное кольцо (см. также рис. 23). © Offering Site Finnestorp.

Рис. 4. Уникальная находка – наконечник ремня со следами ремонта, сделанный из позолоченной серебряной пластины. В отверстии, проделанном в наконечнике ремня, сохранилась небольшая заклепка из позолоченного серебра. © Offering Site Finnestorp.

Рис. 5. Вариант реконструкции узды с накладками, найденными в Финнесторпе, по аналогии с уздой из Хёгома (см. статью Х. Рамквиста в этой книге, рис. 9–14). © Offering Site Finnestorp.

Рис. 6. Крестообразный распределитель ремней, покрытый серебряной пластинкой. Декор состоит из линий вдоль краев. © Offering Site Finnestorp.

Рис. 7. Накладка на ремень из позолоченного серебра с зоной штампованного орнамента. У заклепок – серебряные шляпки. © Offering Site Finnestorp.

Рис. 8. Наконечник ремня из позолоченного серебра с зоной штампованного орнамента. Орнамент нанесен разными видами штампов, включая три изображения звезд пять триквестров, выполненных линзовидным штампом. У заклепок – серебряные шляпки. © Offering Site Finnestorp.

Рис. 9. Округлый распределитель ремней из позолоченного серебра с зоной штампованного орнамента. У заклепок – серебряные шляпки. © Offering Site Finnestorp.

Рис. 10. Округлый распределитель ремней из позолоченного серебра с зоной штампованного орнамента. В центре – фасетированный «умбон щита». У заклепок – серебряные шляпки. Отметим следы рубящих ударов. © Offering Site Finnestorp.

Рис. 11. Длинная накладка не ремень с расширением в центре. Бронзовая основа, покрытая серебряной пластинкой. Разрублена на части. © Offering Site Finnestorp.

Рис. 12. Кольцо удила с двумя зажимами для ремней, один из которых, в форме головы животного, разрублен на две части. У зажимов – фасетированные петли и заклепки с серебряными шляпками. © Offering Site Finnestorp.

Рис. 13. Фрагмент биметаллического трензеля с подвижным кольцом, концом грызла и двумя зажимами для ремней. © Offering Site Finnestorp.

Рис. 14. Два фрагмента поводьев, часть которых, крепившаяся к удилу, представляла собой металлическую цепь. Слева: фрагмент биметаллического трензеля с кольцом удила, концом грызла, крюком для псалия, а также соединители и кольцо цепных поводьев. Справа: кольца и соединители от цепных поводьев. © Offering Site Finnestorp.

Рис. 15. Концы биметаллические грызла, бронза на железной основе. © Offering Site Finnestorp.

Рис. 16. Бронзовый псалий с окончанием в виде повернутой вниз головы хищной птицы. В петле – фрагмент железного грызла и простой бронзовый зажим для ремня. © Offering Site Finnestorp.

Рис. 17. Серебряная оболочка в форме головы хищной птицы, которую можно интерпретировать как оконечность псалия (ср. рис. 16). © Offering Site Finnestorp.

Рис. 18. Корродированная, но почти целая длинная оковка седла, сделанная из железа, с сохранившимися на месте кольцом и крепежным шипом. Отметим остатки заклепок, с помощью которых оковка крепилась к передней луке седла. © Offering Site Finnestorp.

Рис. 19. Отрубленная нижняя часть бронзовой оковки седла. Отметим завершение в виде головы птицы и отверстие для крепежного шипа подпружного кольца. © Offering Site Finnestorp.

Рис. 20. Отломанная верхняя часть бронзовой оковки седла в форме головы животного. © Offering Site Finnestorp.

Рис. 21. Бронзовая оболочка железной оковки седла в форме головы хищной птицы. © Offering Site Finnestorp.

Рис. 22. Неповрежденная бронзовая оковка седла с отверстием для крепежного шипа подпружного кольца. Один конец – в виде головы лошади с изображающими узду мелкими деталями (ср. рис. 5); другой конец, вероятно, должен был изображать круп лошади. © Offering Site Finnestorp.

Рис. 23. Короткая неповрежденная оковка седла с заклепками, подпружным кольцом и крепежным шипом. Обнаружена со вставленным в отверстие шипом и остатками дубового каркаса седла (см также рис. 3). © Offering Site Finnestorp.

Рис. 24. Отрубленная нижняя часть бронзовой оковки седла с отверстием для крепежного шипа подпружного кольца. Декор состоит из простых линий. © Offering Site Finnestorp.

Рис. 25. Отрубленная верхняя часть бронзовой оковки седла. Завершение в виде ящерицы (или дракона) с передними лапами.

Рис. 26. Бронзовое подпружное кольцо, верхняя сторона которого инкрустирована серебряной проволокой. © Offering Site Finnestorp.

Рис. 27. Бронзовая подпружная пряжка с двойным язычком и B-образным неподвижным щитком. © Offering Site Finnestorp.

Рис. 28. Серебряная пельтовидная подвеска в виде полумесяца, прикрепленная к накладке на ремень. Позолоченное серебро с зоной штампованного орнамента. © Offering Site Finnestorp.

Рис. 29. Серебряная открытая пельтовидная подвеска с концами в виде силуэтов птичьих головок. Позолоченное серебро с зоной штампованного орнамента. © Offering Site Finnestorp.

Рис. 30. Серебряная пельтовидная подвеска. Зона позолоты в форме пельты-полумесяца, украшенная штампованным орнаментом. Концы в форме головок хищных птиц. © Offering Site Finnestorp.

Рис. 31. Серебряная пельтовидная подвеска с зоной позолоты в форме пельты-полумесяца в обрамлении штампованного орнамента. Концы в форме обращенных внутрь птичьих головок с открытыми клювами. Инкрустации чернью вдоль края и на птичьих головках.

Sösdala style – Sösdala horizon

Anna Bitner-Wróblewska

The Sösdala style was distinguished by J.E. Forssander in 1937; however, it was never defined sufficiently clearly. In 2001 I proposed establishing a term "Sösdala horizon" designating a group of certain artefacts usually connected with Sösdala style: ceremonial horse bridles, sheet brooches, shield-shaped and biconical pendants, pelta-shaped pendants and mountings. The earliest elements of the Sösdala horizon appeared in phase Scand-C3, but they are generally characteristic of the early Migration Period (phase Scand-D1, beginning of Scand-D2). The Sösdala horizon reflects the far-flung interregional contacts among elites in northern, central and south-eastern Europe.

Bitner-Wróblewska, A. 2017. Sösdala style – Sösdala horizon. In: Fabech, C. & Näsman, U. (eds). *The Sösdala horsemen – and the equestrian elite of fifth century Europe.* Jutland Archaeological Society.

The Sösdala style was distinguished by J.E. Forssander (1937) on the basis of a find at Sösdala in Scania.[1] Similar finds from Fulltofta and Vennebo as well as silver-sheet brooches of Eidsten-Mejlby type were regarded by him as the other elements of a Sösdala style, but Forssander never defined the style clearly. The discussion concerning definition and dating of the Sösdala style was continued by the other scholars (e.g. Norling-Christensen 1949; Voss 1955; Hansen 1970; Magnus 1975; Nielsen *et al.* 1985); see survey by Ulf Näsman in chapter 5. He also reviews the discussion about the origin of the Sösdala style and the impact of Roman and Gothic influences as well as its earlier local tradition of Late Roman Iron Age stamp decoration (e.g. Åberg 1919a; 1956; Forssander 1937).

According to some researchers the style was treated as an indicator of the beginning of the Migration Period in Scandinavia and dated from *c.* AD 400 (e.g. Bakka 1973; 1977). There was a concept of the sequence of styles in Scandinavia: Sösdala, Nydam, Style I – following each other – and a concept of dating based on style history. There was also an opinion that styles in Scandinavia overlapped one another; the beginning of the Sösdala style was placed as early as the end of the 4th century (Näsman 1984:70, fig. 1).

During my studies[1] on the connections between the Baltic lands and Scandinavia in the Migration Period I needed a tool for synchronising the chronology of different areas, with different histories of research, different

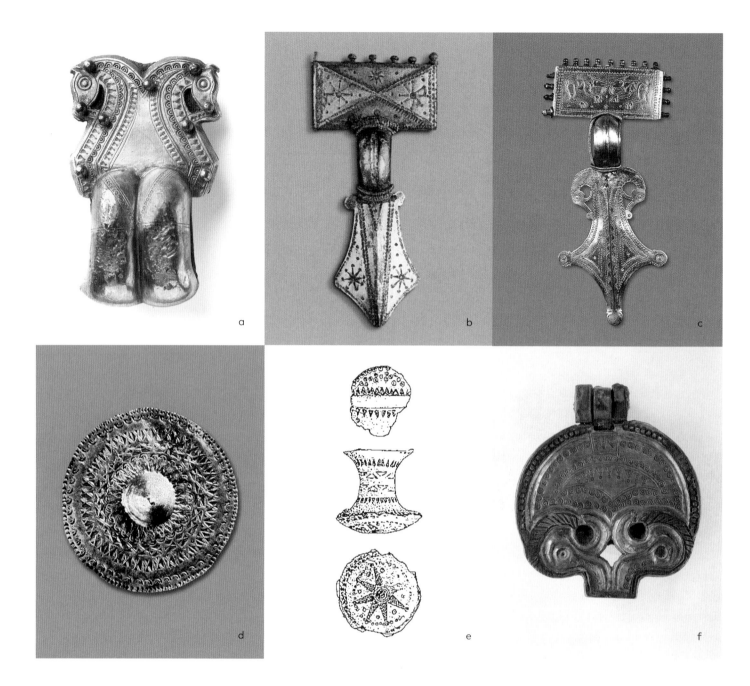

a   b   c   d   e   f

terminology and periodisation (Bitner-Wróblewska 2001, 14–19, fig. 1, plates I, II). Stamp ornamentation occurred in the lands of the Balts, the so-called *Ostpreußische Stern-ornamentik* (Åberg 1919b:29–52) that corresponds to the Scandinavian Sösdala style,[2] and for this reason it was used recurrently as a main tool for correlating the chronology of both sides of the Baltic Sea in the Migration Period (cf. Godłowski 1970, 1974; Nowakowski 1996). In my opinion the largely undefined ornamental Sösdala style was useless for this purpose, because we have incompatible phe-

nomena – on one hand there is a group of specific arte-facts decorated in *Ostpreußische Sternornamentik*, on the other a hardly defined ornamental style. Trying to solve this problem I proposed establishing the term "Sösdala horizon" to designate certain artefact types usually connected with the style in question (Bitner-Wróblewska 2001:89–106, figs 18–26).

Several categories of artefacts may be described as belonging to Sösdala horizon (see Appendix below): elements of ceremonial horse bridles, sheet brooches, shield-

Fig. 1. Sösdala horizon: a) element of ceremonial horse bridle, Sös-dala (photo D. Lindskog); b) sheet fibula type 2, Torstorp Vesterby, grave 3368 (Fonnesbech-Sandberg 1999); c) sheet brooch type 3, Sejl-flod grave DI (Nielsen 2000a); d) shield-shaped pendant, Krosshaug (Magnus 1975); e) biconical pendant, Torstorp Vesterby, grave 3368 (Fonnesbech-Sandberg 2006); f) pelta-shaped pendant, Finnestorp (© Offering Site Finnestorp). – Not to the same scale.

shaped and biconical pendants as well as pelta-shaped pendants (fig. 1). All of them feature an elaborate usually all-over stamped ornamentation and all of them have been described in earlier literature concerning Sösdala style. The style was distinguished based on the Sösda-la deposition, so there is no doubt that among elements of Sösdala horizon I placed ceremonial horse bridles consisting of strap mountings, pendants, strap ends and distributors. There are also pelta-shaped pendants, but I decided to include them as a separate category, because a number of pendants of this type are used in necklaces (e.g. graves DI and IZ at Sejlflod, Jutland) or as decora-tive elements of sword scabbards (e.g. Veien, Norway, and Nydam, Jutland). It would probably be better to call this category of the Sösdala horizon "pelta-shaped pendants and pelta-shaped mountings".

The main group of artefacts traditionally connected with Sösdala style are silver-sheet brooches of the type Kvarmlose-Mejlby with animal heads in profile. I also in-cluded another type of silver-sheet brooches, which are without animal heads in profile, but have rich all-over stamp decoration, often gilt. Scandinavian sheet brooch-es had been divided by Per Ethelberg into two types: type 1 represents brooches with spade-like foot and semicir-cular head, while type 2 has a wide rhomboid foot and semicircular or rectangular head (Ethelberg 1986:25–29). I proposed separating some brooches of type 2 with an-imal heads in profile and described them as type 3 (Bit-ner-Wróblewska 2001:96). Both types 2 and 3 belong to my Sösdala horizon. In a later article Ethelberg added to his types 1 and 2 also type 3 *mit gezipfeltem Fuß*, rectan-gular head-plate and animal heads in profile (Ethelberg 2009:26–27, fig. 12). This classification has been followed by Andreas Rau; however, he named these types different-ly, namely group 1 variant a, group 1 variant b, and group 2 (Rau 2010:66–68), which correspond respectively to types 1, 2 and 3 according to Ethelberg. Among variant 1a in Rau's classification there are also brooches without head-plate treated as *Vorformen* of sheet brooches. He de-scribed groups and variants in question using more ele-ments – except the shape of foot, shape of head, presence or lack of animal heads, also other features were taken into account, such as the number of springs, the cross-section of the bow, the proportions and length of the brooch, the number of different types of stamps. Both Ethelberg and Rau analysed only Danish brooches.

My Sösdala horizon also includes so-called shield-shaped pendants described in literature as "pendants" (Voss 1955; Magnus 1975; Gebers & Hinz 1977), even though it is not really appropriate since the ornaments have no suspension loop or aperture.[3] They look rather like miniature circular shields with a hemispherical or coni-cal boss, and usually have a handgrip at the back. In my study I accepted the term "pendants" as traditionally used in literature. The last but not least category of the Sösda-la horizon consists of hourglass-shaped pendants usually described in literature as "biconical" (Hansen 1971; Niel-sen 2000a:112) or simply as *Hängeschmuck* (Rygh 1885:15; Straume 1987:83).

All elements of the Sösdala horizon feature an elabo-rate almost usually all-over stamped ornamentation with several different stamp motifs on each item such as stars, multiconcentric circles and semicircles, filled triangles and rectangles. In some cases stamped decoration is sup-plemented with the presence of animal heads in profile (mostly horses). Shallow chip-carving and niello inlay are additional decorative techniques. The specimens in question were almost exclusively made of silver, gilt silver, bronze with silver inlay or rarely, gold. In a few cases el-ements of the Sösdala horizon were made as bronze imi-tations of exquisite items. Generally we can treat artefacts of the Sösdala horizon as prestige goods belonging to the elite. This observation seems to be very important, as will be discussed below.

The distribution of elements of the Sösdala horizon is concentrated in southern Scandinavia – in Scania, Västergötland, Zealand, Jutland, south and south-eastern

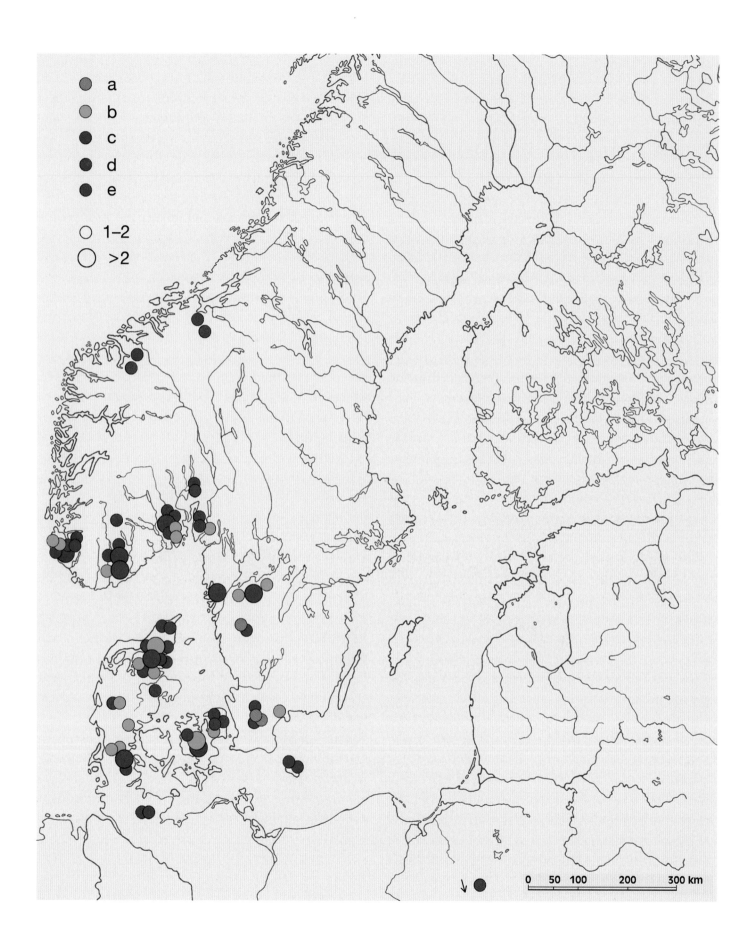

Chapter 12: Sösdala style – Sösdala horizon

Norway. Holstein and Bornholm may be regarded as being on the periphery of the concentration area (fig. 2). An isolated occurrence is recorded at Jakuszowice, southern Poland, in a rich warrior's grave (for references see Appendix).[4]

Many artefacts that belong to the Sösdala horizon occur in graves with other chronological indicators, and it was possible to build combination diagrams both for particular categories of the horizon (except ceremonial horse bridles), and a general one (Bitner-Wróblewska 2001 figs 21, 23, 25–26). The diagrams revealed that the earliest elements of the Sösdala horizon appeared already in phase C3, co-occurring with brooches of Gudumholm, Nydam or Fyn-Nydam types, but objects of the Sösdala horizon are generally characteristic of the Early Germanic Iron Age (Migration Period). At that time the terms "Early Germanic Iron Age" and "Late Germanic Iron Age" were very popular in Danish archaeology (e.g. Hansen 1993; Jørgensen & Nørgård Jørgensen 1997). The early Germanic Iron Age was mostly synchronised with continental phase D (Tischler & Kemke 1902:10–13; Eggers 1951; Godłowski 1970); now Continental phase D is often divided into subphases, which, however, are not synchronic with each other in different regions (Tejral 1992:239–246; Bierbrauer 1992:264ff; Rau 2010 fig. 38,1). For the relation between Scandinavian and Continental chronology see fig. 4 in Introduction.

Single assemblages including elements of Sösdala horizon were found with coins. A grave at Torstorp Vesterby, Zealand, produced a Constantius II *siliqua* (340–350) and a partially gilt elaborately stamp-ornamented silver-sheet brooch type 2 and a rich stamp-decorated biconical silver pendant. In the Høstentorp hoard, Zealand, there were, among other things, eight silver coins or coin fragments (*siliquae*), six of them were identified: one Constantius II (337–361), four Valens (364–378), one uncertain described as Gratian (375–383) or Honorius (395–423) (Breitenstein

1946:22–24; Kromann 1995:355, figs 13:2, 13:4). Almost all of them are rather worn; two of them have a suspension hole (one even pierced twice when the first hole was worn through). The year 395 AD is regarded as *terminus post quem* for the deposition of the hoard. The Høstentorp hoard also contained two categories of the Sösdala horizon, namely a pelta-shaped, partially gilt silver pendant in fragments and fragments of eight silver shield-shaped pendants.

The beginning of the Sösdala horizon could be placed in the second half of the 4th century or probably rather in the third quarter of the 4th century and it flourished in the first half of the 5th century. It is difficult to give the precise absolute dating of the decline of the horizon; but the transition from sheet-brooches to relief ones could be treated as an indicator. We have also to realise that some elements of the Sösdala horizon may persist in use longer, as is perfectly illustrated with a silver-sheet brooch from grave DI at Sejlflod. The grave is one of the latest assemblages of the Sösdala horizon. The brooch belongs to type 3 of sheet brooches. It had been repaired several times – the foot was reinforced with a bronze construction placed on the underside, a bronze catch-plate had also been soldered on, the bow of the brooch was riveted to the foot- and head-plates with bronze sheets (autopsy; also E. Fabech 1985).

Since 2001 not so many studies have appeared concerning Migration Period chronology in Scandinavia which could help us to understanding the Sösdala horizon. The most important is Andreas Rau's book on personal equipment from Nydam where he discusses in details the chronology of south Scandinavia and north Germany (Rau 2010:47–96.). In a combination diagram of Danish (without Bornholm) women's graves from the Late Roman and Migration Periods he distinguished six groups of graves (Rau 2010 Abb. 21[5]). It is hard to compare this very detailed division with my general diagram including finds from Denmark and Norway; however, some observations are worth noting. Some Danish graves which I treated as the earliest, namely Sejlflod grave U, Gudumholm, and Enderupskov grave 136, were placed in group 4 by Rau, synchronised with his phase C3b (Rau 2010 fig. 38,1). Among my latest assemblages, two graves from Sejlflod belong to latest Rau group 6 (grave IZ) or group 5 overlapping group 6 (grave DI), while the Mejlby grave is placed earlier (group 4/5). Group 5 corresponds to his phase D1 and group 6 to his phase D2a (Rau 2010 fig. 38:1).

According to my studies on the Sösdala horizon, the beginning of phase D1 could be defined by the appearance of cruciform brooches, and a developed stage of this phase is marked by pelta-shaped pendants. Sheet brooches type 3 (group 2 according to Rau) are characteristic of the end of phase D1 and beginning of phase D2, as well as cruciform brooches with spade-like foot. The deep relief ornament known already in phase D1 flourishes from phase D2.

A separate discussion is required concerning the grave from Nyrup, Zealand, which plays an important role in the discussion about the Scandinavian transition from the Late Roman Period to the Early Migration Period. Among other things, it produced a partially gilt silver-sheet brooch, which represents type 2 according to Ethelberg's classification and could be treated as an element of the Sösdala horizon; however, its stamp decoration is rather poor. The Nyrup brooch was originally regarded as a kind of *Vorform* of the typical brooches of the Sösdala horizon or as an imitation of a precious masterpiece. I did not include this assemblage in the combination diagram, but discussed its chronology separately, treating it as the earliest grave complex; however, I also expressed my doubts concerning this find as a closed grave (Bitner-Wróblewska 2001:98–99). In Rau's periodisation the Nyrup grave is the last in his group 3 and the earliest in group 4, which actually corresponds with my proposal.[6]

Although Andreas Rau does not use the term "Sösdala horizon" in my sense, his combination diagram ((Rau 2010:63, Abb. 21) confirms that the earliest elements of the Sösdala horizon appear already in phase C3, and that they generally are characteristic of phase D, both stages he introduced (D1 and D2a). It is not possible to compare Jaroslav Tejral's Sösdala-Untersiebenbrunn horizon (1992:240) with my Sösdala horizon as Andreas Rau has done, because it contains rather different phenomena. In Tejral's works his Sösdala-Untersiebenbrunn horizon could be regarded as the chronological horizon of two find complexes – a deposition at Sösdala and graves at Untersiebenbrunn. My Sösdala horizon represents several

categories of artefacts where the objects from the Sösdala deposition represent only one group.

Looking through literature published after 2001, there has not been any comprehensive attempt to define the Sösdala style. Several finds coming from older or new discoveries are described as "decorated in Sösdala style" without further explanation (e.g. Storgaard 2003:123–124; Nordqvist 2013:217)[7], sometimes with the addition that the style is difficult to distinguish and describe without a detailed publication of the Sösdala deposition (cf. Levada 2013). Sometimes just stamp ornamentation with star motifs made researchers include certain artefacts in the Sösdala style. But it is worth remembering that stamp decoration is also known earlier – punch-decorated belt sets dated to the Late Roman Period could be a good example (see Dieter Quast chapter 14). Punched "star ornamentation" appeared in Scandinavia already in the Late Roman Period, probably as a result of influences from provincial Roman workshops (Åberg 1919a). An example is the partly gilt silver bridge mount of a sword scabbard from Tibble, Uppland, which is dated to period C3. It has a rich punch-decoration including punched stars that could be labelled "Sösdala style" (Kazanski & Mastykova chapter 15 fig. 8). However, star motifs were rather rare in the Roman Period (Andersson 1995:183ff, figs 201–203).

For some time three terms have been used in the literature – Sösdala find, Sösdala style, Sösdala horizon – existing beside one another, sometimes overlapping, but they do not mean the same. Maybe we should change our approach to the study of the Sösdala style and stop dating finds by style, and instead date style by finds. There is no doubt that in the Migration Period we can observe a phenomenon of common or very similar types of objects widespread in the north, central and south-eastern Europe, which are decorated in similar design and technique. However, they are not identical; one can observe many similarities among particular group of finds, confirming that the craftsmen that made them may have exchanged experiences and/or that the owner of these objects may have persisted in close connections following the common fashion. Ceremonial horse bridles of Sösdala-Untersiebenbrunn-Coşoveni-Kačin-Jakuszowice type remain one of the good example of the phenomenon in

Chapter 12: Sösdala style – Sösdala horizon

question, while buckles of Zamość-Tiszaladany-Strzego-cice type could be regarded as the other one (Kubitschek 1911; Madyda-Legutko 1978; *Schätze der Ostgoten* 1995 fig. 63; Levada 2011).

The elements of horse bridles from Sösdala, Untersiebenbrunn, Kačin, Coşoveni, and Jakuszowice represent a style with punched decoration and niello inlays, encrustation with silver, sometimes with gilt surfaces. However, each bridle set has also its own feature and they differ in details; for example the horse heads in profile placed on the pendants from Kačin were flat and more simplified compared to the Sösdala ones. Axe-shaped pendants known from Untersiebenbrunn or the swallow-tail-shaped pendants found in Kačin represent forms that are unknown in Sösdala. Also some decorative motifs or techniques recorded in central or south-eastern Europe, such as rosettes of deep almond-shaped punch marks or the composition of ornaments in clear separate sectors are unknown or rather rare in Scandinavia. The recent discovery in Bar district in Ukraine supplements the above-mentioned group of ceremonial horse bridles (Levada 2011:118–119; Kazanski & Mastykova chapter 15 fig. 5–6). The stamp decoration on horse harnesses from Bar is much poorer than on bridles from Untersiebenbrunn or Kačin, but it is clear that the Bar hoard belongs to the same group of prestigious finds. Again we can observe the individual features, but it is also possible to point out similarities such as bird heads in profile on a Bar mount which find their analogues in bird heads on pendants from Kačin.

The example of ceremonial horse bridles confirms the close connections linking interregional elites *inter ambo maria* in the Migration Period. Scandinavian, central and south-eastern European warrior elites remained in lively direct contacts, although based on our earlier knowledge there appeared to be a gap of finds on the way from the Black Sea region towards the Baltic Sea. For a long time almost the only proof of south-north connections was represented by the so-called Olsztyn Group in the Masurian Lakeland, north-eastern Poland, with a remarkable concentration of elements of an interregional Germanic culture (Bitner-Wróblewska 2010:152, earlier literature *ibidem*), the single chieftain's grave at Jakuszowice and the concentration of solidi in Pomerania (Ciołek 2010).

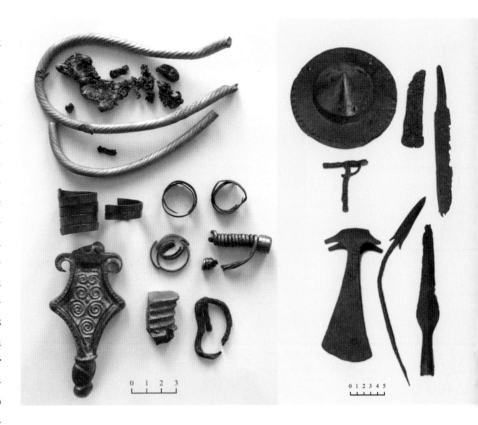

Fig. 3. Sudota, barrow 30, grave 4, east Lithuania (Bliujienė 2013).

New Migration Period discoveries in Masurian Lakeland, Samland and Natangen (now Kaliningrad Oblast'), eastern Lithuania, and last but not least central Poland have changed this picture. It turned out that the well-known Taurapilis grave (Bliujienė & Steponaitis 2009:188–194, figs 6–13) is not the only find confirming connections of east Lithuania with the Danubian area, Scandinavia, and the Black Sea zone; cemeteries e.g. at Pavajonis-Rekučiai, Paduobė-Šaltaliūnė, Sudota or Ziboliškes (fig. 3) also produced such artefacts (Bitner-Wróblewska 2008:99ff.). The recent discoveries in Kaliningrad Oblast', e.g. at Šosseynoe (Skvortsov chapter 13) or Logvino recorded specimens of interregional origin (Skvortsov 2013:357ff.). A fascinating sacrificial bog deposit in Czaszkowo at Nidajno Lake (fig. 4) in Masurian Lakeland has yielded a number of weapons, including precious guard and scabbard mounts, luxury belt sets, elements of horse tack which reflect contacts with the Roman and Byzantine milieu as well as a Germanic en-

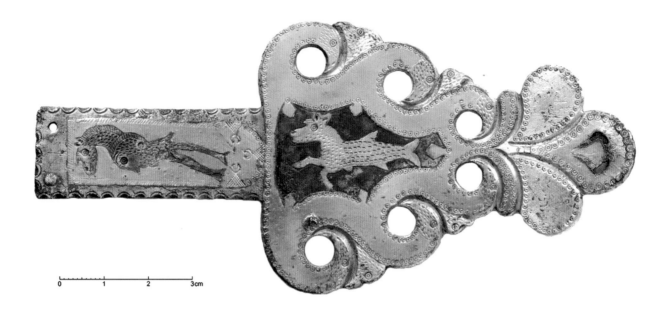

Fig. 4. Large strap mount with a palmetto terminal and large appliqué with hybrids from Czaszkowo at Lake Nidajno (Rzeszotarska-Nowakiewicz & Nowakiewicz 2012).

---

vironment (Rzeszotarska-Nowakiewicz & Nowakiewicz 2012). The finds were probably deposited several times during Late Roman and Migration Periods.[9] Some of them could be connected to a group of officers, the elite of the army. This category of site that is unique in the Baltic lands finds its analogues in Scandinavian depositions of military equipment.

New discoveries in Pomerania such as bracteates from Suchań (Bursche 2014) and a grave at Juszkowo (Kontny & Mączyńska 2015) confirm connections of this region with Scandinavia on one hand and the East Germanic

and nomadic settings on the other. The most unexpected finds appeared in central Poland, previously regarded as a rather empty and poor area with few and dispersed finds and graves dated later than the first half of 5th century (Mączyńska 1998). Especially the Kuyavian region (e.g. settlements at Gąski and Wierzbiczany – Mpov 2016) reveals the totally different picture of the settlement situation between Odra and Vistula.[10]

All these data are very important in any study of the far-flung interregional contacts among the elite in Europe during the Migration Period, and they place the Sösdala deposit and Sösdala style in a different perspective. When we compare the settlement maps published in earlier literature (see Mączyńska 1998) it seemed that in the 5th and 6th centuries only the territory of the Masurian Lakeland (north-eastern Poland) and Pomerania were inhabited rather densely, while other areas of Poland were empty or had only a few dispersed sites recorded. In such a situation it was not easy to explain the lively connections between Scandinavia and south-eastern Europe observed in the material. The impressive increase of archaeological sources from the Migration Period discovered during the last few years in central Poland has changed this picture very much and covered the blank spots of this settlement area.

The mobility of elites supported the dissemination of cultural characteristics and made the cultural communication really very close. It seems that the southern Scandinavian aristocracy that wore or used the objects of the Sösdala horizon described above played an important role in creating the network of contacts among various regions in Barbaricum.

Appendix – Sösdala horizon

References are only given to selected literature – the most important and/or with the best drawings, or the one which collects earlier literature.

Ceremonial finds of horse bridles

- FULLTOFTA, Fulltofta, Scania S – Norberg 1931:105–108, figs 2–3; Fabech 1991:126–128, fig. 4.
- SÖSDALA, Norra Mellby, Scania S – Forssander 1937 figs 1–3; Fabech 1991:123–126, fig. 1a–c (complete literature – see find catalogue, Fabech chapter 1 and Näsman chapter 7).
- VENNEBO[11], Roasjö, Västergotland S – Salin 1904 figs 362, 372.

Pelta-shaped pendants and mountings

- BIRKELAND (ca 16 specimens), Birkenes, Aust-Agder N, grave – Rygh 1885:6, fig. 272; Reichstein 1975:117, Taf. 14.
- BOSAU (2 specimens), Ostholstein, Holstein D, grave – Gebers & Hinz 1977:19, figs 5:1–2, 6:4,6.
- FINNESTORP (7 specimens), Larv, Västergotland S – Hagberg 1957:112–113, fig. 3; Nordqvist 2005:231, fig. 6:1–2 and chapter 11 fig. 28–31.
- FULLTOFTA (2 specimens), Fulltofta, Scania S – Norberg 1931:105, fig. 3.
- HØRUP, Holbæk, Zealand DK – Sørensen 2000:31, fig. 77.
- HØSTENTORP, Ringsted, Zealand DK, hoard – Voss 1955:187–188, fig. 6.

- JAKUSZOWICE, Kazimierza Wielka, Świętokrzyskie PL, grave – Godłowski 1995:155, fig. 4:3.
- NYDAM (4 specimens), Sønderborg, Jutland DK – Jørgensen & Petersen 2003:273.
- SEJLFLOD (4 specimens), Ålborg, Jutland DK, graves DI, IZ – Nielsen 2000a:68,125; 2000b:54,106.
- SKREROS (ca 6 specimens), Vegusdal, Aust-Agder N, grave – Reichstein 1975:117, Taf. 133.
- SÖSDALA, Norra Mellby, Scania S – Norberg 1931:107, fig. 9; Forssander 1937 fig. 3.
- VEIEN (2 specimens), Norderhov, Buskerud N, grave – Rygh 1885:116, pl. 121.
- VENNEBO, Roasjö, Västergötland S – Salin 1904 fig. 362.

Sheet brooches

- BÅSTRUP, Vejle, Jutland DK – Åberg 1924:11,77, fig. 29.
- BRUAREBACKA, Öttum, Västergotland S – Åberg 1924:12,77, fig. 34.
- EIDSTEN, Brunlanes, Vestfold N, grave – Åberg 1924;12,77, fig. 33.
- ENDERUPSKOV, Haderslev, Syddanmark DK, grave – Ethelberg 1986:67–68, fig. 45.
- GRÅLUM, Tune, Østfold N, grave – U. Lund Hansen's archive.
- GUDUMHOLM, Ålborg, Nordjylland DK, grave – Hansen 1971:DK 40.
- HJEMSTED (2 specimens), Tønder, Syddanmark DK, grave 303 – Ethelberg 1986:148–151.
- HÅLAND, Lye, Jæren, Rogaland N – Åberg 1924:10,76.
- KRISTIANSTAD, Kristianstad, Scania S – Åberg 1924:1,76, fig. 27.
- KVARMLØSE (2 specimens), Holbæk, Sjælland DK, grave – Hansen 1970:64–65, fig. 1–2, 8–13; 1971:DK 44.
- KVASSHEIM, Hå, Jæren, Rogaland N – Åberg 1924:10,76.
- LIME, Viborg, Midtjylland DK, grave – Hansen 1971:DK 41.
- MEJLBY (2 specimens), Ålborg, Nordjylland DK, grave – Hansen 1971:DK 43.
- NIKKELVERKET (FOSSVIK), Évje, Aust-Agder N, grave – Reichstein 1975:117, Taf. 6:1–8.
- NYRUP, Holbæk, Sjælland DK, grave – Hansen 1971:DK 42.
- ROLIGHEDEN, Hedrum, Vestfold N, grave – Åberg 1924:12, 77, fig. 36.
- SEJLFLOD (4 specimens), Ålborg, Nordjylland DK, graves DI, OO, U – Nielsen 2000a:38, 67–68, 135–136; 2000b:24, 56, 114.
- TORESTORP, Brun, Västergötland S – Åberg 1924:11, 77, fig. 30.
- TORSTORP VESTERBY, Høje-Taastrup, Hovedstaden DK, grave 3368 – Fonnesbech-Sandberg 1999: 41; 2006:115–166, fig. 6.

Shield-shaped pendants

- Bosau (2 specimens), Ostholstein, Holstein D, grave – Gebers & Hinz 1977:15, 19, figs 5:3–4, 6:1,3.
- Erga, Klepp, Rogaland N, grave – Magnus 1975:51, fig. 22.
- Gjone, Kvelde, Hedrum, Vestfold N, grave – Magnus 1975:49–50, fig. 19.
- Hol, Inderøya, S. Trøndelag N, grave – Magnus 1975:52–53, fig. 24.
- Hole, Grytens, Romsdalen, Möre og Romsdal N, grave – U. Lund Hansen's archive.
- Horr, Hå, Rogaland N – Magnus 1975:52, fig. 23.
- Høstentorp (8 specimens), Ringsted, Sjæland DK, hoard – Voss 1955:189–190, fig. 8–9.
- Krosshaug, Klepp, Rogaland N, grave – Magnus 1975:47, fig. 17.
- Linderup Mark, Hjørring, Nordjylland DK – Voss 1955:190 footnote 113.
- Mejlby (2 specimens), Ålborg, Nordjylland DK, grave – Hansen 1971:DK 43.
- Melsted, Gudhejm, Bornholm, Hovedstaden DK, grave 8 – Klindt-Jensen 1957:234 no 8.
- Mjølhus Vestre, Froland, Aust-Agder N, grave – Magnus 1975:50, fig. 20.
- Nordre Rostad, Rolvsøy, Tune, Østfold N, grave – Magnus 1975:49, fig. 18.
- Råbjerg, Hjørring, Nordjylland DK – Voss 1955:190 footnote 113.
- Rødbjerg/Tornbygård, Bornholm, Hovedstaden DK – Bornholms Museum, BMR 1611x18.
- Sejlflod (2 specimens), Ålborg, Nordjylland DK, graves OO, TR – Nielsen 2000a:136, 178; 2000b:113, 150.
- Skreros (2 specimens), Vegusdal, Aust-Agder N, barrow 2 – Magnus 1975:50–51, fig. 21.

Shield-shaped pendant?

- Hørup, Holbæk, Sjæland DK – Sørensen 2000:29, fig. 69.

Biconical pendants

- Dyster (2 specimens), Ås, Akershus N – Hansen 1971:DK 40 (21).
- Fannerup, Randers, Midtjylland DK – Åberg 1956:182.
- Fullerö, Gamla Uppsala, Uppland S, grave – Arwidsson 1948:41–44; Andersson 1995:39–40, fig. 20.
- Gjerla, Stokke, Vestfold N, mixed grave – Hansen 1971:DK 40 (21); Straume 1987:83–85, Taf. 26:8.

- Gudumholm, Ålborg, Nordjylland DK, grave – Hansen 1971:DK 40.
- Hol, Inderøya, S. Trondelag N, grave – Oldtiden 1912:48–57.
- Kvassheim (3 specimens), Hå, Jæren, Rogaland N, barrow 30 (barrow 77 acc. to G. Lillehammer) – Åberg 1956:183, fig. 196; Lillehammer 1996:172, plate 12d.
- Langlo (3 specimens), Stokke, Vestfold N, barrow 21 – Rygh 1885:14, fig. 281; Åberg 1956:182, 184, fig. 199.
- Mejlby, Ålborg, Nordjylland DK, grave – Hansen 1971:DK 43.
- Nrd. Fevang, Sandefjord, Vestfold N – Hansen 1971:DK 40 (21).
- Nydam, Sønderborg, Syddanmark DK – Engelhardt 1865:64, plate V, 17; Åberg 1956:182, fig. 194.
- Röra socken (3 specimens), Bohuslän S, grave – Åberg 1956:184, figs 197–198.
- Sejlflod (2 specimens), Ålborg, Nordjylland DK, graves IM, NT – Nielsen 2000a:112,130; 2000b:95,109.
- Sætrang (2 specimens), Norderhov, Buskerud N, grave – Rygh 1885:8–9; Åberg 1956:183,185, fig. 195.
- Tokkedalen, Mo, Bratsberg, Telemark N – Hansen 1971:DK 40 (21).
- Torstorp Vesterby, Høje-Taastrup, Hovedstaden DK, grave 3368 – Fonnesbech-Sandberg 2006:117–118, fig. 11–12.
- Tu, Klepp, Jæren, Rogaland N, grave – Åberg 1956:184 footnote 218.
- unknown site, Denmark – Nielsen 1997:32, fig. 3:7.
- Veiberg, Nordalen, Möre og Romsdal N, grave – Åberg 1956:184 footnote 217.
- Vrangstrup, Viborg, Midtjylland DK – Kaul 1990:7–10, figs 2–3.

Notes

1 This article was prepared within the framework of the project "Migration Period between Odra and Vistula", financed by the Polish National Science Centre granted on the basis of decision no. DEC-2011/02/A/HS3/00389.

2 Nils Åberg, who introduced the term *Ostpreußische Sternornamentik* in 1919, noticed the connections with Scandinavia, but he suggested direct contacts between the Baltic lands and the Roman provinces. Of course, he could not know the Sösdala deposition. My studies in 1990s on the Sösdala style and different categories of ornaments common to both the Baltic lands and Scandinavia confirmed the impact of the Sösdala style on *Ostpreußische Sternornamentik* (Bitner-Wróblewska 2001).

3 Two silver pendants from the Bosau grave, Holstein, are completely flat and have no shield-bosses, but their decoration and shape connect them to the Sösdala horizon.

4 In the tarand cemetery at Ketohaka 1, in south-western Finland, fragments of silver plate were found decorated by different stamps such as a star motif, multiconcentric semicircles, filled triangles, rectangles (Schauman-Lönnqvist 1988, 48–50, fig. 46, 5614:3, 5a). It is difficult to identify these fragments, but they probably come from mounts (belt mounts?). The punch decoration connects it to the Scandinavian Sösdala style, but it is not possible to join it to any artefact type of the Sösdala horizon. The character of tarand graves, without closed assemblages, makes the dating difficult. It is supposed that it can be dated to the beginning of the Migration Period.

5 According to Abb. 21 in Rau 2010 a grave from Tåstrupgård, Zealand, contained a sheet brooch of his type 2 but it is not included in his table of sheet brooches Abb. 24. In fact, following Bemmann 1998:227, Abb. 81:2, it is an early relief brooch in Nydam style.

6 Dating Nyrup grave to phase C3 could be confirmed by the analysis of swastika brooches (*Hakenkreuzfibel*) recently performed by Marzena Przybyła (2009). The swastika brooch from Nyrup represents variant Bøttkildegård according to her classification (Przybyła 2009:52, figs 10: 2, 18).

7 Descriptions of finds as "made in Sösdala style" are also common in earlier literature (Godłowski 1980).

8 The evidence of travelling craftsmen has been discussed in literature many times as one aspect of the mobility of people and objects in the past (e.g. Werner 1970; Bitner-Wróblewska 2011; Quast 2011). Support can be found in written sources, namely in Eugippius' work *Commonitorium de Vita Sancti Severini* written at the beginning of 6th century, but concern the life of *Sancti Severini* in Noricum in 5th century (between 453 and 482 AD (*Severin* 1982). There is also information about the Germanic tribes living in the Roman provinces, Rugii and Ostrogoths. Staying at the court of the Rugian king Giso – not of his own free will! – was a foreign jeweller (Eugippius, *Vita Severini* cap. 8).

9 According to recent studies of the materials recorded in Czaszkowo a group of finds could be rather precisely dated to the second half of the 3rd century and the begining of the 4th century. A set of unique specimens without good analogues may have a wider chronological position what would be suggested by 14C datings. Most of the finds were discovered in secondary position, which makes the chronological studies difficult. I would like to thank Dr Aleksandra Rzeszotarska-Nowakiewicz (Institute of Archaeology and Ethnology, Polish Academy of Science) and Dr Tomasz Nowakiewicz (Warsaw University, Institute of Archaeology) warmly for their kind sharing of information.

10 Compare also the hoard from Stare Marzy near Grudziądz dated to the first half of the 5th century, a *Bügelfibel* type Müllhofen at Dźwierzchno near Inowrocław, a settlement in Ostrowo at Gopło Lake dated to the 5th–7th centuries, a brooch of type Daumen/Tumiany at Tarnowo in Great Poland – information kindly shared by Marcin Rudnicki and Prof. Aleksander Bursche from Warsaw University, Institute of Archaeology.

11 A new detector survey indicates that Vennebo cannot be characterised as a "funeral sacrifice" with certainty. See Fabech Chapter 2 note 1.

References

Åberg, N. 1919a. Den germanska stjärnornamentiken under 3- och 400-talet e.Kr. *Antikvarisk tidskrift för Sverige* 21/3: 1–51.

Åberg, N. 1919b. *Ostpreußen in der Völkerwanderungszeit*. Uppsala/Leipzig.

Åberg, N. 1924. *Den nordiska folkvandringstidens kronologi*. Stockholm.

Åberg, N. 1956. *Den historiska relationen mellan senromersk tid och nordisk folkevandringstid*. Stockholm.

Andersson, K. 1995. *Romartida guldsmide i Norden III. Övriga smycken, teknisk analys och verkstadsgrupper*. Uppsala.

Arwidsson, G. 1948. Valsgärde – Fullerö. *Tor* 1948: 34–48.

Bakka, E. 1973. Goldbrakteaten in norwegischen Grabfunden. Datierungsfragen. *Frühmittelalterliche Studien* 7: 53–87.

Bakka, E. 1977. Stufengliederung der norwegischen Völkerwanderungszeit und Anknüpfungen an die kontinentale Chronologie. In: Kossack, G. & Reichstein, J. (eds). *Archäologische Beiträge zur Chronologie der Völkerwanderungszeit*. Bonn: 57–60.

Bemmann, J. 1998. Der Nydam-II-Fund. In: Bemmann, G. & Bemmann, J. 1998. *Der Opferplatz von Nydam. Die Funde aus den älteren Grabungen: Nydam-I and II. Band 1–2*. Neumünster: 217–240.

Bierbrauer, V. 1992. Historische Überlieferung und archäologischer Befund. Ostgermanische Einwanderer unter Odoaker und Theoderich nach Italien. Aussagemöglichkeiten und Grenzen der Archäologie. In: Godłowski, K. & Madyda-Legutko, R. (eds). *Probleme der relativen und absoluten Chronologie ab Latèenzeit bis zum Frühmittelalter*. Cracow: 263–277.

Bitner-Wróblewska, A. 2001. *From Samland to Rogaland. East-West connections in the Baltic basin during the Early Migration Period*. Warsaw.

Bitner-Wróblewska, A. 2008. Observers or participants? The Balts during turbulent epoch. In: Niezabitowska-Wiśniewska, B., Juściński, M., Łuczkiewicz, P. & Sadowski, S. (eds). *The turbulent epoch. New materials from the Late Roman Period and the Migration Period*. Lublin: 97–112.

Bitner-Wróblewska, A. 2010. North-eastern Poland in first centuries AD – a world apart. In: Hansen, U. Lund & Bitner-Wróblewska, A. (eds). *Worlds apart? Contacts across the Baltic Sea in the Iron Age. Network Denmark-Poland, 2005–2008*. Copenhagen/Warsaw: 141–184.

Bitner-Wróblewska, A. 2011. East European enameled ornaments and the character of contacts between the Baltic Sea and the Black Sea. In: Khrapunov, I. & Stylegar, F.-A. (eds). *Inter ambo maria. Contacts between Scandinavia and the Crimea in the Roman Period*. Kristiansand/Simferopol: 11–24.

Bliujienė, A. 2013. *Romėniškasis ir tautų kraustymosi laikotarpiai*. Klaipėda.

Bliujienė, A. & Steponaitis, V. 2009. Wealthy horsemen in the remote and tenebrous forests of east Lithuania during Migration Period. In: Bliujienė, A. (ed.). *The horse and man in European antiquity*. Klaipėda: 185–205.

Breitenstein, N. 1946. De romerske møntfund fra den sjællandske øgruppe. *Nordisk Numismatik Årsskrift*: 1–34.

Bursche, A. 2014. Skarb złotych przedmiotów z okresu wędrówek ludów z Suchania/The Migration Period gold hoard from Suchań. In: Kowalski, K. & Bursche, A. (eds). *Skarby z okolic Suchania/The treasures of Suchań*. Szczecin: 55–60.

Ciołek, R. 2010. Goldene Münzen des 4.-5. Jahrhunderts in den südlichen Ostseegebieten. In: Hansen, U. Lund & Bitner-Wróblewska, A. (eds). *Worlds apart? Contacts across the Baltic Sea in the Iron Age. Network Denmark-Poland, 2005–2008*. Copenhagen/Warsaw: 377–388.

Eggers, H. 1951. *Der römischer Import im freien Germania*. Hamburg.

Engelhardt, C. 1865. *Nydam Mosefund. Sønderjyske Mosefund* II. Copenhagen (reprint Copenhagen 1970).

Ethelberg, P. 1986. *Hjemsted – en gravplads fra 4. og. 5. årh.e.Kr.* Haderslev.

Ethelberg, P. 2009. Die Fibeln. In: Boye, L. & Hansen, U. Lund (eds). *Wealth and Prestige. An Analysis of Rich Graves from Late Roman Iron Age on Eastern Zealand, Denmark*. Kroppedal: 15–36.

Fabech, C. 1991. Neue Perspektiven zu den Funden von Sösdala und Fulltofta. *Studien zur Sachsenforschung* 7: 121–135.

Fabech, E. 1985. Teknisk beskrivelse og vurdering af sølvblikfiblen fra Sejlflod grav DI. In: Nielsen, J.N., Jørgensen, L. Bender, Fabech, E. & Munksgaard, E. En rig germanertidsgrav fra Sejlflod, Nordjylland. *Aarbøger for Nordisk Oldkyndighed og Historie* 1983: 101–122. Summary.

Fonnesbech-Sandberg, E. 1999. Landsby og enkeltgårde. In: Mahler, D.L (ed.). *Høje-Taastrup før Buerne. Glimt af 6000 års historie*. Copenhagen: 26–33.

Fonnesbech-Sandberg, E. 2006. Torstorp Vesterby. A Cemetery from the Late Roman Iron Age. *Journal of Danish Archaeology* 14: 109–125.

Forssander, J.E. 1937. Provinzialrömisches und Germanisches. Stilstudien zu den schonischen Funde von Sösdala und Sjörup. *Meddelanden från Lunds Universitets Historiska Museum*: 11–100.

Gebers, W. & H. Hinz 1977. Ein Körpergrab der Völkerwanderungszeit aus Bosau, Kreis Ostholstein. *Offa* 34: 5–32.

Godłowski, K. 1970. *The Chronology of the Late Roman and Early Migration Periods in Central Europe*. Cracow.

Godłowski, K. 1974. Chronologia okresu późnorzymskiego i wczesnego okresu wędrówek ludów w Polsce północno-wschodniej. *Rocznik Białostocki* XII: 9–109.

Godłowski, K. 1980. Zur Frage der völkerwanderungszeitliche Besiedlung in Pommern. *Studien zur Sachsenforschung* 2: 63–106.

Godłowski, K. 1995. Das "Fürstengrab" des 5. Jhs. und der "Fürstensitz" in Jakuszowice in Südpolen. In: Vallet, F. & Kazanski, M. (eds). *La noblesse Romaine et les chefs barbares du IIIᵉ au VIIᵉ siècle*. Condé-sur-Noireau: 155–179.

Hagberg, U. 1957. Folkvandringstida hängprydnader. *Tor* 3: 108–120.

Hansen, U. Lund 1970. Kvarmløsefundet – en analyse af Sösdalastilen og dens forudsætninger. *Aarbøger for Nordisk Oldkyndighed og Historie* 1969: 63–102.

Hansen, U. Lund 1971. *Danish Grave Finds of the Fourth and Fifth Century AD*. Inventaria Archaeologica. Denmark 8 (DK 40–44). Bonn.

Jørgensen, E. & Petersen, P. Vang 2003. Nydam Bog – New finds and observations. In: Jørgensen, L. et al. (eds). *The spoils of victory. The North in the shadow of the Roman Empire*. Copenhagen: 258–285.

Jørgensen, L. & Jørgensen, A. Nørgård 1997. *Nørre Sandegård Vest. A Cemetery from the 6th–8th Centuries on Bornholm*. Copenhagen.

Kaul, F. 1990. Endnu en grav fra Vrangstrup. *Aarbøger for Nordisk Oldkyndighed og Historie* 1990: 7–11.

Klindt-Jensen, O. 1957. *Bornholm i folkevandringstiden*. Copenhagen.

Kontny, B. & Mączyńska, M. 2015. Ein Kriegergrab aus der frühen Völkerwanderungszeit von Juszkowo in Nordpolen. In: Ruhmann, C. & Brieske, V. (eds). *Dying Gods – Religious beliefs in northern and eastern Europe in the time of Christianisation*. Stuttgart: 241–261.

Kromann, A. 1995. Die römischen Münzfunde von Seeland. In: Hansen, U. Lund. *Himlingøje – Seeland – Europa*. Copenhagen: 347–363.

Kubitschek, W. 1911. Grabfunde in Untersiebenbrunn (auf dem Marchfelde). *Jahrbuch für Altertumskunde* 5: 32–74.

Levada, M. 2011. To Europe via the Crimea. On possible migration routes of the northern people in the Great Migration Period. In: Khrapunov, I. & Stylegar, F.-A. (eds). *Inter ambo maria. Contacts between Scandinavia and the Crimea in the Roman Period*. Kristiansand/Simferopol: 115–137.

Levada, M. 2013. Sösdala. The problem of singling out an artistic style. In: Khrapunov, I. & Stylegar, F.-A. (eds). *Inter ambo maria. Northern Barbarians from Scandinavia towards the Black Sea*. Kristiansand/Simferopol: 213–235.

Lillehammer, G. 1996. *Død og grav. Gravskikk på Kvassheimfeltet, Hå i Rogaland, SV Norge/Death and grave. Burial rituals of the Kvassheim cemetery, Hå in Rogaland, SW Norway*. Stavanger.

Mączyńska, M. 1998. Die Endephase der Przeworsk-Kultur. *Ethnographisch-Archäologische Zeitschrift* 39: 65–99.

Madyda-Legutko, R. 1978. The buckles with imprint ornamentation. *Wiadomości Archeologiczne* XLIII/1: 3–15.

Magnus, B. 1975. *Krosshaugfunnet. Et forsøk på kronologisk og stilhistorisk plassering i 5. årh.* Stavanger.

Mpov 2016. Migration Period between Odra and Vistula. http://www.mpov.uw.edu.pl/en/thesaurus/archaeological-sites – Checked November 2016.

Näsman, U. 1984. Zwei Relieffibeln von der Insel Öland. *Praehistorische Zeitschrift* 59/1: 48–80.

Nielsen, J.N. 1997. Dobbeltkoniske hængesmykker – og andre amuletter fra jernalderen. *Aarbøger for Nordisk Oldkyndighed og Historie 1996*: 21–35.

Nielsen, J.N. 2000a. *Sejlflod – ein eisenzeitliches Dorf in Nordjütland. Katalog der Grabfunde. Band I: Text und Pläne*. Copenhagen.

Nielsen, J.N. 2000b. *Sejlflod – ein eisenzeitliches Dorf in Nordjütland. Katalog der Grabfunde. Band II: Abbildungen und Tafeln*. Copenhagen.

Nielsen *et al.* (Nielsen, J.N., Jørgensen, L. Bender, Fabech, E. & Munksgaard, E.). 1985. En rig germanetidsgrav fra Sejlflod, Nordjylland. *Aarbøger for Nordisk Oldkyndighed og Historie 1983*: 66–122.

Norberg, R. 1931. Moor- und Depotfunde aus dem 5. Jahrhundert nach Ch. in Schonen. *Acta Archaeologica* 2: 104–111.

Nordqvist, B. 2005. Der Kriegsbeuteopferplatz von Finnestorp in Schweden. *Offa* 61/62: 221–238.

Nordqvist, B. 2013. Symbols of Identity. A Phenomenon from the Migration Period Based on an Example from Finnestorp. In: Bergerbrant, S. & Sabatini, S. (eds). *Counterpoint. Essays in Archaeology and Heritage Studies in Honour of Professor Kristian Kristiansen*. Oxford: 213–221.

Norling-Christensen, H. 1949. Germansk jernalders begyndelse i Norden. *Viking* 13: 1–15.

Nowakowski, W. 1996. *Das Samland in der römischen Kaiserzeit und seine Verbindungen mit dem römischen Reich and der barabrischen Welt*. Marburg/Warsaw.

Oldtiden. Tidsskrift for norsk forhistorie 1912. Oslo/Stavanger.

Przybyła, M. 2009. Die Hakenkreuzfibel aus dem Grab 4 aus Engbjerg auf dem Hintergrund anderer pressblechverzierter Hakenkreuzfibeln. In: Boye, L. & Hansen, U. Lund (eds). *Wealth and Prestige. An Analysis of Rich Graves from Late Roman Iron Age on Eastern Zealand, Denmark*. Kroppedal: 37–79.

Quast, D. 2011. The links between the Crimea and Scandinavia. Some jewellery from the third century AD princely graves in an international context. In: Khrapunov, I. & Stylegar, F.-A. (eds). *Inter ambo maria. Contacts between Scandinavia and the Crimea in the Roman Period*. Kristiansand/Simferopol: 198–208.

Rau, A. 2010. *Nydam Mose 1. Die personengebundenen Gegenstände. Grabungen 1989–1999. Text*. Højbjerg/Aarhus. Summary.

Reichstein, J. 1975. *Die kreuzförmige Fibel. Zur Chronologie der späten Kaiserziet und der Völkerwanderungszeit in Skandinavien, auf dem Kontinent und in England*. Neumünster.

Rygh, O. 1885. *Norske Oldsager*. (Former Christiania) Oslo.

Rzeszotarska-Nowakiewicz, A. & Nowakiewicz, W. 2012. *Jezioro Nidajno koło Czaszkowa na Mazurach: niezwykłe miejsce kultu z okresu późnej starożytności/Lake Nidajno near Czaszkowo in Masuria: a unique sacrificial site from Late Antiquity*. Warsaw.

Salin, B. 1904. *Die Altgermanische Thierornamentik*. Stockholm. 2nd ed. 1935.

Schätze der Ostgoten. Eine Ausstellung der Maria Curie Skłodowska Universität Lublin und des Landesmuseums Zamość. 1995. Stuttgart.

Schauman-Lönnqvist, M. 1988. *Iron Age Studies in Salo III. The Development of Iron Age Settlement in the Isokylä Area in Salo*. Helsinki.

Severin: zwischen Römerzeit und Völkerwanderung. 1982. Linz.

Skvortsov, K. 2013. "The amber coast masters". Some observations on rich burials in the Sambian-Natangian Culture ca AD 500. In: Khrapunov, I. & Stylegar, F.-A. (eds). *Inter ambo maria. Northern Barbarians from Scandinavia towards the Black Sea*. Kristiansand/Simferopol: 352–364.

Sørensen, S. 2000. *Hørup – en sjællandsk værkstedsplads fra romersk jernalder*. Holbæk.

Storgaard, B. 2003. Cosmopolitan aristocrats. In: Jørgensen, L *et al.* (eds). *The spoils of victory. The North in the shadow of the Roman Empire*. Copenhagen: 106–125.

Straume, E. 1987. *Gläser mit Facettenschliff aus skandinavischen Gräbern des 4. und 5. Jahrhunderts n. Ch.* Oslo.

Tejral, J. 1992. Einige Bemerkungen zur Chronologie der späten römischen Kaiserzeit in Mitteleuropa. In: Godłowski, K. & Madyda-Legutko, R. (eds). *Probleme der relativen und absoluten Chronologie ab Latènezeit bis zum Frühmittelalter.* Cracow: 227–248.

Tischler, O. & Kemke, H. 1902. *Ostpreußische Altertümer aus der Zeit der grossen Gräberfelder nach Christi Geburt.* Königsberg.

Voss, O. 1955. The Høstentorp silver hoard and its period. A study of a Danish find of scrap silver from about 500 AD. *Acta Archaeologica* 25: 171–219.

Werner, J. 1970. Zur Verbreitung frühgeschichtlicher Metallarbeiten (Werkstatt – Wanderhandwerk – Handel – Familienverbindung). *Antikvariskt Arkiv* 38: 65–81.

Резюме

Стиль «Сёсдала» – горизонт «Сёсдала»

Анна Битнер-Врублевская

Й.-Э. Форссандер выделил стиль «Сёсдала» в 1937 г., но определение этого стиля никогда не было особенно точным. В 2001 г. я предложила термин «горизонт Сёсдала», в который объединила ряд вещей, которые обычно связывают с указанным стилем, поскольку нуждалась в рабочей методике, позволявшей вести сравнительное изучение материалов различных регионов, для исследования связей между Прибалтикой и Скандинавией в Эпоху переселения народов. Горизонт «Сёсдала» включает несколько категорий находок: церемониальные узды, двупластинчатые фибулы, подвески в виде щита и биконические, пельтовидные подвески и накладки. На все предметы исследуемого горизонта, обычно по всей площади, нанесен искусный штампованный орнамент, причем на одном изделии имеются изображения, нанесенные разными видами штемпелей, например, звездочки, концентрические круги и полукружия, заштрихованные треугольники и прямоугольники, по нескольку оттисков каждого штампа. В некоторых случаях штампованный декор дополняют изображения головок животных (как правило, лошадей) в профиль. Кроме того, используются и другие декоративные техники – неглубокий кербшнит и чернение. Почти все эти предметы выполнены из серебра, иногда с позолотой, инкрустированной серебром бронзы или, изредка, из золота. В немногих случаях вещи горизонта «Сёсдала» изготовлены из бронзы и тем самым представляют собой имитации артефактов выдающегося уровня. В целом предметы горизонта «Сёсдала» можно считать престижными предметами, принадлежавшими элите.

Хотя древнейшие элементы горизонта «Сёсдала» появились в периоде C3, в целом они характерны для Эпохи переселения народов (периоды D1 и начало D2). Недавние исследования скандинавской хронологии, проведенные А. Рау, в целом подтвердили результаты моих исследований, однако он не использовал термин «горизонт Сёсдала» в том смысле, который в него вкладываю я.

Изучение литературы, опубликованной после 2001 г., показывает, что с тех пор не было предпринято ни единой попытки дать всестороннее определение стиля «Сёсдала». Быть может, стоит сменить подход к изучению стиля «Сёсдала», прекратив датировать вещи по стилю и начав датировать стиль по вещам. Бесспорно, в Эпоху переселения народов наблюдается феномен существования одинаковых или очень близких типов вещей, с близким декором и техникой исполнения, которые были распространены на севере, в центре и на юго-востоке Европы (например, церемониальные узды типа «Сёсдала – Унтерзибенбрунн – Кошовени – Качин – Якушовице» или пряжки типа «Замостье – Тисаладань – Стшегоцице»). Они отражают непосредственные активные контакты представителей элит в зоне *inter ambo maria*. Мобильность элит способствовала распространению культурных характеристик, сделав межкультурные связи действительно очень тесными. Создается впечатление, что аристократия южной Скандинавии, носившая или пользовавшаяся вещами горизонта «Сёсдала», сыграла важную роль в формировании сети контактов между разными регионами Барбарикума.

Подписи к иллюстрациям

Рис. 1. Горизонт «Сёсдала»: – a) деталь церемониальной узды из Сёсдалы (фото Д. Линдскога); – b) двупластинчатыа фибула типа 2, Торсторп Вестербю, могила 3368 (Fonnesbech-Sandberg 1999); – c) двупластинчатыа фибула типа 3, Сейлфлод, могила DI (Nielsen 2000a); – d) подвеска в виде щита, Кроссхауг (Magnus 1975); – e) биконическая подвеска, Торсторп Вестербю, могила 3368 (Fonnesbech-Sandberg 2006); – f) пельтавидная подвеска, Финнесторп (© место жертвоприношения Финнесторп).

Рис. 2. Распространение элементов типа «Сёсдала»: – a) церемониальные узды; – b) двупластинчатые фибулы; – c) подвески в виде щита; – d) биконические подвески; – e) пельтовидные подвески или накладки (графическое решение Я. Жабко-Потоповича).

Рис. 3. Судота (восточная Литва), курган 30, погребение 4 (Bliujienė 2013).

Рис. 4. Большой наконечник ремня с завершением в виде пальметты и большая накладка с изображением фантастических существ из Чашково на озере Нидайно (Rzeszotarska-Nowakiewicz & Nowakiewicz 2012).

Horse equipment from a double grave at Šosseynoe

(Preliminary report)

Konstantin N. Skvortsov

A short note[1] presents horse tack recently found at Šosseynoe, near Kaliningrad. At one of four horses buried in connection with a cremation grave remains were found of a headstall with a check bar snaffle and saddle mounts. The artefacts reveal close contacts with Scandinavia as well as to Central Europe. The burial dates to the second half of the 5th or the first half of the 6th century.

Skvortsov, K. 2017. Horse equipment from a double grave at Šosseynoe. In: Fabech, C. & Näsman, U. (eds). *The Sösdala horsemen – and the equestrian elite of fifth century Europe*. Jutland Archaeological Society.

A double burial was excavated in the summer of 2012 during rescue archaeology carried out at a burial ground near the village of, Kaliningrad oblast, 1.5 km south of the bank of the Vistula Lagoon (former Frisches Haff). Burial no. 36 was not known before World War II and was discovered in 2006. The partly disturbed grave was found in a sand pit, and appeared to be the cremation burial of two people put into the grave in a wooden box, accompanied by the burial of no more than four horses.

Among the few remains of the cremated grave goods are a silver gilt radiate-headed Purda-type brooch, bronze panelled buckles with oval or B-shaped frames with square plates at the base of the tongue, bronze pincers, a few frag-ments of ceramic vessels, fragments of iron knives and two iron lance heads (Skvortsov 2013 fig. 5).

The horse tack from burial no. 36 was especially wealthy. It included an iron cheek bar snaffle with gilt bronze details and silver damascening (type I in Oexle 1992), 41 silver rivets with hemispherical heads (fig. 1), two gilt bronze pelta-shaped pendants and four gilt bronze strap junctions decorated in Salin's Style I (fig. 2), various saddle fittings of silver plate stamped in Salin's Style I (fig. 3), Haseloff's phase B (Salin 1904:222–223; Haseloff 1981:180–196). The grave goods allow us to date burial no. 36 from the second half of the 5th to the first half of the 6th century (c. AD 475–525). The finds show a

Chapter 13: Horse equipment from a double grave at Šosseynoe

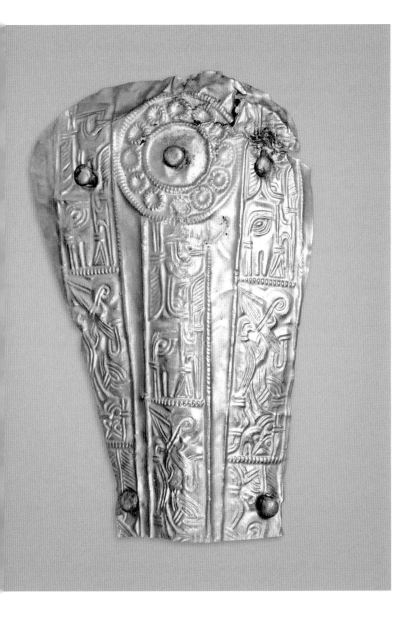

Fig. 4. A reconstruction of the horse tack from burial 36, Šosseynoe.

great many analogies to material in Scandinavia and the Baltic Sea islands.

The reconstruction of the headstall from burial no. 36 was based on remains of metal parts on one of the horse skulls. Some parts of this headstall resemble the headstall from the Langobard burials from Veszkény (Hungary; Gömöri 1988) and Hauskirchen (Austria; Nowotny 2008). In both cases there is a clear similarity in the design of lunula or pelta-shaped pendants and strap junctions, but the quality of the Lombard items is considerably higher. We tend to believe that the Šosseynoe objects represent a revision of the Continental concept, performed by the northern Germans in their own version of the I Germanic animal style.

Concerning the reconstruction of the saddle, there are several possible options, depending on the locations of the saddle horns on the bows (fig. 4). However, we settled on the one that seems to be the most convincing. The central fitting from the rear saddle bow remained fragmentary and probably was originally trapezoid-shaped. In addition to the central plate, three separate fittings from saddle horns have also been found.

Fig. 1. Remains of cheek bar snaffle and headstall from burial 36, Šosseynoe.

Fig. 2. Gilt bronze pelta-shaped pendants and strap junctions from burial 36, Šosseynoe; 1:1.

Fig. 3. Saddle fitting of stamped silver plate, from burial 36, Šosseynoe burial ground; 3:2.

These fittings on the protruding part of the saddle horns had a trapezoidal outline on the bottom, with the narrow part downward, and ended in a semicircle at the top. Only the outer parts of the three-edged wooden saddle horns were decorated with the silver plates, as indicated by the shape of the fittings. Based on the number of discovered fittings from saddle horns it can be assumed that they were all attached to the top of the saddle bow, where a large horn completed the central part of the front saddle bow, while smaller horns were located on the edges of the back bow.

On the basis of this reconstruction, the form of the front saddlebow of this saddle can be compared to the saddle from burial 3 at Ballan (Ballana) in Nubia, dated back to the middle of the 5th century. One can see certain structural similarities to our findings with the reconstruction of the saddles typical of the Scandinavian Migration Period (Horedt & Protase 1972:187-188, Taf. 49-50, 51.1-3; Török 1988:138, 143, Taf. 94.286; Kleemann 2007:134,135, Abb.2c; Norberg 1931 Abb. 14; Fabech & Näsman 2013:93 fig. 11).

Fully preserved saddles have been discovered, dated to the middle of the 6th century, with front and rear bows, completely covered with sheets of silver, found at the local cemeteries of Mitino (2008) and Aleyka-7 (2016). They show that the total covering of saddle bows with silver sheets was a common occurrence, and that the bows were either absolutely straight or slightly tilted outward, to allow the decoration to be seen.

The materials from Šosseynoe, as well as from the several other graves with a comparable wealth of inventory, will be published in detail in a forthcoming book with the working title "Lords of Amber Coast". In this book not only will these discoveries be revealed, but burials of the Aesti elites from the Great Migration era will be presented in general. They are united by the fact that they include a lot of things made in an area from the Danube to Scandinavia. All these sites show us the proximity of artistic ideas and the fact that Germanic fashion was spread from south to north and back by jewellers, merchants and resettled polyethnic groups of people in the era of the Great Migrations.

Note

1   Late in the book production we asked Konstantin Skvortsov to contribute with a short note about Šosseynoe as an example of the important finds of horse tack in Kaliningrad area.

References

Fabech, C. & Näsman, U. 2013. A lonely rider? The finding place of the Sösdala find and the context of its finds In: Khrapunov, I. & Stylegar, F.-A. (eds.) *Inter Ambo Maria: Northern barbarians from Scandinavia towards the Black Sea.* Kristiansand/Simferopol: 84–106.

Gömöri, J. 1988. "Das Langobardische Fürstengrab" aus Veszkény. In: Bott, G. (ed.) *Die Völkerwanderungszeit im Karpatenbecken.* Nuremberg: 105–119.

Haseloff, G. 1981. *Die germanische Tierornamentik der Völkerwanderungszeit 1-3.* Berlin/New York.

Horedt, K. & Protase, D. 1972. Das zweite Fürstengrab von Apahida (Siebenbürgen). *Germania* 50: 174–220.

Kleemann, J. 2007. Bemerkungen zum cloisonnierten goldbeschlag vom Sárvíz. *Archaeologiai Értesítő* 132. Budapest: 123–141.

Norberg, R. 1931 Moor- und Depotfunde aus dem 5. Jahrhundert nach Chr. Schonen. *Acta Archaeologica* 2: 104–111.

Nowotny, E. 2008. Die Ornamentik der Zaumzeugbeschläge von Hauskirchen, Grab 13. In: Bemmann, J. & Schmauder, M. (eds) *Kulturwandel in Mitteleuropa. Langobarden, Awaren, Slawen.* Bonn: 309–318.

Oexle, J. 1992. *Studien zu merowingerzeitlichen Pferdegeschirr am Beispiel der Trensen.* Mainz.

Salin, B. 1904. *Die Altgermanische Thierornamentik.* Stockholm. (2nd ed. 1935).

Skvortsov, K. 2013. "The ambor coast masters" In: Khrapunov, I. & Stylegar, F.-A. (eds) *Inter Ambo Maria. Northern barbarians from Scandinavia towards the Black Sea.* Kristiansand/Simferopol: 352-364. Резюме.

Török, L. 1988. *Late antique Nubia. History and archaeology of the southern neighbour of Egypt in the 4th–6th century AD.* Budapest.

Резюме

Снаряжение коня из парного захоронения с могильника Шоссейное

(Предварительное сообщение)

Константин Скворцов.

Данная короткая заметка посвящена находке конского снаряжения, обнаруженного недавно на могильнике Шоссейное, недалеко от Калининграда. Одно из четырех конских захоронений, сопровождавших парную кремацию, выделялось особым богатством погребального инвентаря, в который входили, в том числе удила, оголовье и оковки седла. Данные артефакты свидетельствуют о тесных контактах со Скандинавией, а также с Центральной Европой. Захоронение датируется 2-й половиной 5-го – 1-й половиной 6-го века.

Подписи к иллюстрациям

Рис. 1. Удила и детали конского оголовья из погребения 36, могильник Шоссейное.

Рис. 2. Бронзовая позолоченная пельтовидная подвеска лунница из погребения 36, могильник Шоссейное; 1:1.

Рис. 3. Элемент серебряной оковки седла из, погребения 36, могильник Шоссейное; 3:2.

Рис. 4. Реконструкция снаряжения коня погребения 36, могильник Шоссейное.

Chapter 14

Sösdala in a western perspective

Dieter Quast

The Sösdala horse tack is normally seen as a result of connections to the middle Danube region. In this article I will show some western connections of the Sösdala material. A critical assessment of the archaeological sources demonstrates how difficult it is to fix the emergence of the Sösdala objects and the "Sösdala style" somewhere in the borderlands of the late Roman Empire. They are part of a widely distributed horizon of sheet metal objects with punch mark decoration.

Quast, D. 2017. Sösdala in a western perspective. In: Fabech, C. & Näsman, U. (eds). *The Sösdala horsemen – and the equestrian elite of fifth century Europe.* Jutland Archaeological Society.

A continental archaeologist naming the find place Sösdala would automatically add another place name that came to his mind, namely Untersiebenbrunn in Austria – in some cases additionally Coşoveni in Romania (recently Tejral 2011:170–186; Nothnagel 2013:90–93). They are combined to describe a "style" (Sösdala-Untersiebenbrunn), which seem to be characteristic of south-eastern Central Europe and Southern Scandinavia. I will use the term Sösdala style simply for the ornamentation with special punch marks knowing that it is not clearly described. This is a little bit unsatisfactory but enough for the purpose of this paper.

Even if this style is not clearly defined (Bitner-Wróblewska 2001:89–90; Levada 2013; Fabech & Näsman 2013:99–102; Tejral 2011:170–185; Nothnagel 2013:90–91)[1] – it is argued on the basis of a special stamped decoration, with special forms of mounts and pelta-shaped pendants for horse tack – we can agree that the offering from Sösdala and the female burial from Untersiebenbrunn are dated in the first half of the 5th century AD (Fabech & Näsman 2013:100); but punched ornaments, e.g. on silver sheet brooches could appear earlier (Bitner-Wróblewska 2001:117–119). Obviously no find place in the west is added to describe this style, and at first sight there is nothing comparable there. That is why the few objects fitting this style in the west, e.g. in the late Roman *burgus* of Gundremmingen, Lkr. Günzburg (fig. 1) and from the hillfort of Wettenburg near Urphar, Main-Spessart-Kreis, are seen as hints of eastern warriors in Roman military service coming to the west (Keller 1986; Neubauer 2007:198–203). The south eastern connection of Sösdala became much pithier when Charlotte Fabech pointed

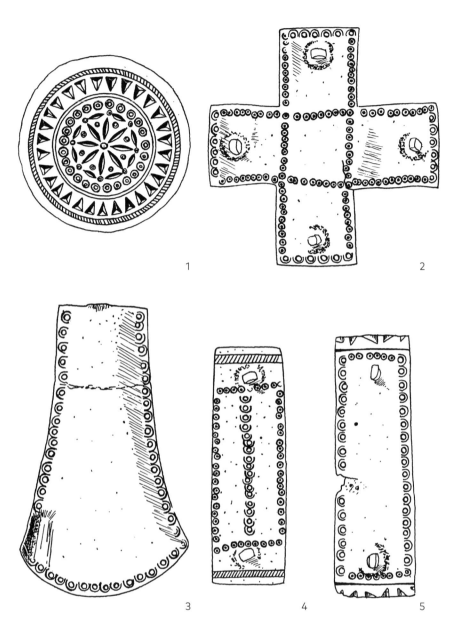

Fig. 1. Gundremmingen (Lkr. Günzburg, D), late Roman burgus "Bürgle". Mounts of a horse headgear, copper alloy. Scale 1:1. After Bersu 1964 pl. 8:1–5.

out that the finds had been a funeral sacrifice or ceremonially deposited horse equipment influenced by nomadic customs in the east (Fabech 1991; Fabech & Näsman 2013:86).

As far as I know, only Helmut Roth (1979) was looking from a western perspective at the Sösdala style, naming it a "derivate of the late Roman military style", which for him was defined by military belt mounts with punched and chip-carved decoration.[2] The punched decoration on the belt mounts, especially the leaf-shaped (*lanzettförmig*) strap ends, had been the prototypes for the characteristic Sösdala-Untersiebenbrunn decoration. Contact zones Roth supposed to be on the Danube in the region of Regensburg, where the eastern border of the distribution of these belt mounts had been set in the 1970s. From here the western influences came to the middle Danube region. The other contact zone was the Elbe-Weser Triangle. From there southern Scandinavia was influenced (Roth 1979:56–58). In his argumentation only the punched decoration was important – all other markers for the style that he mentioned (animal heads, mounts and pelta-shaped pendants from horse tack) were of no importance. And neither in southern Scandinavia nor in the middle and upper Danube are military belts with punched ornamentation known in any numbers. Additionally, no objects with Sösdala-Untersiebenbrunn style are known in the west.

In 2003 Birger Storgaard argued in a contrary way, saying that punch marks and belt mountings and horse-heads were Scandinavian elements on late Roman military belts imparted by northern mercenaries. He based his argumentation on "a new chronology that turned the dating of provincial Roman belt sets upside down" (Storgaard 2003:123–124). But there seem to be a misunderstanding because the new chronology of Horst Wolfgang Böhme – published only in a very short pre-report – is based on chip-carved belt sets. The "older" ones with punch marks are not included. The idea of this chronology was to demonstrate the longer use of the military belts in the 5th century to fill a gap in the archaeological material. Nevertheless punch mark decoration was still established in the second half of the 4th century (Böhme 1974:80 Texttafel A with complexes dated by coins and *Zwiebelknopffibeln* (cross bow brooches). Strap ends with horse heads occur on the continent in the first half of the 5th century – and this means from around AD 400 (Böhme 2008:369–371; cf. additionally below).

In the following article I would like to analyse some Sösdala objects from a western perspective. I will discuss aspects of three criteria: function, form, decoration.

Function

As we find the Sösdala style often as decoration of horse tack, we have to look first at horse tack in the west. This brings us to a problem, because riding equipment was no regular part of grave furniture west of the Rhine. We have richly furnished graves with weapons, belts, brooches etc. but spurs and horse tack are lacking. There is one exception in Burgundy, in Neuilly-lès-Dijon, Dép. Côte-d'Or (fig. 2), but it was detected back in 1857 and not properly excavated. The documented objects were an iron snaffle, an umbo, a sword with silver mounts from the scabbard, a spear heard and a glass bowl, dating the burial to the first half of the 5th century (Baudot 1857–1860:293–297; Oexle 1992:281 Nr. 553). There is another "grave" from the art market, now in Berlin in the Museum für Vor- und Frühgeschichte. There is no final publication, but an iron snaffle is mentioned in a short notice (Bertram 2011:191). Both graves contain only the snaffle, no mounts of the headstall, but it is not sure whether this is a consequence of the non-professional excavation or not. Two other find places with parts of iron snaffles of the first half of the 5th century are known in the west. One is from the hillfort "Lochenstein" in Hausen am Tann, Zollernalbkreis (Oexle 1992, 135–136 Nr. 61 pl. 29), the other one is a Roman villa in Newel, Lkr. Trier-Saarburg, where two identical psaliae (cheek bars) were detected. One was found together with other small finds from the 5th/6th centuries, the other one in a female child grave of the 7th century, probably in secondary position since the burial was dug through older layers (Oexle 1992:207–208 Nr. 286 pl. 131). There are a few other broken parts of horse headgear from other hillforts in the Alamannic region (Hoeper 2003:74–75; Quast 2008:288 fig. 21), but no objects decorated in Sösdala style are known, not even from the hillfort Runder Berg near Urach, Lkr. Reutlingen with its rich material (Quast 2008). But additionally we have to keep in mind that material from the first half of the 5th century in general is rare in Alamannia.

To end this, we can conclude that there is no horse tack with Sösdala style decoration west of Gundremmingen (Bersu 1964 pl. 8:1–5; Fabech & Näsman 2013:101 fig. 22). Is this for real or just caused by the archaeological sources? We have to do a critical assessment of the sources for

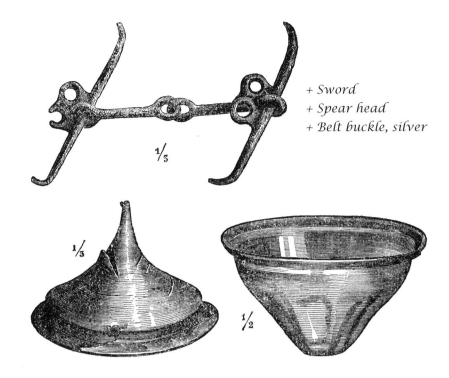

+ Sword
+ Spear head
+ Belt buckle, silver

Fig. 2. Neuilly-lès-Dijon (Dép. Côte-d'Or, F) Grave from 1857. – 1) Snaffle, iron. – 2) Umbo, iron covered with gilded silver sheet. – 3) Glass bowl. After Baudot 1857–1860:294–295.

this and compare the three different regions, Southern Scandinavia, South-Eastern Central Europe, and Western Central Europe (fig. 3:1). If we connect these regions on a map we get a triangle and with this triangle we can visualise the different levels of the sources (fig. 3:2).[3] In Southern Scandinavia horse headgear is known from offerings, in the south east from graves and hoards and in the west from settlements and only one or two undocumented graves. These facts simply demonstrate that there is no good basis for a comparison.

Form

A remarkable "form" in the Sösdala complex is the mounts decorated with pairs of animal heads, most probable horse heads. They are prominent on some bridle parts (nos. I:1, 10, 11) and pendants (nos. I:2–3) in different shapes. Comparable to the bridle is a group of strap ends of late Roman military belts (Steuer 1990:180–195; Böhme 2008:369–372; Tejral 2011:181–182; for the term Rau 2010:279). The

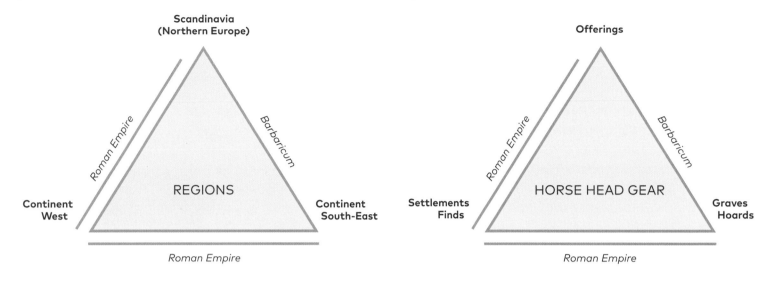

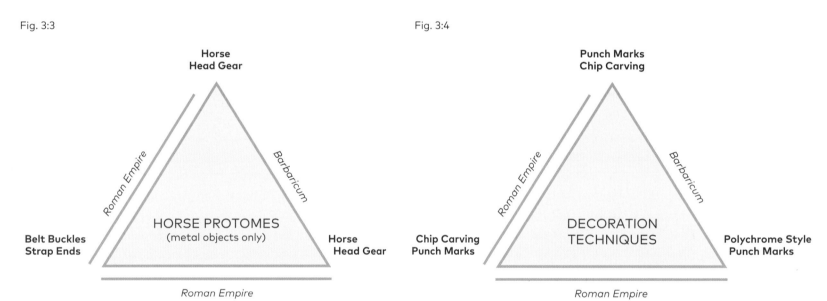

Fig. 3. Triangles schematically showing the connections between the three regions of this paper in the first half of the 5th century. 1) The regions and the "political context". 2) Features with horse tack. 3) Objects with a pair of horse protomes. 4) Main decoration techniques and carriers. Graphics: Michael Ober, RGZM.

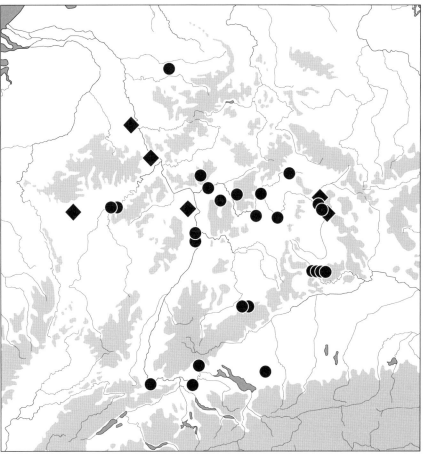

Fig. 4. 1) *Strap end with horse protomes, gilded silver, Babenhausen, Lkr. Darmstadt-Dieburg. Scale 1:1. After Lindenschmit 1870 fasc. XII, pl. 6:4–5. – 2) Belt mounts, silver, Forchheim, Lkr. Forchheim, hillfort Ehrenbürg. Scale 2:3. After Böhme 1977:16, fig. 3.*

Fig. 5. *Distribution map of strap ends with horse protomes (●) and belt mounts of the type "Ehrenbürg-Jamoinge" (◆). Map: Monika Weber, RGZM, redrawn after Böhme 1977:22, fig. 7 and Böhme 2008:372, fig. 3.*

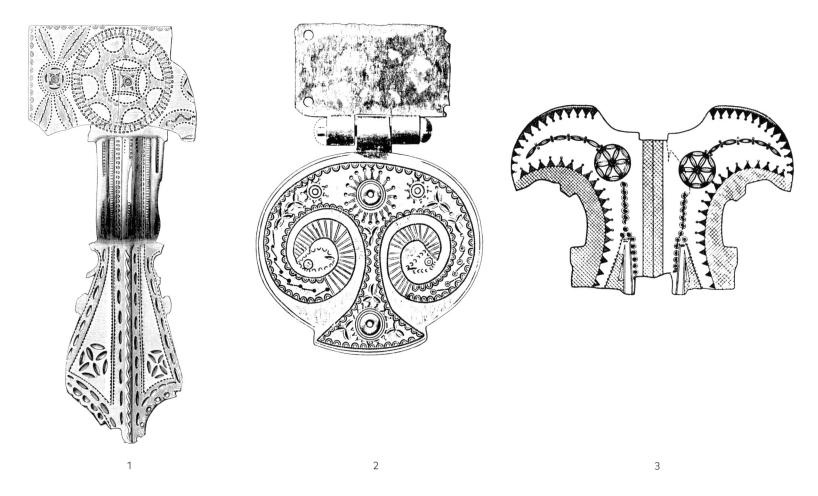

Fig. 6. Objects with punched ornaments. Scale 1:1. 1) Brooch, Bruarebacka, Västergötland. After Åberg 1924:14, fig. 34. 2) Pendant from horse tack, Vennebo, Västergötland. After Werner 1981:251. fig. 14b. 3) Fragment of a brooch, Høstentorp, Zealand. After Werner 1981:251, fig. 14c.

best known example is from Babenhausen, Lkr. Darmstadt-Dieburg (fig. 4:1). A focus in the distribution of this type of strap end is along the Main River, but lots of them are known from the whole of south-western Germany (fig. 5). The dating of those belts is the first half of the 5th century. Comparable to the pendants (nos. I:2–3) is a type of late Roman belt mounts named as "Ehrenbürg-Jamoinge" type (fig. 4:2; Böhme 1977; cf. additionally Tejral 2011:182 fig. 138). The dating is the same, but the distribution differs slightly. The middle Rhine region is more prominent, but this statement is based on only a few type items (fig. 5). Even in the second half of the 5th century and in the 6th century horse protomes were a characteristic form in

the west, as purse mounts of well-furnished weapon graves demonstrate (Windler 1994:71–77), as well as some belt buckle plates (Pesch 2015:398 fig. 13,1). To end this part with a critical assessment of sources (fig. 3:3), horse heads are known in the west in larger numbers from belt mounts, in the north and south-east only from horse tack. These facts likewise demonstrate that there is no good basis for a comparison.

Additionally to the metalwork, pairs of animal heads (but in different configuration) can be found on combs of the first half of the 5th century distributed from Britain to Pannonia, in single cases up to the delta of the Danube (Quast 1993:98 with further reading in footnote 706; Pet-

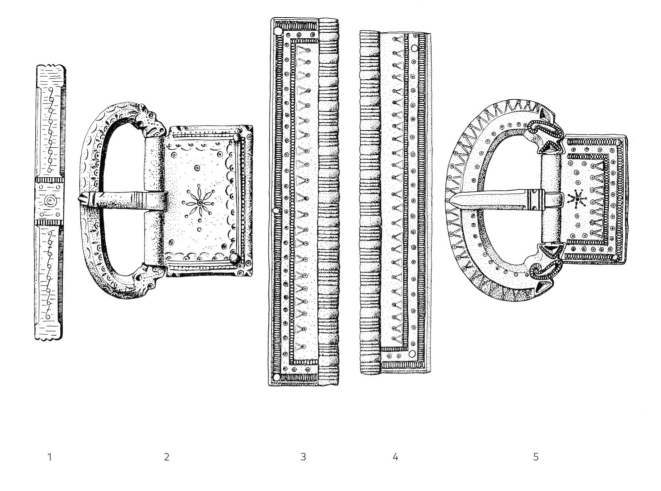

Fig. 7. Late Roman belt mounts with punched ornaments. 1–2) Monceau-le-Neuf, Dép. Aisne. 3–5) Tongrinne, Prov. Namur. Scale 3:4. After Böhme 1974 pl. 108:1–3 and pl. 129:2.5.

ković 1995:26–27, tab. 13a Type VI; Tejral 1997:336; Tejral 2011:182–185).

Decoration

Even if most of the late Roman military belts in the west are decorated with chip-carving there is a group with additional or only punched ornaments. East of Pannonia the late Roman military belts are almost completely absent. This could be for different reasons: They could be made in western workshops only or the distribution is simply caused by the state of the source material. At the eastern Roman border the cemeteries of the fortresses seem to be without furnished male graves. In the nearby Barbaricum the archaeological cultures are also characterised by a lack of well-furnished male graves.

The punched mounts started earlier but were still in use parallel to the chip-carved belts (Böhme 1974:79–90). The items with chip-carving are accepted as the prototypes for the northern Nydam style and the animal style I (Haseloff 1981). But already the punched ornaments of the military belts seem to be important for the development of the Sösdala style. As far as I know there is no systematic analysis of the punched ornaments in late Roman contexts; only Joachim Werner (1981) explored some aspects (for the north cf. Bitner-Wróblewska 2001). Most of the punched elements are (or seem to be) widely distrib-

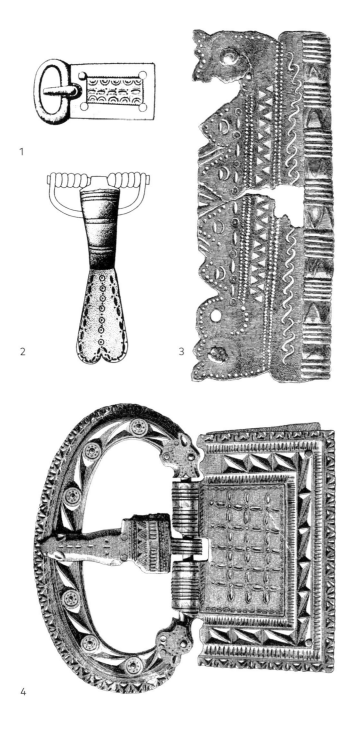

uted. A characteristic punch for Sösdala and Untersieben-brunn is lens-shaped – in German they are named *mandelförmig* ("almond shaped") after the first description of the Untersiebenbrunn burials by Wilhelm Kubitschek (1911:49). Lens-shaped punch marks were combined to rosettes framed by an engraved circle or by a circle made of lens-shaped punches. This decoration was used nearly everywhere (Werner 1981:251–252; Steuer 1990:192–193, also in antler: Petković 1995 pl. XXII:10). In the west it is found especially on mounts and strap ends, e.g. from Gundremmingen (fig. 1:1), Kempten im Allgäu (Werner 1981:247 fig. 12) and Urphar (Neubauer 2007 pl. 36,2–4.6), in the north on the fragment of a silver sheet brooch from Høstentorp, Zealand (fig. 6:3; Voss 1954:195 fig. 13,2; Werner 1981:251 fig. 14:b), on the silver sheet brooch from Bruarebacka, Västergötland (fig. 6:1) (Åberg 1924:14 fig. 34) and lens-shaped punch marks are found on the pelta-shaped pendant in Sösdala itself (nos. I:19–21). Sometimes lens shaped punches were also combined to "stars", e.g. on the buckle plates from Monceau-le-Neuf, Dép. Aisne (fig. 7:2; Böhme 1974 pl. 129:5). Usually stars consist of triangular punch marks, as in Tongerinne, Prov. Namur (fig. 7:5; Böhme 1974 pl. 108:3). This motif is very well known from the "Sösdala horizon" (Bitner-Wróblewska 2001:89–90; Rau 2010:63) in southern Scandinavia, e.g. in Vennebo, Västergötland (fig. 6:2; Werner 1981:251 fig. 14:c) and Sösdala (nos. I:19–21; Salin 1904:156 fig. 362; Åberg 1919).

Special combinations of rows of lens-shaped punches alternating with ring-and-dot punches (fig. 8:2–4) are distributed in a wide area, but they show a clear focus in the Middle Rhine-Main region (fig. 9), in the "Roman-Germanic contact zone" as mentioned by Neubauer (2007:113). From the north examples from Finnestorp, Västergötland (fig. 8:1; Werner 1981:251 fig. 14a), Høstentorp (fig. 6:3) and Bruarebacka (fig. 6:1) are known (Neubauer 2007:233 nos. 19 and 23–33).

There are other types of punch marks occurring on late Roman belt buckles as well as in the Sösdala horizon. Those are different forms of triangles with dots or ring-and-dot punches on the top (Böhme 1974:72 fig. 26). To mention just a few examples I will name the strap ends and buckle plates from Tongeren, Prov. Limburg (Böhme 1974 pl.

Fig. 8. Objects with rows of lens-shaped punches alternating with ring-and-dot punches. Various scales. 1) Finnestorp, Västergötland. After Werner 1981:251, fig. 14a. 2) Urphar, Main-Spessart-Kreis, hillfort Wettenburg. After Neubauer 2007:34:2. 3) Alzey, Lkr. Alzey-Worms. After Lindenschmit 1900 pl. 12:2b. 4) "Rheinhessen". After Lindenschmit 1870 fasc. II, pl. 6:6.

106:11) and Hermes, Dép. Oise (Böhme 1974 pl. 125:2–3) and several times from Sösdala (nos. I:10, 17–18, 41, 65/68) and other Scandinavian find places (Salin 1904:156 fig. 358–359). And to name a last ornament: rows of ring-and-dot punches, connected with diagonal lines. This can be seen on the mount from Wijster, Prov. Drenthe (Böhme 1974 pl. 73:10) and Monceau-le-Neuf, Dép. Aisne (fig. 7:1; Böhme 1974 pl. 129:2) on the belt loop from Herstal, Prov. Liège (Böhme 1974 pl. 92:13). In the north this ornament is known e.g. from a pendant from Vennebo (fig. 6:2).

In the west, punched ornaments are not to be found on late Roman military belts only. In modern Netherlands and north-west Germany there is a horizon of hoards with a special type of neck ring (fig. 10). In most cases there are sets of similar rings in each hoard. They were cast in gold but very thin, looking like gold sheet. The decoration contains punch marks of nearly all types known from Untersiebenbrunn and Sösdala. Those neck rings were called "type Velp" after the eponymous find place in the province of Gelderland north of the IJssel River, meaning outside the Roman Empire. The dating is around the year 400 and the early 5th century (recently Quast 2009:217–220).

To finish this chapter with a short critical assessment of sources, too, we have to assume that punch decoration was very fashionable in the late 4th and early 5th centuries and widely distributed (fig. 3:4). This may be caused by the fact that there was a real horizon of sheet metal during this time and this can be ornamented best with punch marks (Werner 1981; Quast 2009:218). But there are differences between east and west. In the middle Danube area (and east of it) silver sheet brooches were in some cases covered with gold sheet on which precious stones were set. Punch marks are known in this region mostly from the cast ceremonial horse tack of the type Untersiebenbrunn and from some buckle plates (Levada 2011; 2013). In the north we have brooches and ceremonial horse headgear with punch decoration. In the west few brooches with that kind of decoration are known. Here most punch marks are found on late Roman military belts. These facts demonstrate again that there is no good basis for a comparison.

Is there any wise conclusion to be drawn from all this? Not in the sense that allows us to describe the development of the "Sösdala style". What we see is a horizon of

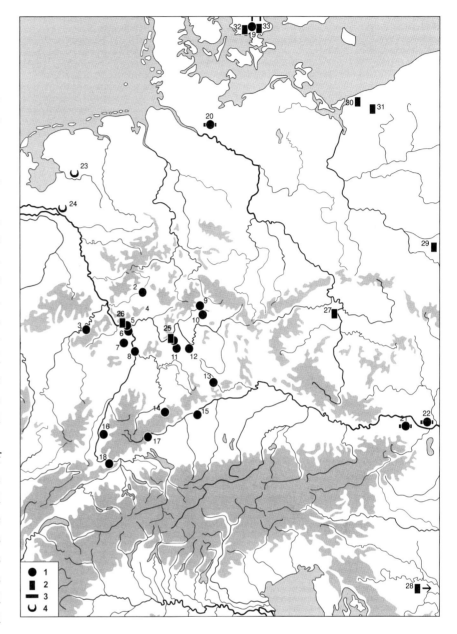

Fig. 9. Distribution of objects with rows of lens-shaped punches alternating with ring-and-dot punches. 1) Belt mounts. 2) Brooches. 3) Horse-tack. 4) Neckrings. After Neubauer 2007:114. fig. 30. Additions: Monika Weber, RGZM.

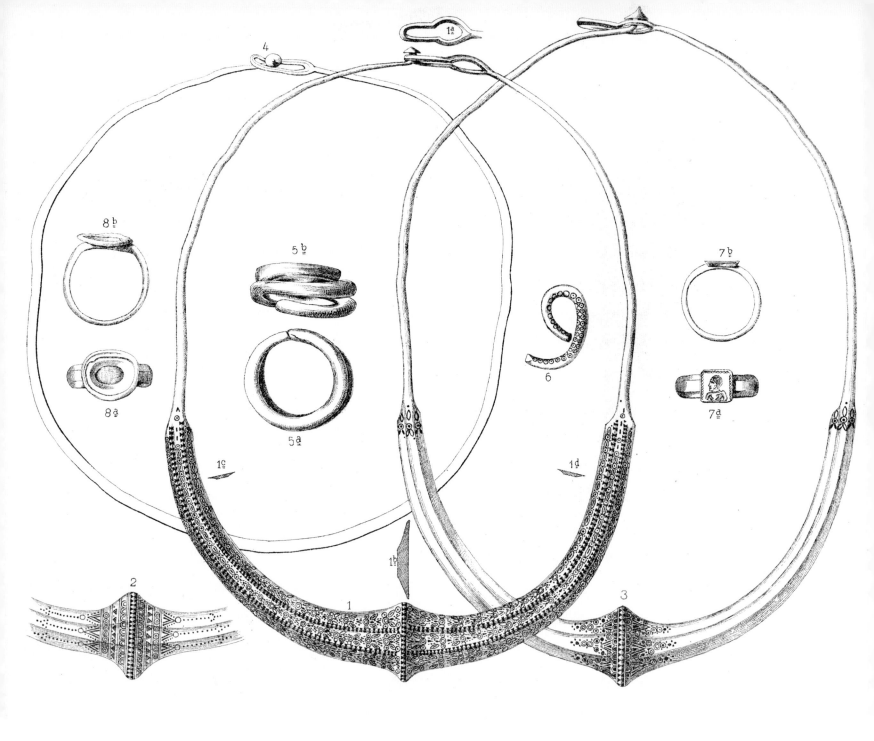

different objects with punched decoration with comparable ornaments. Most probably this is caused by a formation in the borderlands of the late Roman Empire (Steuer 1990:193; Tejral 1997:335–337; Tejral 2011). Different influences from there met in Southern Scandinavia, brought there by returning mercenaries. Those forms of contact with the south-east were analysed several times (e.g. Bemmann 2006; Fischer chapter 16). For the west this context is demonstrated by the derivation of the Nydam style and the animal style I from late Roman chip-carved bronzes

(Haseloff 1981; Bemmann & Bemmann 1998:233–240). But even weapon finds shows connections between the north and the west, especially the region around Trier. A bridge mount of the type Porskær from a sword scabbard was found (together with a comb of Thomas type III "Gotlandic subtype") in Rosport in Luxemburg (Gilles 2006; Thomas 1960:107; Łuczkiewicz 2008:221–222 fig. 3; for map see fig. 11 in chapter 17), a scabbard mouthpiece from a gravel pit in Liedolsheim, Gem. Dettenheim, Lkr. Karlsruhe, (fig. 11:1; Gross 2010:679–681 fig. 3; 2011:334 fig.

2:5) has proportions not fitting the Continental mouth-pieces which are smaller. Additionally the chip-carved scroll ornament shows the best parallels in the north, e.g. in Finnestorp (fig. 11:2; Nordqvist 2005:229 fig. 5:3). Connections can also be seen between some scabbard mouthpieces from Idesheim, Lkr. Bitburg-Prüm (fig. 11:3) and Trier (fig. 11:4; Wieczorek & Périn 1997:859–861 nos. 6–7; Schmauder 2007 fig. 12:28–29) and Nydam, Jutland (fig. 11:5–6). The items from Idesheim, Trier and Nydam IV (fig. 11:5–6) have in common the hanging triangles on the bottom side and the geometric chip-carving; the item from Idesheim shows niello decoration which is characteristic of a group of Scandinavian scabbard mouthpieces, e.g. in Nydam Id, of the first half of the 5th century (Bemmann & Hahne 1994:386; Jørgensen & Petersen 2003:266).

Hoeper (2003:77–80) argues that barbed javelin heads known from several Roman places (*castelli* and settlements) are also of Scandinavian origin, because the types are known in large numbers from Scandinavian bog offerings and weapon graves (in this sense Gross 2010:681; also 2011:334, fig. 3). Bog offerings as well as weapon graves of the 4th and first half of the 5th century are nearly unknown in Alamannia. This we should keep in mind when comparing distribution maps. There is only one little bog offering in Alamannia and this contains a barbed javelin head (Münchhöf: Hoeper 2003:192 no. 11). Even one of the very few weapon graves contained such a weapon (Ihringen: Hoeper 2003:192 no. 9). The items in the Roman contexts could be interpreted to suggest that this type of spear head was usual not only in the north but also in south-western Germany.

Nearly twenty years ago Claus von Carnap-Bornheim (1999) pointed to some "Roman Iron Age Germanic traditions" in the grave of the Frankish king Childeric I. († 481/82), especially on his sword belt. For von Carnap-Bornheim (1999:54–57) the "strap ends with tubular endings" often documented in the bog offerings of southern Scandinavia were prototypes for comparable objects in the king's burial. A few years ago the Museum für Vor- und Frühgeschichte in Berlin bought the grave furniture of a warrior from the first half of the 5th century with a gold grip sword (Bertram 2011), already mentioned above because of the iron snaffle. Even if the find place is unknown, it must be from the Continent. It contains two "strap ends" from the sword belt (Bertram 2011:191 fig. 2) – not similar to Scandinavian ones – but demonstrating that the same system of suspension was used. Some years ago I suggested a new reconstruction of Childeric's sword belt following prototypes of the Scandinavian Roman Iron Age (Quast 2003; 2015:170–172, fig. 2). There are other objects, e.g. the shield bosses with a covering of gilded silver sheet that show a connection between the north and the late antique west (von Carnap-Bornheim 1999:48–53; Bertram 2011:191). One of them was already mentioned above: the one from Neuilly (fig. 2:2). Obviously there are very few late Roman military belt mounts in the north; a few in Jutland but nearly none on Zealand or in Scania (Rau 2010:279–303). As far as I know all of them are with punched decoration – items with chip-carving are missing. Additionally some solidi of western mints could be a hint at western contacts (Metcalf 1995).

To sum up the subject of Sösdala in a western perspective

Of course the connections between Sösdala and Untersiebenbrunn are conspicuous. The lack of comparable horse equipment in the west could be caused simply by the state of the source material. In the west it was not usual to put horse tack into the graves. In the middle Danube area and east of it many male graves with riding equipment are known from the first half of the 5th century (e.g. Anke 1998 pl. 43; 49; 57:12; 82–89; 92–93; 96; 104; 107–109; 112–115; 118; 121–123). The horse tack of the type Untersiebenbrunn is only one of several types – and as remarked by Martina Nothnagel maybe more common in female graves (Nothnagel 2013:90–93). This type of ceremonial horse tack is the only unique feature for the Sösdala-Untersiebenbrunn connection. One single new find could change our image! Punch mark decoration is everything else but unique in late 4th and early 5th century Europe. Along the border of the late Roman Empire it was used for decoration, especially on objects made of sheet

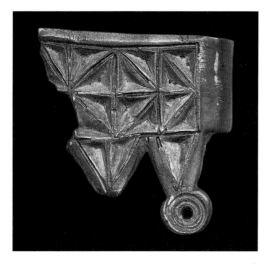

1

2

3

4

5

6

Fig. 11. Sword scabbard mouthpieces. Various scales. 1) Liedolsheim, Gem. Dettenheim, Lkr. Karlsruhe. 2) Finnestorp, Västergötland. 3) Idesheim, Lkr. Bitburg-Prüm. 4) Trier, Viehmarkt . 5) Nydam Id, Jutland. 6. Nydam IV. 1) After Gross 2010:680, fig. 3. 2) After Nordqvist 2005: 229, fig. 5:3. 3–4) Photo: Th. Zühmer, Generaldirektion Kulturelles Erbe Rheinland-Pfalz, Rheinisches Landesmuseum Trier. 5–6) After Jørgensen & Vang Petersen 2003:273, 281.

metal and therefore too thin for chip-carving. The influences and the distribution of punch marks described by Roth (see above) are possible but not provable at present. The chronology does not help to solve this question because the punched decoration on sheet metal is an isochronic horizon. If we just named the "style" Sösdala-Untersiebenbrunn-Velp this would give a broad impression.

Notes

1   Nothnagel 2013:91 mentioned a thesis "on the punched decoration of the Sösdala style" by I. Greußing. As far as I know this thesis is unpublished.

2   Nowadays the term Late Roman Military Style is used in a slightly different way for objects mainly of the male world with garnet cloisonné decoration (von Rummel 2007).

3   These triangles show tendencies only and no absolute figures. There are of course exceptions outside the tendencies.

Acknowledgements

I would like to thank Charlotte Fabech and Ulf Näsman for the invitation to the Sösdala workshop in November 2015 in Lund. Many thanks to the Rheinisches Landesmuseum Trier for photographs and permission to print the Idesheim and Trier scabbard mouthpieces. The graphics and scans for this article were made by Monika Weber and Michael Ober, both RGZM. I owe many thanks to them. For the kind permissions to reproduce images from their works I would like to thank Horst Wolfgang Böhme (Mainz), Uwe Gross (Esslingen), Bengt Nordqvist (Mölndal), Dieter Neubauer (Wiesbaden), Peter Vang Petersen (Copenhagen). In some cases the authors were not alive – I can only hope for their permission to reproduce their illustrations.

References

Åberg, N. 1919. Den germanska stjärnornamentiken under 3- och 400-talet e. Kr. *Antikvarisk Tidskrift för Sverige* 21/3: 1–51.

Åberg, N. 1924. *Den nordiska folkvandringstidens kronologi*. Stockholm.

Anke, B. 1998. *Studien zur reiternomadischen Kultur des 4. bis 5. Jahrhunderts*. Weissbach.

Baudot, H. 1857–1860. Mémoire sur les sépultures des barbares de l'époque mérovingienne, découvertes en Bourgogne, et particulièrement à Charnay. *Mémoires de la Commission des Antiquités du Département de la Côte-d'Or* 5: 127–320.

Bemmann, J. 2006. Eine völkerwanderungszeitliche Bestattung aus Epöl, Kom. Esztergom, mit Schwertriemendurchzügen skandinavischer Form. In: Mihailescu-Bîrliba, V., Hriban, C. & Munteany, L. (eds) *Miscellanea Romano-Barbarica in honorem septagenarii magistri Ion Ioniță*. Bucharest: 217–246.

Bemmann, G. & Bemmann, J. 1998. *Der Opferplatz von Nydam. Die Funde aus den älteren Grabungen: Nydam-I und Nydam-II*. Neumünster.

Bemmann, J. & Hahne, G. 1994. Waffenführende Grabinventare der jüngeren römischen Kaiserzeit und Völkerwanderungszeit in Skandinavien. Studie zur zeitlichen Ordnung anhand der norwegischen Funde. *Bericht der Römisch-Germanischen Kommission* 75: 283–640.

Bersu, G. 1964. *Die spätrömische Befestigung "Bürgle" bei Gundremmingen*. Munich.

Bertram, M. 2011. Das Grab eines "Chef militaire" mit Goldgriffspatha. *Acta Praehistorica et Archaeologica* 43: 189–193.

Bitner-Wróblewska, A. 2001. *From Samland to Rogaland. East-West Connections in the Baltic Basin during the Early Migration Period*. Warsaw.

Böhme, H.W. 1974. *Germanische Grabfunde des 4. bis 5. Jahrhunderts zwischen unterer Elbe und Loire*. Munich.

Böhme, H.W. 1977. Ein germanischer Gürtelbeschlag der Zeit um 400 aus Oberfranken. *Studien zur Sachsenforschung* 1: 13–24.

Böhme, H.W. 1987. Gallien in der Spätantike. Forschungen zum Ende der Römerherrschaft in den westlichen Provinzen. *Jahrbuch des Römisch-Germanischen Zentralmuseums Mainz* 34: 770-773.

Böhme, H.W. 2008. Zur Bedeutung von Aschaffenburg im frühen Mittelalter. In: Ludwig, U. & Schilp, Th. (eds). *Nomen et Fraternitas. Festschrift für Dieter Geuenich zum 65. Geburtstag*. Berlin/New York: 363–382.

Carnap-Bornheim, C. von 1999. Kaiserzeitliche germanische Traditionen im Fundgut des Grabes des "Chef militaire" in Vermand und im Childerich-Grab in Tournai. In: Fischer, T., Precht, G. & Tejral, J. (eds). *Germanen beiderseits des spätantiken Limes*. Cologne/Brno: 47–61.

Fabech, C. 1991. Neue Perspektiven zu den Funden von Sösdala und Full-tofta. In: Häßler, H.-J. (ed.). *Studien zur Sachsenforschung 7*, Hildesheim: 121–135.

Fabech, C. & Näsman, U. 2013. A Lonely Rider? The Finding Place of the Sösdala Find and the Context of its Finds. In: Khrapunov, F. & Stylegar, F.-A. (eds). *Inter Ambo Maria. Northern Barbarians from Scandinavia towards the Black Sea*. Kristiansand/Simferopol: 84–104.

Gilles, K.-J. 2006. Nordseegermanische Siedler im Trevererland? In: Seitz, G. (ed.). *Im Dienste Roms. Festschrift für Hans Ulrich Nuber*. Remshalden: 125–128.

Gross, U. 2010. Militärische Raritäten: zwei Schwertscheidenmundbleche des 5. Jahrhunderts und drei Ortbänder des Hoch- und Spätmittelalters. *Fundberichte aus Baden-Württemberg* 31: 677–686.

Gross, U. 2011. Nördliche Elemente im Fundgut des 4. und 5. Jahrhundert beidseits des Rheins zwischen Mainz und Basel. In: Kasprzyk, M./Kuhnle, G. (eds.), *L'Antiquité tardive dans l'Est de la Gaule. I: La vallée du Rhin superieur et les provinces gauloises limitrophes: actualité de la recherché*. Revue Archéologique de l'Est, Supplément 30. Dijon: 329–338.

Haseloff, G. 1981. *Die germanische Tierornamentik der Völkerwanderungszeit. Studien zu Salin's Stil I*. Berlin/New York.

Hoeper, M. 2003. *Völkerwanderungszeitliche Höhenstationen am Oberrhein. Geißkopf bei Berghaupten und Kügeleskopf bei Ortenberg*. Ostfildern.

Jørgensen, E. & Vang Petersen, P. 2003. Das Nydam Moor – neue Funde und Beobachtungen. In: *Sieg und Triumpf. Der Norden im Schatten des Römischen Reiches*. Copenhagen: 258–284.

Keller, E. 1986. Germanenpolitik Roms im bayerischen Teil der Raetia secunda während des 4. und 5. Jahrhunderts. *Jahrbuch des Römisch-Germanischen Zentralmuseums Mainz* 33: 575–592.

Kubitschek, W. 1911. Grabfunde in Untersiebenbrunn (auf dem Marchfeld). *Jahrbuch für Altertumskunde* 5: 32–74.

Levada, M. 2011. To Europe via the Crimea. On Possible Migration Routes of the Northern People in the Great Migration Period. In: Khrapunov, F. & Stylegar, F.-A. (eds). *Inter Ambo Maria. Contacts between Scandinavia and the Crimea in the Roman Period*. Kristiansand/Simferopol: 115–137.

Levada, M. 2013. Sösdala. The problem of singling out an artistic style. In: Khrapunov, F. & Stylegar, F.-A. (eds). *Inter Ambo Maria. Northern Barbarians from Scandinavia towards the Black Sea*. Kristiansand/Simferopol: 213–235.

Lindenschmit, L. 1870. *Die Alterthümer unserer heidnischen Vorzeit. Zweiter Band*. Mainz.

Lindenschmit, L. 1900. *Die Alterthümer unserer heidnischen Vorzeit. IV. Band*. Mainz.

Łuczkiewicz, P. 2008. Ein völkerwanderungszeitliches Grab (?) aus Spiczyn bei Lublin. In: Niezabitowska-Wiśniewska, B., Juściński, M., Łuczkiewicz, P. & Sadowski, S. (eds). *The Turbulent Epoch. New Materials from the Late Roman Period and the Migration Period*. Lublin: 219–226.

Metcalf, D.M. 1995. Viking Age Numismatics. 1. Late Roman and Byzantine Gold in the Northern Lands. *The Numismatic Chronicle* 155: 413–441.

Neubauer, D. 2007. *Die Wettenburg in der Mainschleife bei Urphar, Main-Spessart-Kreis*. Rahden.

Nordqvist, B. 2005. Der Kriegsbeuteopferplatz von Finnestorp in Schweden. *Offa* 61/62: 221–238.

Nothnagel, M. 2013. *Weibliche Eliten der Völkerwanderungszeit. Zwei Prunkbestattungen aus Untersiebenbrunn*. St. Pölten.

Oexle, J. 1992. *Studien zu merowingerzeitlichem Pferdegeschirr am Beispiel der Trensen*. Mainz.

Pesch, A. 2015. *Die Kraft der Tiere. Völkerwanderungszeitliche Goldhalskragen und die Grundsätze germanischer Kunst*. Mainz.

Petković, S. 1995. *Rimski predmeti od kosti i roga sa teritorije Gornje Mezieje [The Roman Items of Bone and Antler from the Territory of Upper Moesia]*. Belgrade.

Pleyte, W. 1889. *Nederlandsche Oudheden van de vroegste tijden tot op Karel den Grooten. Deel II afbeeldingen, 1989-Gelderland*. Leiden.

Quast, D. 1993. *Die merowingerzeitlichen Grabfunde aus Gültlingen (Stadt Wildberg, Kreis Calw)*. Stuttgart.

Quast, D. 2003. Childerichs Schwertgurt. Ein neuer Rekonstruktionsvorschlag. *Archäologisches Korrespondenzblatt* 33: 597–614.

Quast, D. 2008. Der Runde Berg bei Urach. Die alamannische Besiedlung im 4. und 5. Jahrhundert. In: Steuer, H. & Bierbrauer, V. (eds). *Höhensiedlungen zwischen Antike und Mittelalter von den Ardennen bis zur Adria*. Berlin/New York: 261–322.

Quast, D. 2009. Velp und verwandte Schatzfunde des frühen 5. Jahrhunderts. *Acta Praehistorica et Archaeologica* 41: 207–230.

Quast, D. 2015. Die Grabbeigaben – ein kommentierter Fundkatalog. In: Quast, D. (ed.). *Das Grab des fränkischen Königs Childerich in Tournai und die Anastasis Childerici von Jean-Jacques Chifflet aus dem Jahre 1655*. Mainz: 165–207.

Rau, A. 2010. *Nydam Mose. 1: Die personengebundenen Gegenstände. Grabungen 1989–1999*. Højbjerg/Aarhus.

Roth, H. 1979. Der ältere Völkerwanderungsstil. In: Roth, H. (ed.). *Kunst der Völkerwanderungszeit*. Frankfurt am Main/Berlin/Vienna: 42–58.

Rummel, P. von 2007. *Habitus barbarus. Kleidung und Repräsentation spätantiker Eliten im 4. und 5. Jahrhundert*. Berlin/New York.

Salin, B. 1904. *Die altgermanische Thierornamentik*. Stockholm. – 2nd ed. 1935.

Schmauder, M. 2007. Die Bewaffnung des spätantiken Heeres. In: Demandt, A. & Engemann, J. (eds). *Imperator Caesar Flavius Constantinus – Konstantin der Große* [Exhibition Catalogue Rheinisches Landesmuseum Trier]. Mainz: 147–154.

Steuer, H. 1990. Höhensiedlungen des 4. und 5. Jahrhunderts in Südwestdeutschland. In: *Archäologie und Geschichte des ersten Jahrtausends in Südwestdeutschland*. Sigmaringen: 139–205.

Storgaard, B. 2003. Kosmopolitische Aristokraten. In: Jørgensen, L. *et al.* (eds). *Sieg und Triumpf. Der Norden im Schatten des Römischen Reiches*. Copenhagen: 106–125.

Tejral, J. 1997. Neue Aspekte der frühvölkerwanderungszeitlichen Chronologie im Mitteldonauraum. In: Tejral, J., Friesinger, H. & Kazanski, M. (eds). *Neue Beiträge zur Erforschung der Spätantike im mittleren Donauraum*. Brno: 321–392.

Tejral, J. 2011. *Einheimische und Fremde. Das norddanubische Gebiet zur Zeit der Völkerwanderung*. Brno.

Thomas, S. 1960. Studien zu germanischen Kämmen der römischen Kaiserzeit. *Arbeits- und Forschungsberichte zur sächsischen Bodendenkmalpflege* 8: 54–215.

Voss, O. 1954. The Høstentorp Silver Hoard and its Period. *Acta Archaeologica* 25: 171–219.

Werner, J. 1981. Zu einer elbgermanischen Fibel des 5. Jahrhunderts aus Gaukönigshofen, Ldkr. Würzburg. *Bayerische Vorgeschichtsblätter* 46: 225–254.

Wieczorek, A. & Périn, P. (eds.) 1997. *Die Franken, Wegbereiter Europas.* [Exhibition Catalogue Reiss-Museum Mannheim]. Mainz.

Windler, R. 1994. *Das Gräberfeld von Elgg und die Besiedlung der Nordostschweiz im 5.–7. Jh.* Zürich/Elgg.

Резюме

Сёсдала и ее параллели на Западе

Дитер Кваст

Конская амуниция из Сёсдалы обычно рассматривается как продукт связей между Сканией и Средним Подунавьем, то есть Юго-Восточной Европой. В этой статье я попытался проанализировать некоторые находки из Сёсдалы в западной перспективе, на основании трех критериев – их функций, формы и декора. Основная проблема данного подхода – разное состояние археологических источников. Стиль «Сёсдала» зачастую проявляется в виде декора конской упряжи, однако к западу от Рейна элементы снаряжения для верховой езды обычно не были частью погребального инвентаря. Здесь имеются богатые могилы с оружием, поясами, фибулами и т. д., в которых отсутствуют шпоры и конская амуниция. Детали конской узды в южной Скандинавии известны по находкам приношений, в среднем Подунавье и на юго-востоке Европы – в погребениях и кладах, тогда как на Западе – в очень небольшом количестве экземпляров, происходящих с поселений и из недокументированных погребений. Эти факты сами по себе указывают на отсутствие адекватной базы для сравнительного анализа.

Примечательная форма из комплекса из Сёсдалы – накладки, украшенные парными головками животных, вероятнее всего, коней. Их можно обнаружить на некоторых накладках и деталях узды. Данная узда сопоставима с группой фрагментов позднеримской воинской ременной гарнитуры, распространенных главным образом на берегах реки Майн и на среднем Рейне. На Западе известно множество изображения конских головок на ременной гарнитуре, тогда как на Севере и Юго-Востоке они появляются только на деталях конской упряжи. Эти факты также указывают на отсутствие нормальной базы для сравнительного анализа.

Даже орнаментация в виде отпечатков штампа, характерный элемент вещей из Сёсдалы, – недостаточный материал для анализа, так как она была чрезвычайно популярна и потому широко распространена в конце IV – начале V в. Причем и в этом случае обнаруживаются различия между Востоком и Западом. В среднем Подунавье (и к востоку от него) штампованным орнаментом декорированы некоторые фибулы со щитком, сделанные из серебра и плакированные золотым листом, на который крепились вставки из драгоценных камней. В этом регионе штампованный орнамент известен, главным образом, на церемониальной конской амуниции типа «Унтерзибенбрунн», а также на щитках нескольких пряжек. На Севере же имеются фибулы и фрагменты церемониальной конской узды, украшенные штампованным орнаментом. На Западе известны лишь единичные фибулы с декором этого типа. Большинство находок со штампованным орнаментом в данном регионе – это позднеримские воинские пояса. Кроме того, важен один из типов гривен («Велп»), известных по горизонту кладов на территории современных Нидерландов и в северо-западной Германии. Выполненные в технике литья, они очень тонкие и напоминают листовое золото. В их декоре отмечены практически все виды штампов, известные в Уен-

терзибенбрунне и Сёсдале. Эти гривны указывают на связи между разными регионами.

К сожалению, хорошего решения, которое позволило бы описать развитие «стиля Сёсдала», не существует. Мы видим горизонт разных предметов со штампованным орнаментом, образованным сопоставимыми мотивами. Вероятнее всего, он возник в результате формирования пограничья Позднеримской империи. Если назвать этот стиль «Сёсдала–Унтерзибенбрунн–Велп», то представление о нем станет шире.

Подписи к иллюстрациям

Рис. 1. Гундремминген (округ Гюнцбург, Германия), позднеримский бург Бюргле. Зажим от конской узды из медного сплава. Масштаб 1:1 (по: Bersu 1964 pl. 8: 1–5).

Рис. 2. Нёйи-ле-Дижон (департамент Кот-д'Ор, Франция). Погребение 1857 г. – 1) Удила, железо. – 2) Умбон, железо, плакированное позолоченным серебряным листом. – 3) Стеклянная чаша. (По: Baudot 1857–1860: 294–295).

Рис. 3. Треугольники, схематически показывающие связи между тремя упомянутыми в этой статье регионами в первой половине V в. – 1) Регионы и «политический контекст». – 2) Характеристики конской упряжи. – 3) Вещи с парными протомами коней. – 4) Основные декоративные техники и их носители. (Графика Михаеля Обера, Римско-германский центральный музей в Майнце).

Рис. 4. 1) Наконечник ремня с протомами коней, позолоченное серебро, из Бабенхаузена (округ Дармштадт-Дибург). Масштаб 1:1 (по: Lindenschmit 1870 fasc. XII, pl. 6: 4–5). – 2) Поясная гарнитура, серебро, с городища Эренбюрг (Форхгайм, округ Форхгайм), с. Масштаб 2:3 (по: Böhme 1977: 16, fig. 3).

Рис. 5. Карта распространения наконечников ремней с протомами коней (●) и поясных накладок типа «Эренбюрг–Жамуань" (◆) (карта Моники Вебер, Римско-германский центральный музей в Майнце, по: Böhme 1977: 22, fig. 7 и Böhme 2008: 372, fig. 3).

Рис. 6. Вещи со штампованным орнаментом. Масштаб 1:1. – 1) Фибула из Бруаребакки (Вестергётланд; по: Åberg 1924:14, fig. 34. – 2) Подвеска от конской упряжи из Веннебо (Вестергётланд; по: Werner 1981: 251. fig. 14b). – 3) Фрагмент фибулы из Хостенторпа (Зеландия; по: Werner 1981: 251, fig. 14c).

Рис. 7. Позднеримские поясные накладки со штампованным орнаментом. 1–2) Монсо-ле-Нёф (департамент Эсн). 3–5) Тонгринн (провинция Намюр). Масштаб 3:4 (по: Böhme 1974 pl. 108: 1–3; 129: 2. 5).

Рис. 8. Вещи с рядами линзовидных оттисков штампа чередующихся с мотивом точки в круге. – 1) Финерсторп (Вестергётланд; по: Werner 1981: 251, fig. 14a). – 2) городище Веттенбург (Урпхар, район Майн-Шпессарт; по: Neubauer 2007: 34: 2). – 3) Альцай (округ Альцай-Вормс; по: Lindenschmit 1900 pl. 12: 2b). – 4) «Рейнгессен» (по: Lindenschmit 1870 fasc. II, pl. 6: 6).

Рис. 9. Зона распространения вещей с рядами линзовидных отпечатков штампа, чередующихся с мотивом точки в круге. – 1) Поясные накладки. – 2) Фибулы. 3) – Конская упряжь. 4) – Гривны. (По: Neubauer 2007: 114. fig. 30, с дополнениями Моники Вебер, Римско-германский центральный музей в Майнце).

Рис. 10. Велп, клад 1851 г. с гривнами, украшенными штампованным орнаментом (по: Pleyte 1889 pl. VII).

Рис. 11. Обкладки устья ножен меча. – 1) Лидольсхайм (община Деттенхайм, округ Карлсруэ). – 2) Финнерсторп (Вестергётланд). – 3) Идесхайм (округ Битбург–Прюм). – 4) Площадь Вихмаркт в Трире. – 5) Нидам Id (Ютландия). – 6). Нидам IV. – Разные масштабы. – 1) По: Gross 2010: 680, fig. 3. – 2) По: Nordqvist 2005: 229, fig. 5: 3. – 3–4) Фото Т. Цюмера (Генеральная дирекция культурного наследия Земли Рейнланд-Пфальц, Региональный музей в Трире). – 5–6) По: Jørgensen & Vang Petersen 2003: 273, 281.

Chapter 15

The Sösdala finds in the perspective of Central and South-Eastern Europe

Michel Kazanski & Anna Mastykova

A group of horse tack ornaments, with an engraved or stamped decoration, similar to the mounts discovered at Sösdala, is attested in the "princely" context of the Hun era in Central and Eastern Europe. These are tombs, treasures and isolated discoveries in both nomadic and sedentary environments from Jakuszowice, Kačin, Untersiebenbrunn, Bar and Coşoveni de Jos. These ornaments have common features, but each of them has its individual character and was probably crafted on demand. The Sösdala headstall mounts are part of a large batch of items, usually grouped under the name of Sösdala style, although the use of this term remains subject to discussion. This type of horse tack is attested in a large area from the Middle Danube to the region of Dnieper right bank. The Scandinavian horse ornaments and those of Central and Eastern Europe do not form the same stylistic group, but have the same Roman prototypes and are two parallel lines of shared prestigious fashion among barbaric military elites. Their important place in "princely" rituals is obvious and, most likely, due to Eastern cultural influences, from the steppe and Eastern Germanic environment.

Kazanski, M. & Mastykova, A. 2017. The Sösdala finds in the perspective of Central and South-Eastern Europe. In: Fabech, C. & Näsman, U. (eds). *The Sösdala horsemen – and the equestrian elite of fifth century Europe.* Jutland Archaeological Society.

A group of horse tack ornaments, with an engraved or stamped decoration, similar to the finds of Sösdala, is attested in the "princely" context of the Hunnic era in Central and Eastern Europe. These are tombs, treasures and isolated discoveries from Jakuszowice (fig. 1), Kačin (fig. 2), Untersiebenbrunn (fig. 3 and 4), Bar (fig. 5 and 6) and Coşoveni de Jos (fig. 7), in both nomadic and sedentary environments (Tejral 1973:13,14; Кухаренко 1982; *Germanen* 1987:171, 325; Godłowski 1995; Harhoiu 1998:52, 172, 173, Taf. 37, 38; *L'Or des princes barbares* 2000: n° 6, 9; Tejral

Fig. 1. Bridle mounts from Jakuszowice. Photo Muzeum Archeologiczne w Krakowie.

2011: 167–174; Levada 2011). Thus, items from the steppe civilisation have been found in the tomb of a military leader at Jakuszowice in Poland (Godłowski 1995), and the discoveries at Untersiebenbrunn, Kačin and Bar revealed Eastern Germanic clothing items. Moreover, the discovery in Untersiebenbrunn revealed Pontic items, linked to the mixed civilisation from north of the Black Sea – Greco-Roman on the one hand and Alano-Sarmatian on the other hand (Shchukin, Kazanski & Sharov 2006:200–204). The global feature of this "princely" material culture from Barbaricum, called the "Untersiebenbrunn group/horizon" does not allow a more precise identification of these finds. Thus, we can share Charlotte Fabech's and Ulf Näsman's point of view that the Sösdala finds and the similar discoveries are part of a "supra-regional" princely culture (Fabech & Näsman 2013).

The material culture of mounted barbarian elites

These ornaments have common features, such as cross-shaped appliqués, pelta-shaped pendants, those axe- or fishtail-shaped, horsehead-shaped decorations, bimetallic bits, sometimes with cheek bars with a curved end, and belt buckles with a triangular plate and a disc at the end. However, each of them has specificities, and was probably crafted on demand. Other items of a similar type, especially fibulae and belt buckles, are spread in a very large cultural frame and do not belong to a particular ethnic group. These are part of a prestigious fashion, encompassing barbarians from various origins, especially Germanic peoples, Huns, Alans and Balts, but also spread throughout the Roman Empire and in the Barbaro-Hellenic culture from the North Pontic region.

These ornaments are comparable to Scandinavian finds, the most significant being Sösdala, Fulltofta and Vennebo (Geisslinger 1967:139–140; Bitner-Wróblewska 2001:91, 92, fig. 18). The Scandinavian ornaments come from sacrificial places. Compared to the Central and Eastern Europe finds a difference is the occurrence of hard saddles with metallic mounts. These Scandinavian saddles do not have any direct parallel on the Continent, but their prototypes are known in Scandinavia during the late Roman era, the C2–C3 phases of the European Barbaricum chronology, i.e. roughly 250/260–350/370 (Ørsnes 1994:271–272; Fabech & Näsman 2013; cf. Näsman chapter 7). However, one must note that hard saddles with a metallic mounts existed in the Roman Empire at the same time (4th century), especially in Gaul, in the tomb of Sarry (fig. 11, Chew 1993).

This type of horse tack with engraved and stamped decoration is part of a large batch of items, usually grouped under the name of Sösdala style, although the use of this term remains subject to discussion (see lastly Bitner-Wróblewska 2001:89, 90). The type is attested in a large area from the Middle Danube to the right bank of Dnieper, even though other items of the same style – belt buckles, fibulae, pendants – are spread in an even wider area, from Northern Gaul to the Cimmerian Bosporus and the Don basin (lastly Tejral 2011:174–182; Levada 2011). Jaroslav Tejral gathered Continental "princely" finds, containing items with engraved and stamped decoration, under the

"Kačin-Coşoveni de Jos" group (Tejral 1973:13, 14, 61), belonging to wealthy barbarians of various origins. These finds are part of the "princely" Untersiebenbrunn horizon, from the end of the 4th to the first half of the 5th century, which characterises barbarian elites of various origins.

Horse tack with this type of ornamental mounts date from the Continental D2 period, i.e. in 380/400–440/450 (Tejral 2011:319–321) and are contemporary with Anna Bitner-Wróblewska's phase 2 of the Sösdala style, thus to approx. 375/400–430 (Fabech 1991; Bitner-Wróblewska 2001:118–120, pl. 59; Tejral 2011:174). This date, calculated for Barbaricum, can be confirmed by Roman iconographic data. Thus, the bridge mount from Tibble in Uppland (fig. 8:1, Andersson 1991) with Sösdala style decoration, is comparable, regarding its overall shape, to that of the sword (fig. 8:2) on the diptych from Monza (Kargopoltsev & Schukin 2006:289; for the identification cf. Kiilerich & Torp 1989 [Stilicho]; Bóna 1991:237, 238 [Aetius]).

The background of the mounted elite culture

We may assume that finds such as Untersiebenbrunn or Coşoveni de Jos can be related to Barbarians at the Roman border serving Rome. Other finds, farther from the Roman territory and in the area of the late Černjahov civilisation, as Kačin or Bar, show the "princely" civilisation of the Eastern Germanic satellites of the Huns (Shchukin, Kazanski & Sharov 2006:145–152; Tejral 2011:319–321). Finally, the Jakuszowice tomb most likely belongs to a Hunnic or Germanic leader (Godłowski 1995).

The special role of horse tack in the "princely" rituals is obvious. At the time of the Great Migrations, the presence of horse equipment or even of the horse in the elite tombs is very common and almost ubiquitous in privileged steppe tombs, among Huns and Alans. In a "princely" sedentary Barbaric environment, apart from Untersiebenbrunn and Bar, one may mention the burials of military leaders, containing bits and other horse tack items at Mundolsheim, in Alsace (fig. 9), and Lengueltóti, in Hungary (regarding these tombs, see Kazanski 1990; 1999; Kazanski & Ahmedov 2007). The equestrian equipment from the Hunnic era is sometimes attested in caches of "princely" tombs, especially among Alans, in the tumulus 1 of the necropo-

Fig. 2. Finds from Kačin. After Levada 2011 fig. 3.

lis in Brut-2, North Ossetia (Gabuev 2000). On the other hand, they are part of ritual deposits among the Huns on the Middle Danube, especially in Pécs-Uszög, Pannonhalma, and Szeged-Nágyszéksós (Tejral 2011:332). Tombs and sacrifice deposits, as in Scandinavia, are known, albeit rare and scarce, from the Late Roman period. One may mention the tomb of a leader in Kišpek, in North Caucasus (Бетрозов 1987:15) or the "military" tomb from Sarry already mentioned, in North Gaul (Chew 1993). Saddles in a

Chapter 15: The Sösdala finds in the perspective of Central and South-Eastern Europe

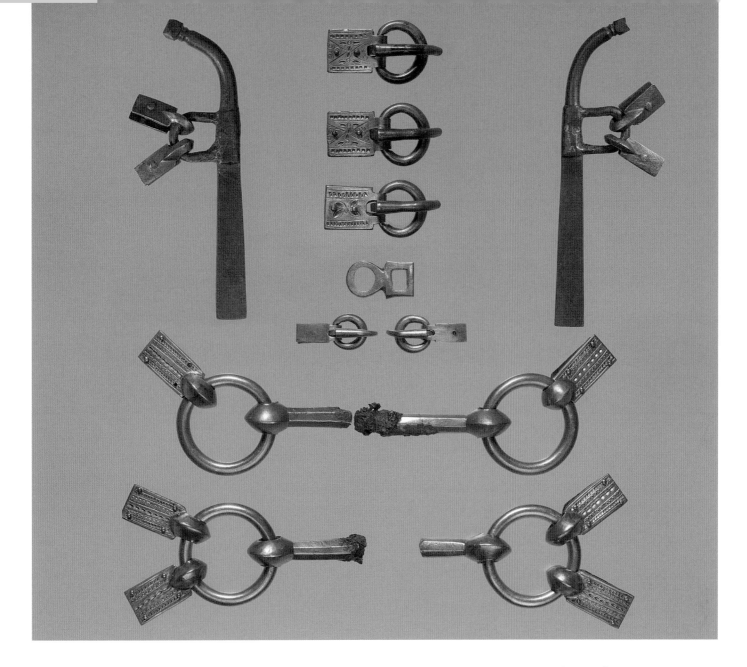

Fig. 3. Bridle mounts from Untersiebenbrunn, see also fig. 4. 1:1. Photo: Kunsthistorische Museum, Wien, KHM-Museumsverband, ref. 1525/2016.

Fig. 4. Bridle mounts from Untersiebenbrunn, see also fig. 3. 3:5. Photo: Kunsthistorische Museum, Wien, KHM-Museumsverband, ref. 1525/2016.

ritual context are more numerous in a steppe environment for the Hunnic era (Засецкая 1994:45–50). Apart from a "nomadic" context, tombs containing a saddle have been discovered among Alans in the North Caucasus, in the necropolis of Lermontovskaja Skala-2, tomb 10 (Рунич 1976),

in the Cimmerian Bosporus (Kertch), in tomb 165.104/ burial 5 and likely in tomb 6.1904 (Шкорпил 1907:49; 1909:3,4; Засецкая 1993: Appendix 3, № 17), in Mundolsheim, in Alsace (fig. 9; Kazanski & Akhmedov 2007) and in the "royal" necropolis of Ballana, in Nubia, in tomb 3, dated to 450/460 (Török 1988:134–144, pl. 94.286).

Tombs containing a horse are also well known in Europe, starting from the Hunnic era, in both steppe nomadic (several examples in Засецкая 1994) and sedentary environment. One must note that in some cases in Eastern Europe several horses were buried outside the burial chamber. We may mention tomb 118 in the Alan necropolis of Zaragiž in the North Caucasus (Atabiev 2000), the burial of a military leader in Lugi in Silesia, the "royal" tu-

steppe tombs for the Hunnic era in Solončanka, in South Ural, and on the other hand of the famous tomb of the Frankish king Childeric (Kazanski & Périn 2005).

We may assume that the presence of horse tack in a "princely" ritual context (tombs or sacrificial sites) and horse deposit in the burial are customs coming from Eastern Europe. Indeed, rich horse tack decorations are part of the items that are usually found in privileged tombs from the late Roman era in both the Alanic steppe (Kazanski 1995) and the Cimmerian Bosporus (Šarov 1994; 2003; Shchukin, Kazanski & Sharov 2006:93–100), but are rare in privileged funerary contexts in Central Europe (e.g. the tomb of the Baltic leader in Szwaicaria, in Suwalki's region, Antoniewicz, Kaczyński & Okulicz 1958). Most likely, during the Great Migration, the "princely" Eastern customs spread widely in Europe with the waves of Hunnic, Alanic and Germanic migrations. It is indeed difficult to determine precisely how these customs arrived in Scandinavia (cf. Fabech chapter 2). The late example of the Heruli (Procopius, *BG* II.15) reveals the existence of dynastic ties between Scandinavian and Danubian/East Germanic royal houses (cf. the Scandinavian [Ranian?]) king Roduulf at the court of Theodoric in Ravenna: Jordanes, *Getica* 24). Thus one can easily imagine that a prestigious fashion also spread in the earlier aristocratic environment. Since no written sources mention Scandinavian warriors serving Rome during the 5th century, it seems very unlikely that this can be explained by the presence of Scandinavian warriors in the Roman army, as is sometimes put forward.

Links between Scandinavian and Continental elites?

Maxim Levada ties the Sösdala style and its presence on the Continent to the spread of Scandinavian items (Levada 2011). We cannot share this point of view. Indeed, the parallels mentioned by Levada are obvious, but we do not know how the items spread – from North to South or from South to North? The concentration of items with stamped

mulus of Žuran in Moravia, tomb 23/11 in the necropolis of Sirenevaja Buhta in Eastern Crimea (Kazanski & Périn 2005:293–295) or the Abkhazian burials in Tsibilium 1 tomb 55, Tsibilium 2 tomb 383, Chapka-Cerkovnyj Holm-4 tomb 5, Chapka-Abgydzrahu tombs 23 and 29, Chapka-Ah'jacarahu tomb 3, Chapka-Apianča tomb 7/22 (Kazanski & Mastykova 2010:60). It should be noted that in two cases, in Žuran and in Sirenevaja Buhta, several horses were buried outside the funerary chamber. This reminds us, on the one hand, of burials of horses around privileged

Fig. 6. Finds from the treasure (?) of Bar, see also fig. 5. After Levada 2011 fig. 5.

decorations in Roman Pannonia may indicate the area of their manufacture (Bóna 1991:261, 262, Abb. 66; cf. Kontny & Mączyńska 2015:250–252, Abb. 10). Thus, it seems more reasonable to assume that they were crafted in Pannonia rather than in Scandinavia.

We think that the Scandinavian horse tack ornaments and those of Central and Eastern Europe do not form the same stylistic group, but have the same Roman prototypes and are two parallel lines of a shared prestigious fashion among barbaric military elites (Кухаренко 1982:240; Tejral 2011:329). Items with stamped decorations are considered as a production of Roman workshops, made on the demand of barbarian chiefs (Tejral 1973:13, 14, 16–18; Кухаренко 1982:240; Tejral 2011:170–174). Indeed, comparable decorations are present on belts in the Western Empire as part of the Late Roman "military" civilisation (e.g. Böhme 1974: Taf. 63:3, 4, 74:1, 2, 7, 90:7–10, 94:13 etc.; Sommer 1984: Taf. 2:5, 3:1, 4, 5, 5:2, 6:1–6 etc.).

Late Roman prototypes

Regarding the direct prototype of horse tack ornaments of the Sösdala type or that of Kačin-Coşoveni, one may mention the discoveries in South Germany, in Bürgle, near Grundremmingen (fig. 10:1–5). Mounts with stamped decorations were discovered in a level of destruction in the Roman fortress. This level is dated to *c.* 400 by coins from 378–383 (Bersu 1964:57, 98, Taf. 8:1–5; Böhme 1988: Abb. 6:7–10, 12). Horst-Wolfgang Böhme regards the mounts from Bürgle as coming from an East Germanic environment (Böhme 1988:28). However, the fortress of Bürgle is older than comparable finds among East Germanic peoples of the Kačin-Coşoveni group. On the other hand, elements of this style, especially C-shaped stamps, are known from the 4th century onwards, e.g. on Roman belts (Sommer 1984: Taf. 3:4,5, 4:3, 5:2 etc.), on a few Pontic items (Beck, Kazanski & Vallet 1988 fig. 2:6) and on those of the Černjahov civilisation (Щукин 1979:19).

Some horse tack parts with stamped decorations have Roman parallels and prototypes, especially the cruci-

form mount found in Bürgle (fig. 10:5). The pattern of the decorations in the shape of a pair of horse heads is well known on Roman belts (e.g. Sommer 1984:53–55) but also on bone combs in Roman tradition with a triangular back (Tejral 1973:17,18; 2011:182–185). The pendants shaped as an elongated trapezium or fishtail, found in Kačin (fig. 2), Coşoveni (fig. 7:5–8) and Untersiebenbrunn (fig. 3), are similar to those from Bürgle, as well as of those from Dahmker (fig. 10:7) on the Lower Elbe (Geisslinger 1961: Abb. 1:1,8).

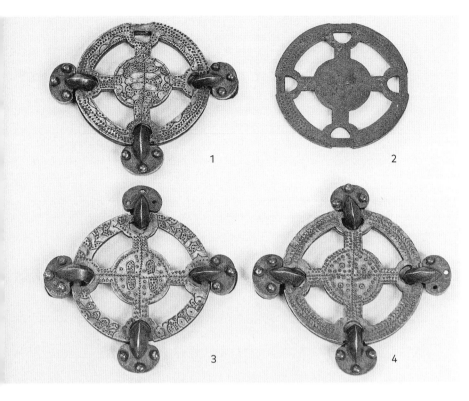

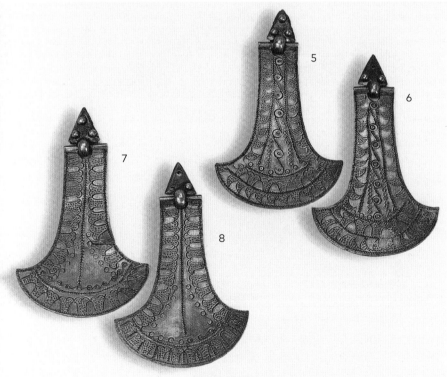

Fig. 7. Bridle mounts from the treasure of Coşovenii de Jos. Various scales. After L'Or des princes barbares 2000 № 6.

Moreover, pendants of the same shape but with a different type of decorations are attested in the late Roman fortress of Oescus on the Danube, and at Kerch in the Crimea, in the aristocratic tombs of 1841 and 24.06.1904 (Tejral 1973:17; Harhoiu 1998:52, 53; Tejral 2011:173–174). Direct prototypes can be found in the Bosporic and Alano-Sarmatian equestrian equipment (Малашев 2000 fig. 10:5, 11:5, 6, 12:Б.7, Г:4, Д:1, Е:5, etc.). However, the pendants found in Bürgle and Dahmker or those from Oescus were, according to their decoration, probably crafted in Roman workshops.

Pelta-shaped pendants are well known in South Scandinavia and on the Continent (Bitner-Wróblewska 2001:92–95, fig. 19), for example in the Jakuszowice tomb (fig. 1). Moreover, comparable pendants have been found at Bosau in Holstein, but these were part of a costume (Gebers & Hinz 1977: Abb. 5:1,2, 11:4). The pelta-shaped pendants have a Roman origin (Hagberg 1957). A pendant found in the Villa of Joannis, Italy (fig. 10:6), in a level with coins of the last quarter of the 4th century, can be mentioned as a possible Roman prototype (Rusconi 1979: tav. 8, 9; Kazanski 1999:302).

Snaffles with cheek bars with curved ends, attested at Untersiebenbrunn (fig. 4), are widely spread across Europe, especially in the Caspian region, but also in Asia Minor, at Sardis, and in Nubia, at Qustul (Akhmedov 2001; 2002). Prototypes are known from the territory of the Roman Empire, for example at Mainz and Cologne (Kazanski 1999:302).

Rectangular strap mounts typical of headstalls with stamped decorations (fig. 1, 2, 4, 5) have prototypes in the Ponto-Caspian region, particularly in the North Caucasus and in the Cimmerian Bosporus, but comparable mounts also exist in the Late Roman Empire (Kazanski 2011:91).

Horse tack strap buckles with an oval frame and a triangular plate with a disc at the end are attested in Kačin (fig. 2) and Sösdala, as well as in other finds of the Hunnic period, including in Árpás, Hungary (Tejral 2011: Abb. 165:3). Prototypes are well known in the 4th century in Gaul, in Italy, in the Danubian provinces and in Moesia (fig. 10:8–10, Vinski 1974:41, tab. 37:3–5,7; Sommer 1984:21,123, Taf. 1:9, 27:2; Tejral 2011: Abb. 188:7). These Roman strap buckles, or rather their imitations, are widely spread in Barbaricum, as far to the east as the Urals (Генинг 1979:98, 99; Кухаренко 1982:241, 243).

Finally, bimetallic bits (fig. 1, 2, 4, 5) are widely spread among both the nomadic and sedentary barbarians during the Hunnic period (Засецкая 1994:40, 41; Kazanski 1991:138, 139; Tejral 2011:169). They can be found on the territory of the Roman Empire, especially in Northern Italy (Kazanski 1991 fig. 9:12). One must note that bimetallic bits already existed in late Roman times as shown by the finds in the tomb from 1841 in Adžimuškaj in the Crimea (Šarov 1994: Abb. 3) and in offerings of military equipment in South Scandinavia as early as the 3rd century AD (Ørsnes 1994:234–235).

Conclusion

A group of horse tack ornaments, with an engraved or stamped decoration, close to the discovery of Sösdala, is attested in the "princely" context of the Hun era in Central and Eastern Europe. These are the tombs, treasures and isolated discoveries from Jakuszowice, Kačin, Untersiebenbrunn, Bar and Coşoveni de Jos, in both nomadic and sedentary environments. These ornaments have common features, but each of them has its own characteristics, and was probably crafted on demand. This type of horse tack mounts, with engraved and stamped decoration, is part of a large batch of items, usually grouped under the name of Sösdala style, although the use of this term remains subject to discussion. The type of decorated mounts mentioned above is attested in a large area from the Middle Danube to the region of the right bank of the Dnieper.

The Scandinavian horse tack ornaments and those of Central and Eastern Europe do not form the same stylistic group, but have the same Roman prototypes and represent parallel lines of the shared prestigious fashion among barbaric military elites. Thus, we can see that both the Scandinavian and Continental mount parts with stamped decorations represent two parallel lines of development of the equestrian equipment with Roman prototypes. Their important place in the "princely" ritual is obvious and, most likely, due to eastern cultural influences, from the steppe and Eastern Germanic environment.

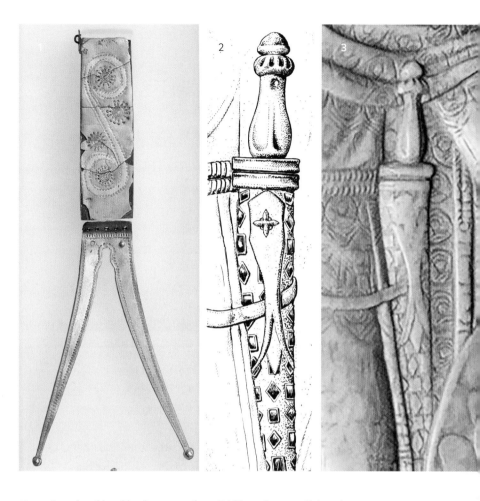

Fig. 8. Sword scabbard bridge mount from Tibble and its parallel on the diptych of Monza. 1) Tibble, SHM Stockholm inv.nr 5089;3:4, photo Gabriel Hildebrand. 2) bridge mount of Monza diptych, detail after Bóna 1991: 34, Abb. 11. 3) Dittico de Stilicone, Photo Museo e Tesoro del Duomo di Monza, detail after Conti 1999 nr 6.

Fig. 9. Finds from the tomb of Mundolsheim. Photo Musée archéologique de Strasbourg.

Chapter 15: The Sösdala finds in the perspective of Central and South-Eastern Europe

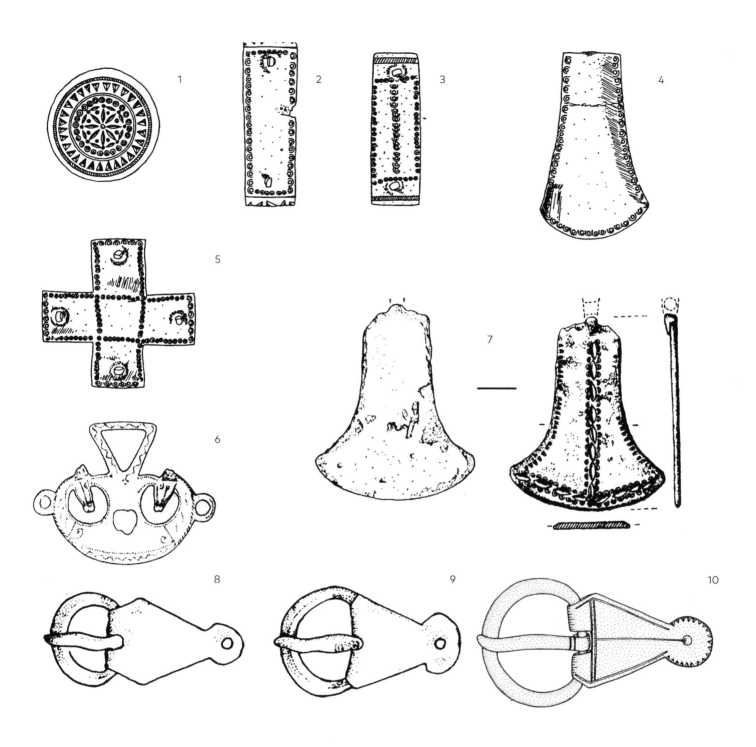

*Fig. 10. Roman prototypes of mounts from the offering at Sösdala. 1–5)
Bürgle, after Bersu 1964 Taf. 8.1–5; 6) Joannis, after Rusconi 1979 tav.
8, 9; 7) Dahmker, after Geisslinger 1961 Abb. 1.1,8; 8, 9) Dunaújváros,
after Vinski 1974 tab. 37.3,4; 10) Vermand, after Sommer 1984 Taf.2.9.*

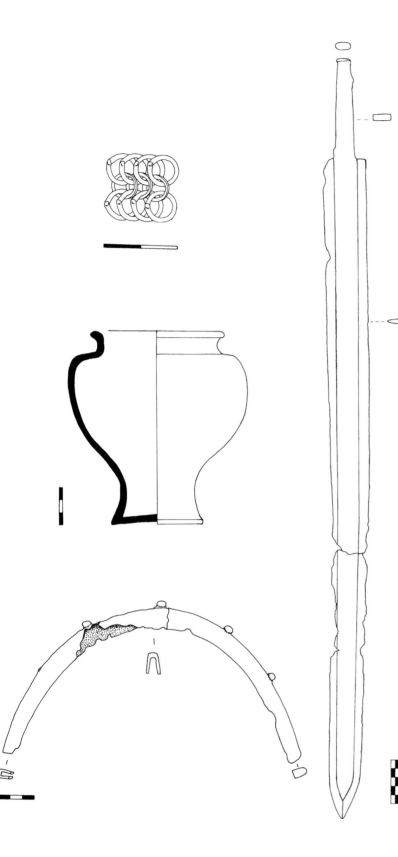

Fig. 11. Objects from the tomb of Sarry. After Chew 1993.

References

Akhmedov, I.R. 2001. New data about the origin of some constructive parts of the horse-harness of the Great Migration Period. In: Istvánovits, E. & Kulcsár, V. (eds). *International Connections of the Barbarians of the Carpathian Basin in the 1st -5th Centuries A.D.* Aszód/Nyíregyháza: 363–388.

Akhmedov, I.R. 2002. Cheek-pieces of harness with zoomorphic decorations in the Great Migrations period. In: Tejral, J. (ed.). *Probleme der frühen Merowingerzeit im Mitteldonauraum.* Brno: 11–30.

Andersson, K. 1991. "Tibblefyndet" – Neues Licht auf einem alten Grabfund im südwestlichen Teil Upplands, Schweden. *Studien zur Sachsenforschung:* 1–10.

Antoniewicz, J., Kaczyński, W. & Okulicz, J. 1958. Wyniki badań przeprowadzonych w 1956 roku na cmentarzysku kurhanowymw wiejsc. Szwajcaria, pow. Suwalki. *Wiadomości Archeologiczne* 25: 22–57.

Atabiev, B. 2000. Tombe 118. Zaragij, Naltchik (Caucase du Nord, République de Kabardino-Balkarie), Russie. In: *L'Or des princes barbares. Du Caucase à la Gaule Ve s. ap. J.-C.* Paris: 162–165.

Beck, F., Kazanski, M. & Vallet, F. 1988. La riche tombe de Kertch du Musée des Antiquités Nationales. *Antiquités Nationales* 20: 63–81.

Bersu, G. 1964. *Die spätrömische Befestigung Bürgle bei Grundremmingen.* Munich.

Bitner-Wróblewska, A. 2001 *From Samland to Rogaland. East-West connections in the Baltic basin during the Early Migration Period.* Warsaw.

Böhme, H.W. 1974. *Germanische Grabfunde des 4. bis 5. Jahrhunderts zwischen unterer Elbe und Loire.* Munich.

Böhme, H.W. 1988. Zur Bedeutung des spätrömischen Militärdienstes für die Stammesbildung der Bajuwaren. In: Dannheimer, H. & Dopsch, H. (eds) *Die Bajuwaren. Von Severin bis Tassilo 488–788.* Munich: 23–37.

Bóna I. 1991. *Das Hunnenreich.* Budapest.

Chew, H. 1993. Une sépulture militaire de l'époque romaine tardive à Sarry (Marne). In: Vallet F. & Kazanski M. (eds). *L'armée romaine et les Barbares du IIIᵉ au VIIᵉ siècle.* Saint-Germain-en-Laye: 313–321.

Conti, R. 1999 (1st ed. 1993). *Il tesoro. Guida alla conoscenza del Tesoro del Duomo di Monza.* Monza.

Fabech, C. 1991. Booty Sacrifices in Southern Scandinavia. A Reassessment. In: Garwood, P. (ed.). *Sacred and Profane.* Oxford: 88–99.

Fabech, C. & Näsman, U. 2013. A Lonely Rider? The Finding Place of the Sösdala Find and the Context of its Finds. In: Khrapunov, I. & Stylegar, F.-A.

(eds). *Inter Ambo Maria. Northern Barbarians from Scandinavia towards the Black Sea*. Kristiansand/Simferopol: 84–106.

Gabuev, T. 2000. Mobilier d'une tombe de cavalier. Brut, Ossétie du Nord, Russie. In: *L'Or des princes barbares. Du Caucase à la Gaule Vᵉ s. ap. J.-C.* Paris: 138–141.

Gebers, W. & Hinz, H. 1977. Ein Körpergrab der Völkerwanderungszeit aus Bosau, Ostholstein. *Offa* 34: 5–39.

Geisslinger, H. 1961. Frühvölkerwanderungszeitliches Zaumzeugzubehör von Dahmker, Kreis Herzogtum Lauenburg. *Offa* 17–18: 175–180.

Geisslinger, H. 1967. *Horte als Geschichtsquelle dargestellt an der völkerwanderungs- und merowingerzeitlichen Funden des südwestlichen Ostseeraumes.* Neumünster.

Germanen, Hunnen und Awaren. Schätze der Völkerwanderungszeit. 1987. Nuremberg.

Godłowski, K. 1995. Das "Fürstengrab" des 5. Jhs. und der "Fürstensitz" in Jakuszowice in Südpolen. In: Vallet, F. & Kazanski, M. (eds). *La noblesse romaine et les chefs barbares du IIIᵉ au VIIᵉ siècle.* Saint-Germain-en Laye: 155–180.

Hagberg, U.E. 1957. Folkvandringstida hängprydnader. *Tor* 3: 108–120.

Harhoiu, R. 1998. *Die frühe Völkerwanderungszeit in Rumänien.* Bucharest.

Jordanes *Getica = Iordanis de origine actibusque Getarum.* Giunta, Fr. & Grillone, A. (eds). Rome 1991.

Kargopoltsev, S. & Schukin, M. 2006. Nouvelles découvertes d'armes occidentales de l'époque romaine tardive en Russie du Nord-Ouest. In: Delestre, X., Kazanski, M. & Périn, P. (eds). *De l'Âge du fer au haut Moyen Age. Archéologie funéraire, princes et élites guerrières.* Saint-Germain-en-Laye: 288–294.

Kazanski, M. 1990. La tombe de cavalier de Mundolsheim (Bas-Rhin). In: Marin J.-I. (ed.). *Attila, les influences danubiennes dans l'ouest de l'Europe au Vᵉ siècle.* Caen: 57–71.

Kazanski, M. 1991. A propos des armes et des éléments de harnachement "orientaux" en Occident à l'époque des Grandes Migrations (IVᵉ–Vᵉ s.). *Journal of Roman Archaeology* 4: 123–139.

Kazanski, M. 1995. Les tombes des chefs alano-sarmates du IVe siècle dans les steppes pontiques. In: Vallet F. & Kazanski M. (eds). *La noblesse romaine et les chefs barbares du IIIe au VIIe siècle.* Saint-Germain-en-Laye: 189–205.

Kazanski, M. 1999. Les tombes des chefs militaires de l'époque hunnique. In: Fischer, T., Precht, G. & Tejral, J. (eds). *Germanen beiderseits des spätantiken Limes.* Cologne/Brno: 293–316.

Kazanski, M. 2011. Kishpek, Ekazhevo and Varpelev. On the Problem of Pontic-Scandinavian Relations in the Late Roman Period. In: Khrapunov, I. & Stylegar, F.-A. (eds). *Inter Ambo Maria. Contacts between Scandinavia and Crimea in the Roman Period.* Kristiansand/Simferopol: 91–101.

Kazanski, M. & Akhmedov, I. 2007. La tombe de Mundolsheim (Bas-Rhin). Un chef militaire nomade au service de Rome. In: Tejral, J. (ed.). *Barbaren im Wandel. Beiträge zur Kultur- und Identitätsumbildung in der Völkerwanderungszeit.* Brno: 173–197.

Kazanski, M. & Mastykova, A. 2010. Les tombes de chevaux chez les fédérés de l'Empire d'Orient sur la côte est de la mer Noire (IIᵉ–VIᵉ s.). In: Urbaniak, A. et alii (eds). *Terra Barbarica.* Łódź/Warsaw: 57–71.

Kazanski, M. & Périn, P. 2005. La tombe de Childéric: un tumulus oriental? *Travaux et Mémoires* 15: 287–298.

Killerich B. & Torp H. 1989. *Hic est: hic Stilicho.* The Date and Interpretation of a Notable Diptych. *Jahrbuch des Deutschen Archäologischen Instituts* 104: 319–371.

Kontny, B. & Mączyńska, M. 2015. Ein Kriegergrab aus der frühen Völkerwanderungszeit von Juszkowo in Nordpolen. In: Ruhmann C. & Brieske V. (eds). *Dying Gods – Religious beliefs in northern and eastern Europe in the time of Christianisation.* Hannover/Stuttgart: 241–262.

Levada, M. 2011. To Europe via the Crimea. On possible migration routes of the northern people in the Great Migration period. In: Khrapunov, I. & Stylegar, F.-A. (eds). *Inter Ambo Maria. Contacts between Scandinavia and the Crimea in the Roman Period.* Kristiansand/Simferopol: 115–137.

L'Or des princes barbares. Du Caucase à la Gaule Vᵉ siècle après J.-C. 2000. Paris.

Ørsnes, M. 1994. Zaumzeugfunde des 1.–8. Jhrh. nach Chr. in Mittel- und Nordeuropa. *Acta Archaeologica* 64/2, 1993: 183–292.

Procopius, III–V. *History of the Wars, Books V–VIII* (éd. H.W. Dewing, Loeb Classical Library). London-Cambridge (Massachusetts), 1962–1968.

Rusconi, M.J. 1979. Scavo di una villa rustica a Joannis. *Aquileia Nostra* 50: 2–119.

Šarov, O.V. 1994. Ein reiches Pferdgeschirr aus Kerč. In: von Carnap-Bornheim, C. (ed.). *Beiträge zu römischer und barbarischer Bewaffnung in den ersten vier nachchristlichen Jahrhunderten.* Lublin/Marburg: 417–428.

Šarov, O. 2003. Die Gräber des sarmatischen Hochadels von Bospor. In: Carnap-Bornheim, C. von (ed.). *Kontakt-Kooperation-Konflikt. Germanen und Sarmaten zwischen dem 1. und dem 4. Jahrhundert nach Christus.* Neumünster: 35–64.

Shchukin, M., Kazanski, M. & Sharov, O. 2006. *Des Goths aux Huns: Le Nord de la mer Noire au Bas–Empire et a l'époque des Grandes Migrations.* Oxford.

Sommer, M. 1984. *Die Gürtel und Gürtelbeschläge des 4. und 5. Jahrhunderts im römischchen Reich.* Bonn.

Tejral, J. 1973. *Mähren im 5. Jahrhundert.* Prague.

Tejral, J. 2011. *Einhemische und Fremde. Das norddanubische Gebiet zur Zeit der Völkerwanderungszeit.* Brno.

Török, L. 1988. *Late Antique Nubia. History and archaeology of the southern neighbour of Egypt in the 4th–6th c. A.D.* Budapest.

Vinski, Z. 1974. Kasnoantički starosjediosci u salonitanskoj regiji prema arheološkoj ostavšini predslavenskog supstrata. *Vjesnik za arheologiju i historiju dalmatinsku* 69: 5–86.

Бетрозов, Р.Ж. 1987. Курганы гуннского времени у селения Кишпек. In: Кузнецов В.А. (отв. ред.). *Археологические исследования на новостройках Кабардино-Балкарии. Т. 3.* Нальчик: 11–39.

Генинг, В.Ф. 1979. Хронология поясной гарнитуры I тысячелетия н.э. (по материалам могильников Прикамья). *Краткие Сообщения Института Археологии* 158: 96–105.

Засецкая, И.П.1993. Материалы Боспорского некрополя второй половины IV–первой половины V вв. *Материалы по Археологии, Истории и Этнографии Таврии* 3: 23–105.

Засецкая, И.П. 1994. *Культура кочевников южнорусских степй в гуннскую эпоху (конец IV–V вв.* Санкт-Петербург.

Кухаренко, Ю.В. 1982. О Качинской находке V в. In: А.К. Амброз, Ф. Эрдели (отв. ред.). *Древности эпохи великого переселения народов V–VIII веков.* Москва: 234–244.

Малашев, В.Ю. 2000. Периодизация ременных гарнитур позднесарматского времени. In: Гугуев Ю.К. (отв. ред.). *Сарматы и их соседи на Дону* (Материалы и исследования по археологии Дона 1). Ростов-на-Дону, 194–232.

Рунич, А.П. 1976. Захоронение вождя эпохи раннего средневековья из Кисловодской котловины. *Советская Археология* 3, 256–266.

Шкорпил, В.В. 1907. Отчет о раскопках в Керчи в 1904 г. *Известия Императорской Археологической Комиссии* 25, 1–66.

Шкорпил, В.В. 1909. Отчет о раскопках в Керчи в 1905 г. *Известия Императорской Археологической Комиссии* 30, 1–50.

Щукин, М.Б. 1979. К вопросу о верхней хронологической границе черняховской культуры. *Краткие Сообщения Института Археологии* 158, 17–22.

Резюме

Находки в Сёсдала и их параллели в Центральной и Юго-Восточной Европе

Михаил Казанский и Анна Мастыкова

В «княжеских» погребениях и кладах гуннского времени в Центральной и Восточной Европе (Качин, Бар, Якушовице, Унтерзибенбрунн, Кошовени де Жос) представлены элементы конского снаряжения, украшенные гравированным и штампованным декором и имеющие параллели в находке из Сёсдалы. Эти детали конской узды встречены в закрытых комплексах, связанных как с оседлыми так и кочевыми варварами, и распространенных на широком пространстве от Нижнего и среднего Дуная до Днепровского Правобережья. Каждый набор имеет свою специфику и вероятно изготовлялся индивидуально, на заказ.

Престижные предметы конского убора с гравированным и штампованным декором принадлежат изделиям так называемого стиля Сёсдала, характерного для эпохи Великого переселения народов. Впрочем само содержание этого термина остается предметом обсуждения. Другие предметы того же стиля – поясные пряжки, фибулы, подвески – известны в широкой зоне от Северной Галлии до Боспора Киммерийского и бассейна Дона. Ярослав Тейрал объединил континентальные «княжеские» находки гуннского времени с вещами, украшенными гравированным и штампованным декором в группу «Качин-Кошовени-де-Жос». Данные находки являются частью «княжеского» горизонта Унтерзибенбрунн (конец IV – первая половина V вв.), характеризующего варварские элиты различного происхождения. Можно предположить, что находки в римском пограничье, такие как Унтерзибенбрунн или Кошовени де Жос принадлежат варварам на римской службе, в то время как находки в глубине Барбарикума, например Бар или Качин на Правобережной Украине, отражают культуру восточногерманских вассалов гуннов. Наконец, погребение в Якушовице, в Южной Польше, может принадлежать как знатному гунну, так и местному варварскому предводителю, связанному с гуннами.

Особая роль конского снаряжения в "княжеском" контексте очевидна. В эпоху Великого переселения народов, наличие конского снаряжения или коня в элитных погребениях отмечается повсеместно в Европе и видимо связано со степным влиянием. Скандинавские и «континентальные» предметы конской экипировки представляют собой две параллельные линии общей престижной моды варварских военных элит и скорее всего являются продукцией разных

ателье, но восходят к общим римским прототипам. Такие прототипы хорошо известны по находкам на территории Римской империи, например в Бюргле (Гундремминген). Концентрация вещей со штампованным и гравированным декором в позднеримской Паннонии может указывать на область производства «континентальных» конских уборов группы Качин-Кошовени-де-Жос. Что касается формы отдельных предметов, составляющих «княжеский» конский убор гуннского времени в Барарикуме, то они также имеют прямые римские прототипы.

Подписи к иллюстрациям

Рис. 1. Предметы конского снаряжения из погребения Якушовице. Фото Археологического музея, Краков.

Рис. 2. Находки из клада Качин. По Levada 2011 fig. 3.

Рис. 3. Предметы конского снаряжения из погребения Унтерзибенбрунн (см. также рис. 4). Фото Музея Истории Искусств, Вена, KHM-Museumsverband, ref. 1525/2016.

Рис. 4. Предметы конского снаряжения из погребения Унтерзибенбрунн (см. также рис. 3). Фото Музея Истории Искусств, Вена, KHM-Museumsverband, ref. 1525/2016.

Рис. 5. Находки из клада (?) Бар (см. также рис. 6). По Levada 2011 fig. 6.

Рис. 6. Находки из клада (?) Бар (см. также рис. 5). По Levada 2011 fig. 5.

Рис. 7. Находки из клада Кошовени де Жос. По L'Or des princes barbares 2000. № 6.

Рис. 8. Портупейная скоба из Тиббле и её параллель с диптиха из Монцы. – А) Тиббле, Исторический Музей, Стокгольм, inv.nr 5089; фото Габриэля Хильдебрандта. – В) портупеная скоба на диптихе из Монцы, деталь, по Bóna 1991: 34, Abb. 11. – С) Диптих Стилихона, фото Музея сокровищ собора в Монце, по Conti 1999 nr 6.

Рис. 9. Находки из погребения Мундольсхейм, Фото Археологического музея, Страсбург.

Рис. 10. Римские прототипы элементов конского снаряжения клада Сёздала. – 1-5) Бюргле, по Bersu 1964, Taf. 8.1-5; – 6) Иоаннис, по Rusconi 1979, tav. 8, 9; – 7) Дамкер, по Geisslinger 1961, Abb. 1.1,8; – 8, 9) Дунайварош, по Vinski 1974, tab. 37.3,4; – 10) Верман, по Sommer 1984, Taf.2.9.

Рис. 11. Вещи из погребения в Сарри. По Chew 1993, pl. 4.

Chapter 16

The material culture of 5th century returning veterans

Svante Fischer

The strongest archaeological evidence for the presence of Scandinavians inside the Western Empire in the 5th century is discussed. The purpose is to address a set of questions related to the return of military veterans from the Continent to the Scandinavian periphery during the 5th century. The key issue here is to discuss whether it is possible to prove the very existence of returning warriors in the Migration Period material culture in Scandinavia by means of die-identical coins found in Continental coin hoards. It is argued that numismatic evidence in the form of die-linked solidi allows us to track at least four different payments in which Scandinavians received gold coins from the main actors in the Late Roman military state apparatus, which were then brought back to Scandinavia. Two or three of these payments in the years AD 465–476 can be described as direct from Italy to South Scandinavia, while an earlier payment after AD 435 can be explicitly linked to the former limes area of Pannonia by means of die-links to solidus hoards found in Slovakia and Hungary, and may be classified as a payment through mid-level intermediaries.

Fischer, S. 2017. The material culture of 5th century returning veterans. In: Fabech, C. & Näsman, U. (eds). *The Sösdala horsemen – and the equestrian elite of fifth century Europe.* Jutland Archaeological Society.

What does the material culture of returning veterans look like in South Scandinavia? It has previously been argued that there must have been stations or provisions ready for private military companies along the great Polish rivers and in the Tatra Mountains prior to the arrival in the former limes area (Herschend 1980). Moreover, it has been argued that these units must have moved on horseback, requiring some kind of agreement with local breeders. Once on horseback, the units could move at an exceptional pace, as evident during World War I (Fischer 2005). It thus very tempting to connect 5th century cavalry equipment in Scania and Västergötland to similar finds on the Continent, and the solidus hoards in Slovakia and Hungary to those of Öland and Bornholm.[1]

A major source-critical problem with deposits of Migration Period cavalry equipment in South Scandinavia remains. It cannot be conclusively proven that equipment was imported as entire sets, or that domestically manufactured kits ever left the region and were brought back again. The link between returning veterans and cavalry equipment is thus quite uncertain. The decoration and style are similar, but not identical, to comparable finds on the Continent. In addition, it cannot be excluded that domestic warfare and ritual depositions were carried out by means of locally manufactured equipment imitating Continental styles (cf. Fabech & Näsman chapter 17).

By contrast, by far the strongest empirical evidence for returning warriors comes from the die-linked Late Roman solidi that have been recovered on Öland and Bornholm.[1] The recorded solidus types show a distinct relationship between settlement patterns and chronology, which cannot be explained by means of trade or secondary circulation, given that the material can be compared to a database of some 7,300 individual solidi and some 23,000 solidi in hoards (Fischer *et al.* 2011; Fischer 2014b; Fischer & Lind 2015).

Theory

The theoretical point of departure of this paper is very simple. It has to do with how people in the past assessed risk in relation to profit and power. It seems reasonable to assume that if people from Scandinavia decided that something was to be gained from investing in a military expedition to the Continent, then when returning they also brought new things back home that would enable them to maximise the return that a homecoming entailed. It is equally reasonable to assume that there was a distinct motive for the return. It had to do with power and ownership. Second and third sons and even the landless among the returning veterans could hope for an increased share of power back in the Scandinavian periphery. This created new challenges within the intellectual realm of ideas and experiences. Yet it also caused a considerable obstacle in very concrete terms (cf. Fabech & Näsman chapter 17).

The return of the veterans meant that all of a sudden there was a distinct new material culture that could only be attained in three ways: 1) by becoming part of the homecomers' network, 2) by going to the Continent oneself, or 3) by depriving a homecomer of his owner-

ship of this new material culture. It follows that an inevitable confrontation and subsequent rejection or integration of these new matters became a real issue for those in charge of the old power structure back home. There are essentially two extremes sides of this phenomenon. Either the society back home makes a concentrated effort to embrace the homecomers. If so, the new ideas and material culture have to become integrated or assimilated. The other scenario is an outright conflict where the leading representatives of the old order have to terminate the returning veterans with extreme prejudice, and either ban or usurp the new ideas and culture and transform the latter to their own needs. It seems reasonable to think that a number of intermediate solutions were attempted, but that the latter conflict scenario was quite often the only option available to the old order (Fabech 2011:34; Näsman 2012:9).

Material

As of September 2016 there are some 365 solidi known from Öland alone. This is roughly a third of the known material from all of Scandinavia (Fischer *et al.* 2011). Solidus hoards on Öland typically date to the period AD 456–480, with only 11 coins struck after AD 476 (Fagerlie 1967). Despite a continuous growth of solidus finds in recent times, this situation has not changed at all in the last half century (Fischer *et al.* 2011; Fischer 2014b; Fischer & López Sánchez 2016). It is thus relatively certain that the influx of solidi to Öland that one can follow with the strict criteria of the empirical method discussed above only lasted one or two generations. In a first analysis, one can see that there are three basic chronological parts, one in the years 435–451, one in the period 451–465, and a final period lasting until the fall of the Western Empire (fig. 1). The subsequent analysis of die-linked coin types on Öland shows that were three different waves of solidi arriving on the island, *c.* AD 465, 473 and 480. The die-linked solidus material divides the island into two distinct parts. In this period, the first wave arrived on the western side of the island around Björnhovda in Torslunda parish (fig. 2). The second and third waves arrived mainly in the parishes of Stenåsa and Sandby on the eastern side of the island (fig. 3).

Network analysis

Behind the solidus finds one can retrace a distribution network of actors, where geographical distance is not the key issue but instead the number of connections between nodes (Latour 2005). This means that the distance between deposited hoards is irrelevant, what matters is how connected the owners must have been at some point. This perspective stems from a long tradition of research on late 5th century Roman solidi in Migration Period Scandinavia as a comparative counterpart to contemporary solidus hoards in Italy. (A succinct historiography of the research on Scandinavian solidus finds from the late 19th century leading up to 1967 can be found in Herschend 1980; the subsequent literature is discussed below.) The comparison between Italy and Scandinavia is inevitable as there are no other regions anywhere else on the European Continent that share so many specific features related to the solidi of the last western emperors.

The fundamental questions of this research tradition can be summarised in two main questions, each raising a following question: why are solidi found outside the Empire, and what does this mean? When and how were they brought to Scandinavia? Basically, there are two schools of thought (referred to below as "the fur trade hypothesis, and "the wage labour hypothesis") that have attempted to explain the commanding presence of late 5th century solidi in South Scandinavia, but neither school has ever attempted to trace the origin of the solidi from all the way out to the periphery back to the imperial mint by means of die-identities as will be done in this paper.

The fur trade hypothesis

The first cohesive theory on the origin of 5th century Roman solidi in Scandinavia as a result of trade was that of Hildebrand (1882). Based on the catalogue work of Janse (1922), Bolin (1926:310) soon thereafter presented an interesting theory that sought to balance trade and warfare. Bolin argued that coins reached Barbaricum by means of Roman trade during times of peace. However, Bolin also believed that there were harsh periods of internal warfare in Barbaricum, when no Roman trade was possible. These periods of inter-barbarian warfare also forced coins to be hoarded and hidden in the ground only to be abandoned.

Fig. 1. Three different waves of solidi arriving on Öland. Blue = hoards with coins struck up to the reign of Marcian (AD 451–457), but mainly from the reigns of Theodosius II (AD 408–450) and Valentinian III (AD 425–455). Green = hoards with coins mainly belonging to the reign of Libius Severus (AD 461–465) and the early reign of Leo I (AD 457–474). Red = hoards with coins mainly belonging to the late reign of Leo I (AD 457–474), the first reign of Zeno (AD 474–476) and Western emperors from Anthemius (AD 467–472) to Romulus Augustus (AD 475–476). Illustration Svante Fischer after Herschend 1980.

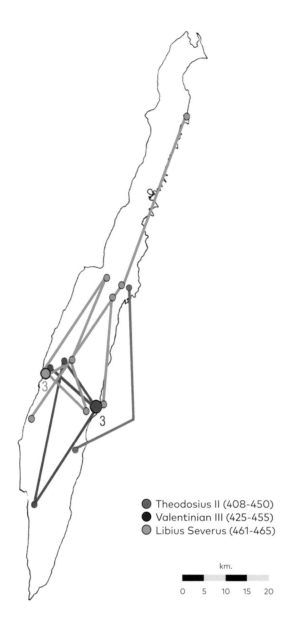

● Theodosius II (408-450)
● Valentinian III (425-455)
○ Libius Severus (461-465)

km.

0   5   10   15   20

● Leo I (457-474)
● Anthemius (467-472)
● Glycerius (473-474)
○ Romulus Augustus (475-476)

km.

0   5   10   15   20

Fig. 2. The first payment in Italy, c. AD 462–465. Illustration Svante Fischer.

Fig. 3. The second and third payments in Italy, c. AD 466–476. Illustration Svante Fischer.

This is an attractive explanation that, while it offers a totality, still remains extremely difficult to verify. Forty years later, Fagerlie (1967) partially followed this line, but with an important reservation: she thought that the key period of peace was that of Theoderic and the Ostrogoths in Italy in the last decade of the 5th century. Moreover, she further argued that solidi subsequently did circulate in trade within a closed Scandinavian circuit, but that solidus hoards were also taken as war booty from Gotland and brought to Helgö. Some 30 years later, Metcalf (1995, 2010) and later Jonsson (2003) argued forcefully for fur trade as the primary reason for the solidus import to Scandinavia, based on their numismatic research on the later Viking Age trade routes to Central Asia and the Middle East.

It should be pointed out that the fur trade theory suffers from the absence of concrete evidence besides a short mention by Jordanes in his *Getica*, stating that amber and fur came from the Baltic (Fagerlie 1967; Metcalf 2010:570). Instead it has to rely on a hypothetical distribution pattern for the exchange of Scandinavian fur for Roman solidi. The question of transport is a key issue here. Following Metcalf (1995:413–441, sec. 4), fur would have been gathered by trappers in the highland forests in the inner parts of Småland, brought to an emporium on the Kalmar Sound, transferred to Öland (presumably to Färjestaden or thereabouts) before reaching Italy. As the 5th century solidus was extremely valuable, the fur trade volume must have been immense to equate the corresponding number of solidi brought back to South Scandinavia.

To prove the fur trade hypothesis, one would have to show why, when and how the fur trade began. It would also be necessary to show if, when, why and how the payment shifted from other currencies or goods to solidi. Thereafter, it must be explained why the customers in Italy paid the Scandinavians with certain types of solidi that fit into long chains of die-links but that are fairly rare elsewhere. Finally, it must be shown when, why and how this fur trade stopped. This is the case, as it follows from the chronology of the Ölandic solidus hoards and from the fur trade hypothesis that huge loads of fur must have been brought down to Italy in trading convoys at the very same time as the one of biggest military enterprises was being carried out by the Roman Empire in AD 468–471, and as the situation in Italy was extremely tense since the military expeditions to Africa and Spain were followed by civil war.

The fur trade theory does not answer any of these questions by means of empirical evidence. It hence is most likely that the fur trade hypothesis remains just that. Rather, there is everywhere reason to suspect that the theory is caught in the constraints of an anachronistic perspective. To be more precise, it would seem that the fur trade theory as formulated by Metcalf (1995) is guilty of prematurely imposing its understanding of the later Viking Age economy on to the Scandinavian Migration Period, essentially in order to get rid of an earlier problem that does not match well with the idea of continuous trade and slow and peaceful monetisation of Scandinavian prehistoric society. But it would still seem that the turbulent 5th century and the nature of the Late Roman solidus economy does not integrate itself into a progressive linear development from Antiquity to the Middle Ages.

The wage labour hypothesis

The second theory, first outlined by Arne (1919), holds the view that 5th century solidi hoards outside the Empire are unlikely to be the result of trade (Herschend 1980; Kyhlberg 1986; Fischer 2005; Ciołek 2007, 2009; Guest 2008). Similarly, Lind (1981, 1988) has argued that the influx of worn Roman denarii to Sweden is a late phenomenon related to warfare in the late 4th century. Rather solidi in Barbaricum pertain to a form of skilled wage labour in the shape of violence – a service sold by private military contractors led by entrepreneurial barbarian warlords or kleptocrats (for a definition of this term, see Fischer 2005:15). The solidi issued by the imperial mints were an important part of the Roman Empire, as they were an a priori urban creation, and their diffusion was part of a larger set of urban dynamics involving wage labour, although this was an unintentional effect.

The solidus had once been conceived as a means of payment that was to circulate within the state apparatus, in sum payments of grain, military salaries and public works. It was imperial gold that would return to the treasury by means of currency exchange within the income tax system (Duncan-Jones 1994). Back in the form of taxes, the solidi would be recast and restruck with different dies and officina marks at the imperial mints. The solidus of the Late Roman Empire must be understood within a much extended framework of urban dynamism in one of the world's largest pre-global economies. The powerful impact of the few imperial mints in a handful of cities extending over the Mediterranean and the Continental hinterland of parts of Africa, Asia and Europe shows that the urban solidus economy extended far beyond mere geographic distances (see fig. 4). This diffusion of solidi meant a steady loss of the purest form of amassed value. This was value meant to run Rome, only to be buried in the soils of Barbaricum. This destruction of monetary value meant that the imperial cities were partially drained of their capacity to manage the state finances by hiring mercenaries from the periphery to protect them.

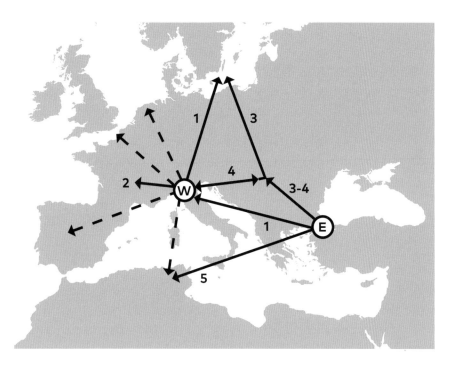

Fig. 4. Distribution routes of gold from the Eastern Empire to the Roman West and Barbaricum. After Fischer & López Sánchez (2016).

Route 1 *Constantinopel > Northern and Central Italy > Pannonia > Barbaricum.*

Route 2 *Constantinopel > Northern and Central Italy > Gaul > Britain and Spain.*

Route 3 *Constantinopel > Balkans > Barbaricum.*

Route 4 *Constantinopel > Balkans > Barbaricum > Northern and Central Italy.*

Route 5 *Constantinopel > Southern Italy, Sicily and North Africa.*

This means that the Late Roman urban economy in Italy was large enough to attract faraway migrant wage labour even during times of crisis, or even because of the crisis. In 5th century Italy, the decaying state military-industrial complex still dominated the wage labour market. The imperial army was always in need of short-contract manpower. By contrast, the reason behind the migrating was to gain closer access to the imperial treasury located in the two largest cities, Rome and Constantinople. Only there could a migrant worker be sure to receive direct cash payment in the highest form of currency, the imperial solidus. But the migrant wages were never put back into the Roman economy again. Instead, the solidus coinage was

taken to Barbaricum and hoarded on the periphery of the monetised economy.

To make an offer of violence in return for solidi must be considered a very cost-effective enterprise compared to the bulky nature of fur trade, especially in situations when the offer cannot be refused. But as pointed out by Fagerlie (1967), the wage labour hypothesis requires concrete evidence, i.e. the presence of various Scandinavian military contractors active on the Continent during the late 5th century. This is a key problem that can be resolved, however. In contrast to the trade hypothesis, the wage labour hypothesis can be verified by the evidence of Scandinavians on the Continent having access to solidi while simultaneously displaying a typically Scandinavian manner of treating solidus coinage in a way peculiar to Scandinavians. The remarkable solidus pendants from Udovice, Serbia, certainly do fulfil these criteria by having a specimen of RIC X 2718 struck for Libius Severus (a type which is very frequent on Öland) attached to a gold filigree work of typical Scandinavian character (Popović 2008; Fischer 2008; Fischer *et al.* 2011). The coin type only occurs in Italy, Scandinavia and the Vedrin hoard in Belgium (Lallemand 1965). This makes it highly unlikely that the coin would have reached a Scandinavian goldsmith through commercial exchange.

The South Scandinavian unit leaders, in turn, were under the command of another migrant or a second-generation migrant who had acquired considerable social status and corresponding Roman rank. To pay the leaders, several of these commanders, notably Ricimer, would have to strike gold coinage in the name of a Roman imperial persona. The men wanted the emperor's money regardless of whether this was the usurper Majorian, the puppet Libius Severus, interoffice adversaries like Anthemius or Glycerius, or merely an effigy of the Eastern Emperor Leo I. As a result, some of the Western issues are evidence of crude artistry indeed.

The onset of solidus hoarding on Öland in significant numbers began only slightly before the extinction of the Theodosian dynasty in AD 457 (Janse 1922; Fagerlie 1967; Herschend 1980; Iluk 2007:92–93; Horsnæs 2010:176–177; Horsnæs 2013:81–86, 94–97). Certainly, there is evidence of gold coinage older than this period in Scandinavia, especially in the area around Gudme, Funen (Kromann 1990). Reasons for the sudden influx of solidi to specific regions in Scandinavia can be varied but it is well known that certain groups in Barbaricum were capable of establishing special relations with specific members of the bureaucratic, military or imperial machinery, and the political situation produced in Italy after the fall of Valentinian III and the new situation in Pannonia after the fall of Attila allowed for new contact networks. Up to AD 465, die-linked coins on Öland are mainly connected to the Björnhovda hoard in Torslunda parish, located in the fertile Mörbylånga Valley along the western shore (fig. 2).

The mid and second half of the 5th century was the time when Visigoths, Burgundians and Vandals, among many other minor ethnic affinities, asserted their power in different regions inside the Empire, establishing the first successor kingdoms. In this context it appears that Öland was the first among other regions in Scandinavia to maintain privileged relations to barbarians inside the Empire. On Öland, there were at least ten important hoards deposited during the two decades spanning from the death of Valentinian III in AD 455 to the abdication of Romulus Augustus in AD 476. The typical Ölandic hoard composition seems to follow the same pattern of subsidies sent from the East in the wake of political emergencies in the West (Fischer 2005, Fischer & López Sánchez 2016).

The hoards probably reflect active Ölandic participation within the shifting and dangerous politics during the third quarter of the 5th century inside the Empire (Fagerlie 1967:155–156). Constantinople is the most important mint of all in the Ölandic hoards. However, almost one third of the solidi of the largest hoard of Åby in the Sandby area on the eastern side of the island has a *tpq* AD 477, Italian mintmarks, a quantity which is close to 40% in the hoard of Björnhovda on the western side of the island. These are similar percentages to those present in the mixed hoard of Bína in Slovakia from the middle of the 5th century, and the large treasure of San Mamiliano in Sovana from *c.* AD 477. Ölandic hoards have similar compositions, divided into two almost symmetrical halves with provenance from the East and the West. All this strongly suggests that Northern Italy and Pannonia are the most likely regions of acquisition for these solidi.

Fig. 5. Solidus pendant from Udovice, Serbia. The coin to the right is a RIC X 2718, struck in the name of Libius Severus (AD 461–465). Photo National Museum, Belgrade, after Lamm 2009: 4.

After AD 476, Bornholm, Gotland and Helgö fill up the void left by Öland (Werner 1949; Fagerlie 1967:156–162; Metcalf 2010). This probably occurred after a major armed conflict on Öland had forced most of the solidi into the ground *c.* AD 490 (Werner 1949). Among the mints, Constantinople increases its dominance (Kyhlberg 1986; Fischer 2014b; Fischer & López Sánchez 2016). Coins struck in Italy represent only 20–25% of the total of the hoarded material up to AD 515/520 (Kyhlberg 1986; Horsnæs 2013:83). After this date, which coincides with the aftermath of the death of Anastasius, Constantinople is of even greater importance and just one eighth of the Botes hoard is composed of Italian coins. Again, the place of their acquisition can still have been the north of Italy or Pannonia. The impression of these hoards, though, is that the gold was

Fig. 6. *The solidus from Skogsby, Öland, Sweden (SHM 17 911). 3:2. Photo Gabriel Hildebrand, courtesy of the Royal Coin Cabinet (KMK), Stockholm.*

mainly Constantinopolitan and that even the Italian mints under Ostrogothic control may have received their supplies from the East.

The fact that the material is divided in this way is a strong argument against a market economy with a secondary coin circulation on Öland. Rather, the martial nature of the solidus import is precisely what prevented market conditions and what also brought about the abrupt end to the short-lived opulence of returning warriors in the Sandby area.

AD 435 – The tenth *vota* of Valentinian III

The first direct payment from the Western Empire to barbarian warriors that can be tracked to South Scandinavia dates to AD 435. A possible background can be found in the preceding years AD 431–434, when a Hunnic unit under Aëtius executed a mopping-up sweep all over Italy neutralising renegade mercenary units and barbarians. Aëtius was made *patricius* in the autumn of AD 434. Afterwards, the Western Emperor wanted to assert his own imperial power, striking the solidus series RIC X 2032–2038, which are easy to track.

In conjunction with the celebration or *vota* on the tenth anniversary of his accession to power, the Western Emperor Valentinian III issued a series of solidi from the mints of Rome and Ravenna, classified as RIC X 2034–2038. The Rome mint produced solidi with at least three obverses and six reverses. The Ravenna mint used at least three obverses and seven reverses, including a re-engraved die from Rome. This could mean that coins were first struck at Rome and that the court transferred back to Ravenna,

where it struck the rest, initially with a recut die (Fischer & Lind 2015).

These types are easily recognised since the emperor is wearing a *chlamys* on the obverse and the reverse sports the legend VOT X (fig. 6). These coins did not circulate for very long and are relatively rare in solidus hoards deposited after AD 450. This allows us to reconstruct the path of these solidi to Scandinavia via frontier areas along the old *limes* in Central Europe. In particular, the Bína hoard from Slovakia (deposited *c.* 450) and the Szikancs hoard in Hungary (deposited *c.* 445) are die-linked to the solidus hoards from Skogsby and Stora Brunneby (*tpq* 451) on south-western and south-eastern Öland respectively and the settlement complex Fuglsangsager in the Sorte Muld area on north-eastern Bornholm (Fagerlie 1967; Kolnikova 1968; Biró-Sey 1976; Kent 1994; Horsnæs 2002, 2009; Fischer *et al.* 2011).

The arguably most important find from this payment is the Fuglsangsager hoard, which contained six looped solidi of which four are die-linked to each other (fig. 7). They have obviously been kept together as the symbolic value of this payment must have been very important to the owners. In addition, the solidi were wrapped up in a silver plate which could also have originated from a direct payment. It is well known from the contemporary written sources, such as the account of the East Roman diplomat Priscus Panites at the court of Attila (Müller 1841:69), that silver plate was a much desired commodity in these transactions (Hobbs 2006; Guest 2008; Depeyrot 2009). Alas, the payments in the years after 435, in particular the great Hunnic tributes from the Eastern Empire up to the death of Attila in AD 454, cannot be directly followed in the Scandinavian material. It is possible that Scandinavians had a very minor role in this period or were simply left out by other larger barbarian actors.

AD 457–465 – Ricimer, Majorian and Libius Severus

The second direct payment from the Western Empire that can be tracked to Öland dates to the reigns of Majorian and Libius Severus (see fig. 1–2). Interestingly enough, there are no intermediate hoards in Central Europe during this period. This means that the old pattern of Scandina-

vians first going to the *limes* area must have disappeared after the downfall of the Hunnic kingdom (Werner 1956; Bóna 1991; Anke & Externbrink 2007). At this point the *limes* area had been abandoned, and the military state apparatus inside the Western Empire was controlled by Ricimer, a barbarian warlord (MacGeorge 2002). It is not unreasonable to see a connection between an agreement reached between Majorian and the Eastern Empire on the Western recruitment campaign of barbarian troops in Pannonia in 456–457, and the subsequent finds of die-linked western solidi on Öland because the relatively rare issues from Arles under Majorian in 461 have been found on Öland. But above all, the apex of die-linked solidi on

Öland is during the reign of Libius Severus. This feature is reflected in the solidus finds from south-western Öland and the Mörbylånga Valley. The Björnhovda solidus hoard and the Färjestaden gold collar could also be connected to the Udovice hoard in Serbia, which may well be a Scandinavian status symbol along the lines of the find from Fuglsangsager. The Udovice pendants are at least a decade later, and must have reached Illyricum via Pannonia in the 470s.

AD 467–472 – The Reign of Anthemius

The third direct payment is a more complicated affaire. It involves substantial Eastern subsidies but above all that largest minting activity in the Western Empire in the entire 5th century. This means that payment to barbarians from the Western military leadership was mixed with Eastern coinage sent to the Westerners, this was financial support meant to pay for specific military campaigns in the Western hemisphere. After AD 465, there is a new influx of solidi and the die-links extend from the Åby hoard in Sandby Parish on the eastern shore. In fact, 36% of all reported solidi on Öland have been found in a 12 km radius around the Sandby Ringfort, an important archaeological site that seems to contain the remains of an armed conflict (Fischer et al. 2011; Dell'Unto & Wilhelmson 2015; Viberg et al. 2014; Fischer & López Sánchez 2016).

This unusual concentration pattern cannot be explained as the result of trade, because trade and circulation would have caused a more evenly distributed pattern. Rather, it would seem that one contingent led by men from the western side left Öland and returned in the late 460s (see fig. 2). Their money ended up in the ground where they settled home. After this, a second contingent led by men from the eastern side left Öland and returned in the late 470s (see fig. 3). This was in all likelihood the last expedition from Öland, because there are so few reported coins that postdate 476. After this, it seems that there was some kind of conflict between different factions on the island, as suggested by the remnants in the Sandby Ringfort, and the many finds of sword beads in Sandby parish. The latter are made of millefiori glass and chalcedony, two materials which had to be imported to the island, and which have distinct counterparts in Continental warrior graves and sacrifices of military equipment such as Skedemosse (Hagberg 1967) and Nydam (Rau 2010).

The solidi struck by Anthemius have been the subject of recent research, and it is certain that the finds in Scandinavia, eastern Öland in particular, are linked to the San Mamiliano hoard in Tuscany, but not to the Case delle Vestali hoard in the city of Rome (Fischer 2014a). The exhaustive catalogue of 49 different solidus hoards and their die-links reveals an almost complete absence of these types of solidi outside Italy and Scandinavia.

The aftermath 473–477

The fourth direct payment is related to the fall of the Western Empire. In the chaotic aftermath that followed the fall of Anthemius, it is clear that people from Öland and to some extent Bornholm were directly involved in Italy (Kyhlberg 1986; Fischer 2014a; Fischer & Lind 2015; Fischer & López Sánchez 2016). Here, it is once again apparent that there are no intermittent hoards between South Scandinavia and Italy at the time; rather the best comparative material is found in the Childeric grave and the Vedrin hoard in Belgium. It is also evident that the passage to and from Öland to Italy closed shortly afterwards. Much like the owners of the Vedrin hoard and Childeric, the Ölandic hoard owners were paid around 476 and then returned back home, burying their hoards for good c. 480–490. What happened here is very uncertain, but a larger conflict c. 490 seems very likely given the finds from the Sandby Ringfort. There is no reliable contemporary account from Italy that can serve to integrate the different forms of evidence, although various events in Pannonia at the time (Lotter 2003) offer a possible, yet highly speculative background without any corresponding numismatic evidence.

Conclusion

The phenomenon of returning veterans in South Scandinavia can be ascertained by means of distinct reciprocity within specific frameworks involving certain artefacts. The Late Roman solidi are indeed such objects. Their die-link patterns allow for the interpretation that there is direct 1:1 evidence of early 5th century returning veterans in Scandinavia, at least on Öland and in the Sorte Muld area on Bornholm. These can be connected to the old *limes* area in Pannonia up to the fall of the Hunnic kingdom in the mid 5th century. However, in the third quarter of the 5th century, the numismatic evidence points to direct involvement in Italy without any certain connections to the *limes* area. Then after 476–477, there is an abrupt disconnection in the case of Öland. Bornholm is thereafter linked to Gotland, Pomerania and later Helgö into the first decades of the 6th century. This can be related to the Ostrogothic presence in Italy.

Fig. 8. The looped solidus pendant from Hol, Västergötland, Sweden (SHM 6 361). 3:2. Photo Gabriel Hildebrand, courtesy of the Royal Coin Cabinet (KMK), Stockholm.

Appendix – Argumentum ex nihilo

Unfortunately, the solidus material from Scania and Västergötland is not very helpful in elucidating specific dates related to the cavalry equipment found in the two regions. On the contrary, coin finds are either of all too frequent types with many different dies, transformed into looped pendants, or they simply belong to another chronological horizon. One case can illustrate this problematic: Solidi are extremely rare in Västergötland – in fact there are only two. The first catalogued solidus from Västergötland (SHM 6361) is from the parish of Hol (fig. 8). The Hol solidus is of the *imp 42 cos 17* type (Kent 1992, 1994). It was struck in AD 441 in Constantinople for Emperor Theodosius II (408–450), and belongs to a very frequent coin type that is closely associated with the

Szikancs hoard in Pannonia. It is very worn and fitted as a pendant with beaded rim and loop. Fagerlie (1967) noted that this was a relatively frequent configuration in areas where minted gold was comparatively scarce in the late 5th century, notably Westphalia, Norway, Medelpad, and, of course, Västergötland. These objects are likely to have been inherited, and it is also quite possible that they may have transferred from the martial male gender to the dominant female gender. It should be noted that the majority of the looped solidi in 5th century Scandinavia are indeed issues of Theodosius II. Meanwhile, the Timboholm gold hoard in Västergötland (Herschend 2001; Lamm 2005) contained 7,081 g unminted gold. It is theoretically plausible that solidi related to the Hunnic tributes of the 430s and 440s AD were melted into ingots, scabbard mounts and rings by returning veterans, as in the Timboholm hoard, and a handful coins were kept as looped heirlooms, such as the Hol solidus. This remains mere conjecture, however, as the hoarded unminted gold in Västergötland could have many different sources.

Note

1   This research has been financed by grants from the Gunnar Ekström Foundation, the Sven Svensson Foundation, the Berit Wallenberg Foundation, the Åke Wiberg Foundation and the Swedish Society for Ancient Monuments.

References

Anke, B. & Externbrink, H. (eds). 2007. *Attila und die Hunnen*. Speyer/Stuttgart.

Arne, T.J. 1919. Solidusfynden på Öland och Gotland. *Fornvännen* 14: 107–111.

Biró-Sey, K. 1976. A Szikancsi V. századi solidus lelet. *Numizmatikai Közlöny*: 74–75: 7–19.

Bolin, S. 1926. *Fynden av romerska mynt i det fria Germanien. Studier i romersk och äldre germansk historia*. Lund.

Bóna, I. 1991. *Das Hunnenreich*. Stuttgart.

Ciołek, R. 2007. *Die römischen Fundmünzen Polens, Pommern*. Wetteren.

Ciołek, R. 2009. Der Zufluss von Solidi in die südlichen Ostseegebiete. In: Wołoszyn, M. (ed.). *Byzantine Coins in Central Europe between the 5th and 10th century*. Kraków: 217–229.

Dell'Unto, N. & Wilhelmson, H. 2015. Virtual taphonomy. A new method integrating excavation and postprocessing in an archaeological context. *American Journal of Physical Anthropology* 157/2: 305–321.

Depeyrot, G. 2009. *Les trésors et les invasions (Les enfouissements d'or et d'orfèvrerie de 379 à 491) I. Introduction, l'Europe oriental et centrale*. Wetteren.

Duncan-Jones, R. 1994. *Money and government in the Roman Empire*. Cambridge 1994.

Fabech, C. 2011. War and rituals. Changes in ritual and transformations of power. In: Panhuysen, T.A.S.M. (ed.). *Transformations in North-Western Europe (AD 300–1000)*. Hannover/Stuttgart: 27–36.

Fagerlie, J. M. 1967. *Late Roman and Byzantine Solidi found in Sweden and Denmark*. New York.

Fischer, S. 2005. *Roman Imperialism and Runic Literacy. The Westernization of Northern Europe 150–800 AD*. Uppsala.

Fischer, S. 2008. The Udovice Solidus Pendants – Late 5th Century Evidence of South Scandinavian Mercenaries in the Balkans. *Fornvännen* 103/2: 81–88.

Fischer, S. 2014a. The solidus hoard of Casa delle vestali in context. *Opuscula* 8: 86–108.

Fischer, S. 2014b. Tracking Solidi from Thessalonica to Hjärpestad. In: Karlsson, L., Carlsson, S. & Blid, J. (eds). *ΛΑΒΡΥΣ. Studies presented to Pontus Hellström*. Uppsala: 153–162.

Fischer, S. & Lind, L. 2015. The Coins in the Grave of King Childeric. *Journal of Archaeology and Ancient History* 14: 1–36. Online: http://www.diva-portal.org/smash/get/diva2:793693/FULLTEXT01.pdf.

Fischer, S. & López Sánchez, F. 2016. Subsidies for the Roman West? The flow of Constantinopolitan solidi to the Western Empire and Barbaricum. *Opuscula* 9: 157–177.

Fischer, S., López Sánchez, F. & Victor, H. 2011. A Result from the LEO-project: The 5th Century Hoard of Theodosian solidi from Stora Brunneby, Öland, Sweden. *Fornvännen* 106: 189–204.

Guest, P. 2008. Roman Gold and Hun Kings: The Use and Hoarding of Solidi in the Late Fourth and Fifth Centuries. In: Bursche, A., Ciołek, R. & Wolters, R. (eds). *Roman Coins Outside the Empire – Ways and Phases, Contexts and Functions*. Wetteren: 295–307.

Hagberg, U.-E. 1967. *The Archaeology of Skedemosse*. Stockholm.

Herschend, F. 1980. *Två studier i öländska guldfynd. I. Det myntade guldet. II. Det omyntade guldet*. (Offprint from *Tor* 18, 1978–1979). Uppsala. Summary.

Herschend, F. 2001. Two "West-Geatish" Greeks. The gold from Vittene and Timboholm. In: Magnus, B. (ed.). *Roman gold and the development of the early Germanic kingdoms*. Stockholm: 103–118.

Hildebrand, H. 1882. Solidus-importen till Sverige under den tidigare jernåldern. *Från äldre tider: kulturvetenskapliga och historiska studier*. Stockholm.

Hobbs, R. 2006. *Late Roman Precious Metal Deposits, c. AD 200–700: Changes over Time and Space*. Oxford.

Horsnæs, H. 2002. New Gold Hoards with Rare Types of Valentinian III Solidi. *Revue Numismatique* 158.

Horsnæs, H. 2009. Late Roman and Byzantine Coins Found in Denmark. In: Wołoszyn, M. (ed.). *Byzantine Coins in Central Europe between the 5th and 10th century*. Kraków: 231–270.

Horsnæs, H. 2010. *Crossing Boundaries. An Analysis of Roman coins in Danish contexts. Vol. 1. Finds from Zealand, Funen and Jutland*. Copenhagen.

Horsnæs, H. 2013. *Crossing Boundaries. An Analysis of Roman coins in Danish contexts. Vol. 2. Finds from Bornholm*. Copenhagen.

Iluk, J. 2007. *Aspects économiques et politiques de la circulation de l'or au Bas-Empire*. Wetteren.

Janse, O. 1922. *Le travail de l'or en Suède à l'époque mérovingienne. Etudes précédées d'un mémoire sur les solidi romains et byzantins trouvés en Suède*. Orléans.

Jonsson, K. 2003. Folkvandringstida guldmynt. B. Radhe (ed). *Klenoder i Gotlands fornsal. Gotländskt arkiv 2003*. 80–81.

Kent, J.P.C. 1992. IMP XXXXII COS XVII PP. When Was It Struck and What Does It Tell Us? Nilsson, H. (ed.). *Florilegium Numismaticum. Studia in honorem U. Westermark edita*. Stockholm. 189–196.

Kent, J.P.C. 1994. *The Roman Imperial Coinage. Volume X*. London.

Kolníková, E. 1968. Nález neskororímskych solidov v Bíni, okres Nové Zámky (K minciadoby sťahovania národnov). *Numismatický sborník* 10.

Kromann, A. 1990. Recent Roman Coin Finds from Denmark. Supplement to Breitenstein and Billing. *Nordisk Numismatisk Årsskrift* 1983–84: 59–122.

Kyhlberg, O. 1986. Late Roman and Byzantine Solidi, An Archaeological analysis of coins and hoards. In: Lundström, A. & Clarke, H. (eds). *Excavations at Helgö X. Coins, Iron and Gold*. Stockholm: 13–126.

Lallemand, J. 1965. Vedrin – Sous d'or de Magnus Maximus à Anastase. *Études Numismatiques* 3: 109–144.

Lamm, J.P. 2005. Timboholm. *Reallexikon der Germanischen Altertumskunde* 30: 612–613.

Lamm, J.P. 2009. Fjernt guldfund. *Skalk* 2009/3: 4–8.

Latour, B. 2005. *Reassembling the Social. An Introduction to Actor-Network-Theory*. Oxford.

Lind, L. 1981. *Roman Denarii Found in Sweden. 2. Catalogue. Text*. Stockholm 1981. (Stockholm Studies in Classical Archaeology, 11:2).

Lind, L. 1988. *Romerska denarer funna i Sverige*. Stockholm 1988.

Lotter, F. 2003. *Völkerverschiebungen im Ostalpen-Mitteldonau-Raum zwischen Antike und Mittelalter (375–600)*. Berlin/New York.

MacGeorge, P. 2002. *Late Roman Warlords*. Oxford.

Metcalf, D.M. 1995. Viking-age Numismatics 1. Late Roman and Byzantine Gold in the Northern Lands. *Numismatic chronicle* 155: 413–441.

Metcalf, D.M. 2010. "First to Öland, then to Gotland". The Arrival and Dispersal of Late Roman and Byzantine Solidi in Sweden and Denmark. In: *Mélanges Cécile Morrisson*. Paris: 561–576.

Müller, K. (ed.) 1841. *Fragmenta historicorum Graecorum* 4: 69–110.

Näsman, U. 2012. Comments on "An Iron Age shock doctrine: The 536–37 event as a trigger of large-scale social change in the Mälaren valley area" by Daniel Löwenborg. *Journal of Archaeology and Ancient History* 4. Uppsala. – Online: http://www.arkeologi.uu.se/Journal/no-4-lowenborg/.

Popović, I. 2008. Solidi with filigreed tubular suspension loops from Udovice in Serbia. *Fornvännen* 103/2: 73–79.

Rau, A. 2010. *Nydam mose 1–2. Die personengebundenen Gegenstände. Grabungen 1989–1999.* Højbjerg/Aarhus. Summary.

Viberg et al. 2014 = Viberg, A., Victor H., Fischer, S., Lidén, K. & Andrén, A. 2014. Archaeological Geophysical Prospection and Excavations at Sandby

Ringfort, Öland, Sweden. *Archäologisches Korrespondenzblatt* 44/3: 413–428.

Werner, J. 1949. Zu den auf Öland und Gotland gefundenen byzantinischen Goldmünzen. *Fornvännen* 44: 257–286.

Werner, J. 1956. *Beiträge zur Archäologie des Attila-Reiches.* Munich.

Резюме

Материальная культура возвращавшихся ветеранов V в.

Сванте Фишер

В данной статье обсуждаются важнейшие археологические свидетельства присутствия скандинавов в Западной Римской империи в V в. Ее цель – рассмотреть ряд вопросов, связанных с возвращением воинов-ветеранов с Европейского континента на скандинавскую периферию на протяжении V в. Можно ли доказать присутствие возвращавшихся воинов в материальной культуре Эпохи переселения народов в Скандинавии по монетам, чеканенным теми же штемпелями, что и попавшие в состав монетных кладов на Континенте? Считается, что нумизматические свидетельства – одноштемпельные солиды – позволяют выявить, по крайней мере, четыре разных платежа, когда скандинавы получили золотые монеты от основных акторов военизированного государственного аппарата Позднеримской империи, а затем принесли их в Скандинавию. Два или три платежа, произведенные в 465–476 гг., могли быть непосредственными, из Италии в южную Скандинавию. Между тем, более ранний платеж, произведенный после 435 г., очевидно, можно связать с зоной бывшего лимеса в Паннонии, учитывая одноштемпельные монеты из кладов солидов, найденные в Словакии и Венгрии, охарактеризовав его как платеж через посредников среднего звена.

Как же выглядела материальная культура ветеранов, возвращавшихся в южную Скандинавию? Как было показано ранее, вниз по течению крупнейших рек Польши и в Татрах должны были быть организованы станции или склады, подготовленные для частных военных компаний, которыми те смогли бы пользоваться до того, как окажутся в зоне лимеса (Herschend 1980). Также было показано, что эти отряды

должны были передвигаться верхом, а это требовало мирных соглашений с местными скотоводами. Верхом эти отряды могли передвигаться очень быстро, как следует из опыта Первой мировой войны (Fischer 2005). Таким образом, весьма соблазнительно будет связать конское снаряжение V в. из Скании и Вестергётланда с близкими находками на Континенте, а клады солидов в Словакии и Венгрии – с найденными на Эланде и Борнхольме.

Остается важнейшая проблема находок конского снаряжения Эпохи переселения народов в южной Скандинавии. Нет убедительных доказательств того, что это снаряжение импортировалось в виде наборов, или же что изготовленные на месте вещи однажды покинули свою родину и затем вернулись обратно. Таким образом, связь между возвращавшимися ветеранами и конским снаряжением весьма проблематична. Его декор и стиль близки, но не идентичны сопоставимым находкам на Континенте. К тому же нельзя исключить, что в местном военном деле и ритуальных приношениях использовались вещи местного производства, имитирующие принятые на Континенте стили.

Напротив, исходя из практического опыта, одноштемпельные позднеримские солиды, найденные на Эланде и Борнхольме, представляют собой куда более существенные данные о возвращавшихся на родину воинах. Документированные типы солидов указывают на явные связи между системами поселений и их хронологией, которые невозможно объяснить как результат торговли или вторичного обращения монет, учитывая возможности сопоставления этих материалов с базой данных, включающей около 7300 солидов из отдельных находок и около 23000 солидов из кладов (Fischer 2011, 2014b; Fischer & Lind 2015).

Теоретически, отправная точка этой статьи очень проста. Она в том, что люди прошлого должны были оценивать риски доступа к прибылям и власти. Разумно будет предположить, раз уж жители Скандинавии посчитали, что военный поход на Континент способен принести им прибыль, то домой они принесли новые вещи, способные сделать возвращение максимально выгодным. Точно также, резонно будет предположить, что у них был очевидный мотив для возвращения, который должен был быть связан с властью и собственностью. Возвращавшиеся домой вторые и третьи сыновья, а также безземельные ветераны могли надеяться на получение большего объема власти на скандинавской периферии. Это создавало новые проблемы в интеллектуальной сфере, связанной с идеями и опытом, равно как и существенные сложности в самых конкретных вещах.

Возвращение ветеранов означало внезапное возникновение совершенно новой материальной культуры, приобщиться к которой можно было тремя способами: 1) став частью возвращавшегося домой коллектива; 2) самостоятельно отправившись на континент; 3) отняв у вернувшегося домой его долю этой материальной культуры. Вследствие этого неизбежная конфронтация и дальнейшее отторжение или интеграция новичков становились реальной проблемой для тех, кто возглавлял старые системы власти на родине. У этого феномена были две прямо противоположные стороны. Оставшееся дома общество могло приложить массу усилий для того, чтобы интегрировать возвращавшихся домой и, в этом случае, интегрировать или ассимилировать новые идеи и новую материальную культуру. Другой сценарий – это открытый конфликт, в котором ведущие представители старого порядка должны были остановить возвращавшихся ветеранов, нанеся им максимальный ущерб, и либо запретить, либо присвоить новые идеи, приспособив последние к собственным нуждам. Кажется разумным предположить, что в реальности возникало множество промежуточных реше-

ний, но последний – конфликтный – сценарий достаточно часто оказывался единственной возможностью для представителей старого порядка (Fabech 2011: 34; Näsman 2012: 9).

За находками солидов может скрываться пространственная система акторов, в которой ключевым показателем являются не географические расстояния, но, напротив, количество связей между узловыми точками. Это значит, что расстояние между кладами не имеет значения, а суть в том, какие связи возникли у их владельцев в том или ином месте. Эта перспектива стала результатом долгой традиции изучения римских солидов конца V в., оказавшихся в Скандинавии Эпохи переселения народов и являющихся сравнительным эквивалентом для кладов солидов в Италии (краткую историографию находок солидов в Скандинавии с конца XIX в. до 1967 г. см в: Herschend 1980). Сравнения между Италией и Скандинавией не избежать, ведь на Европейском континенте нет других регионов, имеющих столько общего в отношении находок солидов, чеканенных последними императорами Западной Римской империи.

Феномен возвращения ветеранов в южную Скандинавию подтверждается наличием очевидного взаимодействия в особых рамках, в которое вовлекались отдельные вещи. К таким вещам, разумеется, относились позднеримские солиды. Наличие одноштемпельных монет позволяет заключить, что эти находки непосредственно связаны с возвращением ветеранов в Скандинавию в начале V в. – по меньшей мере, на Эланд и район Сорте-Мульд на Борнхольме. Их можно связать с древней зоной лимеса в Паннонии, периода до падения гуннского королевства в середине V в. Однако в третьей четверти V в. нумизматические данные указывают на наличие непосредственных контактов с Италией, без каких-либо связей с зоной лимеса. В дальнейшем, после 476–477 гг., связи резко разрываются в случае Эланда. После этого, вплоть до первых десятилетий VI в., Борнхольм был связан с Готландом, Померанией и поздним Хельгё, что можно объяснить присутствием остроготов в Италии.

ПОДПИСИ К ИЛЛЮСТРАЦИЯМ

Рис. 1. Три волны солидов, попадавших в Эланд. Иллюстрация Сванте Фишера (по: Herschend 1980). – Синим показаны клады с монетами, чеканенными вплоть до времени Маркина (451–457 гг.), но главным образом Феодосия II (408–450 гг.) и Валентиниана III (425–455 гг). – Зеленым обозначены клады с монетами, главным образом относящимися ко времени Либия Севера (461–465 гг.) и началу правления Льва I (457–474 гг.). – Красным отмечены клады с монетами, главным образом относящимися к концу правления Льва I (457–474 гг.), первому правлению Зенона (474–476 гг.), а также западных императоров от Антемия (467–472 гг.) до Ромула Августула (475–476 гг.).

Рис. 2. Первый платеж варварам в Италии, ок. 462–465 гг. Иллюстрация Сванте Фишера.

Рис. 3. Второй и третий платежи варварам в Италии, ок. 466–476 гг. Иллюстрация Сванте Фишера.

Рис. 4. Пути распространения золота из Восточной Римской империи на римский Запад и в Барбарикум (по: Fischer & López Sánchez 2016).

Рис. 5. Подвеска из солида из Удовице (Сербия). Справа – монета типа «RIC X, 2718», чеканка Либия Севера (461–465 гг.). Фото Национального музея, Белград (по: Lamm 2009: 4).

Рис. 6. a–b. Солид из Скогсбю (Эланд, Швеция; Шведский исторический музей, № 17 911). Фото Ульрики Борнестаф, с разрешения Королевского кабинета монет (Стокгольм).

Рис. 7. Клад из Фугльсангсагер / Сорте-Мульд II (Борнхольм, Дания). Фото Джона Ли (Национальный музей Дании; № C 34 935 – 34 956).

Рис. 8. a–b. Подвеска из солида с петелькой из Хола (Вестергётланд, Швеция; Шведский исторический музей, № 6 361). Фото Ульрики Борнестаф, с разрешения Королевского кабинета монет (Стокгольм).

Sösdala interpreted in its glocal context

Charlotte Fabech & Ulf Näsman

The three finds of horse tack from Sösdala and Fulltofta can be approached from many different angles. To conclude the publication we have chosen to present reconstructions and comment on chronology, provenance and historical background. The workshop that produced the silver mounts of Sösdala I was probably situated at a centre somewhere in an area circumscribed by Untersiebenbrunn, Coşoveni, Crimea, Kačin and Jakuszowice. The deposition of dismantled horse tack on the top of gravel hills is explainable by references to Nomadic funerary rituals. The paper concludes with a "biography" of the three finds based on written sources and the archaeological record.

Fabech, C. & Näsman, U. 2017. Sösdala interpreted in its glocal context. In: Fabech, C. & Näsman, U. (eds). *The Sösdala horsemen – and the equestrian elite of fifth century Europe.* Jutland Archaeological Society.

The three finds of horse tack from Sösdala and Fulltofta can be approached from many different angles. To conclude the publication we have chosen to present reconstructions and comment on chronology, provenance and historical background. Finally we will write "biographies" of the three finds.

Source criticism

It is an impediment to a proper understanding of the European backdrop of the equestrian equipment from Sösdala and Fulltofta that the character of relevant source materials differs so much in different parts of Europe (Quast chapter 14). In the west a small number of finds come from settlements and a few graves, in eastern Europe from mixed silver hoards (Kačin, Bar, Coşoveni), in central Europe from exclusive graves (Untersiebenbrunn, Jakuszowice) and in South Scandinavia from ritual depositions (e.g. Sösdala, Fulltofta, Vennebo, Finnestorp); a single grave in northern Scandinavia can be added (Högom). Comparison of the presence or absence of finds of horse tack in such different contexts is problematic. Another difficulty is that the awareness of the general public that ancient finds should be reported to museums varies considerably in different countries, not to speak about the willingness to do so. A combination of an increasing antiquities trade and the looting of ancient sites by metal detector users is now leading to a further deterioration of the situation (fig. 1–3).

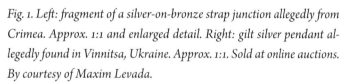

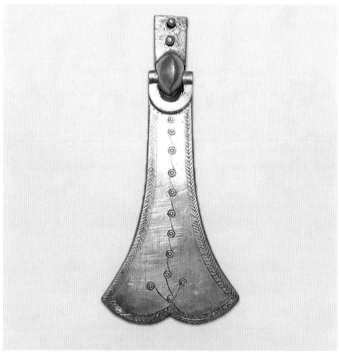

Fig. 1. Left: fragment of a silver-on-bronze strap junction allegedly from Crimea. Approx. 1:1 and enlarged detail. Right: gilt silver pendant allegedly found in Vinnitsa, Ukraine. Approx. 1:1. Sold at online auctions. By courtesy of Maxim Levada.

Reconstructions

In order to understand the function of the many metal mounts we found it necessary to make hypothetical reconstructions. In collaboration with Erika Rosengren we have bridled and saddled a "Sösdala I horse" (fig. 4–5) and bridled horses from Sösdala II (fig. 6) and Fulltofta (fig. 7).

Concerning the parade bridle from Sösdala we find it uncontroversial to attach the pelta-shaped pendant (no. I:19–21) to the browband and the pendant with horse heads (no. I:1) to the noseband. If you assume that all silver mounts from find spot I come from the bridle, the long pendants (nos. I:2,3,4,7) can only be attached to the noseband and browband of the headstall. We find this less likely and instead we have fastened strap ends at the noseband and a martingale to the noseband (fig. 4). The latter is of course very uncertain and is an attempt to find a use for a singular strap buckle (no. I:27) and two odd mounts

(nos. I:12–13). These mounts we associated with the *Kehlbergen* familiar in offerings of military equipment from the Late Roman Iron Age (Lau 2014:144–150). *Kehlbergen* are interpreted as constituents of martingales. The wear on the strap buckle could reflect its use in a two-piece breast collar to control the straps of a martingale (fig. 5). It is not unexpected that a 5th century horseman employed a martingale since the use of martingales is well documented in equestrian equipment of the Late Roman Iron Age (Lau 2014 Abb. 93–94). The depicted Sösdala saddle has mounts from find spot IV applied to a pommel shaped like that of the saddle found in Högom but the cantle is lower and sloping backwards (Näsman chapter 7 figs 24–27 and Ramqvist chapter 10 figs 2–5). We assume that girths, breast collar and breeching were tied to the saddle rings and held the saddle in place. Two girths are in fact used by, for example, Mongolian horseman (Anke & Externbrink 2007:26) and in some Western saddles. Here the long silver pendants are hung in the saddle tack at the shoulder and haunch straps.

Erika Rosengren's reconstruction of the bridle from Sösdala II resembles the reconstruction published the year the find was made (cf. fig. 6 and Näsman chapter 5 fig. 7). A support for this reconstruction is given by mounts

found in situ in an inhumation excavated at Netta, Poland (Bitner-Wróblewska 2007; Näsman chapter 7). The two pendants are placed in the browband and noseband in a way corresponding to the pendants in the parade bridle. The headstall from Fulltofta is reconstructed in two versions, one with the original axe-shaped pendants and a later one where pelta-shaped pendant covers have been added (fig. 7).

Chronology

In all chronological discussions it is problematic that our archaeological dating methods only with difficulty can distinguish between production time and deposition time. A result of this chronological dilemma is the use of periods and phases that cover long time spans.

The bridle found at Sösdala II is dated to period Scand-C3 or c. AD 300–400/410. The Fulltofta bridle in its original condition is likewise possibly from Scand-C3. Later on pendant covers in gilt silver-on-bronze were added to the axe-shaped pendants. Their punched decoration in "Sösdala style" shows that the Fulltofta bridle was deposited in the early Migration Period Scand-D1.

Fig. 2. A number of gilt silver objects including pendants with a miniature yoke, a miniature anvil and a broken key(?). Allegedly from the Volyn district, Ukraine. Approx. 1:1. Sold at online auctions. By courtesy of Maxim Levada.

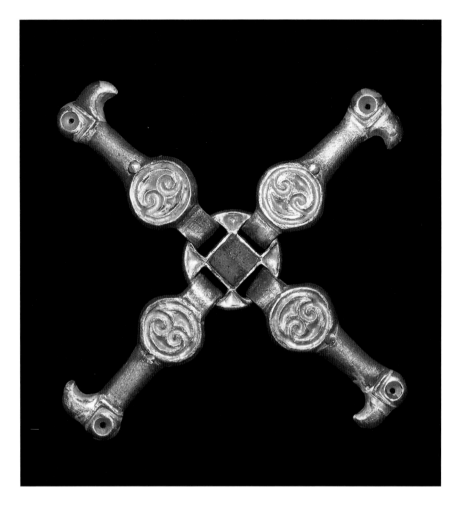

Fig. 3. A strap junction sold as a Merovingian strap distributor from the 6th century at TimeLine Auctions in 2011 with provenance "UK art market, acquired prior to 2000". Approx. 5:4. It is very similar to strap junctions from the Sjörup find, see fig. 8 in chapter 4.

There seems to be consensus that the Sösdala parade bridle belongs to the same period as the bridles from Untersiebenbrunn and that it belongs in the early Migration Period. This corresponds to Scand-D1, in calendar years *c.* AD 400/410–455/465 (Rau 2010:119–120, Abb. 41) or Cont-D2 *c.* AD 380/400–440/450 (Nothnagel 2013:25).

The bridle belongs to a group of exclusive finds that chronologically constitutes an "isochronic horizon" (Quast chapter 14; for a wider "Sösdala horizon" see Bitner-Wróblewska chapter 12) The "Sösdala style" and other contemporary regional styles of punched decoration can be attributed to a *Zeitgeist* (a concept used by An-

dreas Rau in an e-mail 2017), an outcome of both peaceful meetings and military confrontations between various ethnic and cultural groups both outside and inside the long Roman border.

Provenance of the Sösdala parade bridle

Where were the mounts of the parade bridle produced? In Scania, Scandinavia or on the Continent? In one or more places? Discussions about the provenance of the Sösdala bridle often refer to five east European silver bridles: Bar, Coşoveni, Jakuszowice, Kačin and Untersiebenbrunn (Kazanski & Mastykova chapter 15 figs 1–7). They are usually taken as indications that the Sösdala bridle was produced in eastern Europe or strongly influenced from the same quarters. A first problem to solve is whether the four different sets of punches used to decorate the Sösdala mounts represent production at four different workshops or four different craftsmen working at the same workshop (Dal chapter 6 punch groups 1–3; cf. Geisslinger 1967:108–109). It is important to remember that punches with their minute details according to historical traditions were made by the craftsmen themselves and kept as their personal tools.

The headstall was first furnished with mounts made by three different artisans, each with their speciality. The bridle was taken into use and eventually a pendant punched by artisan 1 was lost. It was replaced by a copy made by the skilled artisan 2. Then another pendant was lost but it was replaced by a slipshod copy, probably cut of silver plate in the same workshop but punched by a tyro, the fourth craftsman. More about the "biography" of the bridle is found below.

The quality of the bridle exceeds the best of the very few gilt silver bridles preserved until today. Our view is that the bridle comes from an outstanding workshop, a workshop that furnished "princely" horsemen with bridles in gilt silver. Consequently the Sösdala find is only the tip of an iceberg of contemporary but today unknown bridles. The find spots of silver bridles are widespread and vary the same theme of punch decoration. The variations in shape and decoration show that the finds represent as many workshops/icebergs (Bitner-Wróblewska chapter 12).

Fig. 4. Reconstructions of the parade bridle of Sösdala I, left with long pendants at browband and noseband, right with strap ends at browband and martingale at noseband. Drawing Erika Rosengren.

The exquisite silver bridle of Sösdala I gave the rider a high social status. For instance the silver bridles of a women buried at Untersiebenbrunn belonged to a group of *Fürstengräber*/princely graves (Nothnagel 2013:119–124). Also the warrior grave at Jakuszowice is characterised as a *Fürstengrab* and the power of the buried man seems to have been bolstered by close relations to the Huns (Godłowski 1995; *MPOV* at Jakuszowice).

Several scholars have noted that the decoration of Sösdala I is restrained and conveys a "classical" impression. An excellent example is offered by a comparison of the punched decoration of the pelta-shaped pendant in "Roman" style and that of the Fulltofta pelta in "Sösdala style" (fig. 12). The double horse heads of the Sösdala mounts differ from the "hanging" animal heads of Scandinavian silver sheet brooches in "Sösdala style". In contrast, their similarity to the double horse heads of late Roman strap

ends is obvious (Quast chapter 14 fig. 4). The occurrence of outward-looking animal heads on mounts far from the Roman border at Kačin and Bar in Ukraine is an important indication of relations to south-eastern Europe.

The 27 punch motifs used to decorate the parade bridle are distributed in four different sets of punches. Their singularity is demonstrated by the fact that as many as 18 motifs are present in only one set and among them are the most elaborate punches (Dal chapter 6 fig. 3 nos. 8, 12–22, 24–25). One of the unique punches was used to decorate the noseband pendant (Dal's punch no. 21, fig. 3–4). Perhaps the motif is a pair of outward-looking horse heads. To our knowledge it is only found on one more object, a fragment of a strap junction sold by auction in 2016 and possibly from Crimea (fig. 1). A rich punch decoration with stars is found on a number of auction finds from ?Volyn (fig. 2), finds that give further support to the assumptions of a south-eastern origin.

Fig. 5. Reconstruction of a horse with the parade bridle of Sösdala I with martingale and saddled with saddle 1. Drawing Erika Rosengren.

Otherwise the rich punch ornamentation of Sösdala stands alone in the comparative horse tack material but there are similarities to Scandinavian objects decorated in "Sösdala style". For example the silver sheet brooch from Sejlflod grave DI has along the ridge of the foot plate a double row of triangles composed of 3+2+1 semicircles (Nielsen 2000:56), a punch composition we only know of from five rectangular group 3 mounts from the Sösdala (nos. I:46,48,51,56,60). But the relation between the style of the Sösdala mounts and the "Sösdala style" is far from clear.

In the Sösdala I headstall a noseband mount has as its central piece a three-way connector to which two strap mounts and a pendant are attached. Its fourth side has two outward-looking horse heads. It is an elegant technical solution that we only know one more example of, a loose connector in the already mentioned find from Bar (fig. 8). In this case the connector has a pair of outward-looking bird heads. This similarity between headstall mounts from Sösdala and Bar links the two find spots strongly to one another. The same Sösdala pendant belongs to a small group of Scandinavian Migration Period objects with niello inlays of pure silver sulphide (Dal chapter 6). The result of the niello analysis supports the dating to the 5th century and reveals that the pendant was produced in a workshop that worked in the Roman tradition.

The close relation to late Roman punched decoration (Quast chapter 14) is demonstrated by the six-petal rosettes of two strap junctions from Sösdala I, which are similar to rosettes on strap mounts from Untersiebenbrunn (Näsman chapter 7 fig. 12). Further evidence of a close relation between headstall mounts found in Sweden and Austria comes from Finnestorp. Forssander exemplified the link with the deep lens-shaped punch marks on a strap buckle from Finnestorp and similar punch marks on buckles from Untersiebenbrunn (Näsman chapter 5 fig. 2), and he suggested that the buckle could be either a direct import or a copy. In Sösdala lens-shaped punch marks are found on the pelta-shaped pendant (no. I:19–21). Close relations are also demonstrated by a shield-shaped strap junction from Finnestorp with a facetted "shield boss" similar to the bosses on shield-shaped strap junctions from Untersiebenbrunn (fig. 9). Facetted shield bosses are non-existent among Scandinavian shields but shields with such bosses are found in central and eastern Europe (Kazanski 1988:76 figs 6–7).

Another example of an impact from central and eastern Europe is seen in snaffles with cheek bars, found in Åmossarna and Vennebo, both dated to Scand-D1 (bridle type OI in Ørsnes 1994:278). They are understood as being influenced by snaffles used by mounted nomads, e.g. Keszthely and Lengyeltóti, Hungary (Bóna 1991 Taf. 66, 70) and Untersiebenbrunn (Nothnagel 2013:93–94). Prototypes for the Sösdala buckles with triangular attachment plates are probably late Roman belt buckles with a triangular plate and a disc at the end (Kazanski & Mastykova chapter 15 fig. 8:8–10).

To sum up, there are strong links between Sösdala and central and eastern Europe, links that are based on a long

Fig. 6. Reconstruction of the bridle from Sösdala II. Drawing Erika Rosengren.

history of exchange between South Scandinavia and an area from the Danubian basin to the Black Sea. Furthermore it is important to note that Scandinavian connections to eastern Europe increased considerably in period Scand-D1 and that very few finds indicate comparable connections to western Europe (Rau 2010:483).

We assume that the contacts with south-eastern Europe followed long-established routes and refer to the fact that the distribution of punch-decorated silver bridles is enclosed by the distribution of finds of cut glass vessels, mainly from the 4th century (fig. 10). Relations at a high social level during Late Roman Iron Age periods Scand-C2–C3 are excellently illustrated with a gold hoard from Brangstrup and a rich woman's grave from Årslev, both Funen (Werner 1988; Storgaard 1994). Early gold bracteates demonstrate close links from South Scandinavia to the Danubian basin, exemplified by the A-bracteate

Fig. 7. Reconstruction of the bridle from Fulltofta, left with original axe-shaped pendants at browband and noseband, right with the pendants covered with pelta-shaped silver-on-bronze plates. Drawing Erika Rosengren.

---

from Senoren (Blekinge, Sweden), the frame of which is derived from framed Roman medallions such as those in the Szilágy-Somlyó deposition framed in East Germanic workshops (Bohlin 1981:142; cf. Bursche 1999:43).

At present it seems impossible to narrow down the area further. The workshop that produced the parade bridle was situated at a centre somewhere in an area circumscribed by Untersiebenbrunn, Coşoveni, Crimea, Kačin and Jakuszowice. In this area a multicultural martial elite dominated with prominent Germanic and Nomadic elements (Wieczorek & Périn 2001; Anke & Westernbrink 2007).

Provenance of Sösdala II and Fulltofta

Not a single Scandinavian or Continental bridle is dated to the Late Roman Iron Age, period Scand-C3 (Ørsnes 1994:276–281). Consequently Ørsnes's dating of Sösdala II and Fulltofta to Scand-D1 must be taken with a pinch of salt (Näsman chapter 7). There is almost no comparative material. And in fact there are strong indications that both bridles can be dated to Scand-C3. The decoration with inlaid twisted copper/silver wire in Sösdala II seems restricted to the Roman Iron Age. In Fulltofta the saddle mounts seem to be a missing link between saddle mounts type Ejsbøl from Scand C2/C3 and mounts of Sösdala type from Scand-D1. The lunate pendant in Sösdala II and the axe-shaped pendants in Fulltofta seem to have their best parallels in the Late Roman Iron Age, and originally the two pendant shapes can be traced back to Sarmatian adaptations of Classic apotropaic symbols. The lack of comparative material makes a discussion about provenance difficult. From a technological point of view nothing speaks against a Scanian origin but on the other hand there are indications that open for the possibility that the bridles were made in eastern Europe.

Fig. 8. Three-way mount connectors, 1:1. Left the pendant mount from Sösdala I (no. I:1). Drawing Erika Rosengren. Right a connector from the Bar deposition, Ukraine. After Levada 2011 fig. 10:7.

Fig. 9. Left a strap junction from Finnestorp. Approx. 1:1. © Offering Site Finnestorp. Right a strap junction from Untersiebenbrunn. 1:1. Photo: Kunsthistorische Museum, Wien, KHM-Museumsverband, ref. 1525/2016.

A Scandinavian provenance?

A South Scandinavian provenance of the Sösdala I bridle is an alternative we do not find convincing at present. An important observation is that the bridle was made entirely in silver, also the bit rings. The only parallels to this are found on the Continent. But of course new finds can change the picture. It is a possibility that the bridles discussed above were produced by South Scandinavian craftsmen trained in Roman workshops or by Roman craftsmen brought back to Scandinavia as "war booty" by returning warriors. It was not difficult to find skilled Roman craftsmen, since the late Roman belt sets were produced in many small workshops along the *limes* (Sommer 1984:102–103). Both alternatives are considered reasonable by several scholars (e.g. Strömberg 1961 I:89–90, 183; Haseloff 1974:4, 6; Magnus 1975:38–41). But other scholars reject the idea that Roman craftsmen came to Scandinavia and prefer the hypothesis that Scandinavians returning home with Roman art before their eyes inspired local emulation and transformation (Holmqvist 1952:17–19). However, a domestic provenance finds no support in the interpretation of the three ritual depositions as emulations of Nomadic customs (Fabech chapter 2).

War and social change

Scandinavia was fundamentally changed during the 4th–6th centuries. The Roman Empire, the superpower of the period, disintegrated and the remains of the Western Roman Empire were transformed. This process also influenced the northern part of Europe, where struggles for power were fought and larger polities arose (cf. Näsman 1999; 2012; Rau 2010:483). Wars were waged to gain control of people and wealth. Warriors went to war motivated by stories and myths about the legitimacy of power and the divine descent of their leaders (Fabech 2011). Some young warriors were certainly sent to distant relations to gain experience and knowledge (Herschend 2001:11–38; 2009:294). Back home in Scandinavia they attacked old traditions with new ambitions (Herschend 1992:161–163). Stories about heroic deeds and genealogical myths about divine origins were used by those who defended the *status quo* as well as by those who challenged the existing system.

Spontaneously we assume that the Sösdala and Fulltofta bridles and saddles were used by male warriors, "horsemen", but it is in fact not a matter of course. In Jakuszowice a bridle similar to Sösdala I was found in a rich warrior's grave (Godłowski 1995), but the two loose-ring bridles in

Fig. 10. ● *Find spots of punch decorated silver bridles (early 5th century) on distribution map of cylindrical cut glass vessels of the 3rd–5th centuries AD ("Eggers 230", "type Kowalk"). Glass distribution after Näsman 1984 map 3.*

Untersiebenbrunn were found in a woman's grave (Nothnagel 2013:88–90). The depositions with remains of bridles from Bar and Kačin have a mixed content of male and female. But since pairs of bridles in women's graves represent draught horses we believe that the combination in Sösdala of a single bridle with a saddle supports our warrior interpretation.

War was an important constituent of the social transformations that took place in the Migration Period. The importance of war as cause of social change must not be underestimated (Näsman 1999:5–6; 2006:217–21 with references). Wars created, for example, career opportunities for new leaders. The indicators of war during the Roman Iron Age and the Migration Period are interpreted as evidence of tribal warfare (raids and plunder) to get resources and as wars of conquest. Frands Herschend describes the wars in Scandinavia during the Migration Period as struggles between families of the "upper classes" to gain land and power (Herschend 2009:405).

The Sösdala and Fulltofta depositions were made in a period characterised by endemic warfare (*sensu* Halsall 1989) and frequent battles. Much warfare emanated from the rivalry among elites that easily escalated to struggles for domination and wars of conquest (Ringtved 1999:363–364; Herschend 2003; 2009:405). It is possible that raiding by small parties of mounted warriors is exemplified by Finnestorp (see Nordqvist chapter 11). The Scandinavian evidence consists of offerings of military equipment, fortifications and weaponry. The number of observations in South Scandinavia peaks in period Scand-D1, in the early 5th century AD (Näsman 1994 fig. 8). One may surmise that armed conflicts between neighbouring polities were frequent and we suggest that the martial finds in the Sösdala area are best understood as traces of elite warriors on guard in a border area (Fabech, Helgesson & Näsman chapter 4). The later Sjörup deposition (Scand-D2) is interpreted as a hidden hoard of battlefield spoils and perhaps it is evidence of a battle that took place near the Sösdala area.

Scandinavian participation in events on Continental war theatres is indicated by finds of foreign objects brought back home, such as military belt sets (e.g. Nydam no. 1971-1, Rau 2010:289–291) and solidi (Fisher chapter 16). An example of how integrated Scanian warriors were in the martial elite of *Barbaricum* is given by the Nydam-Porskær type of bridge mounts for sword scabbards. Three Scanian bridge mounts are all of Cu-alloy covered by sheet silver and of high quality. The mount from Tormestorp (Fabech, Helgesson & Näsman chapter 4 fig. 4b) has an exquisite nielloed decoration and represents the highest contemporary quality. The Vätteryd bridge mount is so burnt and fragmented that it cannot be assessed (Fabech chapter 2 fig. 4). The mount from Häckeberga is likewise well made with punched decoration but no niello (Strömberg 1961 Taf. 52:1). This type of suspension mount has a wide distribu-

tion in Europe from Belgium to Ukraine and from Hungary to Medelpad in northern Sweden (fig. 11); today it is assumed to be a Continental form (Rau 2010:486–487). It is noteworthy that the type is completely missing in the many Norwegian weapon graves (Bemmann & Hahne 1994), a fact supporting the surmised south-eastern relation.

How long is the tradition of acquiring martial experience by participating in foreign wars? There is little evidence for the idea of direct participation in Roman wars as early as the 3rd century, but stronger arguments can be presented that direct contact routes existed to the Danubian Basin and the Roman Empire in period Scand-C3, the 4th century (Rau 2012:381,384,389). When an increasing number of young warriors from Scania went to south-eastern Europe around AD 400 they did not enter a *terra incognita* (cf. Bemmann 2006:227-229). Based on the distribution of silver bridles we assume that Scanian warriors probably were found in barbaric troops outside the Roman Empire. A large part of south-eastern *Barbaricum* was controlled by the Huns, but we have to reckon with smaller more or less independent tribal formations on the outskirts of the Hunnic Empire.

Warriors returning from the Continental wars came with new knowledge and valuable experience. Presumably their return brought tension into local communities, with major changes of the ideological and political structures as a result (Fischer chapter 16). Young men returning from the wars easily came into conflict with an old tribal elite, which based its lifestyle on ideals of the Late Roman Iron Age (Fabech 2011:34). They formed a new warrior elite that had served in the Continental wars. They were strongly influenced by an international martial elite dominated by Gepids and Goths, and with prominent Nomadic elements of Alanic, Sarmatian and Hunnic origin. The new elite, the warlords, became not only "makers of manners'" but eventually victors in a struggle for power later in the Migration Period. Warlords became landlords (Herschend 2009:405). It is tempting to consider the finds from Häckeberga, Sösdala, Fulltofta, Tormestorp, and Finnestorp as traces of returning warriors.

The mounted nomads were influential and represented by several different groups: Iranian-speaking Alans and Sarmatians, and Turkic-speaking Huns. But in reality the hordes of mounted warriors were of mixed origin, also in-

Chapter 17: Sösdala interpreted in its glocal context

cluding Germanic-speaking people, so in some contexts "Huns" was rather a politonym than an ethnic designation. The ethnic Huns were the leading faction for a short time only. There was a longer relation between Sarmatians and various Germanic-speaking groups. Contacts could be established in a large area from the Danubian basin to the steppes north of the Black Sea (Istvánovits & Kulcsár 2011; Quast 2011). For example the origin of lunate pelta-shaped pendants and axe-shaped pendants can be sought in Sarmatian contexts on the lower Danube, and the saddle type with high pommel could also be influenced by Sarmatian saddles (Näsman chapter 7; Lau 2014:76–78; 256–258; Rau 2010:486). The ritual depositions at Sösdala and Fulltofta are explained as an adaptation of Nomadic funerary customs (Fabech chapter 2).

The Danubian basin served as a melting pot where various influences were transformed and adapted by different groups in different ways. Some elements of material or immaterial culture were included while other aspects were rejected or fundamentally transformed. We assume a mixed Roman and Nomadic origin of the Scandinavian ring saddle type, which came into existence when saddle rings were added around AD 200. The Sarmatians are mentioned several times in studies of material relevant for the understanding of the bridles from Sösdala II and Fulltofta. When the Huns invaded the plains north of the Black Sea and raided further to the west, groups of peoples such as Alans and Goths fled westward looking for the protection of the Roman Empire where they were accepted as *foederati*. In interaction with Late Roman culture, the so-called Untersiebenbrunn group appeared, representing such *foederati* (Kazanski, Koch and Tejral in Wieczorek & Périn 2001:38–51; Bemmann 2006:226). Common to finds such as Kačin, Bar, Coșoveni, Jakuszowice and Untersiebenbrunn is direct or indirect involvement in the interaction between barbarians and Romans.

Rituals

Barbaric polities were based on values legitimised by a martial culture filled with military rituals and symbols. Ceremonies celebrated after a funeral of a heroic warrior would certainly be an important element. Weapon rituals are a natural constituent of martial societies. The most famous examples of Scandinavian weapon rituals are the offerings of military equipment (e.g. Finnestorp, Nordqvist chapter 11).

The rituals preceding the deposition of horse tack at Sösdala and Fulltofta are unknown; only systematic ritual destruction and deposition can be deduced from the cut-up remains of bridles and saddles. The deposition of dismantled horse tack on the top of gravel hills is explainable by references to studies of Nomadic funerary rituals that followed the death of a prominent warrior. These rituals comprised the transition from one condition to another, more like *rites de passage* than typical sacrifices. The practice is found among mounted nomads such as Sarmatians, Huns and Alans as well as later Nomadic groups. The Fulltofta and Sösdala finds can reflect similar ritual activities. Perhaps Scandinavian warriors attended funerary rituals according to nomadic customs in south-eastern Europe or at least heard about such rituals. The rituals possibly comprised a series of events: *lit de parade*, burial, equestrian ceremonies, funeral feast and arval, ritual destruction of horse tack and the subsequent deposition of the remains. Contemporary sources are indeed few but fortunately we have an eye-witness description of a funeral ceremony.

In *Getica* (§254–259) a summary by Jordanes is preserved of Priscus' own description of the ceremonies performed after the death at Attila, King of the Huns. The corpse of the dead king was placed on a *lit de parade* in a tent. The best horsemen of the Huns rode around the tent in circles performing a dirge about Attila's deeds. After this mourning ceremony a *strava* was celebrated, a revel during which the mourners displayed funeral grief alternating with joy. Then in the night they had the body buried.

After the battle of the "Catalaunian Plains" the Hun camp was besieged by the joint Roman and Visigothic armies. The situation seemed hopeless for the Huns and Attila prepared to take his own life, not to fall in the hands of the enemy alive. He had a funeral pyre erected consist-

Fig. 12. The pelta-shaped pendant covers from Fulltofta (no. F:1) compared with the pelta-shaped pendant from Sösdala I (no. I:19–21). Same size but not to scale. Photo Daniel Lindskog.

ing of a heap of saddles (Jordanes *Getica* 213). It is not possible to conclude whether saddles were chosen as the only fuel available or whether saddles were chosen because of some symbolic meaning.

Surprisingly there is another description of a Migration Period funerary ritual in which riders have a central role. In *Beowulf* (lines 3156–3182) we find a report of the funeral of Beowulf, King of the Geats (*Göter*). The Geats built a large funeral pyre surrounded by shields, helmets and mail coats. After the fire had burnt down the Geats raised in ten days a barrow over Beowulf. Then twelve brave riders rode around the barrow reciting memorial poetry in praise of his deeds, mourning his death.

Obviously horses and horsemen delivered a significant contribution to funerary rituals at high social levels. The similarity between the mourning rituals of Attila and Beowulf may be accidental, but there may also be a link, an impact of Nomadic customs on old Scandinavia as revealed by the Sösdala and Fulltofta finds. The ritual significance of horses in funerary ritual is further demonstrated by the horses buried at the large barrows of King Childeric in Tournai, Belgium, and unknown persons in Žuráň, Czechia (Müller-Wille 1998 Abb. 6, 7, 11; Tejral 2013 fig. 9).

Horses are a regular constituent of elite burials but the concrete way horses were used in funerary rituals varies (Müller-Wille 1972; Jennbert 2011:passim). In some contexts they were killed and buried with or without their tack. Some accounts tell us that after a funeral Nomads killed the horses and ate the meat. We do not know what happened to the horses at Sösdala and Fulltofta. At the Vätteryd cemetery horse bones are present in some of the cremations. The depositions of bridles and saddles at Sösdala I, II and at Fulltofta probably reflect horsemanship influenced by Nomadic culture.

A "biography" of the Sösdala and Fulltofta horse tack

The spectacular parade bridle deposited at Sösdala I is always compared to the remarkable finds from Jakuszowice, Kačin, Untersiebenbrunn, Bar and Coşoveni, which are considered to represent a princely social echelon of south-eastern Europe. Considering the artistic qualities of this outstanding piece of craftsmanship, the Sösdala bridle seems superior. It belongs to the finest art ware of the early fifth century. Bridles of this quality were not obtained on a common market; they were certainly commissioned work from special workshops producing for the elite. Horse tack of this quality was used on horses of the elite or used as diplomatic gifts (Sundkvist chapter 9; Kazanski & Mastykova chapter 15).

But how can we explain why an outstanding bridle appeared in a gravel pit in a remote place in central Scania, over 2000 km from the probable place of production? Since the three finds of horse tack are chronologically and contextually closely related it seems certain that the three horsemen knew each other. For this reason we defy the obvious difficulties with defective and uncertain sources and choose to present our interpretation as a narrative – a "biography" of the horse tack from Sösdala I, embracing Sösdala II and Fulltofta.

The splendid Migration Period finds in the Sösdala-Fulltofta area seem to lack local roots in the preceding Roman Iron Age. The area was settled but not wealthy. In the Migration Period things changed. A new type of large cemeteries with erected stones and stone ships was introduced, Vätteryd being an excellent example. We believe that the area up to the Migration Period became a bone of contention and that powers outside the area took control and planted their own men here. We believe the Sösdala and Fulltofta depositions represent these men. But our story begins far away.

When the 5th century still was young, a king/tribal leader residing somewhere in south-eastern Europe ordered a workshop specialising in horse tack to deliver him an exclusive set. His favourite horse was bridled with it and it was used for display as well as in battle. We know from Procopius' description of the battle at *Busta Gallorum* in AD 552 that Totila, King of the Goths, went to battle in golden armour with helmet and lance with purpled plumes. He rode on his magnificent horse in front of the troops to demonstrate his equestrian abilities and skills in handling a lance (*Gothic Wars* book 4, ch. 31). The story tells us that parade equipment was intended for use as symbol of power and prestige, also in battle.

The horse tack of the narrative's king was damaged at least twice. A pendant lost in battle was replaced with a copy produced in the same workshop by another but skilled craftsman. Then he also lost another pendant. It was replaced, but seemingly in haste, with a pendant decorated by a less skilled craftsman. The reason could be that the king suddenly decided to use a prestigious but defect horse tack to reward a stranger warrior for extraordinary valour. From the story about Beowulf and his heroic deeds we know that his defeat of Grendel and his mother was rewarded by Hrothgar, King of the Danes (*Beowulf* lines 1020–1049). Among the gifts we notice sumptuous weaponry (mail coat, helmet and sword) and eight horses with golden bridles. One had a jewelled saddle. It was King Hrothgar's battle seat. The passage demonstrates that the gifts were not new but taken from the king's armoury. To receive weapons and horse tack loaded with a king's story was even more honourable. Weapons and horse tack with a heroic past were not given to just anybody.

The hero who received the horse tack was a magnate's son from Sösdala. He had been sent on a civilising Grand Tour to acquaintances in south-eastern Europe. It was common that the contemporary elite developed their alliances with marriages and exchange of children who received training in elite behaviour and skills with another family. During his sojourn our hero of course took part in military training and in battles against enemies, which could be Romans, Huns and other barbarian groups. Having distinguished himself with a deed of Beowulfian bravery, our hero received a silver bridle from the king as a reward. Perhaps he also received a bridled horse (Rosengren chapter 8; Sundkvist chapter 9). After some time he returned home with new knowledge and new ideas. We guess he was welcomed in Sösdala with all the attention a hero deserves.

Then his father died. He was the head of the house and the owner of the Sösdala II bridle. We imagine that the son, inspired by his experiences from abroad, gave his father an honourable funeral that at the same time supported our hero's own ambitions and demonstrated his acquired prestige. He arranged the funeral at the new burial ground Vätteryd with pyre, commemorative orations in honour of the deceased, lamentations, and finally the burial of the cremation. The father's favourite horse was killed and cut up. The meat was cooked to be eaten in the arval. The bones were thrown on the pyre. This was possibly the first burial at Vätteryd, a new type of cemetery representing a strengthened social concord. After the burial the mourners went in a procession to the top of a nearby ridge. At a place overlooking the cemetery and with a view to Lönnebjär, the horse tack was ritually killed and deposited on the ground. This was our hero's version of Nomadic customs he had observed during the Grand Tour. Remains of the destroyed bridle were discovered in 1961. Of a saddle nothing is preserved so either it consisted entirely of organic material or the remains were lost in the gravel pit.

The founding of the Vätteryd cemetery as well as the dismantling and deposition of horse tack violated old traditions; a strong signal that a new era had begun was sent. We consider the deposition of Sösdala II as a successor's attempt to strengthen his heritage and to preserve the family's recently acquired power in the area – a forefather was created.

An equal was living at a magnate estate in Fulltofta, 15 km from Sösdala. In his youth at the end of the fourth century AD he also went on a Grand Tour to south-eastern Europe. A keepsake of his adventure was a Sarmatian(?) bridle with axe-shaped pendants. When he years later saw the fine pelta-shaped pendant sported by the Sösdala hero, he decided to upgrade his old headstall and had a skilled craftsmen make pelta-shaped and punch-decorated silver covers (fig. 12). When he died his heirs marked their own position by choosing to arrange his funeral in a way that displayed the father's fame and heroic deeds. Evoking associations with his experiences in south-eastern Europe, they performed a funerary ritual including the Nomadic custom of dismantling of bridle and saddle, the remains of which subsequently were deposited in a gravel hill overlooking a burial ground.

Sometime in the first half of the fifth century our Sösdala hero also died. Obviously it was important for the heirs to use his funeral to support their power and ascendancy by choosing to manifest him in a ritual similar to what he had arranged for his own father. To repeat the ritual deposition of horse tack close to the first deposition was a deliberate act in order to emphasise continuity in heritage and power.

The spectacular qualities of bridle and saddle indicate that the funeral too was magnificent. Based on the excavations at Vätteryd, the stories about the funeral of Attila and Beowulf, and the general knowledge of funeral sacrifices according to Nomadic customs, we imagine the following scenario. The hero from Sösdala was lying on a *lit de parade*, on the pyre that was not yet set on fire. The dead hero was probably fully equipped but all that remains is a bridge mount for a sword scabbard. He was accompanied on the pyre by his horse and dog. We imagine that twelve horsemen of his retinue rode around the corpse. Tales of the hero's deeds were recited and lamentations sung. Now the pyre was set on fire. When the pyre was burning, an arval was held, horse meat was cooked and eaten, mead was drunk, and stories told. Then the heirs led a procession to a top of the ridge, 60 metres opposite the place where their father had deposited the grandfather's bridle. A lance was stuck in the ground as a symbolic marker where the dead man's spirit could wait until received in the other world (Fabech chapter 2). The hero's saddle and bridle were dismantled and cut to pieces. The remains were deposited on the ground. This corresponds to the finds discovered in 1929 and 1930 at find spots I and IV. The twelve saddles of find spots II and III could represent the twelve retainers that destroyed their saddles to honour the deceased and to aid his passage to the other world. Finally the deposition was covered by stones. The mourners returned to the cemetery. After the pyre had burnt out, some of the ashes were gathered and deposed in a stone setting.

Epilogue

The ritual deposition of dismantled horse tack according to Nomadic customs seems to stop after Sösdala I. However, the deposition of mounts of swords and horse tack at Sjörup is considered to signal a continued presence of warrior elite in the area during the second half of the fifth century (Fabech, Helgesson & Näsman chapter 4).

Burial continued at cemeteries in Sösdala and Fulltofta, probably until Christianisation. The excavated remains of burials at Vätteryd contained regularly cremated bones of humans and in some cases horses and dogs. Finds and the many stone ships erected indicate the continued presence of important people. Only an inhumation from the Vendel period that contained a single-edged sword supports our assumption of military power continuity at Sösdala. But only few graves are excavated.

After Christianisation the settlement centre moved from Sösdala to Norra Mellby, and this happened before the parochialisation and the building of stone churches in the 12th–13th centuries (Fabech, Helgesson & Näsman chapter 4). In the eleventh and twelfth centuries written sources and archaeological studies of building remains demonstrate that large royal domains existed in the Sösdala area and that magnate residences existed at Norra Mellby and Häglinge.

References

Anke, B. & Externbrink, H. (eds) 2007. *Attila und die Hunnen*. Speyer/Stuttgart.

Bemmann, J. 1998. Der Nydam-II-Fund. In: Bemmann, G. & Bemmann, J. 1998. *Der Opferplatz von Nydam. Die Funde aus den älteren Grabungen: Nydam-I and -II*. Band 1–2. Neumünster: 217–240.

Bemmann, J. 2006. Eine völkerwanderungszeitliche Bestattung aus Epöl, Kom. Esztergom, mit Schwertriemendurchzügen skandinavischer Form. In: Mihailescu-Bîrliba, V., Hriban, C. & Munteanu, L. (eds). *Miscellane Romano-Barbarica in honorem septagenarii magistri Ion Ioniță oblata*. Iaşi: 217–246.

Bemmann, J. & Hahne, G. 1994. Waffenführende Grabinventare der jüngeren römischen Kaiserzeit und Völkerwanderungszeit in Skandinavien, Studien zur zeitliche Ordnung anhand der norwegischen Funde. *Bericht der Römisch-Germanischen Kommission* 75: 284–640.

Beowulf. A new verse translation, Seamus Heaney 2000. New York/London. – Checked online 2 July 2017.

Bitner-Wróblewska, A. 2007. *Netta. A Balt cemetery in Northeastern Poland*. Warsaw.

Bohlin, P.-O. 1981. *Brakteat-teknik*. [B.A. thesis in archaeology]. Uppsala University.

Bóna, I. 1991. *Das Hunnenreich*. Stuttgart.

Bursche, A. 1999. Die Rolle römischer Goldmedaillone in der Spätantike. In: Seipel, W. (ed.). *Barbarenschmuck und Römergold. Der Schatz von Szilágysomlyó*. Vienna: 39–53.

Fabech, C. 2011. War and rituals. Changes in ritual and transformations of power. In: Panhuysen, T. (ed.). *Transformations in North-Western Europe (AD 300–1000)*. Hannover/Stuttgart: 27–36.

Geisslinger, H. 1967. *Horte als Geschichtsquelle*. Neumünster.

Godłowski, K. 1995. Das "Fürstengrab" des 5. Jhs. und der "Fürstensitz" in Jakuszowice in Südpolen. In: Vallet, F. & Kazanski, M. (eds) *La noblesse romaine et les chefs barbares du IIIᵉ au VIIᵉ siècle*. Condé-sur-Noireau/Saint-Germain-en-Laye: 155–179.

Halsall, G. 1989. Anthropology and the study of pre-conquest warfare and society. The ritual war in Anglo-Saxon England. In: Hawkes. S.C. (ed.). *Weapons and warfare in Anglo-Saxon England*. Oxford: 155–177.

Haseloff, G. 1974. Salin's style I. *Medieval archaeology* 18: 1–15.

Herschend, F. 1992. Beowulf and St. Sabas: the tension between the individual and the collective in the Germanic society around 500 A.D. *Tor* 24: 145–164.

Herschend, F. 2001. *Journey of civilisation. The Late Iron Age view on the human world*. Uppsala.

Herschend, F. 2003. Krig, offerfynd och samhälle i 200-talets Sydskandinavien. *Fornvännen* 98/4: 312–316.

Herschend, F. 2009. *The Early Iron Age in South Scandinavia. Social order in settlement and landscape*. Uppsala.

Holmqvist, W. 1952. De äldsta gotländska bildstenarna och deras motivkrets. *Fornvännen* 47: 1–20. Zusammenfassung.

Istvánovits, E. & Kulczár, V. 2011. From the Crimea to Scandinavia via the Hungarian plain. Traces of Germanic-Sarmatian contacts on the basis of finds of spherical pendants and other phenomena. In: Khrapunov, I. & Stylegar, F.-A. (eds). *Inter Ambo Maria. Contacts between Scandinavia and the Crimea in the Roman Period*. Kristiansand/Simferopol: 80–90. Резюме.

Jennbert, K. 2011. *Animals and humans. Recurrent symbiosis in archaeology and Old Norse religion*. Lund.

Jordanes. The Gothic history of Jordanes. Transl. by C.C. Mierow. Princeton: 1915. Checked online 2 July 2017.

Jordanes Getica. Om goternas ursprung och bedrifter. Översatt av Andreas Nordin. Stockholm: 1997.

Kazanski, M. 1988. Quelques paralleles entre l'armement en Occident et a Byzance (IVᵉ–VIIᵉ s.). In: Landes, C. (ed.). *Gaule mérovingienne et monde méditerranéen*. Lattes: 75–87.

Lau, N. 2014. *Das Thorsberger Moor 1. Die Pferdegeschirre. Germanische Zaumzeuge und Sattelgeschirre als Zeugnisse kriegerischer Reiterei im mittel- und nordeuropäischen Barbaricum*. Schleswig.

Magnus, B. 1975. *Krosshaugfunnet. Et forsøk på kronologisk og stilhistorisk plassering i 5. årh*. Stavanger. Summary.

MPOV Migration Period between Odra and Vistula http://www.mpov.uw.edu.pl/en/thesaurus/archaeological-sites/ Checked 26 October 2016.

Müller-Wille, M. 1972. Pferdegrab und Pferdeopfer im frühen Mittelalter. *Berichten van de Rijksdienst voor het Oudheidkundig Bodemonderzoek* 20-21: 119-248.

Müller-Wille, M. 1998. *Zwei religiöse Welten. Bestattungen der fränkischen Könige Childeric und Chlodwig.* Mainz/Stuttgart.

Näsman, U. 1994. The Iron Age Graves of Öland – Representative of What? In: Stjernquist, B. (ed.). *Prehistoric Graves as a Source of Information.* Stockholm: 15–30.

Näsman, U, 1999. The ethnogenesis of the Danes and the making of a Danish kingdom. In: Dickinson, T. & Griffiths, D. (eds). *The making of kingdoms.* Oxford: 1–10.

Näsman, U. 2006. Danerne og det danske kongeriges opkomst. *Kuml* 2006: 205–241. Summary.

Näsman, U. 2012. Comments on "An Iron Age shock doctrine: The 536–37 event as a trigger of large-scale social change in the Mälaren valley area" by D. Löwenborg. *Journal of Archaeology and Ancient History* 4. Online: http://www.arkeologi.uu.se/Journal/no-4-lowenborg/ – Checked 12 December 2016.

Nielsen, J.N. 2000. *Sejlflod – ein eisenzeitliches Dorf in Nordjütland. 2: Abbildungen und Tafeln.* Copenhagen.

Nothnagel, M. 2013. *Weibliche Eliten der Völkerwanderungszeit. Zwei Prunkbestattungen aus Untersiebenbrunn.* St. Pölten.

Ørsnes, M. 1994. Zaumzeugfunde des 1.–8. Jhrh. nach Chr. in Mittel- und Nordeuropa. *Acta archaeologica* 64/2, 1993: 183–292.

Procopius Cäsariensis. Transl. by D. Coste & A. Ritthaler: *Prokop, Vandalenkrieg – Gotenkrieg.* Munich: 1966.

Quast, D. 2011. The links between the Crimea and Scandinavia: some jewellery from the third century AD princely graves in an international context. In: Khrapunov, I. & Stylegar, F.-A. (eds). *Inter Ambo Maria. Contacts between Scandinavia and the Crimea in the Roman Period.* Kristiansand/Simferopol: 198–308. Резюме.

Rau, A. 2010. *Nydam mose 1–2. Die personengebundenen Gegenstände. Grabungen 1989–1999.* Højbjerg/Aarhus. Summary. Dansk resumé.

Rau, A. 2012. Das nördliche Barbaricum zur Zeit der Krise des 3. Jahrhunderts n. Chr. Einige kritische Anmerkungen zur Diskussion über provinzialrömisch-nordeuropäische Verbindungen. In: Fischer, T. (ed.). *Die Krise des 3. Jahrhunderts n. Chr. und das Gallische Sonderreich.* Wiesbaden: 343–430.

Ringtved, J. 1999: Settlement Organisation in a Time of War and Conflict. In: Fabech, C. & Ringtved, J. (eds). *Settlement and Landscape.* Højbjerg/Aarhus: 361–381.

Sommer, M. 1984. *Die Gürtel und Gürtelbeschläge des 4. und 5. Jahrhunderts im römischen Reich.* Bonn.

Storgaard, B. 1994. The Årslev Grave and Connections between Funen and the Continent an the End of the Later Roman Iron Age. In: Nielsen, P.O. et al. (eds). *The archaeology of Gudme and Lundeborg.* Copenhagen: 160-168.

Strömberg, M. 1961. *Untersuchungen zur jüngeren Eisenzeit in Schonen. I Text, II Katalog und Tafeln.* Lund.

Tejral, J. 2013. The connections between the region north to the Danube and northern Europe. Soma aspects of ethnic and social identity of fifth century elites. In: Khrapunov, I. & Stylegar, F.-A. (eds). *Inter Ambo Maria. Northern barbarians from Scandinavia towards the Black Sea.* Kristiansand/Simferopol: 383–408. Резюме.

Werner, J. 1988. Dančeny und Brangstrup. Untersuchungen zur Černjachov-Kultur und zu den 'Reichtumszentren' auf Fünen. *Bonner Jahrbücher* 188: 241–286.

Wieczorek, A. & Périn, P. (eds) 2001. *Das Gold der Barbarenfürsten.* Stuttgart.

Резюме

Сёсдала: интерпретация в глобальном и локальном контексте

Шарлотта Фабек, Ульф Несман

Три памятника в Сёсдале и Фультофте, где были найдены предметы конской сбруи, можно рассматривать под самими разными углами. Мы решили завершить эту публикацию графическими реконструкциями и комментарием, рассматривающим вопросы хронологии, происхождения и исторической подоплеки данных находок. Наконец, здесь будет представлена «биографии» всех трех комплексов. Характер имеющегося источникового материала сильно различается в разных частях Европы, потому само по себе наличие или отсутствие находок конской сбруи в настолько разных контекстах не показательно. В настоящее время ситуация ухудшается из-за увеличения объема торговли древностями, сочетающейся с разграблением памятников при помощи детекторов металла (рис. 1–3).

Чтобы понять функциональное назначение многих металлических накладок и зажимов, приходится прибегать к гипотетическим реконструкциям. Вместе с Э. Росенгрен мы «оседлали» и «взнуздали» «коня из Сёсдалы I» (рис. 4–5) и «взнуздали» лошадей из Сёсдалы II (рис. 6) и Фультофты (рис. 7). В представленном на рисунке седле из Сёсдалы использованы оковки из места находки IV, прикрепленные к луке, имеющей форму седла из Хёгома, причем задняя лука ниже и наклонена назад.

Кажется, достигнут консенсус, согласно которому парадная уда из Сёсдалы синхронна уздечкам из Унтерзибенбрунна, и что они датируются началом Эпохи переселения народов. Это соответствует периоду D1 по скандинавской хронологии, или времени ок. 400/410–455/465 гг. н. э., или периоду D2 по европейской хронологии, т. е. ок. 380/400–440/450 гг. н. э. Узда из Сёсдалы II относится к периоду C3 по скандинавской хронологии, или 300–400/410 гг. н. э. Узда из Фультофты в своем первоначальном виде датируется периодом C3 по скандинавской хронологии, но подвеска в стиле «Сёсдала» указывает на то, что археологизация находки произошла в начале Эпохи переселения народов, или в период D1 по скандинавской шкале.

Где были сделаны элементы парадной узды – в Скании, Скандинавии или на Европейском континенте? В настоящее время южно-скандинавская локализация не кажется убедительной. Важным представляется то обстоятельство, что элементы парадной узды, а также кольца-ограничители грызл, сделаны из цельного серебра. Это выдающееся произведение искусства относится к группе наиболее тонких изделий начала V в. Можно обнаружить не более пяти параллелей из числа восточноевропейских находок в Баре, Кошовени, Якушовице, Качине и Унтерзибенбрунне. На подвеска из Сёсдалы (№ I.1) имеются вставки черни из чистого сульфида серебра. По данным химического анализа черни, эту подвеску сделали в мастерской, работавшей в русле римских традиций. Она же представляет собой тройной распределитель ремней, напоминающий подвижный распределитель из Барского клада (рис. 8). Из этого сходства становится понятна тесная связь между обеими находками. Мотив на уни-

кальном штампе, с помощью которого декорирована подвеска из Сёсдалы (см. статью Л. Даль в этой книге, штамп № 21), вероятно, изображает головы лошадей, направленные в противоположные стороны. Недавно обнаружен распределитель ремней, вероятно происходящий из Крыма (рис. 1). Богато декорированная штампом находка с Волыни (рис. 2) дает дополнительные аргументы в пользу юго-восточного происхождения этих вещей. На тесную связь с позднеримским штемпельным декором указывают шестилепестковые розетки на распределителях ремней из Сёсдалы I, напоминающие розетки на накладках на ремень из Унтерзибенбрунна (см. статью У. Несмана в этой книге, рис. 12). То же самое демонстрирует и распределитель ремней в форме щита из Финнесторпа с фасетированным «умбоном», напоминающий распределители ремней из Унтерзибенбрунна (рис. 9). Контакты с юго-восточной Европой шли по традиционным путям, на что указывают находки стеклянных сосудов с прошлифованным декором, в основном датирующиеся IV в. (рис. 10). Мастерская, в которой сделана узда из Сёсдалы I, находились где-то посреди области, ограниченной Унтерзибенбрунном, Кошовени, Крымом, Качином и Якушовице. В этой зоне доминировала поликультурная военная элита, включавшая значительный германский и кочевнический элементы. Происхождение уздечек из Сёсдалы II и Фультофты неясно, но есть данные, допускающие их производство в Восточной Европе.

Приношения в Сёсдале и Фультофте были сделаны в период, который характеризовался перманентными вооруженными конфликтами и частыми сражениями. Соперничество элит нередко приводило к эскалации конфликтов в борьбе за господство и завоевательным войнам. Вооруженные конфликты между соседними государственными образованиями случались часто, а потому воинские находки в окрестностях Сёсдалы проще всего объяснить как следы деятельности элитных воинов, охранявших приграничную зону. Более позднее приношение в Шёрупе (период D2 по скандинавской хронологии) можно интерпретировать как клад трофеев, взятых на поле боя, – вероятно, свидетельство сражения, случившегося недалеко от области Сёсдалы.

На то, что скандинавы принимали участие в событиях, разворачивавшихся на театрах военных действий на Континенте, указывают находки привезенных домой вещей иноземного происхождения, например, воинских поясов и солидов. Примером интеграции воинов из Скании в воинскую элиту Барбарикума являются портупейные скобы от ножен меча типа «Нидам-Порскер». Подвесные крепления этого типа были широко распространены в Европе от Бельгии до Украины и от Венгрии до Медельпада на севере Швеции (рис. 11); ныне общепризнано, что это континентальная форма. Распространение серебряных уздечек дает основания предположить, что воины из Скании, вероятно, входили в состав варварских отрядов за пределами Римской империи. Значительную часть юго-восточного Барбарикума контролировали гунны, но нужно учитывать, что на окраинах гуннской империи находились небольшие более или менее независимые племенные образования. Соблазнительно будет считать находки из Сёсдалы и Фультофты следами возвращавшихся воинов.

Неизвестно, какие именно ритуалы предшествовали приношению конской сбруи в Сёсдале и Фультофте; можно определить только, что ритуальное повреждение вещей и принесение их в жертву следовало определенной системе. Помещение поломанной конской упряжи на вершине гравийных холмов можно объяснить, рассмотрев погребальные обряды, которые исполняли кочевники после смерти выдающегося воина. Данная практика обнаруживается у таких кочевников-всадников, как сарматы, гунны и аланы, а также у более поздних групп номадов (см. статью

Ш. Фабек в этой книге). Хотя источников, одновременных описываемым событиям, и немного, к счастью, в нашем распоряжении имеется описание погребальной церемонии, оставленное современником. В «Гетике» (§254–259) сохранилось краткое изложение выполненного Приском описания церемоний, которые осуществили всадники после смерти гуннского царя Аттилы. Как ни странно, есть и еще одно описание погребального обряда, в котором центральную роль играли всадники, – в «Беовульфе» (строки 3156–3182). Сходство между ритуалами оплакивания Аттилы и Беовульфа может быть случайным, но нельзя исключить и связи между ними, в результате влияния кочевнических представлений на древних скандинавов, как следует из находок в Сёсдале и Фультофте. Приношение уздечек и седел в Сёсдале I–II и Фультофте, вероятно, указывают на всадническую культуру, на которую оказала влияние культура кочевников.

Поскольку три находки из Сёсдалы и Фультофты тесно связаны между собой хронологически и по контексту, представляется вероятным, что эти три всадника были знакомы друг с другом. По этой причине мы, несмотря на очевидные сложности, осмеливаемся завершить финальную часть книги рассказом о «биографии» конской сбруи из Сёсдалы I, а также Сёсдалы II и Фультофты.

подписи к иллюстрациям

Рис. 1. Слева: фрагмент распределителя ремней (бронза с серебряным покрытием), предположительно найденный в Крыму. Масштаб ок. 1:1; фрагмент с увеличением. Справа: подвеска из позолоченного серебра, предположительно найденная в Виннице (Украина). Масштаб ок. 1:1. Вещи проданы с аукциона в Интернете (фотографии предоставлены Максимом Левадой).

Рис. 2. Различные изделия из позолоченного серебра, в том числе подвески с миниатюрным ярмом, миниатюрной наковальней и сломанным ключом (?). Предположительно найдены на территории Волынской области (Украина). Вещи проданы с аукционов в Интернете (фотографии предоставлены Максимом Левадой).

Рис. 3. Распределитель ремней, описанный как меровингская находка VI в. при продаже с аукциона «TimeLine Auctions» в 2011 г. О его происхождении было сказано: «Британский рынок предметов искусства, приобретен до 2000 г.». Очень близок распределителям ремней из находки в Шёрупе (см. рис. 8 в статье Фабек, Хельгессона и Несмана в этой книге).

Рис. 4. Реконструкции парадной узды из Сёсдалы I, слева – с длинными подвесками на налобном и носовом ремнях, справа – с наконечниками ремней на налобном ремне и мартингалом на носовом ремне (рисунок Эрики Росенгрен).

Рис. 5. Реконструкция коня с парадной уздой из Сёсдалы I с мартингалом и седлом типа 1 (рисунок Эрики Росенгрен).

Рис. 6. Реконструкция узды из Сёсдалы II (рисунок Эрики Росен-грен).

Рис. 7. Реконструкция узды из Фультофты, слева – с оригиналь-ными топоровидными подвесками на налобном и носовом ремнях, справа – с подвесками с пельтовидными обкладками из серебра и бронзы (рисунок Эрики Росенгрен).

Рис. 8. Тройные распределители ремней. Слева – накладка с зажи-мами из Сёсдалы I (№ I. 1; фото Даниэля Линдского). Справа – распределитель ремней из Барского клада (Украина; фотография предоставлена Максимом Левадой).

Рис. 9. Слева: распределитель ремней из Финнесторпа (© Offering Site Finnestorp). Справа – распределитель ремней из Унтерзи-бенбрунна (фото: Музей истории искусств, Вена; № 1525/2016, KHM-Museumsverband).

Рис. 10. Значком   обозначены находки серебряных деталей узде-чек со штампованным орнаментом (начало V в.), нанесенные на карту распространения цилиндрических стеклянных сосудов со шлифованным орнаментом III–V вв. н. э. (тип 230 по Х. Эггерсу, тип «Ковалк»). Карта распространения стеклянных изделий дана по: Näsman 1984 тар 3.

Рис. 11. Находки портупейных скоб от ножен меча типа «Ни-дам-Порскер». По: Bettmann 1998 Fundliste 9; 2006 Fundliste 1; Rau 2010 Abb. 203; Tejral 2013 fig. 6, дополнено информацией Шар-лотты Фабек о находке на поселении Санда (Уппланд, Швеция) и Максима Левады о двух находках с территории Украины, про-данных с аукциона (Levada 2016).

Рис. 12. Обкладки пельтовидной подвески из Фультофты и пель-товидная подвеска из Сёсдалы I. Размер одинаков; даны не в мас-штабе (фото Даниеля Линдского).

Catalogues

Charlotte Fabech & Ulf Näsman

Concordance

The order of photos in the catalogues follows the numbering of the museum catalogue. The catalogue text of Sösdala I reflects, however, the results of our analysis of find history and our reconstructions of bridle and saddles. The concordance shows where the objects are described.

Catalogue

Sösdala I 1929–1930

LUHM museum number 25 570

This catalogue is based on the catalogue of John-Elof Forssander. He sorted the artefacts in four assumed "find spots" (I, II, III, and IV) according to an interpretation of the information about find circumstances available to him. For a large part it was based on letters from and communication with Carl Mellton, who rescued the find (for find history, see Fabech chapter 1), but also on other sources including his own supplementary investigation at the find place in 1929. The find numbers were written on copies of three photos representing find spots I, II–III, and IV. The photos record how Forssander sorted the artefacts into groups labelled A–D, corresponding to the assumed content of the four find spots (A = I, B = II, C = III, and D = IV). In some cases, however, Forssander included artefacts that, according to information in Mellton's or Rydbeck's letters, were found at another find spot.

Based on our analysis of the information about find contexts and our interpretation of the rituals preceding the deposition of the objects, we have chosen to base the catalogue on artefact types, beginning with the parade bridle (I), and continuing with saddles (find spots II, III, and IV). We use the find numbers assigned to the artefacts by Forssander, but objects of the same type are described together, always with a note about how Forssander arranged them. We have made up our own minds about the attribution of artefacts to the four find spots, not respecting Forssander's opinion when it is contradicted by Mellton's or Rydbeck's letters.

The Parade Bridle (find spot I, 1929)

Most objects that Forssander classified as mounts from a bridle were found by workers in the gravel pit. When Mellton screened the gravel he found only one silver artefact, find no. 37, and three now unidentifiable copper plates, 6–7 cm long and 9–14 mm broad. However, a number of finds that Forssander catalogued as belonging to find spot I were not found in the gravel pit but by Mellton on the top of the ridge where the saddle remains (find spot II) were found. The finds, copper-alloy mounts nos. 74, 81, 82 and 84 as well as Cu-alloy caps nos. 95–99 were recorded by Mellton on a photo and are here moved to Saddles.

Nos. 1–70 represent silver mounts from a parade bridle, to which may be added five decorative silver caps nos. 87 to 91. All (except no. 27) are made of silver sheet or thin silver plate varying from 0.1 mm to 1.9 mm in thickness. All seem to be made by smithery except buckle no. 27, which is cast. The "functional" mounts nos. 1–11, 17–18, 22, 24–26 are thicker (0.8–1.9 mm), while the decorative ones, nos. 28–70, are thinner (0.3–0.6 and usually approx. 0.5 mm). In double mounts, the front plate is thicker and the back plate is thinner. Almost all silver mounts are gilt. With few exceptions the whole front side of the mounts is gilt except where it is worn off by use wear.

To the headstall belongs a snaffle bit with loose rings, nos. 100 to 110.

Almost all silver mounts have punched ornamentation; see contribution by Lovisa Dal on punch ornamentation in chapter 6. The punch marks are placed in rows, mainly along the edges and the central axis of the objects. According to Dal's punch analysis, the material can be sorted into three groups and one unique object.

Punch group 1: nos. 1, 3, 4–6, 10, 11, 17, 18, 22, 24, 25, 26.
Punch group 2: nos. 7–9, 14, 15, 16, 19–21.
Punch group 3: nos. 12, 13 + 245, 27, and all mounts nos. 28–70.
Unique: no. 2.

We suppose that a headstall with ring snaffle is represented by nos. 1, 10, 11, 17, 18, 24, 25, 26, 100–101, 102–105, and 106–110. (For a discussion of the interpretation of the mounts, see Näsman in chapter 7). Most other mounts probably decorated the headstall but some may have adorned the breast collar and/or the breeching of a saddle: nos. 2, 3, 4–6, 7–9, 12, 13, 14, 15, 16, 19–21, 22, 23, 27, and all mounts from no. 28 to no. 70, plus 87–92, and 111. See reconstruction drawings in chapter 17.

No. 1 (incl. 182). Pendant mount consisting of a three-way connector, onto which two attachment plates and a pendant with niello inlay are fixed with loops. Distorted and bent. Overall length from top to bottom is 101 mm, breadth across attachment plates 59 mm. All parts are punch-decorated; the largest number of punches, 12 different, has been used on this object (see Dal chapter 6). It is likely to have been placed in the noseband.

The three-way connector has openings on three sides for two attachment plates and one pendant. The fourth upper side has an extension shaped as two outward-looking horse heads in profile; the bent necks possibly indicate a collected horse. A bridge between nose and neck can be interpreted as reins. At the openings silver strips are soldered on as reinforcement for the wear of attachment plates and pendant; they all have deep wear marks. One was loose when found and recorded as part of the objects from find spot II (no. 182).

The attachment plates are double. The front plate is approx. 18 × 16 mm large and 1 mm thick, the back plate only 0.5 mm. They are attached to the three-way connector with

hollow loops; the back plate was possibly rolled up before or hammered out after being attached to the connector. The straps of the noseband were held in place by rivets in the four corners with domed heads on the front side; judging from the present distance between the plates in which remains of a single leather strap is preserved the strap was at least 2 mm thick.

The pendant is made in open-worked plate. Along the centre an ungilded zone of silver is decorated with a row of three-petal niello inlays (for niello analysis, see Dal chapter 6). The pendant is attached to the three-way connector with a hollow loop that is riveted to the back of the pendant; the head of the rivet is domed.

Nos. 2 and 3. Pendants with attachment plate. Two similar items, bent, hammered and broken into two fitting pieces. Length including attachment plate is 114 and 113 mm. Perhaps they adorned the ends of the noseband of the headstall, but seem better placed on the breast collar.

The triangular attachment plates are double and bent to form a hinge with remains of an axle of iron. On no. 2 it is 20 mm and on no. 3 it is 23 mm long. The mount of no. 2 is undecorated. The decorated attachment plate of no. 3 is broken from the pendant and in the rust of the iron axle a fragment of the pendant loop is preserved. The front plate of no. 2 is 0.8 mm thick, the front plate of no. 3 is 1.5 mm thick; the back plate of both is 0.2 mm thick. Both mounts have three rivets, 4 mm long, with domed heads. The rivet heads of no. 3 were hammered flat during the destruction. The strap was originally approx. 1.5–2 mm thick. A 2 mm thick piece of a single leather strap is preserved in the mount of no. 3. It has two original edges, indicating that the pendant was fastened to a hanging strap. The attachment plate of no. 2 is undecorated, that of no. 3 has punched decoration.

The pendant of no. 2 is broken in two pieces; that of no. 3 is bent and flattened. No. 2 is 0.8–1.2 mm thick, no. 3 1.1–1.4 mm. Both were suspended from the hinge of the attachment plate by a rod bent backwards and soldered on the back to form a loop. They are ridged lengthwise except near the loop where there is a flat triangular field. Along both sides of the lower end there are three upward-looking animal heads (horses?) in openwork. Both pendants have similar punched ornamentation, triangular stamps in the triangular field, lines along the edges and a double row of deeply punched triangles along the central ridge. The neck of the animals is decorated with punched circles. The punching, which is slipshod on no. 2 and well executed on no. 3, reveals that the pendants were made by different craftsmen.

Nos. 4 and 7. Two similar pendants with attachment plate. However, there are so many differences that they are described separately.

No. 4 (incl. 5 and 6). Pendant and attachment plate. Found broken and incomplete; three fitting pieces are preserved; the longest is 97 mm long. The pendant is split along its central ridge. The similar no. 7 was originally approx. 150 mm long. Perhaps the pendants 4 and 7 adorned the end of the browband of the headstall, but seem better placed on the breeching.

The triangular attachment plate is double, 21 mm long and bent to form a hinge with remains of an axle of iron. Three rivet holes and two rivets with domed heads are preserved, 5–6 mm long. The leather strap was originally approx. 2 mm thick. The plate is punch-decorated along the edges.

The pendant was broken and split when found; three bent fitting pieces remain. It is 1.1–1.2 mm thick. It is fastened to the hinge by a rod bent backwards and soldered on the back to form a loop. The pendant is bent lengthwise to form a central ridge, now split. A punched decoration of deep triangles along the ridge is similar to that on nos. 2 and 3. Near the loop the ridge is flattened out in the shape of a triangular field, which is decorated with punched triangles. The pendant ends in flat openwork consisting of four double concentric circles with central dot and between them an open cross-shaped figure; the openwork is decorated with punched circles, dots and triangles. The long edges of the pendant are decorated with a row of openwork circles, 13 on the right side and 14 on the left. They are decorated with punched dots.

No. 7 (incl. 8, 9, and 238). Pendant and attachment plate. Found flattened, broken and incomplete; five fitting pieces are preserved. It was originally approx. 150 mm long. Similar to no. 4.

The triangular attachment plate is single, 31 mm long, and bent to form a hinge with remains of an axle of iron. Three rivet holes with two rivets preserved, 5 mm long, with domed heads. Its punch-decoration is different from that on no. 4.

The pendant was bent and broken when found; five fitting pieces remain. It is 1.0–1.4 mm thick. It is fastened to the hinge by a rod bent backwards and soldered on the back to form a loop. The pendant is bent lengthwise to form a central ridge, now partly flattened. Along the ridge two rows of large punched concentric semicircles. Near the loop is a flat triangular field, decorated with punched concentric semicircles. The pendant ends in flat openwork consisting of four double concentric circles with a central dot and between them an open cross-shaped figure. Rows of punched zigzags decorate the openwork circles. The long edges of the pendant are decorated with a row of 13 openwork circles on the right side and 14 on the left. They are undecorated, but at the first openwork circles below the hinge the craftsman tested one dot and one circle punch but discontinued punching (fig. 12 in Dal chapter 6).

Two small fitting fragments of the openwork (no. 238) came, according to Forssander's catalogue and a letter with photo by Mellton, from find spot IV. But according to a note in Forssander's catalogue it was "later" said that they probably came from find spot I. The fragments came to the museum so late that Forssander could not include them on the photo of find spot I. No. 238 has fittings to no. 7 as well as to nos. 8 and 9. This reveals that no. 7 belongs to this pendant, not to no. 4 as he assumed according to the catalogue photo.

Nos. 10 and 11. Cheekpiece mounts. The two similar mounts probably connected the cheekpieces of the headstall to the bit rings. Both are 54 mm long. The loop of no. 10 is flattened and scratched but the attachment plate is well preserved. No. 11 is wrenched out of shape and marked by several blows, but was once very similar to no. 10. The hollow loop has a rounded cross-section. The gilding ends at crossing lines at the middle of the loop, which is punch-decorated with lines and circles, cf. nos. 17–18 below. Both the front and back plates end in two outward-looking horse heads; the bent necks possibly indicate a collected horse. A bridge between nose and neck can be interpreted as reins. The front plate has varied punch decoration. Nine rivets, all with domed heads and 7 mm long, held the leather strap; a piece of a single 3 mm thick leather strap is preserved between front and back plates. Front plate is 1.1 mm thick, back plate 0.5 mm thick.

Nos. 12 and 13 (probably incl. 245). Mounts. Two similar but incomplete mounts. Function unknown. As 15 mm wide strap-ends they only narrowly pass through buckle no. 26 and not buckle no. 27. So it seems more likely that they were pendants or a kind of strap mount. In the reconstruction drawing they are placed at the end of the martingale straps where they connect to the noseband (fig. 4–5 in chapter 17). The punched ornamentation links the two mounts to punch group 3. As 15 mm wide strap-ends they only narrowly pass through buckle no. 26 and not buckle no. 27. So it seems more likely that they were pendants or a kind of strap mount. On no. 12 the upper end with rivet holes is cut off and missing. The end is preserved on no. 13, which is the upper part of a corresponding mount. Fragment no. 245 is similar to the lower part of no. 12 and could be the end of no. 13; but it does not fit since approx. 20 mm is missing in between. No. 13 was not broken when found according to the first photo but was broken into two pieces in 1967 (see Geisslinger 1967 Taf. 23:13). The upper and lower ends of the mounts are not gilt. At the upper end are two rivet holes with traces after silver caps, 5 mm in diameter. At the lower end an openwork roundel with a central hole (for a rivet?). No. 12 is now 99 mm long, no. 13 is 54 mm and no, 245 is 30 mm. Comparison between nos. 12 and 13 indicates that both probably were approx. 105 mm long originally. They are 15 mm broad and 0.5–0.6 mm thick.

Fragment no. 245, which arrived late at the museum together with finds from find spot IV, was sketched by Forssander on the catalogue photo of find spot I. The fragment is absent on Mellton's photo of finds from find spot IV, but was added later according to a find list by Rydbeck.

No. 14. Strap junction. Cross-shaped plate, when found broken in 3, now in 4, fitting pieces. Small remains of a back plate of Cu-alloy. The object is 40 × 43 mm large, 0.4 mm thick. The cross-arms are 20 mm broad. Two riv-

et holes in each cross-arm and one in the centre, 6 rivets with domed heads are preserved, 6 mm long. Punched ornamentation in four concentric zones, alternately gilt and ungilt. Punch marks form a star motif in the centre. On the back a pentagram is incised in a circle; its centre is a pentagon (Dal chapter 6 fig. 14).

Nos. 15 and 16. Strap junctions. Two similar cross-shaped plates. No. 16 is battered but obviously quite similar to no. 15. No. 15 is 39 × 41 mm large, 0.5–0.7 mm thick. No. 16 is 40 mm long. The cross-arms are 22 mm broad. Two rivet holes in each cross-arm and one in the centre. Remains of rivets with domed heads are preserved, 6–7 mm long. On the front a wide circle is punched, inside which six lanceolate petals surround a six-petal rosette; the leaves are gilt, the spaces in between are ungilt creating a six-armed cross. On the back of no. 15 a whirl is incised with 12 curved spokes. On the back of no. 16 is incised the same motif as on the front, but the leaves have incised pinnate venation (Dal chapter 6 fig. 14).

Two strap junctions probably connected the headpiece, cheekpieces, noseband, and throatlash to one another, the two others connected the noseband to the cheekpieces.

Nos. 17 and 18. Rein mounts. Two similar mounts that probably connected reins with bit rings. No. 17 is battered and 53 mm long but no. 18 is undamaged, 47 mm long and 25 mm broad. Both mounts are worn. The hollow loops are rounded in cross-section. Gilt as far as cross-lines at the middle of the loop, which is punch-decorated with lines and circles like nos. 10–11. The attachment plates are shaped as isosceles triangles with cut-off corners at the base. No. 17 is punch-decorated along the edges with triangles and concentric semicircles, no. 18 the same but reverse order. Front plate is 1.9 and 1.4 mm thick and back plate is 0.5 and 0.2 mm thick. Five rivets with domed heads are preserved, 8 mm long.

No. 19 (incl. 20 and 21; probably also no. 185). Pelta-shaped pendant and attachment plate. Bent and broken in 4 fitting pieces; small fragments missing. In all 86 mm from top to bottom. It is likely to have been placed in the browband.

The attachment plate (no. 19) is approx. 30 × 30 mm large, bent and broken into 3 fitting pieces. The front plate,

1.5 mm thick, is bent over to form a hinge and a short back plate that ends after the first pair of rivets. Four rivet holes with 3 rivets, 6 mm long, preserved with domed heads. Punched borders and in the centre a punched star of concentric circles, radiating triangles ending in a dot of concentric circles.

The pelta-shaped pendant (nos. 20–21) is crumpled up and broken in 2 fitting pieces. It is 0.8–1.0 mm thick. Originally it was approx. 60 mm across. The ends of the pelta are shaped like heads of a bird of prey, bent inwards. The opening of the pelta is filled with openwork, now broken, consisting of a bow, and a narrow bridge that originally connected the two bird heads. Rich punch-decoration including a row of four-petal flowers of deep lens-shaped punch marks.

A silver knob made of a profiled silver ribbon is folded around an iron axle (no. 185). Its circular base is decorated by a line. Then follows a gilt moulding and it ends in a domed head in silver. It is 9 mm long and 5.6 mm in diameter. Its original position was likely at the axle of the pendants nos. 19–21 (above). According to Forssander's catalogue it was found at find spot II.

No. 22. Buckle with triangular attachment plate. The buckle has no tongue. Total length 49 mm, the frame is 44 × 21 mm large. The oval frame is made of a bent rod, with a long scarf below the loop of the plate. The frame is not gilt. It has deep wear marks, especially in the loop (cf. cross-section) but also on the front side at both ends. The attachment plate is double and shaped as an isosceles triangle with cut-off corners at the base. It is punch-decorated with a row of triangles along the edges and a triangular field of circles at the loop. The plate has a tubular loop for the frame. Most of the gilding on the loop is worn off. The front plate is 1.4 mm thick, the back plate only 0.3 mm thick. Five rivets 5 mm long, with domed heads are preserved, three at the end and one at each corner. Function unknown; a strap slider of the parade bridle? or a mount of a breast collar with martingale in saddle tack?

Nos. 23 and 111. Integral plate strap buckles. Both are undecorated and not gilt. No. 23 is 29 mm long, no. 111 is 27 mm long, and both are 22 mm wide. The oval frames

have facetted cross-sections. The plates are rounded with bevelled edges. They are 15 and 16 mm broad respectively. Both once had 3 rivets, 2 at the frame are made of silver; one at the end is made of Cu-alloy. The rivets of no. 23 are 5 mm long; those of no. 11 7 mm long. All silver rivets are hammered flat with the plate except one on no. 111 which has a domed head, a repair? The pins are flat with bevelled edges except at the loop which is decorated with a notch. Neither the mounts nos. 12, 13, nor the strap ends nos. 35, 36, and 38 can pass through the frame of these buckles, the inner openings of which are 13 and 12 mm respectively. No. 111 is one of the objects that were taken from the find spot by private persons and bought back by Carl Mellton in 1929 so its original context is unknown.

Nos. 24 and 26. Strap buckles with triangular plate. Two similar buckles but the rounded D-shaped frame of no. 24 is compressed like no. 25 below. No. 24 is now 42 mm long and the attachment plate is 22 x 17 mm large. The length of well-preserved no. 26 is 43 mm; the length of the attachment plate is 22 mm and it is 17 mm broad. The width of the frame is 25 mm. The base of the 21 mm long tongues is rounded with a single moulding, which is gilt; the rest is plain and, like the frame, not gilt. The attachment plates are shaped as an isosceles triangle with cut-off corners at the hinge at the base and a roundel at the end. They are double with a 1–1.1 mm thick front plate and a 0.2 mm thick back plate. The plates have rivets at the corners and the roundel at the end. Three rivets with domed heads are preserved, 5 mm long. In the back plate of no. 26, an empty extra rivet hole in the roundel indicates a repair. Both attachment plates are punch-decorated with lines and concentric semicircles.

Strap ends 35, 36, and 38 can pass through the frame of these buckles.

No. 25. Strap buckle with triangular plate. The rounded D-shaped frame is compressed; the hinge is distorted. It is now 44 mm long. The attachment plats is 27 x 18 mm large. Original shape of frame and attachment plate similar to nos. 24 and 26, but the gilt base of the tongue is box-shaped, not rounded. Also the ornamentation of punched rows of triangles along the edges differs from nos. 24 and 26.

No. 27. Integral plate strap buckle. Slight damage at a corner, but otherwise intact. The buckle is cast. The inner side of the frame and the tongue are not gilt. Buckle length 54 mm, width 21 mm. It is 2 mm thick. The frame has a rounded-oval D-shape. It has a triangular cross-section and an external moulding, which is gilt. The flat tongue is bent around the frame and has bevelled edges and a box-shaped base above the axle, with a characteristic decoration of double lines and notches. The plate is an irregular-ridged triangle ending in a roundel, 10 mm across. There is a flat triangular field at the frame, similar to pendants nos. 2, 3, 4, and 7, although there is no punch relation to these. Three Cu-alloy rivets held the strap and buckle together. Two rivets at the frame are hammered in level with the plate and gilt. The third rivet at the centre of the roundel is not visible on the front side because of gilding and circular punch marks. The concentric circles are the centre of a punched star with radiating waffled triangles. Decorated with rows of punched dots and concentric semicircles along edges and central ridge. Strap ends nos. 35, 36 and 38 can pass through this buckle.

Nos. 28–70. Strap mounts, ring-link connectors, and strap ends that are similar: 23 or 24 are simple rectangular mounts, six mounts and one loose ring represent ring-link connectors, and there are three strap-ends. The mounts have two rivets at each end; the distance between them vary between 6 mm and 9 mm. The average of 46 cases is 6.9 mm.

According to Dal's punch analysis all mounts are linked to one another by identical punch marks. Based on the punch marks along the edges they can be sorted in six groups, plus a few more loosely attached mounts.
Concentric semicircles: nos. 12, 13 + 245, 29, 35, 36 + 37 + 69 + 70, 47, 50, and 57.
Concentric semicircles with dotted outline: 33, 34, 39 + 67, 52, 53, 58, 59, 62, and 64.
Concentric moulded semicircles with dotted outline and inner spiny half-circle: 43 and 49.
Concentric semicircles arranged 3 + 2 + 1 as a triangle: 46, 48, 51, 56, and 60 + 66.
Concentric semicircles arranged 3 + 2 + 1 in a triangle of dotted lines: 32, 40, 42, 44, 45, 54, and 55.
Double triangles: 28 + 61, 31, 41, and 65 + 68.

A single punch motif links strap buckle no. 27 to these strap mounts and the fragmented strap end no. 38 is linked to strap end no. 35.

Eleven different punch motifs are used to decorate all these mounts. The punch-decoration connects the mounts to one another in spite of the fact that there are 14 different combinations. Unique punch combinations are found on only a few mounts: nos. 36, 47, and 60 + 66. Sets of similar punch marks are found on two mounts in seven cases, each with different combinations (nos. 12 and 13; nos. 35 and 38; nos. 28 and 31; nos. 32 and 40; nos. 41 and 65; nos. 43 and 49; nos. 50 and 57). One set of similar punch marks is found on three mounts: nos. 33, 34, and 59. Another set of similar punch marks is found on four mounts: nos. 46, 48, 51, and 56. A set of similar punch marks on five mounts: nos. 42, 44, 45, 54, and 55; and another set on six mounts: nos. 39, 52, 53, 58, 62, and 64.

Nos. 28 (incl. 61 and 174), 29, 30, 31, 32, 33, and 34. Ring-linked strap connectors. The nine fragments represent at least 3 complete ring-link connectors. The mounts are hammered, twisted, and cut into pieces. The ring of ring-link connector no. 33cum34 was cut into two parts that fit one another. No. 174 is the loop and short back plate that fits the front plate no. 28. According to Forssander's catalogue it came from find spot II.

The ring-link connectors consisted of two rectangular strap mounts connected by a ring. The mounts consist of a front plate which is bent back to form a loop and a short back plate which ends after the first pair of rivets. Fragments of a back plate of Cu-alloy are preserved at the loops of nos. 31, 32, 33, 34 (see photos of backs and cross-section). The length of the front plates including loop varies between 69 and 73 mm, the breadth between 14 and 15 mm, and the thickness of the plate varies between 0.4 and 0.6 mm. Four rivets held the strap in place. Rivet length is approx. 7 mm. The space for a leather strap indicates a leather thickness of 2–3 mm. In some cases domed silver caps are preserved, 5 mm in diameter.

The front plates are gilt and punch-decorated; the loops are decorated with lines and a central moulding; only the moulding is gilt. Nos. 28 and 31 have the same punch marks and probably belong to the same ring-link connector, no. 28cum31. The remains of a connecting ring that is preserved in the loops of nos. 33 and 34 fit one another, making it certain that no. 33cum34 is another set of ring-link connectors. Both are decorated with the same punches, which are different from the connector no. 28cum31. Mount no. 32 is decorated with a third set of punch marks from a third ring-link connector.

The rings are approx. 27 mm in diameter. They have a deep external moulding that is gilt and punch-decorated. The punch used is the same as that used on mounts nos. 12–13 and strap ends 35–38, and the strap mounts nos. 39–68.

Nos. 35, 36 (incl. 37, 69 and 70), and 38. Three strap ends. No. 35 is bent. Fragment no. 37 was found by Mellton when he was screening gravel in the gravel pit and it has fittings to other fragments from find spot I (nos. 36 and 69–70). Only the upper end remains of no. 38. The strap ends were originally 56–57 mm long and 12 mm broad; the plate is 0.5 mm thick. The upper part has two rivets, 5 mm long. The rivets on nos. 35 and 38 have conical heads, but on no. 36 they have been flattened. On the back there is a short back plate of silver; the distance between front and back plates indicates that the leather strap was approx. 2 mm thick. A short upper part with rivets is separated from a long lower part by two notches. The punch marks on no. 38 are similar to those on no. 35. The punch-decoration of no. 36 is unique.

The three strap ends pass through the three strap buckles nos. 24–26 as well as no. 27 but not the buckles nos. 23 and 111. The punches are identical to the ones that punched the mounts nos. 12–13, the ring-link connectors nos. 28–34 and the strap mounts nos. 39–68.

No. 39 (incl. 67). Double strap mount. Two fitting fragments. The longer fragment no. 39 was broken after 1930 but before 1967 (see Geisslinger 1967 Taf. 11:16–17). The mount is made from a silver strip bent to form a longer front plate and a shorter back plate, connected by a tubular loop. The tube is not gilt. The preserved part of the front plate is 32 mm long; the breadth is 10 mm. The back plate is only 11 mm long and ends after the preserved rivet with conical head, 6 mm long. The distance between front and back plates indicates that the mount held an object (a

strap?) 4–5 mm thick. The internal diameter of the tube is 5 mm. No wear is recorded in the tube.

The shape and dimensions of the mount are unique and its function unknown, but the punch marks are similar to no. 52 so presumably it was part of the parade bridle. A number of mounts of Cu-alloy also have one end bent to form a tube. They were catalogued by Forssander as part of finds from find spot I because of their similarity to no. 39. But they have other dimensions and the rivet is placed in the opposite end. They are here treated as part of the saddle context (see nos. 72, 74, 79, 81, 82 and 246 below at Copper alloy mounts).

Nos. 40–60, 62–66, and 68 plus 241. Strap mounts. 27 find numbers, 15 of which are relatively well-preserved mounts; 6 are more or less battered and 6 are fragments. Nos. 60 and 66 as well as nos. 65 and 68 are fitting fragments of two different mounts. Nos. 62 and 64 can be from the same mount. No. 63 is missing today but was perhaps present in more fragmented condition on the photo Geisslinger 1967 Taf. 15:32. According to Forssander's catalogue it was 23 mm long, 14 mm broad and similar to no. 41 . In all 23 or 24 different mounts of the same type are represented. The well-preserved mounts are between 59 and 61 mm long, 13–15 mm broad, and 0.3–0.6 mm thick; ten mounts are 59–60 mm long, 14 mm broad and 0.5 mm thick. No. 59 is shorter than the rest, approx. 45 mm long. The mounts have rivets in the four corners, in some cases 6–8 mm long rivets are preserved (nos. 42–43, 45–46, 48–52, 55–60), and some still have a domed silver cap, 6 mm in diameter (nos. 45–46, 50–52, 58, 60; however, some of the caps are absent on early photos and were probably later glued in place at the museum. Three silver caps no. 241 were joined to no. 46 according to Forssander's catalogue). Fragments of back plates of Cu-alloy are preserved in three cases (nos. 45, 51 and 52). The leather strap was originally approx. 3 mm thick.

The punch marks of the ornamentation appear more or less clearly on the back of the mounts. For punch marks, see contribution by Lovisa Dal chapter 6.

Nos. 71, 73, 75, 76, 77, 78, 80, 83, 85, and 86. Mounts, Cu-alloy. All more or less fragmentary, possibly as suggested in

Forssander's catalogue back plates to strap mounts like nos. 28–34, 40–65. They are 13–14 mm broad and approx. 0.5 mm thick. Only two are preserved in full length; no. 73 is only 40 mm long and no. 77 is 49 mm long. Both have 3 rivets or rivet holes preserved. The distance between rivets in a pair is 7–8 mm and between pairs of rivets no. 73 has 31 mm and no. 77 37 mm. The other fragments vary between 18 and 55 mm. The ten finds represent at least eight mounts. Most have 1–3 rivet holes preserved, a few with remains of rivets. However, fragments of sheet Cu-alloy from similar mounts with remains of rivet holes are also recorded among the finds from find spot II; see nos. 192 and 196 below under Saddles, Miscellaneous.

Nos. 87–91. Five domed rivet caps decorated with a four-petal flower or a Mantuan cross. All five have marks of hammer blows, two have cracked. Only one is fairly well preserved. The flower or Mantuan cross is created by crosswise punched pointed ovals with lines along the edges; four similar ovals follow the edge of the caps. The sunken pointed ovals/petals of the flowers are gilt, the cross arms are not. The diameter of the caps was originally 17 mm, the height 7 mm, and the thickness 0.5–0.7 mm. The cavity of no. 87 is partly filled with an unidentified substance in which is a rectangular hole, possibly left by a kind of nail (see cross-section). It is unclear whether the decorative caps adorned the parade bridle or a saddle.

No. 92. Rod-shaped mount. Ungilt and undecorated. Three 5 mm long rivets with flat heads held something approx. 1 mm thick in place. On the side of the rivets the corners of one long side are much worn. The mount is 37 mm long, 7 mm broad and 3 mm thick. Function unknown.

No. 93. Leather strap. A 43 mm long piece of a strap of two layers of leather, a core of thicker leather covered by thinner leather, held together by seams along both edges. A proteomic analysis (see Dal chapter 6) revealed that the thin leather is ovine (sheep/goat). Small remains of thread. The breadth of the strap is 14 mm (too narrow for the 14 mm broad ring-link connectors nos. 28–34 and the strap mounts nos. 40–68). In present condition the strap is 4 mm thick. For other remains of leather straps in the context of the bridle, see nos. 3, 10, and 94 and in the context of saddles, see nos. 133, 148–149, 183–184, and 229.

No. 94. Leather strap. A 14 × 15 mm large and 1 mm thick piece of a strap. No seams visible. A proteomic analysis shows that the leather came from cow (see Dal chapter 6). Two rivet holes, 9 mm apart, have impressions of washers, one square, and one round. A preserved rivet is 6 mm long, cf. the preserved piece of leather strap on hook no. 133. For other remains of leather straps, see no. 93 above.

Nos. 100–101, 102–105 and 106–110. Bimetallic single-jointed loose-ring snaffle. The jointed mouthpiece consists of two rods of iron, square in cross-section, linked to one another by loops. At the other end the rods are bent to form loops for the loose bit rings. One of the iron rods is broken in two pieces without preserved fitting; if the bit was symmetrical approx. one cm is lost, but an original asymmetry is plausible. Straightened out the snaffle was approx. 209 mm long, including missing piece perhaps 220 mm. Bit breadth was approx. 148 mm. The looped ends of the iron bit are encased in silver, 3 mm thick; a rounded casing covers the loop of the bit end and also part of the bar of the bit is covered by a cylindrical silver casing with ridges and mouldings. The 34 mm long silver casings are battered and cracked; iron rust has widened the cracks from within. The free central iron part of the bit was approx. 80 mm long.

Loose bit rings nos. 102 (incl. 103–105) and 106 (incl. 107–110). Made of a silver rod with round cross-section, 8 mm thick. Bit ring no. 102 was cut into 4 fitting pieces. The diameter was originally 82 mm. Bit ring no. 106 was cut into 5 pieces and bent out of shape; only nos. 108 and 109 fit one another. It had probably the same diameter as no. 102.

Saddle Tack
(find spots II–III 1929 and find spot IV 1930)

According to Mellton, workers found many Cu-alloy objects at a second find spot, about 3 m east of the place where they had found silver mounts (find spot I) Forssander classified the objects as mounts from saddles. The material from find spot II consists of at least five different saddles cut in pieces: The remains are fragmented, and four of the saddles are very incomplete. The material from find spot II has links to better-preserved saddles from find spots III and IV.

When Mellton screened the dug-up gravel on the top of the ridge at find spot II, he found a number of identifiable finds (photo 21 June mailed to Lund 24 June 1929). Forssander nevertheless interpreted and catalogued them as related to mounts of the parade bridle at find spot I: four Cu-alloy mounts (nos. 74, 81, 82, and 84) and five Cu-alloy caps (nos. 95–99). Other finds found by Mellton on the same occasion and obviously from saddles were however all catalogued as belonging to find spot II; mount no. 131, rivet no. 177, and rivets nos. 186–189. In our opinion all Mellton's finds are part of saddle tack and thus catalogued below.

Mellton investigated the area where the workers had dug for treasure, and found and recorded a third find spot some 3 m further to the east. From his plan and photo one can imagine how a saddle was cut into pieces and left here (nos. 201–206). Similarities to two saddle mounts and two saddle rings in find spot II (nos. 125–126, 170–171) make it probable that the two find spots in reality are constituents of one single ritual event.

After 1929 the museum in Lund made no further investigations in Sösdala. Then on 9 April 1930 unattended workers found splendid saddle mounts and other small finds at what came to be called find spot IV, about 3 m north of find spot I and north-west of find spot II (fig. 9 in chapter 1). The find has a very homogeneous composition, evidently an almost complete set of silver decorated Cu-alloy mounts for a saddle: two long saddle mounts and one short saddle mount, and six saddle rings with staples (nos. 207–217). To this saddle set various small finds are added, nos. 229–247, many linked to saddle remains, a few to the parade bridle in nearby find spot I.

According to a letter written 25 June 1930 Rydbeck assumed that a group of finds labelled B also came from find spot IV. But Forssander catalogued them as part of find spot II. Rydbeck's summary find list does not allow us to identify all objects but it is certain that two hooks nos. 132–133 were included, and it seems reasonable to assume that strap mounts nos. 134–144 were, and probably also the gilt silver mount no. 245. Two pieces of leather cannot be identified but could be either nos. 148–149 or nos.

183–184. Nevertheless, Forssander catalogued all these finds (except no. 245) as coming from find spot II. In spite of the uncertainty we follow Rydbeck and treat them as having been found in relation to the saddle mounts of find spot IV; for no. 245 see no. 13 at Parade Bridle above.

The many artefacts numbered in the catalogue 115–247 came to the museum in several batches. There is some confusion between the information in Mellton's letters and reports to the museum and the way Forssander arranged the material in the catalogue. Obviously artefact fragments were mixed up during both the 4th-century rituals and the 20th-century recovery, both at the find place and in the handling at the museums in Lund and Stockholm. As a consequence of this, we have chosen to treat the artefacts from find spots II, III, and IV as one unit, subdivided into Saddles and Miscellaneous.

According to generally accepted reconstructions of saddles of the period, they had a carcass of two boards on the back of the horse, connected by pommel and cantle. It can be assumed on the basis of the only saddle found at Högom in a roughly contemporary grave (see Ramqvist 1992 and chapter 10) that the longer Sösdala saddle mounts were fastened to the pommel and the shorter ones to the cantle. Based on the Högom saddle and the almost complete set of saddle mounts and rings found in 1930 (below saddle 1) it can be assumed that each saddle had four or six rings. (For discussion and reconstruction of the Sösdala saddles, see Näsman chapter 7).

In his catalogue of find spot II Forssander included silver fragments nos. 174 and 182 that both fit finds from find spot I (we assume that no. 185 can also be linked to find spot I, see no. 19). Saddle mounts nos. 125–126 and saddle rings nos. 170–171 are similar to the saddle remains that Mellton found in situ at find spot III; they are all treated together as saddle 2 below. In the museum catalogue a lance head of iron was included in the lot from find spot II as no. 172. But according to Forssander it was found about 50 m from find spot II, thrown among stones removed from the find spot by the workers.

Saddle 1

The fourth find that was made in 1930 has a very homogeneous composition, evidently an almost complete set of silver decorated Cu-alloy mounts for a saddle: two long saddle mounts, one short saddle mount, and six almost identical saddle rings and staples (Näsman chapter 7 fig. 24). Only a short mount is missing. To this set various small finds from the same context can be added, nos. 229–247. Two fragments belong to the parade bridle from find spot I (nos. 238, 245). Based on a letter with find list by Rydbeck we assume that some objects that Forssander catalogued as coming from find spot II were in fact part of the saddle tack from find spot IV: two hooks (nos. 132 and 133) and eleven fragments of double strap mounts (nos. 134–144). Two fragments of leather straps are also mentioned but they cannot be identified, so all leather fragments (nos. 148–149 and 183–184) are treated below under Miscellaneous.

Saddle 1: Long saddle mounts

No. 213 (incl. 176, 214, 218, 224, 225, 236). Long saddle mount broken in two fitting pieces (nos. 213 and 214). No. 213 is 159 mm long and no. 214 is 130 mm long. The mount was originally about 290 mm long and is similar to no. 215. Cast in Cu-alloy with inlays of silver wire and details covered by silver sheet or silver caps. The ornamentation of the upper side of the rod consists of parallel silver wires along the whole length of the rod. The two sides have similar ornamentation consisting of wires straight across, crossing wires, slanting wires between circle-and-dots, a long row of circle-and-dots, treble wires slanting left or right, alternately. Possibly the surface between silver sheets at the end of no. 214 is silver-plated.

Secondary deep cuts are found on the rod-shaped mount, which is 9 × 10 mm in cross-section. The curve of the rod seems to reflect the shape of the pommel it once was attached to. The lower end, no. 214, is shaped as a flat plate with curved edges and a central hole for the saddle-ring staple. The mount was fastened to the pommel with 5 rivets and the staple. Two rivets were placed in rounded projections at the upper end, two in the "eyes" of animal-head-shaped projections at the middle, and a single rivet was placed at the lower end point. One of two preserved rivets is 39 mm long and has a Cu-alloy rove, 6 mm in diameter (cf. nos. 232 and 233 below). It went through a material 31 mm thick. The domed silver caps are 11 mm in diameter. A similar rivet, no. 236, with domed silver cap, 11 mm in diameter, is now loose but belongs to no. 213 according to Forssander's catalogue. The silver caps are filled with an unknown substance to affix it to the rivets. The animal-shaped projections and the flat plate were covered by silver sheets. A triangular silver sheet covered the upper end of the rod. Silver sheet covers nos. 176 (from find spot II), 218, 224, and 225 were loose when catalogued by Forssander, but later glued in place at the museum. They are 0.3–0.4 mm thick.

No. 215 (incl. 216, 221–223, 226–228, 230, 234–235). Long saddle mount, broken and repaired. Similar to no. 213, but bent out of shape. Deep cuts across. No. 215 overlaps an old repair, no. 216, which is a new plate replacing the lost lower end of no. 215. No. 216 was riveted to the broken end of no. 215 with four rivets. No. 215 is 245 mm long and no. 216 is 74 mm long but without overlap only 55 mm. So the whole mount was originally approx. 300 mm long. Rod-shaped, 9 × 9 mm in cross-section. The mount was fastened to the pommel in the same way as no. 213 but a rivet hole is missing at the end of no. 216. Some Cu-alloy rivets with domed silver caps (nos. 230, 234, 235) were loose according to Forssander's catalogue, but at the museum glued in place. The silver caps are 11 mm in diameter. They are filled with an unknown substance to affix it to the rivet. Silver sheet covers are placed as on no. 213. Silver covers nos. 222–223, and 226–227 were loose when found but were glued into place at the museum. Still loose silver covers are nos. 221, 41 mm long, 0.4 mm thick, and 228, 40 mm long, 0.3 mm thick; both silver covers of no. 216. The inlaid silver wire ornamentation on the sides of the rod differs a bit from that of no. 213; two circle-and-dots placed vertically replaced the circle-and-dots with slanting wires in between.

Saddle 1: Short saddle mount

No. 217 (incl. 219, 220, 237). Short saddle mount, obviously related to the long saddle mounts nos. 213 and 215 above. It is only 118 mm long, but was once approx. 140 mm long straightened out. It has deep cuts across and one cut hit the upper end, which is cut off, approx. 15 mm is missing. The point and a possible rivet hole are missing at the lower end. Rod-shaped, 8 × 8 mm in cross-section. Its bend is probably original. Fastened to the saddle in the same way as nos. 213 and 215, but it has only one pair of rivet projections at the upper end. The domed silver caps on the Cu-alloy rivets are 11 mm in diameter. The silver cap is filled with an unknown substance to affix it to the rivet. Silver sheet covers nos. 219 and 220 were loose when recorded the first time, but glued into place at the museum. A rivet with silver cap, no. 237, was loose when found and glued in place at the museum.

The silver sheet covers at the upper end of the rod and at the widened back plate are similar to those of nos. 213 and 215. The inlaid silver wire ornamentation is similar but differs a little from nos. 213 and 215. On the front side of the rod the ornamentation consists of wires straight across and of crossed wires. On the side wires are inlaid as crosses and as wires slanting alternately to the left or right.

Saddle 1: Loose silver sheet covers, rivets, and caps to the saddle mounts

Among the fragments from find spot IV are silver sheet covers and silver caps that were loose already when the finds were recorded the first time. Some silver sheet covers and rivets with caps were still joined to the saddle mounts in 1930 and most of the rest were later put in place at the museum. For a small silver mount without obvious connection to saddles, see Miscellaneous below (no. 239). Still loose sheets and caps may be from these mounts or the missing short mount.

No. 175 is a folded fragment, 10 × 8 mm, 0.2 mm thick, recorded as coming from find spot II. Silver cover of saddle mount? Cf. no. 240 from find spot IV, below.

No. 240. Silver sheet fragment, 12 × 10 mm large, 0.3–0.5 mm thick. Similar too silver sheets nos. 218–228 above and probably a fragmented silver cover of a saddle mount.

No. 241. Domed silver caps. According to Forssander's catalogue no. 241 consists of six different silver caps, 0.6 cm in diameter, of which three were joined to the rectangular mount no. 46 of the bridle, and one to strap mount no. 229, see below. Two caps not accounted for are probably joined to other objects and not identified.

Nos. 230, 231, 232, 233, 234, 235, 236, 237 are rivets of Cu-alloy and/or domed silver caps. The silver caps are approx. 12 mm in diameter. Nos. 230 and 235, according to Forssander's catalogue, are joined to saddle mount no. 215, no. 236 to mount no. 213, and no. 237 to mount no. 217. No. 231 is not identified. No. 234 is now found on no. 215. Two fragmentary rivets are still loose: no. 232, now 14 mm long, head is broken off, rove of Cu-alloy, 6 mm in diameter, – no. 233, rivet, now 13 mm long, with flat-hammered end, 5–6 mm in diameter.

Saddle 1: Saddle rings and staples

Nos. 207, 209, 211, 212. Four saddle rings and staples. Only no. 207 lacks a staple. All staple legs are more or less twisted and their ends are sometimes missing, probably damaged when the staples were pulled out of the saddle. The length of the legs varies between 46 and 82 mm. High-quality inlays of silver wire are found on both rings and staple loops. On the loops parallel wires follow the edges. Only the upper side of the rings has inlays. Radially laid wires start at an external equator. The inlays are well preserved and only on nos. 207 and 211 have some ends loosened. The rings are 46–47 mm in diameter and 13–14 mm thick with a 14 mm broad staple loop.

Nos. 208 and 210. Two saddle rings and staples. The rings are identical to the four above but smaller, only 42–43 mm in diameter and 12–13 mm thick. Their staple loops are 13 mm broad. So it seems that two smaller and four larger saddle rings belong to saddle 1 from find spot IV.

Saddle 1: Strap hooks

The two Cu-alloy hooks in find spot II are not exactly similar but probably fulfilled the same function in the saddle gear. Similar hooks are included among the saddle mounts found at Fulltofta (see catalogue at nos. F:16 and F:17). Remains of leather straps and the shape of the hooks make it reasonable to assume that they were used to fasten straps of breast collar and/or breeching to the saddle rings.

Forssander catalogued them as part of find spot II, but according to a letter by Otto Rydbeck the hooks may come from find spot IV and belong to saddle 1.

No. 132. Strap hook. The hook is 48 mm long and has a square plate, 30 × 25 mm large. To its back a leather strap was once fastened by two rivets, 12 mm apart; only one is preserved. The plate is 3 mm thick but only 2 mm thick at the flat end where two rivets were placed. A ridge on its front side continues into the hook, but after the bend the hook is flat. The opening is now approx. 9 mm wide. The preserved rivet has a domed head on the front side and an irregular rove, 9 x 10 mm large, on the back where the strap was fastened. The strap was originally about 4 mm thick.

No. 133. Strap hook. The hook is 55 mm long and its plate is square, approx. 32 × 25 mm large; it passes evenly over to the hook. A double leather strap was fastened to the back by two rivets, 13 mm apart, with flat heads on the front and flat roves on the back, a square of Cu-alloy 7 x 7 mm large, and a round of iron, approx. 9 mm in diameter, and a repair? The upper strap is double, 25 mm broad and 3 mm thick with seams along the edges and in the middle like strap no. 229 (below). The lower leather is single and thin. The front side of the mount as well as the beginning of the hook are ridged but from the bend the hook is flat. The opening is 12 mm wide.

Saddle 1: Double mounts of breast collar and/or breeching
A number of mounts of Cu-alloy with silver sheet cover were riveted to leather straps. As evidenced by no. 229 (below) small Cu-alloy rivets with silver caps adorn the edges of the straps and silver-capped rivets were also placed between the mounts. The double mount no. 113 comes from an uncertain context but is possibly from find spot II. Nos. 134–144 were catalogued by Forssander as from find spot II, but according to a letter from Rydbeck it seems more probable that they were part of the saddle tack found at find spot IV, where in fact similar double strap mounts were found. No. 229 is present on Mellton's photo of the first finds from 1930 and nos. 242, 243, and 247 were later added to this find according to both Forssander's catalogue and Rydbeck's find list. In total the fragments represent at least eleven double mounts and all are included in the description here and assumed to belong to straps belonging to saddle 1.

Nos. 134–144 plus 113, 229, 242, 243, and 247 are fragments of double strap mounts. Remains of a leather strap, no. 229 below, demonstrate that the mounts decorated 28 mm wide leather straps surrounded by small rivets with silver caps. The mounts consist of a Cu-alloy plate, 0.5–1.2 mm thick, covered by a 0.1–0.2 mm thick silver sheet. Four well-preserved mounts, nos. 113, 134, 229, 242, are all similar and 59 mm long and 13–14 mm broad at the pointed widening at the middle. At each end there was a Cu-alloy rivet; preserved rivets are 6–8 mm long. In a few cases domed silver caps are preserved. Nos. 135–139, 243, and 247 are loose silver sheet covers and nos. 140–144 are loose Cu-alloy mounts.

No. 229 (incl. 181 and 241) is a similar double strap mount still riveted to a leather strap end, which is 75 mm long and narrowing from 28 to 10 mm in breadth. It is decorated along the edges by small Cu-alloy rivets with domed silver caps, 4 mm in diameter, one from no. 241. Three larger rivets, 8 mm long, with silver caps, 7 mm in diameter, are placed across the broad end. One of them is no. 181. The strap consists of a core of thick leather covered by thinner leather, held together by seams along both edges and in the middle. The end of another narrower strap, 19 mm broad and 3 mm thick, was riveted to the underside of the strap by two Cu-alloy rivets; one end of this strap is original, the other is torn off. This strap too consists of two layers of leather seamed together; a thicker covered by a thinner. The function of the strap is unclear, but the broad strap could be the end of a breast collar or breeching and the narrow strap could have been used for binding the breast collar/breeching to a saddle ring, see reconstruction drawing (see Fabech and Näsman chapter 17).

Saddle 2

On 21 June 1929 Carl Mellton himself found saddle mounts roughly 3 m east of find spot II during his investigation at the site; it was labelled find spot III (Fabech chapter 1 fig. 6). His record supports the assumption that parts of a saddle cut to pieces were deposited here. Similarities to two short mounts and two saddle rings from find spot II make it probable that this saddle is represented by a complete set: two long mounts, two short mounts, and four larger and two smaller saddle rings (Näsman chapter 7 fig. 29).

Saddle 2: Long saddle mounts

Nos. 201 and 202. Long saddle mounts. They are approx. 270 mm long. No. 201 is bent out of shape and both have deep cuts across. The bend of no. 202 seem to be almost original and reflects the bend of the pommel of the saddle. The mounts were hammered out of a thick Cu-alloy rod, 7 × 11 mm in cross-section. The upper end is flattened to a round plate with a rivet hole. The lower end is shaped as a pointed oval with an oval hole for a saddle-ring staple and a rivet hole in a roundel at the end point. A third rivet/nail hole is placed in the convex upper part of the rod. The two saddle mounts undoubtedly belong to the same saddle.

Saddle 2: Short saddle mounts

The lower ends of the long saddle mounts are shaped in the same way as on two short saddle mounts found at find spot II, nos. 125–126. They are probably from the same saddle.

Nos. 125–126. Two saddle mounts hammered out from a 4–5 × 8 mm flat rod. They have probably kept the original bend given to fit the cantle. The lower end is widened with an oval hole for a saddle-ring staple. The upper end is widened and has a rivet/nail hole; a second rivet/nail hole is found in a roundel at the lower end point. Straightened out they are short: approx. 118 mm (no. 126) and 122 mm (no. 125).

Saddle 2: Saddle rings and staples

Nos. 203 and 204 plus 170 and 171. The legs of the staples are cut off. The loops of the staples are decorated with 2 × 3 lines. The rings have an external single moulding. They are 38–39 mm in diameter. All rings are worn, much wear on no. 170. Mellton's sketch and photo record how the saddle rings nos. 203–204 were found together with the long saddle mounts nos. 201 and 202. The similar rings nos. 170–171 from find spot II probably belonged to this saddle.

Nos. 205 and 206. Saddle rings and staples. The plain rings are narrow, only 26–27 mm in diameter. The staples are made of a ribbon-shaped rod and have only one leg, 45–46 mm long. No other staple in the Sösdala find is made like this. According to Mellton's sketch and photo they were found only 22 cm from the long saddle mounts nos. 20 and 202 and probably belong to the same saddle. Thus

like saddle 1, saddle 2 had possibly six saddle rings, four larger and two smaller.

Saddle 3

This saddle is represented by two long saddle mounts. Perhaps the fragmentary saddle mount no. 127 belongs to this saddle as one of two shorter cantle mounts (Näsman chapter 7 fig. 30).

Nos. 117 (incl. 118) and 119 (incl. 120). Long saddle mounts. The mounts are cast in Cu-alloy and the well-preserved no 117cum118 is 293 mm long. The distorted and broken no. 119cum120 is only 233 mm. The back of the basically rod-shaped mount is hollowed. Both mounts were bent out of shape, cut into pieces and damaged by deep cuts. The two fitting pieces nos. 117 and 118 form a complete mount, while the upper end of mount no. 119 is missing; the other end fits no. 120. The upper end of both mounts is shaped like a lizard with two legs ending in paws. On no. 117 the head is preserved. Its projecting eyes are worn and without inlays of any kind. Double grooves follow the front edges of the rod. At the nose of the lizard is a rivet/nail plate. The lower end is widened to a triangular shape with a central hole for a (now missing) saddle-ring staple. The mounts were fastened to the pommel by four rivets and the staple of the saddle ring. Rivets were placed at each end and at a pair of projections below the legs of the lizard. A saddle ring and staple are seen in place in the hole of no. 120 on a photo taken by Mellton 11 June 1929 after he had gathered objects at both find spots I and II. This combination is also present on an old photo in the museum archives. Unfortunately it is not possible to identify the ring and staple with certainty, but it could be no. 162 (a ring unfortunately without equals).

No. 127. Saddle mount. Upper end cut off. Deep cut marks. Cast in Cu-alloy. The back of the basically rod-shaped mount is hollowed. Double cast grooves follow the upper edges of the rod. The lower end is widened to a triangular shape with a central hole for a (now missing) saddle-ring staple. At the end point a rivet/nail hole. The present length is 75 mm. No. 127 is similar in detail to the long mounts 117 and 119, so it is possible that it was a short mount and belonged to the same saddle.

Saddle 4

Nos. 122 and 129 are probably a pair of long mounts for the pommel of the same saddle. The short saddle mount no. 124, which has a lower end shaped in a similar way, probably belonged to the same saddle at the cantle.

No. 122 (incl. 123 and 128). Long saddle mount. Bent out of shape and broken in three fitting pieces; the upper end is missing. Present length is 243 mm. Straightened out the three pieces are together 280 mm long; a complete mount was probably approx. 300 mm long (see similar no. 129 below). Undecorated and shaped from 5 × 10 mm square rod. Slightly widened towards the upper end; the lower triangular end has a square central hole for the staple of the saddle ring. Broken at a rivet/nail hole in the middle of the rod. Fastened to the pommel by this rivet/nail and probably another at the missing upper end and by the saddle-ring staple in the lower end.

No. 129 (incl. 130). Long saddle mount. Bent out of shape and broken in two fitting pieces. At present the length of nos. 129–130 is 241 mm but was probably, like no. 122, approx. 300 mm. The lower end with the hole for a saddle-ring staple is missing. Shaped like no. 122, above, but made from a 4 × 9 mm square rod. It was fixed to the pommel by a rivet/nail at the upper end, another at the fracture in the middle of the rod and by the staple in the missing lower end.

No. 124. Short saddle mount. Hammered out from a 4–5 × 8 mm flat rod. It probably kept its original bend to fit the cantle. Straightened out it is approx. 130 mm long. The lower end is widened with a square central hole for a saddle-ring staple. The upper end is widened and has a rivet/nail hole. It has only one rivet hole in the upper widened end. It lacks an equal; since its lower end is similar to that of the long mounts nos. 122 and 129, it could be a short mount for the same saddle.

Saddle 5

Saddle mount no. 115 has no equal and represents what is left of one saddle (Näsman chapter 7 fig. 31).

No. 115 (incl. 116). Long saddle mount. The mount is 293 mm long. Cast in Cu-alloy with silver ornamentation. The mount had been broken in two pieces and repaired. The two pieces were held together by rivets in holes bored through each part of the mount and by Cu-alloy plates placed over and under the fracture. When delivered to the museum the two parts were again separated, but the old repair was renewed at the museum by a new rivet replacing a missing one. The triangular lower part is bent out of shape and two rivet/nail holes torn open.

The mount consists of an upper part (no. 115), slightly widened towards the end and a lower triangular part (no. 116) with a hole for a (now missing) saddle-ring and staple. It was fastened to the pommel with 10 rivets and the staple: only remains of rivets are preserved: three without preserved silver caps at the upper end, four at two pairs of projections, and three in holes at the three points of the triangular lower part. Remaining silver caps decorating the rivets are 6 mm in diameter.

The upper end is accurately decorated with incrusted silver, at the top an M-shaped silver sheet from which incrusted silver wires cross one another diagonally in a square net, followed by a section with a long wire along the axis of the mount, other wires straight across, and diagonal wires in between forming acute angles, then a section with a row of crosses and wires across that ends at the widened and undecorated lower part. Possibly the flat end above the staple hole was silvered but it is now covered by verdigris.

Saddle 6

No. 121. Long saddle mount with saddle ring and staple. It has no equal and represents all what is left of one saddle. Fragmentary, the upper part is missing. Cast in Cu-alloy. The only mount found with saddle ring and staple still in situ. Rod-shaped with widened triangular lower end with a central hole for the staple of the saddle ring. The end point is shaped as an animal nose and the side projections end as roundels. The present length is 162 mm. The ring has an external moulding between lines. Its outer diameter is 38–39 mm. The staple is made of a plain rod. It is not worn. The ends are splayed at an acute angle that reflects how it was fastened to the pommel of the saddle. The thickness of the wooden part of the pommel was originally approx. 27 mm.

Saddle 7

No. 131 has no equal and represents what is left of one saddle.

No. 131. Long saddle mount. Only the upper part is preserved of a long mount found by Mellton when screening at find spot II. Cast in Cu-alloy. The central part is rod-shaped, 7 × 9 mm thick with flat underside with tool marks. The front side is rounded and decorated by lines along the edges and double lines across at the rivet holes at the end. Another rivet hole was placed at the middle of the rod. It is curved and 129 mm long, straightened out 138 mm.

Saddle rings and staples

The total number of saddle rings with or without staple is 33 (23 rings in find spot II, 4 rings in III, and 6 rings in IV). Twelve rings could be attributed to saddles 1 and 2 and were described above. A unique saddle ring is still attached to a mount of saddle 6, see above no. 121. Below saddle rings are treated that cannot be related to specific saddle mounts. Similar rings are grouped together, assuming that similar rings come from the same saddle (Näsman chapter 7 fig. 32). In all five or six different saddles are represented by these rings. Five saddle rings and staples lack equals and each may represent one saddle. So the number of dismantled saddles was at least 13.

Many rings were wrenched off the saddles and the staples became more or less twisted in the process: only the staple in no. 121 (saddle 6) seems to be almost intact. Other rings were cut off with a sword or an axe, so most staples have fragmentary legs or the legs are simply cut off. When they seem well preserved their length is noted below.

Nos. 151 and 152. Two similar saddle rings. One has preserved the loop of the staple. It is decorated by a threefold moulding. The rings are heavy with triangular cross-section, 14 × 8 mm. External diameter of rings 38–40 mm. Probably from the same saddle.

Nos. 153, 160, and 168 (incl. 200). Three saddle rings and staples. The staples are plain. The approx. 14 mm broad loops are broader than the 7–9 mm broad legs. The length of the best-preserved legs (nos. 153 and 160) is approx. 70 mm. The legs of no. 160 are twisted and there is

wear on its loop. The rings are plain and 38 mm in diameter. These simple rings and staples possibly come from the same saddle. Forssander identified no. 200, a twisted Cu-alloy rod, as a 32 mm long leg fragment of staple no. 168. Possibly the loops once had a silver cover similar to no. 158 below.

Nos. 154, 155, 156, and 157. Saddle rings and staples. The loops of the staples are covered by silver sheet and decorated by two single and one central double moulding. The legs of the staples are broken off and the loop of no. 155 is wrenched out of shape. The rings have an external single moulding between lines; they are 38–39 mm in diameter. The four rings and staples are almost identical and probably a full set from the same saddle.

No. 158. Saddle ring and staple with silver covered loop. The legs of the staple are broken off. In dimensions and shape both ring and staple are similar to nos. 153, 160, and 168, but the plain loop of the staple is covered by silver sheet that has partly loosened from the loop. So it is possible that the loops of nos. 153, 160, and 168 likewise were once silver-covered; if so, the four rings and staples belong to the same saddle. Wear from the loop visible in the ring.

Nos. 159 and 112. Saddle rings and staples. The loops of the staples are covered by silver sheet, decorated by lines and a double moulding. The staple legs of no. 159 are twisted and 59 mm long. The rings have an external single moulding. Ring no. 112 is heavily worn. External diameter of rings 30–32 mm. Probably from the same saddle. – **No. 164** Saddle ring without staple. The ring has an external single moulding and is 33 mm in diameter. It lacks an exact equal but resembles the rings nos. 112 and 159, and the three are possibly from the same saddle.

Nos. 161 and 146–147. Saddle ring and staples. The staples are plain and the legs are fragmentary; the legs of nos. 146–147 are 38 and 41 mm long. The ring of no. 161 has an external single moulding and is 27 mm in diameter. It lacks an equal, but staple no. 146 could represent a similar set.

No. 162. Saddle ring and staple. The loop of the staple is decorated by a central ridge and double mouldings. The legs are broken off. The ring is plain and 28 mm in diameter. It lacks an equal. It could be the ring that on early photos is placed in the hole of saddle mount no. 117, see Saddle 3.

Nos. 163, 165, and 166. Saddle rings and staples. No. 165 lacks a staple and the legs of staples nos. 163 and 166 are cut off. The two preserved loops are decorated by a convex honeycomb pattern between grooves along the edges. The rings are plain and 29 mm in diameter. The three rings and staples probably belong to the same saddle.

No. 167. Saddle ring and staple. The legs of the loop are twisted and broken off. The loop is decorated with three narrow mouldings. The ring has an external single moulding and is 33 mm in diameter. It lacks an equal.

No. 169. Saddle ring and staple. The legs of the staple are broken off. The loop is decorated by three narrow mouldings leaving two central ridges. The ring has an external single moulding and is 34 mm in diameter. It lacks an equal.

No. 190. Rod, Cu-alloy. Similar to no. 199. Probably a fragment of a saddle-ring staple. 22 mm long, rectangular cross-section 2–3 × 1.5 mm.

Nos. 198–199. Rods, Cu-alloy. Two fragments of a saddle-ring staple. 19 and 20 mm long, rectangular cross-section 3–4 × 1.3–1.8 mm.

Copper alloy mounts

Nos. 72, 74, 79, 81, 82, and 246. Copper alloy mounts. The finish and preservation of these mounts is much better than the Cu-alloy mounts recorded by Forssander as part of the bridle at find spot I, no. 71 etc. above. Another difference is that they are decorated with lines along the edges, are bent over at one end to form a tube (broken off in no. 82), and that at the other end there is a rivet. Forssander assumed in the catalogue that the Cu-alloy mounts belong to gilt silver mounts like no. 39 and for this reason he placed them in find spot I. Only for no. 74 have we certain information that it came from find spot II (letter with photo by

Mellton). No. 246 was catalogued as part of find spot IV but this is uncertain. We have chosen to place them all together with no. 74, the only mount for which find context seems certain.

Mounts 72 and 79 are 49 mm long, no. 246 is 39 mm, no. 74 is 35 mm, and no. 81 is 20 mm long. The long mounts are 10–15 mm broad and 0.3–0.5 mm thick; the two short ones are 9 mm broad and 0.3 mm thick. The tube is approx. 4 mm in diameter. On the front side there are thin lines along the edges, possibly decoration or guiding lines when cutting out the mounts. Unknown function but probably part of saddle tack.

Domed rivet caps of copper alloy

Nos. 95, 96, 97, 98, 99. Five domed rivet caps of Cu-alloy, undecorated. Three are well preserved, two slightly flattened. The cavity of three caps has a verdigrised substance with an impression of a rivet. Three caps are 16 mm in diameter and 5 mm high, 0.4–0.5 mm thick; two are 22 mm in diameter, 8 mm high, and 0.3 mm thick. The function of the probably decorative rivet caps is unknown. All five caps were found by Mellton when he screened gravel at find spot II; probably Forssander catalogued them as belonging to the bridle of find place I because he associated them with the five silver caps nos. 87–91.

Copper alloy rivets

No. 145 and no. 244. Rods/long rivets? Made from rolled-up Cu-alloy sheets. One end is shaped as a thicker head. No. 145 is 40 mm long 2,5 mm thick, head 5 mm in diameter; no. 244 is 45 mm long 3 mm thick. No. 145 came from find spot II; 244 from find spot IV. Could be rivets of saddle mounts.

Nos. 186–189. Rivets, Cu-alloy. The four rivets are 16, 18, or 19 mm long with domed heads, 11 mm in diameter, and square roves of iron 15 × 18, 16 × 18, or 17 × 19 mm large. The distance between head and rove is 10, 11, or 14 mm. Around the shaft are traces of two layers of leather with remains of wood in between. Probably decorative rivets of one of the saddles.

Nos. 186–189 were found by Carl Mellton when screening at find spot II.

Remains of leather straps

In the material from find spot II Forssander catalogued four leather fragments. In a letter Rydbeck assumed that two leather fragments came from find spot IV. Since it cannot be settled whether nos. 148–139 or 183–184 came from find spot IV and thus probably from saddle 1, the four fragments are placed here.

No. 148. Leather stump. 21 × 15 mm, very thin. Holes left by seam in the middle. Two rivet holes 7 mm from each other; impressions left by round roves. Uncertain impression left by a square end of a mount.

No. 149. Leather strap stump. 19 × 28 mm, approx. 3 mm thick. Holes left by seams in the middle and along one edge. A proteomic analysis shows that the leather came from cow (see Dal chapter 6). Four rivet holes set in a square; distance between rivets 12 mm. Remains of Cu-alloy rivets and impressions left by round roves. A pair of Cu-alloy rivets closer to one another in-between.

Nos. 183–184. Leather strap stumps. Irregular. No. 183 is 15 × 9 mm large and 2 mm thick. It has a rivet hole. Fragment no. 184, 18 × 8 mm large and 2 mm thick, has an impression of a large rivet head, approx. 14 mm in diameter. Could perhaps fit a rivet like no. 177 below, or rivet caps like 95–99 in find spot I.

Miscellaneous

Nos. 84, 191, 193–195, and 197. Fragments of Cu-alloy sheet. Nos. 84, 193, and 195 have sparsely punched concentric semicircles along one side or two (no. 84); for stamps see Dal chapter 6. No. 84 is 0.2 mm thick and 32 × 14 mm large. The other fragments are from 7 × 8 to 12 × 18 mm large, 0.4–0.6 mm thick. The fragments represent some kind of mount with unknown function. According to a letter with photo, no. 84 was found by Mellton when screening at find spot II. So it probably belongs to the same context as nos. 193 and 195 but Forssander catalogued it for unknown reasons as part of the finds from find spot I.

No. 114. Carl Mellton bought four objects from private persons who had taken them from the find place in 1929

(letter 20/1/1930, Fabech chapter 1). Forssander numbered them 111–114 and labelled them AB, indicating that they could come from either find spot I(A) or II(B). Buckle **no. 111** is similar to buckle no. 23 and described above; they probably came from the same bridle. The saddle ring and staple **no. 112** is an equal to no. 159 from find spot II and described above. Double strap mount **no. 113** is similar to a number of mounts described above as part of saddle straps, see Saddle 1. **No. 114.** A ribbon-shaped rod of Cu-alloy bent to form a loop, and according to Forssander in his catalogue it resembles the pin of a buckle. It is 20 mm long, 2 × 1 mm in cross-section. Its original context is unknown.

In Forssander's catalogue various small finds and fragments from find spots II and IV were grouped in three number series, nos. 145–150, 172–200 and 230–247; those that could not be attributed to saddles above are presented below.

No. 150. Silver mount. Undecorated silver sheet, 29 mm long, 0.1 mm thick. A rivet hole in each end. Has no equal. Function unknown.

No. 172. Lance head, found some 50 m from find spot II thrown among stones removed from the find spot by the workers. Very corroded iron with broken point and damage on blade and socket. In the socket a rivet with domed head. The present length is 170 mm, diameter of socket 18 mm, cross-section at transition to blade 4 × 9 mm, at the broadest part of the blade 4 × 12 mm. When Forssander measured it the length was 175 mm, the diameter of the socket 20 mm, cross-section at the transition to blade 7 × 10 mm, the breadth of the blade 18 mm. Typologically it is too corroded to be evaluated with certainty but it could have been a point of Ilkjær's type 19 or a short type Kragehul, and could belong to weapon group 12 or period Scand-D1 (see Fabech 2016 with refs.).

No. 173. Silver mount. Upper front side gilt. Fragmented, it is 17 × 12 mm large, 0.5 mm thick and 4 mm high. Broken at one end but possibly symmetrical. The preserved end is bent down and out in acute angles. Here two silver rivets with domed heads, 7 mm long. If it is a symmetrical strap mount it could have served to hold a <12 mm broad strap. Has no equal.

No. 177. Rivet, Cu-alloy, 18 mm long. Flat head, 12 mm in diameter. Has no equal. Found by Mellton in gravel screened at find spot II.

Nos. 178–180. Three rivets with silver caps. Only short fragments of the Cu-alloy rivets. The silver caps are domed, 9 mm in diameter. They are filled with an unidentified substance. Probably from saddle mounts but their diameter does not fit those found on mounts above.

Nos. 192 and 196. Mount fragments, Cu-alloy. No. 192 has remains of 2 rivet holes and no. 196 remains of 2 rivets, one of which has a domed head. No. 192 is 17 × 12 mm large and no. 196 13 × 10 mm large. Both are 0.5 mm thick. Similar fragments were catalogued as back-plates of silver mounts of the bridle from find spot I, see no. 71 etc. above.

No. 239. Mount, a cupped 14 mm long silver sheet with a rivet hole in each end. One end broken. It is 5 mm broad and 0.1 mm thick. It has no equal. Unknown function.

Among the finds he collected Mellton mentioned two rusty fragments of iron. He suggested they could be remains of a strap buckle. The fragments are not recorded in Forssander's catalogue and seem to have been lost, but are perhaps depicted in Geisslinger 1967 Taf. 15:28–30. Several fragments found on Geisslinger's photos (1967) are not identified above: Taf. 15:14, 28, 29, 30, Taf. 16:33, 40, 41, 42, 53, 54, 55, 58.

References

Fabech, C. 2016. Krig, vapen och Vång. In: Henriksson, M. & Nilsson, B. (eds). *Vikten av Vång*. Karlskrona: 41–50 + 113–114.

Geisslinger, H. 1967. *Horte als Geschichtsquelle*. Neumünster.

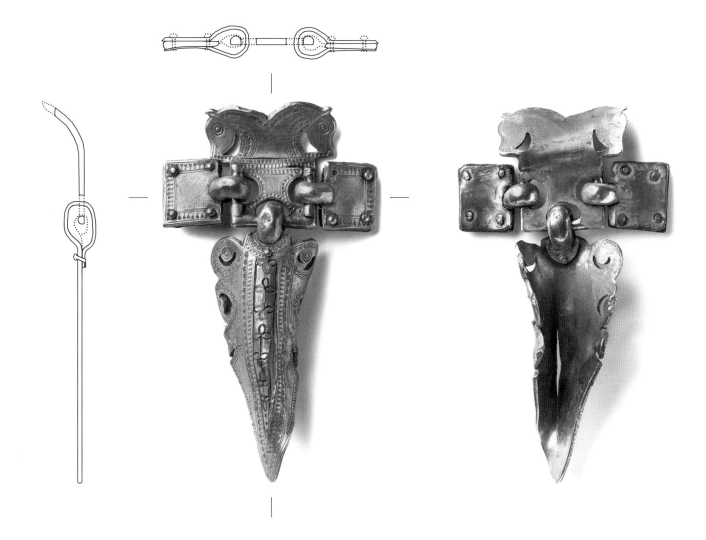

No. 1

No. 2

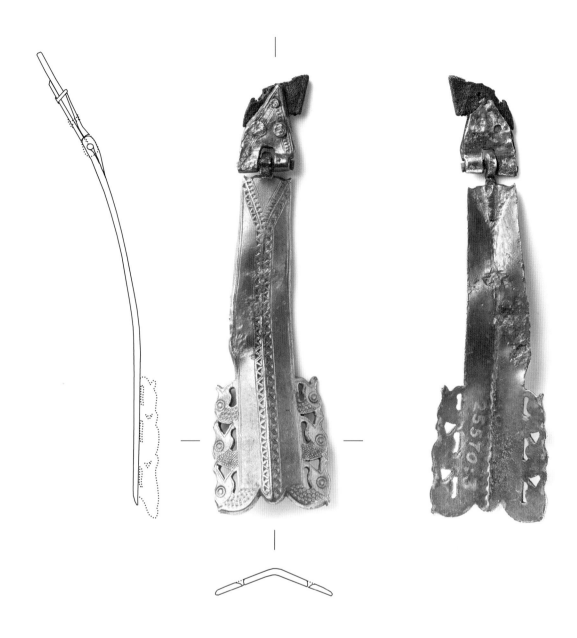

No. 3

No. 4

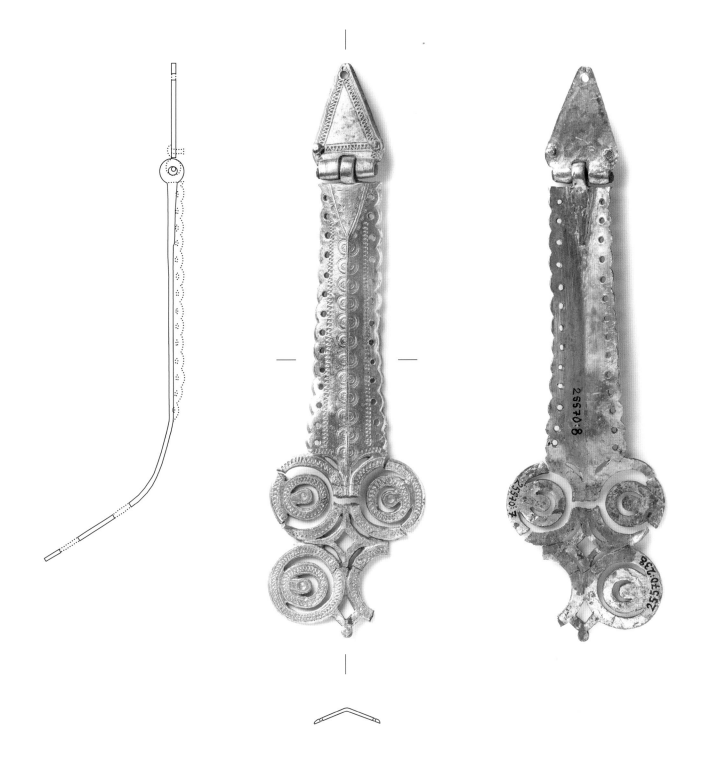

No. 7

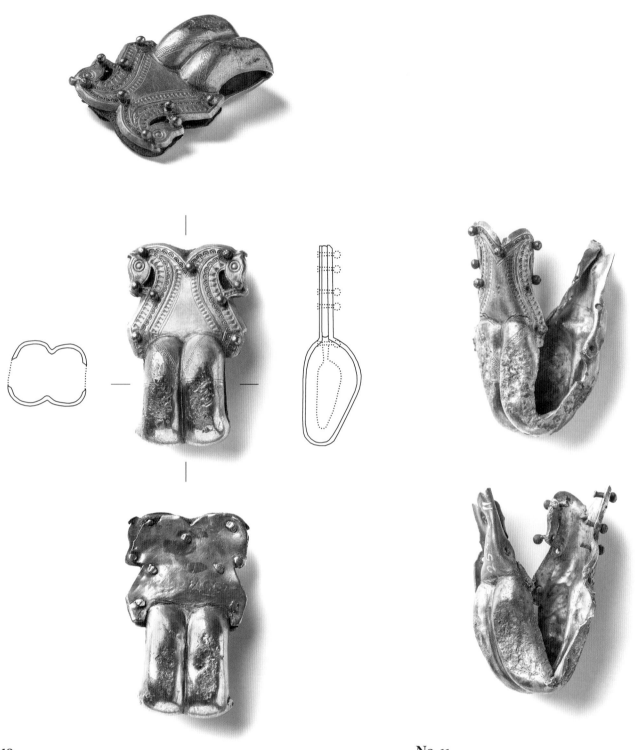

No. 10

No. 11

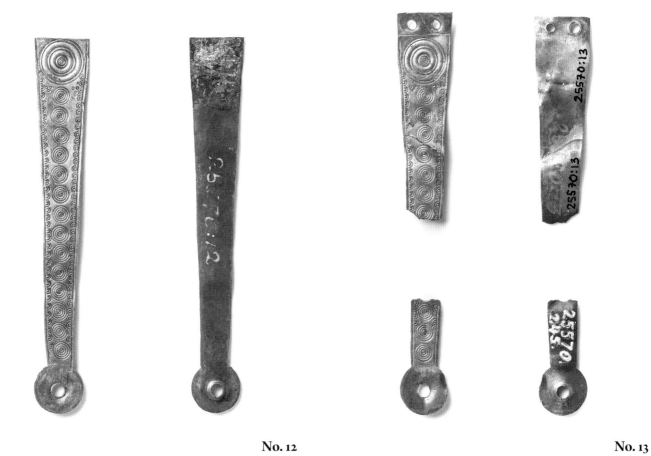

No. 12

No. 13

No. 14

No. 15

No. 16

No. 17

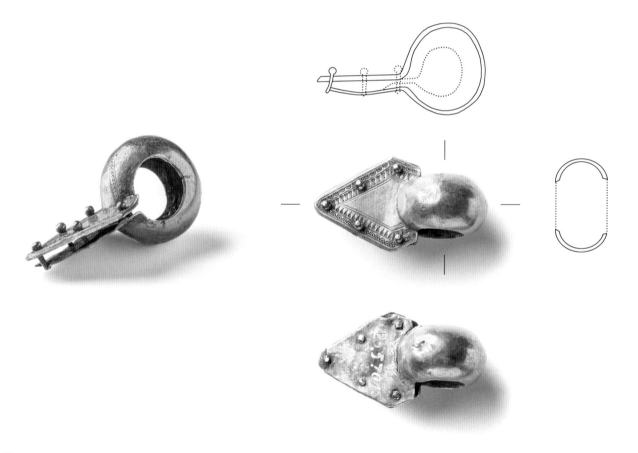

No. 18

No. 19

Nos. 19, 20 and 21

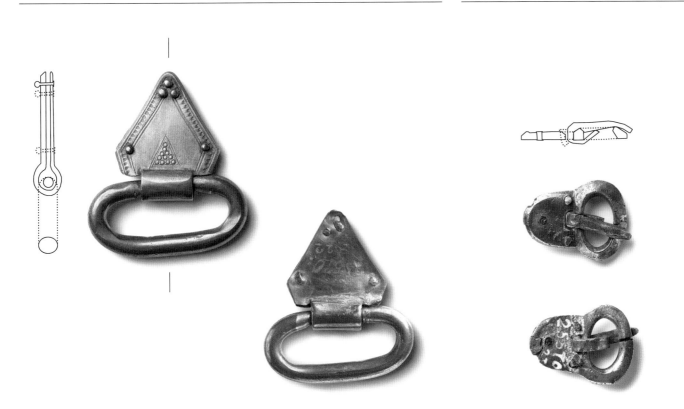

No. 22

No. 23

No. 24

No. 25

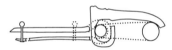

No. 26

No. 27

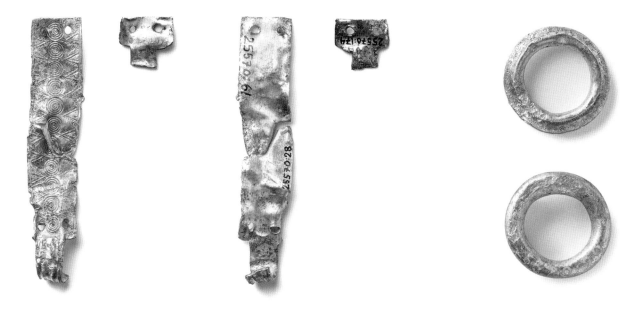

Nos. 28, 61 and 174

No. 29

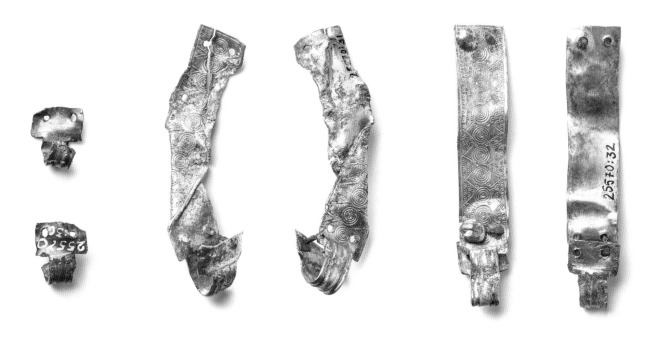

No. 30

No. 31

No. 32

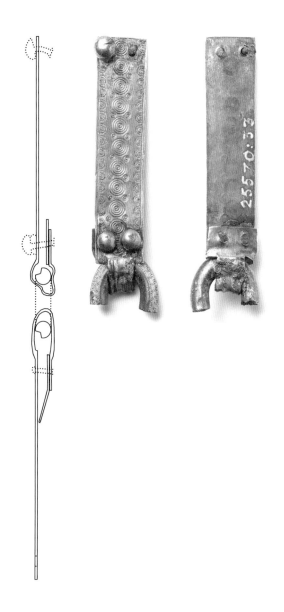

No. 33

Nos. 33 and 34

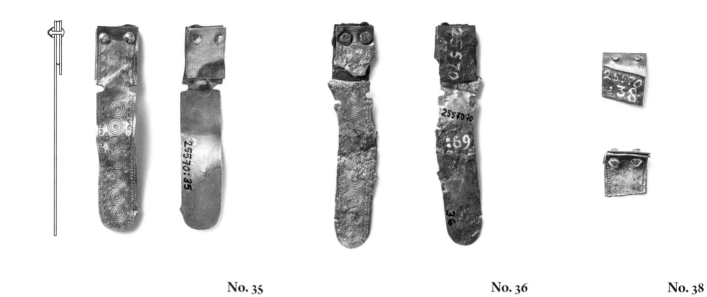

No. 35   **No. 36**   **No. 38**

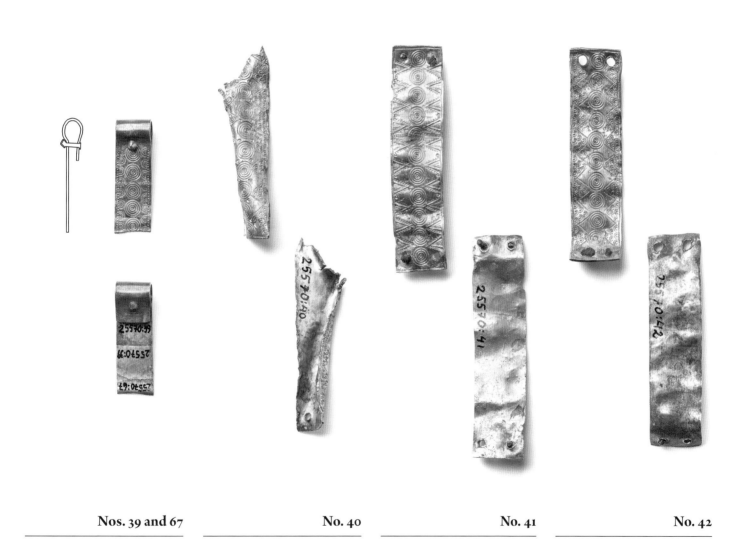

Nos. 39 and 67   **No. 40**   **No. 41**   **No. 42**

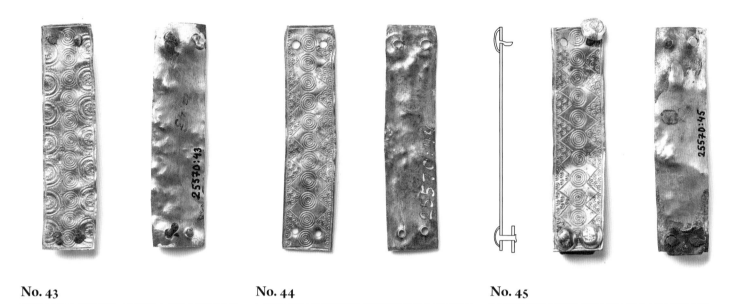

No. 43

No. 44

No. 45

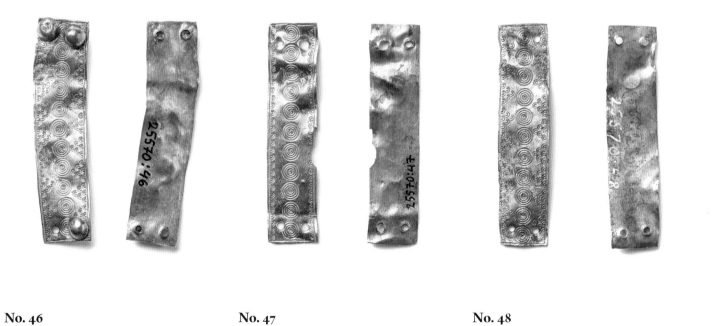

No. 46

No. 47

No. 48

No. 49 **No. 50** **No. 51**

No. 52 **No. 53** **No. 54**

No. 55

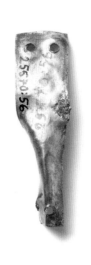

No. 56

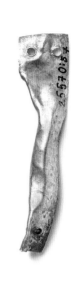

No. 57

No. 58

No. 59

Nos. 60 and 66

No. 62

No. 64

Nos. 65 and 68

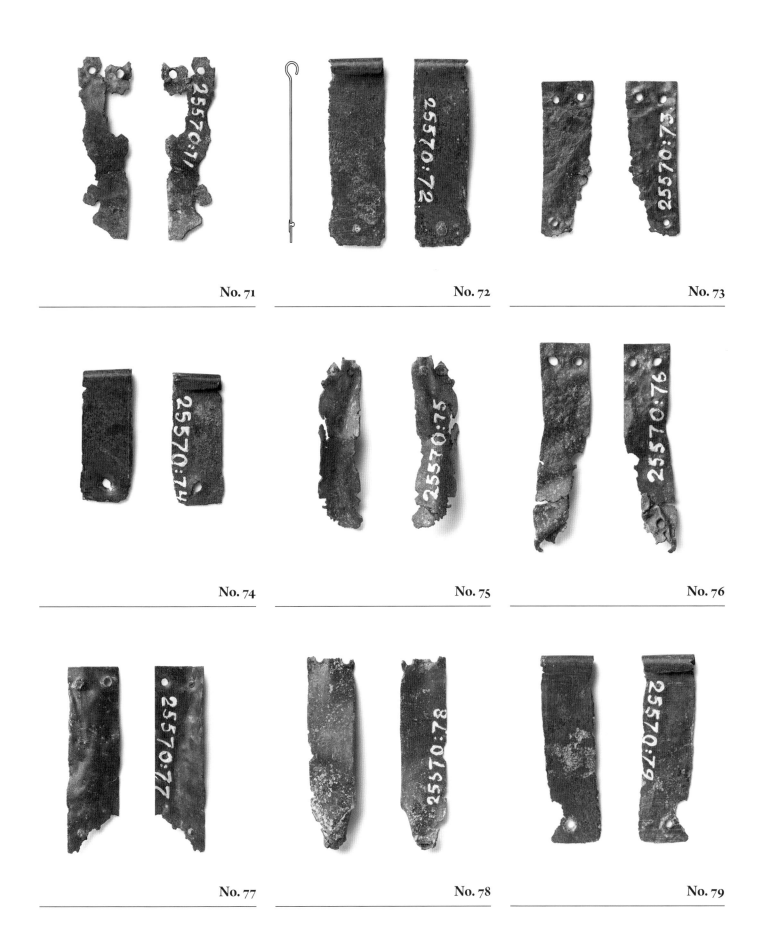

No. 71

No. 72

No. 73

No. 74

No. 75

No. 76

No. 77

No. 78

No. 79

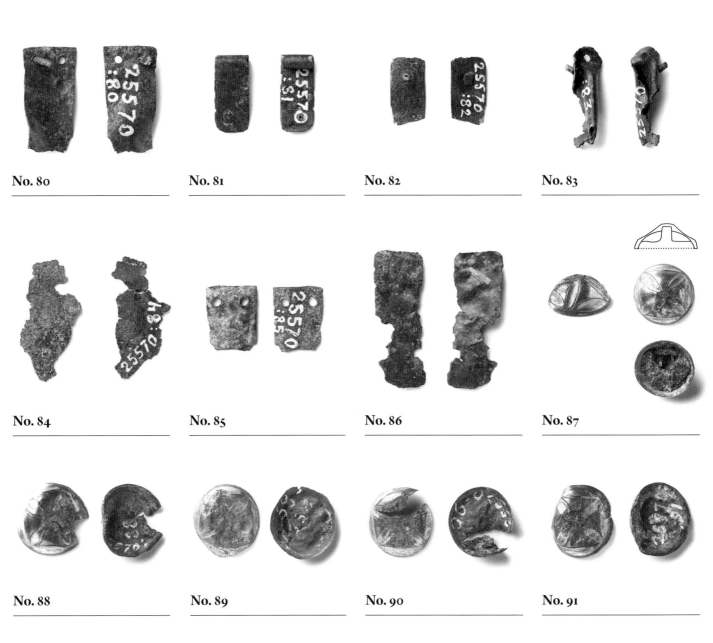

No. 80

No. 81

No. 82

No. 83

No. 84

No. 85

No. 86

No. 87

No. 88

No. 89

No. 90

No. 91

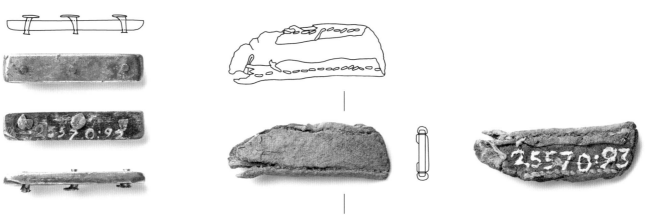

No. 92

No. 93

No. 94

No. 95

No. 96

No. 97

No. 98

No. 99

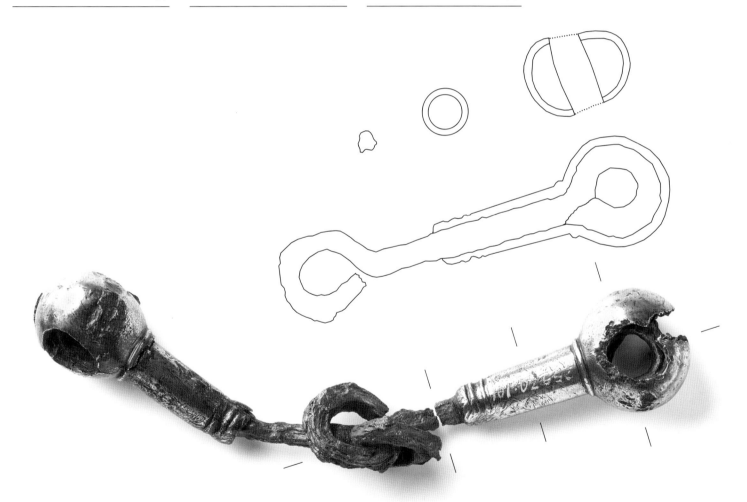

Nos. 100 and 101

Nos. 102-105

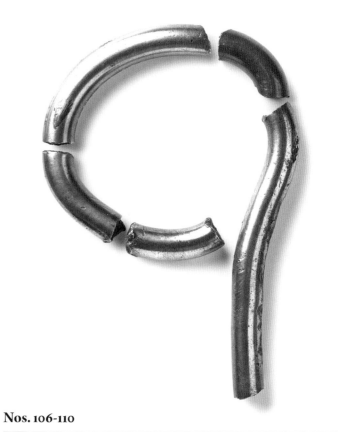

Nos. 106-110

No. 111

No. 112

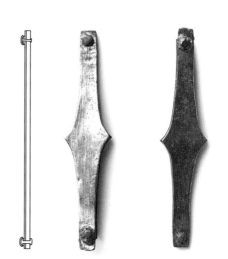

No. 113

No. 114

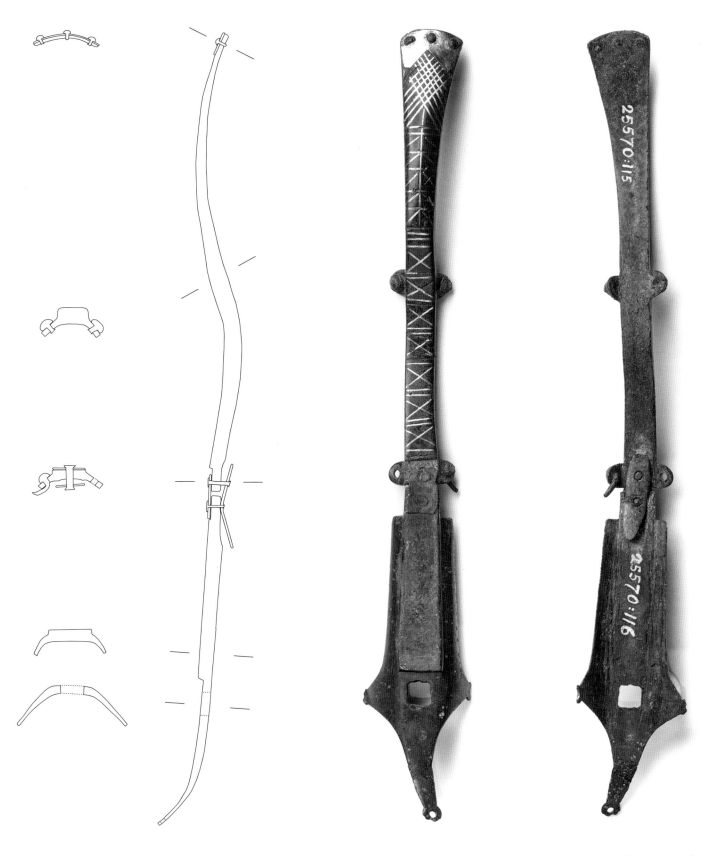

Nos. 115 and 116 (scale: 75%)

Nos. 117 and 118 (scale: 75%)

Nos. 119 and 120 (scale 75%)

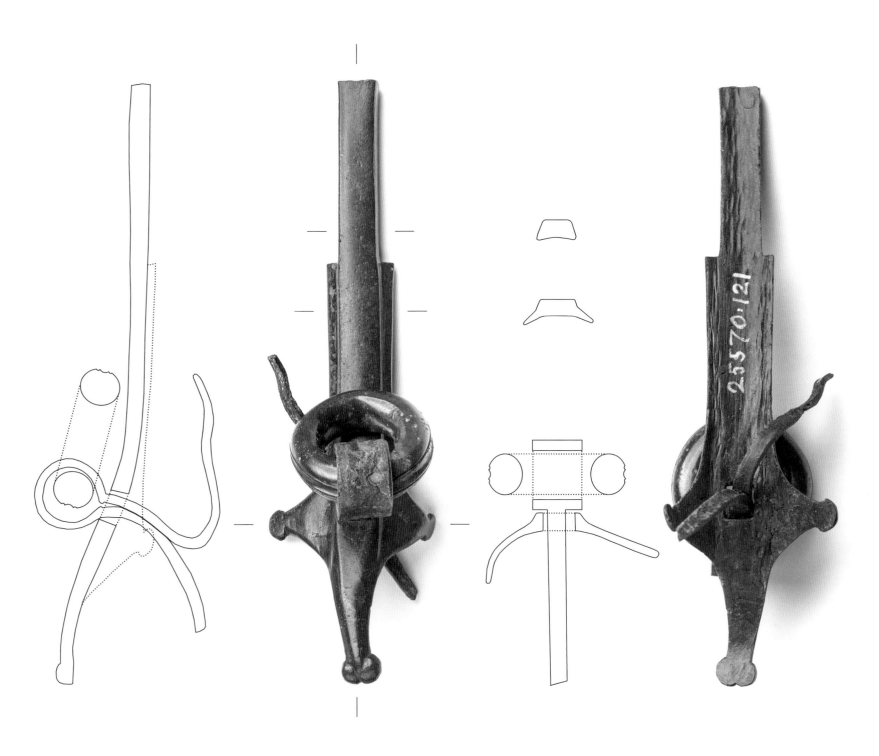

No. 121

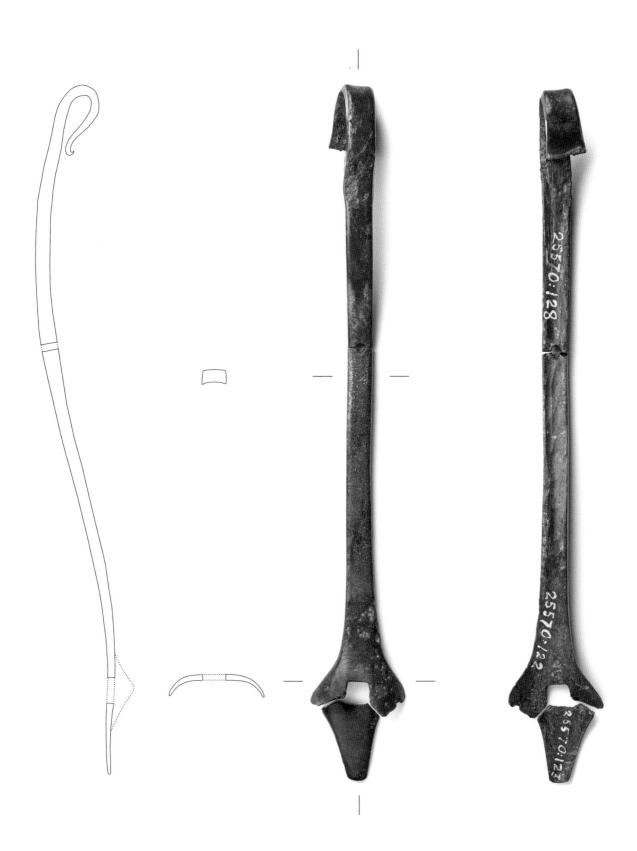

Nos. 122, 123 and 128 (scale: 75%)

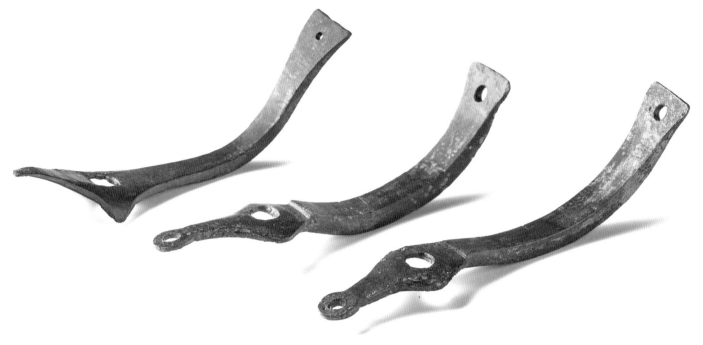

Nos. 124, 125 and 126

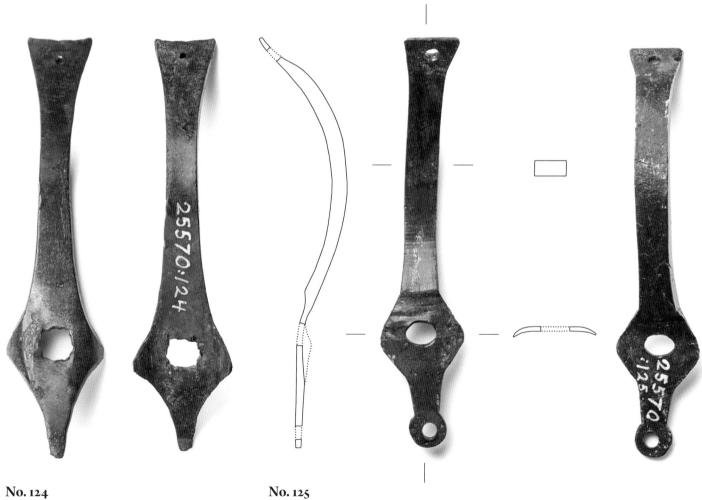

No. 124

No. 125

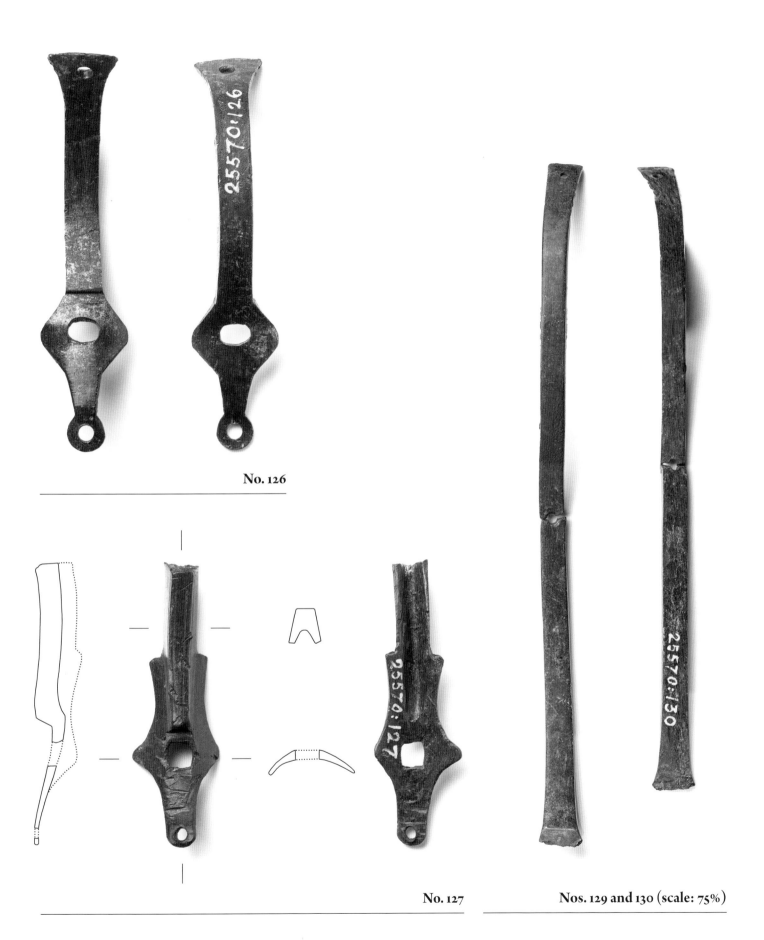

No. 126

No. 127

Nos. 129 and 130 (scale: 75%)

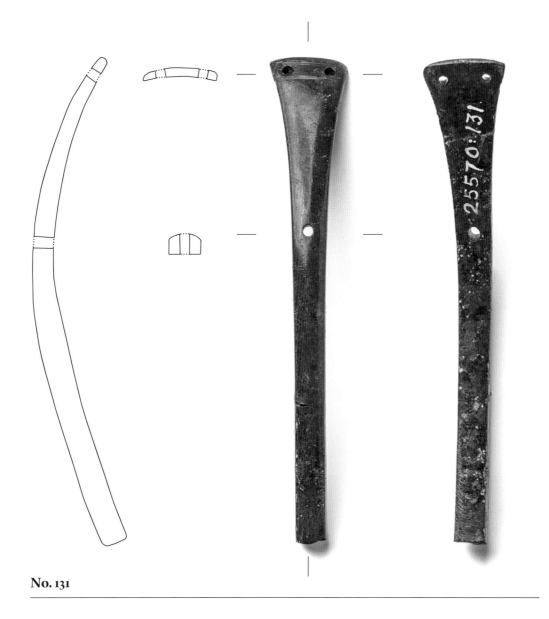

No. 131

No. 132

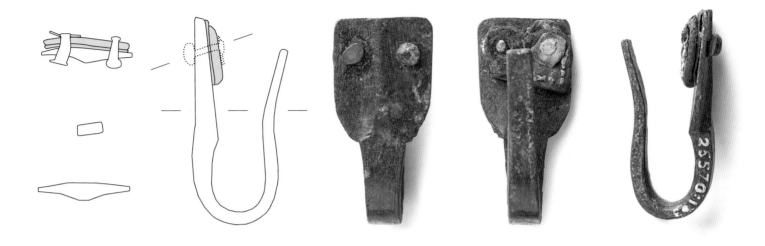

No. 133

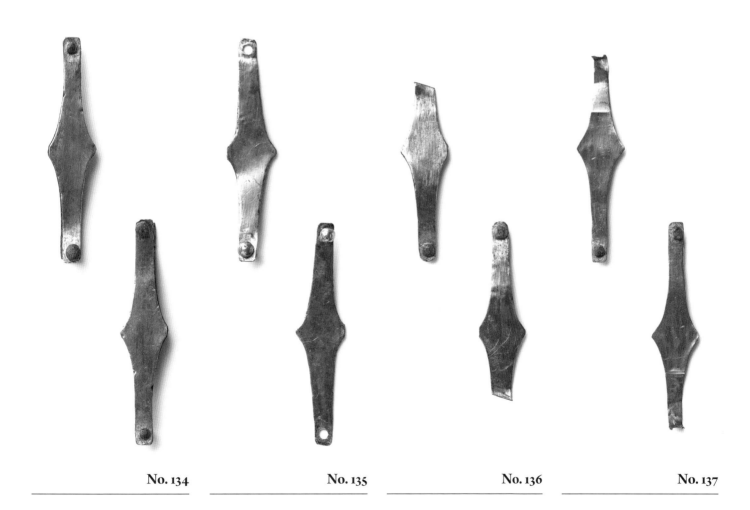

No. 134 **No. 135** **No. 136** **No. 137**

No. 138

No. 139

No. 140

No. 141

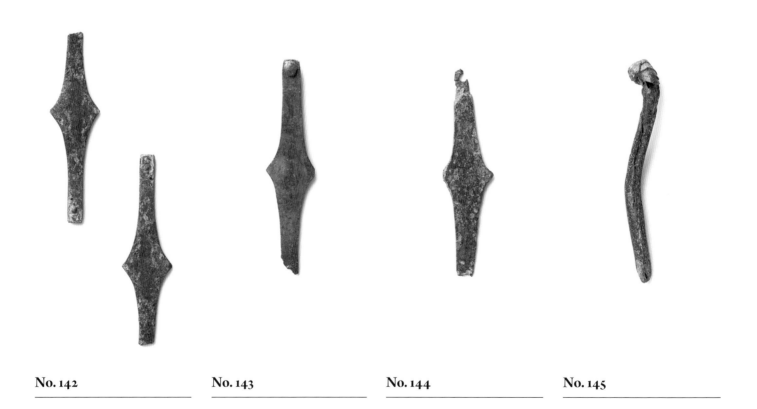

No. 142

No. 143

No. 144

No. 145

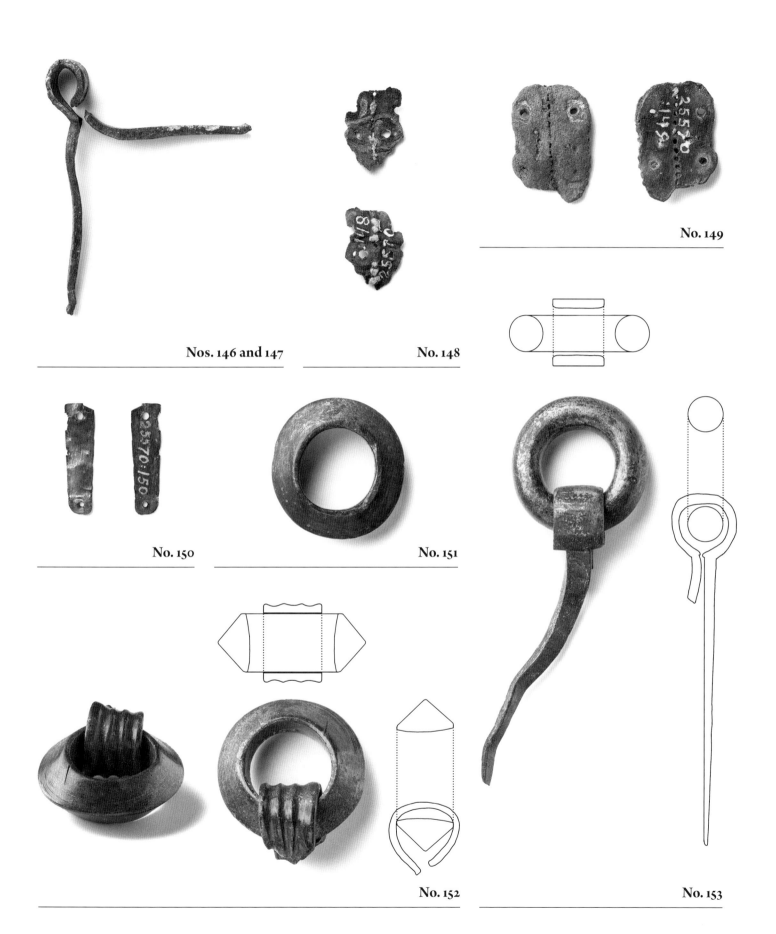

Nos. 146 and 147

No. 148

No. 149

No. 150

No. 151

No. 152

No. 153

No. 154

No. 156

No. 155

No. 157

No. 158

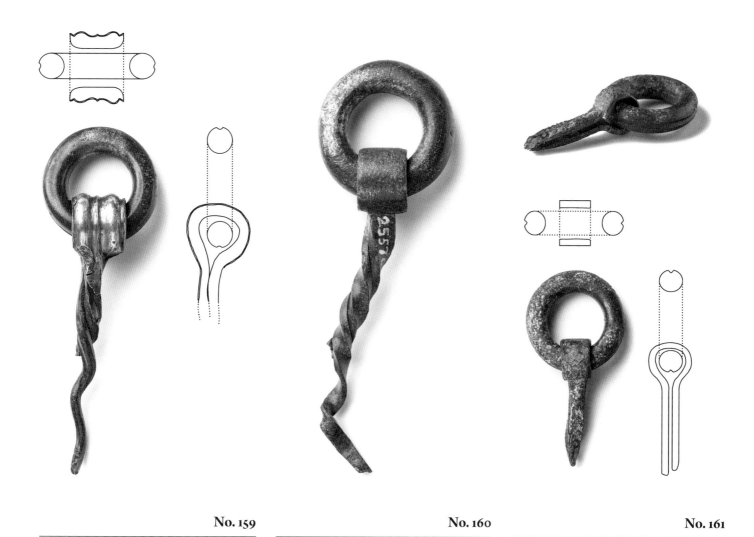

No. 159   No. 160   No. 161

No. 162

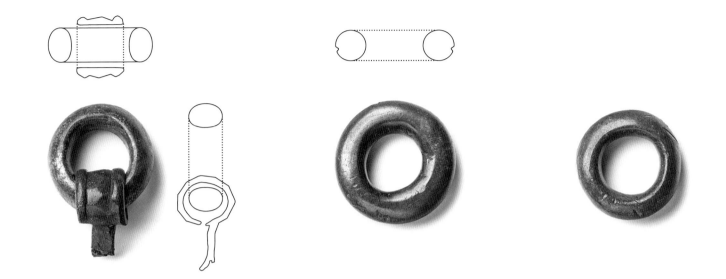

No. 163 **No. 164** **No. 165**

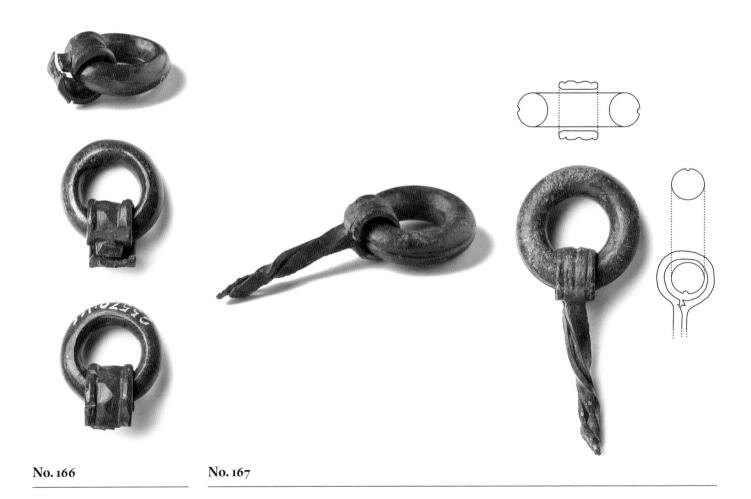

No. 166 **No. 167**

Nos. 168 and 200   **No. 169**

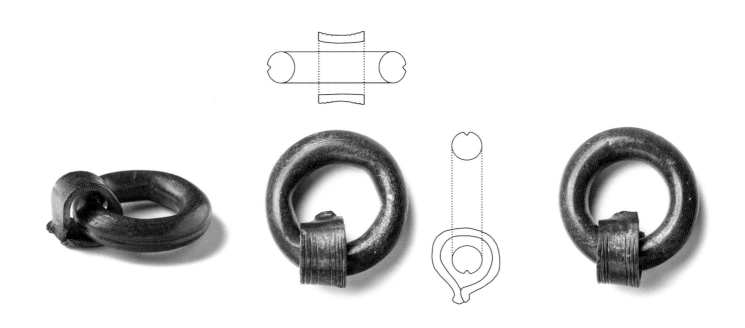

No. 170   **No. 171**

No. 172

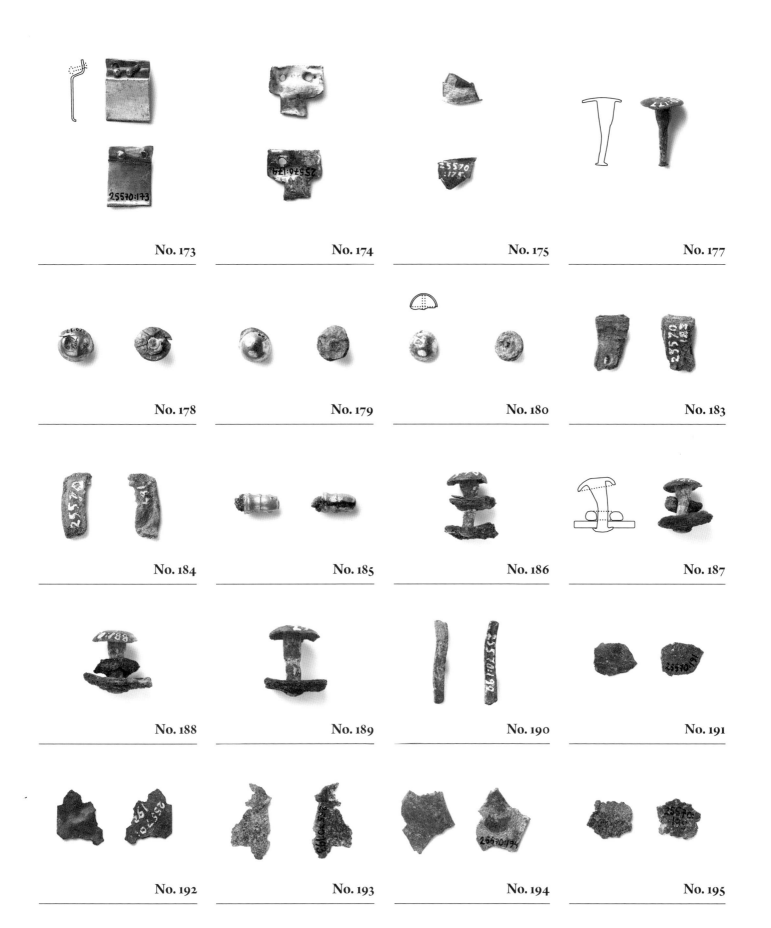

No. 173

No. 174

No. 175

No. 177

No. 178

No. 179

No. 180

No. 183

No. 184

No. 185

No. 186

No. 187

No. 188

No. 189

No. 190

No. 191

No. 192

No. 193

No. 194

No. 195

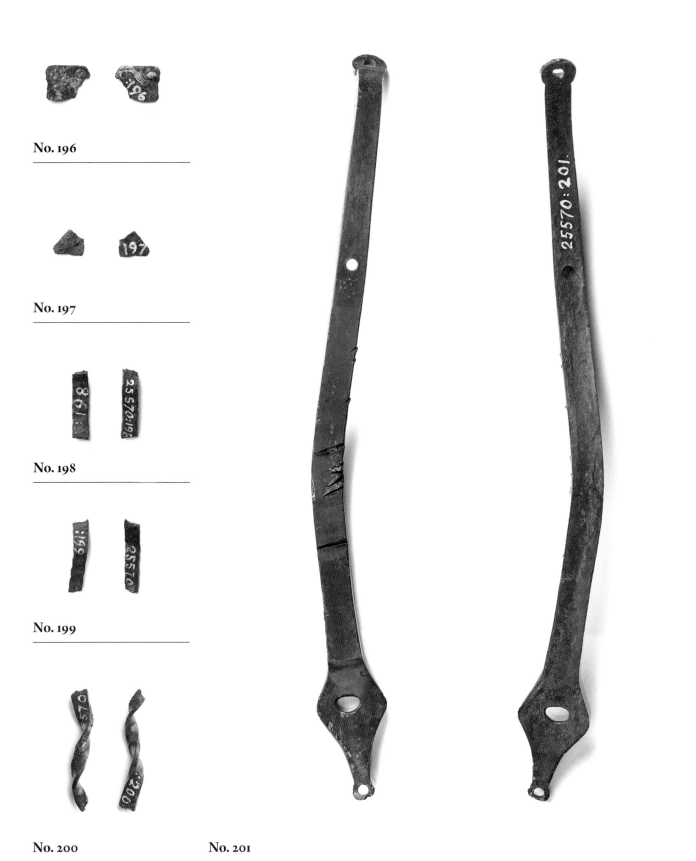

No. 196

No. 197

No. 198

No. 199

No. 200

No. 201

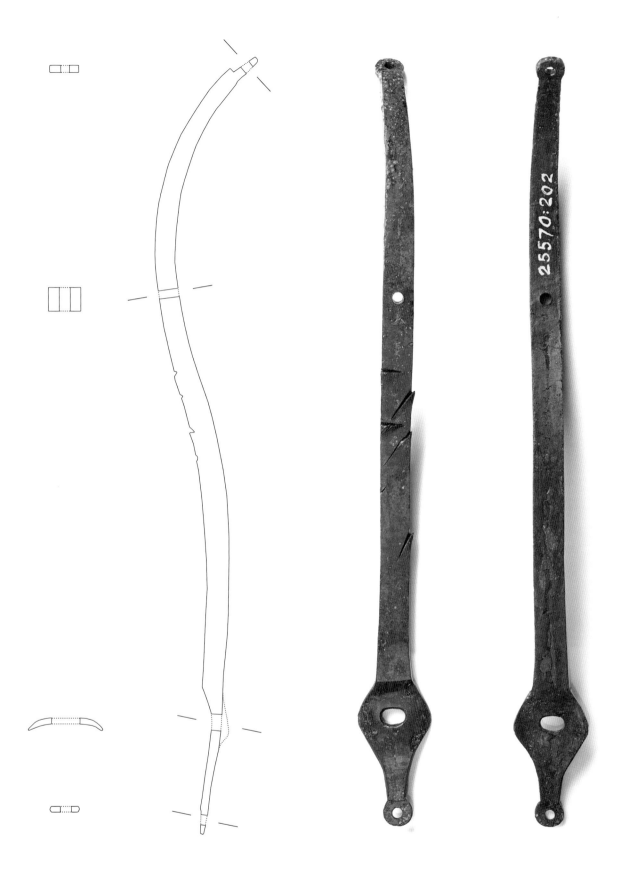

No. 202

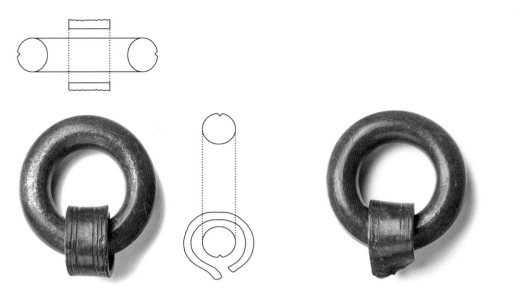

No. 203

No. 204

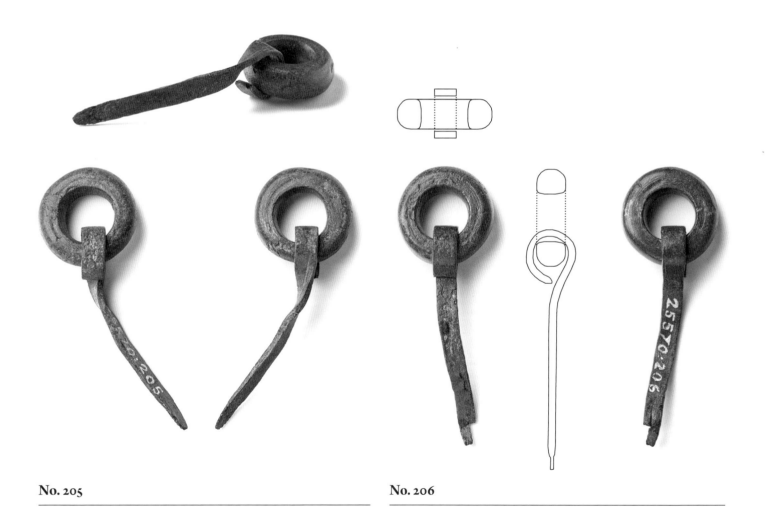

No. 205

No. 206

No. 207

No. 208

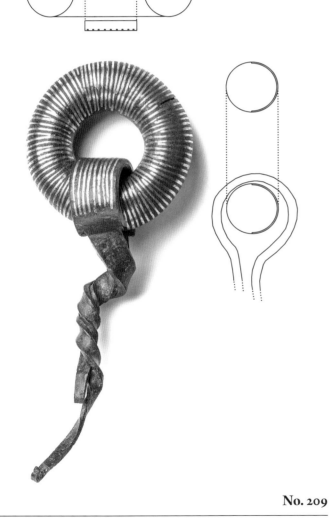

No. 209

No. 210

No. 211

No. 212

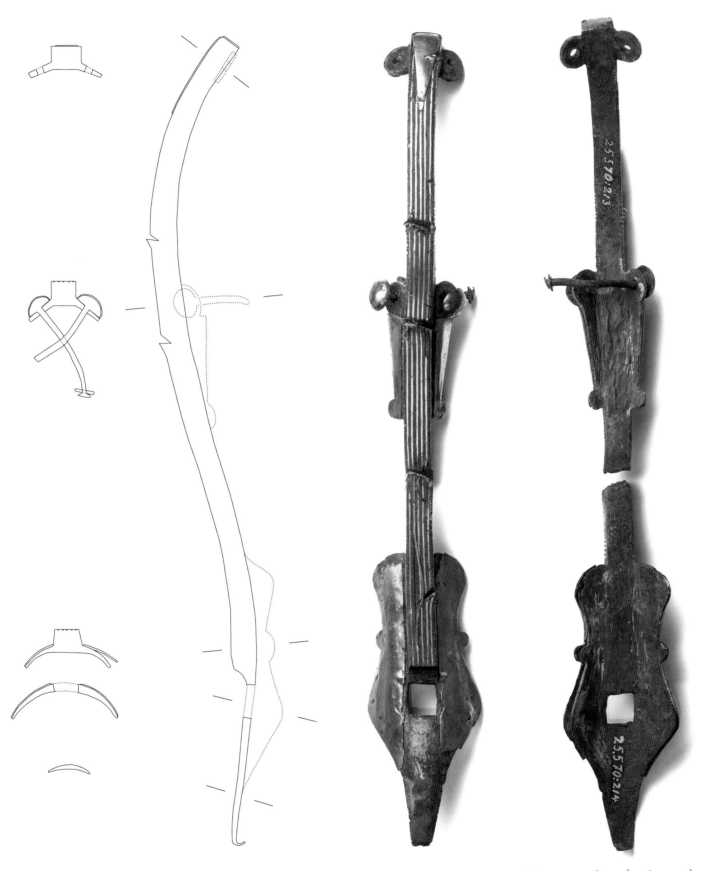

Nos. 213 and 214 (scale: 75%)

Nos. 215 and 216 (scale: 75%)

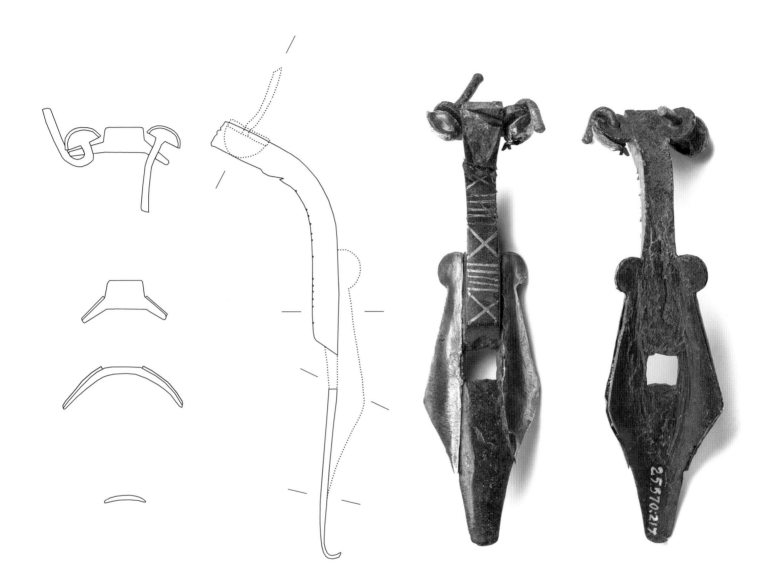

Nos. 213, 215 and 217

No. 221   No. 228

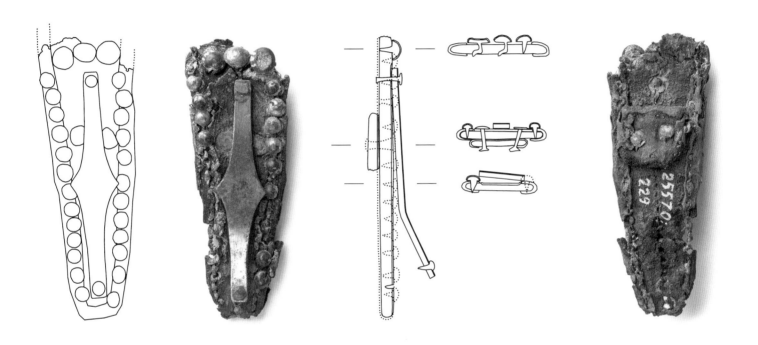

No. 229

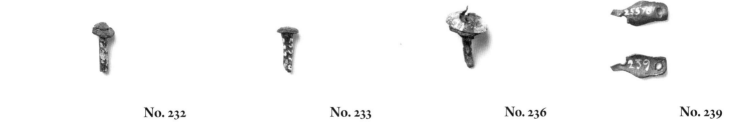

No. 232   No. 233   No. 236   No. 239

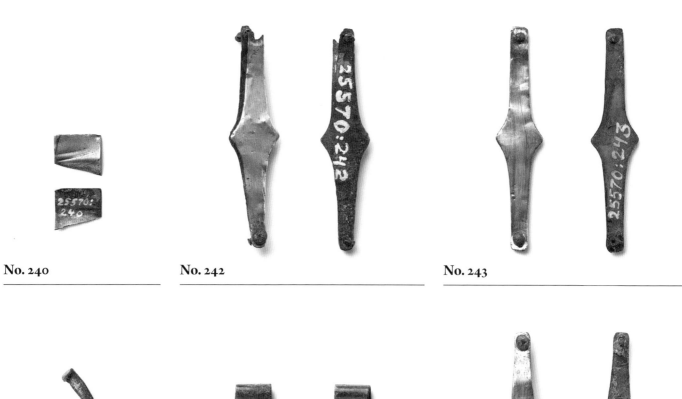

No. 240   No. 242   No. 243

No. 244   No. 246   No. 247

Catalogue

Sösdala II 1961

LUHM museum number 32 492

After 1930 the museum heard nothing from the gravel pit at Sösdala until August 1961, when a new find was reported. It consists of mounts from a headstall and a loose-ring snaffle. It was rapidly published by Carin Bunte as Sösdala II with a full description (A New Bridle Find from Sösdala. *Meddelanden från Lunds universitets historiska museum* 1961: 194–207). Bunte made an investigation at the find place and found some more items but nothing in situ. The find was made about 60 m north of the 1929–1930 find spot. It is evident that some deposited objects were lost, for example a strap junction like no. 3.

For detailed descriptions of the objects, see Bunte's publication, which is in English. For the comparison of the bridles 1929 and 1961 some further comments are made here. The finds are listed below with new photos and the terminology used in the descriptions of Sösdala I.

The bimetallic loose-ring snaffle has a strong construction with an iron bit, the ends of which are cased in cast Cu-alloy. The loose bit rings are of good quality. Also the strap buckles nos. 19–20 and the pendant strap-end no. 26

are cast. But the attachment plates are hammered out of Cu-alloy rods and seem to be remarkably weak. They are slipshod products. The hammer blows are very visible on nos. 15–17. The double attachment plates are bent to form a loop and a wide front and a narrow back plate. The ribbon-shaped back plates are fastened to the roundel of the triangular front plates by a rivet at the end. The strap was held in place by two rivets through the broad end of the front plate and an extra strip of Cu-alloy placed across the back plate (see cross-sections and photos of the underside of the mounts).

Silver strips placed below the two rivets at the broad end of the attachment plates are decorated with edge lines. The rivets heads are covered by domed silver caps; those at the end roundel are wider in diameter than the two at the broad end. The leather strap was originally approx. 3 mm thick.

The mounts are worn and repaired, see for example no. 3. The snaffle was destroyed by heavy cuts and hammer blows or broken in pieces.

Nos. 1 and 2. Bimetallic double-jointed snaffle with loose bit rings and headstall connectors with double attachment plates. Bit breadth 120 mm. Bunte 1961 fig. 1–2.

No. 3. Strap junction consisting of a cast ring and 4 double attachment plates. Note that two of the back plates are broken and repaired. Bunte 1961 fig. 3.

Nos. 4–9 and 11–18. Ring-link connectors consisting of a cast ring and two double attachment plates. No. 4. Bunte 1961 fig. 4:5 – No. 5. Bunte 1961 fig. 4:1 – No. 6. Bunte 1961 fig. 5:2 – No. 7. Bunte 1961 fig. 5:1. – No. 8. Bunte 1961 fig. 6:2. – No. 9. Note that one of the lower plates is broken and repaired. Bunte 1961 fig. 6:1. – No. 11. Bunte 1961 fig. 5:3. – No. 12. Bunte 1961 fig. 4:3–4. – No. 13. Bunte 1961 fig. 4:6.

– No. 14. Bunte 1961 fig. 6:18. – No. 15. Bunte 1961 fig. 6:9. – No. 16. Bunte 1961 fig. 6:8. – No. 17. Bunte 1961 fig. 6:10. – No. 18 Various small fragments of rivets and attachment plates. Bunte 1961 fig. 4:2, 6:13–15–17, 6:20.

No. 10. Lunate pendant on ring-link connector similar to no. 4. The pendant is cut out of a Cu-alloy plate and filed in shape. Bunte placed it in the browband. Bunte 1961 fig. 7 and 10.

Nos. 19 and 20. Integral plate strap buckles. Bunte 1961 fig. 6:3–4. The frame openings are 12 mm wide. Instead of a Cu-alloy rivet in the roundel no. 19 has one of iron, a repair? The Cu-alloy rivets of no. 20 are virtually invisible on the front side. The upward angle of the frame in relation to the plate made Bunte interpret them as buckles used to connect the reins to the bit rings (Bunte 1961:204). Two stumps of leather straps, nos. 29–30, come from the buckles; the rivet holes of no. 29 fit the rivets of buckle no. 19. The strap is 14/15 mm broad and longer than the attachment plate; this supports Bunte's interpretation that the buckles connected reins to bit rings as in her fig. 9.

Nos. 21–25. Ring mounts. All rings are worn. They were once attached to a leather strap approx. 2 mm thick, by simple ribbon-shaped double mounts. – No. 21. Bunte 1961 fig. 6:6. – No. 22. Bunte 1961 fig. 5:5. – No. 23. Bunte 1961 fig. 6:5. – No. 24. Only a ring. Bunte 1961 fig. 6:7. – No. 25. Bunte 1961 fig. 5:4.

No. 26. Pendant with double attachment plate. Cast with a hinge with bored holes for the separately made axle. Animal-head-shaped end with eyes marked by point circles. Perhaps silver wire was inlaid in three double circle-and-dots. The front of the attachment plate was covered by a silver sheet and is decorated by double circles-and-dots around the four rivets that held the leather strap; no silver caps preserved. The leather strap was originally approx. 2 mm thick.

Nos. 27–28. Mounts. Square, 16 × 12 mm and 17 × 13 mm large.

No. 29. Stump of single leather strap. Rivet holes fit to strap buckle no. 19. Length 28 mm. Approx. 3 mm thick.

No. 30. Stump of single leather strap. Length 9 mm.

No. 1 p.t.o.

Nos. 1 and 2

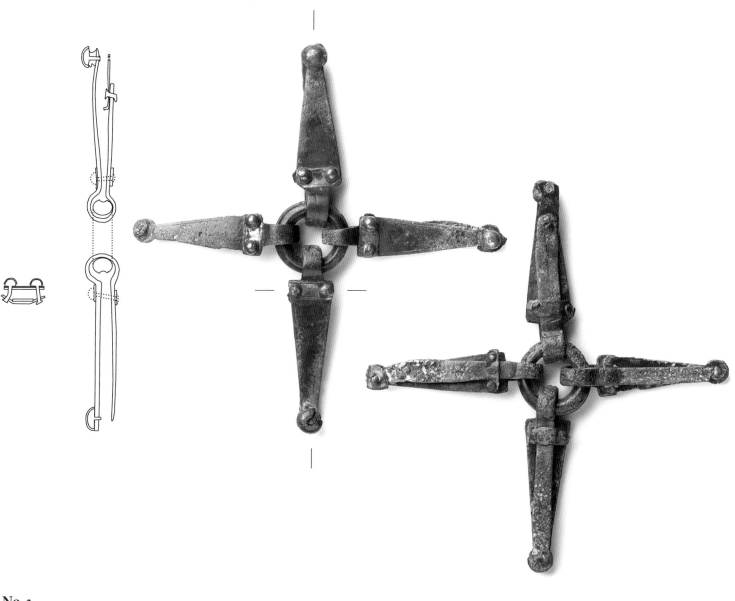

No. 3

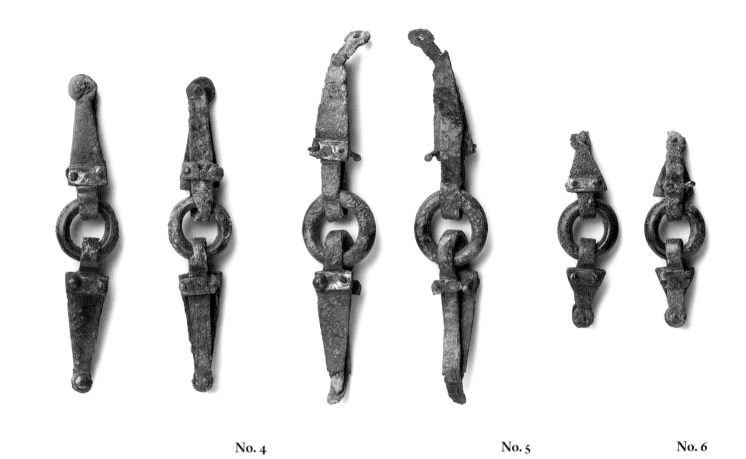

No. 4   No. 5   No. 6

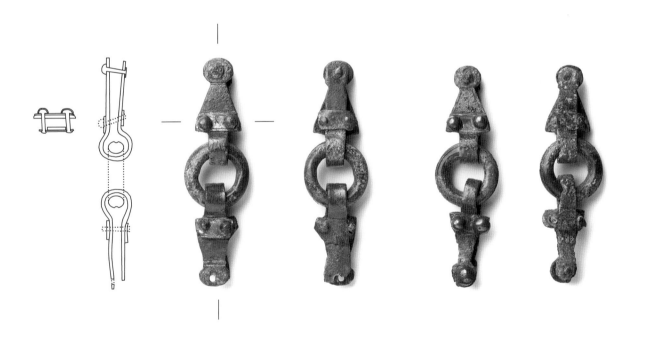

No. 7   No. 8

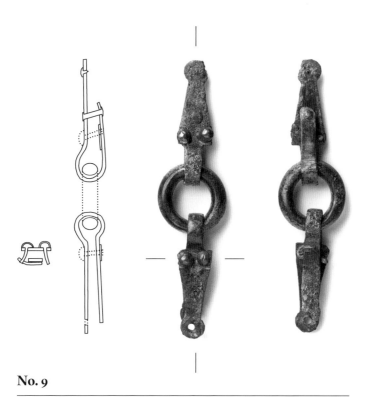

No. 9

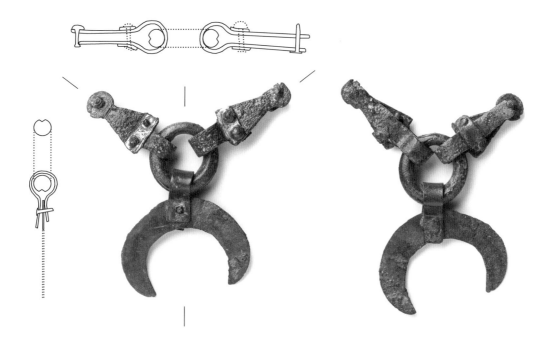

No. 10

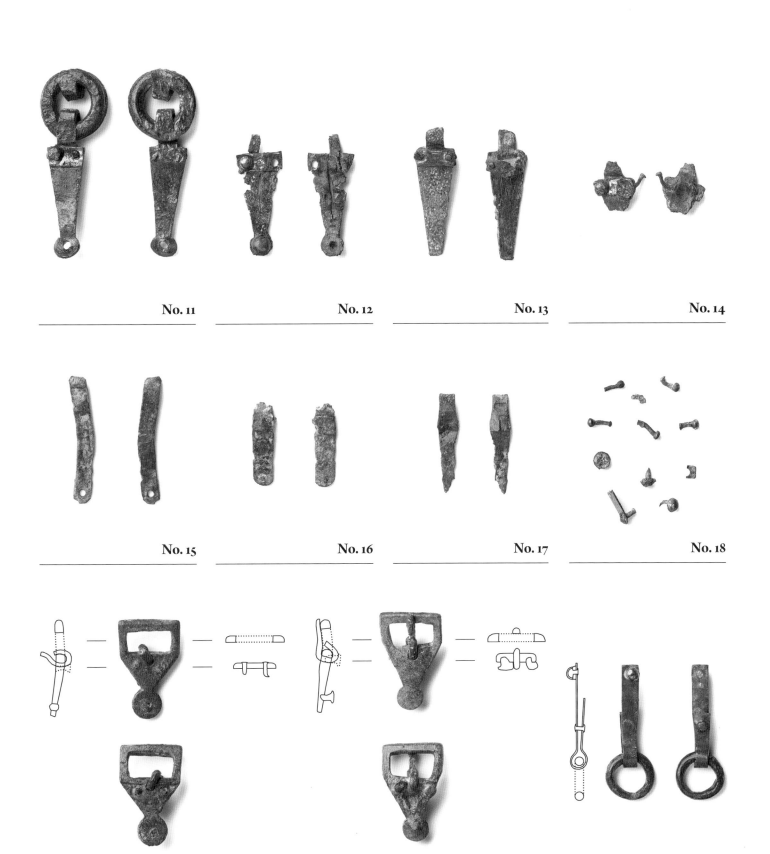

No. 11   No. 12   No. 13   No. 14

No. 15   No. 16   No. 17   No. 18

No. 19   No. 20   No. 21

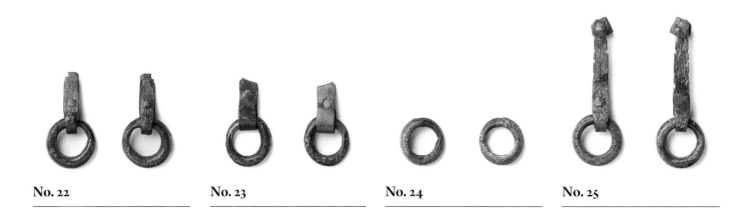

No. 22

No. 23

No. 24

No. 25

No. 26

No. 27

No. 28

No. 29

No. 30

Catalogue

Fulltofta gård 1896

LUHM museum number 14 080

The following catalogue of the finds from Fulltofta is based on Sven Söderberg's never published descriptions and sketches from 1897 for the catalogue at Historical Museum at Lund University as well as on our own autopsy in 2015. It is remarkable that Söderberg does not have a single word to suggest that the objects belong to horse tack.

The find, incomplete remains of a saddle and a headstall, was made by Måns Olsson (for find history, see Fabech chapter 1). Much of what once was deposited was lost; the snaffle, three of the saddle mounts and two saddle rings and three staples are missing. Many years later in 2002 one fragment belonging to the same headstall and a part of one of the missing saddle mounts were found by Jonas Paulsson in an authorised metal-detecting survey. They are included below as nos. 24 and 25. The find spot was surveyed again in 2017 by Jonas Paulsson but only two insignificant fragments of attachment plates were found.

A number of mounts probably belong to a headstall (nos. 1–15, 18–19 and 25); the snaffle is missing. Some other mounts represent the remains of a saddle cut to pieces (nos. 16–17 and 21–24).

Headstall (nos. 1–15, 18–19 and 25)

No. 1. Ornamental pelta-shaped pendant cover, partly gilt silver sheet on Cu-alloy plate. The plate is 68 × 53 mm large and 0.7–0.9 mm thick (thinner silver sheet, thicker sheet of Cu-alloy). The ends of the pelta are shaped like gilt bird heads turned inwards; their beaks are not gilt. The ornamentation of the pelta was marked by incised lines before punching. The edge is punch-decorated and gilt. The triple concentric semicircles are the same as on strap end no. 13. Inside the gilt border is a pelta-shaped silver surface, the centre of which is dominated by a large circle subdivided by curved spokes into a whirl with three punch-decorated gilt fields and three fields that are left as blank silver. On both sides of the whirl there are three smaller punched circles; the one in the middle has dotted outline and is gilt. The plate probably once covered one of the axe-shaped Cu-alloy pendants, nos. 5 or 6, but it is probably a later addition and not an original feature. On the back remains of glue reveal that it was fastened at the museum to the axe-shaped pendant of no. 5 (see photo in Norberg 1931, fig. 3). However, nothing in Söderberg's record reveals whether this is correct or how it was placed; see more at no. 2 below.

Nos. 2 and 25. Two fragments of ornamental pelta-shaped pendant cover, similar in shape and size to no. 1. The fragments are between 0.5 and 1.2 mm thick (thinner silver sheet, thicker sheet of Cu-alloy). The punched decoration is not exactly the same as on no. 1; for instance, of the three smaller circles the central gilt one is larger than the two others, which not are gilt. Of the large central motif only the gilt punched border is preserved; its central motif is lost but it was probably not similar to the whirl on no. 1. On the back of no. 2 differences in the verdigris reveal that it once was fastened to the axe-shaped pendant of nos. 5 or 6 and that the bird heads turned downwards, like the pelta-shaped pendant in Sösdala I, nos. 19–21. But it does now reveal whether it is a later addition or an original feature.

Nos. 3–10. Hinge-linked strap connectors. All are cast in Cu-alloy with hollow backs. Added details are in sheet silver. The mounts consist of a separately cast square central piece with two, three, or four hinges. Those with two or four hinges are linked to two or four attachment plates. All four mounts with three hinges are linked to two attachment plates but in two cases a pendant is attached to the third hinge and in two cases to a snaffle ring connector. The mounts thus consist of 3, 4, or 5 separate parts held together by Cu-alloy axles in the hinges. The central piece is covered by a silver sheet, 11 × 14, 13 × 14, 13 × 17, 14 × 14, or 15 × 15 mm large, decorated with a simple incised four-petal flower on nos. 9–10; on nos. 3–4 the centre of the four-petal flower is a triple concentric circle with a dot and on nos. 5–8 the centre of the four-petal flower is a double concentric circle with a dot. The attachment plates have the shape of a long-legged ridged triangle with hinge and two rivets at the broad end and a roundel with a larger rivet at the narrow end. The rivets are approx. 10 mm long and leave approx. 2 mm for the leather strap. The large rivets have had a Cu-alloy rove 7–8 mm in diameter. The rivet heads are covered by silver caps; the smaller ones are 5–6 mm in diameter, the larger ones 9–10 mm. The attachment plates are decorated by simple lines along ridge and edges.

No. 3. Four-armed hinge-linked trap junction. Five separate pieces joined by hinges. The junction is 129–130 mm large across two arms. One attachment plate is broken in the hinge. Another mount has instead of a cast loop a rod that is bent over the axle of the hinge and held in place by a plate and two rivets (see photo of back); probably a broken mount has been replaced. Connected cheekpiece, throatlash, headpiece and browband.

No. 4. Four-armed hinge-linked strap junction, as no. 3 but one attachment plate is broken in the hinge and two lack the roundel at the end. Connected cheekpiece, throatlash, headpiece and browband.

No. 5. Two-armed hinge-linked strap connector with axe-shaped pendant. Four pieces joined by hinges. The overall present length is 121 mm but it was originally approx. 125 mm. The central piece has three hinges and on the fourth side there is a triangular projection with lines along the edges. Two hinges hold attachment plates; the third an undecorated axe-shaped pendant. One attachment plate is broken and the roundel at the end is broken off and now missing (it is present on old photos; see Norberg 1931 fig. 3). The pendant is bent. At the museum the pelta-shaped silver plate, no. 1, was glued to the pendant (by Norberg??), but Sven Söderberg did not mentioned this possibility in his description in 1897. He only made a general remark that the axe-shaped pendant could have been covered with silver. New observations on the back of no. 2 indicate that the pelta-shaped silver sheets once covered the axe-shaped pendants but it is uncertain whether this was a later addition or an original feature.

No. 6. Two-armed hinge-linked strap connector with axe-shaped pendant. Like no. 5. One attachment plate lost its end roundel with rivet already in the Migration Period; a secondarily bored hole at the broken end represents an ancient repair; the preserved length is 120 mm. The triangular projection is broken off and missing. The axe-shaped pendant is damaged and fragmented. The original green verdigris is miscoloured by some later act of preservation.

No. 7. Three-armed hinge-linked snaffle ring connector. Four pieces joined by hinges. The overall length was approx. 125 mm, height is 77 mm. In two hinges there are attachment plates for straps to the noseband and cheekpiece, respectively; in the third is a mount that connected the headstall to the snaffle ring. On the fourth side is a triangular projection like nos. 5–6, but here it turned downwards. The loop that held the snaffle ring is broken open. One attachment plate is broken at the hinge. The other lacks the roundel at the end. The axe-shaped projection is damaged.

No. 8. Three-armed hinge-linked snaffle ring connector. Similar to no. 7 but more damaged. The connector arm that held the snaffle ring is missing and the other two arms are bent.

Nos. 9–10. Two-armed hinge-linked strap connectors. Each consists of three pieces joined by hinges. The overall length is now 108 mm but was probably approx. 127 mm. On both connectors one mount lacks the end roundel with rivet. The central piece is rectangular and covered with 11 × 14 mm large sheet silver.

No. 11. Pendant hinged in attachment plate. Cu-alloy plate covered with sheet silver. The pendant is 98 mm long, the mount 26 mm long and 12 mm broad. The pendant has double-curved edges. The now loose silver sheet is undecorated. Hung with a simple loop on a Cu-alloy axle in the hinge of the double mount. The front of the mount is also covered by sheet silver. The leather strap was originally approx. 2.5 mm thick and held in place by one Cu-alloy rivet with silver cap. The Cu-alloy pendant is 1.7 mm thick, the sheet silver 0.3–0.4 mm thick.

No. 12. Fragmentary pendant hinged in strap mount. Only the loop of a pendant is preserved in the hinge of the attachment plate; it probably looked like pendant no. 11. The strap mount is like that of no. 11, but has an axle of iron. The Cu-alloy rivet has lost its silver cap. The mount is 26 mm long and 12 mm broad. The leather strap was originally about 3 mm thick.

No. 13. Strap end. Cu-alloy with cover of sheet silver. Overall the strap end is approx. 107 mm long and 15 mm broad. Square upper end fastened to a leather strap by two Cu-alloy rivets with silver caps. The upper end is separated from the rest by a recess at both sides; incised lines along the edges and across. The lower part has curved edges ending in a roundel, which has lost the silver sheet cover. The edges are decorated with punched quadruple semicircles (the same punch as on nos. 1 and 2cum25). The silver sheet has loosened from the Cu-alloy but is still held in place by the rivets at the upper end. At the back of the upper end there are remains of a thin Cu-alloy back plate; the leather strap was once in-between. The Cu-alloy mount is 1.6 mm thick; the silver sheet is 0.4 mm thick.

Nos. 14–15. Two double strap mounts. The mounts consist of two 30 × 14 mm large Cu-alloy plates joined by a rivet in each corner. No. 14 is well preserved except that only traces are left of silver caps on the rivet heads; silver caps are preserved on two rivets on no. 15. Incised lines follow the long sides of no. 14. The front plate of no. 15 is decorated with edge lines and a large triple concentric circle with dot. The rivets are 7 mm long; the leather strap was originally approx. 3 mm thick. The silver caps are 5 mm in diameter.

Nos. 18–19. Integral plate strap buckles. The buckles are 31 mm long and 19–20 mm broad. The square frames have concave bevelled sides and a notch for a simple ribbon-shaped tongue. The tongues are broken on both buckles. The attachment plates are square with two Cu-alloy rivets and a rounded projection for a third rivet at the end. The rivets have no head and are flush with the plate. Rivets are 4–5 mm long, leaving approx. 2 mm for the leather strap. The buckles probably belong to the headstall or attached reins to bit rings.

No. 20. Fragment of rod-shaped object. Originally more than 29 mm long. One end is broken, the other flattened into a roundel with a broken Cu-alloy rivet with silver-capped head. The rod-shaped part has bevelled edges. Unknown function.

Saddle (nos. 16–17 and 21–24)

Nos. 16–17. Two strap hooks. The hook were fastened to a leather strap, of which very small remains are preserved at one of four rivets in a square plate, 25 × 30 mm large, 2.7 mm thick. The Cu-alloy rivets are 11 mm long, their heads covered by silver caps, 5 mm in diameter. Three preserved on no. 16, two on no. 17. Use has worn a hole on top of four of the silver caps. The leather strap was fastened to the inside of the plate and was originally 4–5 mm thick. The hooks have a rounded shape, approx. 16 mm in inner diamter, and have similarities to the snaffle ring mounts nos. 7–8. The hook on no. 17 is secondarily bent.

Nos. 21–22. Saddle rings and staple. Only saddle ring no. 21 has preserved its staple. The well preserved ring is 39 mm in diameter. The loop of the staple is decorated with 3 × 2 narrow ridges with convex mouldings in-between. The now 56 mm long legs of the staple are broken. The ring has an external single moulding and has deep wear marks left by the staple. The saddle ring no. 22 is cut open and has deep cut marks. It is similar to no. 21 with an external single moulding. Its diameter was approx. 40 mm.

No. 23. Short saddle mount. Bent out of shape and cut in two fitting pieces with cut marks. The lower end is 58 mm long, the upper part 54 mm. Straightened out it is approx. 152 mm long. The lower end point is bent back. Made of a cast ribbon-shaped rod, 11–12 mm wide and 3.5–3.7 mm thick. Fastened to the cantle of a saddle by a rivet (missing) at the upper end and the staple in the lower widened part that ends in a point. The wings of the lower part, which is 32 mm broad, are decorated with single and triple drawn lines. On the front side is a central furrow, the upper end of which is closed by a separately cast ribbon-shaped piece. The raised edges are decorated by a single drawn line and the cross-piece with three parallel lines. In the furrow a row of rivet holes, three of which still have a Cu-alloy stud with its head covered by lens-shaped silver cap. The studs are flush with the back of the mount. The missing rivet probably had a similar head and silver cap.

No. 24. Long saddle mount. The upper end of a long saddle mount is similar to the short saddle mount no. 23. The missing lower part probably was similar to the lower end of no. 23. The present length is 185 mm but the total length can be estimated at approx. 280 mm (corresponding long mounts in Sösdala I are approx. 290 mm long). The mount is damaged by deep cuts. It is a cast ribbon-shaped rod, 12 mm wide and 4–5 mm thick; at the preserved end it is widened to 18 mm. On the front is a deep furrow along its length, the upper end of which is closed by a separately cast ribbon-shaped 18 mm long piece. The raised edges are decorated with a single drawn line and the cross-piece with three parallel lines. In the furrow seven Cu-alloy studs are riveted to the mount in groups of three (3 + 3 + 1 plus 2 missing at cut-off end). The groups are separated by rivets that fastened the mount to the pommel (now only the rivet holes remain). The studs as well as (probably) the rivets were once covered by lens-shaped silver caps, now fragmented by use-wear.

No. 1

Nos. 2 and 25

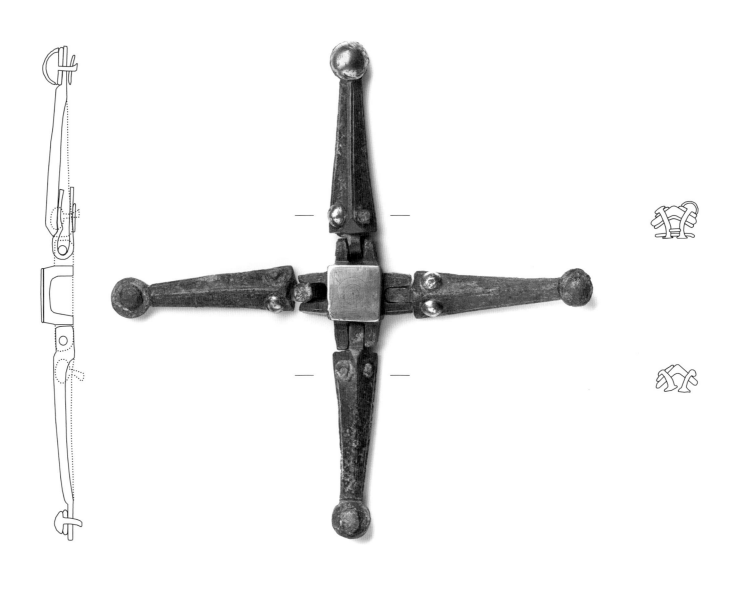

No. 3

No. 4

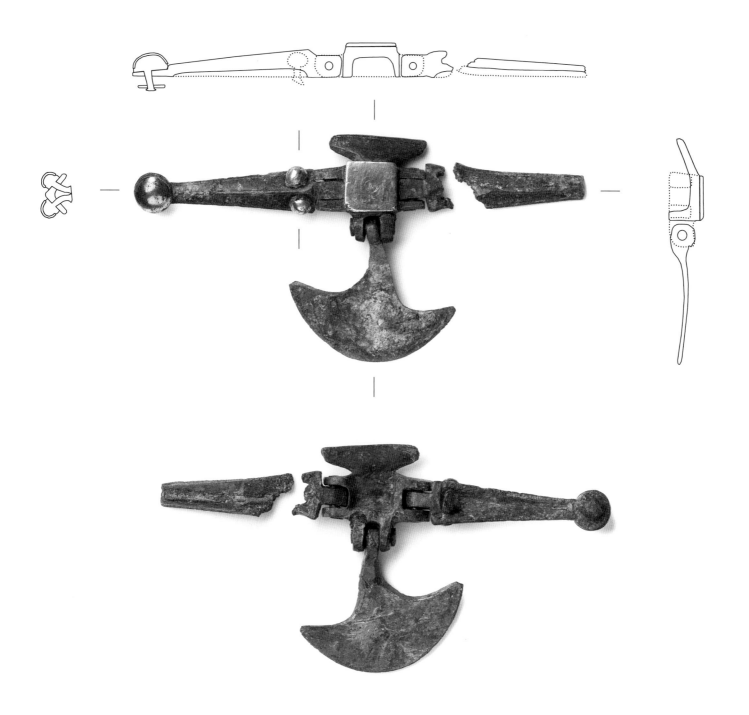

No. 5

No. 6

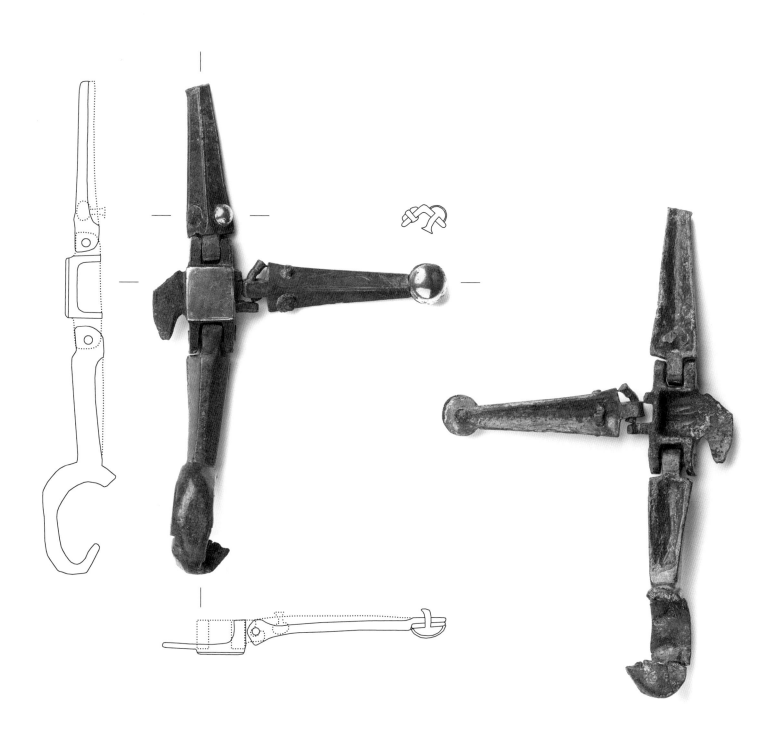

No. 7

No. 8

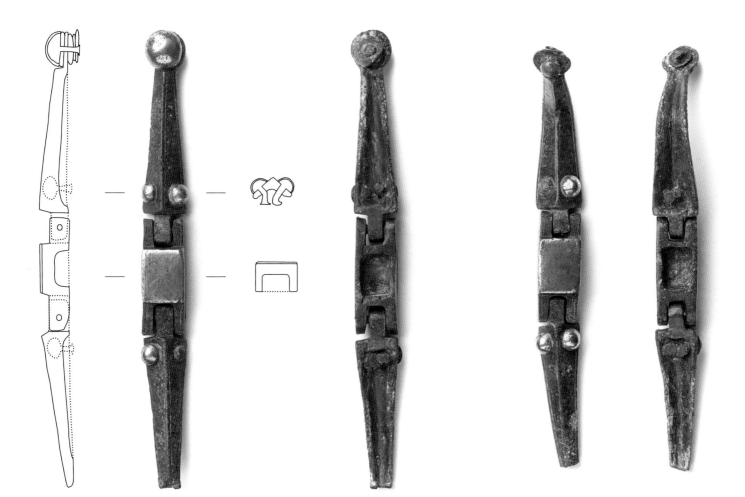

No. 9   No. 10

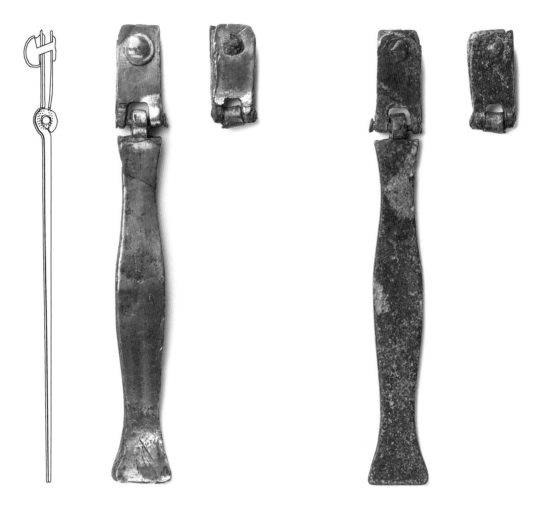

Nos. 11 and 12

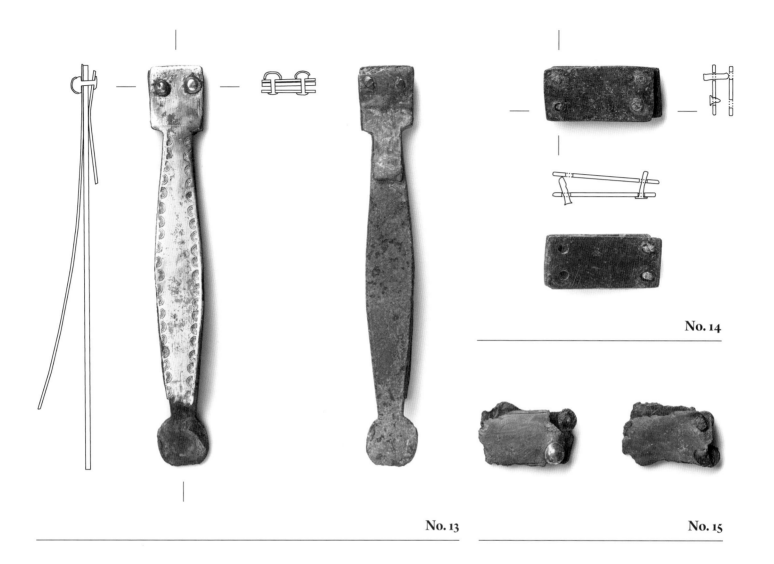

No. 14

No. 13

No. 15

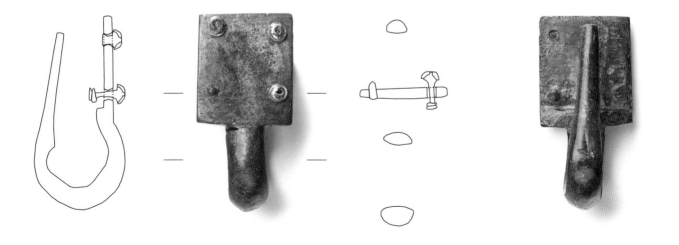

No. 16

No. 17

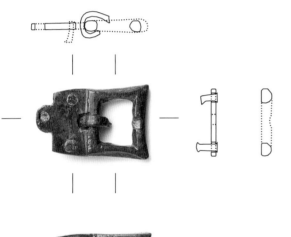

No. 18

No. 19

No. 20

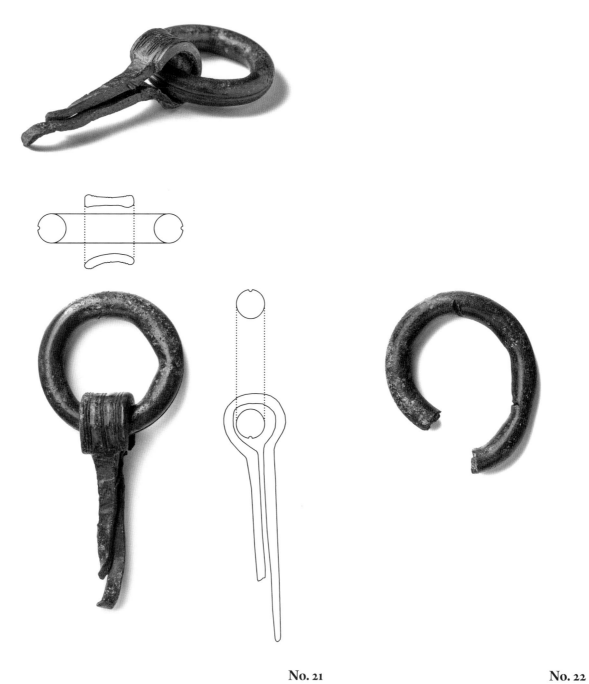

No. 21

No. 22

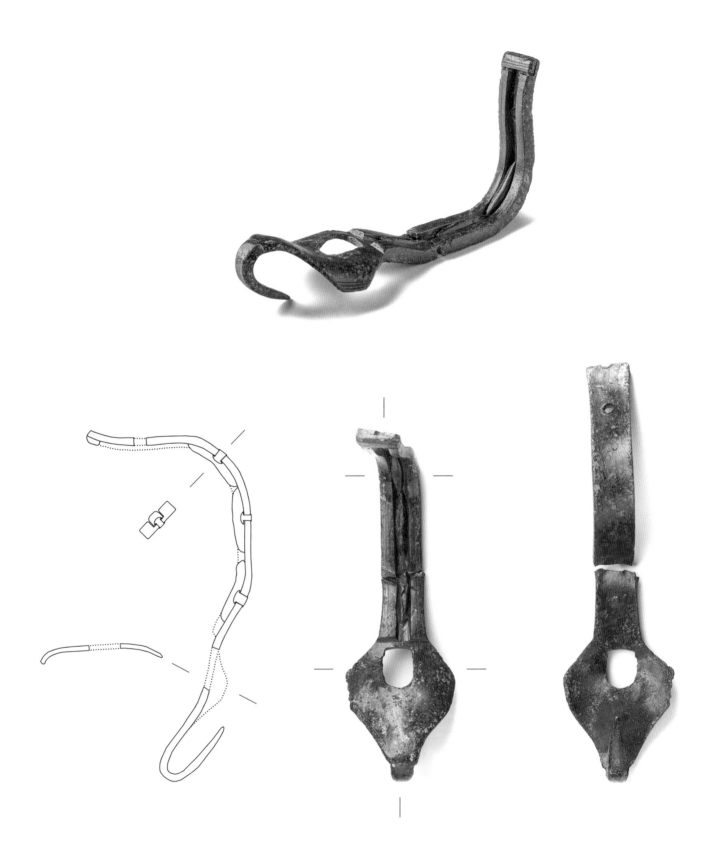

No. 23

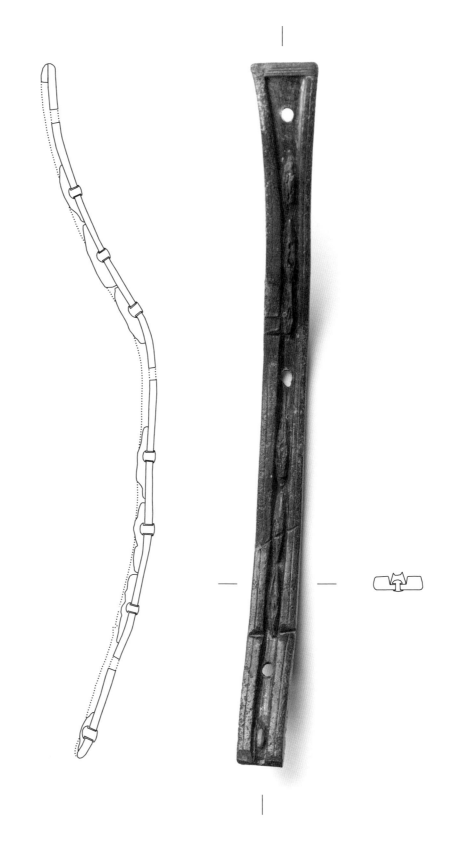

No. 24

Frontispieces

Chapter 1 – The Sösdala gravel pit 1929. Photo Carl Mellton.

Chapter 2 – Cheekpiece mount, Sösdala I no. 11. Photo Daniel Lindskog.

Chapter 3 – Scanian reconnaissance map 1812-1820. Part of map sheet IVÖ 201. Names added.

Chapter 4 – The Sjörup hoard. Detail of fig. 8. Photo Sören Hallgren, SHM.

Chapter 5 – Photo reconstruction of pendant Sösdala I no. 19–21. Photo Daniel Lindskog.

Chapter 6 – Strap junction, Sösdala I no. 15. Photo Daniel Lindskog.

Chapter 7 – Saddle ring, Sösdala I no. 208. Photo Daniel Lindskog.

Chapter 8 – Pendant, Sösdala I no. 3. Photo Daniel Lindskog.

Chapter 9 – Cheekpiece mount, Sösdala I no. 10. Photo Daniel Lindskog.

Chapter 10 – Strap mounts, Sösdala I no. 41, 43 and 45. Photo Daniel Lindskog.

Chapter 11 – Strap junction, Sösdala I no. 14. Photo Daniel Lindskog.

Chapter 12 – Pendant cover, Fulltofta no. 1. Photo Daniel Lindskog.

Chapter 13 – Strap buckle, Sösdala I no. 22. Photo Daniel Lindskog.

Chapter 14 – Strap buckle, Sösdala I no. 27. Photo Daniel Lindskog.

Chapter 15 – Strap buckle, Sösdala I no. 26. Photo Daniel Lindskog.

Chapter 16 – Pendant, Sösdala I no. 7. Photo Daniel Lindskog.

Chapter 17 – Pendant, Sösdala I no. 1. Photo Daniel Lindskog.

Catalogues – Strap fragment, Sösdala I no. 229. Photo Daniel Lindskog.

List of Contributors

Anna Bitner-Wróblewska, Państwowe Muzeum Archeologiczne, Warsaw

Lovisa Dal, Historical Museum at Lund University, Lund

Charlotte Fabech, emerita at Sydsvensk arkeologi, Malmö

Svante Fischer, Uppsala University, Uppsala

Bertil Helgesson, emeritus at Sydsvensk arkeologi, Kristianstad

Per Karsten, Historical Museum at Lund University, Lund

Michel Kazanski, Centre national de la recherche scientifique, Centre d'Histoire et de Civilisation de Byzance, Paris

Anna Mastykova, Russian Academy of Sciences, Institute of Archaeology, Moscow

Ulf Näsman, emeritus at Linnaeus University, Kalmar

Bengt Nordqvist, National Historical Museum, Mölndal

Dieter Quast, Römisch-Germanisches Zentralmuseum, Mainz

Per H. Ramqvist, Silvermuseet, Arjeplog; emeritus at Umeå University, Umeå

Erika Rosengren, Historical Museum at Lund University, Lund

Konstantin Skvortsov, Russian Academy of Sciences, Institute of Archaeology, Moscow

Anneli Sundkvist, Societas Archaeologica Upsaliensis (SAU), Uppsala

Ola Svensson, PhD at Linnaeus University, Växjö